WORLD SCIENTIFIC ENCYCLOPEDIA OF BUSINESS SUSTAINABILITY, ETHICS AND ENTREPRENEURSHIP

Volume 1: Environmental and Social Entrepreneurship

WORLD SCIENTIFIC ENCYCLOPEDIA OF BUSINESS SUSTAINABILITY, ETHICS AND ENTREPRENEURSHIP

Volume 1: **Environmental and Social Entrepreneurship**

Editor-in-chief
Gideon Markman
Colorado State University, USA
Gent University, Belgium
Audencia Business School, France

Edited by
Peter Gianiodis
Duquesne University, USA

Maritza Espina
St. Ambrose University, USA

William R Meek
Bucknell University, USA

NEW JERSEY · LONDON · SINGAPORE · BEIJING · SHANGHAI · HONG KONG · TAIPEI · CHENNAI · TOKYO

Published by

World Scientific Publishing Co. Pte. Ltd.
5 Toh Tuck Link, Singapore 596224
USA office: 27 Warren Street, Suite 401-402, Hackensack, NJ 07601
UK office: 57 Shelton Street, Covent Garden, London WC2H 9HE

Library of Congress Control Number: 2021046136

British Library Cataloguing-in-Publication Data
A catalogue record for this book is available from the British Library.

WORLD SCIENTIFIC ENCYCLOPEDIA OF BUSINESS SUSTAINABILITY, ETHICS AND ENTREPRENEURSHIP
(In 3 Volumes)
Volume 1: Environmental and Social Entrepreneurship
Volume 2: Sustainable Development Goals (SDGS)
Volume 3: Spirituality, Entrepreneurship and Social Change

Copyright © 2022 by World Scientific Publishing Co. Pte. Ltd.

All rights reserved. This book, or parts thereof, may not be reproduced in any form or by any means, electronic or mechanical, including photocopying, recording or any information storage and retrieval system now known or to be invented, without written permission from the publisher.

For photocopying of material in this volume, please pay a copying fee through the Copyright Clearance Center, Inc., 222 Rosewood Drive, Danvers, MA 01923, USA. In this case permission to photocopy is not required from the publisher.

ISBN 978-981-124-158-1 (set_hardcover)
ISBN 978-981-124-884-9 (set_ebook for institutions)
ISBN 978-981-124-885-6 (set_ebook for individuals)

ISBN 978-981-124-208-3 (vol. 1_hardcover)
ISBN 978-981-124-886-3 (vol. 1_ebook for institutions)

ISBN 978-981-124-209-0 (vol. 2_hardcover)
ISBN 978-981-124-887-0 (vol. 2_ebook for institutions)

ISBN 978-981-124-210-6 (vol. 3_hardcover)
ISBN 978-981-124-888-7 (vol. 3_ebook for institutions)

For any available supplementary material, please visit
https://www.worldscientific.com/worldscibooks/10.1142/12405#t=suppl

Desk Editors: Balamurugan Rajendran/Sylvia Koh

Typeset by Stallion Press
Email: enquiries@stallionpress.com

Printed in Singapore

© 2022 World Scientific Publishing Company
https://doi.org/10.1142/9789811248863_fmatter

About the Editors

Peter Gianiodis is the Inaugural Holder of the Merle E. Gilliand Professorship. He received his PhD from the Terry College of Business at the University of Georgia. He researches at the intersection of entrepreneurship, technology management, and strategy. His scholarly work has appeared in the *Academy of Management Review*, *Organization Science, Journal of Management Studies*, *Journal of Management, Journal of Business Venturing*, and the *Academy of Management Perspectives*. He serves on the board of several journals, including *Academy of Management Perspectives*, *Journal of Management Studies*, and *Group & Organization Management*, and is currently on the board of directors of the Sustainability, Ethics & Entrepreneurship (SEE) Conference.

Maritza I. Espina, a Transformational Leader, has served as Dean of the College of Business at St. Ambrose University since 2018. Maritza is also the Executive Director and Program Chair for the *Sustainability, Ethics, and Entrepreneurship* (SEE) Conference & Consortium. From its inception in 2012, the SEE continues to build a worldwide community connecting entrepreneurship scholars who recognize that sustainability and ethics are growth engines, not just acts of compliance.

Dr. Espina received a PhD in Management and a Master's in Operations Research and Statistics from Rensselaer Polytechnic Institute in New York. The integration of business and technology has been a common thread through her research projects, including the intersections of intellectual property, entrepreneurship, and social innovation. Recently, she edited the volume *Social Innovation and Sustainable Entrepreneurship*, part of The Johns

Hopkins University series on Entrepreneurship. Her research has been presented at international academic conferences including the Academy of Management, Strategic Management Society, and Babson College Entrepreneurship Research Conference and published in the Academy of Management Perspectives, the Journal of Management, and others.

William R (Bill) Meek is the Campbell Rutledge Jr. and Eleanor Rutledge Endowed Chair in Management and Entrepreneurship and a Professor of Management and Organizations in the Freeman College of Management at Bucknell University. He studies social and sustainable entrepreneurship, academic entrepreneurship, and gender and entrepreneurship. Dr. Meek has published in top entrepreneurship journals such as *Journal of Business Venturing, Journal of Business Venturing Insights, Entrepreneurship Theory and Practice, Journal of Technology Transfer, International Journal of Entrepreneurial Behavior and Research,* and *Journal of Business Research.*

About the Contributors

Geoff Archer is an Associate Professor at Royal Roads University in Victoria, BC Canada. He has been invited to give conference presentations all over the world and has authored numerous academic works on the topics of entrepreneurial thinking, experiential learning, microfinance and sustainable business. Archer holds the first utility patent granted to a Royal Roads faculty member. In addition to his professorial responsibilities, Archer is also the director of the Eric C. Douglass Centre for Entrepreneurial Studies. In this capacity he has mentored myriad entrepreneurial students and alumni and connected investors to Royal Roads stakeholders with practical business models that make a difference. Archer is a former senior vice president of Partnerships for the International Council for Small Business and Entrepreneurship and a past president of the Canadian Council for Small Business and Entrepreneurship.

Archer holds a Bachelor of Arts in Public Policy from Duke University's Terry Sanford Institute (1994), a Master of Environmental Management from Duke University's Nicholas School of the Environment (1995), a Master of Business Administration from Cornell's Johnson Graduate School of Management (1999) and a PhD in Business Administration from the Darden Graduate School of Business at the University of Virginia (2009).

Felix Arndt is the John F. Wood Chair in Entrepreneurship at the University of Guelph, a Research Fellow at the Center for Business and Sports of the Stockholm School of Economics, Sweden, and a Visiting Professor at the University of Agder, Norway.

Dr Arndt's research intersects strategy, entrepreneurship, and innovation. He looks at how firms use organizational renewal and technological innovation to stay ahead of the competition (dynamic capabilities, ecosystems, business models). A second field of interest is best captured by the question how entrepreneurs overcome extreme challenge. His research extends to the emerging market context and corporate social responsibility. His work has been published in the *Academy of Management Review*, the *Journal of Business Ethics*, the *Journal of Business Venturing Insights, Industrial and Corporate Change, Entrepreneurship and Regional Development, Technological Forecasting and Social Change, Technovation* among others.

Felix is an active entrepreneur and investor. As an engineer by training, he is fascinated by new technologies and their application. He has held patents, has experience as an entrepreneur, as a consultant and as a lobbyist. Felix is a recognized executive and start-up coach, provides consulting services to the private sector and policy advice to the government.

James E. Austin is the Eliot I. Snider and Family Professor of Business Administration, Emeritus, Harvard Business School, his third chaired professorship. He is a Co-Founder of the School's Social Enterprise Initiative, which has played since its founding in 1993 a significant role in the development of the social entrepreneurship field. His research has focused on social enterprise, cross-sector collaboration, management in developing countries, nutrition policy and management, and agribusiness.

Patricia (Trish) Doyle Corner is a Full Professor at the University of British Columbia, Okanagan. She earned her PhD from Arizona State University in the US and has published in top journals including *Journal of Business Venturing, Entrepreneurship, Theory, and Practice, Organization Science, Journal of Business Ethics, International Small Business Journal*, and *Entrepreneurship Research Journal*. Her current research interests include social and commercial entrepreneurship and advancing human knowledge.

Rosanna Garcia is Professor of Marketing and Walter Koch Endowed Chair of Entrepreneurship at the University of Denver in Colorado. Her current research is focused on diversity in entrepreneurship and the legitimacy of benefit corporations. She previously held the position of Chancellor's Faculty of Excellence in Innovation + Design at North Carolina State University from 2014–2017. She was also an Associate Professor of Marketing in the Poole College of Management and was the college's Faculty Director of the Business Sustainability Collaborative. Dr. Garcia's research is published in *Management Science, Marketing Science, Decision Sciences, Sloan Management Review*, and other journals. She is co-founder and current treasurer of the B Academics, a global organization focused on teaching on research on purpose-driven enterprises. She has received grants from the National Science Foundation, the HASTAC/MacArthur Foundation, the Marketing Science Institute, and the Product Development Management Association for her work on diffusion and agent-based modeling.

Richard T. Harrison is Professor of Entrepreneurship and Innovation at University of Edinburgh Business School. He researches the nature of the entrepreneurial process — in social and corporate as well as new venture contexts — as it is reflected in business development (particularly in the financing, by business angels and VCs, of innovation and growth), and in the implications of research and theorizing for practice and public policy. Current research includes the entrepreneurial response to climate change (he is co-editing a *Special Issue of Leadership* on this), identity and identity work (he co-edited a *Special Issue of Entrepreneurship and Regional Development* [vol 28(3/4), April 2016] *on Identity*), entrepreneurial finance (he is founding co-editor of *Venture Capital: An International Journal of Entrepreneurial Finance*), entrepreneurial learning and leadership (he has edited *Special Issues of Leadership* [vol 11(4) November 2015] *on leadership, authority and crisis, and Entrepreneurship Theory and Practice* [vol 29(4) July 2005] *on entrepreneurial learning*), entrepreneurship and innovation in China, the nature of peace entrepreneurship in conflict societies (including Rwanda and Democratic Republic of Congo), and the post-Bourdieusian analysis of gender and entrepreneurship. In recognition of the importance of his angel finance research, he was the 2015 recipient of the UK Economic and Social Research Council Award for Outstanding Research Impact on Business, and 2018 recipient of the Academy of Management Award for Impact on Entrepreneurial Practice.

Kate Kearins is Deputy Dean and Professor of Management at Auckland University of Technology in Auckland, New Zealand. Kate's PhD is from the University of Waikato in New Zealand. She has published on a wide range of accounting and management topics. Her research is currently focused on what it takes to advance sustainability in business and organizational contexts.

Herman B. "Dutch" Leonard is George F. Baker Jr. Professor of Public Management at the Kennedy School, Eliot I. Snider and Family Professor of Business Administration, and Cochair of the Social Enterprise Initiative at Harvard Business School. He teaches leadership, organizational strategy, crisis management, and financial management. His current research concentrates on crisis management, corporate social responsibility, and performance management. He is a Member of the Board of Directors of Harvard Pilgrim Health Care, a 1-million-member Massachusetts HMO. He was Formerly a Member of the Board of Directors of the ACLU of Massachusetts, the Hitachi Foundation, the Massachusetts Health and Education Facilities Authority, and Civic Investments, a nonprofit organization that assists charitable enterprises with capital financing; a Member of the Research and Education Advisory Panel of the General Accounting Office; a Member of the Massachusetts Performance Enhancement Commission; and a Member of the Alaska Governor's Council on Economic Policy.

Wentong Liu is a Lecturer (Assistant Professor) in Management at the School of Business Administration, Zhongnan University of Economics and Law, China. He holds a PhD and MSc in Entrepreneurship and a BSc in Japanese. His research interests are social entrepreneurship and social innovation, high-tech entrepreneurship and strategic management, especially in the emerging economies. He is currently researching about how high-tech businesses contribute to society and civilization. His work has been published in journals including the Technological Forecasting & Social Change. His work has also been presented at various leading academic conferences, and he has won the best paper award in the 2019 annual conference of Frontiers of Business Research in China.

Thomas B. Long is Assistant Professor of Sustainable Entrepreneurship at the University of Groningen's Campus Fryslân Faculty, and a Member of the Centre for Sustainable Entrepreneurship. Tom's research interests focus on responsible innovation in contexts of sustainable entrepreneurship, entrepreneurship in nature and heritage protection areas, and business models for sustainability. These themes are pursued through several funded research projects, including the Interreg funded PROWAD Link: Protect and Prosper and Erasmus+ Teaching Entrepreneurship for Sustainability. Tom co-directs and coordinates the Sustainable Start-up Academy at Campus Fryslân, an initiative in collaboration with Founded in Friesland to support students in launching their own sustainable ventures. See his profile on www.rug.nl/staff/t.b.long/ and www.researchgate.net/profile/Thomas_Long2

Anne H. Reilly is Professor of Management in the Quinlan School of Business at Loyola University, Chicago. Her academic background includes a PhD in organizational behavior from Northwestern University (Kellogg), an MBA in finance from the University of Iowa (Tippie), and a BA in economics, summa cum laude, from Knox College. Dr. Reilly's research interests address organizational change, including sustainability & crisis management, gender & careers, and teaching methods. She has published extensively in both scholarly and practitioner journals, such as *Strategic Management Journal*, *Academy of Management Journal*, *Journal of Organizational Behavior*, *Business Horizons*, and *Journal of Management Education*.

In addition to her teaching and research responsibilities, she has served in multiple administrative positions including Associate Dean of the Graduate School of Business, Assistant Provost for Faculty Administration in Loyola's Office of the Provost, and Associate Dean for Faculty and Research at Quinlan. rior to her academic career, she worked in the financial services industry.

Fiona Robinson has a strong entrepreneurial background that includes running her own design and marketing agency, corporate consulting and providing coaching and mentoring support to small business entrepreneurs and not-for-profit leaders. She taught as Visiting Professor in the Social Entrepreneurship Department at Rollins College and as associate faculty at Royal Roads University.

Robinson received her Masters in Environmental Design from the University of Calgary and is completing her Doctorate in Social Sciences at Royal Roads University with a focus on creative entrepreneurship and self-sufficiency. Prior to this, she studied environmental and social justice issues while completing a BSc in Environmental Planning at the University of Northern British Columbia.

Sumita Sarma is an Assistant Professor of Management at California State University, Bakersfield. She received her PhD in Entrepreneurship and Innovation from the University of Missouri-Kansas City. Prior to her PhD, Dr. Sarma had extensive industry work experience in multi-functional roles. Before joining the industry, she completed her Bachelor of Engineering in Electronics and Telecommunications in India, and her Master's from France. Sarma has lived and worked in three countries — USA, France, and India, and has rich industrial work experience in multi-functional roles. Her main teaching and research interests include entrepreneurship and innovation, and strategic management. Dr. Sarma has published in the *Asia Pacific Journal of Management, Business Horizons, Entrepreneurship Research Journal, Asia Pacific Journal of Marketing and Logistics*, and *Journal of International Consumer Marketing* on areas of entrepreneurship and firm-level strategies. She has presented several of her research papers at national-level conferences such as the *Academy of Management, Babson Conference, Sustainability Ethics and Entrepreneurship*, and *USASBE*. Sarma is a Member of the Academy of Management and Strategic Management Society and has served as ad-hoc reviewer for multiple journals such as *Research Policy, Journal of Small Business Management, Asian Pacific Journal of Marketing and Logistics, Asian Journal of Management Science and Applications, and Academy of Management*.

Katrin Schaefer gained her PhD from Auckland University of Technology in Auckland, New Zealand. She has previous degrees from her native Germany and her new home country, New Zealand, along with work experience promoting sustainability in business. Her current interest lies in the potential for coaching to enhance metacognition and to contribute to personal and societal transformational change.

Sharon A. Simmons holds a PhD in Entrepreneurship and Emerging Enterprises from Syracuse University, a Juris Doctor and Master's in Accounting from the University of Virginia and a BS in Accounting from Hampton University. She has also practiced as a Certified Public Accountant. Her research is published in *Journal of Business Venturing, Organizational Research Methods, Small Business Economics, Journal of Small Business Management, Venture Capital*, and other highly ranked peer-reviewed journals. Dr. Simmons has global experience working with public and private institutions in the United States and its Territories, China, Scotland, London, France, Australia, and Bahamas. She is an accomplished entrepreneur who is skilled at opportunity identification, exploration, and exploitation.

Sanwar A. Sunny is an Assistant Professor of Entrepreneurship at the R. G. Merrick School of Business at University of Baltimore. He received a PhD in entrepreneurship and innovation and Master of Public Administration (MPA) from the University of Missouri-Kansas City (UMKC) and a Bachelor of Science degree in Mechanical Engineering from the University of Kansas (KU). His publications appear in the *Academy of Management Review, Small Business Economics, Journal of Small Business Management, International Business Review,* and *Business Horizons.*

Preeti Tiwari is an Assistant Professor of Entrepreneurship at the School of Management and Entrepreneurship, IIT JODHPUR, Rajasthan, India. She received her PhD in Social Entrepreneurship from Birla Institute of Technology & Science (BITS), Pilani. Her area of interest is Entrepreneurship and Social Entrepreneurship. Social entrepreneurship is a part of entrepreneurship.

Lilach Trabelsi is a Management Scholar with a finance background. Her research focuses on the link between corporate strategy and sustainability. The research aims primarily at enhancing our understanding of strategic decision-making and the role of stakeholders in the area of corporate sustainability, in order to better understand how companies and industries address global grand challenges. Lilach obtained her PhD in Business Administration and Management from Bocconi University. Prior to joining academia, she has held various positions in the private and public sectors.

Gladis Cecilia Villegas-Arias, Ph.D. served as Professor of Management at the Facultad de Ciencias Económicas y Administrativas at the Universidad de Medellín. Dr. Villegas received a Ph.D. in Management, a Master of Engineering in Industrial and Management Engineering, and a Master of Business Administration in Management from the Rensselaer Polytechnic Institute in New York. She also received postdoctoral training in Business/Organizational Anthropology at Wayne State University, Detroit. She holds a Bachelor's degree in Systems Engineering from Universidad Eafit in Medellín, Colombia.

Dr. Villegas has worked, researched, presented, and published on topics such as dangerous waste management, business integration supported by IT, bankruptcy and critical success factors, and recently on sociotechnical issues in management. Her research interests include Process Modeling for Resiliency in Business models, and Human Issues and Management.

Megan Epler Wood is the Director of the International Sustainable Tourism Initiative (ISTI) at the Harvard T.H. Chan School of Public Health, where she is managing a comprehensive research program to place a value on the unaccounted for public health and environmental burdens tourism generates in destinations worldwide. ISTI also is working with the Harvard Graduate School of Design on geographic information systems (GIS) applications for tourism master planning and with the Harvard Kennedy School on policy research to help local governments to manage tourism in the era of growing impacts from climate change. Since 2003, Epler Wood has led the international consulting practice EplerWood International, fostering sustainable tourism and ecotourism development in Africa, Asia, and Latin America, working for the US Agency for International Development, the World Bank group, the Inter-American Development Bank, and the Planeterra Foundation. Epler Wood is a the managing director of the Sustainable Tourism Asset Management Program (STAMP) at the Cornell Center for Sustainable Global Enterprise in the SC Johnson College of Business, which supports the development of applied research, curriculum resources, and outreach activities that will increase collective knowledge and understanding of how to more effectively manage tourism destination assets over time in the face of rapidly growing tourism pressure, endemic poverty, ecosystem degradation, and climate change.

William Young is Professor of Sustainability and Business with over 25 years working with industry to develop sustainable solutions. His areas of expertise are ethical consumer behavior, sustainability behavior change, product sustainability standards and sustainability strategies in retailing research focused on consumer and organizational behavior around sustainability issues. He develops real-world experiments to test behavior change interventions and then measure the resulting behavioral and sustainability impacts. Current major research funding is focused on working with international datasets on actual consumer behavior on sustainability issues through the ESRC Consumer Data Research Centre. William is currently Editor of the *Resources, Conservation, and Recycling Journal* as well as on the journal Editorial Boards of *Corporate Social Responsibility & Environmental Management and Social Business*. William is co-organizer of the annual Corporate Responsibility Research Conference along with Kedge Business School in France.

© 2022 World Scientific Publishing Company
https://doi.org/10.1142/9789811248863_fmatter

Contents

About the Editors		v
About the Contributors		vii
Chapter 1	Introduction — The State of the Art in Environmental and Social Entrepreneurship Research *Peter Gianiodis, Maritza I. Espina and William R. Meek*	1
Part I	**Sustainable Venturing Across Global Contexts**	**15**
Chapter 2	Responding to Climate Change by Developing a Low-Carbon Economy Through Innovation: An Entrepreneurial Ecosystem Perspective *Richard T. Harrison*	17
Chapter 3	Supply Chain Climate Change Mitigation Strategies and Business Models *Thomas B. Long and William Young*	49
Chapter 4	Corporate Sustainability, Stakeholder Orientation, and Collaboration between Competitors: What Lies Beneath *Lilach Trabelsi*	89
Chapter 5	Beyond Goal Hybridity: How Multilevel Actor Networks Can Scale Climate Impact *Sanwar A. Sunny*	119
Chapter 6	Value Creation through Environmental Entrepreneurship *Geoff Archer, Felix Arndt and Fiona Robinson*	157

Chapter 7	Key Success Factors in Environmental Entrepreneurship: The Case of Wilderness Safaris *James E. Austin, Megan Epler Wood and Herman B. Leonard*	175

Part II Social Entrepreneurship and Impact — **197**

Chapter 8	Societal Attitudes Toward Corporate Responsibility and Social Entrepreneurship *Sumita Sarma and Sharon A. Simmons*	199
Chapter 9	How Social Entrepreneurs' Metacognition Shapes Socioeconomic Change Toward Sustainability-as-Flourishing *Katrin Schaefer, Patricia Doyle Corner and Kate Kearins*	225
Chapter 10	How a Prosocial Personality is Helpful in Predicting Social Entrepreneurial Intentions *Preeti Tiwari*	255
Chapter 11	Changing the World Under Limitations: The Role of Resource in Social Enterprise *Wentong Liu*	283

Part III Social Entrepreneurship and Impact — **335**

Chapter 12	Sustainability Leadership: Innovation in Governance and Gender *Anne H. Reilly*	337
Chapter 13	The Language of Entrepreneurship: An Exploratory Gender-Coding Study *Rosanna Garcia*	357
Chapter 14	Where to Fall Dead: A Comparative Analysis of the Death Care Industry *Gladis Cecilia Villegas-Arias*	391

Index — 411

Chapter 1

Introduction — The State of the Art in Environmental and Social Entrepreneurship Research

Peter Gianiodis,[*,§] Maritza I. Espina[†,¶] and William R. Meek[‡,||]

[*]Duquesne University, Pittsburgh, Pennsylvania, USA

[†]St. Ambrose University, Davenport, Iowa, USA

[‡]University of Dayton, Dayton, Ohio, USA

[§]gianiodisp@duq.edu

[¶]espinamaritza@sau.edu

[||]wmeek1@udayton.edu

1.1. Introduction

Welcome to the volume on environmental and social entrepreneurship as part of the *World Scientific Encyclopedia of Business Sustainability, Ethics, and Entrepreneurship*. This volume is the culmination of many discussions among the editors over the years, especially at the *Sustainability, Ethics and Entrepreneurship (SEE) Conference*, related to the growth and institutionalization of environmental and social entrepreneurship. Research on these two forms of entrepreneurial action has tried to keep pace with what is occurring in the field. While the research is diverse, attracting scholars across many disciplines and from all parts of the world, it is still in the formative stages. This volume seeks to take stock of the literature and report the state of the art in environmental and social entrepreneurship. In particular, it seeks to explore new theoretical directions that blend traditional notions of economic efficiency and social welfare and new ways of measuring and empirically testing these phenomena. The chapters in this volume demonstrate the diverse philosophical, methodological, and theoretical techniques to studying these forms of entrepreneurship.

This volume does not aim to cover all the many creative ways researchers are investigating these forms of entrepreneurship around the world. Indeed, environmental and social entrepreneurship is accelerating at such a rapid pace worldwide that researchers are struggling to build generalizable models. Hence, much of the research remains descriptive. Yet, this does not prevent contributors of this volume to attempt theory building or approaches to theory building, which we illustrate in this introduction. We expect this volume will contribute to this burgeoning research and that researchers will engage in theory development for the foreseeable future, as new business models are developed, tested, abandoned, and evolved.

The proliferation of environmental and social entrepreneurship research has been aided by better measuring techniques by government agencies, non-profit organizations (NGOs), industry associations, as well as firms themselves. Two recent developments exemplify the progress on measurement. First, the United Nations Sustainable Development Goals (SDGs) set in 2015 has been a catalyst for governments, NGOs, and the industry to begin/intensify data collection, which can then be measured and assessed against the SDGs. Likewise, the growth and influence of scaled philanthropy (e.g. Bill and Melinda Gates Foundation) has provided entrepreneurs extensive funding and made the organizations more disciplined because the funding decisions are outcomes-based. The combination of outcome-driven funding and specific targets provided in the SDGs has attracted numerous environmental and social entrepreneurs across the globe. These entrepreneurs have experimented with modern techniques of venture formation, such as the lean start-up, with initial venture concepts designed to pivot in response to feedback learned in the field. Ventures generally go through multiple iterations after a series of experiments, gaining legitimacy from the myriad of stakeholders who sponsor their work and/for whom their work serves. Thus, these ventures focus on sustainability of the business model within their context, rather than on "off-the-shelf" solution for broad social issues.

Despite access to better data, research still employs methods that are mostly descriptive in nature, with authors relying on field research and qualitative approaches, such as case reports, which can support primary data collection from surveys and interviews. More recently, researchers have applied new, richer data sets to investigate environmental and social entrepreneurship across a myriad of settings — from urban greenhouses to rural organic cooperatives. Increasingly, this research is leveraging large-scale data, especially in sustainable venturing financing and social impact, drawing from government, NGO, and industry data in public health, infrastructure, clean energy, and climate change. However, data that compares to traditional forms of entrepreneurial action (e.g. Kauffman Foundation) is still sparse, mostly because environmental and social ventures continue to be small, with private ownership structures. The popular press, such as

Inc. magazine, have begun reporting on venture-backed social enterprises, but these data skew to larger firms and in market domains that already have high levels of visibility (e.g. alternative energy). Researchers await access to large-scale data in emerging market domains, such as rare diseases, poverty eradication, and sustainable farming.

1.2. State of the Field

Prior to introducing the chapters in this volume, we briefly assess the state of the field for environmental and social entrepreneurship research. As noted, the field has significantly progressed since the early days of the sustainability and social impact movement. Yet, there is much work to be done and a better accounting to the predictive power and impact of the research. In this section, we consider areas where there are opportunities to advance the field by building upon the depth and breadth of research to resolve three pressing needs in the literature: contextuality, scalability, and stakeholder management. Table 1.1 provides an overview of these critical research challenges and opportunities for entrepreneur scholars.

1.2.1. *Contextuality*

Research has acknowledged the many contextual differences related to environmental and social entrepreneurship. At the micro level, environmental and social entrepreneurs vary greatly depending upon their motivation, interests, skills, and identity (Douglas and Prentice, 2019; McMullen and Bergman, 2017; Shepherd and Patzelt, 2011). This research applies much of the learnings from mainstream entrepreneurship research, with the individual or team central to the venturing process. Supplementing this work are the distinct nuances related to multi-mission and goal venturing that is emblematic to this form of venturing. While identifying and categorizing at the micro level, contextual differences are important, and the field urgently needs theory that predicts and explains how contextual differences explain the emergence, growth, and impact of ventures.

At the macro level, regional and institutional conditions vary greatly across settings, and act as spurs to, and impediments against, environmental and social venturing (*cf.* Dean and McMullen, 2007; Henrekson and Sanandaji, 2011; Meek *et al.*, 2010; Pathak and Muralidharan, 2016; Sud *et al.*, 2009). Much of this research would argue that regional, national, and institutional forces have a greater influence on venturing than it does on primarily commercial ventures. This is due to the competing logics, social norms prevalent in a region, myriad of stakeholders and their many potential conflicts, and the limited infrastructure developed to support non-commercial venturing (*cf.* Lumpkin *et al.*, 2013; Muñoz & Dimov,

Table 1.1. Opportunities for environmental and social entrepreneurship research.

Challenge	Progress to Date	Work to Be Done	Representative Research Questions
Contextuality	– Identify of micro- and macro-contextual differences – Categorize these differences at different levels of analysis: individual, organizational, institutional, country, etc. – Explain the primary antecedents to and outcomes of environmental/social venturing	– Determine importance of context to the growth and impact of ventures – Predict how contextual differences impact relevant outcomes related to environmental/social entrepreneurship – Explain not just the primary antecedents to and outcomes of venturing, but important interactions within and across levels of analysis	– To what extent do entrepreneurs' motives, experiences, skills, etc. change over time, and how does this influence the social impact of the venture? – How does the geographic location of an environmental or social venture interact with the venture's mission/ and or purpose itself to impact success, longevity, or outright failure of the venture? – How does the geographic location of an environmental or social venture interact with the venture's mission/ and or purpose itself to impact success, longevity, or outright failure of the venture? – Research has surfaced many of the primary factors that predict venture creation, growth, and impact, but what (if any) are the important interaction effects of these primary factors within and across levels of analysis?
Scalability	– Identify the founding conditions of environmental and social ventures – Categorize the growth modes and trajectories of ventures	– Identify the conditions for venture growth; how do environmental and social ventures manage growth – Explain the varying modes and likely outcomes of venture growth – Predict and explain the exiting process of venturing — individual, organizational, and institutional exits	– What are the risks, and more specifically the fault lines related to scaling up environmental/social enterprises? – What modes — e.g. strategic alliances — do enterprises use to scale up; how do they impact performance? – How can limitations in one type of capital (e.g. financial, physical, human, and social) be partially or fully overcome by strengths in another type of capital?

Stakeholder Management	– Identify key stakeholders of environmental and social ventures – Categorize the key stakeholders to determine their varying motivations/concerns, and how they influence the venture process	– Explain the why, how and when of stakeholder management; how do these ventures manage the myriad of stakeholders given multifaceted missions/goals – Predict and explain how stakeholders influence venturing — the formation, growth, and exiting of the venture related to micro, macro, and institutional decisions	– Do legal or business structure limitations (e.g. B-corp) impact the ability of ventures to scale up and grow? And if so, how do these differ across country contexts? – What does exit look like for environmental and social enterprises — how are they similar/dissimilar to pure commercial ventures? – What is the optimal mode and timing for stakeholder engagement in environmental/social enterprises? – What are the institutional challenges related to stakeholder management, especially when the enterprise cuts across industry/sector, regional and national boundaries? – Besides mission drift, what are the primary risks to undermining stakeholder–organization alignment? – Do external shocks from government institutions such as rolling back environmental standards or declining access to healthcare coverage incentivize existing stakeholders to become more deeply involved in social and environmental ventures?

2015). For example, there is generally tension between the community that is spurred to action through social ventures and the communities in which these ventures serve (Markman et al., 2019). Research needs to surface the distinct nuances related to operating multi-mission and goal ventures in varying contexts, while appeasing both active and passive stakeholders.

While we acknowledge the progress to date, here is just a sample of research questions that should drive future research. How do entrepreneurs' motives, experiences, skills, etc. influence the aspirations and likely impact of the venture? To what extent are these motives, experiences, skills, etc. dynamic, and how does their change influence the strategy, mission, and impact of the venture? How does the geographic location of an environmental or social venture interact with the venture's mission and/or purpose itself to impact success, longevity, or outright failure of the venture? How do factors such as religious affiliation, and individual belief systems/structures impact the acceptability of certain types of social and environmental ventures? Lastly, research has surfaced many of the primary factors that predict venture creation, growth, and impact, but what (if any) are the important interaction effects of these primary factors within and across levels of analysis?

1.2.2. *Scalability*

Research has acknowledged the challenges to scaling environmental and social ventures (e.g. Islam, 2020). These types of ventures, especially purely social ventures, are charged with creating higher social value in general, by serving greater number of communities and their beneficiaries, and specifically solving a protracted social problem (Markman et al., 2019). Improving social impact through scaling relies on securing access to more capital, including financial, physical, human, and social capital. Table 1.2 provides a summary of four forms of capital — financial, physical, human, and social capital — and their importance to the growth of environmental and social enterprises. Prior research has generally emphasized financial and social capital, especially at founding as a means for ventures to gain legitimacy (Lounsbury and Glynn, 2001; Nicholls, 2010). Yet, there is much less research on gaining access to physical and human capital, especially for enterprises operating in distressed communities. In addition, the resource accumulation orientation is generally focused on early-stage venturing, with limited attention to capital access at later stages to support scaling and fuel growth.

The importance of understanding the micro-foundations of scalability — motivations, structures, processes, policies, etc. — that support venturing strategies cannot be overstated. Below are sample research questions that will help surface relevant micro-foundations, and thus progress the literature. What are the optimal conditions under which environmental and social enterprises can grow? What are the likely risks, and more specifically the fault lines, related to scaling

Table 1.2. Challenges to resource accumulation for ventures in distressed environments.

Capital Type	Definition	Manifestations
Financial Capital	Tangible assets (funds) that support mission-critical functions & prevent insolvency	Access to banking services, funds provided by investors and/or donors to fuel growth; necessary to transition from early-stage to scaling
Physical Capital	Tangible assets — land, office space, equipment, etc. — that support critical functions	Access to adequate space and equipment; buildings can be outdated or even dilapidated in communities served; scaling may be muted by lack of physical space & equipment
Human Capital	Intangible assets — knowledge, skills, abilities, etc. — embedded in the employees of the organization that support critical functions	Access to a pool of qualified, dedicated human resources that share the organization's mission — skilled workers to alleviate pressure on the founders — and support growth; may need to "import" human capital from outside of the community
Social Capital	Intangible assets — network of relationships — embedded in the employees of the organization	Access to a social network containing mentors as well as individuals who "open doors"; difficult to engage influential people who make the connections

up environmental and social enterprises? What are the modes — e.g. strategic alliances — these enterprises take to scale up, and what are the implications to commercial and non-commercial performance? How can limitations in one type of capital (e.g. financial, physical, human, and social) be partially or fully overcome by strengths in another type of capital? How does the process of raising financial capital evolve in social and environmental firms as the organization matures and attempts to scale up? How do social and environmental firms use appeals for social good to gain access to different types of capital? Do legal or business structure limitations (e.g. B-corp) impact the ability of ventures to scale up and grow? And if so, how do these differ across country contexts? Lastly, what does exit look like for environmental and social enterprises — how are they similar/dissimilar to pure commercial ventures?

1.2.3. Stakeholder management

Critical to their formation, growth, and impact is how well environmental and social enterprises build legitimacy and align with the myriad of stakeholders. An important consideration is the potential for mission drift (Ramus and Vacacaro, 2017). In particular, the relationship between enterprise scaling and stakeholder management is critical. Scaling ensures the enterprise's survival and prosperity, but it also may change the balance of power within the enterprises' set of stakeholders. No wonder many social enterprises grow slowly and remain highly localized, albeit sacrificing the opportunity to create (Islam, 2020). Current research has explored who the key stakeholders are and how their motives differ, but there is still much work to be done about explaining the why, how, and when of stakeholder management for environmental and social enterprises (Tang and Tang, 2012). This is a critical feature in determining whether society can promote and secure what Lumpkin and Bacq (2019) describe as *civic wealth creation* — the social, economic, and communal endowments generated by local communities through the work of socially oriented entrepreneurial enterprises.

Applying this civic wealth creation framework, here are sample research questions that will advance the literature. What is/are the optimal mode(s) and timing for stakeholder engagement in environmental and social enterprises? Under what positive and negative societal events or shocks are additional stakeholders more likely to become engaged in environmental and social enterprises? Do external shocks from government institutions, such as rolling back environmental standards or declining access to healthcare coverage, incentivize existing stakeholders to become more deeply involved in social and environmental ventures? Furthermore, how do ventures engage stakeholders during shock events, such as natural disasters and public health crises, and does conflict increase or decrease stakeholder engagement in social and environmental firms? What are the institutional challenges related to stakeholder management, especially when the enterprise cuts across industry/sector, regional, and national boundaries? Besides mission drift, what are the primary risks to undermining stakeholder–organization alignment?

1.3. Organization of the Volume

This volume features research that was initially presented at the *SEE Conference*, which promotes emergent research in environmental and social venturing. The volume is organized in three parts. The first part reports on sustainable venturing across a myriad of global contexts, which integrate the importance of contextualizing environmental entrepreneurial research. There are seven chapters in this section. Chapter 2, by Harrison, illustrate how the development of a low-carbon economy poses a number of challenges and opportunities, which require a systematic and integrated response. In this study, the author draws from the entrepreneurial ecosystems framework (i.e. the development of new business models in the context of the availability and interdependence of the resources) and a strategic leadership perspective (the ability to think strategically), to examine five key issues related to infrastructure that must be addressed in responding to the low-carbon challenge. Those five issues relate to coordination of actors, development of multifaceted enabling partnerships, experimentation of funding models, the hybridization of business modes through public–private partnerships, and the creation of a fully functioning innovation and entrepreneurial ecosystem that leverages all of the actors and resources to respond to this challenge. The author concludes by proposing three non–mutually-exclusive options for addressing environmental degradation through a low-carbon economy: (1) public–private partnerships in the development and deployment of new, cost-effective, low-carbon solutions; (2) strategic industry partnerships to mobilize resources and complementary strengths and link established players with entrepreneurial low-carbon actors; and (3) financial innovation to accelerate the development and deployment of novel technologies by creating a new asset class for low carbon and providing for the securitization of low-carbon project investments. This study addresses all three pressing themes of the research — contextuality, scalability, and stakeholder management. It is important in a low-carbon economy to deftly manage stakeholder as they will have to change the ways in which they operate, and thus, the methods of funding their operations.

Chapter 3, by Long and Young, focuses on the sustainability of firms' supply chains, which contains a high proportion of the total greenhouse gas (GHG) emissions associated with products and services. Employing an exploratory qualitative approach, the authors explore the objectives and activities involved in managing supply chain GHG emissions, and how these impact the underlying business models and sustainable value creation opportunities. Specifically, they interviewed 31 expert informants in both the private and public sectors over two phases. Their findings point to the importance of design changes within the supply chain to decrease GHG emissions. Further, firms' existing strategies for integrating their supply chains often overlook entrepreneurial opportunities and thus impede their value creation from sustainable business practices. In fact, the *scalability* of sustainable business model archetypes, which emphasize maximizing efficiency and creating value from waste, are consistent with supply chain GHG emission management.

Chapter 4, by Trabelsi, applies a corporate stakeholder orientation lens to explore how firms' consideration of stakeholders' perspectives, interests, and needs influence their decision to participate in multistakeholder initiatives (MSIs). The aim of these MSIs is to address grand challenges related to sustainability and environmental entrepreneurship alongside their competitors. The importance of the stakeholder orientation of firms is revealed through the uncovering of contextual factors, both at the firm and the industry level. This study highlights the role of the orientation of individual firms vis-à-vis their suppliers, customers, competitors, regulators, and society, in incentivizing participation in MSIs. The study uses a qualitative analysis of 26 semi-structured interviews conducted with knowledgeable professionals. The findings reveal the primary importance of firm orientation toward suppliers in the goods sector, and customers in the services sector, in the decision of firms to participate in MSIs. This chapter's primary concern is *stakeholder management* as MSIs, by definition, require stakeholder engagement. However, the authors also consider how stakeholder management of MSIs is a means to achieve greater *scalability* at the organizational and ecosystem level. This is an important insight and offers interesting paths for future research.

Chapter 5, by Sunny, starts with a call for sustainable entrepreneurs and corporations to act to address the damages from climate change. It then elaborates a framework that integrates disparate perspectives and theories that heretofore have guided sustainable entrepreneurial action. To advance the field, the author proposes an actor–action–outcome framework that clarifies the distinct nature of agency and its relationship regarding the magnitude or direction of environmental impact from organizational actors and their actions. The framework applies a *stakeholder management* lens as it attempts to (1) uncover key attributes of the current structure, (2) reflect on the nature of heterogeneity in different outcome measures across groups of multilevel actors, and (3) clarify how a multilevel network model explains the heterogeneity of impact given structural limitations and mismatched motivations across system levels. As a result, the framework explains the value-creation processes at different structural contexts — i.e. at the micro-level to the global, macro-level — and highlights conceptualizations of economic growth and sustainable development. Thus, it sheds light on the perceived trade-offs and their sources, especially involving stakeholder management.

Chapter 6, by Archer, Arndt, and Robinson, identifies three classes of value creation for entrepreneurs participating in sustainable venturing. The authors apply a two-stage approach. First, they advance a taxonomy of general entrepreneurial opportunity that provides the foundation for further inquiry. The second stage describes a pragmatic tool that enables the authors to distinguish entrepreneurial opportunities that are always good for the planet from those which are only good conditionally. This framework contributes to the field by providing an organized platform for future scholarship into the overlap between entrepreneurship, opportunity, social objectives, sustainability and the natural environment. Importantly, their framework considers *scalability* — there are challenges of scaling a sustainable venture as certain opportunities may have diminishing returns to the planet as they reach scale. In this case, the authors advocate "micro-opportunities" that are specific to the geographical context.

Chapter 7, the last chapter in the first section on environmental entrepreneurship, is by Austin, Wood, and Leonard. These authors apply a contextual perspective to analyze opportunity recognition and the evolution of the Wilderness Safaris (WS) ecotourism enterprise operating in eight African countries. WS has grown to be one of the largest and most successful ecotourism enterprises internationally. The case illustrates the micro-foundations of social venture scaling, as the WS' innovative business model deviated from the prevailing tourism approach, first focusing on wildlife rather than the common hunting safaris. *Scalability* in this context was shifting from a value-destroying to value-preserving orientation, specifically, attracting a new market segment of customers who would be attracted not only for viewing wildlife but doing this in a way that would be distinctive from current practice and through a model that would enable different economic and conservation outcomes. The chapter illuminates a series of factors that contribute to positive environmental impact as well as financial profitability and sustainability.

A second set of chapters adjusts the focus from environmental ventures to more general social entrepreneurship. Chapter 8, by Sarma and Simmons, considers the role of societal attitudes about corporate social responsibility and its influence on the entry and performance of social ventures. Foundational to this study is its *contextuality*, specifically at the macro- and institutional level. A number of ecosystem factors affect the market entry decisions of individual entrepreneurs, but chief among them are the societal attitudes of the communities supporting the venture. The authors find a gap in the literature related to the lack of understanding about the effects of different societal attitudes on entrepreneurial behaviors of individuals. Drawing on Situationism Theory, the authors test for relationships between societal attitudes about corporate social responsibility and individual-level engagement in social entrepreneurship. They use a unique dataset for 26 countries built from the Global Entrepreneurship Monitor, Flash Eurobarometer, and World Bank Doing Business Reports to test their theory. Findings suggest the importance of contextuality in explaining social entrepreneurship, as being well informed is associated with the likelihood of individual-level engagement in social entrepreneurship. This has implications for research on stakeholder theory in entrepreneurship because community stakeholder attitudes will significantly affect entrepreneurial action.

Chapter 9, by Schaefer, Corner, and Kearins, examines social entrepreneurs' metacognition — awareness and regulation of thoughts and feelings — and its effect on the entrepreneurial process of social ventures. Specifically, how social entrepreneurs' environmental value creation supports positive socioeconomic change toward sustainability-as-flourishing, which is an inspirational vision of a possible future where humans, animals, and plants thrive indefinitely. The authors suggest that social entrepreneurship is a promising and useful business approach to bring about such change. They conduct an inductive design that yields patterns across five German cases of social entrepreneurship at different levels of analysis. Findings at the individual level reveal social entrepreneurs' metacognitive abilities facilitated awareness of discontent about social and environmental problems. Findings at the enterprise level show how social entrepreneurs resolved conflicts with recalcitrant external stakeholders by calming stakeholders' anxieties and negativity. At a societal level, social entrepreneurs were shown to co-create change by consciously investing in and empowering external stakeholders. This study emphasizes the importance of *stakeholder management* as it is the foundation for creating *civic wealth creation* (Lumpkin and Bacq, 2019), and thus a strong predictor of venture success. It offers insights to predict social entrepreneurs' behavior while considering their metacognition as a subjective dimension.

Chapter 10, by Tiwari, explores the prosocial personality traits, characteristics, and social entrepreneurial intentions. Specifically, the study identifies the role of empathy, moral obligation, and sense of responsibility — which are prosocial personality traits — on the formation of social entrepreneurial intentions among the students of a premier multi-campus technical university in India. It examines the *contextuality* of social entrepreneurial behavior through the lens of theory of planned behavior. Empathy was found to be the strongest affecting antecedent, followed by social responsibility. Findings of this research will be helpful in predicting how the prosocial personality traits affect the formation of the intention of Indian students. It also provides a platform to test the theory across various contexts in the developing world.

Chapter 11, by Liu, advances research on social entrepreneurship by examining the similarities and differences between social entrepreneurship and the social enterprise. Specifically, given that social entrepreneurship is in a pre-paradigmatic state, there may be a disconnect between fast-growing but early-stage researching and the proliferation of social enterprises. To bridge this possible disconnect, the author proposes a typology of social enterprise resource typology that includes strategies for social venturing. In particular, the chapter considers the antecedents to resource acquisition by social enterprises — considering the sources of and mechanisms for acquiring resources. This typology addresses the *contextuality* and *scalability* concerns that plague the social entrepreneurship research, as the resource acquisition mechanisms likely generalize across time and space. Importantly, the typology in this chapter integrates important research streams from traditional entrepreneurship research such as bricolage, adaptability, and commitment. Lastly, the chapter highlights the importance of institutional differences in explaining resource acquisition by social enterprises.

Finally, the last part of this edited book includes three chapters that explore research at the intersection of sustainability — social entrepreneurship and gender studies. Chapter 12, by Reilly, is an empirical study with a multidisciplinary focus, exploring the intersection of sustainability leadership, innovative corporate governance, and gender diversity. Specifically, it empirically tests sustainability leadership within 194 multinational enterprises based in the US using metrics compiled from corporate social responsibility (CSR) reports, 10-K documents, company websites, and the Global Reporting Initiative (GRI). Further, it explores firm engagement in sustainability reporting through CSR reports and GRI participation, as well as key elements of sustainability governance and leadership. The presence of sustainability leadership is critical to the *scalability* of sustainable venturing; the presence of board-level committees with specific mandates for sustainability oversight, the proportion of women chairs of those committees, the number of chief sustainability officers present across firms, and whether men or women hold those positions are critical in predicting the launch and survival of corporate sustainable ventures. In fact, the chapter makes several recommendations for firms positioning sustainability as an important element of their strategy, including benchmarking exemplar firms (i.e. ones that support gender diversity and sustainability initiatives) and creating career paths for high-potential women and minorities.

Chapter 13, by Garcia, examines the dearth of female-led entrepreneurial ventures, as women are less likely to engage in entrepreneurial activity. This chapter examines the role of language in promoting female-led entrepreneurship. Specifically, it uses a sample of entrepreneurs and non-entrepreneurs of both genders to examine how success in business is linguistically expressed. Webpages of university entrepreneurship programs are then assessed for gender-coding. Results suggest that gender is not the delineating factor in masculine and feminine approaches to entrepreneurship; instead a strong distinction exists between entrepreneurs, who have a more masculine viewpoint, and non-entrepreneurs, who have a balanced viewpoint. In addition, universities provide a more balanced gender approach in webpage text than in visuals.

Chapter 14, the final chapter written by Villegas-Arias, examines the death care industry and the unique services it provides to society. The industry offers services that often have deep ritualistic and religious overtones. Yet, the end product of these services produces hazardous anatomical waste, which has a negative impact on the earth's environment. The author first reviews the evolution of socio-cultural factors related to death services and then conducts a comparative case analysis of the industry in Spain, the US, and Columbia. The analysis includes the various traditional and sustainable business models applied in the industry, the implications of these various model, and the resources exploited in the environment. The chapter ends with brief recommendations for research, policy, and practice.

Overall, the 14 chapters contained in this volume represent the diversity of research examining the intersection of sustainable and social venturing. These chapters advance some outstanding scholarship, but more importantly, provide specific paths forward to address the three challenges facing the field — contextuality, scalability, and stakeholder management. We hope the entrepreneurial community benefits from these chapters as much as we enjoyed working with their respective authors. We are grateful to all of the contributors for their hard work, persistence, and passion.

References

Dean, T. J., & McMullen, J. S. (2007). Toward a theory of sustainable entrepreneurship: Reducing environmental degradation through entrepreneurial action. *Journal of Business Venturing*, **22**(1), 50–76.

Douglas, E., & Prentice, C. (2019). Innovation and profit motivations for social entrepreneurship: A fuzzy-set analysis. *Journal of Business Research*, **99**, 69–79.

Henrekson, M., & Sanandaji, T. (2011). The interaction of entrepreneurship and institutions. *Journal of institutional Economics*, **7**(1), 47–75.

Islam, S. M. (2020). Unintended consequences of scaling social impact through ecosystem growth strategy in social enterprise and social entrepreneurship. *Journal of Business Venturing Insights*, **13**, e00159.

Lounsbury, M., & Glynn, M. A. (2001). Cultural entrepreneurship: Stories, legitimacy, and the acquisition of resources. *Strategic Management Journal*, **22**(6–7), 545–564.

Lumpkin, G. T., Moss, T. W., Gras, D. M., Kato, S., & Amezcua, A. S. (2013). Entrepreneurial processes in social contexts: how are they different, if at all? *Small Business Economics*, **40**(3), 761–783.

Lumpkin, G. T., & Bacq, S. (2019). Civic wealth creation: A new view of stakeholder engagement and societal impact. *Academy of Management Perspectives*, **33**(4), 383–404.

Markman, G. D., Waldron, T. L., Gianiodis, P. T., & Espina, M. I. (2019). E Pluribus Unum: Impact entrepreneurship as a solution to grand challenges. *Academy of Management Perspectives*, **33**(4), 371–382.

Meek, W. R., Pacheco, D. F., & York, J. G. (2010). The impact of social norms on entrepreneurial action: Evidence from the environmental entrepreneurship context. *Journal of Business Venturing*, **25**(5), 493–509.

McMullen, J. S., & Bergman Jr, B. J. (2017). Social entrepreneurship and the development paradox of prosocial motivation: A cautionary tale. *Strategic Entrepreneurship Journal*, **11**(3), 243–270.

Muñoz, P., & Dimov, D. (2015). The call of the whole in understanding the development of sustainable ventures. *Journal of Business Venturing*, **30**(4), 632–654.

Nicholls, A. (2010). The legitimacy of social entrepreneurship: Reflexive isomorphism in a pre–paradigmatic field. *Entrepreneurship Theory and Practice*, **34**(4), 611–633.

Pathak, S., & Muralidharan, E. (2016). Informal institutions and their comparative influences on social and commercial entrepreneurship: The role of in-group collectivism and interpersonal trust. *Journal of Small Business Management*, **54**(sup1), 168–188.

Shepherd, D. A., & Patzelt, H. (2011). The new field of sustainable entrepreneurship: Studying entrepreneurial action linking "what is to be sustained" with "what is to be developed." *Entrepreneurship Theory and Practice*, **35**(1), 137–163.

Sud, M., VanSandt, C. V., & Baugous, A. M. (2009). Social entrepreneurship: The role of institutions. *Journal of Business Ethics*, **85**(1), 201–216.

Tang, Z., & Tang, J. (2012). Stakeholder–firm power difference, stakeholders' CSR orientation, and SMEs' environmental performance in China. *Journal of Business Venturing*, **27**(4), 436–455.

Part I
Sustainable Venturing Across Global Contexts

© 2022 World Scientific Publishing Company
https://doi.org/10.1142/9789811248863_0002

Chapter 2

Responding to Climate Change by Developing a Low-Carbon Economy Through Innovation: An Entrepreneurial Ecosystem Perspective

Richard T. Harrison

University of Edinburgh Business School, Edinburgh, UK

r.harrison@ed.ac.uk

Abstract

We examine the challenges of global warming as a "hyperobject," an entity of such vast temporal and spatial dimensions that it defeats traditional ideas of what a thing is in the first place, and discuss the implications of the development of a low-carbon economy. Against the background of the application of carbon capture, utilization and storage technologies (CCUS) in the Chinese iron and steel sector, we examine the dynamics and challenges of moving to a low-carbon economy as an entrepreneurial and innovation-based response to the global warming hyperobject. We argue that the development of a low-carbon economy requires a systematic and integrated approach to innovation and entrepreneurship, through the identification and exploitation of new opportunities, development of new business models, acquisition of resources and recognition and exploitation of interdependencies. We identify three non-mutually exclusive policy options: public–private partnerships in the development and deployment of new cost-effective low carbon solutions; strategic industry partnerships to mobilize resources and complementary strengths and link established players with entrepreneurial low carbon actors; and financial innovation to accelerate the development and deployment of novel technologies by creating a new asset class for low carbon and providing for the securitization of low-carbon project investments.

Keywords: Global warming; super-wicked problems; hyperobjects; low-carbon economy; carbon capture, utilization and storage (CCUS); China; entrepreneurship and innovation.

Only a god can save us now

Heidegger (1976)

We just don't know what sort of god

Morton (2013)

2.1. Introduction

Climate change, as a wicked problem (Lazarus, 2003; Grint, 2010; Levin *et al.*, 2012), represents a tragedy of the commons, as economic development based on fossil fuel use has generated benefits in the developed nations at the expense of global environmental destruction (Wright and Nyberg, 2019). As a threat to human well-being, climate change is a defining symptom of our times (Eraut and Segnit, 2006; Stafford-Smith *et al.*, 2011) and arguably the greatest challenge facing humanity (IPCC, 2014; Mann and Kemp, 2015; New *et al.*, 2011). In seeking to address this challenge, the scale of the response required is enormous (Wright and Nyberg, 2019): the radical decarbonizing of global energy, industrial, and transport systems; the mass replacement of oil, coal, and gas by renewables such as solar and wind; and the reinvention of established economic and political conventions (Angus, 2016; Klein, 2014; Wright and Nyberg, 2015).

In this chapter, we examine the nature and challenges of global warming/climate change as the basis for a discussion of the nature of the requirements for the development of a low-carbon economy. Against the background of a discussion of the development and application of carbon capture and storage technologies as applied to the iron and steel sector in China, we argue that the development of a low-carbon economy requires the adoption of a strategic leadership perspective to navigating the unknown (Beckert and Bronk, 2018) through the refinement of the skills of anticipating, challenging, interpreting, deciding, aligning, and learning. It also requires a systematic and integrated response to innovation and entrepreneurship, taking an integrated entrepreneurial ecosystems approach to the identification and exploitation of new opportunities through the development of new business models, acquisition of resources, and recognition and exploitation of interdependencies.

2.2. Climate Change, Global Warming, Super-Wicked Problems, and Hyperobjects

The scale of climate change, as a long-term phenomenon, is clearly demonstrated by the data on global warming (Figure 2.1): relative to baseline data for the period 1951–1980, the global annual mean land–ocean temperatures have been steadily increasing for over a century. Increasingly, global warming is being construed as more than a wicked problem — a problem that one can understand perfectly but for which there is no rational solution (Rittel and Webber, 1984). Rather, it is a super-wicked problem, i.e. a wicked problem "for which time is running out, for which there is no central authority, where those seeking the solution to it are also creating it, and where policies discount the future irrationally" (Morton, 2013: 135; Levin *et al.*, 2010).

As such, global warming is perhaps the most dramatic example of a "hyperobject," an entity of such vast temporal and spatial dimensions that it defeats traditional ideas of what a thing is in the first place. For Morton (2013), hyperobjects share a number of properties. They are *viscous*, in that they "stick" to beings that are involved with them; they are *non-local*, in that local manifestations of the hyperobject are not the hyperobject itself; their effects are demonstrated *interobjectively*, in that they can be detected in a space that comprises interrelationships among aesthetic properties of objects; and they are *futural*, in the sense that they represent the future beamed into the present and "scoop out the objectified now of

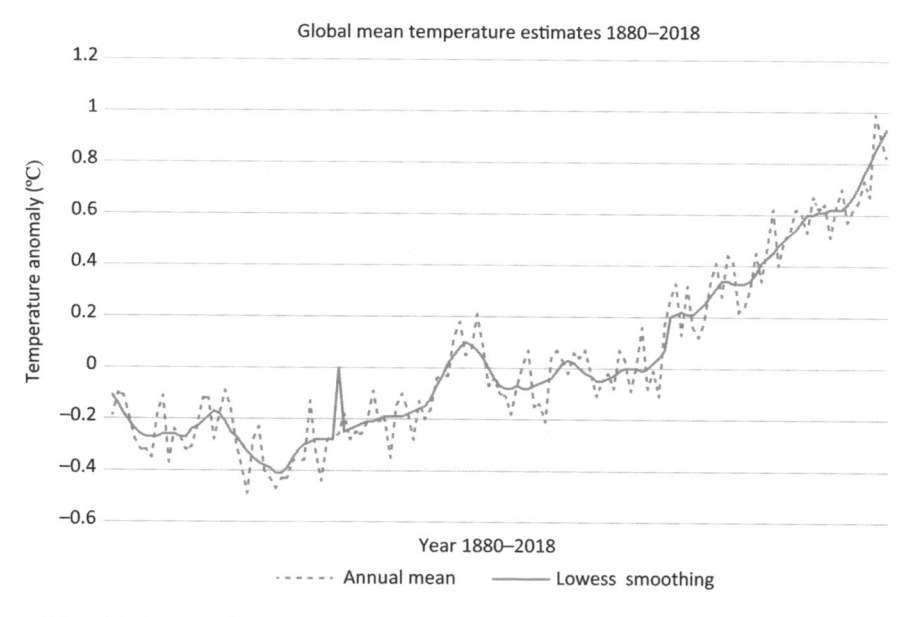

Figure 2.1. Global warming trends 1880–2018.
Source: NASA Godard Institute for Space Studies.

the present moment into a shifting uncertainty" (Morton, 2013: 122). As such, hyperobjects are not just collections, systems, or assemblages of other objects; neither are they figments of the (human) imagination. Rather, they are objects in their own right; they are real whether or not someone is thinking of them (Morton, 2013: 1–2).

As a contemporary "grand challenge" (George et al., 2016), the global warming/climate change hyperobject is social and political, not just a technical problem, which requires a focus on social and environmental concerns beyond profit maximization, where the demand for action is coming more from social movements than from government or business, and which poses clear ethical concerns and social justice imperatives (Wright and Nyberg, 2019). In this, the terminology used takes on instrumental significance: the beyond questioning of the reality of global warming and subsequent drastic climate change is accompanied by uncertainty over its precise scope. In calling this "climate change" rather than "global warming," there has been a significant impact on social and political discourse in two respects. First, there has been a decrease in appropriate levels of concern, a form of denial of the radical trauma of unprecedented global warming, and a cynical recourse to the argument that "climate has always been changing" as a justification for doing nothing (Morton, 2013, pp. 7–8).[1] Second, the emphasis on "climate change" rather than global warming draws attention to the search for scientific and technocratic solutions at the expense of an appropriate level of shock and anxiety about a specific and era-defining ecological trauma: given the unstoppable effects of global warming (Rockström et al., 2009), the 2009 UN Copenhagen Climate Change Conference identified mitigation and resilience as ways of providing strategies for dealing with these effects (Andersson, 2018). This includes a package of strategies in which contemporary markets and financial actors are centrally involved (Mirowski, 2014) in the production of legitimacy around the continuation of key types of economic activity. In so doing, climate change is being reimagined from an ecological disaster to a set of economic promises in a process of "eco-modernization" (Baker, 2007), an economization of the future through which market processes are used to reconcile conflicting future values (Andersson, 2018, p. 92).

We address some of these mitigation and resilience strategies below. The immediate context is that in a volatile, uncertain, complex, and ambiguous (VUCA) world (Bennett and Lemoine 2014; Elkington et al., 2017; Mack et al., 2016) characterized by super-wicked problems defined by their scale, complexity, and incomprehensibility (Brown et al., 2010), the global warming/climate change hyperobject is "too big." Such problems and environment are characterized by

---

[1] As Morton (2013: 8) argues, using *climate change* as a substitute for *global warming* is like using "cultural change" as a substitute for *Renaissance* or "change in living conditions" as a substitute for *iHolocaust*.

complex and systematic change that crosses traditional institutional and disciplinary boundaries (Kangas *et al.*, 2019): the atomization and specialization of academic knowledge, however, militate against the development of appropriate analysis of and response to these challenges. Specifically, in the crisis literature, there is event-focus but not process-orientation. This diverts attention from slow-burn gradual crises that are endemic and constitutive and unfold on a grand scale over a significant time period (e.g. global warming) to low-probability/unexpected/unpredictable but time-limited events with antecedents and consequences that can be measured (e.g. hurricanes, tsunamis, earthquakes) (O'Reilly *et al.*, 2015). There is, in other words, a focus on the epiphenomena, not the phenomenon itself (Williams *et al.*, 2017; Bazerman and Watkins, 2004; Weick *et al.*, 1999).

More often than not, couched in the apocalyptic language of abrupt, non-linear, and potentially calamitous ruptures (Steffen *et al.*, 2011), the advocates of immediate and far-reaching measures to address global warming as manifest in dramatic climate change emphasize the importance of leadership, reflected in resource capabilities, legitimacy, and credibility (Karlsson *et al.*, 2011), as critical to addressing the crisis of governance (Young *et al.*, 2007) facing the Earth's natural systems (Case *et al.*, 2015). Much of this debate is predicated on a "great man" perspective, relying on "the exceptional few" (Scheffer *et al.*, 2003, p. 493) or "moral entrepreneurs" (Harrison, 2020) responding entrepreneurially to catalyze opinion and drive effective change (Karlsson *et al.*, 2011). Given the failures to deliver on climate change policies, others have called for a more "grass-roots" perspective, grounded in sub-national, often local and community-based, initiatives (Ostrom, 2012) and incorporating a co-production (Jasanoff and Kim, 2015) approach to the involvement of multiple stakeholders, the generation of symbolic legitimacy, and the development of dominant images, or narratives (Beckert, 2016), of the future.

Alongside these wider studies, there has been an emerging mainstream interest in global warming, climate change, and the low-carbon economy in the organization and management studies (e.g. special issues of *Business and Society* [2012]; *Organization Studies* [2012]; *Organization* [2013]). This is reflected in studies of the role and functioning of carbon markets (Böhm *et al.*, 2012), mitigation strategies (Schwarhoff *et al.*, 2017), ethics (Le Menestrel *et al.*, 2002), corporate political strategy and engagement (Levy and Egan, 2003; Nyberg *et al.*, 2013), and the creation of new organizational landscapes (Okereke *et al.*, 2012; Wittneben *et al.*, 2012; Wright *et al.*, 2013). It has been accompanied by studies of, for example, policy entrepreneurship (Mintrom and Luetjens, 2017), institutional entrepreneurship (Wijen and Ansari, 2007), urban climate change entrepreneurs (Schroeder *et al.*, 2013), governance entrepreneurship (Boasson and Huiteman, 2017), and climate change entrepreneurship (Kaesehage *et al.*, 2019). This chapter adds to this literature by examining some of the dynamics and challenges of moving to a low-carbon economy as an entrepreneurial and innovation-based response to the global warming hyperobject (Autio and Webb, 2015).

2.3. Developing a Low-Carbon Economy

There are two aspects of hyperobjects in particular that make attempts to address them difficult. First, as one only sees pieces of a hyperobject at any given moment (their local manifestation), thinking of them is "intrinsically tricky" (Morton, 2013, p. 4). Second, they are time-stretched to a vast extent, making them, never mind solving them, almost impossible to hold in mind. Figure 2.1 shows global warming over a century. The 2015 Paris Agreement set out a global action plan to limit long-term global warming levels to below 2°C compared with pre-industrial levels and to reduce per capita global emissions by around 70% by 2050 (Liang et al., 2019). For individual humans, these timescales are beyond our direct experience — what was economy and society like in the late 1800s? What will the economy and society look like in the mid-21st century?[2] Historically, these questions are beyond our apperception; in terms of futurality, we may consider them with respect to the life experience and constraints/opportunities available to our children and grandchildren. However, it has been estimated that 75% of global warming effects will persist until 500 years from now, 25% of carbon compounds will still be in the atmosphere 30,000 years from now, and 7% of global warming effects will still be occurring 100,000 years from now (Archer, 2008) — what Morton (2013, pp. 58–59) refers to as the *horrifying*, the *terrifying*, and the *petrifying* timescales of global warming. In the face of these timescales, there is a radical asymmetry between the urgency, passion, and horror we feel when confronted with global warming and its consequences for life on Earth and our sense of cognitive weirdness in attempting to solve the problem: doing nothing is self-evidently not an option, but equally, possible actions (driving a Prius, using solar panels, extending nuclear power, overthrowing the state) seem inconsequential at the individual and the societal level in the face of the sheer numbers with which global warming is forced on us (Morton, 2013, p. 136).

Given this, the development of a low-carbon economy as a response to and mitigation of global warming poses a number of challenges and opportunities which require a systematic and integrated response. Until recently, and particularly in emerging economies, environmental degradation and climate change have been seen as part of the price necessarily paid to promote economic growth and alleviate poverty (Yang et al., 2016; Jiang et al., 2020). However, over the past decade in particular, carbon capture, utilization, and storage (CCUS) has attracted

---

[2]Here, we may look to science fiction, and especially "hard" science fiction based on exploring technological possibilities (Westfahl, 1996), as a potentially more insightful guide than conventional science-based scenario development and forecasting (Jameson, 2005).

increasing attention nationally and internationally as a priority technology for global warming mitigation and the move to a low-carbon economy (Schwarhoff et al., 2017) and is predicted to contribute up to 32% of carbon dioxide (CO_2) emission reductions by 2050 (Jiang et al., 2020). In parallel, CCUS moved to the center of climate policy debates and negotiations. Research on CCUS is developing on two fronts (Backstrand et al., 2011): (1) analyzing how societies are engaging with CCUS as a mitigation option and (2) exploring both basic technology developments for mitigation and how these are being aligned with the needs of the climate and environmental policy community (Schwarhoff et al., 2017). Cutting across both of these is a three-way focus on cross-cutting themes: first, the role of CCUS in the emergence of long-term climate and energy strategies; second, issues of regulation, policy instruments, and public acceptance; and third, the international politics of CCUS in developing countries. This chapter seeks to build on these developments by focusing in particular on the development and evaluation of innovative and sustainable technology and entrepreneurial business solutions for CCUS, and on the application of these in a major developing economy, namely China.

2.4. CCUS and the Iron and Steel Sector in China

The application of CCUS to large-scale industrial facilities, particularly to fossil fuel power generation and high-energy consuming industrial plants, is reflected in the construction of large-scale demonstration plants as a bridge to full commercial deployment (IEA, 2007, 2008a, 2008b, 2009), and the pace, orientation, and scale of CCUS deployment will depend not just on engineering advances and the evolution of comparative costs but also on the identification and development of innovative entrepreneurial solutions to the new opportunities that will arise (in addition to other issues, including agreement on international emissions abatement efforts, the rate of economic growth, attitudes toward risk, and the efficacy of policy and regulatory frameworks) (see Coninck et al., 2009a, 2009b; Gilotte and Bossetti, 2007; Shackley et al., 2009). The Global Carbon Capture and Storage Institute has identified 43 large CCUS projects worldwide as of 2018, of which 18 have entered commercial operation, 5 are under construction, and 20 are at different stages of deployment (Jia et al., 2019, p. 56). More recent data suggest that there are 23 identifiable CCUS projects in China, of which 15 are operational (5 pilot, 7 demonstration, and 3 large-scale), concentrated in the power generation, chemical (including fertilizer), and natural gas sectors (Table 2.1). However, there are very few CCUS projects in the iron and steel sector: Liang et al. (2019), for example, identify only two integrated large-scale iron/steel CCUS projects worldwide, and none in China.

Globally, the iron and steel industry is estimated to be responsible for around 5% of overall global CO_2 emissions (IEA, 2008): energy use in the global steel

Table 2.1. Key CCUS projects in China funded by the government or domestic companies.

Project	Year of operation	Main area	Scale	Capture capacity (Mt/year)	Status	Industry
Sinopec Zhongyuan Carbon Capture Utilization and Storage Pilot Project	2006	Capture and CO_2-EOR	Pilot	0.12	Operational	Chemical Production
Sinopec Shengli Oilfield Carbon Capture Utilization and Storage Pilot Project	2008	Capture and CO_2-EOR	Pilot	0.04	Operational	Natural Gas Processing
Huaneng Gaobeidian Power Plant Carbon Capture Pilot Project	2008	Capture and utilization	Pilot	0.003	Completed	Power Generation
Jilin Oil Field EOR Demonstration Project	2008	CO_2-EOR	Demonstration	0.10–0.35	Operational	Natural Gas Processing
Shanghai Shidongkou 2nd Power Plant Carbon Capture Demonstration Project	2009	Capture	Demonstration	0.10–0.12	Operational	Power Generation
Chongqing Hechuan Shuanghuai Power Plant CO_2 Capture Industrial Demonstration Project	2010	Capture and utilization	Demonstration	0.10	Operational	Power Generation
Sinopec Shengli Oilfield Carbon Capture Utilization and Storage Pilot Project	2010	Capture and CO_2-EOR	Pilot	0.03–0.04	Operational	Power Generation
Shenhua Group Ordos Carbon Capture and Storage (CCS) Demonstration Project	2011	Storage	Demonstration	0.1	Completed	Coal-to-liquids
ITRI Calcium Looping Pilot	2013	Capture (cement industry)	Pilot	1 tonne/hour	Operational	Cement Production
Daqing Oil Field EOR Demonstration Project	2014	CO_2-EOR	Demonstration	0.20	Operational	Chemical Production

Project	Year	Type	Scale	Size (Mt/yr)	Status	Industry
Karamay Dunhua Oil Technology CCUS EOR Project	2015	CO_2-EOR	Demonstration	0.10	Operational	Chemical Production
PetroChina Changqing Oil Field EOR CCUS	2017	CO_2-EOR	Demonstration	0.05–0.10	Operational	Coal-to-liquids
CNPC Jilin Oil Field CO_2-EOR	2018	Full-chain	Large-scale	0.60	Operational	Natural Gas Processing
Haifeng Carbon Capture Test Platform	2018	Capture	Large-scale	0.03	Operational	—
Beijing Shuangang LanzaTech New Energy Technology	2018	Utilization	Large-scale	0.09	Operational	Iron and Steel Production
Sinopec Qilu Petrochemical CCS	2019	Full-chain	Large-scale	0.40	In Construction	Chemical Production
Guohua Jinjie CCS Full Chain Demonstration	2019	Full-chain	Large-scale	0.15	Advanced Development	Power Generation
Yanchang Integrated CCUS Demonstration	2020–2021	Full-chain	Large-scale	0.41	In Construction	Chemical Production
Sinopec Eastern China CCS	2020s	Full-chain	Large-scale	0.50	Early Development	Fertilizer Production
Sinopec Shengli Power Plant CCS	2020s	Full-chain	Large-scale	1.00	Advanced Development	Power Generation
Shenhua Ningxia Coal-to-liquids Project	2020s	Full-chain	Large-scale	2.00	Early Development	Coal-to-liquids
China Resources Power (Haifeng) Integrated CCS Demonstration	2020s	Full-chain	Large-scale	1.00	Early Development	Power Generation
Huaneng GreenGen IGCC Large-scale System (Phase 3)	2020s	Full-chain	Large-scale	2.00	Early Development	Power Generation

Source: Jiang et al. (2020: 12)

industry accounted for 22% of total industrial energy use, and the sector's carbon emissions accounted for 31% of total industrial direct emissions (Jia *et al.*, 2019, p. 47). Steel production based on the blast furnace and basic oxygen furnace-based route is the main technology corresponding to the growth in global steel production, and this technology route is also the main source of CO_2 emissions in the iron and steel industry (Arasto *et al.*, 2013). The iron/steel sector is one of the most energy- and carbon-intensive sectors, producing a global average of around 1.3 tonnes of CO_2 per tonne of crude steel produced, representing around 7%–9% of direct carbon emissions from the use of fossil fuels; the most recent data for China suggests the production of around 2.18 tCO_2/t (Liang *et al.*, 2019, p. 3716). The magnitude of the task ahead, and the scale of the interventions necessary to deal with the global warming hyperobject, is exemplified by the European Union Roadmap for Low Carbon, which has set a target for 2050 of global emissions intensity of less than 0.2 tCO_2/t (EU Commission, 2011). The combination of this with continued increase in the global steel production, from 0.85 billion tons in 2000 to 1.8 billion tons in 2018, and the emergence of China as a dominant player in the global iron/steel industry (accounting for 12% of world steel production in 2000 and for 51% in 2018), represents a major challenge for the application of environmentally friendly and low-carbon technologies in the sector (Figure 2.2).

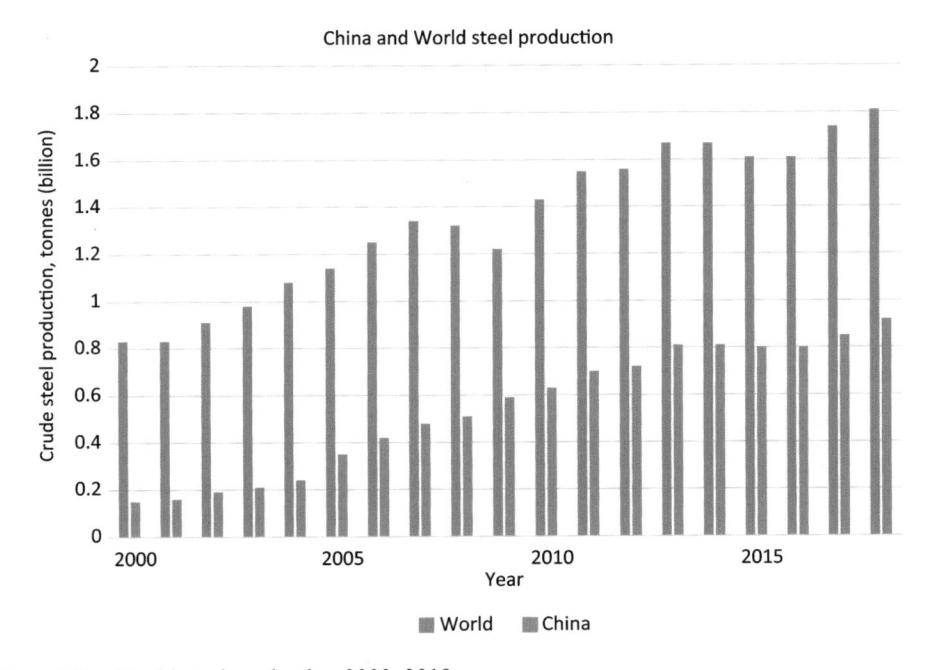

Figure 2.2. World steel production 2000–2018.
Source: World Steel Association (2020).

In China, the pursuit of CCUS in the foreseeable future is being driven by interest in technology R&D to underwrite a future export market. In this respect, the interests of China and all developed countries with regard to CCUS R&D may intersect based on interest in developed economies in facilitating the emergence of low-cost offset opportunities through the deployment of CCUS in developing countries including China (Wilson et al., 2011; Jaccard and Tu, 2011; Chen and Xu, 2010; Liu and Gallaher, 2009). There are a number of effective energy-saving technology options in the iron and steel industry to reduce carbon emissions (Napp et al., 2014): upgrading production systems to improve energy efficiency and waste energy utilization; improving the recovery rate of waste gas and waste heat; adopting improved production processes in rough steel production; and CCUS. At present, energy-saving is the most important carbon emission reduction technology in the current steel production process (Jia et al., 2019). However, the Asian Development Bank has suggested that new-build steel mills in China should be designed to be CCUS-ready (Liang et al., 2019: 3716).

There are a number of reasons for developing CCUS technologies. First, CCUS has a proportionately larger impact than other technologies in emissions reduction. Second, although they incur relatively high capital costs, first-of-a-kind CCUS technologies are competitive in terms of the cost of CO_2 avoided, as recent techno-economic appraisals have demonstrated (Liang et al., 2019). Third, without deployment of CCUS, the cost of limiting atmospheric CO_2 concentration to <450 ppm, necessary to meet global warming targets, has been estimated to be 138% higher than where CCUS is available (IPCC Fifth Assessment Report, 2014). Fourth, in only 36% of scenarios examined by IPCC could this climate change target be met without CCUS (and in industrial applications such as steel and cement, CCUS is currently the only means to make significant emissions reductions). Fifth, decarbonizing energy-intensive industries requires transformational changes to products and production processes — incremental innovation is not sufficient (Napp et al., 2014).

Accelerating the implementation and scale-up applications of CCUS to large-scale industrial plants, such as those in the iron/steel industry, requires four conditions to be met. First, the construction of pilot projects, large-scale demonstration plants, and first-of-a-kind commercial scale operations as a bridge to commercialization. Second, the grounding of policies in effective, long-term strategies as the basis for developing the understanding of and planning for CCUS and the transparency required for its further deployment. Third, political and regulatory alignment along multiple dimensions, including international agreement on emissions abatement, the efficacy of policy/regulatory efforts, economic growth rates, and risk attributes. Fourth, development of innovative entrepreneurial responses to new opportunities as they arise.

At present, relative to the position in many other countries, the policy and regulatory environment in China is not conducive to the rapid adoption of CCUS technologies — there is a lack of an enforceable legal framework, insufficient information for the operationalization of projects (although this is being addressed to some extent [Huang *et al.*, 2014; Liang *et al.*, 2019; Jia *et al.*, 2019]), weak market stimulus, and a lack of financial subsidies (Jiang *et al.*, 2020). As a result, there is a low participation rate of Chinese companies in CCUS and little public understanding of what the technology offers. Even if issues of wider policy and regulatory frameworks are addressed, the issues of weak market stimulus and a lack of financial subsidies remain significant constraints. In this context, a direct stimulus policy for CCUS, for example, in the form of a US-style tax credit, can go some way to offsetting the high capital cost of CCUS, which remains a major barrier to its implementation (Fan *et al.*, 2019). Furthermore, there is scope for institutional innovations to overcome these constraints. One such is the development of a Special Purpose Vehicle (SPV), modeled on examples from Norway and Japan (Liu *et al.*, 2020) but adapted to fit Chinese conditions (e.g. in the international comparators, the CCUS SPVs are directly government-funded, but the Chinese government will not own a SPV, which will therefore have to be set up by the steel plant owners). The SPV would own the assets of the CO_2 capture facilities at the steel plant and, as a legal entity and operational body of the CCUS project, can receive domestic financial and policy support from the government, sign contracts (e.g. for construction of the facilities and with transport and oil companies to deploy a full-chain CCUS project), enter into agreements with international and national research institutes to develop CCUS R&D, and attract CCUS-related private companies to participate in the project.

2.5. Responses and Requirements

Initiatives such as those discussed in Section 2.4, important though they are, are only partial solutions to the carbon emissions challenge of the steel industry in China in policy, technical and economic terms (Figure 2.3). If CCUS, as part of a wider move to a low-carbon economy as the basis for sustainable development and building an "ecological civilization" (Du *et al.*, 2020b), is to be effectively developed, a number of constraints will have to be overcome (Viebahn *et al.*, 2015). These include issues of technical, legal, economic, and social acceptance of CCUS in China; the non-existence of a nationwide CO_2 pricing structure, which challenges the economic viability of CCUS; further increases in the negative social and environmental effects of industrialization; and the resulting overall delayed commercial viability of CCUS initiatives. Addressing these issues within the context of continuing, if slowing, economic growth requires institutional change, in terms of cooperation between industry, government, and society, and systemic innovation and entrepreneurship, in terms of the development and application of the game-changing technologies that will underpin the transition to a low-carbon energy system.

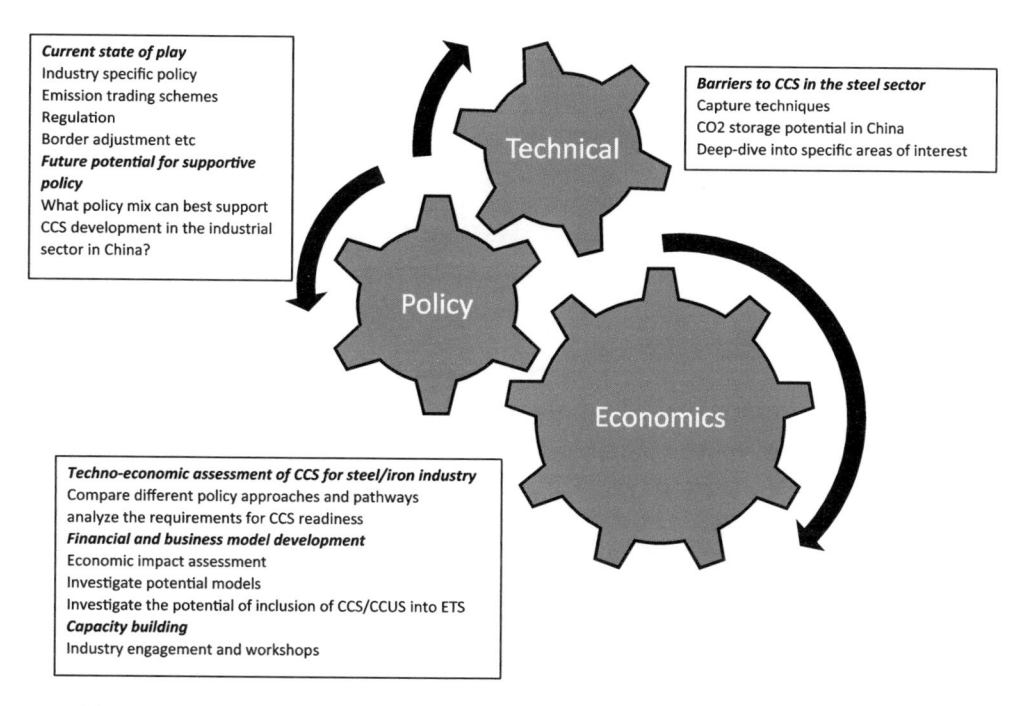

Figure 2.3. Deployment challenges for industrial carbon capture and storage in China.

Given the relatively low starting point, in terms of policy and practice in China, this requires addressing four key issues: the development of a comprehensive innovation system; adoption of an integrated systemic approach; enabling partnerships; and long-term funding commitments.

2.5.1. *Innovation system*

Central to the development of an effective CCUS implementation is an innovation strategy that bridges science and commercialization by coordinating the efforts and interests of multiple players (Figure 2.4). Loosely based on the triple helix model (Etzkowitz and Zhou, 2017), this links the interests of the scientific community across a wide range of disciplines (including engineering, geosciences, finance, accounting, politics, law, innovation, and entrepreneurship), the industry community (large companies, state-owned enterprises, new entrepreneurial businesses, and the finance industry), and the government community at intergovernmental, international, national, regional, and municipal levels. This innovation system perspective provides a focus on more than just the development of CCUS technologies. For example, notwithstanding the existing commitment to pilot and demonstration projects, there is still a pressing need for innovation in the accounting and measurement

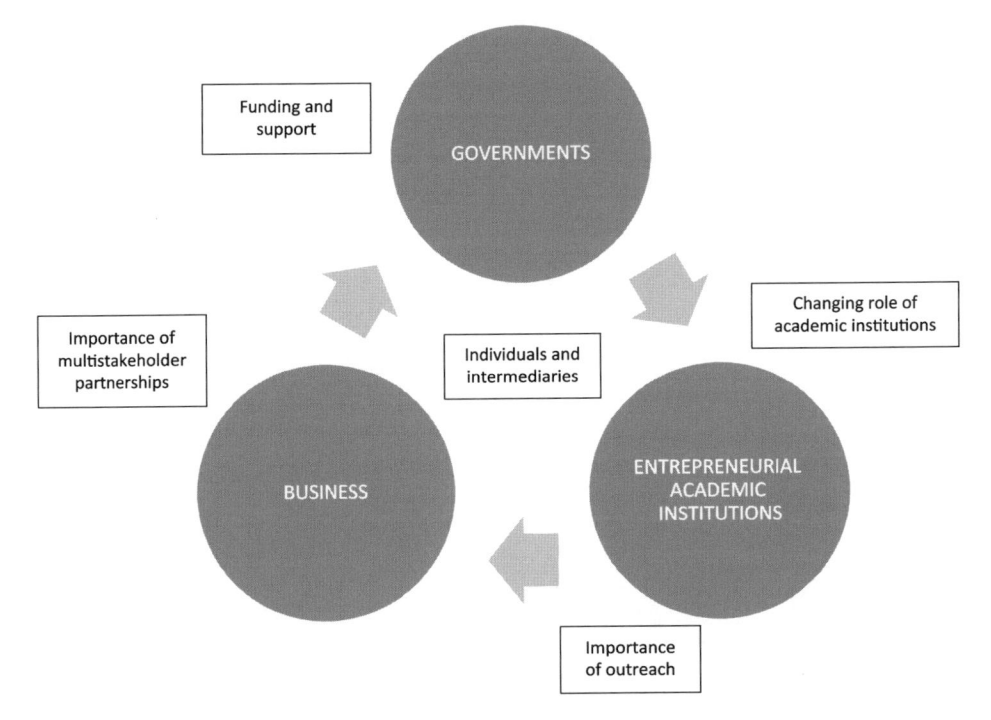

Figure 2.4. The innovation cycle.

practices to determine and quantify the benefits of CCUS technologies (Zakkour *et al.*, 2018). There is also a need to recognize that the CCUS investment sits within a wider low-carbon market in which low-carbon investment is moving downstream in response to the limits of the traditional venture capital/limited partner model (in terms of the appetite for funding large-scale investments and the long time-to-market cycles for low-carbon technologies) (Du *et al.*, 2020a; Viebahn *et al.*, 2015; Li *et al.*, 2016; Lacy *et al.*, 2020). From an entrepreneurial perspective, therefore, we can identify two types of challenges: (1) downstream, where the emerging focus is on the exploitation of technical innovations already in the market (and the key requirements are technology vetted, market-based product development and engineering) and (2) upstream, where the focus is increasingly on developing novel, next-generation, low-carbon technologies.

2.5.2. *Systemic approach*

A full value chain analysis of CCUS as part of the wider shift to a low-carbon economy also requires the application of integrative systemic thinking. This is reflected in the growing interest in entrepreneurial ecosystems, defined as all the independent actors and factors — including policy, finance, culture, support professions, human capital, and markets — that enable and constrain entrepreneurship in particular territories, sectors, and technologies (Stam and Van de Ven, 2019). While appealing, the entrepreneurial ecosystem metaphor is problematic in conceptual, theoretical, methodological, and empirical terms (Kuckertz, 2019). It is, for example, somewhat tautological (entrepreneurial ecosystems produce successful entrepreneurship and successful entrepreneurship is evidence of a strong entrepreneurial ecosystem) and taxonomic (offering no more than a "laundry list" of relevant factors without clear reasoning as to their cause and effect (Stam and Van de Ven, 2019).

Increasingly, however, there have been explicit attempts to develop a dynamic, process-oriented approach to entrepreneurial ecosystems, viewing them as complex systems of interactions and interdependencies that evolve over time (Spigel and Harrison, 2018). Specifically, there has been a renewed focus in recent discussions on the ecosystem (ecological system) as a co-evolutionary system based on four factors: institutional arrangements that legitimate, incentivize, and regulate entrepreneurial activity; public resource endowments on basic scientific knowledge, finance, and pools of competent labor; market demand of informed consumers; and proprietary business activities, including R&D, manufacturing, marketing, and distribution (Stam and Van de Ven, 2019, p. 4). Based on recent work in ecological economics (Kallis and Norgaard, 2010), the potential of a co-evolutionary framework for analyzing a transition to a low-carbon economy as a long-term industrial change has been suggested (Foxon, 2010). This recognizes that the co-evolution of technologies and institutions has led to the lock-in of high-carbon technological systems, and that the co-evolution of physical and social technologies and business strategies has generated significant material and welfare benefits for inhabitants of industrialized countries. It also provides a framework for developing more sustainable, low-carbon economies that could overcome this lock-in. The four systems — technologies, institutions, business strategies, and user practices — that comprise the ecological system (or "ecosystem") broadly correspond with those identified by Stam and Van de Van (2019) (Figure 2.5). Each functions as a separate system, and innovation and key events in the transition to a low-carbon economy can occur both within each system and through their interactions. At all levels, this framework allows for the role of agency, i.e. for actors to actively influence change, while acknowledging that the consequences of any individual action will always be uncertain, mediated as it is through interaction with existing structures (Foxon, 2010: 15). One of the benefits of this approach, beyond examination of the innovation and deployment of individual technologies, is the scope for improving the "understanding of the processes by which systemic change in systems of energy technologies and supporting institutions could occur" (Foxon, 2010, p. 17). While much of the low-carbon transition literature focuses on the role of entrepreneurial small actors (Autio and Webb, 2015), the co-evolutionary framework also accounts for lobbying efforts of

- Methods and designs for transforming matter, energy and information from one state to another in pursuit of a goal or goals

- Ways of structuring human interactions.

Technologies | Institutions

Ecological system

Business Strategies | User Practices

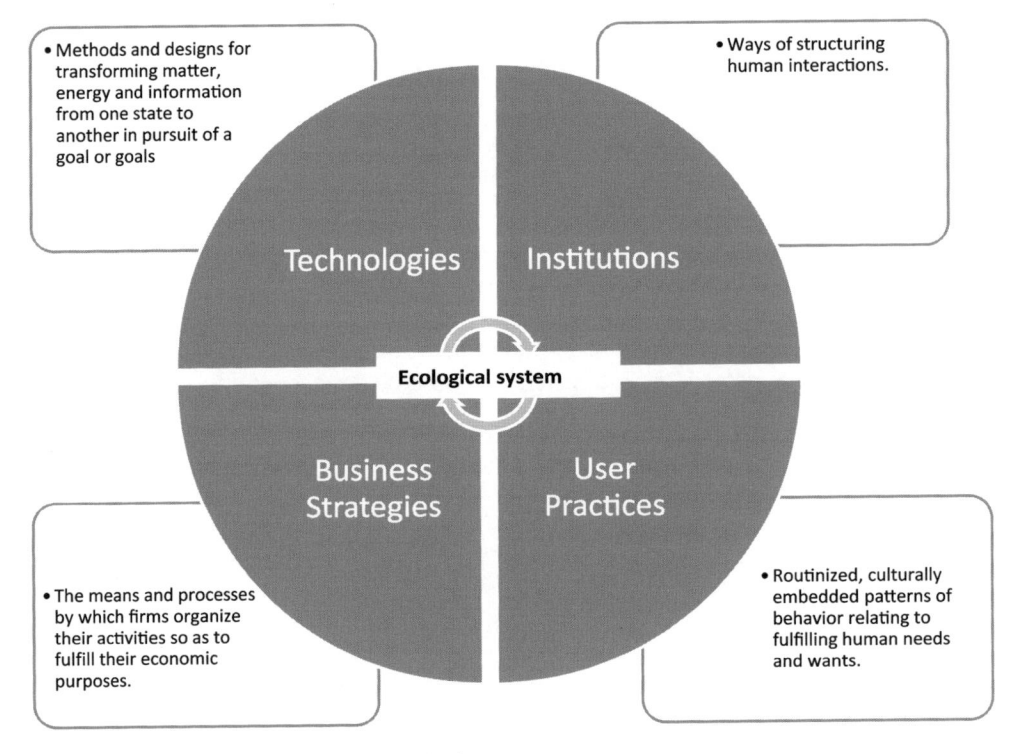

- The means and processes by which firms organize their activities so as to fulfill their economic purposes.

- Routinized, culturally embedded patterns of behavior relating to fulfilling human needs and wants.

Figure 2.5. The co-evolutionary ecological system.
Source: Based on Foxon (2010).

larger firms for greater government support for the demonstration of CCUS technologies, which "may be seen as attempting to enhance the replicative capacity of the current dominant regime, as these large-scale technologies require investment from the incumbent firms" (Foxon, 2010, pp. 17–18).

2.5.3. *Enabling partnerships*

The systemic entrepreneurial ecosystem/co-evolutionary ecological system approach highlights that innovation in addressing global warming and the emissions crisis through the development and deployment of new technologies is not just the domain of new firms and market entrants but can, and in some cases, must involve sometimes radical innovation by incumbent firms. Given the lock-in of current unsustainable systems of production and consumption at firm as well as system levels (Kallis and Norgaard, 2010), this will require the development of multifaceted enabling partnerships for innovation in new products, remediation technologies, and markets to identify and exploit new market opportunities and pursue high-potential/high R&D cost, next-generation, low-carbon innovative

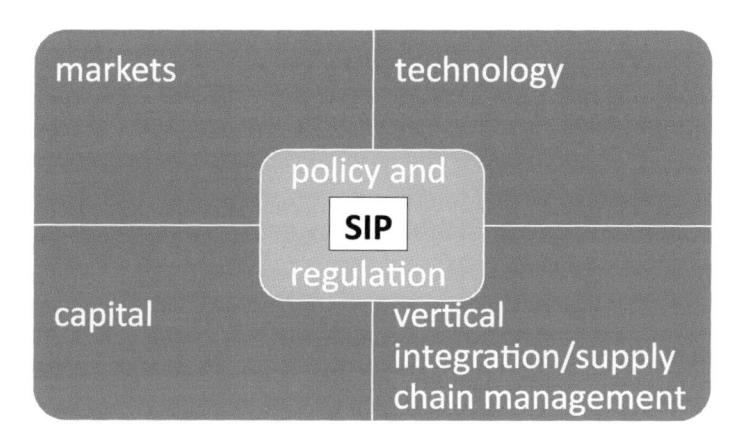

Figure 2.6. Strategic industry partnerships.
Source: Adapted from Murphy *et al.* (2014) and Adams *et al.* (2016).

supply and remediation technologies embodying sophisticated engineering, novel material combinations, and new hardware. The development of SPVs as a mechanism to take steel sector CCUS projects forward in the China context has already been referred to above as a viable means of mitigating risk; managing the design, implementation, and running of CCUS facilities; and mobilizing investment from private-sector players, state-owned enterprises, and municipal, regional, and national governments.

More generally, one potential opportunity for taking these projects forward — and for bridging resources and eliminating the investment gaps that characterize the sector (see below) — is the pursuit of large strategic industry partnerships (SIPs) (Figure 2.6). These can leverage a significant resource base, including marketing, capital, technical, manufacturing, and supply chain expertise, and as such SIPs can provide more industry stability, alignment, and commitment and can often provide more patient capital than other sources and vertically integrate needed resources (Adams *et al.*, 2016; Murphy *et al.*, 2014). Many of the benefits of SIPs are already being seen in areas such as clean energy, where the emergence of strategic investors and partners in recent years has opened up new business opportunities, and novel models for commercialization acceleration are emerging involving new alliances among clean energy companies, R&D support systems, and strategic customers, with firms from various industries, including real estate, finance, manufacturing, and transport, showing a growing interest (Adams *et al.*, 2016). The development of SPVs as discussed above provides one potential anchor point for the development of SIPs for CCUS that can offer a broad spectrum of resources that span a range of upstream and downstream needs (Li *et al.*, 2016; Lacy *et al.*, 2020). However, as with SPVs, and for CCUS investments in general (Jaing *et al.*, 2018), in order for strategic partnerships to be successful,

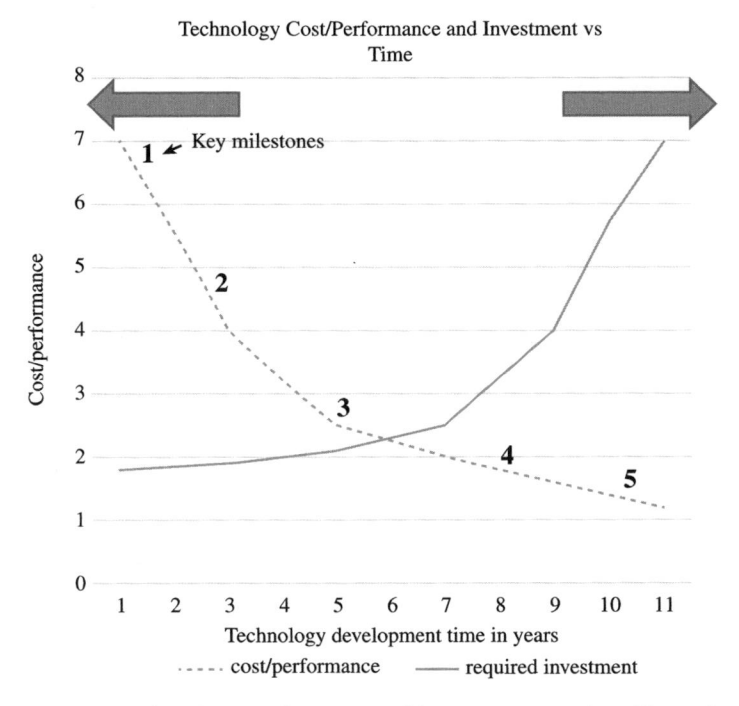

Figure 2.7. Technology/cost performance and investment over time: Key milestones.

SIPs will require good visibility of potential future revenue streams with a transparent path toward sustained profitability.

2.5.4. *Long-term funding*

In the evolution of new technologies, industries, and markets, it is the intersection of innovative policy, venture capital, and strategic corporate investment that facilitates sector-wide learning, with each component contributing critically to the advancement of innovation (Gompers and Lerner, 2001; Rai *et al.*, 2015). However, in the case of low-carbon development in general and CCUS in particular, the absence and/or underdevelopment of sources of capital investment is a major obstacle to technology and infrastructure development and scale-up (Lacy *et al.*, 2020; Wang *et al.*, 2018). In part, this reflects the nature of the technology (Figure 2.7). Over the medium to long term, the technology cost/performance relationship falls, albeit at a decreasing rate, while the investment requirements and risk increase over time as a project develops: a new technology may be shown to be feasible in the laboratory or prototype stage at relatively low cost and timescale, but may require 10 times the investment and significantly more time for a small pilot/demonstration project. The challenge is to demonstrate scalability at a given cost and performance level in a robust manufacturing/engineering environment, which might require up to 100 times the cost of a pilot plant (Jiang et al., 2018; Wang et al., 2018). In terms of the schematic in Figure 2.7, each development milestone (1 — basic technical feasibility; 2 — laboratory scale prototype; 3 — pilot prototype; 4 — scale-up/performance reliability demonstration; 5 — commercial plant) is associated with increased performance at lower per unit cost. It is also, however, associated with increased investment requirements to realize these cost/performance benefits.

This disjoint between cost/performance and investment requirements disincentivizes providers of both debt and equity finance (Jiang et al., 2018): given the limitations of current funding models, there is a need for new approaches to long-term finance to address the long time-to-market cycles for low-carbon technologies (Lacy et al., 2020). In so doing, two issues need to be addressed (Figure 2.8). First, there is a (early stage) technology "valley of death" as project promoters require capital to develop, test, and refine technologies and demonstrate technology and market viability. The long development and time-to-market horizons and high technical, market, and management risks at this stage — reflected in investor concerns about time-to-return, capital intensity, time-to-exit, and policy risks (Rai et al., 2015) — preclude the involvement of most market-based financiers (Jenkins and Mansur, 2011). Government general funding for R&D and, in the case of CCUS projects, "internal" funding from the companies themselves provides the feedstock for the technology development process as part of the corporate technology strategy. At present, there is little identifiable financing support for prototype/proof of concept work in CCUS technology development and implementation, which is likely to be covered by extensions of company R&D expenditure together with ad hoc local government funding. Funding for pilot and demonstration projects is actually or potentially available from commercial bank debt (although there is evidence to suggest that the banks have an appetite for no more than around 25% of overall project development costs — Jiang et al., 2018), co-financing by technology vendors (often to verify their own technologies) is increasing at the pilot stage, and new initiatives such as green finance from state-owned banks and climate loans and climate bonds are under consideration. In terms of public finance, local governments are more likely to offer support for CCUS development through both grants/direct investment and favorable tax treatment.

Second, there is a late-stage commercialization valley of death between the demonstration and commercialization stages of technology development. This reflects the preference of project financiers to finance commercial-scale projects for proven technologies with less risk. In situations where technologies have successfully completed the proof-of-concept phase and have moved into the pilot/demonstration phase, the large capital investment requirements for commercialization are beyond the risk tolerance and timelines of most debt and equity market participants, restricting the availability of funds to support the scale-up of these

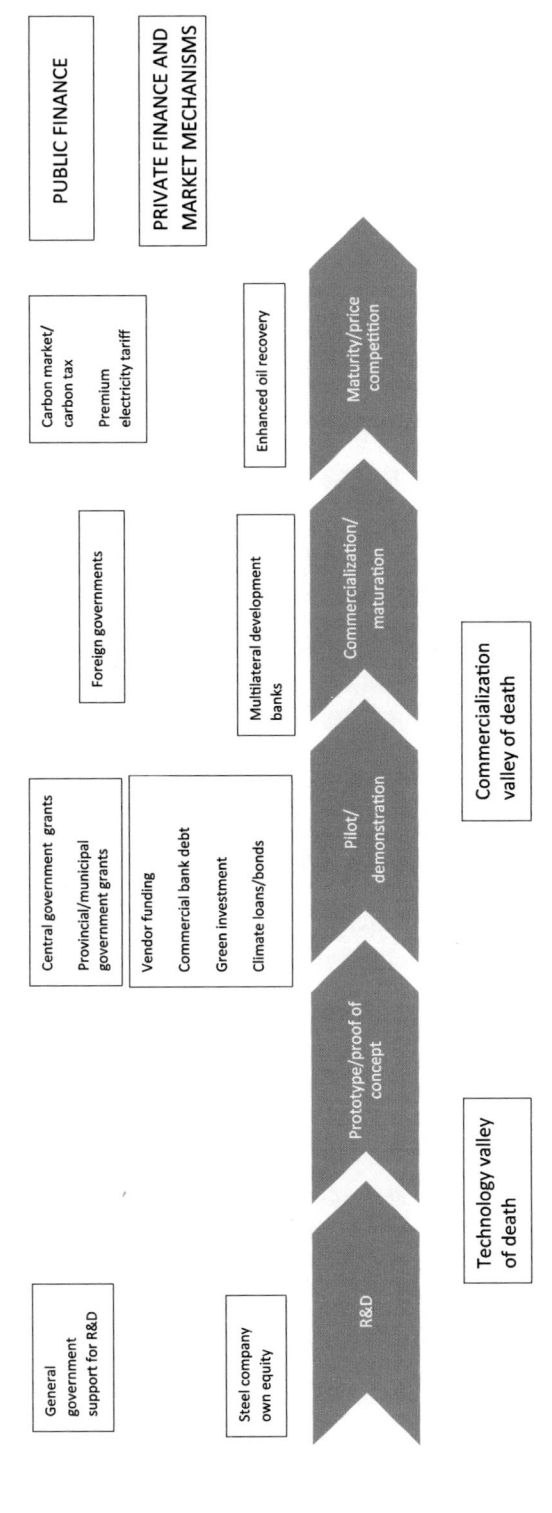

Figure 2.8. The CCUS innovation and technology development cycle and funding the "valleys of death."
Source: Developed from material in Jenkins and Mansur (2011) and Jiang *et al.* (2018).

projects. However, there is some emerging evidence to suggest that international climate change policy perspectives are increasingly recognizing the importance of Chinese CCUS projects to controlling carbon emissions and meeting greenhouse gas reduction targets, and international bilateral and multilateral scientific and industrial project collaborations may potentially provide support for CCUS commercialization in China (subject to the additional caveat that the involvement of international actors significantly increases the lead times for decisions and action) (Jiang *et al.*, 2018). Similarly, multilateral development banks and related funding sources (including Asian Development Bank, World Bank, UNFCCC Strategic Climate Fund, and OCGI's Mission Innovation) may play an increasing role in funding the commercialization of CCUS, and it is likely to be on the basis of part-funding in partnership with other players, re-emphasizing the importance of strategic partnership development discussed above. One of the key barriers to large-scale investment at the level required for CCUS technology deployment to make a significant contribution to addressing global warming is the uncertainty of returns on investment. In this respect, the use of market mechanisms such as enhanced oil recovery (where the use of near-to-exhaustion oil aquifers for CO_2 storage enables additional oil production), the development of a carbon market and carbon tax regimes, as in the piloting of emission trading schemes, and sector-specific premium electricity tariff regimes may help address the ongoing maturity of the technology (Jiang *et al.*, 2018).

In short, addressing the technology and commercialization valleys of death in the exploitation of CCUS and other technologies will require new and innovative public–private and strategic industry partnerships to develop and deploy new and effective Low carbon (LC) solutions, identify emerging entrepreneurial LC actors, and effectively mobilize an LC asset class to attract investors. These challenges require an integrated approach, not a piecemeal one: the development of an LC economy requires the development of a fully functioning innovation and entrepreneurial ecosystem that leverages all of the actors and resources to respond to this challenge.

2.6. Conclusion

To conclude, drawing on the example of CCUS technology development and adoption in China, as well as more general evidence on the low-carbon technology shift, as a response to the challenge of global warming, this chapter has identified a number of fundamental challenges to be conquered. Three non-mutually exclusive options for addressing these challenges from an integrative innovation and entrepreneurial ecosystems perspective have been developed: public–private partnerships in the development and deployment of new, cost-effective, low-carbon solutions; strategic industry partnerships to mobilize resources and complementary strengths and link established players with entrepreneurial low-carbon actors; and financial innovation to accelerate the development and deployment of novel technologies by creating a new asset class for low carbon and providing for the securitization of low-carbon project investments.

Certainly, there is a need for the development and deployment of new, breakthrough, low-carbon technologies. However, there is also a need to recognize that many of the technologies required by energy-intensive industries for a near-zero emissions world already exist at small scale (e.g. hydrogen-based steel making). The challenge is not one of invention but of scale and diffusion of innovation. In this, there is a need for not only new production processes but also new and upgraded infrastructure, which requires strategic investment from the "entrepreneurial state" (Mazzucato, 2013). Given that LC technologies carry high abatement costs, often significantly higher than the visible carbon price generated by emissions trading systems, there remains a need to scale-up from pilot projects, enable learning effects to reduce capital costs of highly capital-intensive investments, facilitate companies to maintain a high sustained cash flow, and develop the necessary network externalities (the infrastructure requirements of scaling-up) through focused policy intervention and support. As policy continues to evolve in this area, there are a number of possible policy instruments to support LC innovation in general and CCUS innovation in particular: public procurement (especially developmental procurement to support creating markets and diffusing new products and services); public–private partnerships (long-term contracts with public counterparties, e.g. capacity auctions or contracts for difference); industrial partnerships (long-term contracts with private counterparties, e.g. power purchase agreements); carbon cost integration mechanisms (regulatory flexibility through transferring a liability to reduce compliance costs and deploy LC investments); and a technology choice mechanism (transparent framework, set of criteria and choice mechanism to select technologies for financial support).

The complexity of these technology and policy development options reflects the underlying scale and complexity of the global warming/climate change issue they are designed to address. For the optimist, the technological, economic, and social elements that will permit the "great transformation" to a global low-carbon economy, comparable to the Neolithic Revolution or Industrial Revolution, are already emerging, albeit acknowledging that the speed and geographical spread of low-carbon dynamics remain insufficient to avoid dangerous climate change (Leggewie and Messner, 2012). More pessimistic commentators on the "great derangement" (Ghosh, 2016) point to our inability to understand the scale and violence of the environmental crisis and to the limits of present value systems — including the belief in continuous progress — that inhibit politicians, industrialists, and economists from moving toward a genuinely sustainable society (Montagnino, 2020). Accordingly, the detailed scientific analysis of the crisis continues to be rejected in favor of irrational short-term utilitarian behaviors that fundamentally prevent the change necessary for sustainable development (Montagnino, 2020).

However, science itself is increasingly contested, confronted by hypercomplex systems and super-wicked problems, and no longer provides an unequivocal or binding basis for action and policy design, especially in areas such as the economy (the core driver of climate change) where epistemic subjects and objects are entangled in a co-evolutionary relationship (Herrmann-Pilath, 2019) and subject to the unpredictable exigencies of life in the Anthropocene (Micky, 2016).

In many ways, this brings us back to where we started, to Morton's (2013) formulation of global warming as a hyperobject, an entity that is massively distributed in time and space relative to humans. In charting a path between the Scylla of optimism and the Charybdis of pessimism, the hyperobject frames and contextualizes the specific policies, actions, and initiatives discussed in this chapter. While not without criticism (Frantzen and Bjering, 2020), the global warming hyperobject is not something out there that I can avoid, ignore or circumvent but is something that I am embedded in. It "defines and affects my daily life, … how I understand myself … we find ourselves already enmeshed in an environment affected by oil spills, the burning of fossil fuels, and deforestation — all of which shape my existence in the deepest ways possible" (Daves, 2019, p. 526). In other words, we both define and are defined by them (Morton, 2013, p. 32). The implication is clear — if we wish to change "global warming," we need, in addition to the development of techno-scientific "solutions" such as CCUS, to change ourselves, to seek (as in the co-evolutionary perspective on systemic change discussed earlier) to realize our agentic potential within the multiplicitous structural constraints that govern us.

One of the challenges in responding to the threat and actuality of global warming is that hyperobjects are non-local and do not occupy a particular or easily identifiable region of space. There is, in other words, no single definable object to which we can point and say "there is global warming"; we can only ever catch glimpses or pieces of it at any given time (Morton, 2013, p. 70). As global warming "is something that takes place all over the world and is recorded only through data collected over a vast period of time, I do not see the entirety of it … and yet I find myself always already capturing glimpses of global warming through its effects on my daily activities. It is both there and not there" (Daves, 2019: 526). As we experience the hyperobject global warming and address it and its consequences through specific actions such as described in this chapter, we do so in the knowledge that "it is not the object in its entirety that is being experienced but always only the system of effects that make up the atmosphere, both literally and figuratively, of my environment" (Daves, 2019, p. 528).

The more we know about the global warming hyperobject in all its transdimensional greatness, the more we realize we are enmeshed in it and the more we know that we do not and cannot know of its vastness. Using reason, the endless parsing of the data and production of maps and charts is not wrong but is no longer adequate in dealing with objects this huge, this massively distributed, counterintuitive, and transdimensional: "we need to get out of the persuasion business and start getting into the magic business, or the catalysis business, or the magnetizing business or whatever you want to call it" (Morton, 2013, p. 181).

References

Adams, R., Pless, J., Arent, D. J., & Locklin, K. (2016). Accelerating clean energy commercialization. A strategic partnership approach (No. NREL/TP-6A60-65374). National Renewable Energy Lab (NREL), Golden, CO, USA.

Andersson, J. (2018). Arctic futures: Expectations, interests, claims, and the making of Arctic territory, In J. Beckert, and R. Bronk (eds.). *Uncertain Futures: Imaginaries, Narratives and Calculation in the Economy* (Oxford: Oxford University Press), pp. 83–101.

Angus, I. (2016). *Facing the Anthropocene: Fossil Capitalism and the Crisis of the Earth System* (New York: Monthly Review Press).

Arasto, A., Tsupari, E., Kärki, J., Sihvonen, M., & Lilja, J. (2013). Costs and potential of carbon capture and storage at an integrated steel mill. *Energy Procedia*, **37**, 7117–7124.

Archer, D. (2008). *The Long Thaw: How Humans are Changing the Next 100,000 Years of Earth's Climate* (Princeton, NJ: Princeton University Press).

Autio, E., & Webb, R. (2015). Engineering growth: Enabling world-class UK entrepreneurship in the low-carbon economy. Available at https://papers.ssrn.com/sol3/papers.cfm?abstract_id=2609726. Accessed on 26 August 2020.

Backstrand, K., Meadowcroft, J., & Oppenheimer, M. (2011). The politics and policy of carbon capture and storage: Framing an emergent technology. *Global Environmental Change*, **21**, 275–281.

Baker, S. (2007). Sustainable development as symbolic commitment: Declaratory politics and the seductive appeal of ecological modernization in the European Union, *Environmental Politics*, **16**, 297–317.

Bazerman, M. H., & Watkins, M. (2004). *Predictable Surprises: The Disasters You Should Have Seen Coming, and How to Prevent Them* (Boston, MA: Harvard Business Press).

Beckert, J. (2016). *Imagined Futures. Fictional Expectations and Capitalist Dynamics* (Cambridge MA: Harvard University Press).

Beckert, J., & Bronk, R. (eds.) (2018). *Uncertain Futures: Imaginaries, Narratives and Calculation in the Economy* (Oxford: Oxford University Press).

Bennett, N., & Lemoine, G. J. (2014). What VUCA really means for you? *Harvard Business Review*, **92**(1/2), 27.

Boasson, E. L., & Huitema, D. (2017). Climate governance entrepreneurship: Emerging findings and a new research agenda. *Environment and Planning C: Politics and Space*, **35**(8), 1343–1361.

Böhm, S., Misoczky, M. C., & Moog, S. (2012). Greening capitalism? A Marxist critique of carbon markets. *Organization Studies*, **33**, 1617–1638.

Brown, V. A., Harris, J. A., & Russell, J. Y. (eds.) (2010). *Tackling Wicked Problems Through the Transdisciplinary Imagination*, (London: Earthscan).

Business and Society (2012). Climate change: Challenging businesses, transforming politics. *Special Issue*, **51**, 7–210.

Case, P., Evans, L. S., Fabinyi, M., Cohen, P. J., Hicks, C. C., Rpideaux, M., & Mills, D. J. (2015). Rethinking environmental leadership: The social construction of leaders and leadership in discourses of ecological crisis, development, and conservation. *Leadership*, **11**, 396–423.

Chen, W., & Xu, R. (2010). Clean coal technology in China. *Energy Policy*, **38**, 2123–2130.

Coninck, H. D., Stephens, J. C., & Metz, B. (2009a). Global learning on carbon capture and storage: A call for strong international cooperation on CCS demonstration. *Energy Policy*, **37**, 2161–2165.

Coninck, H. D., Flach, T., Curnow, P., Richardson, P., Anderson, J., Shackley, S., Sigurthorsson, G., & Reiner, D. (2009b). The acceptability of CO_2 capture and storage (CCS) in Europe: An assessment of the key determining factors. Part 1. Scientific, technical and economic dimensions, *International Journal on Greenhouse Gas Control*, **3**, 333–343.

Daves, S. (2019). Hyletic phenomenology and hyperobjects. *Open Philosophy*, **2**(1), 525–538.

Du, X., Zhou, D., Chao, Q., Wen, Z., Huhe, T., & Liu, Q. (2020a). *Overview of Low-carbon Development* (Singapore: Springer).

Du, X., Zhou, D., Chao, Q., Wen, Z., Huhe, T., & Liu, Q. (eds.) (2020b). Strategic goals of low-carbon development in China, in *Overview of Low-Carbon Development* (Singapore: Springer). https://doi.org/10.1007/978-981-13-9250-4_6.

Elkington, R., van der Steege, M., Glick-Smith, J., & Moss Breen, J. (2017). *Visionary Leadership in a Turbulent World: Thriving in the New VUCA Context* (Bingley, England: Emerald Publishing).

Eraut, G., & Segnit, N. (2006). *Warm Words: How are We Telling the Climate Story and Can We Tell It Better?* (London: Institute for Public Policy Research).

Etzkowitz, H., & Zhou, C. (2017). *The Triple Helix: University–Industry–Government Innovation and Entrepreneurship*, (London: Routledge).

EU Commission (2011). *The Roadmap for Transforming the EU into a Competitive, Low-Carbon Economy By 2050* (Brussels: European Commission).

Fan, J.-L., Xu, M., Yang, I., Zhang, X., & Li, F. (2019). How can carbon capture, utilization and storage be incentivized in China? A perspective based on the 45Q tax credit provisions. *Energy Policy*, **132**, 1229–1240.

Foxon, T. J. (2010). A coevolutionary framework for analysing a transition to a sustainable low carbon economy. *Ecological Economics*, **70**, 2258–2267.

Frantzen, M. K., & Bjering, J. (2020). Ecology, capitalism and waste: From hyperobject to hyperabject, *Theory, Culture & Society*, **37**, 87–109.

George, G., Howard-Grenville, J., Joshi, A., & Tihanyi, L. (2016). Understanding and tackling societal grand challenges through management research. *Academy of Management Journal*, **59**, 1880–1895.

Ghosh, A. (2016). *The Great Derangement: Climate Change and the Unthinkable* (Chicago: University of Chicago Press).

Gilotte, L., & Bossetti, V. (2007). The impact of carbon capture and storage on overall mitigation policy. *Climate Policy*, **7**, 3–12.

Gompers, P. A., & Lerner, J. (2001). *The Money of Invention* (Boston: Harvard Business School Press).

Grint, K. (2010). Wicked problems and clumsy solutions: The role of leadership. In Brookes, S. and Grint, K. (eds). *The New Public Leadership Challenge* (London: Palgrave Macmillan), pp. 169–186.

Harrison, R. T. (2020). The moral entrepreneur in social and sustainable entrepreneurship. Paper presented to *Sustainability, Ethics and Entrepreneurship Conference*, Puerto Rico, February 2020.

Herrmann-Pillath, C. (2020). The art of co-creation: An intervention in the philosophy of ecological economics. *Ecological Economics*, **169**, 106526.

Huang, Y., Guo, H., Liao, C., Zhao, D., Zhou, D., Liu, Q., Li, X., Liang, X., & Li, J. (2014). Study of a roadmap for carbon capture and storage development in Guangdong Province, China. *International Journal of Sustainable Energy*, **35**, 1–17.

IEA (2007). Near term opportunity for carbon dioxide capture and storage. Summary Report of Global Assessment Workshop, Paris.

IEA (2008a). *CO2 Capture and Storage, A Key Carbon Abatement Option* (Paris: OECD/IEA).

IEA (2008b). *Summary Document: International Energy Agency's Launch of International CCS Regulators's Meeting* (Paris: IEA). Available at: http://www.iea.org/Textbase/work/2008/ccs/summary.pdf.

IEA (2009). *Technology Roadmap Carbon Capture and Storage* (Paris: OECD/IEA).

IPCC (2014). *Climate Change 2013: The Physical Science Basis, Fifth Assessment Report of the International Panel on Climate Change* (Cambridge, MA: Cambridge University Press).

Jaccard, M., & Tu, J. (2011). Show some enthusiasm but not too much: CCS development prospects in China. *Global Environmental Change*, **21**(2), 402–412.

Jameson, F. (2005). *Archaeologies of the Future: The Desire Called Utopia and Other Science Fictions* (London: Verso).

Jasanoff, S., & Kim, S.-H. (eds.) (2015). *Dreamscapes of Modernity: Sociotechnical Imaginaries and the Fabrication of Power* (Chicago, IL: University of Chicago Press).

Jenkins, J., & Mansur, S. (2011). Bridging the clean energy valleys of death: Helping American entrepreneurs meet the nation's energy innovation imperative. Oakland, CA: Breakthrough Institute. https://thebreakthrough.org/articles/bridging-the-clean-energy-vall.

Jia, F., He, J., Yang, J., Liang, X., Wang, L., Cao, J., Chen, P., Wu, S., Liu, M., Zhang, Y., Zhang, Q., Guan, D., & Fu, X. (2019). 2019 Climate Investment and Finance Case Studies: Research Report, Center for Environmental Education and Communications of Ministry of Ecology and Environment, Beijing.

Jiang, M., Liang, X., Liu, Q., Liu, C., & Chen, X. (2018). Manage multiple policy instruments in financing CCUS case study of Guangdong, *14th Greenhouse Gas Control Technologies Conference,* Melbourne 21–26 October (GHGT-14). Available at: https://ssrn.com/abstract=3365787.

Jiang, K., Ashworth, P., Zhang, S., Liang, X., Sun, Y., & Angus, D. (2020). China's carbon capture, utilization and storage (CCUS) policy: A critical review. *Renewable and Sustainable Energy Reviews*, **119**. https://doi.org/10.1016/j.rser.2019.109601.

Kaesehage, K., Leyshon, M., Ferns, G., & Leyshon, C. (2019). Seriously personal: The reasons that motivate entrepreneurs to address climate change. *Journal of Business Ethics*, **157**(4), 1091–1109.

Kallis, G., & Norgaard, R. (2010). Coevolutionary ecological economics. *Ecological Economics*, **69**, 690–699.

Kangas, A., Kujala, J., Lönnqvist, A., Heikkinen, A., & Laihonen, H. (2019). Introduction: Leadership for dealing with complex changes, *Leading Change in a Complex World: Transdisciplinary Perspectives*. Tampere, Finlamd, Tampere University Press, 7–23.

Karlsson, C., Parker, C., Hjerpe, M., & Linnér, B.-O. (2011). Looking for leaders: Perceptions of climate change leadership among climate change negotiation participants. *Global Environmental Politics*, **11**, 89–107.

Klein, N. (2014). *This Changes Everything. Capitalism vs the Climate* (New York: Simon & Schuster).

Kuckertz, A. (2019). Let's take the entrepreneurial ecosystem metaphor seriously! *Journal of Business Venturing Insights*, **11**, e00124.

Lacy, P., Long, J., & Spindler, W. (eds.) (2020). Oil & Gas (O&G) Industry Profile, in *The Circular Economy Handbook* (London: Palgrave Macmillan), pp. 99–108.

Lazarus, R. J. (2009). Super wicked problems and climate change: Restraining the present to liberate the future. *Cornell Law Review*, **94**, 1155–1234.

Le Menestrel, M., van den Hove, S., & de Bettignies, H. C. (2002). Processes and consequences in business ethical dilemmas: The oil industry and climate change. *Journal of Business Ethics*, **41**, 251–266.

Levin, K., Cashore, B., Bernstein, S., & Auld, G. (2010). Playing it forward: Path dependency, progressive incrementalism, and the "super wicked problem" of global climate change. Available at: https://iopscience.iop.org/article/10.1088/1755-1307/6/50/502002/meta. Accessed 3 March 2021.

Levin, K., Cashore, B., Bernstein, S., & Auld, G. (2012). Overcoming the tragedy of super wicked problems: Constraining our future selves to ameliorate global climate change. *Policy Sciences*, **45**, 123–152.

Levy, D. L., & Egan, D. (2003). A neo-Gramscian approach to corporate political strategy: Conflict and accommodation in the climate change negotiations. *Journal of Management Studies*, **40**, 803–830.

Leggewie, C., & Messner, D. (2012). The low-carbon transformation—A social science perspective. *Journal of Renewable and Sustainable Energy*, **4**(4), 041404.

Li, Q., Wei, Y. N., & Chen, Z. A. (2016). Water-CCUS nexus: challenges and opportunities of China's coal chemical industry. *Clean Technologies and Environmental Policy*, **18**(3), 775–786.

Liang, X., Lin, Q., Muslemani, H., Lei, M., Liu, Q., Li, J., Wu, A., Liu, M., & Ascui, F. (2019). Assessing the economics of CO_2 capture in China's iron/steel sector: A case study. *Energy Procedia*, **158**, 3715–3722.

Liu, H., & Gallager, K. S. (2009). Driving carbon capture and storage forward in China. GHGT-9. *Energy Procedia*, **1**, 3877–3844.

Liu, M., Liang, X., Lin, Q., Harrison, R., & Muslemani, H. (2020). Developing a special purpose vehicle to support CCS in the steel industry, Working Paper, University of Edinburgh Business School.

Mack, O., Khare, A., Krämer, A., & Burgartz, T. (2016). *Managing in a VUCA World* (Heidelberg, Germany: Springer).

Mann, M. E., & Kump, L. R. (2015). *Dire Predictions: Understanding Climate Change* (New York: DK Publishing).

Mazzucato, M. (2013). *The Entrepreneurial State* (London: Anthem Press).

Micky, S. (2016). *Coexistentialism and the Unbearable Intimacy of Ecological Emergency* (New York: Lexington Books).

Mintrom, M., & Luetjens, J. (2017). Policy entrepreneurs and problem framing: The case of climate change. *Environment and Planning C: Politics and Space*, **35**(8), 1362–1377.

Mirowski, P. (2014). *Never Let A Serious Economic Crisis Go To Waste: How Neoliberalism Survived the Financial Meltdown* (London: Verso).

Montagnino, F. M. (2020). Beyond the "great derangement": Will the humanities lead ecological transition? In Formica, P. and Edmondson, J. (eds.). *Innovation and the Arts: The Value of Humanities Studies for Business* (Emerald Publishing Limited), pp. 111–142.

Morton, T. (2013). *Hyperobjects. Philosophy and Ecology After the End of the World* (Minneapolis MN: University of Minnesota Press).

Murphy, L M., Ondecheck, R, Bracho R, & McKenna, J. (2014). Clean Energy — Bridging to Commercialization: The Key Potential Role of Large Strategic Industry Partners. FEEM Working Paper No. 092.2014. http://dx.doi.org/10.2139/ssrn.2520343.

Napp, T. A., Gambhir, A., Hills, T.P., Florin, N. and Fennell, P. S. (2014) A review of the technologies, economics and policy instruments for decarbonising energy-intensive manufacturing industries. *Renewable and Sustainable Energy Review*, **30**, 616–640.

NASA Godard Institute for Space Studies (2020). Global annual mean surface air temperature change. Available at: https://data.giss.nasa.gov/gistemp/graphs_v3/ (accessed 26 August 2020).

New, M., Liverman, D., Schroeder, H., & Anderson, K. (2011). Four degrees and beyond: The potential for a global temperature increase of four degrees and its implications.

Philosophical Transactions of the Royal Society A: Mathematical, Physical and Engineering Sciences, 369, 6–19.

Nyberg, D., Spicer, A., & Wright, C. (2013). Incorporating citizens: Corporate political engagement with climate change in Australia. *Organization*, 20, 433–453.

O'Reilly, D., Leitch, C. M., Harrison, R. T., & Lamprou, E. (2015). Leadership, authority and crisis: Reflections and future directions. *Leadership*, 11, 489–499.

Okereke, C., Wittenben, B., & Bowen, F. (2012). Climate change: Challenging business, transforming politics. *Business and Society*, 51, 7–30.

Organization (2013). Future imaginings: Organizing in response to climate change. *Special Issue*, 20, 647–776.

Organization Studies (2012). Climate change and the emergence of new organizational landscapes. *Special Issue*, 33, 1431–1638.

Ostrom, E. (2012). Green from the grassroots. *Project Syndicate*. Available at http://www.Project-syndicate.org/commentary/green-from-the-grassroots (accessed 27 June 2019).

Rai, V., Funkhouser, E., Udwin, T., & Livingston, D. (2015). Venture capital in clean energy innovation finance: Insights from the U.S. market during 2005–2014, *Social Science Research Network* (October). http://dx.doi.org/10.2139/ssrn.2676216.

Rittel, H., & Webber, M. (1984). Dilemmas in a general theory of planning, In Cross, N. (ed.), *Developments in Design Methodology* (Chichester, UK: Wiley), pp. 155–169.

Rockström, J., Steffen, W., Noone, K., Persson, Å., Chapin III, F. S., Lambin, E. F., Lenton, T. M., Scheffer, M., Folke, C., Schellnhuber, H. J., Nykvist, B., de Wit, C. A., Hughes, T., van der Leeuw, S., Rodhe, H., Sörlin, S., Snyder, P. K., Costanza, R., Svedin, U., Falkenmark, M., Karlberg, L., Corell, R. W., Fabry, V. J., Hansen, J., Walker, B., Liverman, D., Richardson, K., Crutzen, P., & Foley, J. A. (2009). A safe operating space for humanity. *Nature*, **461**(7263), 472–475.

Scheffer, M., Westley, F., & Brock, W. (2003). Slow response of societies to new problems: Causes and costs. *Ecosystems*, 6, 493–502.

Schroeder, H., Burch, S., & Rayner, S. (2013). Novel multi-sector networks and entrepreneurship in climate change governance. *Environment and Planning C: Government and Policy*, 31, 761–768.

Schwarhoff, G., Kornak, U., Lessmann, K., & Pahle, M. (2017). Leadership in climate change mitigation: Consequences and incentives. *Journal of Economic Surveys*, 32, 491–517.

Shackley, S., Reiner, D., Upham, P., Coninck, H. D., Sigurthorsson, G., & Anderson, J. (2009). The acceptability of CO_2 capture and storage (CCS) in Europe: An assessment of key determinant factors. Part 2. The social acceptability of CCS and the wider impacts and repercussions of its implementation. *International Journal of Greenhouse Gas Control*, 2, 344–356.

Spigel, B., & Harrison, R. (2018). Toward a process theory of entrepreneurial ecosystems. *Strategic Entrepreneurship Journal*, 12(1), 151–168.

Stam, E., & van de Van (2019) Entrepreneurial system elements. *Small Business Economics*, https://doi.org/10.1007/s11187-019-00270-6.

Stafford-Smith, M., Horrocks, L., Harvey, A. et al. (2011). Rethinking adaptation for a 4°C world. *Philosophical Transactions of the Royal Society*, **369**, 196–216.

Steffen, W., Persson, A., Deutsch, L. et al. (2011). The Anthropocene: From global change to planetary stewardship. *Ambio*, **40**, 739–761.

Viebahn, P., Vallentin, D., & Höller, S. (2015). Prospects of carbon capture and storage (CCS) in China's power sector–An integrated assessment. *Applied Energy*, **157**, 229–244.

Wang, H., Zhong, P., Zhang, X., Diao, Y., Consoli, C., & Yang, Y. (2018). Carbon Sequestration Leadership Forum (CSLF) Capacity Building Program: Exploring CCUS Financing Roadmap for China. In *14th Greenhouse Gas Control Technologies Conference* Melbourne 21–26 October (GHGT-14). Available at: https://ssrn.com/abstract=3365613.

Weick, K. E., Sutcliffe, K. M., & Obstfeld, D. (1999). Organizing for high reliability: Processes of collective mindfulness, In B. M. Staw and R. I. Sutton (eds.), *Research in Organizational Behavior* (Greenwich, CT: JAI Press), pp. 81–123.

Westfahl, G. (1996). *Cosmic Engineers: A Study of Hard Science Fiction* (Westport, CT: Greenwood Press).

Wijen, F., & Ansari, S. (2007). Overcoming inaction through collective institutional entrepreneurship: Insights from regime theory. *Organization Studies*, **28**(7), 1079–1100.

Williams, T. A., Gruber, D. A., Sutcliffe, K. M., Shepherd, D. A., & Zhao, E. Y. (2017). Organizational response to adversity: Fusing crisis management and resilience research streams, *Academy of Management Annals*, **11**(2), 733–769. doi:10.5465/annals.2015.0134

Wilson, E., Zhang, D., & Zheng, L. (2011). The socio-political context for deploying CCS in China and the U.S. *Global Environmental Change*, **21**(2), 324–335.

Wittneben, B. B. F., Okereke, C., Banerjee, B. et al. (2012). Climate change and the emergence of new organisational landscapes. *Organization Studies*, **33**, 1431–1450.

World Steel Association (2020). Available at: https://www.worldsteel.org/steel-by-topic/statistics/steel-data-viewer/P1_crude_steel_total/CHN/WORLD_ALL (accessed 30 August 2020).

Wright, C., & Nyberg, D. (2015). *Climate Change, Capitalism and Corporations: Processes of Creative Self-destruction* (Cambridge, MA: Cambridge University Press).

Wright, C., & Nyberg, D. (2019). Climate change and social innovation, In G. George, T. Baker, P. Tracey, and H. Joshi (eds.), *Handbook of Inclusive Innovation. The Role of Organizations, Markets and Communities in Social Innovation*, (Cheltenham: Edward Elgar), pp. 47–60.

Wright, C., Nyberg, D., De Cock, C. et al. (2013). Future imaginings: Organizing in response to climate change. *Organization*, **20**, 647–658.

Yang, L., Zhang, X., & McAlinden, K. J. (2016). The effect of trust on people's acceptance of CCS (carbon capture and storage) technologies: Evidence from a survey in the People's Republic of China. *Energy*, **96**, 69–79.

Young, O. R., Osherenko, G., Ogden, J. et al. (2007). Solving the crisis in ocean governance: Place-based management of marine ecosystems. *Environment*, **49**, 21–32.

Zakkour, P., Cook, G., Akai, M., Itaoka, K., Chae, S. O., & Kemper, J. (2018). Towards greenhouse gas accounting guidelines for carbon dioxide capture and utilisation technologies, *14th Greenhouse Gas Control Technologies Conference*, Melbourne. Available at: https://www.researchgate.net/profile/Paul_Zakkour/publication/336114875_Towards_Greenhouse_Gas_Accounting_Guidelines_for_Carbon_Dioxide_Capture_and_Utilisation_Technologies/links/5d8eff0992851c33e9430435/Towards-Greenhouse-Gas-Accounting-Guidelines-for-Carbon-Dioxide-Capture-and-Utilisation-Technologies.pdf (Accessed September 1, 2020).

© 2022 World Scientific Publishing Company
https://doi.org/10.1142/9789811248863_0003

Chapter 3

Supply Chain Climate Change Mitigation Strategies and Business Models

Thomas B. Long[*,†,§] and William Young[‡,¶]

[†]*Centre for Sustainable Entrepreneurship, University of Groningen/Campus Fryslân, The Netherlands*

[‡]*Sustainable Research Institute, University of Leeds, Leeds, United Kingdom*

[§]*t.b.long@rug.nl*

[¶]*C.W.Yound@leeds.ac.uk*

Abstract

The supply chains of large organizations contain a high proportion of the total greenhouse gas (GHG) emissions associated with products and services. This has implications for climate mitigation and the sustainability strategies of "focal" firms that lead and control supply chains. This research explores the objectives and activities involved in managing supply chain GHG emissions, and how these impact underlying business models and sustainable value creation opportunities.

An exploratory qualitative approach is undertaken, involving interviews with 31 expert informants, through two phases. Of interviewees, 20 are from focal organizations in the public or private sectors. This data is coded to identify specific supply chain GHG emission management activities and, separately, the objectives they fulfil. Matrices are used to link activities with the different supply chain GHG emission management objectives.

The results show that the most direct way to achieve supply chain GHG emission reductions is through design changes. It is also found that current

---
[*]Corresponding author.

strategies often miss sustainable value-creating opportunities. Sustainable business model archetypes such as "maximizing efficiency," "creating value from waste," and "industrial symbiosis" may be consistent with supply chain GHG emission management.

This chapter deepens understanding of the supply chain as an area of action for organizational climate change strategy, providing new granularity to existing models. A tentative contribution is made on the relationship between supply chain management and business models, where the chapter shows how which sustainable business model archetypes may be applicable to supply chain GHG emission management.

Keywords: Climate change; supply chain climate mitigation objectives; business models for sustainability.

3.1. Introduction

Climate change presents severe risks and challenges to populations and ecosystems globally. Climate change mitigation, one of the two complementary routes to reduce the risks posed by climate change, involves managing and reducing greenhouse gas (GHG) emissions (Füssel, 2007; Yohe and Strzepek, 2007). Businesses and other large organizations largely accept that they have a role to play in tackling climate change and wider sustainability issues (Kolk and Pinkse, 2008). This is in part due to the increasing role and value of brands and associated reputational risk from not engaging in climate change mitigation activities, as well as evidence of improved financial performance from being proactive (Porter and Kramer, 2006).

Organizations have various ways to respond to sustainability concerns, from operational adjustments to more fundamental changes to underlying logics. For example, corporate social responsibility (CSR) extends philanthropic approaches and is associated with smaller incremental changes, such as the introduction of Environmental Management Systems (EMS). A sustainable business approach goes further, involving more fundamental alterations to an organization, including the redesign and creation of business models for sustainability (BMfS) (Boons and Lüdeke-Freund, 2013; Schaltegger *et al.*, 2016). Innovation of the business model itself can enhance value creation not only for the organization but also for stakeholders and the natural environment (Evans *et al.*, 2017). This thinking follows concepts such as shared value creation and sustainable value creation, which explore the rationale for a business to engage with sustainability issues for its own benefit (Porter and Kramer, 2011; Hart and Milstien, 2003). The creation of shared or sustainable value often involves innovation of the business model, and where a business model does not change, for instance, as with CSR, there is the possibility of missed value creation opportunities for the leading supply chain organizations and the wider society (Yang *et al.*, 2017). Business engagement with sustainability has also broadened, from looking internally, for instance at efficiency improvements, to including sustainability impacts occurring outside the traditional boundaries of organizations, including in the supply chain (Kovács, 2008; Lüdeke-Freund *et al.*, 2016).

Just as climate change and wider sustainability has become a strategic concern for business, supply chain management has also increased in importance. This is partly because supply chains have become longer and more internationalized through outsourcing, which has made managing sustainability issues more complex (Preuss, 2005). These changes mean direct GHG emissions associated with organizations have decreased, while the GHG emissions located in the supply chains have increased. The supply chains of consumer goods firms, manufacturers, and high-tech firms can contain between 40%–60% of the overall GHG footprint associated with their goods or services, while this figure can be over 80% for retailers (Brickman and Ungerman, 2008; Oracle, 2008). High GHG emissions within supply chains presents a CSR and potential future regulatory risk (Brickman and Ungerman, 2008). Hence, organizations are increasingly engaging with their supply chain GHG emissions, through programs such as the Carbon Disclosure Project (CDP, 2013) and Courtauld Commitment (WRAP, 2013).

The organizations that lead and control supply chains, and the emissions embodied within them, are known as "supply chain leading organizations" or "focal organizations" (this chapter adopts the latter term) (Seuring and Müller, 2008). These organizations represents an avenue for climate change mitigation efforts (Long and Young, 2015) and allow GHG emissions to be aligned more closely with consumption, linking to concepts such as consumer responsibility (Munksgaard and Pedersen, 2001) and ecological footprint (Wackernagel and Rees, 1996). This also improves management by localizing GHG emissions and assigning responsibility to "focal organizations," allowing a larger proportion of GHG emissions to be targeted through a single actor (Mózner, 2013; Nishitani *et al.*, 2016). Sole enterprises lack the knowledge, skills, and resources to tackle grand challenges, and supply chain GHG emissions are no different (Markman *et al.*, 2019). Engagement with the supply chain also provides an avenue to additional support and resources.

Understanding how firms manage GHG emissions in their supply chains is an important research topic. Climate change requires a coordinated global response. No single actor can provide a solution, and sustainable supply chain management (SSCM) facilitates wider inter- and intra-firm management (Lambert and Cooper, 2000), which helps in managing sustainability impact beyond organizational boundaries (Kovács, 2008; Nishitani *et al.*, 2016). We focus our analysis on the organizational and supply chain level, while recognizing the role that individuals, community, and civic perspectives increasingly play in terms of sustainable business and entrepreneurship (Lumpkin and Bacq, 2019; Markman *et al.*, 2019). Previous research examined corporate engagement with climate change mitigation objectives and the management of environmental and sustainable objectives in supply chains (e.g. see Chaabane *et al.*, 2012; Côté *et al.*, 2008; Hsu *et al.*, 2011; Lee, 2011). This has included how supply chain emissions are measured (also known as Scope 3 emissions), which also impacts decision-making (Downie and Stubbs, 2013). However, these studies have either looked at corporate engagement with climate change in general, and thus include non-supply-chain–related aspects at the expense of detail, or in the case of Downie and Stubbs (2013), have focused on particular aspects of management, such as the assessment strategies in particular and not management and reduction efforts.

As such, a research problem exists in terms of developing a clear and combined picture of how large organizations manage GHG emissions in their supply chains, among their supplies, and the extent to which these activities can be integrated into organizational sustainability strategy and contribute to sustainable value creation. By examining and combining SSCM and organizational engagement with climate change and BMfS approaches, synergies can be identified that could be beneficial to the individual fields and the research problem overall. For instance, the integration of a business model approach helps to explore if additional value can be created through business model innovation (Lüdeke-Freund *et al.*, 2016). Approaches found within the SSCM domain have neither previously been incorporated into corporate climate change mitigation strategy nor explored in terms of implications for BMfS, thereby creating potential for theoretical contributions as well (Lüdeke-Freund *et al.*, 2016).

In order to explore the extent to which supply chain GHG emission management can be integrated into organizational strategy and create sustainable value, this research identifies the key objectives of focal organizations attempting to manage the GHG emissions embodied in their supply chains and the activities used to fulfil these objectives. These aims are achieved by collecting and analyzing data from semi-structured interviews ($n = 31$) with actors involved in supply chain GHG emission management. This data is analyzed thematically and through a matrix to link specific supply chain GHG emission management objectives and activities.

The results indicate that many of the activities used to manage supply chain GHG emissions are of an operational nature and therefore fail to create sustainable value for organizations. The central way to manage supply chain GHG emissions that creates sustainable value and enhances the strategic position of an organization is through design changes. On a more practical level, the results also provide a better understanding of how GHG emissions are managed in the supply chain, including how activities contribute to different aims and objectives, and the implications for organizational strategy. Without this research, we would not have an initial understanding of the synergies and links between SSCM, organizational engagement with climate change, and BMfS, including how the identified management activities and approaches impact business model value creation, capture, and delivery. Our contribution includes a practical consideration, including the how and why of organizational strategy in relation to supply chain GHG emissions, as well as a theoretical element showing how SSCM can influence organizational strategy through the business model.

This chapter proceeds by first reviewing the literature in Section 3.2 on organizational engagement with climate change, the management of sustainability and environmental objectives in supply chains, and the BMfS literature. Next, in Section 3.3, we outline our research approach, how we collected our primary data, and the analysis techniques used. Section 3.4 contains the results of the coding, which sought to identify key objectives and management activities in relation to supply chain GHG emissions, and the extent to which these represented innovations consistent with BMfS. In Section 3.5 we discuss the findings, and finally, in Section 3.6 we provide our conclusions.

3.2. Literature Review

3.2.1. *Organizational engagement with climate change*

Organizations have used several different strategies to manage their GHG emissions; the high number of responses is due to flexibility within regulatory regimes (Kolk and Pinkse, 2005). This means managers are faced with choices, for example, between GHG emission reductions versus offsetting or trading (Weinhofer and Hoffman, 2010). We examine these strategies through the literature to establish a knowledge base and to contextualize our research.

Organizational action can take both an internal and external focus. For example, one area of action is process and supply improvements, which include actions to manage and reduce supply chain GHG emissions (external) but could also include internal actions. Examples include the reuse of materials or enhanced recycling (Olah *et al.*, 2008). Table 3.1 provides an overview of the different activities undertaken by organizations to manage their GHG emissions.

Initial efforts will involve some scoping, measurement, and identification of hotspots. This is followed by internal efficiency improvements and offsetting and trading (Hoffman, 2006; Lash and Wellington, 2007). Increasingly, the total GHG emissions involved in the production of a product or service (i.e. both direct and indirect emissions) are now seen as important for both mitigation and wider CSR goals (i.e. GHG emissions located up and downstream in the supply chain). This has led to actions such as supplier selection based on GHG emission performance (Enkvist *et al.*, 2008) and the integration of climate change mitigation objectives with supply chain management.

Table 3.1. Activities for environmental and sustainable supply chain management.

Activities	Source
Reducing packaging and waste	Walker et al. (2008)
Supplier/vendor environmental assessments, evaluation, auditing	Ciliberti et al. (2008); Walker et al. (2008); Lamming and Hampson (1996)
Eco-friendly product design	Walker et al. (2008); Donnelly et al. (2006)
Eco-efficiency initiatives	Donnelly et al. (2006)
Life Cycle Assessment	Lamming and Hampson (1996)
Product stewardship, i.e. "cradle-to-grave" or "cradle-to-cradle" thinking and design	Lamming and Hampson (1996)
Supplier enabling, capacity building, and coaching	Ciliberti et al. (2008); CIPS (1998)
Supplier requirements, such as codes of conduct	Ciliberti et al. (2008); Preuss (2010)
Involvement of procurement or supply chain managers with environmental or sustainability programs	Preuss (2005)
Supplier forums — discussion/reporting of progress, annual benchmarking, and to outline future strategies	Keating et al. (2008)
CSR management systems and standards — e.g. SA8000, ISO14001	Ciliberti et al. (2008)

Although climate change mitigation policies do exist (e.g. the EU Emissions Trading Scheme), many organizational climate change strategies occur in the absence of direct regulation. Concepts such as "early mover advantage" or shared value creation explain why organizations act voluntarily (Porter and Kramer 2011). While "win-win" outcomes are presented as a rationale for business action (Lash and Wellington, 2007; Porter and Reinhardt, 2007), improvements in environmental performance can create costs and "trade-offs" exist (Hahn et al., 2010).

Different drivers for engagement with supply chain GHG emissions create different aims and objectives for strategies. These range from seeking an understanding of GHG emissions through assessment and quantification (Lovell and MacKenzie, 2011), to reporting and disclosure in response to stakeholder demand through schemes such as the CDP (Knox-Hayes and Levy, 2011). The rationale for these activities includes cost reductions, reputation, or fulfilling stakeholder expectations (Yunus et al., 2016; Busch and Schwarzkopf, 2013; Sullivan, 2010). The objectives and activities pursued are influenced by political and national jurisdiction (Weinhofer and Hoffman, 2010), industry type and company size (Lee, 2012), corporate governance (Galbreath, 2010), and the type of stakeholders and their specific demands, such as investors and their requests for disclosure and reporting (Boiral *et al.*, 2012; Sprengel and Busch, 2010).

3.2.2. *Environmental and SSCM*

As GHG emissions are viewed as an environmental impact, we draw primarily on environmental supply chain management (ESCM) to explore the existing knowledge for the management of supply chain GHG emissions. Srivastava (2007, pp. 53–54) defines ESCM as:

> [I]ntegrating environmental thinking into supply-chain management, including product design, material sourcing and selection, manufacturing processes, delivery of the final product to the consumers as well as end-of-life management of the product after its useful life.

ESCM has many synergies with SSCM, with the latter including social and economic elements. Focal organizations often lead initiatives to manage sustainability in supply chains because they govern the supply chain, provide direct contact to customers, and often design the product or service (Seuring and Müller, 2008).

The drivers for focal organizations to manage issues within their supply chain beyond that as required by law fit into two categories: (1) stakeholder pressure versus traditional management of efficiency and (2) supply variability. Stakeholder pressures link to specific customer demands, reputation, and brand image objectives (Beske *et al.*, 2014; Kovács, 2008; Stiller and Gold, 2014; Walker *et al.*, 2008), whereas efficiency and variability reasons include desires to reduce costs, enhance product quality, or manage (environmental) risks (Pagell and Wu, 2017; Turker and Altuntas, 2014; Walker *et al.*, 2008). Proactive focal organizations go beyond basic requirements, often for financial reasons, until they achieve a competitive advantage-seeking stage (Porter and Kramer, 2006).

SSCM, and by extension, ESCM, involve two types of activities: (1) those concerned with supplier evaluation for risk and (2) performance and management for "sustainable" products (Seuring and Müller, 2008). Table 3.1 provides an overview of activities used for ESCM and SSCM. These activities help highlight what can be expected when attempting to manage GHG emissions in the supply chain.

3.2.3. *Comparative analysis*

The above review illustrates that common objectives exist between organizational engagement with climate change and SSCM, such as stakeholder engagement and the management of reputational and brand factors (see Table 3.2)

Table 3.2. Comparison of aims and objectives.

Aims and objectives: Organizational engagement with climate change	Aims and objectives: Sustainable and environmental supply chain management
To assess and quantify GHG emissions	
For reporting and disclosure of GHG emissions via sustainable reports, disclosure programs (i.e. CDP) or in response to regulation	To manage environmental impacts and risks
To participate in offsetting/trading mechanisms	To respond to customer demands or societal pressures
To achieve GHG emission reductions	To enhance product quality
	To reduce costs
To enhance credibility and reputation	To improve competitive position/as a differentiator
To fulfil stakeholder expectations	Reputation and brand image improvements

(Lüdeke-Freund, 2009; Lüdeke-Freund *et al.*, 2016; Schaltegger and Wagner, 2011). A range of activities for managing climate change mitigation objectives are also evidence. Many activities go beyond the supply chain and involve internal actions of a strategic nature, such as seeking new markets. In comparison, activities noted for SSCM are more specific and less strategic in nature. Indeed, "process and supply improvements" noted in relation to organizational engagement with climate change could encompass nearly all the activities associated with SSCM (see Table 3.3). This observation is important in moving forward to explore how focal organizations currently manage supply chain GHG emissions and the extent to which they create and capture value consistent with a BMfS approach.

Next, we explore thinking and research around value creation for strategy and sustainability. This will help us to consider the extent to which action to manage supply chain GHG emissions creates values and is representative of BMfS.

3.2.4. *Value creation and business models for sustainability*

Traditional concepts of value creation focused on shareholders and owners. CSR, shared value creation, and sustainable value concepts expand the scope of value creation, creating arguments for the creation of value for wider stakeholders, society, and even the environment (Porter and Kramer, 2006; Hart and Milstein, 2003). These concepts helped change the debate over the role of business and established a rationale for why business should also create value for society (Porter and Kramer, 2006). Indeed, it is increasingly realized that businesses (enterprises) are critical to social change initiatives, which are most effective through the cooperation

Table 3.3. Comparison of corporate climate change mitigation and SSCM activities.

Corporate climate change mitigation engagement	SSCM
Product choice editing (i.e. limiting the choices available to consumers).	Product stewardship, i.e. "cradle-to-grave" or "cradle-to-cradle" thinking and design
Emission reduction commitments	Supplier requirements, such as codes of conduct
Product development (i.e. design/redesign of products to reduce embodied and/or in use GHG emissions)	Eco-friendly product design
Process and supply improvements (i.e. reduction of GHG emissions in the supply chain or organizational processes)	Reducing packaging and waste
	Supplier/vendor environmental assessments, evaluation, auditing
	Eco-efficiency initiatives
	Life Cycle Assessment
	Supplier enabling, capacity building, and coaching
	Involvement of procurement or supply chain managers with environmental or sustainability programs
	Supplier forums — discussion/reporting of progress, annual benchmarking, and to outline future strategies
Entry into new markets	N/A

of three key actors — community, regimes of support (donors, corporations, etc.), and enterprise (Lumpkin and Bacq, 2019).

Within mainstream business logics, to legitimately engage in sustainable value creation requires the development of a "business case" or rationale, highlighting how social and environmental action will also be beneficial for business (Schaltegger et al., 2012). Business case drivers illustrate how the business will benefit, be it through reduced costs, improved reputation, or enhanced innovation opportunities. A key assumption in this thinking is that voluntary social or environmental activities by business are driven by an instrumental motivation, i.e. that business will benefit. This link between voluntary action and business benefit is not automatic, meaning that strategic business objectives and activities (including the business model) have to be oriented toward the triple bottom line. This shows the importance in understanding the objectives of business actions, in response to drivers such as cost or risk reduction, and the activities used, when considering the development of shared or sustainable value.

Change to the business model can indicate the development of business cases for sustainability (Schaltegger *et al.*, 2012), highlighting a role for the business model as a type of indicator. The degree the business case is integrated into strategy and the business model can vary (Aragón-Correa and Rubio-López, 2007):

- Defensive orientation: driven by cost constraint and is little more than compliance with official or civic regulation. This approach is narrow in scope, meaning the chances of value-creating opportunities being missed is high.
- Accommodative orientation: integration of management control systems into key processes, but in a cautious way: for instance, for environmental protection or eco-efficiency. The core business logic is not changed.
- Proactive orientation: environmental or social aspects fully integrated into the business. All processes directed toward sustainability.

The development of the strongest and most proactive business cases involves changes to the business model, and the development of a business model for sustainability will largely involve a proactively orientated business case (Lüdeke-Freund, 2009). Conversely, an unchanged business model will constrain opportunities to develop value. As such, for effective and value-creating supply chain GHG emission management, changes in the business models should be evident. The identification and generation of value is not automatic and can be "missed" (Yang *et al.*, 2017).

To consider the extent to which supply chain GHG emission management strategies create value, we need knowledge of the objectives of action, the activities undertaken, and the degree to which these activities impact the business model. Where the business model is not impacted, and where they represent more operational-effectiveness–type measures, then value creation may have been missed (Yang *et al.*, 2017).

Previous research categorized the types of BMfS, highlighting technological, social, or organizational types (Bocken *et al.*, 2014; Bocken and Short, 2016; Young and Tilley, 2006). BMfS also provide a conceptual link between organizational engagement with climate change and SSCM literature. A comparison of SSCM and BMfS highlights that both involve bringing multiple stakeholders together (beyond consumers and suppliers) and reacting to their demands (Lüdeke-Freund *et al.*, 2016). This shows that SSCM, organizational engagement with climate change, and BMfS aim to provide both business and sustainable value (in the form of reduced GHG emissions). However, the degree of sustainable value generation is critical. Where these initiatives do not involve changes to business models, value may have been missed. Potentially relevant BMfS for the management of supply chain GHG emissions, including product stewardship and enhanced supplier engagement (noted as supplier enabling), can be linked to

BMfS archetypes, such as encouraging sufficiency, maximizing efficiency, and creating value from waste (Bocken and Allwood, 2012; Bocken *et al.*, 2014).

3.3. Methods

This chapter seeks to explore the extent to which supply chain GHG emission management strategies create sustainable value. To do this, we identify and categorize supply chain GHG emission management objectives, the activities undertaken to achieve them by focal organizations in the UK, and the extent to which these lead to business model innovations. A matrix analysis links specific activities with objectives, which is followed by a consideration of which activities and strategies constitute BMfS.

To achieve these objectives, we used a qualitative research approach. This was due to the "how" and "why" nature of the research aims, the in-depth data required for the answering of the research questions, and the lack of sufficient secondary data on GHG emission management approaches. We collected data through semi-structured interviews with both the public and private sectors as well as information from independent experts. Secondary data was collected where available, such as environmental/CSR reports, environmental policy documents, supplier evaluation questionnaires, internal policy documents, and external media sources (Walker *et al.*, 2008). Du to anonymity requirements, we do not refer to specific secondary data.

Data from multiple perspectives allowed data triangulation to increase validity (Guion, 2008); this included the use of secondary data. The number of interviews conducted also affects validity. Within a homogenous group of participants, 10–15 interviews are felt sufficient, but within a heterogeneous group, more may be needed (Mason, 2010). The length of the interview can also influence validity. All interviews within our sample were concluded until respondents were no longer providing additional information, generally between 40 min and 1 hour. Due to the non-probabilistic and purposive sampling strategy undertaken (as explained in Sections 3.1 and 3.2), and the heterogeneous nature of the participants, data was collected until data saturation was achieved, i.e. when no new insights were being obtained through additional data/interviews (Green and Thorogood, 2013). Due to the relative lack of knowledge regarding supply chain GHG emission management efforts, two research phases were required: an initial scoping, exploratory phase and then a main exploratory and explanatory phase, termed Phases One and Two.

The aim of Phase One was to provide an overview of current supply chain GHG emission management efforts within the UK. Participants external to organizations undertaking supply chain GHG emission management initiatives were interviewed (see Table 3.4), and asked to provide an overview of current initiatives, the key actors involved, and overarching drivers and barriers. This provided a working structure from which to launch the second phase. Phase Two sought an

Table 3.4. Phase One interview participants.

Interview Code/Number	Participant Job Title	Organization Type	Type and length
A01	Senior Policy Advisor	Business Representation Organization	57 minutes/in person
A02	Head of Corporate Relations	Local Business Support and Representation Organization	36 minutes/in person
A03	Operations Director	Regional Business Support Organization	58 minutes/in person
A04	Senior Account Manager	Solution Based NGO	44 minutes/in person
A05	Program Manager	Regional Intelligence Network	36 minutes/in person
A06	Research Fellow	Policy Think Tank	34 minutes/telephone
A07	Environmental Campaign Organizer	Regional Business Support Organization	42 minutes/in person
A08	Corporate Strategy Consultant	Global Management Consultancy	28 minutes/in person
A09	Post-Doctoral Researcher	Academic Institution	50 minutes/in person (notes only)
A10	Senior Strategy Manager	National Low Carbon Business Support Organization	28 minutes/telephone
A11	Senior Sustainability Manager	Sustainability Think Tank	32 minutes/telephone

insider perspective from participants within focal organizations engaging with supply chain GHG emissions. An overview of the research phases is provided in Figure 3.1. This shows how the literature review contributed to the scope of the research and its design as well as the different research and analysis phases.

The UK was chosen as the context for the research, partly due to the location of the researchers themselves and due to discussions at the time for the mandatory reporting of supply chain GHG emissions by the UK government (Defra, 2011). This meant many focal organizations had been "primed" to start to manage supply chain GHG emissions, providing a natural research sample.

3.3.1. *Phase One interviews*

Table 3.4 shows the respondents for Phase One; they included individuals from academia, business support organizations, and NGOs that had engaged with the topic. As such, we considered them independent expert informants. To be included

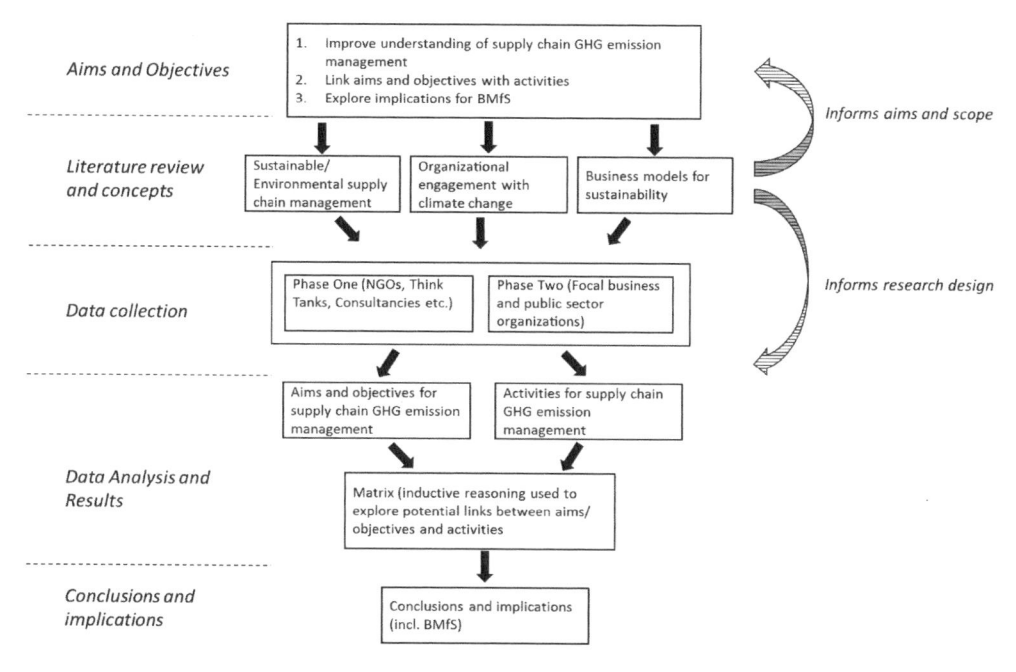

Figure 3.1. Overview of research stages and design.

in the sample, the participant had to have three years' experience in a relevant position; this acted as a validation criterion for the participants and the data they provided.

Phase One results indicated that supply chain GHG emission management efforts were developed, or at least administered, by companies at the head of supply chains. Subsequently, focal organizations formed the focus of this second stage of the research.

3.3.2. Phase Two interviews

A definition of focal organizations was adapted from Seuring and Müller (2008), as those organizations that led or controlled their supply chain, often designing the product or service being offered and being positioned next to, or one supply chain stage away from consumers. This definition was used in participant recruitment during this phase. We sought a diversity of cases to examine the phenomenon in a broad spectrum of settings. For example, we included cases from both the public sector and private sector, involving different industries and different types of initiatives. The same participant recruitment and qualification criteria used in Phase One was also applied to Phase Two.

Data was collected through semi-structured interviews with key individuals who had experience within the organizations attempting to manage their supply chain GHG emissions. As such, they provided an internal and more in-depth perspective. Table 3.5 provides an overview of the interview respondents, including their roles. Secondary data, where available, are also noted. The anonymity afforded to the cases helped tackle response bias. Secondary sources were used to check the veracity of the primary data provided, rather than directly contribute to the categories developed.

3.3.3. *Analysis*

Two analysis techniques were used in this research. First, we coded the transcribed interviews using Nvivo, creating the data for this initial phase (i.e. transcripts). A thematic coding approach was used (Boyatzis, 1998), meaning the first round of coding involved noting factors that were significant and important. For example, a broad theme of "management" was developed, with all references to the management of supply chain GHG emissions included within this broad category. Similar broad thematic categories included "primary aims and objectives." The next round of coding then explored within these broad categories for more detailed patterns. For example, within the "management" theme, we found that activities could be categorized according to their location in the supply chain, such as upstream, downstream, or in-house. Finally, specific management actions were coded and developed into the categories presented in the results. This can be characterized as a process of abstraction (empirical to conceptual) and generalization (seeking invariances common in the data). The results of this first analysis are a set of categories outlining the aims and objectives of supply chain GHG emission management and the various activities undertaken to achieve them. To enhance reliability, the results were shared with the respondents for corroboration, while the purposive sampling technique helped provide a suitable sample and reduce potential bias.

The second analysis technique sought to explore possible relationships between the categories developed, through the use of inductive reasoning and a matrix analysis (Johnson and Christensen, 2010). In this second analysis phase, we used data display analysis techniques, taking the form of a matrix analysis. For this, two sets of categories were plotted onto the axes of a matrix, allowing cross-referencing to identify any possible causal relationships between the two sets of categories. Once the data categories were plotted onto the matrixes, inductive reasoning was used to extrapolate new patterns and interrelationships. The matrix analysis used both sets of categories developed (i.e. aims and objectives, and activities).

Table 3.5. Phase two interview participants.

Interview Code/Number	Participant Job Title	Secondary data collected	Organization Type	Total time of interview
B01	(Interview involved two participants) Head of CSR Strategy & Policy for Procurement; Climate Change & Sustainability Officer	Supplier questionnaire design and results. Corporate sustainability report.	Multinational Telecoms Service Provider	29 minutes/telephone
B02	Associate Director of Brownfield and Sustainability	None.	British House Building Company	37 minutes/telephone
B03	Science & Technology Leader	Corporate sustainability report.	Multinational Consumer Goods Company	45 minutes/telephone
B04	VP of Sustainability	Corporate sustainability strategy from website.	Multinational Pharmaceutical and Consumer Healthcare Goods Company	32 minutes/telephone
B05	Executive Director	None.	Regional Social Enterprise	41 minutes/telephone
B06	Capability Manager	None.	British Water Utility Company	44 minutes/in person
B07	Group Environment Health and Safety manager for the UK subsidiary	Corporate sustainability report.	Dairy Products Company	55 minutes/in person
B08	Head of Sustainability	None.	Construction, Property & Housing Company	42 minutes/telephone
B09	Senior Sustainability Manager	Corporate sustainability report. Internal sustainability strategy documents. Internal sustainability "toolbox."	Multinational Construction & Development Company	1 hour 04 minutes/in person

(Continued)

Table 3.5. (Continued)

Interview Code/Number	Participant Job Title	Secondary data collected	Organization Type	Total time of interview
B10	Regional Manager, North of England	None.	Multidisciplinary Consultancy Company	18 minutes/telephone
B11	Head of Supply Chain Carbon Reduction	Access to supplier sustainability forum materials.	Multinational Grocery and General Merchandise Retailer	37 minutes/telephone
B12	Sustainability Officer	None.	County Council	40 minutes/in person (notes only)
B13	Low Carbon Consultant	None.	Global Consultancy and Professional Services Firm	38 minutes/telephone
B14	Responsible Procurement Manager	None.	Top-tier Regional Administrative Body	49 minutes/in person
B15	Head of Supply Chain Research	Consultancy Report.	Environmental Consultancy	43 minutes/in person
B16	(2x Participants) Environmental Advisor (Construction); Sustainable Procurement Advisor	None.	Government Agency	47 minutes/in person
B17	Climate Change Officer	None.	County Council	10 minutes/telephone + email correspondence
B18	(2x Participants) Environment and Sustainability Officer; Research Fellow	Report on University Scope 3 GHG emissions.	University	58 minutes/in person
B19	Sustainability Officer		University	33 minutes/in person
B20	Operations Director		Sustainability Unit of National Public Service Provider	26 minutes/telephone

3.4. Results

3.4.1. *Objectives of supply chain GHG emission management*

Analysis of the interview data identified two broad themes regarding the objectives of focal organizations engaging with supply chain GHG emissions:

(1) *Measurement and scoping* efforts provided data for reporting and disclosure requirements and/or to for internal management purposes. One aim was to provide information for management, e.g. supply chain mapping, and could be done through supplier reporting and disclosure or modelling.

> *So, the old adage that says "to measure is to manage" is true, so you have to start measuring their carbon emissions in order to manage and reduce them eventually. (A04)*

An additional aspect of scoping and measurement objectives was for the disclosure and reporting of supply chain GHG emissions via organizational sustainability reports, or for example, through the CDP. Such reporting could be either at the supply chain or product level, with the latter allowing per product GHG emission labelling — for instance, the amount of GHG emissions associated with a liter of milk. Where measurement was used for reporting purposes, value could be created via transparency and reputational impacts.

> *[A] lot of the supermarkets are competing on this issue, the wider sustainability issue, and carbon is a part of that. [Large UK supermarket] are probably ahead of everyone due to the fact that they are footprinting some of their products. (A06)*

(2) *Supply chain GHG emission reduction* was the second broad objective identified, which focused on reducing the level of GHG emissions within the supply chain. By doing so, focal organizations could create environmental value.

> *But, that idea of using the data to implement carbon reduction plans is something that I try follow up with some of the London authorities, who were part of [project], and in fact, I found out this afternoon who is actually using the data to influence their supply chain. (B14)*

The data analysis identified a range of secondary objectives and outcomes from efforts to manage supply chain GHG emissions. These included efficiency gains and cost reductions, increased resilience and health of the supply chains, improved supply chain dynamics and relationships, as well as other context-specific benefits. Table 3.6 details the primary and secondary objectives and outcomes identified.

Table 3.6. Overview of primary and secondary objectives and outcomes of supply chain GHG emission management efforts.

Objective		Details	BMfS/value creation potential
GHG emission measurement and scoping		Reporting and disclosure through CSR reports, NGO organizations, or regulatory schemes	Accommodative: Where value propositions included transparency aspects, could impact business models.
		Non-reporting: i.e. for internal measures and strategy	Defensive: no impacts to business model. Could be used as a supporting measure.
Supply chain GHG emission reductions		Aim to reduce supply chain GHG emissions	Accommodative/Proactive: where reduced embodied emissions or in use emissions included in value proposition.
Secondary objectives and outcomes	Efficiency gains/ cost reductions	Actions to reduce GHG emissions also increase efficiency and/or producing cost saving	Defensive/accommodative: operational impacts, rather than to business model.
	Increase financial resilience/ health of suppliers and supply chain	Efficiency increases for SC, reduces costs, increasing financial resilience of the supply chain	Defensive/accommodative: operational impacts, rather than to business model.
	Improve supply chain relations and dynamics	Collaboration enhances supplier relationships, to benefit of future business	Defensive/accommodative: operational impacts, rather than to business model.
	Other	Other context-specific benefits	Defensive/accommodative: operational impacts, rather than to business model.

3.4.2. *Activities for the management of supply chain GHG emission*

Activities were first categorized according to where in the supply chain they occurred: upstream, in-house, as well as downstream. An overview of the activities and their location is provided in Table 3.7 and the category descriptions are provided in the following sections.

3.4.3. *Upstream supply chain GHG emission management activities*

(1) *Information sharing and dissemination* was coded as an activity because while several other activities involved information flows, in this category, the sharing of information was undertaken as an activity in isolation. These information flows were diverse, flowing from focal organization to the supply chain, vice versa, or between suppliers. The content included specific GHG emission data or advice to suppliers.

So, we thought to try and just link [suppliers] up, we'll share a load of our information with them, we'll run fortnightly webinars, we'll run site visits etcetera. (B11)

Table 3.7. Overview of supply chain GHG emission management activities developed through the coding.

Location of activities in the supply chain	Activity categories developed through coding
Upstream activities	1. *Information sharing and dissemination*
	2. *GHG emissions inclusion in contracts and tendering processes*
	3. *Collaboration and partnering agreements*
	4. *Direct supplier interventions*
	5. *Management standards and verification activities*
	6. *Supplier involvement in design*
	7. *Supplier training and schools*
In-house activities	1. *Supply chain GHG emission modelling*
	2. *Design changes*
	3. *Training and information provision*
	4. *Embedding of supply chain GHG emission management into commercial teams*
Downstream activities	1. *R&D on consumers*
	2. *Influencing customer use of products*

So, we actually contacted most of our big suppliers and asked them how much we bought from them. We knew how much we spent with them but didn't necessarily track the amount of stuff. (B03)

(2) *GHG emission inclusion in contracts and tendering processes* could include requiring GHG emission reporting to the focal organization or mandatory reductions over the course of a contract. This activity put formal requirements onto suppliers and could be used in decisions.

Some of the procurement teams I've been working with have started to put more language into their producer codes, and their specifications for tender, about disclosure and about Scope Three emissions to their suppliers. (B13)

(3) *Collaboration and partnering agreements* applied to primary, "top," or preferred suppliers. This contrasts with the previous two activities, which were often undertaken with all suppliers. Due to the closer supply relationship, more influence could be exerted, which aided the collecting of supplier GHG emission information.

The top 50 are managed through supplier relationship management. They are assessed against their performance, including sustainability criteria, among other things, and are scored on a quarterly basis and they go into a league table. (B06)

(4) *Direct supplier interventions* could include free supplier GHG emission assessments or, in some cases, capital investments into suppliers by focal organizations. Where interventions included more substantial action, financing could be provided.

We have a thing called an "energy kisan," which was developed in-house, which means we can go into one of our own factory's and find 30% of savings with a 5-year investment plan, and we're starting to take that into our supply chain. (B04)

(5) *Management standards and verification activities* were applied to ensure consistent measurement and management of GHG emissions across the supply chain. In some cases, third parties verified these management standards. The use of standards and verification led to greater confidence in the data, enhancing decision-making.

So, if we take carbon, we're active members of CEMARS, by Achilles Information Ltd — it is something that we helped develop with Achilles and we encourage suppliers, not just top 50, but all of our suppliers, to sign up to something like CEMARS. (B06)

(6) *Supplier involvement in design* meant more extensive collaboration with the supply chain. The activity sought to utilize supplier knowledge and insights into production processes to reduce embodied GHG emissions through design changes. Supplier innovation competitions were also organized, enabling an approach similar to crowdsourcing to solve problems.

Then when they actually come to work for us, because we're carbon footprinting projects from the design stage, right the way through and as we've got the targets to reduce the carbon, we've got to engage with the supply chain at a very early point to try and get these reductions. (B09)

(7) *Supplier training and schools* ensured the supply chain had needed capabilities to manage GHG emissions. In one example from the construction industry, a supplier school was created focusing on those contractors unable to fulfil environmental management requirements required by the focal organization.

So, last year, we ran a program of five workshops for suppliers, co-hosted with the carbon trust on that very subject. (B01)

We're looking to set up, what we call a supply chain school. We've got an application into the government for funding, to set this up. (B09)

3.4.4. *In-house supply chain GHG emission management activities*

In-house management activities were undertaken by the focal organizations internally, without supplier engagement.

(1) *Supply chain GHG emission modelling* enabled internal calculation with little or no direct input from the supply chain, using financial receipts or data collected through supplier disclosures. This allowed focal organizations to identify hotspots and points of influence. This approach avoided costly supplier engagement but lacked accuracy as it used conversion factors.

If we start with the upstream scope 3 emissions, what we had to do was start to calculate them, or rather start to estimate them; estimate is a better term than calculate. So, we contacted most of our big suppliers and asked them how much we bought from them. We knew how much we spent with them but didn't necessarily track the amount of stuff. (B03)

(2) *Design changes* involved altering the fundamental design of products and services, therefore changing the production processes used and reducing

embodied and/or in-use GHG emissions. While this activity would influence the supply chain, it is an activity conducted internally within the focal organization without supplier involvement.

We often focus on mitigation, so we're trying to reduce that in our design, so low carbon design, that sort of thing. So that would be our design work. (B10)

And we're already doing that with the big stuff, which you do at the planning stage, like all the equipment providers ... especially as that equipment will knock onto our scope 1 and 2 emissions. (B07)

(3) *Training and information provision* enhanced the internal competencies of the focal organization and was needed due to the cross-cutting nature of supply chain GHG emission management within focal organizations. For example, it is likely that procurement, supply chain management, and environmental management departments are all involved.

On our intranet, we have a section called the "[REDACTED]," which has loads of environmental stuff on it — and that's how we share best practice. (B09)

(4) *Embedding of supply chain GHG emission management into commercial teams* allowed supply chain GHG emission management to be "mainstreamed." This involved integrating GHG emission criteria into commercial relationships and treating it as any other supply chain management objective.

The third piece is what we describe as "trying to mainstream carbon" into the commercial relationship. (B11)

Well, I think it's maturing now for us like I say it's becoming part of our culture from a supply chain point of view. (B06)

3.4.5. Downstream supply chain GHG emission management activities

These activities involved working with or influencing actors downstream of the focal organization.

(1) *Research and Development (R&D) on consumers* aimed to understand downstream GHG emissions. This was common where the "in-use" emissions of a product or service were a high proportion of the overall GHG emissions.

[A]nd there's downstream: we have a particular product which is [specific product]. So, they are about a third of our footprint, so to be an honest, we're just concentrating to a large extent on the downstream emissions. (B04)

(2) *Influencing customer use of products* was undertaken where a focal organization took responsibility for downstream GHG emissions. This activity utilized strategies such as carbon labelling on products (in order to guide consumers to lower GHG emission options). These approaches sought to target consumer behavior.

We are in the process of thinking hard about how we can make labelling more effective, as not that many consumers really understand the Carbon Trust label. (B11)

3.4.6. *Linking objectives with supply chain GHG emission management activities: Matrix analysis*

Earlier, we identify the primary objectives of supply chain GHG emission management efforts, as well as the activities undertaken by focal organizations. Using inductive reasoning (as a way of identifying generalized causation), we explore which activities contribute to specific objectives. We did this through several matrices, which allowed each activity to be cross-referenced and compared with outcomes/objectives (Johnson and Christensen, 2010).

In doing so, we generate a clearer picture of the business case drivers and the impacts on the core business logic and business model. In turn, this allows consideration of what value is created or missed in the different supply chain GHG emission management strategies.

In total, three matrices were produced, one for each area of action in the supply chain (i.e. upstream, in-house, or downstream). The specific activities were plotted vertically on the matrices, whilst objectives were plotted on the horizontal axis (see Appendix section for matrices).

When analyzing the relationships between the activities and objectives, it becomes clear that activities have different levels of impact in terms of achieving different objectives. Some activities would not be able to achieve an objective in isolation but would contribute toward it. For example, the use of 'management standards and verification activities' contributed toward "GHG emission reductions" by improving management techniques, but in isolation would not lead to GHG emission reductions.

In other instances, activities would only achieve an objective or contribute toward one under certain conditions. For example, "direct supplier interventions" could directly achieve "GHG emission reductions," where funds for capital works were provided, but not where the intervention only involved a free GHG emission assessment. Due to these observations, four types of relationship between activities and objectives/outcomes were established:

(1) "Direct" = activity is central to the fulfillment of the objective or outcome, e.g. see Table 3.6.
(2) "Contribute" = activity contributes toward an objective or outcome, but in isolation would be unable to fulfill objective or outcome.
(3) "Conditional Contribution or Conditional Direct" = where activity could, if designed and applied appropriately, directly fulfil objective/contribute to the fulfillment of the objective.
(4) "None" = no relationship between activity and outcome/objective.

Figures 3.2 and 3.3 illustrate which activities directly fulfill the different objectives of supply chain GHG emission measurement versus supply chain GHG emission reduction. We only explore activities deemed with a direct relationship here; the full matrices are available in the Appendix section. To illustrate the reasoning used, we provide examples of where no direct relationship was found with conditional or contributory relationships.

Upstream in supply chain
Activities:
- Information Sharing and Dissemination
- Management Standards and Verification Activity

Rationale for why activities facilitates achievement of objective
- *Information sharing and dissemination* directly facilitates supply chain GHG emission scoping and measurement objectives by enabling information sharing by suppliers. This sharing provides focal organisations with the data required for reporting and disclosure.
- *Management stands and verification activites* directly facilitates supply chain GHG emission scoping and measurement objectives by providing a structured and sometimes certified management system (i.e. CEMARS) for suppliers. This system produces more reliable GHG emission data for focal organisation, directly fulfilling reporting and disclosure efforts.

Inhouse Activities
Activities:
- Supply chain GHG emission Modelling & Assessment

- *Supply chain GHG emission Modelling & Assessment* directly facilitates supply chain GHG emission scoping and measurement objectives by enabling emissions to be calculated through the modelling of finanicial receipts. This directly provides focal organisations with data required for reporting and disclosure requirements without involving suppliers directly.

Downstream in supply chain
Activities:
- No activities.

- *No acivities directly facilitates the measurement or scopig of GHG emissions in the supply chain.*

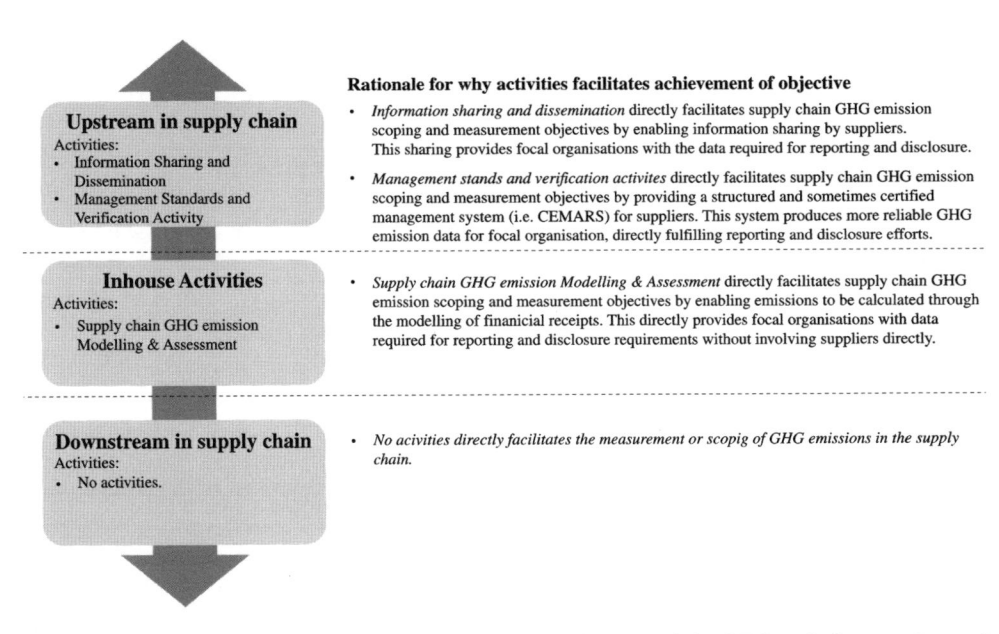

Figure 3.2. Activities that directly fulfill the objective of supply chain GHG emission scoping and measurement objectives. These activities are categorized according to their location in the supply chain.

3.4.7. *Activities for measurement and scoping and value creation*

Figure 3.2 shows activities that were central to the fulfillment of supply chain GHG emission measurement and scoping objectives. Upstream activities found to have a direct impact on objective fulfillment included "*information sharing and dissemination*" and "*management standards and verification.*" Information sharing and dissemination is designated as a direct impact as it is central to data collection from suppliers and can achieve the objective. Management standards and verification are included as a direct relationship as they ensure data is collected in a structured way, sometimes through certified management systems for suppliers (e.g. CEMARS). This system produces more reliable GHG emission data for the focal organization, fulfilling reporting and disclosure efforts (Downie and Stubbs, 2012).

In-house activities found to have a direct impact on the fulfillment of the measurement and scoping only included supply chain GHG emission modelling and assessment. As noted in Section 5.2.2, this often involved modelling supply chain emissions using financial receipts. This directly provides focal organizations with data required for reporting and disclosure requirements without involving suppliers directly. No downstream activities were found to directly fulfill this objective of measurement and scoping. Consumer R&D could enable measurement and scoping where this activity included data collection, but often as this was not central to the activity, it was only included as a conditional activity (see appendix).

Supply chain GHG emission measurement and scoping aimed to provide data for reporting and disclosure requirements and/or to provide information for internal management purposes. This involved a range of upstream and in-house activities, including information sharing, management standards, and internal modelling. Most changes are to business processes and align to an accommodative approach to sustainability. This suggests that business logic remains the same (unchanged), but that management systems are integrated into key processes. This perspective suggests value creation could be missed.

It is possible, however, that shared value is created, depending on the drivers for these aims and if they develop a business case for sustainability (Schaltegger *et al.*, 2012). On the one hand, if the aim of assessing supply chain emissions is for internal management purposes, no additional value is created, and indeed, value creation is missed (Yang *et al.*, 2017). However, if measuring specifically to report emissions for users or other key stakeholders, a business case exists in terms of reputation and regulatory risk reduction. In this case, although it is accommodative, it may create shared value and alter value propositions.

3.4.8. *Activities for reductions and value creation*

The activities that directly fulfilled the achievement of supply chain GHG emission reduction are illustrated in Figure 3.3. Only design changes to products or production processes directly reduce emissions. This is a direct relationship because design changes fundamentally change a product or process, including the embodied emissions of production and/or use. Influencing the downstream activity of customer use of products is not included as a direct relationship due to the difficulties in influencing consumers and measuring outcomes. For these reasons, this activity was assigned as a contributing or conditional relationship. Figure 3.4 provides an overview of the activities contributing to both GHG emission reduction and scoping and measurement.

The matrices used to conduct the analysis, which include reasons for the absence of relationships, can be found in the Appendix. The Appendix also includes a wheel outlining all direct and contributing relationships for the two-supply chain GHG emission management objectives shown in Figure 3.4.

GHG emission reductions present a more compelling case for the creation of shared value and the development of a BMfS. However, this is still dependent on the business case drivers developed. Changing design and reducing embodied GHG emissions are likely to be in response to customer demands and are also likely to involve more profound changes to other parts of the business model, such

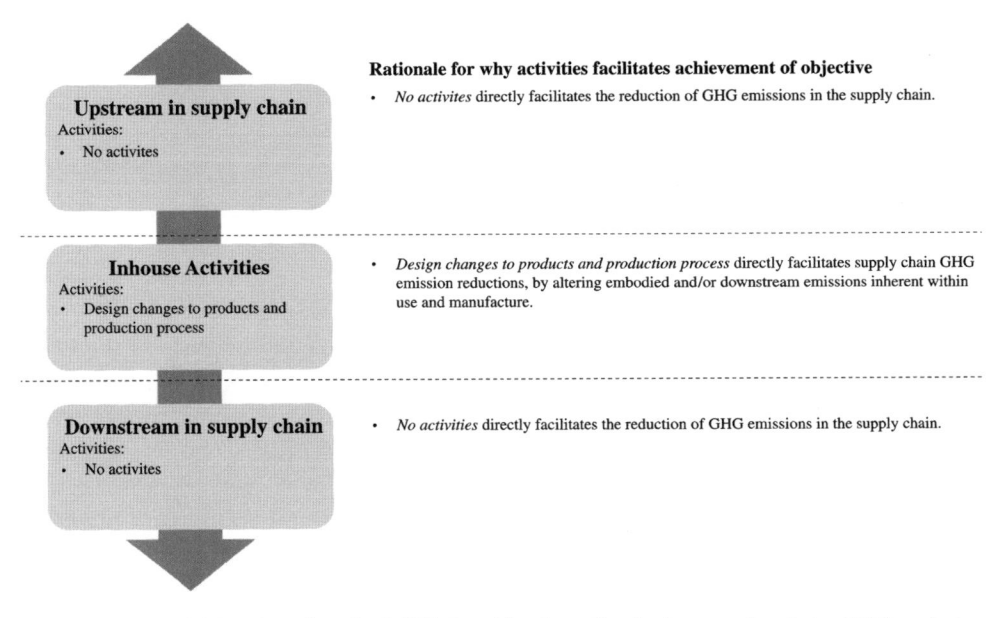

Figure 3.3. Activities that directly fulfill the objective of reducing supply chain GHG emission reductions. These activities are categorized according to their location in the supply chain.

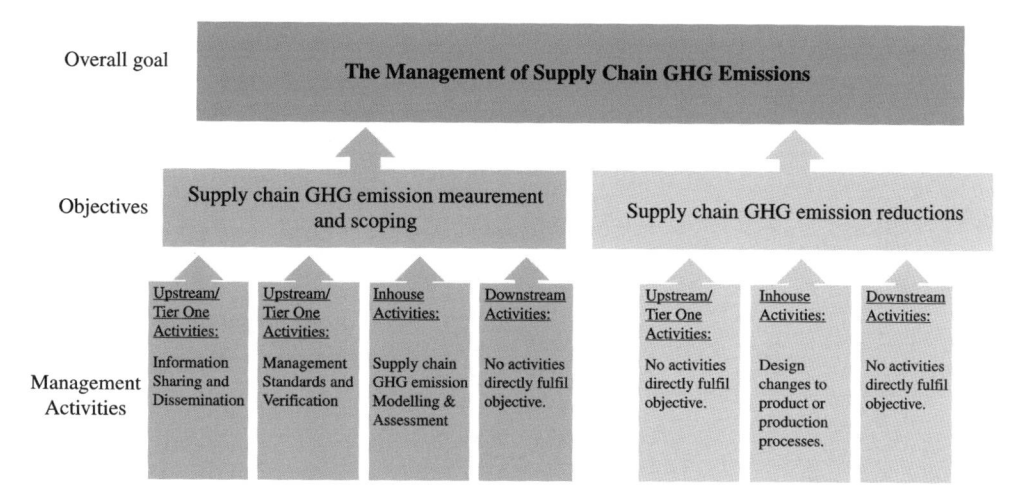

Figure 3.4. Simplified overview of the activities that directly fulfil the management of focal organizations supply chain GHG emissions. Non-direct relationship activities excluded.

as key activities and channel operation (Bocken et al., 2016; Prendeville and Bocken, 2017). These changes align well with previously identified types of BMfS. For instance, reducing in-use or embodied GHG emissions would be consistent with maximizing energy and material efficiency and encouraging sufficiency archetypes (Bocken et al., 2014). It is also important to note that many of the activities identified through the analysis contribute toward design changes; for instance, design changes are likely not to be possible without some engagement with supplier or understanding of where in the supply chain GHG emissions are located. Therefore, while much of our analysis focuses on the "directly" involved activities, readers should consult the matrices produced during analysis to get a better overview of all activities involved in achieving a particular objective.

3.5. Discussion

3.5.1. *Supply chain GHG emission management strategies and their potential to create sustainable value*

Aside from identifying key objectives and activities for supply chain GHG emission management strategies, we wanted to identify which activities used to manage GHG emissions could be used within organizational strategies to create sustainable value. Where activities did not change business logics or business models, it was likely that sustainable value was being missed, and that organizational engagement with supply chain climate change mitigation was sub-optimal from a sustainable strategy point of view. Answering this practical question would also help shed light on important questions around how sustainable value creation is linked to (a type of) SSCM.

We found that supply chain GHG emission efforts can create sustainable value, indicated by their alignment with some types of BMfS. The creation of this value was dependent on the nature of the objective, the scale of activity, as well as the underlying motivation. It is also clear that the more tactical nature of supply chain GHG emission management (and SSCM in general) means it can be practiced at a level below that which impacts the business model. In this way, not all actions to manage supply chain GHG emissions create sustainable value, and where this is the case, organizations are missing value creating opportunities.

We find that BMfS archetypes associated with maximizing efficiency and encouraging sufficiency are linked to the aim of GHG emission reductions, via design changes. However, it is likely that other BMfS archetypes may also be relevant and could be used to better manage and reduce supply chain GHG emissions (Bocken et al., 2014). For instance, creating value from waste archetypes, circular economy, and cradle-to-cradle and industrial symbiosis approaches lead to fundamental redesigns of supply chains consistent with the design change activities highlighted within our results. These approaches enhance the reduction and management of GHG emissions that lie beyond organizational boundaries (Garnett, 2011; Govindan et al., 2015; Talbot et al., 2007). For example, the construction firms included within this sample may reduce embodied GHG emissions by reusing excavation tailings for building aggregates. Leading supply chain organizations should explore these strategies to take their supply chain GHG emission activities further and avoid situation where value is missed (Yang et al., 2017).

We can also ask which BMfS would be most effective at managing supply chain GHG emissions. For example, functionality archetypes, including product service system (PSS) approaches could enhance the control that focal organizations have over their products, and so also over the embodied GHG emissions (Li and Found, 2016; Mont and Lindhqvist, 2003). These business models can reduce the distance between the embodied emissions and the focal organization, easing measurement and management.

Stewardship archetypes and specifically models aimed at providing "radical transparency" link well to the scoping and measurement activities highlighted within these results. Although the aim of scoping and measurement was seen as accommodative and unlikely to create sustainable value directly, this type of business model shows that these activities could be value creating. They would be important in a radical transparency business model. Such business models hold promise in terms of improving customer relations and understanding of market demands (Prahalad and Ramaswamy, 2004; Smith and Tabibnia, 2012).

Our results highlight that management of supply chain GHG emissions may involve alterations to business models and that some BMfS archetypes could offer guidance in a way that enhances business and societal value. This is important, as previous research has shown that attempting to manage sustainability issues in a "bolt-on" and incremental manner can be detrimental to outcomes and business performance (Pagell and Wu, 2009). Our results also advance understanding in terms of the links between (a type of) SSCM and BMfS. We explore empirically how different SSCM approaches influences the business model; for instance, we show that many SSCM activities do not influence the business model and as such, can create a "value missed" scenario. In doing so, we provide additional understanding of two key variables of sustainable strategy, i.e. the link between SSCM and BMfS.

3.5.2. *Theoretical and practical implications of linking supply chain mitigation objectives with management activities*

Section 3.4.1 highlighted that the two key objectives were measurement and scoping as well as GHG emission reductions.

These results provides new detail to the management of climate change mitigation objectives in supply chains. The models advanced by scholars exploring corporate engagement with climate change objectives, such as Lee (2012) and Kolk and Pinkse (2005), operate at a higher level, looking at internal and external GHG emissions, the development of new "climate-friendly" products, and the competitive opportunities these bring. These models lacked specificity with regards to supply chain GHG emissions. Without our results, we would lack detail of actions to achieve climate change objectives in the supply chain. As such, these results provide detail and granularity for both practitioners and existing conceptual models for managing organizational climate change mitigation goals.

In addition to the central objectives (measurement and reduction), this research also identified a range of additional outcomes which extends the literature (Preuss, 2005; Walker *et al.*, 2008), such as improved supplier relationships and supply chain dynamics, cost reductions or efficiency gains, enhanced supply chain resilience, and context-specific benefits. This is important, as it shows that engagement with supply chain GHG emissions can provide unexpected "windfalls." This strengthens the case for focal organizations to engage with this issue, which could in turn further contribute to climate change mitigation objectives.

3.6. Conclusions

Our exploratory research highlighted how supply chain GHG emission management strategies undertaken by focal organizations are often missing sustainable value-creating opportunities, and that several BMfS archetypes are potentially applicable to this area of organizational strategy. We also identified and categorized supply chain GHG emission objectives and the management activities.

A range of activities, if applied correctly, can also fulfil GHG emission reductions. These include stipulating supplier GHG emission reduction targets (through contracts) and providing help through information provision and dissemination or through supplier training. In addition, the research highlights the potential for such actions to constitute business model alterations consistent with BMfS, as well as highlighting how different types of BMfS could be applied to the challenge of managing supply chain GHG emissions.

This chapter has contributed to knowledge by deepening the understanding concerning the supply chain as an area of action for corporations engaging with climate change objectives (Hoffman, 2006; Kolk and Pinkse, 2005; Lee, 2012). It has illustrated which activities contributed to core climate change mitigation objectives, providing a guide to managers and practitioners as to which activities should be focused on when attempting to achieve specific goals. The results also provide additional detail to existing conceptual models of organizational engagement with climate change mitigation objectives and for SSCM approaches in terms of the management of gaseous wastes (Lee, 2012; Seuring and Müller, 2008). This chapter also explores the extent to which current approached may miss sustainable value-creating opportunities and which archetypes of BMfS are potentially applicable to the sustainability challenge of supply chain GHG emission management (Bocken et al., 2014; Lüdeke-Freund, 2009; Schaltegger et al., 2016).

Due to the small sample size and qualitative approach, this chapter has not answered questions of "how much." Although schemes such as the CDP indicate current engagement levels, several participants interviewed noted that their efforts were for internal use and not for reporting purposes. A quantitative survey of large focal organizations could provide answers to these questions. If such an investigation took place, questions such as the impact of different management activities could also be included, as well as drivers and barriers experienced. This research was also limited in the types of industries it sampled, raising questions over the influence of specific sectoral factors and the applicability of the results to different sectors.

BMfS offer a key avenue for the integration of supply chain GHG emissions into the core of organizations, taking it from CSR more toward genuinely sustainable business conceptions. This is a critical insight. The management of GHG emissions across supply chains represents an opportunity to manage a larger proportion of the GHG emissions associated with products and services, compared to targeting the internal emissions of any one single organization. Large public- or private-sector organizations control substantial amounts of resources and can influence numerous actors and many elements of the systems central to modern production and consumption. This research has demonstrated how the potential of large organizations to contribute positively to contemporary problems and their potential contribution, when considered in terms of embodied environmental impacts through supply chains, increases significantly.

Acknowledgments

This study was undertaken as part of a PhD studentship by T. B. Long, funded by the White Rose University Consortium, a strategic partnership between the UK Universities of Leeds, Sheffield, and York. The authors thank the anonymous reviewers of the chapter for their comments that significantly improved the chapter.

References

Aragón-Correa, J. A., & Rubio-Lopez, E. A. (2007). Proactive corporate environmental strategies: Myths and misunderstandings. *Long Range Planning*, **40**(3), 357–381.

Barnett, J. (2003). Security and climate change. *Global Environmental Change*, **13**, 7–17.

Beske, P., Land, A., & Seuring, S. (2014). Sustainable supply chain management practices and dynamic capabilities in the food industry: A critical analysis of the literature. *International Journal of Production Economics*, **152**, 131–143.

Bocken, N. M., de Pauw, I., Bakker, C., & van der Grinten, B. (2016). Product design and business model strategies for a circular economy. *Journal of Industrial and Production Engineering*, **33**, 308–320.

Bocken, N. M. P., & Allwood, J. M. (2012). Strategies to reduce the carbon footprint of consumer goods by influencing stakeholders. *Journal of Cleaner Production*, **35**, 118–129.

Bocken, N. M. P., & Short, S. W. (2016). Towards a sufficiency-driven business model: Experiences and opportunities. *Environmental Innovation and Societal Transitions*, **18**, 41–61.

Bocken, N. M. P., Short, S. W., Rana, P., & Evans, S. (2014). A literature and practice review to develop sustainable business model archetypes. *Journal of Cleaner Production*, **65**, 42–56.

Boiral, O. (2006). Global warming: Should companies adopt a proactive strategy? *Long Range Planning*, **39**, 315–330.

Boiral, O., Henri, J.-F., & Talbot, D. (2012). Modeling the impacts of corporate commitment on climate change. *Business Strategy and the Environment*, **21**, 495–516.

Boons, F., & Lüdeke-Freund, F. (2013). Business models for sustainable innovation: State-of-the-art and steps towards a research agenda. *Journal of Cleaner Production*, **45**, 9–19.

Boyatzis, R. E. (1998). *Transforming Qualitative Information: Thematic Analysis and Code Development* (London, UK: Sage).

Brickman, C., & Ungerman, D. (2008). Climate change and supply chain management. *The McKinsey Quarterly*. July, 1–2.

BSR (2010). The Business Case for Supply Chain Sustainability, In BSR (ed.). BSR, New York.

BSR (2015). *The State of Sustainable Business 2015* (New York: BSR).

Busch, T., & Schwarzkopf, J. (2013). Carbon management strategies — A quest for corporate competitiveness. *Progress in Industrial Ecology, an International Journal*, **8**, 4–29.

CDP (2013). *What We Do — Catalyzing Business and Government Action* (London: CDP).

Chaabane, A., Ramudhin, A., & Paquet, M. (2012). Design of sustainable supply chains under the emission trading scheme. *Advances in Optimization and Design of Supply Chains*, **135**, 37–49.

Ciliberti, F., Pontrandolfo, P., & Scozzi, B. (2008). Investigating corporate social responsibility in supply chains: A SME perspective. *Journal of Cleaner Production*, **16**, 1579–1588.

CIPS. (1998). *Buying into a Green Future: Partnerships for Change*. London: Business in the Environment (BIE); Publisher: Chartered Institute of Purchasing and Supply (CIPS) and Business in the Community (BITC), UK.

Côté, R. P., Lopez, J., Marche, S., Perron, G. M., & Wright, R. (2008). Influences, practices and opportunities for environmental supply chain management in Nova Scotia SMEs. *Journal of Cleaner Production*, **16**, 1561–1570.

Defra (2011). *Measuring and Reporting and Greenhouse Gas Emissions by UK Companies: A Consultation on Options*. Department for Environment, Food and Rural Affairs (HMG) London.

Donnelly, K., Beckett-Furnell, Z., Traeger, S., Okrasinski, T., & Holman, S. (2006). Ecodesign implemented through a product-based environmental management system. *Journal of Cleaner Production*, **14**, 1357–1367.

Downie, J., & Stubbs, W. (2012). Corporate carbon strategies and greenhouse gas emission assessments: the implications of scope 3 emission factor selection. *Business Strategy and the Environment*, **21**(6), 412–422.

Enkvist, P., Nauclér, T., & Oppenheim, J. M. (2008). Business strategies for climate change. *The McKinsey Quarterly*, **2**, 24–33.

Evans, S., Vladimirova, D., Holgado, M., Van Fossen, K., Yang, M., Silva, E. A. & Barlow, C. Y. (2017). Business model innovation for sustainability: Towards a unified perspective for creation of sustainable business models. *Business Strategy and the Environment*, **26**(5), 597–608.

Füssel, H. M. (2007). Adaptation planning for climate change: concepts, assessment approaches, and key lessons. *Sustainability Science*, **2**, 265–275.

Galbreath, J. (2010). Corporate governance practices that address climate change: An exploratory study. *Business Strategy and the Environment*, **19**, 335–350.

Garnett, T. (2011). Where are the best opportunities for reducing greenhouse gas emissions in the food system (including the food chain)? *Food Policy*, **36**, S23–S32.

Gillespie, B., & Rogers, M. M. (2016). Sustainable supply chain management and the end user: Understanding the impact of socially and environmentally responsible firm behaviors on consumers' brand evaluations and purchase intentions. *Journal of Marketing Channels*, **23**, 34–46.

Govindan, K., Soleimani, H., & Kannan, D. (2015). Reverse logistics and closed-loop supply chain: A comprehensive review to explore the future. *European Journal of Operational Research*, **240**, 603–626.

Green, J., & Thorogood, N. (2013). *Qualitative Methods for Health Research* (Sage). In European Operation Management Association (EurOMA) Conference.

Guion, R. M. (2008). Validity and reliability. In G. Rogelberg (ed.), *Handbook of Research Methods in Industrial and Organizational Psychology* (Malden, USA: Blackwell Publishing).

Hart, S. L. and Milstein, M. B. (2003). Creating sustainable value. *Academy of Management Perspectives*, **17**(2), 56–67.

Hahn, T., Figge, F., Pinkse, J., & Preuss, L. (2010). Trade-offs in corporate sustainability: You can't have your cake and eat it. *Business Strategy and the Environment*, **19**, 217–229.

Hoffman, A. J. (2005). Climate change strategy: The business logic behind greenhouse gas reductions. *California Management Review*, **47**, 21–46.

Hoffman, A. J. (2006). Getting ahead of the curve: Corporate strategies that address climate change. PEW Centre on Global Climate Change, Arlington, VA, USA.

Hsu, C.-W., Kuo, T.-C., Chen, S.-H., & Hu, A. H. (2011). Using DEMATEL to develop a carbon management model of supplier selection in green supply chain management. *Journal of Cleaner Production*, **56**, 164–172.

Johnson, B., & Christensen, L. (2010). *Educational Research: Quantitative, Qualitative and Mixed Approaches* (Thousand Oaks, USA: Sage).

Keating, B., Quazi, A., Kriz, A., & Coltman, T. (2008). In pursuit of a sustainable supply chain: Insights from Westpac Banking Corporation. *Supply Chain Management: An International Journal*, **13**, 175–179.

Kim, Y., Yun, S., Lee, J., & Ko, E. (2016). How consumer knowledge shapes green consumption: An empirical study on voluntary carbon offsetting. *International Journal of Advertising*, **35**, 23–41.

Knox-Hayes, J., & Levy, D. L. (2011). The politics of carbon disclosure as climate governance. *Strategic Organization*, **9**, 1–9.

Kolk, A., Levy, D., & Pinkse, J. (2008). Corporate responses in an emerging climate regime: The institutionalization and commensuration of carbon disclosure. *European Accounting Review*, **17**, 719–745.

Kolk, A., & Pinkse, J. (2005). Business responses to climate change: Identifying emergent strategies. *California Management Review*, **47**, 6–20.

Kolk, A., & Pinkse, J. (2008). Corporate responses in an emerging climate regime: The institutionalization and commensuration of carbon disclosure. *European Accounting Review*, **17**, 719-745.

Kovács, G. (2008). Corporate environmental responsibility in the supply chain. *Journal of Cleaner Production*, **16**, 1571–1578.

Lambert, D. M., & Cooper, M. C. (2000). Issues in supply chain management. *Industrial Marketing Management*, **29**, 65–83.

Lamming, R., & Hampson, J. (1996). The environment as a supply chain management issue. *British Journal of Management*, **7**, S45–S62.

Lash, J., & Wellington, F. (2007). Competitive advantage on a warming planet. *Harvard Business Review*, **85**, 95, 723–740.

Lee, K. (2011). Integrating carbon footprint into supply chain management: The case of Hyundai Motor Company (HMC) in the automobile industry. *Journal of Cleaner Production*, **19**, 1216–1223.

Lee, S.-Y. (2012). Corporate carbon strategies in responding to climate change. *Business Strategy and the Environment*, **21**, 33–48.

Li, A. Q., & Found, P. (2016). Lean and green supply chain for the Product-Services System (PSS): The literature review and a conceptual framework. *Procedia CIRP*, **47**, 162–167.

Long, T.B., Tallontire, A., & Young, W. (2015). CSR, voluntary standards and sustainability. In H. Kopnina, and E. Shoreman-Ouimet (eds.), *Sustainability — Key Issues* (UK: Routledge).

Long, T.B., & Young, W. (2015). An exploration of intervention options to enhance the management of supply chain greenhouse gas emissions in the UK. *Journal of Cleaner Production*.

Lovell, H., & MacKenzie, D. (2011). Accounting for carbon: The role of accounting professional organisations in governing climate change. *Antipode*, **43**, 704–730.

Lüdeke-Freund, F. (2009). Business model concepts in corporate sustainability contexts: From rhetoric to a generic template for "Business Models for Sustainability." Centre for Sustainability Management (CSM), Leuphana Universität Lüneburg.

Lüdeke-Freund, F., Gold, S., & Bocken, N. M. P. (2016). Sustainable business model and supply chain conceptions — Towards an integrated perspective. In L. Bals, and W. Tate (eds.), *Implementing Triple Bottom Line Sustainability into Global Supply Chains* (Sheffield, UK: Greenleaf), pp. 337–363.

Lumpkin, T. & Bacq, S. (2019). Civic wealth creation: A new view of stakeholder engagement and societal impact. *Academy of Management Perspectives*, **33**(4), 383–404.

Markman, G., Waldron, T., Gianiodis, P., & Espina, M. (2019). E Pluribus Unum: Impact entrepreneurship as a solution to grand challenges. *Academy of Management Perspectives*, **33**(4), 371–382.

Mason, M. (2010). Sample size and saturation in PhD studies using qualitative interviews. In Forum qualitative Sozialforschung/Forum: qualitative social research **11**(3).

Mont, O., & Lindhqvist, T. (2003). The role of public policy in advancement of product service systems. *Journal of Cleaner Production*, **11**, 905–914.

Mózner, Z. V. (2013). A consumption-based approach to carbon emission accounting — sectoral differences and environmental benefits. *Journal of Cleaner Production*, **42**, 83–95.

Munksgaard, J. & Pedersen, K. A. (2001). CO2 accounts for open economies: Producer or consumer responsibility? *Energy Policy*, **29**, 327–334.

Nishitani, K., Kokubu, K., & Kajiwara, T. (2016). Does low-carbon supply chain management reduce greenhouse gas emissions more effectively than existing environmental initiatives? An empirical analysis of Japanese manufacturing firms. *Journal of Management Control*, **27**, 33–60.

Oracle (2008). The shape of tomorrow's supply chains: The science of sustainability, The Future Laboratory Oracle, Reading, UK.

Pagell, M., & Wu, Z. (2009). Building a more complete theory of sustainable supply chain management using case studies of 10 exemplars. *Journal of Supply Chain Management*, **45**, 37–56.

Pagell, M., & Wu, Z. (2017). Business implications of sustainability practices in supply chains. In Y. Bouchery, C. J. Corbett, J. C. Fransoo, & T. Tan (eds.), *Sustainable Supply Chains: A Research-Based Textbook on Operations and Strategy* (Cham., Springer International Publishing), pp. 339–353.

Porter, M. E., & Kramer, M. R. (2006). Strategy and society: The link between competitive advantage and corporate social responsibility. *Havard Business Review*, **84**, 78–92.

Porter, M. E., & Reinhardt, F. L. (2007). A strategic approach to climate. *Harvard Business Review*, **85**, 22–26.

Porter, M. E., & van der Linde, C. (1995). Green and competitive. *Havard Business Review*, **73**, 120–134.

Porter, M. E., & Kramer, M. R. (2011). Creating shared value: redefining capitalism and the role of the corporation in society. *Harvard Business Review*, **89**(1/2).

Prahalad, C. K., & Ramaswamy, V. (2004). Co-creating unique value with customers. *Strategy & Leadership*, **3**, 4–9.

Prendeville S., & Bocken N. (2017). Design for Remanufacturing and Circular Business Models. In Matsumoto M., Masui K., Fukushige S., and Kondoh S. (eds). *Sustainability Through Innovation in Product Life Cycle Design*. EcoProduction (Environmental Issues in Logistics and Manufacturing). Springer, Singapore. https://doi-org.proxy-ub.rug.nl/10.1007/978-981-10-0471-1_18.

Preuss, L. (2005). Rhetoric and reality of corporate greening: A view from the supply chain management function. *Business Strategy and the Environment*, **14**, 123–139.

Preuss, L. (2010). Codes of conduct in organisational context: From cascade to latticework of codes. *Journal of Business Ethics*, **94**, 471–487.

Reid, E. M., & Toffel, M. W. (2009). Responding to public and private politics: Corporate disclosure of climate change strategies. *Strategic Management Journal*, **30**, 1157–1178.

Rockstrom, J., Steffen, W., Noone, K., Persson, A., Chapin, F. S., Lambin, E. F., Lenton, T. M., Scheffer, M., Folke, C., Schellnhuber, H. J., Nykvist, B., de Wit, C. A., Hughes, T., van der Leeuw, S., Rodhe, H., Sorlin, S., Snyder, P.K., Costanza, R., Svedin, U., Falkenmark, M., Karlberg, L., Corell, R. W., Fabry, V.J., Hansen, J., Walker, B., Liverman, D., Richardson, K., Crutzen, P., & Foley, J. A. (2009). A safe operating space for humanity. *Nature*, **461**, 472–475.

Schaltegger, S., Lüdeke-Freund, F., & Hansen, E. G. (2016). Business models for sustainability: A co-evolutionary analysis of sustainable entrepreneurship, innovation, and transformation. *Organization & Environment*, **29**(3), 264–289.

Schaltegger, S., & Wagner, M. (2011). Sustainable entrepreneurship and sustainability innovation: categories and interactions. *Business Strategy and the Environment*, **20**, 222–237.

Schaltegger, S., Lüdeke-Freund, F., & Hansen, E. G. (2012). Business cases for sustainability: The role of business model innovation for corporate sustainability. *International Journal of Innovation and Sustainable Development*, **6**(2), 95–119.

Schultz, K., & Williamson, P. (2005). Gaining competitive advantage in a carbon-constrained world: Strategies for European business. *European Management Journal*, **23**, 383–391.

Seuring, S., & Müller, M. (2008). From a literature review to a conceptual framework for sustainable supply chain management. *Journal of Cleaner Production*, **16**, 1699–1710.

Smith, R., & Tabibnia, G. (2012). Why radical transparency is good business. *Harvard Business Review*, October 11.

Soosay, C. A., Hyland, P. W., & Ferrer, M. (2008). Supply chain collaboration: Capabilities for continuous innovation. *Supply Chain Management: An International Journal*, **13**, 160–169.

Sprengel, D. C., & Busch, T. (2010). Stakeholder engagement and environmental strategy — The case of climate change. *Business Strategy and the Environment*, **20**, 351–364.

Srivastava, S. K. (2007). Green supply-chain management: A state-of-the-art literature review. *International Journal of Management Reviews*, **9**, 53–80.

Stiller, S., & Gold, S. (2014). Socially sustainable supply chain management practices in the Indian seed sector: A case study, *Supply Chain Forum: An International Journal*, pp. 52–67.

Sullivan, R. (2010). An assessment of the climate change policies and performance of large European companies. *Climate Policy*, **10**, 38–50.

Talbot, S., Lefebvre, É., & Lefebvre, L. A. (2007). Closed-loop supply chain activities and derived benefits in manufacturing SMEs. *Journal of Manufacturing Technology Management*, **18**, 627–658.

Turker, D., & Altuntas, C. (2014). Sustainable supply chain management in the fast fashion industry: An analysis of corporate reports. *European Management Journal*, **32**, 837–849.

Wackernagel, M., & Rees, W. E. (1996). *Our Ecological Footprint: Reducing Human Impact on the Earth* (Gabriola Island, BC: New Society).

Walker, H., Di Sisto, L., & McBain, D. (2008). Drivers and barriers to environmental supply chain management practices: Lessons from the public and private sectors. *Journal of Purchasing & Supply Chain Management*, **14**, 69–85.

Weinhofer, G., & Hoffman, V. H. (2010). Mitigating climate change — How do corporate strategies differ? *Business Strategy and the Environment*, **19**, 77–89.

WRAP (2013). Information sheet — Courtauld Commitment (Banbury, UK: WRAP).

Yang, M., Vladimirova, D., & Evans, S. (2017). Creating and capturing value through sustainability: The Sustainable Value Analysis Tool. A new tool helps companies discover opportunities to create and capture value through sustainability. *Research-Technology Management*, **60**(3), 30–39.

Yohe, G., & Strzepek, K. (2007). Adaptation and mitigation as complementary tools for reducing the risk of climate impacts. *Mitigation & Adaptation Strategies for Global Change*, **12**, 727–739.

Young, W., & Tilley, F. (2006). Can businesses move beyond efficiency? The shift toward effectiveness and equity in the corporate sustainability debate. *Business Strategy and the Environment*, **15**, 402–415.

Yunus, S., Elijido-Ten, E., & Abhayawansa, S. (2016). Determinants of carbon management strategy adoption: Evidence from Australia's top 200 publicly listed firms. *Managerial Auditing Journal*, **31**, 156–179.

Appendix

Matrices used during analysis can be seen in Tables A1–A3. The supply chain GHG emission management objectives can be seen on the top/columns, whilst the different management activities are presented on the left/rows. Where an objective

Table A1. Matrix: Activities within Tier One suppliers.

Objectives Impacted → Management Activities ↓	GHG Emission Scoping and Measurement	GHG Emission Reduction
Information Sharing & Dissemination	Direct (GHG emission information provided by suppliers required for reporting and disclosure).	Conditional Contribution (where information provided by suppliers is used to enable GHG emission reductions).
GHG Emissions Inclusion in Tenders and Contract	Conditional Direct (where GHG emission reporting and disclosure specified).	Conditional Direct (where GHG emission reductions stipulated).
Collaboration and Partnering Agreements	Conditional Direct (where agreement includes reporting and disclosure requirements).	Conditional Direct (where agreements include reduction requirements).
Direct Supplier Interventions	Conditional Direct (with interventions such as free GHG emission assessments, which provide GHG emission data from suppliers).	Conditional Direct (where focal organization funds contribute to capital works that reduce GHG emissions).
Management Standards & Verification Activities	Direct (i.e. B06 and their use of CEMARS with suppliers).	Contribution (improves the management of GHG emissions within the supply chain).
Supplier Involvement in Design	None	Contribution (supplier input able to reduce GHG emission of supply chain).
Supplier Schools & other Training	Conditional Direct (if supply chain is trained in how to conduct GHG emission assessment and report data).	Conditional Direct (if supplier trained in reducing GHG emissions).

Table A2. Matrix: Activities within focal organization.

Objectives Impacted → Management Activities ↓	GHG Emission Scoping and Measurement	GHG Emission Reduction
Supply Chain GHG Emission Modelling & Assessment	Direct (Provides unverified supply chain GHG emission information, suitable for some reporting requirements).	Conditional Contribution (where modelling used to identify hotspots, and enable reduction actions).
Design Changes to Reduce supply chain GHG emissions	None	Direct
Internal Training and Information Provision	Conditional Direct (where information needs to be shared internally).	Conditional Contribution (where information needs to be shared internally).
Embedding of Supply Chain GHG Emissions into Commercial Teams	Conditional Contribution (where this mainstreaming improves collection of information from supply chain).	Contribution (eases efforts to engage with, and influence, suppliers toward these aims).

Table A3. Matrix: Activities downstream in supply chains.

Objectives Impacted → Management Activities ↓	GHG Emission Scoping and Measurement	GHG Emission Reduction
Influencing Customer Use of Products for GHG Emission Reductions	Conditional Contribution (only in relation to product labelling efforts, which could involve data collection from suppliers).	None
Research on Consumers Use of Products	Conditional Contribution (where focal organization includes downstream GHG emissions within its reporting).	Conditional Contribution (where consumer use highlights changes that can reduce supply chain GHG emissions).

intersects with a management activity the type of relationship is noted with a brief reasoning.

There are four types of relationship between activities and objectives/outcomes were established:

(5) "Direct" = activity is central to the fulfillment of the objective or outcome, for example, see Table A3.

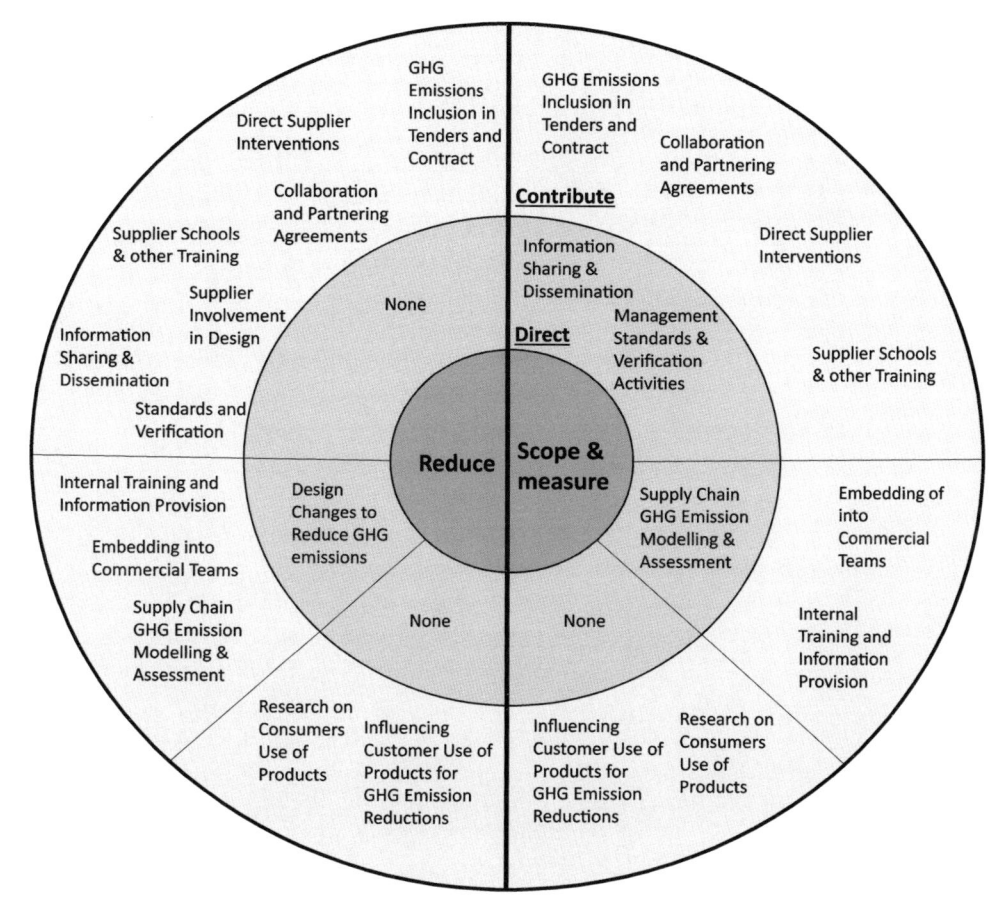

Figure A1. Wheel illustrating the ranges of activities that directly fulfilled or contributed (conditionally or directly) to the fulfillment of the different objectives. The two objectives, including the reduction of supply chain GHG emissions and the measurement of scoping of supply chain GHG emissions, are located in the center. The location of an activity on the left or right indicates the different objectives, while location on inner or outer ring indicates whether there is a direct (inner) or contributory (outer) relationship.

(6) "Contribute" = activity contributes towards an objective or outcome, but in isolation would be unable to fulfil objective or outcome.
(7) "Conditional Contribution or Conditional Direct" = where activity could, if designed and applied appropriately, directly fulfil objective/contribute to fulfillment of objective.
(8) "None" = no relationship between activity and outcome/objective.

More detailed information regarding the objectives can be found in section 3.4.1 and section 3.4.2 contains more detailed information on the different activities (see Figure A1).

© 2022 World Scientific Publishing Company
https://doi.org/10.1142/9789811248863_0004

Chapter 4

Corporate Sustainability, Stakeholder Orientation, and Collaboration between Competitors: What Lies Beneath

Lilach Trabelsi

University of Geneva, Geneva, Switzerland
Webster University, Geneva

lilach.trabelsi@unige.ch

Abstract

This study applies a corporate stakeholder orientation lens to explore how firms' consideration of stakeholders' perspectives, interests, and needs influence their decision to participate in multi-stakeholder initiatives (MSIs) aimed at tackling grand challenges in the sustainability realm alongside their competitors. The importance of the stakeholder orientation of firms is revealed through the uncovering of contextual factors, both at the firm and the industry level. In particular, this study highlights the role of the orientation of individual firms vis-à-vis their suppliers (through supply chain awareness and supplier overlap), customers (through customer overlap), competitors (through perceived level of competition), regulators and civil society (through antitrust apprehension and sustainability regulation), and out-of-industry actors (through industry stigma), in incentivizing firms to participate in MSIs. To uncover the contextual factors, a qualitative analysis of twenty-six semi-structured interviews conducted with knowledgeable professionals working in US and European firms and MSIs is undertaken. Interview analysis is followed by a qualitative comparative analysis (QCA), which provides a clearer understanding of whether and how the various contextual factors relate to each other. The QCA analysis points to the primary importance of firm orientation towards suppliers in the goods sector, and customers in the services sector, in the decision of firms to participate in MSIs.

Keywords: Corporate sustainability; stakeholder orientation; competitor collaboration; multi-stakeholder initiatives; decision-making.

4.1. Introduction

Over recent decades, businesses have seen growing concern and attention being paid to their ability to secure a future for the next generations. Increased awareness of sustainability-related issues has led to increased pressures on businesses to act in a more sustainable manner (Freeman *et al.*, 2010). Today, firms take a more systemic approach to sustainability, as it is increasingly integrated throughout firms (Ernst and Young, 2011).

Firms can use sustainability as a strategic tool to provide increased value to their stakeholders (Malik, 2015). Firms that have relatively advanced sustainability strategies can collaborate with stakeholders such as regulators, communities, and civil society, and form strategic alliances with major competitors to address complex sustainability problems (Buysse and Verbeke, 2003; Gray and Stites, 2013).

Effectively, in recent decades, deficits in global business regulation of sustainability-related concerns, coupled with the understanding that unilateral firm actions may be insufficient, resulted in a decline in the command-and-control mode of regulation and the rise of global governance initiatives, often referred to as multi-stakeholder initiatives (MSIs), that try to regulate global business (Baek, 2017; Mele and Schepers, 2013; Voegtlin and Pless, 2014). An MSI is an entity that works with multiple stakeholders (e.g. businesses, civil society, regulators) to solve sustainability problems that cannot be solved at an individual-firm level (Baumann-Pauly *et al.*, 2017). Within the framework of MSIs, firms try to address a variety of environmental and social issues across and between industries (Castka and Corbett, 2016). Over recent decades, many MSIs have been developed to support firms in their sustainability efforts (Runhaar and Lafferty, 2009). Regardless of which sector initiates the initiative, firm participation in these initiatives is indispensable (Mele and Schepers, 2013).

By and large, MSIs have emerged as an important empirical phenomenon in global governance processes that is of high practical relevance. They help provide a response to pressing, global sustainability challenges. As part of these initiatives, firms co-create and voluntarily commit to new sustainability standards, compensating for governance gaps and going beyond existing regulation (Zeyen *et al.*, 2016).

Thus, MSIs have become an integral and vital part of organizational sustainability efforts (Moog *et al.*, 2015), yet they remain underexplored (Baumann-Pauly *et al.*, 2017).

Participation in MSIs may help firms manage and facilitate their transition toward more stakeholder-oriented and sustainable forms of enterprise. The corporate sustainability context is especially pertinent for evaluating the attitudes of firms toward their stakeholders as the impacts of firms' actions on their social and environmental performance are seen as proxies for organizational effectiveness for becoming more stakeholder-oriented, and hence satisfying various stakeholders' needs and interests. To do so, firms may need to undergo fundamental changes in their core purpose and identity, as their processes, outcomes, and strategies become more stakeholder-oriented (Zollo *et al.*, 2016). Working with competitors within the framework of MSIs may be an indication of the willingness of firms to take actions toward the achievement of such fundamental changes.

Despite their prevalence and importance, collaborations between competitors arising in the context of sustainability appear to have been understudied. This study aims to enhance our understanding of the role of the stakeholder orientation of firms in their decision to collaborate with their competitors within the framework of MSIs. Employing a stakeholder-orientation lens, this qualitative study discusses contextual factors, both at the firm and the industry level, that incentivize or deter firms from collaborating with their competitors within the framework of MSIs. These factors, indicative of the stakeholder orientation of firms, include supply chain awareness, supplier overlap, customer overlap, perceived level of competition, antitrust apprehension, sustainability regulation, and industry stigma.

The study highlights the role of the orientation of individual firms vis-à-vis their suppliers (through supply chain awareness and supplier overlap), customers (through customer overlap), competitors (through perceived level of competition), regulators and civil society (through antitrust apprehension and sustainability regulation), and out-of-industry actors (through industry stigma), in incentivizing firms to participate in MSIs. Conclusions are also drawn with respect to how the contextual factors relate to each other, as well as their relative importance. These point to the primary role of firm orientation toward suppliers in the goods sector, and customers in the services sector, in the decision of firms to participate in MSIs.

To uncover the contextual factors indicative of the stakeholder orientation of firms, a qualitative analysis of 26 semi-structured interviews conducted with knowledgeable sustainability professionals working in US and European firms and MSIs is undertaken. To obtain a more holistic view of the findings, the qualitative interview analysis is followed by a qualitative comparative analysis (QCA). The QCA facilitates a clearer understanding of whether and how the contextual factors relate to each other in influencing firms to join MSIs and collaborate with their competitors.

Taking an explorative, cross-industry approach toward an enhanced understanding of the importance of the collaboration of firms with competitors within the framework of MSIs for their ability to address systemic sustainability challenges, this study reinforces the general notion that MSIs are an important tool for tackling various sustainability challenges (Seitanidi and Crane, 2014). Enhancing our understanding of how the stakeholder orientation of firms may influence their decision to join MSIs and collaborate with their competitors is of interest not only to scholars studying the transformation of the business models of firms toward greater sustainability but also for managers and practitioners interested in creating and being a part of more sustainable enterprises.

From a managerial perspective, the resulting insights may help draw the attention of managers to the link between the stakeholder orientation of their firms vis-à-vis various stakeholder groups, and their willingness to take advantage of participation in MSIs as a means to assist them on their path toward becoming more sustainable enterprises. This may assist managers in better understanding under what circumstances involvement in MSIs alongside competitors may make more or less sense for their firm and could potentially trigger a need to reevaluate the way in which their firm prioritizes the needs of stakeholders and firm participation in MSIs.

4.2. Literature Review

Sustainability has been increasingly highly placed on research agendas. The sustainability literature attempts to highlight that firm obligations should go beyond financial considerations and include obligations to society, as it discusses the purpose of the firm and how it can achieve what may be perceived as multiple and separate goals (Freeman *et al.*, 2010). It has been argued that "doing good [...] leads to doing better" (Lindgreen and Swaen, 2010), and that, in today's society, "good ethics is good business" (Van Beurden and Gössling, 2008). Increased awareness of sustainability-related issues has led to increased pressures on businesses to act in a more sustainable manner (Freeman *et al.*, 2010).

Hence, in recent years, investors have been perceiving a strong link between corporate sustainability and financial performance. They are more likely to use Environmental, Social, and Governance (ESG) firm data to make investment decisions. Investors believe that greater potential for long-term value creation, improved revenue potential, and operational efficiency, provide business value to firms that invest in sustainability. Importantly, investors are increasingly likely to divest firms that have a poor sustainability track record. Indeed, evidence that sustainability-related activities are material to the financial success of a company over time has become more prevalent, and investors are more likely to believe that the sustainability actions of firms can create tangible value for the firms (MIT and BCG, 2016). Furthermore, executives understand that sustainability is important for business and perceive sustainability as increasingly vital for firm strategy as they incorporate it into the business. There is also indication of a growing perception that sustainability should be a top CEO priority, as executives see an important business role for sustainability (McKinsey, 2014).

Over time, firms have been taking a more systemic and proactive (rather than reactive) approach to sustainability (Ernst and Young, 2011; Utting, 2005). While it is often difficult for firms to observe the effectiveness of their sustainability efforts, sustainability is perceived "as a mechanism to energize and motivate stakeholders, as well as manage societal perceptions and expectations on the role and utility of businesses in societies and communities" (Wang *et al.*, 2016, p. 534). By integrating it at the strategic level, firms can use sustainability as a tool to provide greater value to their stakeholders (Malik, 2015).

As concerns related to the sustainability of firms persist, three types of solutions to alleviate those concerns may come to mind. The most prevalent one in the past followed the command-and-control route, where governments impose regulations on firms. A second solution is the reliance on market incentives. A third solution is self-regulation by firms (Argandoña, 2004). Given economic globalization, and the global nature of sustainability issues, both command-and-control and individual-firm-level approaches appear to be insufficient. Actors from different sectors started referring to the need for a cooperative paradigm (Lund-Thomsen and Lindgreen, 2014). Whether trying to address social concerns, such as the implementation of responsible labor standards in the entire value chain (Lin-Hi and Blumberg, 2017), or environmental ones, such as the generation of environmental standards (Buysse and Verbeke, 2003), collective action was called for (Lin-Hi and Blumberg, 2017).

In effect, increasingly, global competition is not purely competitive. Firms may simultaneously compete and collaborate with the same rival or rivals (Luo, 2007). Already a couple of decades ago, Lado *et al.* (1997: 111) stated that "success in today's business world often requires that firms pursue both competitive and cooperative strategies simultaneously," and that, "cooperation can enhance the competitive position of a firm." This is because competitors are more likely to be facing similar market conditions, customer needs, and uncertainty concerns, facilitating the generation of a common understanding of the issues faced by the various competing organizations and potential solutions to said issues (Bouncken *et al.*, 2015).

Considering the deficits in global business regulation of sustainability-related concerns together with the understanding that unilateral firm actions may be insufficient, more encompassing global governance initiatives, often referred to as MSIs have been established to try to remedy global governance gaps and regulate global business (Baek, 2017; Mele and Schepers, 2013; Voegtlin and Pless, 2014). MSIs are thus located between command-and-control regulatory approaches and single-firm undertakings aimed at addressing sustainability issues (Baumann-Pauly *et al.*, 2017).

An MSI is an entity that works with multiple stakeholders (e.g. businesses, civil society, regulators) to solve sustainability problems that cannot be solved at an individual-firm level (Baumann-Pauly *et al.*, 2017). MSIs try to address a variety of environmental and social issues across and between industries (Castka and Corbett, 2016). Many initiatives have been developed to support firms in their sustainability efforts over recent decades (Runhaar and Lafferty, 2009) as firm-level solutions started being perceived as inadequate, while the understanding of the usefulness of the inclusion of additional stakeholders started gaining traction (Baumann-Pauly *et al.*, 2017).

A collaboration continuum ensuing from the analysis of the more general area of cross-sector partnerships suggests that there are four types of collaborations: philanthropic, transactional, integrative, and transformative (Austin and Seitanidi, 2012; Gray and Stites, 2013; Seitanidi and Crane, 2014). Focusing on MSIs, this study is concerned with collaborations that fall under the integrative and transformative categories, and that include firms as key actors. These types of collaborations have a relatively wide scope and high levels of shared ownership and responsibility of actors. Firms in such initiatives try to balance their financial, social, and environmental concerns, with firms in transformative initiatives also deliberately trying to integrate stakeholder expectations (Gray and Stites, 2013). Firm participation in these MSIs is indispensable (Mele and Schepers, 2013).

Existing studies point to several benefits that firms participating in MSIs may enjoy. Adherence to these initiatives can generate economic, reputational, and legitimacy benefits, as well as learning, cooperation, and networking opportunities (Arevalo and Aravind, 2017; Berliner and Prakash, 2015; Cetindamar, 2007; Mele and Schepers, 2013; Runhaar and Lafferty, 2009). Participation enables stakeholders to observe the sustainability actions and performance of participating firms (hence enhancing firm transparency), and stakeholders may react accordingly (Baek, 2017; Janney *et al.*, 2009; Runhaar and Lafferty, 2009). For instance, regulatory agencies may reduce regulatory pressure, investors may show confidence in firms leading to better market performance, consumers may demonstrate increased loyalty, and the firm may enjoy more goodwill and be able to sell products at higher prices (Baek, 2017; Cetindamar, 2007; Janney *et al.*, 2009). Firms may therefore enjoy a range of benefits, including those related to regulatory expectations, market opportunities, operations, and customer relationships (Bowler *et al.*, 2017). The impact of participation on individual firms can vary among participants (O'Faircheallaigh, 2015).

While increasing in popularity, MSIs are also facing criticism when compared to other approaches. One such criticism is that following this approach means that firms are regulating themselves. This poses the risk that firms may be choosing to take actions that would be considered too lenient compared with other regulatory approaches, which would result in the rejection of such approaches by regulators and society (Argandoña, 2004). Additionally, member firms may enjoy enhanced reputation without making substantial changes to their operations (Perez-Batres et al., 2012).

MSIs are particularly important for addressing sustainability challenges, given the nature of the issues to be resolved. Sustainability issues are often complex, broad, and systemic in nature, and firms within the same industry often face similar sustainability issues. Solving these types of issues requires competitors to collaborate, especially when a problem is faced by an industry as a whole (Buysse and Verbeke, 2003; NBS, 2017). An observed rise in simultaneous collaborative and competitive approaches over time in the sustainability context may be due to growing interdependence among global competitors and an increase in the need for collective action, risk-sharing, and strategic flexibility (Bouncken et al., 2015; Luo, 2007). The interdependency between competing firms is an important feature of the reality that competing firms face as they attempt to tackle sustainability concerns.

A special emphasis may be placed on the role of indirect links between competitors passing via several stakeholders (i.e. suppliers, customers, regulatory bodies), as well as the common use of external limited resources. It is therefore paramount to view the firm as part of a world encompassing itself, its stakeholders (including its competitors), the stakeholders of its competitors, and a limited amount of external resources. External resources provided by the earth, for instance, are not only limited at any given point in time, their availability is also changing due to external factors, such as climate change. Other resources, such as qualified labor, are also expected to be in short supply in some cases. This may be because the demand for a certain input is growing while the quantity of qualified labor is not, and/or because qualified labor no longer finds the provision of the input profitable and moves away from it towards other sources of income.

Hence, links are found between firms and their stakeholders, but importantly, between stakeholders of different competing firms, and between individual stakeholders and multiple competing firms (see Figure 4.1 for a simplified illustration). Not only do firms in the same industry face similar issues, they also share stakeholders, and therefore the very same stakeholder-related issues.

Therefore, MSIs are particularly important due to two main reasons. The first one is the inability of firms to tackle sustainability issues on their own, given the complex and systemic nature of similar sustainability issues that firms in the same industry face. The second one is the interdependency between competing firms that are indirectly linked to each other through their stakeholders and the common use of limited external resources. Existing literature evaluating firm motivations to participate in cross-sector collaborations, in particular with social organizations, classifies firm motivations to collaborate by placing firms in a

External environment

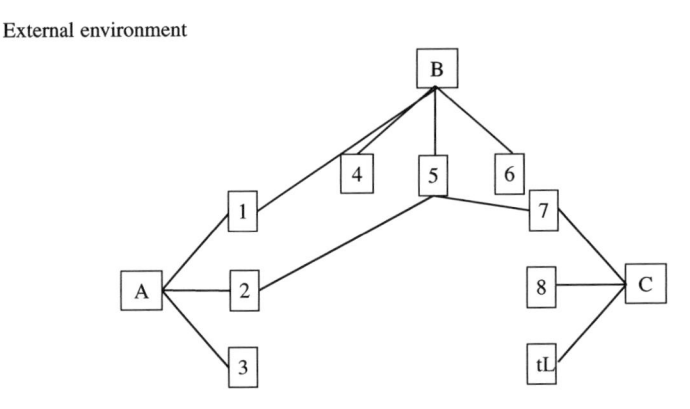

Figure 4.1. Simplified view of the firm's world.

Note: Letters represent competing firms, numbers represent stakeholders, and lines represent ties. Each firm has internal resources. External resources are found in the external environment and are limited. Stakeholder 1 is a direct stakeholder of both firms A and B. Stakeholders 2, 5, and 7 are directly and indirectly connected to different firms and are also either directly or indirectly connected to each other.

framework, with one axis representing the degree to which firm motivations are altruistic (as opposed to self-interested), and a second axis representing the degree to which firm motivations are utilitarian (as opposed to idealistic) (Austin and Reficco, 2005). The motivations of firms are expected to be predominantly utilitarian and self-interested as they try to improve their triple bottom line (Austin and Reficco, 2005). This, however, does not prevent firm actions from potentially benefiting more generally the environment and society as a whole, creating a win-win situation. According to the classification by Gray and Stites (2013), the motivation of firms to collaborate, mainly with other sectors, can be classified into four categories: legitimacy-oriented, competency-oriented, resource-oriented, and society-oriented motivations. In this study, a stakeholder-orientation lens is applied to enhance our understanding of factors taken into account during the decision-making process behind the willingness of firms to collaborate with their competitors within the framework of MSIs to advance a sustainability agenda.

4.3. Methods

This study explores the decision-making of firms with regard to their participation in MSIs. To generate insights on the phenomenon at hand, namely, the participation of firms in MSIs to tackle sustainability issues together with their competitors, an insider's view was sought. This study first takes a qualitative approach and then complements it using QCA.

In an effort to gather data, firms and relevant MSIs were contacted to obtain interviews with knowledgeable individuals. In total, 26 semi-structured interviews were conducted between October 2016 and May 2017. Some interviewees are sustainability professionals working predominantly for firms in the textile/apparel, food and beverages, and finance industries (with the exception of one interviewee holding the position of CEO). Other interviewees are sustainability professionals working for relevant MSIs, also related to a range of industries, henceforth referred to as "experts."

The textile/apparel industry is an important one to examine as it has been the focus of media and civil society attention for several years, mainly due to poor working conditions along the supply chain. The food and beverages industry caters to the fulfillment of some of the basic needs of an ever-growing world population with increasingly limited earthly resources. Finally, the finance industry is a key intermediary providing firms with means to carry out various activities and is uniquely positioned in such a way that it can act as a "gatekeeper," promoting or prohibiting the undertaking of certain activities.

In preparation for the interviews, several informal discussions were held with knowledgeable individuals, and online research on the topic and relevant organizations was conducted to help ensure that pertinent questions would be asked. The average interview length is around 50 minutes, average interviewee tenure with his/her organization is 7.4 years, and all but one interviewee work directly on corporate sustainability matters, with the remaining interviewee holding the position of CEO. Most of the firms interviewed are some of the largest in the world, while the membership size of the MSIs whose employees were interviewed exceeds 100.

All interviews were recorded, transcribed, and analyzed. Data was inserted into and coded using the NVivo software. A vertical reading of the interviews for the coding of the data was followed by a horizontal reading of the interviews to compare the data and generate insights, as well as for the categorization of the codes. No additional interviews were sought once information of only marginal value was generated via later interviews relative to previously collected data (i.e. emerging theoretical categories appeared to be "saturated").

More specifically, for every transcribed interview, data analysis began with a reading of the interview from beginning to end, and the coding of every piece of text found in the interviewee's answers. Hence, a code reflecting the subject matter discussed was attached to every piece of text using the NVivo software. All the pieces of text describing or discussing a similar topic were given the same code. This vertical reading and coding of the data was followed by a horizontal reading of the data, or, in other words, the comparison of the information provided by the different interviewees that was grouped under the various individual codes. This facilitated a more in-depth discovery of insights that transpire from the data in relation to the individual codes, going beyond the more superficial understanding obtained through the generation of the various codes. Furthermore, at the end of the coding process, and based on the understanding of the insights generated through the analysis of the data found under the various codes, the codes were grouped into categories, where relevant. For example, the codes "supply chain location," "supply chain structure," and "supplier power," were all placed under the category "supplier overlap."

Interviews with firms mainly centered around the individual firm's approach to sustainability, how sustainability is incorporated into the firm, internal and external pressures on the firm to behave in a sustainable manner, motivation for collaborating with competitors and perceived risks, and how collaborations come about. Interviews with MSI employees revolved around initiative members' motivation to collaborate, benefits and downsides to collaborations, differences between firms and/or industry characteristics and how they might affect firm likelihood to join and benefit from collaborations, as well as how collaboration actually happens. Table 4.1 provides an overview of the interviews conducted. Given that all MSIs in the sample of this study cater to more than 100 members, all MSIs are categorized as large.

QCA can complement the type of qualitative research conducted in this study. It helps provide a more complete view of the data that is both interpretable and does not ignore relatively rare data, does not require a large number of cases to produce meaningful results, and is therefore effective even when analyzing a relatively small number of cases (Lacey and Cohen, 2015). It facilitates the discovery of different combinations of causal variables that lead to a certain outcome and can help test models in which there are multiple interacting variables (Longest and Vaisey, 2008). Additionally, QCA allows for the examination of how effects combine and interact across levels (Lacey and Fiss, 2009). This is helpful seeing as some of the contextual factors that were uncovered are at the firm level and others are at the industry level.

To perform a QCA using the interview data, qualitative data was converted into quantitative data. For every interview, participation in an initiative (the outcome variable) and the presence of the different contextual factors (supply chain awareness, supplier overlap, customer overlap, perceived level of competition, antitrust apprehension, sustainability regulation, and industry stigma) were coded. The variables were coded in the following manner:

Participation: A value of 1 was given if a firm generally participates in MSIs or if the interviewed employee works for an MSI; a value of 0.7 was given if a firm is mostly favorable to participation in MSIs; a value of 0.3 was given if a firm is mostly not favorable to participation in MSIs; and a value of 0 was given if a firm does not participate in MSIs.

Contextual factors: For every contextual factor, a value of 1 was given if the factor was mentioned during the interview, and 0 otherwise.

Table 4.1. Interview overview.

Interview #	Organization type	HQ location	Industry	Organization age (in years)	Firm size (2016 revenues in billions of USD)	Management level/location within firm
1	MSI	Europe	Cross-industry	Between 51–99	—	—
2	Firm	Europe	Healthcare	20 or below	20 or below	Senior/Main office
3	Firm	US	Diversified industrials	Over 100	Over 100	Middle/HQ
4	MSI	Europe	Cross-industry	20 or below	—	—
5	Firm	US	Diversified industrials	Over 100	Over 100	Middle/Subsidiary
6	Firm	Europe	Finance	20 or below	20 or below	Senior/HQ
7	Firm	US	Tobacco	Over 100	Between 51 and 99	Middle/HQ
8	Firm	Europe	Food & beverages	Over 100	Between 51 and 99	Senior/HQ
9	Firm	US	Food & beverages	Between 51–99	Between 21 and 50	Middle/Regional office
10	MSI	US	Cross-industry	Between 21–50	—	—
11	Firm	Europe	Finance	Over 100	Between 21 and 50	Senior/HQ
12	MSI	Europe	Single industry	20 or below	—	—
13	MSI	Europe	Cross-industry	Between 51–99	—	—
14	MSI	Europe	Single industry	20 or below	—	—
15	MSI	Europe	Single industry	20 or below	—	—
16	MSI	US	Cross-industry	Between 21–50	—	—
17	Firm	US	Finance	Over 100	Between 51 and 99	Senior/HQ
18	MSI	Europe	Cross-industry	Over 100	—	—
19	Firm	Europe	Food & beverages	Over 100	20 or below	Senior/HQ
20	Firm	US	Apparel	Over 100	20 or below	Middle/Regional office
21	Firm	US	Finance	Over 100	Between 51 and 99	Senior/Main office
22	Firm	Europe	Retail	Between 51–99	20 or below	Middle/HQ
23	MSI	Europe	Single industry	Over 100	—	—
24	MSI	Europe	Cross-industry	Over 100	—	—
25	MSI	Europe	Single industry	Over 100	—	—
26	MSI	US	Cross-industry	Over 100	—	—

Note: MSI stands for multistakeholder initiative; in the Industry column, the industry is provided for firms, and only an indication of whether the initiative covers one or more industries is provided for initiatives. This is to help preserve responders' anonymity.

Having converted the qualitative data into quantitative data, the entire sample composed of coded data from the 26 interviews was analyzed using the fuzzy command in Stata to gain a more in-depth understanding of the qualitative findings (Longest and Vaisey, 2008).

4.4. Findings

The stakeholder theory acknowledges that firms are accountable not only to their shareholders but also to a wide range of stakeholders. Stakeholders are "groups and individuals who have a stake in the success or failure of a business." The stakeholder theory suggests that, to succeed, a firm needs to be able to manage its relationships with multiple stakeholders (Van Beurden and Gössling, 2008). It has also been argued that sustainability requires a "mechanism for balancing stakeholders' interests" (Freeman *et al.*, 2010).

Thus, this study employs a stakeholder-orientation lens to enhance our understanding of how individual firms react to and take various stakeholders into consideration when deciding whether to join an MSI and work with competitors on the advancement of a sustainability agenda, as they attempt to become more sustainable enterprises. The discussion about the stakeholder orientation of firms is based on the understanding of seven contextual factors uncovered by the qualitative analysis of the semi-structured interviews. These factors are indicative of the orientation of firms vis-à-vis several stakeholders. In particular, the orientation of firms toward their suppliers, customers, competitors, regulators and civil society, and a more general group of out-of-industry actors is revealed by discussing the following contextual factors: supply chain awareness, supplier overlap, customer overlap, perceived level of competition, antitrust apprehension, sustainability regulation, and industry stigma. The contextual factors influencing the willingness of firms to participate in MSIs are found both at the firm and the industry level. Firm-level factors refer to internally generated firm perceptions and realities. Industry-level factors refer to industry-level realities or ways of doing business (see Figure 4.2).

As can be seen in Figure 4.2, the orientation of firms vis-à-vis their suppliers as well as regulators and civil society is influenced by both internally generated perceptions and industry-level realities. The orientation of firms toward customers and out-of-industry actors is influenced by industry-level realities, whereas their orientation toward competitors is affected by internally generated perceptions.

In this section, following the discussion of the link between the contextual factors and the stakeholder orientation of firms below, the findings of the QCA analysis are assessed. The QCA analysis enriches our understanding of how the different contextual factors relate to each other, which are perceived as more important, and enables the drawing of additional conclusions in relation to the stakeholder orientation of firms.

```
                    ┌─────────────────────────────┐
                    │ SUPPLIERS                   │
                    │ Supply chain awareness (+)(F)│
                    │ Supplier overlap (+)(I)     │
                    └─────────────────────────────┘
┌──────────────────────────┐                      ┌──────────────────────────┐
│ OUT-OF-INDUSTRY ACTORS   │                      │ CUSTOMERS                │
│ Industry stigma (+)(I)   │                      │ Customer overlap (+)(I)  │
└──────────────────────────┘    FOCAL FIRM        └──────────────────────────┘
┌──────────────────────────────────┐  ┌────────────────────────────────────┐
│ REGULATORS and CIVIL SOCIETY     │  │ COMPETITORS                        │
│ Antitrust apprehension (−)(F)    │  │ Perceived level of competition (−)(F)│
│ Sustainability regulation (+)(I) │  │                                    │
└──────────────────────────────────┘  └────────────────────────────────────┘
```

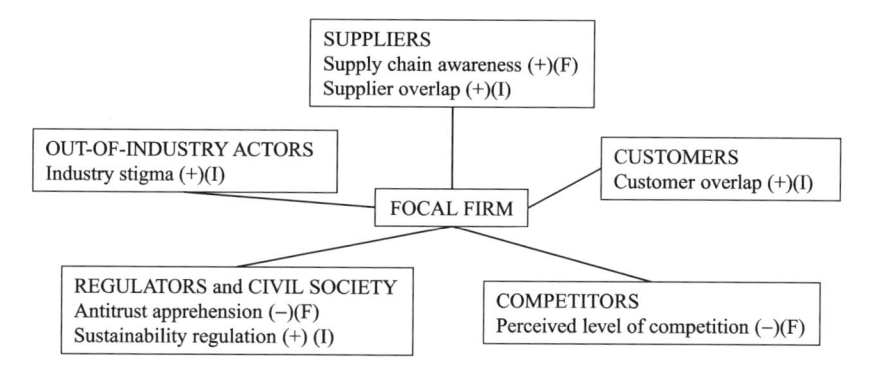

Figure 4.2. The stakeholder orientation of firms.

Note: (+) and (−) indicate the direction in which a factor is expected to influence the likelihood of firm participation in MSIs. (F) and (I) indicate whether a factor is at the firm level (F), or at the industry level (I).

The analysis below centers around the different stakeholders that firms take into consideration when they decide whether to participate in MSIs. The orientation of firms toward the various stakeholder groups and the relevant contextual factors supported by interview data are elaborated on.

4.4.1. *Suppliers*

The orientation of firms toward their suppliers is evidenced by two factors. The first one is the need for firms to have basic awareness of what their supply chain looks like, which many firms lack, and can motivate them to join MSIs. *Supply chain awareness* is therefore internal to the firm and is a firm-level factor. The higher the awareness of firms of what their supply chains looks like, the higher the likelihood that they would be willing to join relevant MSIs. The second factor is related to the way in which supply chains function at the industry level. In different industries, such as the textile/apparel and the food and beverages industries, firms share suppliers, creating *supplier overlap*. When there is supplier overlap, firms are incentivized to collaborate with their competitors toward finding solutions to sustainability concerns. Supply-chain-related issues seem to be of general concern, as they were mentioned often both by experts and by sustainability professionals working for goods-producing firms.

4.4.1.1. *Supply chain awareness*

The supply chains of many firms today are very intricate and span across multiple locations and geographies. At the same time, many firms are not aware of the different parts of their supply chain. In fact, "most companies […] have limited understanding of all the links in their supply chain" (interview 13). This is why MSIs may "engage with companies that don't have good understanding. [They] have to map their supply chain" (interview 13). Not only are firms not aware of the different elements in their supply chain, they sometimes do not even realize that they should learn about their supply chain. Indeed, "until very recently [firms] thought that the only thing they need to be worried about is the direct suppliers, and little by little they realize that there are many other direct and indirect links that they need to watch out for" (interview 18).

While "usually [firms] think that the conditions [in the supply chain] are better than they actually are" (interview 4), a need to better understand their supply chain can arise when stakeholders put pressure on firms via "a media exposé" (interview 4). "In those sectors, [firms] would be more aware than in many other sectors" (interview 4), even though they still "tend not to agree too much" (interview 4) about the conditions. Sometimes the pressure is anticipated by firms, as was the case with cotton, where firms may have "anticipated that eventually they will be under pressure, that cotton will be the next thing, so they tried to take measures in advance" (interview 23).

By joining MSIs, firms can learn how to "map the supply chain and then learn about how to deal with issues [...] How do I react in a way that is responsible, respecting the people [in the supply chain] but also my own company" (interview 18). For example, in the textile industry, "the supply chain is really not transparent. So the problem is that we have direct contracts with our suppliers, but the supplier so many times is just an agency or just a person that then outsources all the contracts, all the orders, and then you already lose control of who he is sourcing it out to. [...] So it's really easy to just completely lose control over the supply chain. [...] In working together there is a much better way to somehow get more transparency into the supply chain and get back the control" (interview 22). By collaborating, firms "gain knowledge about their supply chain, and get an understanding of it. [...] Also as a result, they start thinking more strategically about their supply chain" (interview 23).

Hence, once firms become aware of the need to better understand their supply chain, they can join MSIs and work with competitors to learn about and work on improving sustainability along their supply chain. The higher the awareness of firms of what their supply chain looks like, the higher the likelihood that a firm would be willing to join an MSI, as higher awareness results in a better understanding of the need to address sustainability challenges along the supply chain. An assessment of the interviews shows that references made to supply chain awareness (or lack thereof) were made by experts, indicating that supply chain awareness is a general concern, while it also seems to be of particular concern in the textile/apparel industry. The textile/apparel industry is also a particularly striking example of an industry with substantial supplier overlap, the second contextual factor indicative of firm orientation toward suppliers.

4.4.1.2. Supplier overlap

In some industries, firms that want to improve sustainability along their supply chain may find that they are unable to do so without working together with some of their competitors toward that end. The need to collaborate with others stems from the inability of individual firms to influence their suppliers on their own. As a group, firms can increase their influence over their suppliers. Collaborations can be useful when (i) suppliers are co-located and (ii) suppliers cater to an array of customers with different sustainability-related requirements. Furthermore, the need to improve sustainability along the supply chain likely depends on whether the part of the supply chain to be improved is located in developed or developing countries. Supplier-overlap-related issues appear to be of general concern.

Supplier co-location may refer to suppliers being co-located in the same building, as is often the case in the textile industry. When suppliers are co-located in this way, a single firm may find it very difficult to make a difference. If a firm wishes to improve the working conditions of its suppliers, but these suppliers work in the same building as several other suppliers that have different customers, the firm on its own may not be able to improve working conditions sufficiently as some changes would need to be made to the building as a whole. By "working together, there is a much better way [for firms] to somehow get more transparency into the supply chain and get back the control over where [they] are actually producing" (interview 22).

Supplier co-location may also occur when suppliers are located in the same geographic region. Issues may arise if actions of individual suppliers affect the ability of other suppliers to provide adequate working conditions to their employees (e.g. by causing pollution), or even the suppliers' incentive to improve the working conditions of their employees. Along the supply chain, the awareness of suppliers of the need to provide adequate working conditions may be very low. Firms may "have to build [the suppliers'] capacity sometimes because they might not even know what protective equipment should look like. Sometimes firms don't even realize that taking passports from workers is not legal. But when you are in the rural areas of Honduras, Nicaragua, Thailand, or India, there's very little consideration given to a lot of things" (interview 25). In fact, it appears that some "production areas are horrifying, it's really bad for the people working. You could imagine people killing themselves, or their children die because they get water in a pesticide bottle. So really some of the conditions are so bad that even the smallest improvement gets big results" (interview 23).

Under such circumstances, it is the need for firms to work together with other firms to obtain results that drives firms toward collaboration. A lack of effort on behalf of competitors to improve conditions along their supply chain can affect the supply chain conditions of a focal firm. "When [the companies] are able to collaborate, they are able to leverage their influence and make a greater impact in the industry itself" (interview 25). Through collaborations, firms can work together to better understand how to approach suppliers and come up with streamlined, coherent requirements for suppliers to follow. They can create a minimal benchmark (e.g. standard) to try to improve overall sustainability levels. For example, one of the MSIs hopes "to push the sector out of this era of the last ten years where every company and every government is doing their own thing, thinking that they're doing the right thing" (interview 12). By collaborating, firms can more easily and consistently communicate with suppliers, while exercising stronger influence on them than they would have been able to otherwise through the generation of collective demands.

This holds true when suppliers work with an array of firms that individually purchase only a small portion of the suppliers' output, yet have different sustainability-related requirements for suppliers to follow. In these cases, the individual efforts of a focal firm to improve supplier conditions are likely to be insufficient, as firms may "really have a hard time with low volumes to have control over the suppliers" (interview 22). Sometimes, "the way the whole industry is structured creates a need for cooperation" (interview 14). Firms need to "join up against the supplier together" (interview 22). Hence, if a sustainability mindset is not advocated by multiple customers, non-sustainable conditions will likely persist. If, however, several firms, which individually represent a small portion of the suppliers' output, approach suppliers as a group representing a larger share of the output with clear, agreed-upon requirements, the suppliers are more likely to pay attention to the requests and make the necessary adjustments. Collectively, firms can exercise stronger influence.

Issues relative to supplier overlap may arise regardless of whether supply chains are fragmented or more consolidated. When the supply chain is fragmented, "[collaborative] initiatives raise the commitment and trust within the supply chain in a way. You see that this supplier could provide you with a better, more sustainable material, and as a result they might go up in your rank of suppliers and eventually you get a stronger relationship" (interview 23). Sometimes, parts of the supply chain can be consolidated, such that "there are certain big companies that it seems everyone is sourcing from" (interview 7). Even though the firms may only be working directly with a small number of suppliers, indirectly they are likely to be sourcing from an extensive array of suppliers through their direct suppliers. Direct suppliers "may be sourcing from millions and millions of [suppliers], but at the higher levels it's quite consolidated" (interview 9). Regardless of the consolidation level of the supply chain, firms (and their suppliers) can become more efficient and effective if they work together to agree on certain ways of undertaking some activities. This can be done using standards, or by aligning training needs and provision to avoid supplier confusion and inefficient work processes.

Whether supplier overlap may or may not be of concern to firms depends to a certain extent on the geographic location of their suppliers. Very large firms may have "global exposure" (interview 11). However, even when firms spread across a small number of countries, they may employ many small suppliers. It is possible for a single firm to "source from 450,000 farms in 30 countries and have 2.5 million workers in the supply chain" (interview 7). Either way, supply chains are often "not local" (interview 9), and "every country has been different. [For example,] Europe has a lot more visibility to the farm level than other parts of the world right now" (interview 9). Given the different conditions across countries, some firms "might have a policy to source in lower-risk countries. And then there's of course less of a need to invest in changes" (interview 14). Firms may choose to work "only with companies that are in OECD countries or the US" (interview 2).

Essentially, the extent to which a supply chain is located in developing as opposed to developed countries is likely to be indicative of the working conditions along the supply chain. Parts of supply chains that are located in developing countries tend to have poorer working conditions and therefore require more of the firms' attention and efforts, relative to parts of supply chains that are located in developed countries. Reality is such that "in low cost countries, developing countries, […] you have a lot of health and safety issues, you have a lot of issues with respect to freedom of association, you have some discrimination issues, and there tend to be quite a lot of informal systems, so things are not as properly documented in terms of payment and working hours" (interview 4). The need for firms to collaborate toward the creation of more sustainable supply chains therefore seems to be more pertinent when the supply chains of firms operate in developing countries.

4.4.2. Customers

The orientation of firms toward their customers is evidenced in their willingness to work together with their competitors when there is *customer overlap* (i.e. when firms share customers). Customer overlap is a reality that firms in certain industries, such as the finance industry, face. "Oftentimes, financing is a collaborative thing, and very few banks do deals on their own" (interview 17). As firms pursue business opportunities, they are more likely to collaborate with their competitors when there is customer overlap.

When the needs of individual customers require multiple competing firms to work together on the same project, good communication among participants greatly facilitates the work. It is more efficient and effective for firms to present a united front. Through MSIs, a common language can be created in the form of an agreed-upon standard that competing firms agree to, and maybe even help develop.

To create a standard, which may be especially useful when a product category is in its infancy, firms need to collaborate with each other to first create a common view and understanding of the product category, which can then result in a standard that customers can refer to. The clarification of the product category, such as that of green bonds, can attract customers, enhance customer confidence, and help grow the market for the product category, to the benefit of all firms offering this type of product. By setting industry standards together with competitors, firms "make sure that [they] are pushing clients, everyone, to do the same thing" (interview 21), and that helps to "develop a whole marketplace" (interview 17).

4.4.3. Competitors

A contextual factor that is indicative of the orientation of individual firms toward their competitors, and can dissuade firms from collaborating with them, is the extent to which firms perceive the competition level in their industry as high. This view is internal to individual firms. Research on managerial cognition shows that CEOs from the same industry and that evolve in the same environment may have different perceptions of industry trends and levels of uncertainty (Sund, 2013). Similarly, managers from different firms evolving in the same industry may perceive different levels of competitive tension or intensity.

When the competitive tension is perceived as being high, managers may be more susceptible to psychological barriers, such as increased levels of difficulty to cede control. These barriers can prevent firms from collaborating with their competitors, even if the information shared within the framework of the MSI is expected to be non-strategic (or pre-competitive). Indeed, it may be "difficult to imagine sitting with the people that you battle so brutally with every day on the commercial side, and at the end of the day you sit together and you strategize how to ensure, let's say, the most sustainable basil for everyone in the world" (interview 8). Therefore, when "the competitive dynamic is much more pronounced [...] companies will only go so far" (interview 13).

Existing studies on technological environments name actual (not perceived) competitive intensity as a factor influencing firm collaboration likelihood (Ang, 2008; Sakakibara, 2002). Even though the issue of *perceived level of competition* has only rarely been referred to in the interviews, this contextual factor is attention-worthy. This is because the perceived level of competition by a focal firm may potentially be an important barrier to collaborations between competitors in the sustainability context, which could help explain why there are different levels of collaborations within and across industries.

4.4.4. Regulators and civil society

Regulation plays an important role in the ability of firms to conduct their business and can greatly influence the way in which they do so. It is therefore in the interest of firms to be attentive to both existing and potential future regulatory frameworks that could affect their business operations. To do so, firms should pay attention not only to existing regulations that regulatory bodies expect them to follow but also to civil society pressures and any processes that could result in new regulations that could affect their business. This is reflected in two contextual factors that can be associated with the orientation of firms toward regulators and civil society.

The first contextual factor is *antitrust apprehension*. It is indicative of the reluctance of firms to join MSIs for fear of being perceived as breaching antitrust laws. This contextual factor is therefore at the firm level. The second factor, *sustainability regulation*, which is at the industry level, is the extent to which firms are expected to implement existing sustainability-related regulation coupled with industries' anticipation of future regulation. The need to address existing regulatory frameworks and the desire to prevent, act ahead of, or influence future regulation provide an incentive for firms to collaborate with their competitors within the framework of MSIs.

Regulatory concerns appear to be top-of-mind. Both antitrust considerations and the extent and expectation of industry-level, sustainability-related regulation seem to be of general concern across industries, as they were mentioned often both by experts and sustainability professionals working within firms.

4.4.4.1. *Antitrust apprehension*

The concerns of firms about how their actions may be viewed by regulators and civil society are reflected in their reluctance to join MSIs if this may be viewed by those stakeholders as a potential breach of antitrust laws. Antitrust law is meant to regulate anticompetitive firm behavior, preventing the collusion of competing firms on matters such as price. Research suggests that collaborations between competitors may lead to anticompetitive collusion on the part of participating firms (Walley, 2007). This is because one of the risks linked to collaboration is the potential oversharing of information.

According to interviewees, firms collaborating on sustainability issues should not be in violation of antitrust laws, given the pre-competitive nature of the topics discussed. Nevertheless, firms that evolve in environments in which their participation in MSIs may be perceived as a possible act of collusion, may "have concerns about antitrust" (interview 1). Indeed, "antitrust considerations [are] certainly something that companies need to be aware of, and [they need to] be careful not to cross the line of antitrust collusion" (interview 13). Firms may refrain from participating in MSIs for fear of negative repercussions from regulators and civil society, who may mistakenly perceive firm participation in an MSI as an act of participation in collusive activities.

To try to mitigate such concerns, often, MSI participants "sign an antitrust agreement, that means that [...] competitive elements cannot be talked about and it's purely a non-competitive environment" (interview 12). Before becoming a member of an MSI, firms may "need to go internally through a long process of internal stakeholder engagement" (interview 21) related to antitrust, as "the anti-competitive law is one of the first things that you have to check" (interview 21).

4.4.4.2. Sustainability regulation

In addition to antitrust apprehension, firms pay attention to existing and potential future sustainability-related regulation that is relevant for their industry. Hence, firms care not only about the extent to which their industry is already regulated but also about industry expectations of future regulation and act accordingly. The more regulation firms have to comply with, and the more concerned they are about future regulation, the higher their incentive to join MSIs and collaborate with their competitors. Firms that are more aware of the need to address existing regulatory frameworks and to anticipate or preempt future regulation are those that have a higher stakeholder orientation vis-à-vis regulators and civil society.

In general, "sustainability-linked topics [...] have increasingly become a regulatory topic. There is standardization when the regulator is more sensitive to the topic" (interview 6). Since firms tend to work on similar issues, once regulation is in place, they can collaborate to understand how different firms are "going about implementation and to share best practices" (interview 17). This is especially important given the "great and very rapid changes in the way sustainability was dealt with, let's say ten years ago, and how it's dealt with now. [...] Ten years ago it was not whatsoever related to laws and now more and more soft laws and hard laws are getting issued in different countries" (interview 18). Even when trying to understand broad guidelines, such as the UN Guiding Principles, firms may turn to their competitors to "try to understand [the principles], because [they] are not specific to sectors like other standards, and they cover both the regulation and the voluntary side" (interview 6).

Given the costs involved in understanding and implementing new regulation, it can be more efficient for firms to join their efforts to understand and agree on how to address regulatory constraints that are already in place. Sometimes, "voluntary collaborations are a way to preempt regulation" (interview 10). Firms can work together to "try to understand how they can anticipate legal requirements" (interview 6), "rather than waiting for regulation" (interview 11). Firms may prefer to "start acting instead of waiting for bigger requirements" (interview 6). This approach is in line with existing literature suggesting that firms may collaborate in an attempt to manage risk and avert regulatory or stakeholder action (Austin and Reficco, 2005; King *et al.*, 2012).

If firms work together to preempt future regulation by showing that they are taking action, they can avoid being dictated to on how to address sustainability concerns. At the very least, firms can influence future requirements, even if they do become anchored in governmental regulations. Sometimes, firms may even be incentivized to collaborate with governmental bodies. For example, in the apparel industry "there are initiatives promoted by the European Union [...] that [firms] cannot avoid being involved with because the outcomes will probably become laws that [firms] will need to follow in the future. So it's better to be part of this kind of initiative to influence it from the inside" (interview 20).

4.4.5. *Out-of-industry actors*

Out-of-industry actors are those stakeholders who are not part of the industry that the focal firm belongs to, whether they be civil society representatives, suppliers, or other firms. These actors may have an unfavorable attitude toward collaborations with firms in stigmatized industries. Organizational stigma has been defined as "a label that evokes a collective stakeholder group-specific perception that an organization possesses a fundamental, deep-seated flaw that deindividuates and discredits the organization." As a result, organizational stigma can have a negative impact on stakeholder interaction with a stigmatized organization (Devers *et al.*, 2009, p. 155). It is argued that the definition of organizational stigma could be extended to and applied at the industry level, such that firms in a stigmatized industry would incur a lack of willingness on the part of out-of-industry stakeholders to collaborate with them. *Industry stigma* affects industries such as the tobacco, arms, and gambling industries.

Effectively, stigmatized firms may find it very difficult to collaborate with stakeholders other than their competitors as other stakeholders "do not want to be associated" with them (interview 7). Stakeholders, and more specifically firms, external to a stigmatized industry may fear that their reputation would be tarnished if they work with stigmatized firms (interview 8). Stakeholders may even be dissuaded from collaborating with stigmatized firms by inter-governmental bodies such as the UN, even though firms in the stigmatized industry could "have more impact if other stakeholders helped [them]" (interview 7). "Sometimes [stigmatized companies] don't get the recognition because if [other stakeholders] do recognize [those] companies it can create a lot of difficulties. [...] It has always been so difficult for [stigmatized companies] to work with other stakeholders" (interview 7).

Whereas by being part of non-stigmatized industries, firms can reach out to and try to collaborate with non-competitors to address sustainability issues, the default solution for firms in stigmatized industries is to work with their competitors. It therefore transpires that industry stigma can be a powerful contextual factor pushing firms to orient themselves toward and collaborate with their competitors. As firms in stigmatized industries cannot count on external stakeholder collaboration to help them find and advance solutions to address sustainability-related concerns, they are likely to turn to and collaborate with each other.

4.5. Configurations of Contextual Factors

Having discussed how the orientation of firms toward various stakeholder groups relates to the various contextual factors that firms take into consideration when they decide whether to join MSIs, the section below discusses how the contextual factors relate to each other by examining the results obtained through QCA. The QCA facilitates the generation of a more holistic view of the findings.

To generate insights using the QCA, the entire sample of semi-structured interviews was considered. First, the total number of configurations was found, followed by the visual inspection of the coincidence score and the sufficiency and necessity matrix. This inspection confirmed that the variables overlap with the outcome measure, namely, participation, and that the variable sets are related. Then, reduced common sets were analyzed. These were obtained after specifying two conditions — that the y-consistency score be above 0.7 and above the n-consistency score.

The results indicate that there is some overlap between the configurations of different interviews. Out of a total of 15 configurations, 8 appear only once, but 4 appear twice, 2 appear 3 times, and 1 appears 4 times. Overall, there are 11 common sets in total, reduced to 7 configurations, with a total coverage score of 0.727 (see Table 4.2). Four of the configurations include a mix of firm- and industry-level contextual factors, and the other three highlight the key role of two industry-level factors — supplier overlap and customer overlap. The configurations are discussed below. When discussing the seven configurations, the contextual factors that appear in a final configuration as having been mentioned in interviews are mentioned explicitly, as well as any factors that were dropped from the final configuration. Those that are not explicitly mentioned are those that are part of the configuration but were not mentioned in interviews.

Table 4.2. QCA final reduction set.

Set	Raw coverage	Unique coverage	Solution consistency
$t*u*v*W*X*y*z$	0.045	0.045	1.000
$t*u*V*w*x*Y*Z$	0.045	0.045	1.000
$T*u*V*W*x*Y*z$	0.045	0.045	1.000
$t*u*v*x*Y*z$	0.227	0.227	0.833
$t*U*v*w*y*z$	0.136	0.091	1.000
$t*U*v*x*y*z$	0.091	0.045	1.000
$T*u*v*w*X*Y$	0.182	0.182	1.000

Note: T = supply chain awareness; U = customer overlap; V = perceived level of competition; W = antitrust apprehension; X = sustainability regulation; Y = supplier overlap; Z = industry stigma. Only capital letters are indicative of the mentioning of a factor in interviews. Total coverage = 0.727.

Of the seven configurations, two relate solely to the services sector. In both cases, customer overlap is the only factor that is explicitly mentioned. However, antitrust apprehension is omitted from one of the configurations, and sustainability regulation is omitted from the second configuration, indicating that some of the initial configurations coupled customer overlap with regulatory concerns. These results highlight not only the key role played by customer overlap in the decision-making of firms in the services sector but also its possible coupling with antitrust apprehension and sustainability regulation as part of the decision-making process. A third configuration highlights the presence of regulatory concerns further, combining the presence of antitrust apprehension and sustainability regulation. It appears that, while issues related to antitrust apprehension are acknowledged, they do not necessarily prevent firms from collaborating with their competitors and participating in MSIs. Instead, participating firms are likely to take measures to mitigate this risk.

All of the remaining four configurations include supplier overlap, a factor that was frequently mentioned both by experts and by sustainability professionals working within firms. Supplier overlap appears to be the most prominent factor in the decision-making process of firms when they contemplate whether they should participate in MSIs. In one of the configurations, supplier overlap appears on its own, and antitrust apprehension is dropped. In a second configuration, supplier overlap is coupled with perceived level of competition and industry stigma. Supplier overlap and perceived level of competition appear together in a third configuration, this time alongside supply chain awareness and antitrust apprehension. The final configuration includes supplier overlap, supply chain awareness, and sustainability regulation. Industry stigma is omitted from this final configuration. Hence, while supplier overlap is important on its own, more generally, supply-chain-related determinants, which include supplier overlap but also supply chain awareness, as well as regulatory factors, which combine in different ways, appear to play key roles in understanding firm motivation to participate in MSIs. These factors are especially relevant for the goods sector. Notably, even though two of the factors, namely, antitrust apprehension and perceived level of competition, are expected to reduce the likelihood of firm participation in MSIs, the findings suggest that while firms take these factors into account, they may not necessarily act as a "deal breaker" with regards to firm participation in MSIs.

Based on the findings, in the services sector, firm orientation vis-à-vis customers is key to understanding the inclination of firms to join MSIs, while the orientation of firms toward regulators and civil society also plays a significant role. In the goods sector, the orientation of firms toward their suppliers appears to play a fundamental role in understanding the inclination of firms to join MSIs, with their predisposition toward understanding the expectations of regulators and civil society playing a notable role. The findings also underscore that, predominantly, firms take into account both firm- and industry-level contextual factors when deciding whether to join MSIs, highlighting the importance of both levels in the decision-making processes of firms.

4.6. Discussion and Conclusions

It is becoming increasingly difficult to argue against the need for firms to act responsibly by paying heed not only to their financial outcomes but also to their social and environmental impacts. What tools do firms have at their disposal to achieve their sustainability goals? The intricate and systemic nature of sustainability concerns calls for collaborative efforts as a means to this end. In particular, firms may find that they need to talk not only to stakeholders such as suppliers, customers, regulatory bodies, and civil society but also, importantly, to their competitors, if they wish to address some of their sustainability concerns and improve their social and environmental bottom lines.

This study takes an explorative, cross-industry approach toward an enhanced understanding of the importance of the participation of firms in MSIs together with their competitors for their ability to address systemic sustainability challenges. It studies MSIs that bring together a number of competitors. These MSIs often try to tackle broad sustainability concerns, the possible resolution of which requires a multilateral approach.

By collaborating with their competitors, firms can drive change by working together to understand sustainability-related issues and come up with and implement solutions that may lead to more efficient and effective outcomes, market growth, and enhanced firm credibility and reputation. Collaborations between competitors can therefore be an important means for firms to advance their sustainability agendas. The findings of this study reinforce the general notion that MSIs are an important tool for tackling various sustainability challenges (Seitanidi and Crane, 2014).

Studies have found that the levels of collaboration and competition between competitors may change over time, as responses change in accordance with the internal and external environments of firms (Luo, 2007). Relatedly, this study highlights the presence of both firm- and industry-level contextual factors, uncovered through the qualitative analysis of semi-structured interviews with sustainability professionals. Firm-level factors are indicative of internally generated perceptions and realities, whereas industry-level factors are related to the ways in which business is conducted in an industry.

Firms may be more or less prone to participating in joint efforts to solve sustainability issues depending on the various firm- and industry-level factors. The decisions of firms are likely to be affected by firm-level factors such as supply chain awareness, their perceived level of competition in the industry, and their apprehension of antitrust-related issues. Customer overlap with other competitors, sustainability regulation, supplier overlap, and industry stigma are industry-level factors that are likely to play a role in the decision of a firm to collaborate with its competitors within the framework of an MSI. These factors are revealing of the stakeholder orientation of firms.

The contextual factors point to the orientation of firms toward their suppliers, customers, competitors, regulators and civil society, and out-of-industry actors. From the QCA, it transpires that, in the goods sector, the orientation of firms toward their suppliers is a vital determinant in their decision to join MSIs, while in the services sector, the orientation of firms toward their (joint) customers is essential to understanding the motivation of firms to collaborate with their competitors. It is important for all firms to be aware of existing and potential regulatory concerns. Firms should be alert and tend to concerns raised by regulators and civil society. Regulations may take the form of "hard laws" (e.g. governmental regulations) or "soft laws" (e.g. UN voluntary principles). Finally, firms take into account internally generated perceptions (firm-level factors) and industry-level realities (industry-level factors) simultaneously when deciding whether to participate in MSIs, underscoring the importance of both levels in the decision-making process of firms.

The uncovered contextual factors indicative of the stakeholder orientation of firms represent different degrees of the extent to which firms may be willing to take substantive action to address the needs of their stakeholders. Perceived level of competition and antitrust apprehension both relate to firms' internally generated perception of the environment and are indicative of a lack of willingness of firms to take action with regards to their advancement of a sustainability agenda within the framework of MSIs. These are factors that may potentially dissuade some firms from participating in MSIs. The other factors, however, suggest a more objective awareness of the sustainability issues that need to be addressed and the environment in which firms operate, which can then prompt concrete actions by firms, such as joining MSIs to work on the resolution of sustainability issues. These include supply chain awareness, supplier overlap, customer overlap, sustainability regulation, and industry stigma.

It has been acknowledged that industry transition toward more sustainable practices depends on the contributions of multiple stakeholders, as these come together, whether in a joint or in a complementary manner, to tackle widespread concerns (Jones et al., 2019). Whereas it is firms that are at the center of this study, the findings insinuate that their ability to advance sustainability agendas depends not only on their ability to collaborate with each other but also on their ability to work with or alongside prominent stakeholders, including suppliers, customers, and regulators and civil society. Collaboration with additional stakeholders is important when implementing potentially viable solutions and best practices that arise from firm collaboration, as a refusal on the part of additional stakeholders to partake in the implementation of solutions could prevent firms from moving forward.

From a managerial perspective, this study emphasizes that collaborations between competitors within the framework of MSIs can serve as a tool to help firms address some of their sustainability concerns — especially those that cannot be addressed by firms single-handedly. Importantly, contextual factors are discussed for managers to consider when contemplating entry into a collaboration with their competitors in the sustainability context.

This study has various limitations. First, interviews were conducted with firms and MSIs that, although they are international, are headquartered in Europe or the US. This may create a bias in the perception and understanding of interviewees as to why firms collaborate with their competitors within the framework of MSIs. Second, the data analyzed is likely to be more relevant for large-sized organizations than small- and medium-sized ones. Further discussions with sustainability experts in smaller-sized firms may unveil additional perspectives. Third, even though multiple industries were addressed via the interviews, not all industries were covered, and the list of factors highlighted is likely not exhaustive. It is acknowledged that different industries and sectors have different dynamics, and that some insights are more relevant for some than they are for others, limiting the generalizability of the findings.

Furthermore, additional fine-tuning at the MSI level may be fitting, as there are different types of MSIs. For example, MSIs may include only peers or additional stakeholders as well, be led by the industry or a third party, and be formal or informal. Distinguishing between different types of MSIs may help us understand whether different types of MSIs are preferred by different types of firms or industries, and whether they are used to address different issues. This study therefore represents only a step toward a better understanding of the phenomenon discussed. It appears that much more about this phenomenon and its implications for firms is yet to be uncovered.

References

Ang, S. H. (2008). Competitive intensity and collaboration: Impact on firm growth across technological environments. *Strategic Management Journal*, **29**(10), 1057–1075.

Arevalo, J. A., & Aravind, D. (2017). Strategic outcomes in voluntary CSR: Reporting economic and reputational benefits in principles-based initiatives. *Journal of Business Ethics*, **144**(1), 201–217.

Argandoña, A. (2004). On ethical, social and environmental management systems. *Journal of Business Ethics*, **51**(1), 41–52.

Austin, J., & Reficco, E. (2005,). Motivation and the cross-sector alliance, January 10. Available at: https://hbswk.hbs.edu/item/motivation-and-the-cross-sector-alliance. Accessed December 2, 2018.

Austin, J. E., & Seitanidi, M. M. (2012). Collaborative value creation: A review of partnering between nonprofits and businesses: Part I. Value creation spectrum and collaboration stages. *Nonprofit and Voluntary Sector Quarterly*, **41**(5), 726–758.

Baek, K. (2017). The diffusion of voluntary environmental programs: The case of ISO 14001 in Korea, 1996–2011. *Journal of Business Ethics*, **145**(2), 325–336.

Baumann-Pauly, D., Nolan, J., van Heerden, A., & Samway, M. (2017). Industry-specific multi-stakeholder initiatives that govern corporate human rights standards: Legitimacy assessments of the Fair Labor Association and the Global Network Initiative. *Journal of Business Ethics*, **143**(4), 771–787.

Berliner, D., & Prakash, A. (2015). "Bluewashing" the firm? Voluntary regulations, program design, and member compliance with the United Nations Global Compact. *Policy Studies Journal*, **43**(1), 115–138.

Bouncken, R. B., Gast, J., Kraus, S., & Bogers, M. (2015). Coopetition: a systematic review, synthesis, and future research directions. *Review of Managerial Science*, **9**(3), 577–601.

Bowler, K., Castka, P., & Balzarova, M. (2017). Understanding firms' approaches to voluntary certification: Evidence from multiple case studies in FSC certification. *Journal of Business Ethics*, **145**(2), 441–456.

Buysse, K., & Verbeke, A. (2003). Proactive environmental strategies: A stakeholder management perspective. *Strategic Management Journal*, **24**(5), 453–470.

Castka, P., & Corbett, C. J. (2016). Governance of eco-labels: Expert opinion and media coverage. *Journal of Business Ethics*, **135**(2), 309–326.

Cetindamar, D. (2007). Corporate social responsibility practices and environmentally responsible behavior: The case of the United Nations Global Compact. *Journal of Business Ethics*, **76**(2), 163–176.

Devers, C. E., Dewett, T., Mishina, Y., & Belsito, C. A. (2009). A general theory of organizational stigma. *Organization Science*, **20**(1), 154–171.

Ernst and Young, 2011, Six growing trends in corporate sustainability. Available at: http://www.ey.com/us/en/services/specialty-services/climate-change-and-sustainability-services/six-growing-trends-in-corporate-sustainability_overview. Accessed November 12, 2016.

Freeman, R. E., Harrison, J. S., Wicks, A. C., Parmar, B. L., & De Colle, S. (2010). *Stakeholder Theory: The State of the Art* (Cambridge: Cambridge University Press).

Gray, B., & Stites, J. P. (2013). Sustainability through Partnerships: Capitalizing on Collaboration (London, Ontario: Networks for Business Sustainability).

Janney, J. J., Dess, G., & Forlani, V. (2009). Glass houses? Market reactions to firms joining the UN global compact. *Journal of Business Ethics*, **90**(3), 407–423.

Jones, J., York, J., Vedula, S., Conger, M., & Lenox, M. (2019). The collective construction of green building: Industry transition toward environmentally beneficial practices. *Academy of Management Perspectives*, **33**(4), 425–449.

King, A., Prado, A. M., & Rivera, J. (2012). Industry self-regulation and environmental protection. In *The Oxford Handbook of Business and the Natural Environment* (Oxford, UK: Oxford University Press), pp. 103–121.

Lacey, R., & Cohen, L. (2015). Using Qualitative Comparative Analysis (QCA) as a descriptive numerical method in support of narrative methods. In Kimberly D. Elsbach and Roderick M. Kramer (eds.), *Handbook of Qualitative Organizational Research: Innovative Pathways and Methods* (Abingdon: Routledge), pp. 362–370.

Lacey, R., & Fiss, P. C. (2009). Comparative organizational analysis across multiple levels: A set-theoretic approach. In Brayden King, Teppo Felin, and David A. Whetten (eds.), *Studying Differences Between Organizations: Comparative Approaches to Organizational Research* (Bingley, UK: Emerald Group Publishing Limited), pp. 91–116.

Lado, A. A., Boyd, N. G., & Hanlon, S. C. (1997). Competition, cooperation, and the search for economic rents: A syncretic model. *Academy of Management Review*, **22**(1), 110–141.

Lin-Hi, N., & Blumberg, I. (2017). The power(lessness) of industry self-regulation to promote responsible labor standards: Insights from the Chinese toy industry. *Journal of Business Ethics*, **143**(4), 789–805.

Lindgreen, A., & Swaen, V. (2010). Corporate social responsibility. *International Journal of Management Reviews*, **12**(1), 1–7.

Longest, K. C., & Vaisey, S. (2008). fuzzy: A program for performing qualitative comparative analyses (QCA) in Stata. *Stata Journal*, **8**(1), 79–104.

Lund-Thomsen, P., & Lindgreen, A. (2014). Corporate social responsibility in global value chains: Where are we now and where are we going? *Journal of Business Ethics*, **123**(1), 11–22.

Luo, Y. (2007). A coopetition perspective of global competition. *Journal of World Business*, **42**(2), 129–144.

Malik, M. (2015). Value-enhancing capabilities of CSR: A brief review of contemporary literature. *Journal of Business Ethics*, **127**(2), 419–438.

McKinsey. (2014, July). Sustainability's Strategic Worth. Available at: http://csr-raadgivning.dk/wp-content/uploads/2016/02/Sustainabilitys-strategic-worth-McKinsey-Global-Survey-results-McKinsey-July-2014.pdf. Accessed April 1, 2017.

Mele, V., & Schepers, D. H. (2013). E Pluribus Unum? Legitimacy issues and multi-stakeholder codes of conduct. *Journal of Business Ethics*, **118**(3), 561–576.

MIT and BCG. (2016). Investing for a sustainable future. Available at: http://csr-raadgivning.dk/wp-content/uploads/2016/06/Investing-For-a-Sustainable-Future-Survey-BCG-and-MIT-May-2016.pdf. Accessed April 1, 2017.

Moog, S., Spicer, A., & Böhm, S. (2015). The politics of multi-stakeholder initiatives: The crisis of the Forest Stewardship Council. *Journal of Business Ethics*, **128**(3), 469–493.

NBS (2017). Solving complex problems requires competitors to collaborate, September 28. Available at: https://nbs.net/p/solving-complex-problems-require-competitors-to-collabo-53084055-6ecf-49e8-92e7-8cfd4ac268b4. Accessed October 31, 2017.

O'Faircheallaigh, C. (2015). Social equity and large mining projects: Voluntary industry initiatives, public regulation and community development agreements. *Journal of Business Ethics*, **132**(1), 91–103.

Perez-Batres, L. A., Doh, J. P., Miller, V. V., & Pisani, M. J. (2012). Stakeholder pressures as determinants of CSR strategic choice: Why do firms choose symbolic versus substantive self-regulatory codes of conduct? *Journal of Business Ethics*, **110**(2), 157–172.

Runhaar, H., & Lafferty, H. (2009). Governing corporate social responsibility: An assessment of the contribution of the UN Global Compact to CSR strategies in the telecommunications industry. *Journal of Business Ethics*, **84**(4), 479-495.

Sakakibara, M. (2002). Formation of R&D consortia: Industry and company effects. *Strategic Management Journal*, **23**(11), 1033–1050.

Seitanidi, M. M., & Crane, A. (eds.). (2014). Social partnerships and responsible business: What, why and how? In *Social Partnerships and Responsible Business: A Research Handbook*. (Abingdon and New York, NY: Routledge), pp. 1–12.

Sund, K. J. (2013). Scanning, perceived uncertainty, and the interpretation of trends: A study of hotel directors' interpretation of demographic change. *International Journal of Hospitality Management*, **33**, 294–303.

Utting, P. (2005). Rethinking business regulation. *From Self-Regulation to Social Control, UNRISD*. Geneva, Switzerland.

Van Beurden, P., & Gössling, T. (2008). The worth of values–a literature review on the relation between corporate social and financial performance. *Journal of Business Ethics*, **82**(2), 407–424.

Voegtlin, C., & Pless, N. M. (2014). Global governance: CSR and the role of the UN Global Compact. *Journal of Business Ethics*, **122**(2), 179–191.

Walley, K. (2007). Coopetition: An introduction to the subject and an agenda for research. *International Studies of Management & Organization*, **37**(2), 11–31.

Wang, H., Tong, L., Takeuchi, R., & George, G. (2016). Corporate Social Responsibility: An overview and new research directions thematic issue on corporate social responsibility. *Academy of Management Journal*, **59**(2), 534–544.

Zeyen, A., Beckmann, M., & Wolters, S. (2016). Actor and institutional dynamics in the development of multi-stakeholder initiatives. *Journal of Business Ethics*, **135**(2), 341–360.

Zollo, M., Bettinazzi, E. L., Neumann, K., & Snoeren, P. (2016). Toward a comprehensive model of organizational evolution: Dynamic capabilities for innovation and adaptation of the enterprise model. *Global Strategy Journal*, **6**(3), 225–244.

© 2022 World Scientific Publishing Company
https://doi.org/10.1142/9789811248863_0005

Chapter 5

Beyond Goal Hybridity: How Multilevel Actor Networks Can Scale Climate Impact

Sanwar A. Sunny
*Department of Marketing and Entrepreneurship,
R. G. Merrick School of Business,
University of Baltimore, Baltimore, MD, USA*

ssunny@ubalt.edu

Abstract

Will environmental entrepreneurs and corporate responses to climate change save the natural environment? This simple question cannot be answered given the current state of fragmentation in the perspectives and theories that are needed to form an appropriate response. Duality of goals and complex multi-faceted interactions between multiple actors at different levels limit the ability to provide robust conjectures regarding the magnitude or direction of environmental impact from organizational actors and their actions. In this chapter, using an actor-action-outcome framework, I clarify the distinct nature of agency and its relationship to impact. Using recent examples from firms, investor funds, and government programs, the framework introduced in this chapter uncovers (1) key attributes of the current structure, (2) observes the nature of heterogeneity in different outcome measures across groups of multi-level actors, and (3) clarifies how a multilevel network model explains the heterogeneity of impact given the structural limitations and mismatched motivations across system levels.

Keyword: Sustainable entrepreneurship; agency; action-action-outcome framework; environmental impact; climate change.

5.1. Introduction

Climate change mitigation as a public good concept is a case of the "tragedy of the commons" (IPCC 5th Assessment, 2014) with each agent — individuals, households, firms, and governments — needing to overcome the "rational" pressures to act independently in their own self-interest, and instead act collectively to attain a higher-level outcome. Potential technology solutions to this global problem include propositions to stabilize the atmospheric concentrations of greenhouse gas emissions. A key agent playing a significant role are environmental entrepreneurs, who despite lacking direct focus in these discussions, have been developing low-carbon technology solutions as well as propagating sustainable lifestyle and behavioral choices aimed at collective and corrective action.

While most discussions and framework have historically resided at the macro level, environmental entrepreneurs present an interesting case using *actor*-based *outcomes* framework to expand on micro-foundations of their *actions*, i.e. changes necessary and their sociopolitical and technical mechanisms. In particular, the duality of organizational actions creating both environmental and economic values, and the implied potential tradeoff in meeting such simultaneous goals, is problematic due to the absence of a multilevel perspective in situating the role of such agents and their actions to the global public good outcomes and discussions.

This current chapter bridges the two interrelated discussions — the agency of the environmental entrepreneurs and their value creation processes at different structural contexts, i.e. at the micro level to the global macro level, and highlights conceptualizations of economic growth and sustainable development. In doing so, we shed light on the perceived tradeoffs and their sources, if considered according to this framework. Current conceptualization of macro-level economic growth and sustainable development takes on a false narrative of tradeoffs — mutually exclusive outcomes where a balance needs to be struck. Here contribution to production, or legitimized growth metrics that increase national or regional economic performance, provides reinforcements to ignore production-related degradation to the natural environment, such as emissions at different levels.

Concepts and theories that depend on economic outcomes as impact measures, such as GDP as a metric for economic growth or development when formed as the basis for global corrective policies, may in fact misdirect initiatives to reduce environmental externalities. Arguably, this has led to the tradeoff mentality, which has served as a cognitive barrier at multiple levels of analysis hindering effecting implementation of emissions-reduction strategies and policies among organizations and globally. This chapter explores how environmental entrepreneurs, with their value creation processes underscored by both sustainability and innovation, are a rare agent that, in both theory and practice, can and do simultaneously increase outcomes on both dimensions, and thereby overcome the paradox.

Discussions on corrective top-down policies to synergistically enhance bottom-up processes are also explored.

5.1.1. *Background*

Scholars in different fields are increasingly studying topics at the intersection of organizational research and environmental impact with great interest (George *et al.*, 2016; George *et al.*, 2015; Howard-Grenville *et al.*, 2014; Lenox and Chatterji, 2018). Streams within these fields have emerged as exciting areas of academic enquiry, namely environmental entrepreneurship, sustainable entrepreneurship, and corporate sustainability (Cohen and Winn, 2007; Dean and McMullen, 2007; Hall *et al.*, 2010). In spite of growing interest in such topics, most studies have focused on strategic or economic attributes, rather than the environmental dimension — surprising, given the operative word of the fields' specialization.

Naturally, studies on ecological outcomes are often not a part of what management researchers study, highlighting the disconnect between economics and ecology (Starik and Kanashiro, 2013). For example, most prior research on the subject tend to focus on the economic aspects of global commitments, such as the Paris Treaty or the Kyoto Protocol, centering on the best way to react to perceived fiscal shocks that will be associated with the implementation of clean energy transitions, etc. (Arent, 2017), not the environmental benefits. Actors such as entrepreneurs in new startup ventures and managers in incumbent organizations are looking to lessen their environmental impact (Lenox and Chatterji, 2018). However, how their actions relate to environmental impact is often left unexplored — yet the overarching question remains. If the conceptualization or operationalization of ecological impact is erroneous, it can amount to subsequent limitations in understanding the set of conditions under which organization actions are ecologically impactful from a performance outcomes perspective. This is particularly so when considering the timeline of the global transformations necessary due to climate change.

Understandably, scholars trained in the social sciences, such as psychology, sociology, or economics, may not be comfortable spanning boundaries to include tenets of the natural sciences (Starik and Kanashiro, 2013); however, for topics such as environmental sustainability, such interdisciplinary enquiry on environmental impacts are a necessary next step (Cohen and Winn, 2007; Hall *et al.*, 2010; Lenox and York, 2011; Thompson *et al.*, 2011).

If not, the sole reliance on financial performance and economic outcomes driving climate-change–related actions may have organizations, knowingly or unknowingly, seeking "impact" in the wrong place. This process that has been impossible to detect and thereby correct, given that a framework did not exist to guide organizational actions or investments. If organizations are to move beyond a normative reasoning or instrumental choice framing for climate change mitigation actions, a collective reorientation of our perspectives is needed, such that organizational choices and their outcomes are situated within the broader natural processes.

The author proposes a multilevel framework from systems ecology, which espouses that both conceptualizations of impact are jointly necessary, yet independently insufficient to solve the problem of climate change on their own. The current chapter also seeks to visualize this framework in the context of management research, making climate change and its corrective solutions virtually undeniable. This insight helps charts pathways to synchronize the activities of actors within planetary system boundaries, thereby fostering ecologically meaningful actions and impact. The chapter also visually illustrates this framework across many levels, making climate change and its corrective solutions virtually undeniable.

In order to achieve its goals, this chapter is structured in the following way: it begins by discussing the nested actor hood across multiple levels. Socially constructed or economically motivated problematization of environmental problems, such as that of global climate change, impacts the framing and subsequent optimality of organizational options and entrepreneurial solutions when viewed by the actors. The author contrasts a natural-science–based discussion of impact, borrowing from systems ecology to currently existing theorizing in environmental sustainability. By introducing the new joint-impact framework, the author reframes and discusses key takeaways for organizations and institutional actors across multiple levels, with relevant implications for entrepreneurs, managers, policymakers, and scholars as they collaborate on finding and applying solutions to pressing global issues.

5.2. Hierarchical Structure and the Nature of System Components

To simplify and model a complex system, some elements of ontological reductionism can be beneficial. For instance, assuming that a real system can be modelled as a composition of a minimum number of kinds of entities, we can create hierarchical and nested set of classifications. As such, one can argue that the systemic emergence to be observed is an epistemological phenomenon that exists only through a modeled description of a system (Silberstein and McGeever, 1999). It follows, thus, that each perceivable type of item is a sum of items, or types of items, with a lesser degree of complexity. Beyond ontological reductionism, advances in methodological reductionism have attempted to reduce explanations to smallest possible entities of an observed system. For example, within sciences, certain topics of enquiry are arranged within areas that study smaller spatial scales and organization units to higher-level ones. Examples include particle physics, chemistry, to molecular to cellular biology, to physiology, psychology, and onto the social sciences. At each of these stages, entirely new laws, concepts, generalizations, and theories are needed (Anderson, 1972), where proponents of a reductionist view support organizational hierarchies, with each level being simply described in terms of objects one level below it, and moving up in levels of abstraction as one goes higher up — such as individual decision-makers, to groups, to organizations, to a group or organizations at the local level, and eventually toward global decision-makers.

The acceptability of behavioral sciences as a genuine field of enquiry to environmental outcomes and impacts, under such a condition, would mean that tenets within the social sciences are formed more or less based on a lower level of enquiry, such as genetic biology (Dawkins, 1986). The issue with this approach, however, would limit the study of the emergent properties of complex systems. That is, although we can study top-down relationships, from top-down governance, to bottom-up emergence, as in how larger scales of organization influence smaller ones, independent and non-linear feedback loops may hide a true representation of the effects under study. As a result, for certain topics, it is impossible to replicate the relevant ecological phenomenon without influencing or changing the system, such as under laboratory conditions (Jørgensen, 2002). At these levels of organizations, such as for ecosystems and society, a large number of diverse components are linked with multiple feedback loops (Clayton and Davies, 2006). Given that emergence is particularly relevant when systems are affected by historicity and path-dependence is studied (Longo *et al*., 2012), organizational studies often divert from law-like natural process models.

In fact, in ecology and the social sciences, complex and non-linear interactions characterize the nature of relationships between system components, at different levels and over time, such as technology regimes and cities with national economies, including the biosphere (Odum *et al*., 2000). For this reason, emergent properties that arise at the higher levels cannot be appropriately predicted by analyzing the micro-level parts in isolation (Harding, 2006). Doing so would impose a theoretical limit on the very ability to understand systemic behavior of agents beyond a certain level. For instance, in complex social human systems, a detailed understanding of individual human behavior alone cannot predict group-level behavior that results at the emergent collective level. The topic of climate change as a planetary problem has been especially deemed "wicked" as a result — i.e. the multitude of micro-level actions and impact cannot be aggregated to global scales of impact.

5.2.1. *Multiple levels of system action and response*

A specific focus, not on top-down transitions from policy instruments, but bottom-up processes of social movements and technological change, is noticed as the process of innovation transformation as industrial mutation revolutionizes the economic structure from within (Schumpeter, 1942, pp. 82–83). This could broadly be construed as the innovative entry of sustainable and environmental entrepreneurs, who produce environmental solution sets and bring about these transitions with efficiency improvements (Sunny, 2020), which then creates new institutions that significantly differ from technological, organizational, and regulatory paradigms of previous states (Sidak and Teece, 2009).

In other words, together these dynamics represent innovation in technologies and behavior by incumbent organizations and nascent entrepreneurs, enabling innovations by targeting relevant market failure through corrective approaches and methods. By influencing organizational behavior to reduce environmental impact through enacting appropriate strategies, policy-making also influences market solutions. Although these effects have originated from different theories at different levels of analysis and are studied by different streams, an outcome measure unifies the environmental dimension of different organizational activities driven by these set of organizational actors.

When top-down climate mitigation policies are considered in a more practical manner, it is increasingly common to see regulations, from nearly every level of government around the world, attempting to curb consumption-based externalities that contribute to climate change, even though a central authority does not exists to align or oversee such forces (Wright and Nyberg, 2017). Additionally, regional social movement organizations and other stakeholders are gaining momentum in pressuring lower-level entities, such as organizations, to reduce their use of fossil fuels (Eesley and Lenox, 2006). These meso-level social movement organizations are simultaneously incentivizing clean energy companies to enter, replace, and scale within the economic system (York and Lenox, 2014). Fluctuating markets and changing social institutions accelerate this induced transformation and entry of environmental entrepreneurs (Geels *et al.*, 2017). Governmental intervention and other institutional efforts drive this entry, aimed at internalizing various negative externalities for many lower-level actors. These actors then leverage new knowledge to drive innovations that impact the existing economic order to cause systemic change.

Consider Figure 5.1, where greenhouse gas emissions, particularly carbon dioxide, need to be reduced over time, according to a set reduction strategy. Let us say $\Phi(t)$ represents the amount of carbon dioxide being emitted by an actor, be it an individual, firm, or region, in a given time t. Over n years (or longer, m years), this actor plans to enact strategies and actions that reduce the emissions to $\Phi(t + n)$. The reduced degradation due to these actions is thus the impact, δ_N. Figure 5.2 shows the different actions that collectively engender an outcome, O.

5.2.2. *System barriers across levels*

The costs and benefits of climate change mitigation are quite uncertain, unevenly distributed, and accrue primarily to future generations over time (Pachauri *et al.*, 2014).

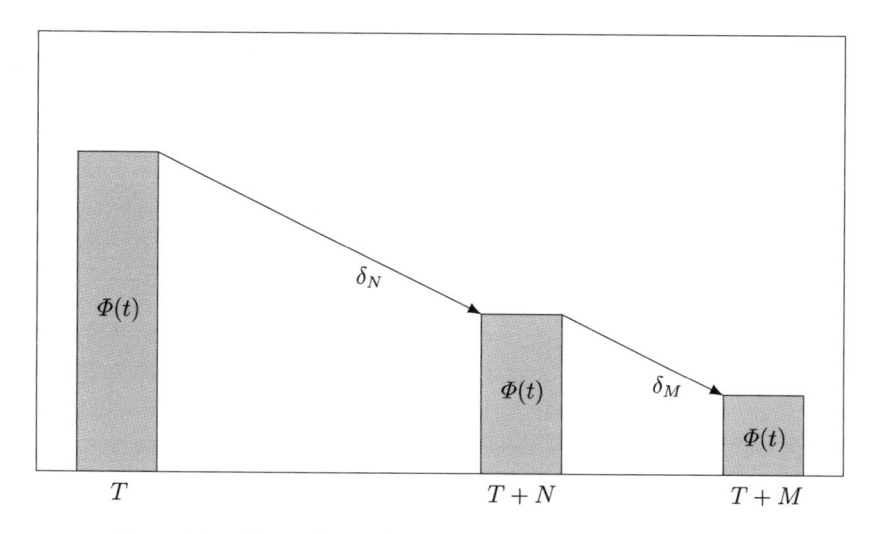

Figure 5.1. Measuring environmental impact for each actor-level.

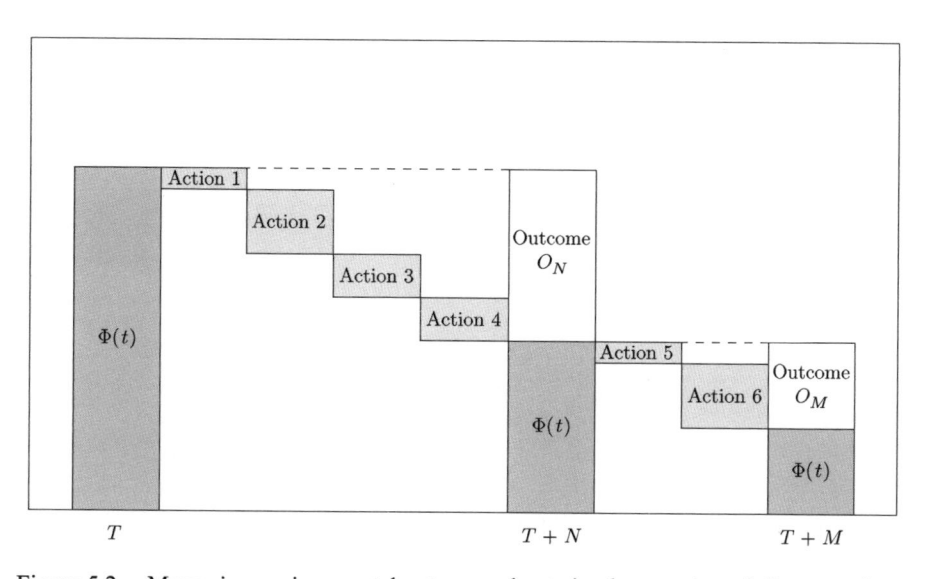

Figure 5.2. Measuring environmental outcomes due to implementation of climate actions.

Although postponing action policy interventions that facilitate the transition is considered costly (Acemoglu *et al.*, 2012; Kalkuhl *et al.*, 2012; Gawel *et al.*, 2016), traditional public choice perspectives also shows political vulnerability in being captured by vested, top-level interests (Arrow, 2012; Black, 1958; Buchanan and Tullock, 1962; Downs, 1957; Stigler, 1971). In other words, policy-makers at higher levels may favor flexible economic instruments over more naturally meaningful or effective regulatory instruments that reduce externalities (Bueb *et al.*, 2016).

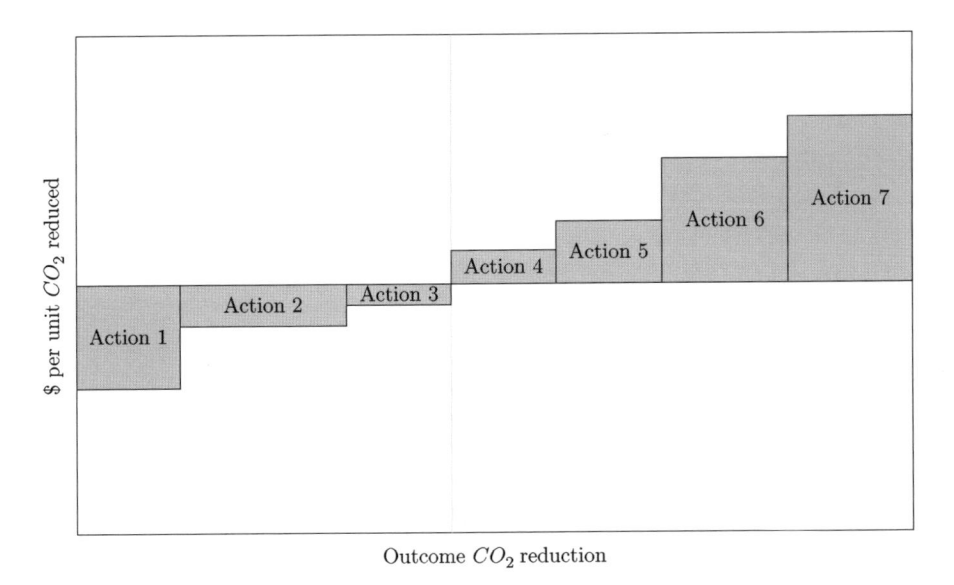

Figure 5.3. Marginal abatement cost curve for implementing impactful climate actions.

Instead of acting on minimizing environmental degradation, policy-makers may thus be enacting policies that minimize economic impacts on businesses and households instead. Figure 5.3 shows the actions from previous figures in terms of ecological outcomes, namely carbon emissions in metric tons, along costs needed to implement them. Ideally, the actions on the left-side of the graph optimizes selection through least-cost, high-impact outcomes.

Whether or not such flexible regulations went on to internalize emissions, and thereby created social or ecological value, does not receive the same attention given the paucity of appropriate frameworks that can show this divergence across levels.

This implies that a robust and well-accepted trajectory or pathway for achieving decarbonization goals is missing. Even if such a path were to exist, a transition involving such shifts of resources between competing economic sectors and political constituencies alongside changes in institutional and policy frameworks would attract scrutiny and possible inaction from top- as well as bottom-up processes (Arent et al., 2017). Table 5.1 shows existing solutions that different actors can implement to successfully drawdown carbon emissions (Hawken, 2017). Ideally, the entities in previous tables would implement the listed actions and reduce their emissions, thereby creating impact.

The progress on this, however, is slow. By strategically minimizing cost burdens on important sectors who ought to be implementing these solutions, the majority of policies may be redistributing rents, not to create impact, but in ways that secure a politically durable coalition (Jesse and Valerie, 2017). In fact, voters

Table 5.1. Impactful actions that drawdown carbon emissions globally.

Actions	Outcome, $O - CO_2$ reduction (Gigatons)	Cost ($) per unit outcome (MT)	Economic savings ($B)
Bike Infrastructure	2.31	−877.48	400.47
Cars	4	−149.67	1761.72
Commercial LED Lighting	5.04	−40.68	1089.63
Geothermal	16.6	−9.37	1024.34
Solar Farms	36.9	−2.18	5023.84
Landfill Methane	2.5	−0.73	67.57
Nuclear	16.09	0.05	1713.4
Solar Water	6.08	0.49	773.65
Small Methane Digesters	1.9	8.16	13.9
Onshore Wind Turbines	84.6	14.48	7425
Building Automation	4.62	14.74	880.55
Rooftop Solar	24.6	18.42	3457.63
Heat Pumps	5.2	22.83	1546.66
Large Methane Digesters	8.4	23.98	148.83
Smart Thermostats	2.62	28.31	640.1
Waste-to-Energy	1.1	32.73	19.82
Offshore Wind Turbines	14.1	38.67	762.5
Residential LED Lighting	7.81	41.42	1729.54
Wave and Tidal	9.2	44.77	−1004.7
District Heating	9.38	48.73	3543.5
In-Stream Hydro	4	50.63	568.36
Biomass	7.5	53.64	519.35
Telepresence	1.99	64.18	1310.59
Cogeneration	3.97	70.34	566.93
Trucks	6.18	87.95	2781.63
Electric Bikes	0.96	111.20	226.07
Ships	7.87	116.38	424.38
Concentrated Solar	10.9	121.07	413.85
Airplanes	5.05	131.17	3187.8
Water Distribution	0.87	157.90	903.11
Micro Wind	0.2	180.60	19.9
Smart Glass	2.19	425.71	325.1
Insulation	8.27	442.07	2513.33
High-speed Rail	1.52	683.17	368.1
Electric Vehicles	10.8	1310.00	9726.4
Trains	0.52	1555.08	313.86
Green Roofs	0.77	1809.47	988.46

frequently express limited tolerance for internalization measures, such as carbon tax or energy price increases, which impact private welfare at micro levels (Kotchen *et al.*, 2013; Nemet and Johnson, 2010). Such vested interests and institutional inertia have hampered effective policy design and implementation at both ends of the multilevel actor spectrum (e.g. Helm, 2010; Spash, 2010; Gawel *et al.*, 2016). If policy effectiveness is the degree to which "achieved outcomes correspond to the intended goals of the policy instrument" (Mickwitz, 2003, p. 426), the ecological impact of environmental policy goals is currently at risk of becoming secondary to only economically feasible and instrumental outcomes. The resulting incongruence between political action and environmental impact often embodies the difference between the actual levels of reductions needed, such as under global agreements like the Kyoto Protocol or Paris Climate Accord, which vary significantly from the required level of organizational commitment to limit climate-change–contributing emissions (Agu and Ogbeide-Osaretin, 2016).

Common antecedents to sustainability outcomes, such as macro-level institutions and micro-level actor interests or processes which underpin them, have often been discussed in a non-systemic manner (Ćetković *et al.*, 2016). Often organizational theorists and management scholars study firm actions and responses under different research contexts but primarily by operationalizing outcomes along mainly commercial or strategic dimensions (Starik and Kanashiro, 2013). Table 5.2 shows some meso-level impact planning to reduce carbon emissions from major US cities and counties, also shown on a map in Figure 5.4.

Although policies may be initiated by federal or state governments, implementation often rests at more regional levels (Autio *et al.*, 2014). Scholars even claim that cities at the meso level will need to become far more resource efficient, and global groups of megacities, such as C40, are already acting locally and collaboratively with organizations and entrepreneurs to lessen the environmental damages (Howard-Grenville *et al.*, 2014). Emergent research in smart cities are infusing technological advances and higher citizen support for fundamental changes in energy, transportation, and infrastructure (Sarma and Sunny, 2017). While the top-down approach is based on policy elements that originate from an overall strategic intent such as carbon emission reductions, bottom-up approaches focus on the nexus of different levels, such as the focal impact domain or geographic region (North Carolina Clean Energy Technology Center *et al.*, 2016; Ossenbrink *et al.*, 2018).

5.2.3. *Interaction between system levels*

Macro-level institutions often drive the distribution of resources across meso-groups and the design of organizational infrastructure that ultimately supports economic activities, transactions, and collective actions at micro levels. To overcome the current stalemate, a regional-level outcome of environmental value can

Table 5.2(a). Cities and counties in the US with decarbonization strategies and implementing actions to create impact.

Meso-level actors	T	$\Phi(t)$	δ_N	$\Phi(t+n)$	N	δ_M	$\Phi(t+m)$	M
Boulder County, CO	2005	5021236	45	2761680	25	90	502124	45
Broward County, FL	2010	22177409	10	19959668	10	80	4435482	40
City of Alameda, CA	2005	367294	25	275471	15	—	—	—
City of Ann Arbor, MI	2000	1681926	25	1261445	25	90	168193	50
City of Baltimore, MD	2005	10708828	25	8031621	15	—	—	—
City of Benicia, CA	2000	426735	10	384061	20	—	—	—
City of Boston, MA	2005	7653810	50	3826905	25	100	0	45
City of Boulder, CO	2005	1846217	80	369243	45	—	—	—
City of Brisbane, CA	2005	72072	15	61261	15	—	—	—
City of Charlottesville, VA	2000	470024	10	423022	35	—	—	—
City of Chicago, IL	2005	36869456	26	27283397	20	—	—	—
City of Chula Vista	2005	1339993	15	1138994	15	—	—	—
City of Cincinnati, OH	2006	9300000	40	5580000	24	84	1488000	44
City of Cleveland, OH	2010	12834200	16	10780728	10	80	2566840	40
City of Culver City, CA	2005	492561	26	364495	20	—	—	—
City of Cupertino, CA	2010	307288	15	261195	10	83	52239	40
City of Denver, CO	2005	10410000	80	2082000	45	—	—	—
City of Dublin, CA	2010	328155	15	278932	10	—	—	—
City of Dubuque, IA	2003	1266234	50	633117	27	—	—	—
City of Easton, PA	2016	350900	80	70180	34	—	—	—
City of Emeryville, CA	2004	167071	40	100243	26	—	—	—
City of Evanston, IL	2005	1056169	28	760442	20	80	211234	45
City of Fort Collins, CO	2005	2472391	20	1977913	15	100	0	45
City of Fremont, CA	2005	1659020	25	1245000	15	—	—	—
City of Fresno, CA	1990	3334214	27.2	2427308	30	—	—	—
City of Greensboro, NC	2007	5365412	0	5365412	13	—	—	—
City of Hayward, CA	2005	1175665	20	940532	15	—	—	—
City of Huntington Beach, CA	2005	1699610	15	1444668	15	53.33	793208	35
City of Indianapolis, IN	2010	52651586	100	0	40	—	—	—
City of Iowa City, IA	2005	1285168	28	925321	20	80	257034	45
City of Key West, FL	2005	400000	15	340000	10	—	—	—
City of Knoxville, TN	2005	4507885	20	3606308	15	—	—	—
City of Lakewood, CA	2007	2646240	20	2116992	18	50	1323120	43

Table 5.2(b). Cities and counties in the US with decarbonization strategies — *continued*.

Meso-level actors	T	$\Phi(t)$	δ_N	$\Phi(t+n)$	N	δ_M	$\Phi(t+m)$	M
City of Louisville, KY	2016	16000537	80	3200107	34	—	—	—
City of Medford, OR	2015	465879	100	0	35	—	—	—
City of Minneapolis, MN	2006	5173279	15	4397287	9	80	1034656	44
City of New Haven, CT	1999	1625057	55	731276	31	—	—	—
City of Northampton, MA	2010	316858	80	63372	40	—	—	—
City of Oakland, CA	2005	2992735	36	1915350	15	—	—	—
City of Palo Alto, CA	1990	765920	80	153184	40	—	—	—
City of Philadelphia, PA	2006	21067224	28	15168401	19	80	4213445	44
City of Piedmont, CA	2005	48818	40	29291	25	—	—	—
City of Pittsburgh, PA	2003	4837715	20	3870172	22	50	2418858	27
City of Portland, OR	1990	8989869	80	1797974	60	—	—	—
City of Providence, RI	2010	2652837	100	0	40	—	—	—
City of Reno, NV	2008	2751879	80	550376	42	—	—	—
City of Richmond, VA	2008	3370527	80	674105	42	—	—	—
City of Rochester, NY	2010	1800000	40	1080000	20	—	—	—
City of San Francisco, CA	1990	6201949	25	4651462	27	80	1240390	60
City of San Jose, CA	2014	6900000	88	828000	36	—	—	—
City of San Leandro, CA	2005	675800	25	506850	15	—	—	—
City of Santa Cruz, CA	1990	427280	30	299096	30	80	85456	60
City of Santa Monica, CA	1990	1386640	15	1178644	25	—	—	—
City of Seattle, WA	2008	3708000	58	1557360	22	100	0	42
City of Somerville, MA	2014	651426	100	0	36	—	—	—
City of St Louis, MO	2005	8081418	80	1616284	45	—	—	—
City of Tacoma, WA	2000	1658939	80	331788	50	—	—	—
City of West Hollywood, CA	2008	583213	25	437410	27	—	—	—
City of West Palm Beach, FL	2013	1484767	25	1113575	12	100	0	37
Washington, DC	2006	10535018	50	5267509	26	100	0	44
City of Kansas City, MO	2000	11300000	30	7910000	20	—	—	—
King County, WA	2007	20100000	50	10050000	23	80	4020000	43
New York City, NY	2005	61060000	40	36636000	25	80	12212000	45
Salt Lake City, UT	2009	4943904	80	988781	31	—	—	—
Town of Blacksburg, VA	2017	438641	100	0	33	—	—	—
Town of Lexington, MA	1990	526705	80	105341	60	—	—	—

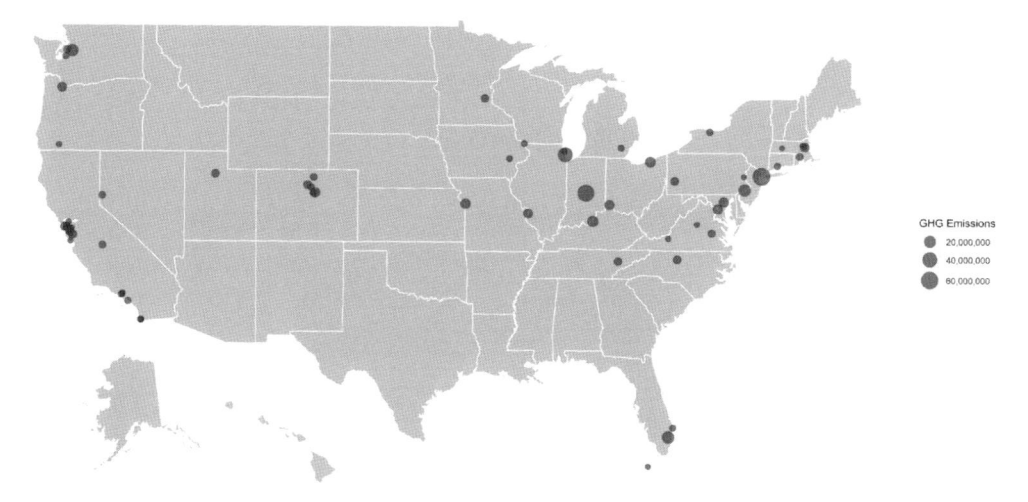

Figure 5.4. Greenhouse gas emissions of selected US cities and counties who have committed to reductions.

guide institutional interventions, as in missing an ecological link, actors collectively lack the necessary tools and frameworks to judge the efficacy of institutional pressures, such as policies or activism, in relation to induced transformation necessary from a policy and landscape perspective (Geels et al., 2017). This hinders the ability to understand the mechanisms for optimal response of the multilevel system. There is thus some promise in having an appropriate framework to relate institutional forces, not only to symbolic or preferably economic mediating actions but also to the eventual outcome in terms of the natural or ecological impact of said micro-level actions and macro-level policy (Geels et al., 2017).

At the micro level, individuals who are nested within consuming households and firms are also generally observed collectively to view and understand group dynamics and its effects on decision-making. Management theories view households from sociology and microeconomics frames. Thus, at the individual level, the consumers are crucial in our understanding of how artifacts they own or use are produced at any given time and the impact they have on the natural environment (Sunny, 2016). These micro-level interactions of actors with artifacts manifest collectively at more macro-level structural changes.

At the macro level, however, the mainstream framework that dominates such systemic and structural changes is theorized based on macroeconomics, and thereby, global mechanisms, such as the Paris Climate Talks or United Nations (UN) directives on economic growth and climate impact, make its way to lower levels, such as regional scales, groups, or individuals, as top-down directives. At this level, political science, public administration, macroeconomics, or international relations view structural and aggregate developments on consumption and strategies to curb them, relying on frameworks to evaluate long-term policy options or to explain mechanisms that link global economic growth to climate change — and not to individual agency.

In monitoring progress of global issues, it is important to have a multilevel viewpoint, although integration is difficult given that the fields from technological, scientific, and social arenas need to be restructured (Lam et al., 2014). However, the recent models of sustainability draw from environmental, economic, and social outcomes and are often idealized at multiple levels (Schoolman et al., 2012), from global communities and transnational bodies to the firm-level for business aspirations, e.g. the triple bottom line (Elkington, 2013). In judging organizational actions on climate change issues, rarely do practitioners or organizational scholars invoke an environmental impact-based, interdisciplinary perspective.

Generally, internal, psychological, and sociological views with the external world are used to understand the individual's relationship with the artificial world, where the economic sciences use price and quantity to answer the questions of who it is produced for, how, and at what quantities, but not how it impacts the natural environment, as a result. Within groups, where such individuals are nested, prior experience imprinting and socializing bias can affect decision-making — a key attribute often unaccounted for when aggregating individual actions to higher levels.

As it currently stands, it is difficult for macro-level actors and policy-makers to design, implement, or evaluate the effectiveness of environmental interventions. The question that needs answering is whether organizations that adopt environmentally friendly behaviors are, in fact, actually helping the environment. Without an appropriate framework, current theory or existing measures limit our ability to appropriately answer that question. Beyond government responses to highlighted global environmental challenges like climate change, George et al. (2016) point out the role of informal institutions, such as social movements. For instance, without an appropriate lens, how does one theorize and extend our understanding of how meso-level advocacy organizations may shape action on sustainability shifts in augmenting the role of governments at the macro level and firms at the micro level? An explicit outcome variable once again is needed, both for environmental entrepreneurship and corporate environmentalism alike, in order to judge the efficacy of firm actions, institutional policies, or the "success" of social movements and campaigns with regard to climate change.

It can be argued that a multilevel framework may enable both traditional institutional theorists and phenomenon-driven scholars to finally provide relevant and robust boundary conditions to the applicability of existing theoretical perspectives to ecological research contexts in ways that make climate-change–related mitigation efforts less uncertain than they currently are.

5.3. Assessing System-wide Impact on the Natural Environment

It is clear that recent interest on the role of businesses in combating environmental degradation or responding to climate change has been considerable in both academic and media outlets (Lenox and Chatterji, 2018). Scholars are not only encouraged to expand the link between ecological and economic outcomes but also look to place businesses at the forefront in the fight against global environmental degradation (Hall *et al.*, 2010). This is because the locus of most anthropogenic drivers of such issues lie within the subjects of management research (Dean and McMullen, 2007; Lenox and York, 2011). For example, the burning of fossil fuels by corporate actors disproportionately contributes to increased concentration of harmful greenhouse gases (Pachauri *et al.*, 2014) which contributes to global warming — considered one of the most crucial social issues of our time (Solomon, 2007). The foundational challenge has been the fact that most management theories that are widespread in prior literature have systematically overlooked the inherent embeddedness of the *natural* environment, despite recent calls to integrate the two (see Starik and Kanashiro, 2013, for details). In order to first understand and address the complex and interlinked issues of environmental sustainability, diversity of knowledge and methods of inquiry is crucial to uncover various barriers (Schoolman *et al.*, 2012).

Environmental sustainability studied by organizational scholars resides at the intersection of ecological and social sciences. Yet, in both these broad fields, complex and non-linear interactions characterize the nature of relationships between system components, at multiple different levels, and over time (Odum *et al.*, 2000). For this reason, emergent properties that arise at the higher levels are seldom appropriately predicted by analyzing the parts in isolation (Harding, 2006). Doing so would impose a theoretical limit on the very ability to understand systemic behavior beyond a certain level.[1] The confluence of interdependencies has resulted in the topic of climate change as a planetary problem to have been especially deemed "wicked," as a result. Additionally, studying climate change through socioeconomic lens, without a commensurate emphasis on a natural or ecological one, significantly obscures corrective action. Extant research in environmental sustainability, be it as a completely new phenomenon or interesting context, seldom distinguish the natural processes from normative or instrumental motivations behind organizational actions. Despite it being true that organizations and their environments are sometimes "talked into existence" (Weick *et al.*, 2005, p. 409) there exists a real, natural impact exerted by each organization and actor. Different, and often underutilized, lens may inform the wider management research in

---

[1] For instance, in complex social human systems, detailed understanding of individual human behavior alone cannot predict group-level behavior that results at the emergent, collective level.

understanding the natural *why* behind environmentally responsible behavior beyond socially constructed, overtly commercial, value-laden, or contentious ones. This framework provides ideas on ways to link economic activity to the subsequent environmental impacts and outcomes at multiple levels and thereby bridge two different conceptualizations of *impact*.

As global communities and actors at every level collectively design and implement different directives under climate scenarios, scholars can assist in efforts by further incorporating such natural-system requirements and understand limitations of overly socialized views of climate change mitigation or adaption across levels. Scholars have noted the tension inherent in this duality in balancing divergent tensions and expectations, from taking ideas within the natural sciences, to applications within the social sciences (Thompson *et al.*, 2011). Historically, there has been reasons for this duality, as both forms of performance measures have developed in parallel and rarely juxtaposed, which is why the split between natural and social sciences seem to expand, despite calls for management scholars to be more integrative within the Anthropocene (Hoffman and Jennings, 2016) or reforming measures and sustainability conceptualizations (Peloza, 2009; Wood, 2010).

This chapter recognizes this difficulty, as there has been considerable challenge given the rarity in cross-pollination across distant categories, and the general fragmentation of such knowledge, both in terms of its classification, production, and organization, as well as its usage in academic, professional, and societal arenas (Porter and Chubin, 1985). Compounded with distinct values, identities, and beliefs, it is understandable why efforts to combine different scientific perspectives by integrating cross-disciplinary tenets have traditionally been faced with fundamental obstacles in such research (Evans and Marvin, 2006).

Despite these challenges, an increasing number of scholars have recently taken to exploring shifts in production and consumption as well as the emergence and adoption of new and impactful ideas introduced by sustainable entrepreneurs (George *et al.*, 2015) recognizing that economic factors or market mechanisms are not the only ones at play in society (Howard-Grenville *et al.*, 2014; Thompson *et al.*, 2011). Although these sustainable ventures are said to create micro- or meso-level environmental solutions, it is still not clear what role it plays in system-wide or higher level sustainability shifts (George *et al.*, 2015; Hall *et al.*, 2010; Howard-Grenville *et al.*, 2014) and whether actors spearheading sustainable market actions actually reduce environmental degradation and create ecological impact or value (Thompson *et al.*, 2011; Wry and Haugh, 2018).

This framework reorients existing perspectives by explaining how what had seemed to be assorted, socially constructed, and heterogenous sets of recommendation on climate actions, can in fact, be composed of a single element with robust grounding in systems ecology with a long tradition. In exposing such different traditions of equilibrium, what may have seemed to be an individual or disjointed phenomenon is really a global and holistic set of axioms; and what may have seemed to be a changing set of assumptions and conditions in environmental sustainability may actually be a stable set of natural laws, constant over time, but has been systematically overlooked and thus left unintegrated.

In order to understand the idiosyncratic challenges of environmental sustainability, the field must first elaborate on the outcomes of such commercial and ecological logics and organizational choices. While the former is well defined and widely accepted, the latter is not. If arguably topics such as environmental entrepreneurship and corporate sustainability are theoretically distinct from wider management sciences, what limits this argument further is a general lack of agreed-upon outcome criteria and an absence of an appropriate "impact" variable.

Put another way, although means to such sustainable ends may vary in economic systems, the ends themselves are rather parsimonious in natural systems. Juxtaposing the goals allow actors in practitioner communities to judge the relative contribution of their actions, both in terms of direction and magnitude. Such topics from environmental science, which has governed natural systems for longer than humanity's ascension to earth's domination, may provide prominent areas and perspectives to draw from for management scholars and organizational scientists studying topics of environmental sustainability.

5.3.1. *Environmental entrepreneurs and the value they create*

The burning of fossil fuels contributes to climate change through increased concentration of greenhouse gases (Pachauri *et al.*, 2014). Fossil fuels, such as coal, natural gas, and oil, emit a large proportion of the anthropogenic carbon emissions that can be supplemented by or replaced with renewable energies, such as solar, wind, biomass, geothermal, and hydroelectric (Stocker *et al.*, 2013). Such cleaner energy technologies, which can reduce the severity of human-induced climate change, are being introduced by environmental entrepreneurs and adopted by organizations (Lenox and York, 2011). Environmental entrepreneurs, as changemakers, are thus mobilizing resources toward the proliferation of such technologies, and in the process creating ecological value by lessening global environmental degradation (Russo, 2003; York *et al.*, 2016). This exogenous, global climate change regime necessitates structural modifications to the global economic system, both from a demand side (consumption) and supply side (production) perspectives, across nearly all levels, from micro- and product-level to macro- or global-level actions.

Environmental entrepreneurs develop new products, services, and business models that minimize environmental degradation (York *et al.*, 2016). Examples of ecological impact include Tesla Motors attempting to reduce the consumption of hydrocarbon fuels in passenger vehicles, or SolarCity attempting to propagate the mass adoption of solar energy to shift residential homes and commercial offices from consuming electricity generated by coal-fired power plants. Regardless of the motivation of the founders to start these ventures, or the financial performance of the firms, the eventual outcomes of both these ventures' innovation or business model is to intentionally reduce the consumption of fossil fuels that contribute to carbon emissions (Edenhofer *et al.*, 2011; Stocker *et al.*, 2013). This stream of research takes place under the broad banner of environmental and sustainable entrepreneurship literature, as the environmental impact of such entrepreneurs distinguish them from other forms of value creation (Dean and McMullen, 2007; York and Lenox, 2014).

5.3.2. *Emergent drivers at different levels*

Both macro- and meso-level feedback loops, such as government regulations and other social norms, can impact their trajectory. In fact, Thompson *et al.* (2011) posits that entrepreneurs at the micro level deal with environmental degradation in a manner different from institutional response by governments at the macro level. There has been much research in terms of how micro-level factors might influence opportunity recognition and motivate entrepreneurs in the sustainability context. What an entrepreneur perceives as risky or rewarding is thus dependent on market, regulative, cultural, or demographic contexts (Klewitz, 2017; Hechavarría *et al.*, 2017; Urban and Nikolov, 2013; Mioara and Mihai, 2014) much of which social movements or government interventions at meso- and macro-level drive (Sunny and Shu, 2019). Therefore, the way in which an entrepreneur experiences the external environment varies according to their individual perceptions as in how the various contextual, institutional, and social drivers are perceived by the entrepreneur.

Generally, environmental and social values are a crucial factor for sustainable entrepreneurship (Gast *et al.*, 2017; Klewitz and Hansen, 2014; Spence *et al.*, 2011; Stevens *et al.*, 2015; Patzelt and Shepherd, 2011). In order to recognize opportunities, entrepreneurs need the right cognitive framework (Baron and Ensley, 2006) and in the sustainability context, a favorable attitude toward sustainability is a pre-requisite for sustainable self-efficacy (Koe *et al.*, 2015). Sustainable and environmental entrepreneurs not only need general entrepreneurial knowledge, and managerial competence[2] (Lans *et al.*, 2014) but also commercial and

---

[2] Entrepreneurial competences are also required and are multidimensional in nature — encompassing social, business, and industry-specific competences (Lans *et al.*, 2014). A low perceived social status of conventional entrepreneurship may also engender a more environmental business orientation (Hörisch *et al.*, 2017). As such, prior startup experience, although typically critical for traditional entrepreneurs, may not affect environmental or social entrepreneurs the same way (Hosseininia and Ramezani, 2016) although empirical findings tend to be mixed regarding this (Choongo *et al.*, 2016).

environmental knowledge (Gast *et al.*, 2017) — an infusion of micro-foundations of opportunity, as well as meso-level ecosystem resources to exploit said opportunities (Sun *et al.*, 2019).

From the perspective of sustainable and environmental entrepreneurs and new ventures, opportunities are geared toward attempting to reduce the consumption of energy and lowering emissions through the proliferation of their core innovation, products, or business models (Cohen and Winn, 2007; York *et al.*, 2016). The point of departure in this assessment, in contrast to existing or prior research in mainstream entrepreneurship, is that instead of measuring sales as a strategic performance outcome, the focus is on the environmental benefits of the products (Thompson *et al.*, 2011). It has to be explicitly stated here that whether a firm is commercially viable is a rather different question than if their products and services are environmentally impactful. It is possible to have an environmentally impactful product that is not commercially viable or vice versa. As such, this present dissertation only explicitly centers on the environmental impact, while setting aside the commercial outcomes that have been the focus of studies elsewhere within the entrepreneurship field. Therefore, one of the assumptions made in this research work is that it is possible, and is often the case, that environmental entrepreneurs are motivated by not only environmental reasons but also commercial ones.

Entrepreneurs often have immaterial motives (Hahn and Ince, 2016) as well as goal heterogeneity in improving sustainability or creating sustainable value (Jolink and Niesten, 2015). Socio-environmental mission, to a certain extent, drive such entrepreneurs relating to their goals, normative identities, and desire to create value (Stevens *et al.*, 2015). Besides entrepreneurial orientation and innovative orientations, socio-environmental orientation positively affects sustainable entrepreneurship (Crnogaj *et al.*, 2014; Hooi *et al.*, 2016) through scanning and interacting with the macro-environment. Sustainable entrepreneurs, perhaps more so than traditional or conventional entrepreneurs, need to be skillful seekers of legitimacy in ways that balance their own values to stakeholders in their social environment (Choi and Gray, 2008). The balance of values between self and the other impact the propensity to launch sustainable ventures as opposed to conventional entrepreneurship — a key differentiator between ecological and commercial logics driving processes and outcomes.

Each individual entrepreneur often acts in line with their self-perception of their own identity, which could vary between being utilitarian or commercial, or normative, socio-ecological (York *et al.*, 2016). As such, entrepreneurs also face tradeoffs between perceptions of sustainability-oriented outcomes, such as environmental and economic logics (Hahn and Ince, 2016). How they prioritize these different logics depends on these identities and their strengths as well as how entrepreneurs engage one or the other or both through coupling. Some believe that such coupling may enable them to catalyze a larger societal change and impact than forms of organizing can (Simon *et al.*, 2013). In short, it is true that both forms of value creation, namely commercial and ecological, are at play across such contexts, and coupling configurations can impact the trajectory of societal or environmental value, as a function of the macro–meso institutional setting.

5.3.3. *How environmental entrepreneurs create value*

Existing literature also claim that entrepreneurs can potentially resolve problems of market failure such as environmental issues (Dean and McMullen, 2007) and thus, sustainable and environmental entrepreneurship may be able to slow or reverse environmental degradation (Cohen and Winn, 2007; Russo, 2003; York *et al.*, 2016). This theory of sustainable and environmental entrepreneurship thus attempts to explain the role entrepreneurs play in creating a more socially and environmentally sustainable economy (Dean and McMullen, 2007). Although there have been such attempts to explain how environmental entrepreneurship can reduce or eliminate environmental problems (Dean and McMullen, 2007), there has been very little theoretical or empirical work on, if in fact, entrepreneurship influences environmental sustainability (Dean and McMullen, 2007). As a result, prior work has been more prescriptive than descriptive (Hall *et al.*, 2010). By putting forth a framework showing how sustainable entrepreneurs can replace unsustainable practices with sustainable technologies and business models, this chapter contributes to a rich and diverse stream of future research (Cohen and Winn, 2007) regarding system-wide transitions to environmental sustainability.

However, such a sustainable transition is only possible with significantly dramatic innovation and adoption across multiple sectors around the world, across levels, and at the same time (Lenox and Chatterji, 2018). Private, public, and not-for-profit organizations are increasingly called to collaboratively engage a suite of approaches in order to usher in the necessary transformation subsequently needed in the global economy. By building a model of environmental sustainability using systems concepts, this framework provides grounding to prevalent organizational discussions at different levels of analysis and system boundaries, a key gap needing to be bridged for future research.

For instance, we can attribute the central role of sustainable and environmental entrepreneurship and their innovations as driving these multilevel trends where all major stages of necessary technological change, such as invention, innovation, and diffusion of clean energy technologies and artifacts, can be analyzed against the heterogenous backdrop and economic, technological, and sociological contexts (Río González, 2009; Rogge and Reichardt, 2016). In fact, the issue of global challenges, e.g. climate change, is so pervasive that its root causes and consequences manifest at every level of analysis of interest to management and organizational scholars researching social, political, and economic choices (Howard-Grenville *et al.*, 2014).

Sustainable entrepreneurship also includes such aspects under the banner of corporate social (CSR) (Shepherd and Patzelt, 2011) also commonly called corporate sustainability (Hall *et al.*, 2010). Similar to examples given in Chapter 2, one of the mechanisms such actor groups would implement, for example, include Google Inc trying to reduce the gasoline consumption of its corporate fleet vehicles or switching to rooftop solar energy in powering its multitude of datacenters. Again, their micro-level organizational decision to adopt these technologies could be influenced by macro-level institutional measures such as the efficiency standards of California Air Resources Board (CARB), or partnerships with the SunShot program from the US Department of Energy (DoE).

The nexus manifests in such a way that potential solution for Google to reduce its gasoline usage or increase its solar energy consumption could be realized by adopting innovations in the product classes offered by Tesla Motors and SolarCity, the environmental entrepreneurs, respectively. This developed framework, which can help model the interaction of these actor effects over time, illustrates how processes and mechanisms scholars study can impact the natural environment.

5.4. Environmental Entrepreneurs: The Action, the Actor, and the Impact

The role of government interventions on macrostructures play a critical role. The literature on existing sustainable and environmental entrepreneurship explain that there exists a negative externality to market transactions given that pricing mechanisms work imperfectly for environmental goods (Cohen and Winn, 2007). For instance, non-renewable resources are priced incorrectly, while renewable resources are often undervalued (Lenox and York, 2011). Mispricing of resources and market failures create opportunities for environmental entrepreneurs, which is why policy-makers are crucial for sparking sustainable entrepreneurship (Dean and McMullen, 2007). For these reasons, this research stream views macro-level institutions, such as polices and other corrective mechanisms for environmental market failures, as an antecedent to meso- and micro-level environmental and sustainable entrepreneurship.

A measure of ecological value creation could thus help in testing the efficacy of different policies enacted by institutional actors, such as regulative policy-makers, as they design and implement public policy aimed at fixing market imperfections — manifesting as opportunities for sustainable entrepreneurs (Cohen and Winn, 2007). As such, regulatory intervention has historically been the primary solution to environmentally relevant market failures (Dean and McMullen, 2007), which is why the role of macro-level actors, such as governments, has taken center stage for the initial discussion of topics of sustainable and environmental entrepreneurship. From earlier examples, the introduction of CARB emissions reduction strategies aims to reduce the consumption of hydrocarbon fuels due to toxic emissions, or introduction of SunShot program by the US DoE increases the cost-effectiveness of solar electricity for consumption by households and offices, thereby reducing the amount of carbon emissions. In this way, the macro-level inputs to the system impact lower-level trajectories. Compared to the first set of micro-level actors, who are environmental and sustainable entrepreneurs, these macro-level institutional actors engender a different mechanism through CARB and SunShot, which are designed to generate the same outcome as Tesla and Solar City, respectively — i.e. reducing the consumption of fossil fuels in transportation and increasing the consumption of renewable energy in the built environment.

It comes as no surprise that policy-makers have recently started collaborating with businesses to improve collective environmental performance (Cohen and Winn, 2007). However, without a multilevel framework, questions still remain regarding the mechanisms in which public policy may influence the incidence of such entrepreneurship (Hall *et al.*, 2010) or to what extent entrepreneurs and policy-makers can together lead the fundamental societal transformation in the production and consumption of resources, such as energy, toward sustainable economies (Hall *et al.*, 2010).

Besides a lack of theoretical connection between outcomes, subsequent empirical research on actual impacts of environmental entrepreneurship are particularly limited. Most quantitative studies have ignored attempts to model or test direct environmental impacts, resorting to using environmental entrepreneurship itself as the dependent variable (Lenox and York, 2011). Similarly, most studies at the institutional level focus on the effect of different policies and instruments on the likelihood of firm action, such as the probability of firm responses to external pressure, or the aggregate level of firm entry, given the external environmental or landscape (Russo, 2003; Sine and Lee, 2009; Sunny and Shu, 2019). Although it is important to understand such influencing factors, the environmental impact of the resulting action or outcome is far more crucial, especially for the field of environmental entrepreneurship or corporate environmentalism (Hall *et al.*, 2010; Thompson *et al.*, 2011). This is despite recent interest regarding the notion that the addition of environmental consequences offers a significantly expanded definition for the field of entrepreneurship (Cohen and Winn, 2007).

Major gaps still exist as to how the process of entrepreneurship driving sustainability transitions will unfold (Hall *et al.*, 2010). Therefore, large-scale econometric analysis of the role of the entrepreneur in understanding how entrepreneurial entry impacts society beyond economic growth and job creation will contribute to our existing knowledge of sustainable and environmental entrepreneurship, as a subset of the broader concept of sustainable entrepreneurship (Dean and McMullen, 2007; Thompson *et al.*, 2011). Knowing that sustainable entrepreneurs are driven not just by an economic perspective, but from an environmental or social perspective as well, it is surprising that virtually no research exists that empirically tests the latter (Cohen and Winn, 2007).

This is problematic, as scholars have recently claimed entrepreneurship research that focuses only on economic outcomes without sustainability outcomes cannot be considered sustainable entrepreneurship research (Shepherd and Patzelt, 2011). Instead of a push to create "more" entrepreneurial entry, scholars previously agreed that studies should thus rather view how entrepreneurial entry can create social value (Kirzner, 1990; Eckhardt and Shane, 2003; Thompson *et al.*, 2011). If entry does relate to ecological benefit, what are some conditions or factors that moderate this relationship? A framework that links economic theorizing to more nuanced ecological impacts could hold promise for guiding institutional forces at multiple levels, as argued above, which would in turn allow more expositions of research questions of recent interest within management scholarship.

This further illustrates the necessity and importance of a measure of environmental impact to varying groups of stakeholders and actors across multiple levels. Although finding such an appropriate dependent variable that is able to adequately capture the role of organizations in creating environmental value is a formidable challenge (Cohen and Winn, 2007), scholars argue that future research should nonetheless examine whether environmental entrepreneurs actually yielded positive environmental outcomes (Thompson *et al.*, 2011).

In an effort to test such processes, new frameworks need to emerge that facilitates and unifies such multitude of research designs. Given that the link between the natural environment and economic systems lacks theoretical robustness, empirical testing abilities of the above research questions have been nearly non-existent. As a result, most of the open questions which represent the current research gap continue to go unbridged. In order to address this, a framework focusing on such multilevel dynamics and dual outcomes can address the gaps on the topic of environmental sustainability within management more broadly.

5.5. Corporate Sustainability

Current paradigms create new, yet similar questions — are firm actions improving the natural environment? Answers to such questions are rare in relevant literature. To appropriately answer such questions, a measurement reform within CSR needs to take place (Peloza, 2009; Wood, 1991) which can begin to open the "social" black box. Scholars are increasingly scrutinizing the flexibility organizations currently have in doing socio-environmental good only in ways that suits them (Brammer *et al.*, 2012; Margolis and Walsh, 2003). Prior research explored and elaborated on how firms engage with these landscape actors and for what reasons

(Durand *et al.*, 2019). Yet much is to be known about how these actions impact the sought-after environmental outcome.

Consider the example of organizational emissions of carbon dioxide. The use of carbon data to inform mitigation activities is generally measured in a unidimensional manner, such as in weight equivalents, or derivatives such as firm-level carbon intensity ratios, and as such is largely interchangeable. However, the actions or choices themselves, such as divestment strategies or reduction, consists of clean energy or efficiency investments, limiting clear benchmarks when comparing one of these initiatives or strategies to another. Efforts by institutional investors to decarbonize at the portfolio level are categorized along multiple and confusing dimensions of coverage. Questions arise on issues such as whether it is the proportion of the portfolio, subject, or focus; if it is outcome-quantified as reduction in business unit-, firm-, or portfolio-level emissions or other metrics, such as societal decarbonization; and the timeframes on long-term vs. short-term horizons on actions and steps to decarbonization. In other words, there is currently no consensus on how to calculate emissions offsets along different dimensions over a multitude of levels, i.e. the lifecycle of a project, firm activities, or investment timeframes across industries. Articulation of a few of these dimensions, to the exclusion of others, results in a deficient strategy which may lack clarity, compounding the further non-comparability of efforts both within and between portfolios, assets, or entire organizations.

5.5.1. *Toward a multilevel impact corporate framework*

For instance, a new measure can instead be denoted by the level to which a given firm, portfolio, business unit or asset reduces their fossil-fuel usage or natural resource consumption by intentionally allocating effort and resources, thereby reducing system-wide emissions. Similar to the supply-side examples, it can also be the extent to which environmental entrepreneurs, such as a clean energy company, integrates renewable energy with the economic system, thereby replacing fossil fuel usage and reducing the subsequent degradation or negative impacts. In the same vein that prior studies have previously explored the conditions under which change-makers, such as environmental entrepreneurs, enter the marketplace, the majority of research work continues to lack an understanding related to the conditions under which such actors and corporations create environmental value.

Normative theories of sustainability (e.g. Porter and Kramer, 2006; Eccles and Serafeim, 2013) allow decision-makers to make choices in selecting sustainable practices that help them, not the environment (Margolis and Walsh, 2003) — a micro-level economic gain rather than a macro-level ecological gain. Without an ecological reasoning, this process risks being used as a political tool by resource-rich actors for strategic and economic gains only. Current management theories, as a result, provide a considerably weak, highly fragmented, and relatively untested link between organizational actions and environmental sustainability, due to the multiple levels of analysis and perspectives used to previously theorize or study them. The present framework posits the ecological framework to augment such rich discussions, i.e. although scholars within corporate sustainability research observes organizational actions to be in line with lowering their environmental impact (Hall *et al.*, 2010), many do not currently question the specific ecological impact of such actions. Rather, they focus on the economic rationale for partaking in actions and behavior, or the motivational factors that drive actors to act.

Firms and organizations are under significant public and regulatory pressures to reduce the production and consumption of fossil fuels and to reduce their carbon footprint, which they can do so through the adoption of cleaner, renewable energy. However, this shift can be thought of by some in terms of opportunities for new value creation (Aguinis and Glavas, 2012; Winston *et al.*, 2017, Sunny *et al.*, 2018) while for others, it manifests as a perceptual risk (Wood, 1991; Orlitzky and Benjamin, 2001). Table 5.3 shows select Fortune 100 firms committed to addressing climate change with impact, but through the same framework.

In fact, industry is often considered one of the largest contributors to environmental degradation (Cohen and Winn, 2007), deriving the same private or micro-level benefits while incurring meso- and macro-level social costs of economic production (Dean and McMullen, 2007). Driven by such forces, companies are often also being accused of distorting public policies by using industry lobbying to protect the status quo. Firms respond with CSR initiatives to appease stakeholder expectations by engendering "greenwashing" or other symbolic efforts, intentionally or not, by reducing little to no environmental degradation (Delmas *et al.*, 2016; Laufer, 2003). The macro–micro divide shows the externalities of their production processes; a micro-level interaction represents a considerable hidden cost to society, aggregated at the macro level, that firms readily derive their profits at the expense of (Pearce *et al.*, 1996).

For future research through the application of the framework to guide impactful organizational-level actions, one can quantify organizational-level ecological impact through tangible actions, investments, strategies, or programs, while exploring how organizations respond to existing and future institutional pressures in reducing their own impact. In line with the framework, the author quantifies impact as the organizational-level adoption and intentional use of clean energy technologies and related changes in behavior that tangibly draws down greenhouse gases and carbon emissions. In doing so, we objectively test the ecological value creation construct from the perspective of organizations trying to reduce the consumption of their energy for operational processes, which gives off carbon emissions.

Table 5.3. Corporations at the microlevel with decarbonization strategies.

Micro-level actors	T	$\Phi(t)$	δ_N	$\Phi(t+n)$	N	δ_M	$\Phi(t+m)$	M
Allstate	2007	188715	20	150972	—	—	13	—
American International Group	2010	5190	20	4152	—	—	10	—
Apple	2012	160400	61	62556	—	—	8	—
Bank of America Corp	2010	1819036	50	909518	100	0	10	30
Boeing	2017	1006000	25	754500	—	—	8	—
Citigroup	2005	1090651	35	708923	80	218130	15	45
Comcast	2009	105839	10	95255	—	—	11	—
CVS Caremark	2010	1766531	36	1130580	56	777274	20	40
General Electric	2011	3635617	20	2908494	—	—	9	—
General Motors Company	2010	6173746	31	4259885	—	—	20	—
Goldman Sachs Group	2013	249112	15	211745	50	124556	7	23
Google	2015	1451418	100	0	—	—	10	—
Hewlett-Packard	2015	388700	60	155480	—	—	10	—
Humana	2017	67712	10.5	60602	—	—	5	—
Intel	2012	1275000	62	484500	—	—	8	—
International Business Machines (IBM)	2005	2028000	40	1216800	—	—	20	—
Johnson & Johnson	2010	1343105	20	1074484	80	268621	10	40
JP Morgan Chase & Co	2005	1392704	50	696352	—	—	15	—
Lockheed Martin	2010	1271358	35	826383	—	—	10	—
Lowe's	2016	2498134	40	1498880	—	—	14	—
Merck	2015	1458500	40	875100	—	—	10	—
MetLife	2012	176955	10	159260	—	—	8	—
Microsoft	2013	920143	75	230036	—	—	17	—
Morgan Stanley	2012	357990	90	35799	—	—	10	—
Oracle	2015	459516	26	340042	65	160831	10	35
PepsiCo	2015	5484701	20	4387761	—	—	15	—
Pfizer	2012	2131885	20	1705508	—	—	8	—
Philip Morris International	2010	914050	40	548430	60	365620	20	30
Procter & Gamble	2010	5422275	30	3795593	50	2711138	10	20
Prudential Financial	2016	9609	18	7879	—	—	4	—
Target	2017	2817713	30	1972399	—	—	13	—
United Technologies	2015	2049836	15	1742361	—	—	5	—
UnitedHealth Group	2017	95079	3	92227	—	—	6	—
Verizon Communications	2018	4418820	100	0	—	—	17	—
Wal-Mart Stores	2015	19629573	18	16096250	—	—	10	—
Walt Disney	2012	1742927	50	871464	—	—	8	—
Wells Fargo	2008	1953466	45	1074406	—	—	12	—

Note: Only selected Fortune 100 companies are shown here.

To counter the growing trend, corporate greening strategies, such as corporate environmental programs and sustainability initiatives, are on the rise (Cohen and Winn, 2007). For commercial and industrial economic sectors at the meso level, we can aggregate and detail out the role of organizations and their level of clean energy adoption in line with the ecological value creation measure, as part of their sustainability initiatives for CSR, while being in line with macro-level transition plans, like Science Based Targets initiative (SBTi).

5.6. Discussion

As a research community, it is time we take a wider look toward extended outcomes at various levels, rather than relying solely on economically motivated performance metrics. We may answer how and why different actions by firms lead to specific environmentally sustainable outcomes from a natural sciences perspective. Similar to the proposal by Dacin et al. (2011) that entrepreneurship research focus on social "consequences" of entrepreneurship, perhaps it is now time to look at more ecological consequences of entrepreneurial activity as well. Instead of a push to create "more" entrepreneurial entry of environmental solutions, we may look to understand how entrepreneurial entry can create more *environmental* value (Thompson et al., 2011). If the promise of our discussions is to develop theory that encompasses both economic and non-economic outcomes (Venkataraman, 1997), one can readily see that prior research in the field is disproportionately skewed to the former, i.e. the economic implications of organizational actions. The importance of both economic and environmental perspectives within our discussions of sustainable transitions, and to bring the two streams together, is paramount.

This chapter contributes to existing literature and practice by heeding recent calls to extend current theories in sustainable and environmental entrepreneurship and corporate sustainability (Howard-Grenville et al., 2014). The framework posits practical implications in a way that entrepreneurs, such as founders and managers of clean energy companies, and policy-makers at different levels can understand the process of ecological value creation and the role they play in it. Such nuance may highlight ways to collaboratively align initiatives and activities in creating ecological value at different levels.

A broad ecosystem of actors, including inventors, executives, customers, investors, activists, and governments, need to play a role in sustainably growing the economy, in a way that better manages *both* ecological and economic outcomes, where the latter does not limit the former. This plurality informs the complex and collaborative efforts required from multiple groups across levels to appropriately address the current environmental crisis (Lenox and Chatterji, 2018). The theoretical gap introduced here exists at the crossroads of different intellectual domains and analysis levels, roughly grouped herein as organizational-level and institutional-level processes. At the firm or organization level, both supply-side and demand-side determinants shape their corresponding ecological outcomes. At the institutional level, particularly for formal and regulative institutions, regional, state, and national actors and policy-makers are designing and managing interventions. This is primarily to influence organizational-level behavior on both demand- and supply-side market strategies. Different theoretical traditions within management have previously observed such complex phenomena in isolation, despite sharing inherent similarities.

In order to illustrate and fill the gap, the framework highlighted some recent, cross-level understanding for future management scholars. On the supply-side organizational level, researchers can explore recent calls in the entrepreneurship field, starting with Thompson *et al.* (2011), where scholars ask the basic question of whether environmental entrepreneurship reduces, or have reduced, environmental degradation.

In this chapter, the author highlights how management scholars do not typically ask research questions related to an organization's environmental impact. Rather, most assume that firm actions, if carried out or taken, should somehow logically lead to impact. However, prior literature has to date not elaborated the mechanism through which this occurs, neither have they fully exposited on how to quantify the impact (Wry and Haugh, 2018). If organizations do create positive impact, what are the enabling conditions under which the roles of environmental entrepreneurs, are most salient (George *et al.*, 2015)? Others ask similar questions on the role that entrepreneurs specifically play in sustainability shifts necessary to respond to global climate change (George *et al.*, 2015; Hall *et al.*, 2010; Howard-Grenville *et al.*, 2014). Howard-Grenville *et al.* (2014) specifically question the underlying technological facets of such changes, such as how new technologies by entrepreneurs and other innovators can be used to influence such large-scale shifts and adaptation.

Overall, researchers have been encouraged to explore such production and consumption shifts, as it relates to the emergence and adoption of new environmentally benign technologies and practices. Despite such calls, the existing aspects of these mechanisms interacting differently under different levels and contexts, in addition to a reliance on historic economic or strategic outcomes, oversimplify the theoretical nuance by overlooking ecological ones.

These limitations represent not only differences in intervention studied by different disciplines but also hinder both streams from collaboratively reflecting on potential outcomes of different processes. Such processes together play a key role in the global sustainability shift and transformations but cannot single-handedly drive the transition. For some of these groups, an incentive system exists, while for others, institutional change can overcome voids to make the process more efficient (Lenox and Chatterji, 2018). Moving forward, a framework that combines both of the performance dimensions and views the system across levels is necessary to facility these discussions.

Besides managerial or entrepreneurial implications for sustainable innovations or CSR at both the organizational and regional levels, the framework's application can provide insights on influencing effective practical interventions, particularly for implementing the different strategies considered among global frameworks, such as the Paris Climate Accord and others at different level of analyses. In responding to the effects of climate change, almost all countries and organizations are setting goals to achieve their carbon reduction contributions in their own ways by 2020–2050. Their means for achieving these ends, however, may vary enormously (Arent *et al.*, 2017). Investing in clean energy innovation or imposing regulations on high-emitting sectors are ambiguous policy mandates that may manifest differently for different countries, economies, or regions, but a disproportionate attention to means — the strategic actions, and policy instruments, rather than the congruence with the ends, i.e., the environmental impact of such intervention — may give a misleading account of such processes that underlie such outcomes. By adding contextual clarity to the role and agency of organizations and governments under global and regional reduction strategies, this framework moves the dial in one of the most pressing issues of our time.

5.7. Conclusion

While climate change can be disastrous to human societies and global economy, it also presents a major opportunity for entrepreneurs and innovators to design and scale solutions (Wry and Haugh, 2018; Wiklund *et al.*, 2018). Akin to Schumpeter's gale, climate change may very well necessitate the destruction of existing business conditions, paving the way for future innovations. The actors involved in these very mechanisms are entrepreneurs in new startup ventures, policy-makers, and managers in incumbent organizations who are increasingly acting to lessen their impact on the environment by reducing externalities (Lenox and Chatterji, 2018). The extent of such reductions is ambitious and radical but justified if disastrous effects are to be limited to targets within international negotiations (Howard-Grenville *et al.*, 2014).

These reductions also imply considerable and structural economic shifts that need to take place — raising concerns over the competitiveness of existing businesses and costs to consumers (Howard-Grenville *et al.*, 2014). Investors and funds also raise concerns regarding the instability faced by the private sector in these public policy responses and subsequent cost incurred in adjusting to rapidly changing regulations. Nuanced theories can begin to understand the promises and threats of competing interventions and mechanisms.

The current gap in existing theoretical perspectives limit the appeal of environmental entrepreneurship and corporate environmentalism as a delineated research phenomenon or lens to view solutions to large-scale environmental issues. To build on extant theories and help inform the actors in practitioner communities who are involved in large-scale, socioeconomic transformation, the current chapter conceptualizes and derives ecological value creation as an outcome within a framework at the regional (macro, meso) and micro and organization levels. It incorporates institutional factors theorized in recent research work and presents conjectures regarding the effects of environmental intervention by organizations. Thereby, a model can be based on existing theory by linking possible effects from the spatial and temporal heterogeneity within different institutional and organizational configurations, but from the standpoint of natural environmental impact.

Understanding such conditions will allows scholars to build and test more nuanced theories and engage with practitioners to answer open research questions (Howard-Grenville *et al.*, 2014; George *et al.*, 2016; George *et al.*, 2015). By integrating a more explicit, theoretical focus on ecological outcomes, organizational actions across levels can be made less ambiguous and more impactful. This chapter helps researchers, academics, entrepreneurs, managers, and policy-makers to better understand their role and engage each other to respond strategically and with impact, in line with large-scale sustainability shifts (Hall *et al.*, 2010).

References

Acemoglu, D., Aghion, P., Bursztyn, L., & Hemous, D. (2012). The environment and directed technical change. *American Economic Review*, **102**(1), 131–66.

Agu, D. O., & Nwamaka Ogbeide-Osaretin, E. (2016). An inquiry into the political economy of the global clean energy transition policies and Nigeria's federal and state governments' fiscal policies. UNU-WIDER, Helsinki, Finland.

Aguinis, H., & Glavas, A. (2012). What we know and don't know about corporate social responsibility: A review and research agenda. *Journal of Management*, **38**(4), 932–968.

Anderson, P. W. (1972). More is different. *Science*, **177**(4047), 393–396.

Arent, D. (2017). *The Political Economy of Clean Energy Transitions* (Oxford, UK: Oxford University Press).

Arrow, K. J. (2012). *Social Choice and Individual Values*. Vol. 12 (London, UK: Yale University Press).

Autio, E., Kenney, M., Mustar, P., Siegel, D., & Wright, M. (2014). Entrepreneurial innovation: The importance of context. *Research Policy*, **43**(7), 1097–1108.

Baron, R. A., & Ensley, M. A. (2006). Opportunity recognition as the detection of meaningful patterns: Evidence from comparisons of novice and experienced entrepreneurs. *Management Science*, **52**(9), 1331–1344.

Black, D. (1958). The Theory of Committees and Elections (Cambridge, UK: Cambridge University Press).

Brammer, S., Jackson, G. & Matten, D. (2012). Corporate social responsibility and institutional theory: New perspectives on private governance. *Socio-Economic Review*, **10**(1), 3–28.

Buchanan, J., & G. Tullock (1962). *The Calculus of Consent: Logical Foundations of Constitutional Democracy* (Ann Arbor, MI: University of Michigan Press).

Bueb, J., Hanania, L., & Le Clézio, A. (2016). Border adjustment mechanisms elements for economic, legal, and political analysis. Report 020, World Institute for Development Economic Research (UNU-WIDER).

Ćetković, S., Buzogány, A., & Schreurs, M. (2016). Varieties of clean energy transitions in Europe: Political-economic foundations of onshore and offshore wind development. WIDER Working Paper No. 2016/18.

Choi, D. Y, and Gray, E. R. (2008). Socially responsible entrepreneurs: what do they do to create and build their companies? *Business Horizons*, **51**(4), 341–352.

Choongo, P., Van Burg, E., Paas, L. J., & Masurel, E. (2016). Factors influencing the identification of sustainable opportunities by SMEs: Empirical evidence from Zambia. *Sustainability*, **8**(1), 81.

Clayton, P., & Davies, P. (eds.) (2006). *The Re-emergence of Emergence: The Emergentist Hypothesis from Science to Religion*, No. 159 (Oxford, UK: Oxford University Press).

Cohen, B., & Winn, M. I. (2007). Market imperfections, opportunity and sustainable entrepreneurship. *Journal of Business Venturing*, **22**(1), 29–49.

Crnogaj, K., Rebernik, M., Hojnik, B. B., & Omerzel Gomezelj, D. (2014). Building a model of researching the sustainable entrepreneurship in the tourism sector. *Kybernetes*, **43**(3/4), 377–393.

Dacin, M. T., Dacin, P. A., & Tracey, P. (2011). Social entrepreneurship: A critique and future directions. *Organization Science*, **22**(5), 1203–1213.

Dawkins, R. (1986). *The Blind Watchmaker: Why the Evidence of Evolution Reveals a Universe Without Design* (New York, NY: WW Norton & Company).

Dean, T. J., & McMullen, J. S. (2007). Toward a theory of sustainable entrepreneurship: Reducing environmental degradation through entrepreneurial action. *Journal of Business Venturing*, **22**(1), 50–76.

Delmas, M., Lim, J., & Nairn-Birch, N. 2016. Corporate environmental performance and lobbying. *Academy of Management Discoveries*, **2**(2), 175–197.

Downs, A. (1957). An economic theory of political action in a democracy. *Journal of Political Economy*, **65**(2), 135–150.

Durand, R., Hawn, O., & Ioannou, I. (2019). Willing and able: A general model of organizational responses to normative pressures. *Academy of Management Review*, **44**(2), 299–320.

Eccles, R. G., & Serafeim, G. (2013). The performance frontier. *Harvard Business Review*, **91**(5), 50–60.

Eckhardt, J. T., & Shane, S. A. (2003). Opportunities and entrepreneurship. *Journal of Management*, **29**(3), 333–349.

Edenhofer, O., Pichs-Madruga, R. Sokona, Y., Seyboth, K., Matschoss, P., Kadner, S., Zwickel, T. *et al*. (2011). IPCC Special Report on Renewable Energy Sources and Climate Change Mitigation. Technical report. Intergovernmental Panel on Climate Change.

Eesley, C., & Lenox, M. J. (2006). Firm responses to secondary stakeholder action. *Strategic Management Journal*, **27**(8), 765–781.

Elkington, J. (2013). Enter the triple bottom line. In *The Triple Bottom Line* (Oxfordshire, UK: Routledge), pp. 23–38.

Evans, R., & Marvin, S. (2006). Researching the sustainable city: Three modes of interdisciplinarity. *Environment and Planning A*, **38**(6), 1009–1028.

Gast, J., Gundolf, K., & Cesinger, B. (2017). Doing business in a green way: A systematic review of the ecological sustainability entrepreneurship literature and future research directions. *Journal of Cleaner Production*, **147**, 44–56.

Gawel, E., Strunz, S., & Lehmann, P. (2016). Support policies for renewables instrument choice and instrument change from a public choice perspective. Report 006. World Institute for Development Economic Research (UNU-WIDER). Available at: https://www.wider.unu.edu/publication/support-policies-renewables. December 6, 2019.

Geels, F. W., Sovacool, B. K., Schwanen, T., & Sorrell, S. (2017). Sociotechnical transitions for deep decarbonization. *Science*, **357**(6357), 1242–1244.

George, G., Howard-Grenville, J., Joshi, A., & Tihanyi, L. (2016). Understanding and tackling societal grand challenges through management research. *Academy of Management Journal*, **59**(6), 1880–1995.

George, G., Schillebeeckx, S. J., & Liak, T. L. (2015). The management of natural resources: An overview and research agenda. *Academy of Management Journal*, **58**(6), 1595–1613.

Hahn, R., & Ince, I. (2016). Constituents and characteristics of hybrid businesses: a qualitative, empirical framework. *Journal of Small Business Management*, **54**, 33–52.

Hall, J. K., Daneke, G. A., & Lenox, M. J. (2010). Sustainable development and entrepreneurship: Past contributions and future directions. *Journal of Business Venturing*, **25**(5), 439–448.

Harding, S. (2006). *Animate Earth: Science, Intuition, and Gaia* (Cambridge, England: Chelsea Green Publishing).

Hawken, P. (2017). *Drawdown: The Most Comprehensive Plan Ever Proposed to Reverse Global Warming* (London, UK: Penguin).

Hechavarría, D. M., Terjesen, S. A., Ingram, A. E., Renko, M., Justo, R., & Elam, A. (2017). Taking care of business: The impact of culture and gender on entrepreneurs' blended value creation goals. *Small Business Economics*, **48**(1), 225–57.

Helm, D. (2010). Government failure, rent-seeking, and capture: The design of climate change policy. *Oxford Review of Economic Policy*, **26**(2), 182–196.

Hoffman, A. J., & Jennings, P. D. (2015). Institutional theory and the natural environment: Research in (and on) the Anthropocene. *Organization & Environment*, **28**(1), 8–31.

Hooi, H. C., Ahmad, N. H., Amran, A., & Rahman, S. A. (2016). The functional role of entrepreneurial orientation and entrepreneurial bricolage in ensuring sustainable entrepreneurship. *Management Research Review*, **39**(12), 1616–38.

Hörisch, J., Kollat, J., & Brieger, S. A. (2017). What influences environmental entrepreneurship? A multilevel analysis of the determinants of entrepreneurs' environmental orientation. *Small Business Economics*, **48**(1), 47–69.

Hosseininia, G., & Ramezani, A. (2016). Factors influencing sustainable entrepreneurship in small and medium-sized enterprises in Iran: A case study of food industry. *Sustainability*, **8**(10), 1–20.

Howard-Grenville, J., Buckle, S. J., Hoskins, B. J., & George, G. (2014). Climate change and management. *Academy of Management Journal*, **57**(3), 615–623.

Jesse, D. J., & Valerie, J. K. (2017). Carbon pricing under political constraints. In *The Political Economy of Clean Energy Transitions* (Oxford University Press), pp. 39–59.

Jolink, A., & Niesten, E. (2015). Sustainable development and business models of entrepreneurs in the organic food industry. *Business Strategy and the Environment*, **24**(6), 386–401.

Jørgensen, S. E. (2002). *Integration of Ecosystem Theories: A Pattern* (Heidelberg, Germany: Springer Science & Business Media).

Kalkuhl, M., Edenhofer, O., & Lessmann, K. (2012). Learning or lock-in: Optimal technology policies to support mitigation. *Resource and Energy Economics*, **34**(1), 1–23.

Kirzner, I. M. (1990). Self-interest and the new bashing of economics: A fresh opportunity in the perennial debate? SSRN Working paper series. SSRN Scholarly Paper ID 1626931.

Klewitz, J., & Hansen, E. G. (2014). Sustainability-oriented innovation of SMEs: A systematic review. *Journal of Cleaner Production*, **65**, 57–75.

Klewitz, J. (2017). Grazing, exploring and networking for sustainability-oriented innovations in learning-action networks: An SME perspective. *Innovation: The European Journal of Social Science Research*, **30**(4), 476–503.

Koe, W.-L., Omar, R., & Sa'ari, J. R. (2015). Factors influencing propensity to sustainable entrepreneurship of SMEs in Malaysia. *Procedia-Social and Behavioral Sciences*, **172**, 570–577.

Kotchen, M. J., Boyle, K. J., & Leiserowitz, A. A. (2013). Willingness-to-pay and policy-instrument choice for climate-change policy in the United States. *Energy Policy*, **55**, 617–625.

Lam, J. C., Walker, R. M., & Hills, P. (2014). Interdisciplinarity in sustainability studies: A review. *Sustainable Development*, **22**(3), 158–176.

Lans, T., Blok, V., & Wesselink, R. (2014). Learning apart and together: Towards an integrated competence framework for sustainable entrepreneurship in higher education. *Journal of Cleaner Production*, **62**, 37–47.

Larson, A. L. (2000). Sustainable innovation through an entrepreneurship lens. *Business Strategy and the Environment*, **9**(5), 304.

Laufer, W. S. (2003). Social accountability and corporate greenwashing. *Journal of Business Ethics*, **43**(3), 253–261.

Lenox, M., & Chatterji, A. (2018). *Can Business Save the Earth? Innovating our Way to Sustainability* (Palo Alto, CA: Stanford University Press).

Lenox, M., & York, J. G. (2011). Environmental entrepreneurship. In Pratima Bansal and Andrew J. Hoffman (eds.), *The Oxford Handbook of Business and Natural Environment* (Oxford, UK), pp. 70–92.

Lenox, M. J., & Chatterji, A. (2018). *Can Business Save the Earth? Innovating Our Way to Sustainability* (Stanford, CA: Stanford Business Books).

Longo, G., Montévil, M., & Kauffman, S. (2012). No entailing laws, but enablement in the evolution of the biosphere. *Proceedings of the 14th Annual Conference Companion on Genetic and Evolutionary Computation*, July, pp. 1379–1392, ACM.

Margolis, J. D., & Walsh, J. P. (2003). Misery loves companies: Rethinking social initiatives by business. *Administrative Science Quarterly*, **48**(2), 268–305.

Mickwitz, P. (2003). A framework for evaluating environmental policy instruments: Context and key concepts. *Evaluation*, **9**(4), 415–436.

Mioara, B., & Mihai, T. (2014). Incidence of green business on developing the entrepreneurial environment from metropolitan area of IASI. *Procedia Economics and Finance*, **15**, 1201–1208.

Nemet, G. F. & Johnson, E. (2010). Willingness to pay for climate policy: A review of estimates. SSRN Working paper series. SSRN Scholarly Paper ID 1626931.

North Carolina Clean Energy Technology Center, Proudlove, A., Daniel, K., Lips, B., Sarkisian, D., *et al.* (2016). The 50 States of Solar: Q2 2016 Quarterly Report Executive Summary. Raleigh: NC Clean Energy Technology Center.

Odum, H. T., Brown, M. T., & Williams, S. B. (2000). Handbook of Emergy Evaluation: A Compendium of Data for Emergy Computation Issued in a Series of Folios. Folio# 1. Introduction and Global Budget, 32611−6450. US EPA Handbook: https://archive.epa.gov/emap/aed/html/collaboration/web/pdf/folio2.pdf.

Orlitzky, M., & Benjamin, J. D. (2001). Corporate social performance and firm risk: A meta-analytic review. *Business & Society*, **40**(4), 369–396.

Ossenbrink, J., Finnsson, S., Bening, C. R., & Hoffmann, V. H. (2019). Delineating policy mixes: Contrasting top-down and bottom-up approaches to the case of energy-storage policy in California. *Research Policy*, **48**(10), 103582.

Pachauri, R. K., Allen, M. R., Barros, V. R., Broome, J., Cramer, W., Christ, R., ... & Dubash, N. K. (2014). Climate change 2014: synthesis report. Contribution of Working Groups I, II and III to the fifth assessment report of the Intergovernmental Panel on Climate Change, IPCC, p. 151.

Patzelt, H., & Shepherd, D. A. (2011). Recognizing opportunities for sustainable development. *Entrepreneurship Theory and Practice*, **35**(4), 631–652.

Pearce, D. W., Clince, W. R., Achanta, A. N., Fankhauser, S., Pachauri, R. K., *et al.* (1996). The social costs of climate change: Greenhouse damage and the benefits of control. In J. P. Bruce, H.-s. Yi, and E. F. Haites (eds.), *Climate Change 1995: Economic and*

Social Dimensions of Climate Change (Cambridge, England; New York: Published for the Intergovernmental Panel on Climate Change, Cambridge University Press).

Peloza, J. (2009). The challenge of measuring financial impacts from investments in corporate social performance. *Journal of Management*, 35(6), 1518–1541.

Porter, A. L. D. E., & Chubin, D. (1985). An indicator of cross-disciplinary research. *Scientometrics*, 8(3–4), 161–176.

Porter, M., & Kramer, M. (2006). Strategy and society. *Harvard Business Review*, 84(12), 42–56.

Rogge, K. S., & Reichardt, K. (2016). Policy mixes for sustainability transitions: An extended concept and framework for analysis. *Research Policy*, 45(8), 1620–1635.

Russo, M. V. (2003). The emergence of sustainable industries: Building on natural capital. *Strategic Management Journal*, 24(4), 317–331.

Sarma, S., & Sunny, S. A. (2017). Civic entrepreneurial ecosystems: Smart city emergence in Kansas City. *Business Horizons*, 60(6), 843–853.

Schoolman, E. D., Guest, J. S., Bush, K. F., & Bell, A. R. (2012). How interdisciplinary is sustainability research? Analyzing the structure of an emerging scientific field. *Sustainability Science*, 7(1), 67–80.

Schumpeter, J. A. (1942). *Capitalism, Socialism and Democracy* (Oxfordshire, UK: Routledge).

Shepherd, D. A., & Patzelt, H. (2011). The new field of sustainable entrepreneurship: studying entrepreneurial action linking "what is to be sustained" with "what is to be developed." *Entrepreneurship Theory and Practice*, 35(1), 37–63.

Río González, P. (2009). The empirical analysis of the determinants for environmental technological change: A research agenda. *Ecological Economics*, 68(3), 861–878.

Sidak, J. G., & Teece, D. J. (2009). Dynamic competition in antitrust law. *Journal of Competition Law & Economics*, 5(4), 581–631.

Silberstein, M., & McGeever, J. (1999). The search for ontological emergence. *The Philosophical Quarterly*, 49(195), 201–214.

Simon, M., Miree, C., & Dule, M. (2013). La vida local: Planting the seeds for growing an organic food delivery business. *Entrepreneurship Theory and Practice*, 37(3), 641–660.

Sine, W. D., & Lee, B. H. (2009). Tilting at windmills? The environmental movement and the emergence of the US wind energy sector. *Administrative Science Quarterly*, 54(1), 123–155.

Solomon, S. (ed.) (2007). *Climate Change 2007-The Physical Science Basis: Working Group I contribution to the Fourth Assessment Report of the IPCC*, Vol. 4 (Cambridge University Press).

Spash, C. L. (2010). The brave new world of carbon trading. *New Political Economy*, 15(2), 169–195.

Spence, M., Boubaker Gherib, J. B., & Ondoua Biwolé, V. (2011). Sustainable entrepreneurship: Is entrepreneurial will enough? A North–South comparison. *Journal of Business Ethics*, 99(3), 335–367.

Starik, M., & Kanashiro, P. (2013). Toward a theory of sustainability management: Uncovering and integrating the nearly obvious. *Organization & Environment*, **26**(1), 7–30.

Stevens, R., Moray, N., & Bruneel, J. (2015). The social and economic mission of social enterprises: Dimensions, measurement, validation, and relation. *Entrepreneurship Theory and Practice*, **39**(5), 1051–1082.

Stigler, G. J. (1971). The theory of economic regulation. *The Bell Journal of Economics and Management Science*, **2**(1), 3.

Stocker, T. F., Qin, D., Plattner, G. K., Tignor, M., Allen, S. K., Boschung, J., Nauels, A., Xia, Y., Bex, V., & Midgley, P. M. (2013). IPCC, 2013: Climate Change 2013: The Physical Science Basis. Contribution of Working Group I to the Fifth Assessment Report of the Intergovernmental Panel on Climate Change (Cambridge, UK; New York: Cambridge University Press).

Sun, S. L., Chen, V. Z., Sunny, S. A., & Chen, J. (2018). Venture capital as an ecosystem engineer for regional innovation in an emerging market. *International Business Review*, **28**(5), 101485.

Sunny, S. A. (2016). Instantaneous "figures of merit" for conducting autonomous systematic meta-energy-economic analyses-numerically verifiable emission reduction devices. *Current Environmental Engineering*, **3**(1), 38–60.

Sunny, S. A. (2017). Systemic emergence under transitional uncertainty: The dynamic role of energy technology innovation. *Kybernetes*, **46**(9), 1527–1541.

Sunny, S. A., & Shu, C. (2019). Investments, incentives, and innovation: Geographical clustering dynamics as drivers of sustainable entrepreneurship. *Small Business Economics*, **52**(4), 905–927.

Sunny, S. A., Ali, M. I. N., & Chowdhury, R. R. (2018). A stakeholder synergy perspective of ecological value creation. *Academy of Management Proceedings*, Vol. 2018, No. 1, p. 16460. Briarcliff Manor, NY 10510: Academy of Management, July.

Sunny, S. A. (2019). Of floods and gales: Environmental value creation due to creative destruction. Doctoral dissertation, University of Missouri, Kansas City, Kansas, USA.

Sunny, S. A. (2020). "Nature Cannot Be Fooled": A Dual-Equilibrium Simulation of Climate Change. *Organization & Environment*, 1086026620937461.

Surroca, J., Tribó, J. A., & Waddock, S. (2010). Corporate responsibility and financial performance: The role of intangible resources. *Strategic Management Journal*, **31**(5), 463–490.

Wry, T., & Haugh, H. (2018). Brace for impact: Uniting our diverse voices through a social impact frame. *Journal of Business Venturing*, **33**(5), 566–574.

Thompson, N., Kiefer, K., & York, J. G. (2011). Distinctions not dichotomies: Exploring social, sustainable, and environmental entrepreneurship. In *Social and Sustainable Entrepreneurship* (Emerald Group Publishing Limited), pp. 201–229.

Urban, B., & Nikolov, K. (2013). Sustainable corporate entrepreneurship initiatives: A risk and reward analysis. *Technological and Economic Development of Economy*, **19**(sup1), S383–S408.

Venkataraman, S. (1997). The distinctive domain of entrepreneurship research. *Advances in Entrepreneurship, Firm Emergence and Growth*, **3**(1), 119–138.

Weick, K. E., Sutcliffe, K. M., & Obstfeld, D. (2005). Organizing and the process of sensemaking. *Organization Science*, **16**(4), 409–421.

Wiklund, J., Wright, M., & Zahra, S. A. (2018). Conquering relevance: Entrepreneurship research's grand challenge. *Entrepreneurship Theory and Practice*, **43**(1), 1–18.

Winston, A., Favaloro, G., & Healy, T. (2017). Energy strategy for the C-Suite. *Harvard Business Review*, **95**(1), 139–146.

Wood, D. J. (1991). Corporate social performance revisited. *Academy of Management Review*, **16**(4), 691–718.

Wood, D. J. (2010). Measuring corporate social performance: A review. *International Journal of Management Reviews*, **12**(1), 50–84.

Wright, C., and Nyberg, D. (2017). An inconvenient truth: How organizations translate climate change into business as usual. *Academy of Management Journal*, **60**(5), 1633–1661.

York, J. G., & Lenox, M. J. (2014). Exploring the sociocultural determinants of de novo versus de alio entry in emerging industries. *Strategic Management Journal*, **35**(13), 1930–1951.

York, J. G., O'Neil, I., & Sarasvathy, S. D. (2016). Exploring environmental entrepreneurship: Identity coupling, venture goals, and stakeholder incentives. *Journal of Management Studies*, **53**(5), 695–737.

© 2022 World Scientific Publishing Company
https://doi.org/10.1142/9789811248863_0006

Chapter 6

Value Creation through Environmental Entrepreneurship

Geoff Archer[*,§], Felix Arndt[†,¶] and Fiona Robinson[‡,∥]

[*]Royal Roads University, Victoria, BC, Canada

[†]De Montfort University, Leicester, UK

[‡]Winnipeg, Manitoba, Canada

[§]Geoff.Archer@RoyalRoads.ca

[¶]ffarndt@gmail.com

[∥]fiona@gluehq.com

Abstract

This chapter identifies three classes of value-creating opportunities for environmental entrepreneurship. This is achieved with a two-stage analysis. First, answering Venkataraman's (1997) timeless call to refine the domain of entrepreneurship research, a taxonomy of general entrepreneurial opportunity is distilled. Second, we craft a pragmatic tool that enables us to distinguish entrepreneurial opportunity that is always good for the planet from that which is only good conditionally. This framework contributes to the field by providing an organized platform for future scholarship into the overlap between entrepreneurship, opportunity, social objectives, sustainability and the natural environment.

Keywords: Environmental entrepreneurship; value creation; entrepreneurial opportunity; social objectives; sustainability-as-flourishing.

6.1. Divining Strong Opportunity for Environmental Entrepreneurship

Entrepreneurship is a powerful force for solving the most pressing problems that face mankind. The natural environment offers the basis for life, and the health of the natural environment is a precondition for successfully addressing the goals set through the UN Sustainable Development Goals (SDGs). This chapter aims to classify environmental opportunities for sustainable entrepreneurship.

In their definitional work, management scholars and economists have distinguished several greener sub-categories of entrepreneurship, including, among others, social entrepreneurship, sustainable entrepreneurship, and environmental entrepreneurship (Austin *et al.*, 2006; Dean and McMullen, 2007; Cohen and Winn, 2007). Opportunities in these areas have been defined using convergent and divergent elements, motivating our inquiry to more explicitly identify the playing ground for environmental entrepreneurship and related research opportunities.

Neatly modifying the Venkataraman (1997) locution, Cohen and Winn (2007, p. 35) defined sustainable entrepreneurship as "the examination of, 'how opportunities to bring into existence future goods and services are discovered, created and exploited, by whom, and with what economic, psychological, social, and *environmental* consequences.'" Like Austin *et al.* (2006, p. 3), they asserted that, "Market failure will create differing entrepreneurial opportunities for social and commercial entrepreneurship"; specifically, market failure will result in opportunities to improve environmental conditions while generating entrepreneurial rents. Dean and McMullen (2007, p. 58) narrow down environmental entrepreneurship as a subset of sustainable entrepreneurship that focuses on "the resolution of market failures which result in environmental degradation." York *et al.* (2016, p. 725) further clarify that environmental entrepreneurs use both "commercial and ecological logics to address environmental degradation through the creation of financially profitable organizations, products, services, and markets." The possibilities of this domain offer an optimistic alternative to business-as-usual, in which business is often pitted against the environment. Indeed, Schaefer *et al.* (2015) suggest that sustainable entrepreneurship may be a process to achieve *sustainability-as-flourishing*, a transformative ideal where the balance between nature, society, and economic activity is restored through radical intervention.

In delineating these opportunities, both Cohen and Winn (2006) and Dean and McMullen (2007) specify precisely which market failures yield what sort of entrepreneurial opportunity. More important to the field, however, is a look at the overlap between these two lists of environmental entrepreneurship opportunities and the venerable categories previously elucidated by classical entrepreneurial theorists, including Schumpeter (1976), Hayek (1945), Baumol (1990), and Drucker (1985). The big question here is whether these emergent theories of where the environmental entrepreneurship opportunity is found or created were unique with regard to each other and in relation to the bigger picture classics.

Certainly, we expect environmental entrepreneurship opportunities to be associated with a different range of outcomes.

To answer this question, and shake the golden nuggets out from these turbid waters, we will first develop a typology of entrepreneurial opportunity. In Section 6.2, we will do just that through a theoretical evaluation of 25 potentially unique conceptions of environmentally relevant opportunity proposed in 7 different works over the course of more than 9 decades. We start where it, i.e. our field, all began. The choice set from which we begin our analysis is that venerable group of authors who anchor everyone's entrepreneurship doctoral program. From there, our literature review expands to include the major environmentally relevant papers contributed in top journals in the past two decades. We select these papers based on our judgement on their impact to advance thinking on entrepreneurial opportunities in general and environmental opportunities more specifically. We assess these papers on their convergent and divergent elements. Predictably, a great number of them show convergent elements, leaving us with a manageable synthesis of a MECE[1] typology of entrepreneurial opportunity.

While this typology alone would be of great value to the field, our quest beckons further inquiry. It is clear at this point that many of the surviving types of entrepreneurial opportunity can sometimes be good for the natural environment and bad for it otherwise. Therefore, we craft a pragmatic tool in the form a simple question that enables us to divine those few activities from this typology that represent strong opportunity for environmental entrepreneurship. In other words, we believe that we have distinguished a few types of environmental opportunity that are not only conditionally good for the natural environment but that *action undertaken to exploit a particular type of entrepreneurial opportunity would be easily imagined to be good for the natural environment in general, regardless of one's intentions, slogans, or political affiliations*. We believe that this framework will contribute to the field by: (1) bringing older theory (e.g. classic Schumpeter, Hayek, Drucker, and the notorious Baumol) into the current dialogue about environmental entrepreneurship; (2) identifying redundancy between extant theories of entrepreneurial opportunity; and (3) providing an organized platform for future scholarship into environmental entrepreneurship as well as the broader field of sustainable entrepreneurship.

6.2. Review of Typologies of Entrepreneurial Opportunities

6.2.1. *Schumpeter*

Schumpeter's work has shaped the discussion of entrepreneurship like no other. While he is ostensibly better known for the widely accepted dogma of

---

[1] MECE = Mutually Exclusive, Categorically Exhaustive.

"creative destruction," entrepreneurship scholars have drawn other durable and parsimonious insights from his several long socio-political manifestos, including *Capitalism, Socialism and Democracy*, which was first published in 1942. With the following short quotation from a re-published edition of his seminal text, he boldly grounds our list of entrepreneurial opportunity:

> The function of entrepreneurs is to reform or revolutionize the pattern of production by exploiting an invention or, more generally an (1) untried technological possibility for producing a new commodity or (2) producing an old one in a new way, by (3) opening up a new supply of materials or (4) a new outlet for products, by (5) reorganizing an industry and so on (Schumpeter, 1976, p. 132).

Regardless of whether or not any subsequent scholar's entrepreneurial philosophy was resource-based or Austrian, made or found, toward equilibrium or away, the above quote started the conversation, and still ring true. As Table 6.1 depicts, these five categories have recurred in slightly different prose in other Schumpeter works. Later scholars have proposed additions to these categories but none succeeded in reducing the quorum around this seminal section of text (Baumol, 1990). Biased toward getting the "cash value[2]" out of research, we assert that Joseph Schumpeter began this typology of entrepreneurial opportunity nearly a century ago.

6.2.2. *Hayek*

In 1945, another Austrian economist, Friedrich Hayek (1945, p. 522), proffered the sixth unique type of entrepreneurial opportunity when he said that, "to know of and put to use a machine not fully employed, or somebody's skill, which could be better utilized, or to be aware of a surplus stock which can be drawn upon during an interruption of supplies, is socially quite as useful as the knowledge of better alternative techniques." Continuing Hayek's original quote, an alert reader could even pick up more than a hint environmentally relevant content in his very first example:

> And the shipper who earns his living from using otherwise empty or half-filled journeys of tramp-steamers, or the estate agent, whose whole knowledge is almost exclusively one of temporary opportunities, or the arbitrageur, who gains from local differences of commodity prices, are all performing imminently useful functions based on special knowledge of circumstances of the fleeting moment not known to others.

---

[2] "You must bring out of each word its practical cash value, set it at work within the stream of your experience" (James, 1997, p. 98).

Table 6.1. Entrepreneurship concept environmental entrepreneurship example.

1.	**UNTRIED TECHNOLOGICAL POSSIBILITY FOR PRODUCING A NEW COMMODITY** "the introduction of a new good — that is one with which consumers are not yet familiar — or of a new quality of a good (Schumpeter,[a] 1934)."	The Green Microgym power-generating exercise equipment http://www.thegreenmicrogym.com/ Tesla "Supercharger" stations for electric cars https://www.tesla.com/supercharger Harbour Air all-electric airline https://www.harbourair.com/harbour-air-and-magnix-partner-to-build-worlds-first-all-electric-airline/
2.	**PRODUCING AN OLD (COMMODITY) IN A NEW WAY** "The introduction of a new method of production, that is one not yet tested by experience in the branch of manufacture concerned, which need by no means be founded upon a discovery scientifically new, and can also exist in a new way of handling a commodity commercially (Schumpeter, 1934)."	Square Watermelons http://www.snopes.com/photos/odd/watermelon.asp Bakeys edible cutlery http://www.bakeys.com Biofuel from natural beer waste http://www.dbexportbeer.co.nz/db-export-brewtroleum
3.	**OPENING UP A NEW SUPPLY OF MATERIALS** "The conquest of a new source of supply of raw materials or half-manufactured goods, again irrespective of whether this source already exists or whether it first has to be created (Schumpeter, 1934)."	Bamboo as an ethical clothing supply http://www.onyamagazine.com/australian-affairs/environment/a-material-world-how-bamboo-went-from-eco-alternative-to-global-trend/ Algae as a biofuel https://cla.auburn.edu/ces/energy/algae-as-energy-a-look-to-the-future/ Urine as plant fertilizer https://www.sciencenewsforstudents.org/article/recycling-urine-may-be-way-boost-plant-growth
4.	**OPENING UP A NEW OUTLET FOR PRODUCTS** "The opening of a new market, that is a market into which the particular branch of manufacture of the country in question has not previously entered, whether or not this market has existed before (Schumpeter, 1934)."	Facebook drones for global Internet access https://www.theguardian.com/technology/2017/jul/02/facebook-drone-aquila-internet-test-flight-arizona Rugged, affordable, connected laptops for children in developing countries by One Lap Top Per Child http://one.laptop.org/about/mission Omlet urban chicken coops https://www.omlet.co.uk/shop/chicken_keeping/
5.	**REORGANIZING AN INDUSTRY** "The carrying out of the new organization of any industry, like the creation of a monopoly position (for example through trustification) or the breaking up of a monopoly position.[b] (Schumpeter, 1934)."	Rideshare transportation with Uber https://www.uber.com The rise of coworking as an alternative to traditional commercial leasing http://www.deskmag.com/en/coworking-spaces Solar energy savings through Sungevity http://www.sungevity.com/#start

(Continued)

Table 6.1. (Continued)

6.	**INFORMATION** "To know of and put to use a machine not fully employed, or somebody's skill, which could be better utilized, were to be aware of a surplus stock which can be drawn upon during an interruption of supplies, is socially quite as useful as the knowledge of better alternative techniques. And the shipper who earns his living from using otherwise empty or half-filled journeys of tramp-steamers, or the estate agent, whose whole knowledge is almost exclusively one of temporary opportunities, or the arbitrageur, who gains from local differences of commodity prices, are all performing imminently useful functions based on special knowledge of circumstances of the fleeting moment not known to others (Hayek, 1945)."	Donating unused truck space to charity through Trucks For Change http://trucksforchange.org ThredUp upcycling and consigning high-end used clothes https://www.thredup.com Increasing high occupancy ride-sharing with smart-phone app, Carma https://www.gocarma.com/what-we-do
7.	**WASTE EQUALS FOOD** "the process by which entrepreneurs in resource-poor environments were able to render unique services by recombining elements at hand for new purposes that challenged institutional definitions and limits (Baker & Nelson, 2005)." "...opportunities relating to efficiency imperfections...will commonly be 'recognized' by combining known supply and demand elements of a market in more efficient ways (Cohen & Winn, 2007)."	Workspaces in empty buildings https://www.fastcompany.com/3041551/unconventional-ideas-for-using-empty-office-buildings Using plastic bottles to make homes https://insteading.com/blog/plastic-bottle-homes/ Last resource for otherwise non-recyclable household waste https://www.terracycle.com/en-CA/
8.	**EXTERNALITIES** "Innovative firms able to recognize and create opportunities to reverse existing negative environmental externalities can generate triple bottom line results… (Cohen & Winn, 2007)." "Environmental entrepreneurs can capture economic value and reduce environmental degradation by reducing the transaction costs associated with environmentally relevant externalities (Dean & McMullen, 2007)."	Colibri silicon straws to replace single-use plastic straws http://nivervillecitizen.com/news/local/st-adolphe-sisters-sip-up-sales-with-silicone-straws Carbon Credit Solutions for legitimate carbon trading https://www.carboncreditsolutions.ca Government fees to dispose of tires https://archive.epa.gov/epawaste/conserve/materials/tires/web/html/laws.html
9.	**PUBLIC GOODS** "Coasian entrepreneurs translate public goods into excludable private ones through both political and technological mechanisms (Dean & McMullen, 2007)."	Ecotourism with Sea Lion Caves http://www.sealioncaves.com/ Harvesting salt for sale https://www.visaltco.com Privatization of national parks https://www.nps.gov/articles/park-concessions-historic-privatization.htm

[a] All Schumpeter quotes are as they appeared in Baumol, but rearranged to match the more commonly quoted sequence found in, "Capitalism, Socialism and Democracy."
[b] Emphasis not in the original.

As delineated in Table 6.1, more than a half a century later, we observe a new wave of start-ups focused on eliminating wasteful dead-heading of trucks and container ships, and even offering optimized, loyalty-group–affiliated, smartphone-enabled hitchhiking optimization. Hayekian information entrepreneurship, like Schumpeter's original five types, is clearly not good for the natural environment in all circumstances, but as these examples show, it can be.

6.2.3. *Drucker*

Peter Drucker's renowned work in the 1980s does not seem to have anything to add to our typology, despite the blatant intentions of his chapter entitled, "Purposeful Innovation and the Seven Sources for Innovative Opportunity." Drucker (1985, pp. 27, 31) asserts that, "Entrepreneurs innovate. Innovation is the specific instrument of entrepreneurship" and that, "entrepreneurs will have to learn to practice systematic innovation."

> Specifically, systematic innovation means monitoring seven sources for innovative opportunity. The first four sources lie within the enterprise, whether business or public service institution, or within an industry or service sector. They are therefore visible primarily to people within that industry or service sector. They are basically symptoms. But they are highly reliable indicators of changes that have already happened or can be made to happen with little effort. These four source areas are:
>
> - *the unexpected* — the unexpected success, the unexpected failure, the unexpected outside event;
> - *the incongruity* — between reality as it actually is in reality as it is assumed to be or as it "ought to be";
> - *innovation based on process need*;
> - *changes in industry structure or market structure* that catch everyone unawares.
>
> The second set of sources for innovative opportunity, a set of three, involves changes outside the enterprise or industry:
>
> - *demographics* (population changes);
> - *changes in perception, mood, and meaning*;
> - *new knowledge*, both scientific and nonscientific.
>
> ... the order in which these sources will be discussed is not arbitrary. They are listed in descending order of reliability and predictability (Drucker, 1985, pp. 31–32).

It is not that his list does not appear to be useful; it is simply redundant. Although nicely packaged for a practitioner audience, Drucker's seven sources — (1) unexpected occurrences, (2) incongruities, (3) process needs, (4) industry and market changes, (5) demographic changes, (6) changes in perception, and (7) new knowledge — collapse all too easily into Schumpeter's and Hayek's prior theoretical art. Drucker's first, second, and seventh innovation sources describe quintessential INFORMATION opportunities. His third is trumped by Schumpeter's NEW METHODS OF PRODUCTION. In addition, by virtue of the fact that he is writing specifically about change, and thereby new information, the fourth, fifth, and sixth on this list are covered in part by Hayek, de facto. They are also conceptually redundant with several of Schumpeter's five original categories.

It is probably just as well that Drucker fails to earn a spot on our list. His few words on the natural environment were harsh (and hopefully satirical.)

> Innovation, indeed, creates a resource. There is no such thing as a "resource" until man finds a use for something in nature and thus endows it with economic value. Until then, every plant is a weed and every mineral just another rock. Not much more than a century ago, neither mineral oil seeping out of the ground or bauxite, the ore of aluminum, were resources. They were nuisances; both ran to the soil in for tile. The penicillin mold was a pest, not a resource (Drucker, 1985, p. 27).

Although this extreme anthropocentrism has actually been used as the basis for at least one environmental ethic (Baxter, 1995), the irony of that thought experiment is not enticing to revisit.

6.2.4. *Baumol*

> This paper proposes a rather different set of hypotheses, holding that entrepreneurs are always with us and always play some substantial role. But there are a variety of roles among which the entrepreneur's efforts can be reallocated, and some of those rules do not follow the constructive and innovative script is conventionally attributed to that person. Indeed, at times the entrepreneur may even lead a parasitical existence that is actually damaging to the economy. How the entrepreneur acts at a given time and place depends heavily on the rules of the game-the reward structure in the economy-that happened to prevail. Thus the central hypothesis here is that it is the set of rules and not the supply of entrepreneurs or the nature of their objectives that undergoes significant changes from one period to another and helps dictate the ultimate effect on the economy via the allocation of entrepreneurial resources (Baumol, 1990, p. 894).

Readers familiar with this interesting work might find it counter-intuitive inspiration for this chapter on environmentally beneficial entrepreneurship. Yet, it was indeed Baumol's 1990 article, "Entrepreneurship: Productive, Unproductive, and Destructive," that kicked off this list-making effort. Perhaps easily lost in the provocative nature of his prose, the mechanics of Baumol's actual argument relied strongly on an expansion of Schumpeter's five original categories. Specifically, he proposes:

(1) **Technology Transfer:** "[T]echnology transfer that takes advantage of opportunities to introduce already-available technology (usually with some modification to adapt it to local conditions) to geographic locales whose suitability for the purpose had previously gone unrecognized or at least unused."
(2) **Rent-Seeking Innovation:** "[I]nnovations in rent-seeking procedures, for example, discovery of a previously unused legal gambit that is effective in diverting rents to those who are first in exploiting it" (Baumol, 1990, p. 897).

Baumol's first suggestion is essentially impossible to justify as a new theoretical claim. It appears to be a modern paraphrasing of Schumpeter, yielding clear precedence to him. Baumol's second suggestion suffers a similar fate, albeit at the hand of Hayek. While it might not have been widely discussed until the 1990s, Hayekian INFORMATION entrepreneurship staked this ground in the 1940s. Given Baumol's controversial nature, it is just as well that Baumol did not make our list. Importantly, the potentially negative ramifications (and intentions) of entrepreneurship that Baumol brings to light certainly underscore the conditional nature of the environmental benefits of Schumpeter and Hayek:

> If entrepreneurs are defined, simply, to be persons who are ingenious and creative in finding ways that add to their own wealth, power and prestige then it is to be expected that not all of them will be overly concerned with whether an activity that achieves these goals adds much social product or, for that matter, even whether it is an actual impediment to production.... (Baumol, 1990, p. 898).

6.2.5. *Baker and Nelson*

In their 2005 ASQ article, "Creating Something from Nothing: Resource Constraints and Entrepreneurial Bricolage," Ted Baker and Reed Nelson describe how, "A field study of 29 resource-constrained firms that varied dramatically in their responses to similar objective environments is used to examine the process by which entrepreneurs in resource-poor environments were able to render unique services by recombining elements at hand for new purposes that challenged institutional definitions and limits." In so doing, they co-opt a disused term from the famous French anthropologist Claude Levi-Strauss: *bricolage*. They go on to explain that *bricolage*, "a common correlate of improvisation," involves three elements:

(1) Making do which they define as, "a bias for testing received limitations";
(2) Combination of resources for new purposes, meaning a "combination and reuse of resources for different applications than those for which they were originally intended or used" (Baker and Nelson, 1995, p. 335); and
(3) The resources at hand — "In defining resources at hand, we included resources that are available very cheaply or for free, often because others judge them to be useless or substandard" (Baker and Nelson, 2005, p. 336).

With a nod to Edith Penrose's[3] precedent in the larger management context, we submit to you that *bricolage* is in fact the seventh unique category of entrepreneurial opportunity to make our list:

> Because bricolage often draws on degraded, fallow, and otherwise undeveloped resources to construct new combinations, it represents a form of value creation that does not depend on the Schumpeterian assumption that assets are withdrawn from one activity for application in another (Baker and Nelson, 2005).

With regard to the natural environment, bricolage is a pioneer in our typology in that it would seem that most acts of bricolage do benefit the natural world. From simple materials reused in a bike shop to methane-powered farming and brownfield reclamation, nearly all of the firms in Baker and Nelson's (2005) sample demonstrated a net environmental benefit, even though an environmental motive was described for none of them. For example:

> Both Biggs Dig (#4) and Tim Grayson (#7) drew on toxic waste products as part of a process of bricolage that created new value. In other cases, bricolage called forth hidden and seemingly unrelated resources that would otherwise not have been put to any productive application (Baker and Nelson, 2005).

---

[3]"Since attempts to achieve a balance in the utilization of resources can never reach the continually receding goal, some resources will only be partly used and some will be used less efficiently than they would have been in the absence of the restriction on the firm's expansion. Idle services range from those available from resources which could be **byproducts** or which are in fact treated as waste product and thrown away or dumped because the firm cannot organize the profitable exploitation of them and is unable to sell them to idle man or machine hours at various points in the production process and in the managerial staff. **Byproducts** and certain other types of potential joint products have in fact provided an important basis for expansion some firms, once the energies of management could be released to the task of expanding the firm's primary lines" (Penrose, 1995, p. 70).

In *Rubbish! The Archaeology of Garbage*, authors William Rathje and Cullen Murphy (2001) state that such resourcefulness is hardly a recent phenomenon. It appears to be driven in some part by that element of human nature best captured by the old adage, "one man's trash is another man's treasure."[4] In fact, it is not hard to imagine such a driver catalyzing a Kirznerian[5] entrepreneurial alertness:

> Long before the recent spate of recycling laws; long before the creation, in October of 1970, the Environmental Protection Agency; and long before the celebration, on April 22 of that same year, of the first Earth Day, that chronometric marker for the environmental movement as a whole — before all of this, there existed a breed of entrepreneur whose chief aim in business was to collect material objects that had been thrown away and sell them to people who had a use for them. These entrepreneurs, ... are the scrap metal and secondary materials dealers... (Rathje and Murphy, 2001, p. 201).

6.2.6. *Sarasvathy*

Whereas Baker and Nelson (2005) considered the material world of bricolage as a source of entrepreneurial opportunity, Sarasvathy (2001) detailed the inner world of effectual logic that applied resourcefulness toward creating entrepreneurial opportunity. The Bird In Hand principle (Sarasvathy, 2011) invites a deconstructive reflection of *who I am*, *what I know* and *who I know* to reimagine combinations of previously and potentially unusual aspects of identity into potential entrepreneurial beginnings. Additionally, the Patchwork Quilt principle stimulates reconsideration of self-selected stakeholders in one's network where the relationship value was previously unrealized while the Lemonade principle repositions contingencies as opportunities and "potential clues to create new markets" (Sarasvathy, 2011, p. 2).

---

[4] "Two garbage Project researchers, Paul Freidel and Bruce Douglas, were detailed to Tucson's Los Reales landfill for a week and told to keep a record of all the major appliances and big pieces of furniture that were hauled to the site. As it turned out, few of the targeted items ever appeared. And, tellingly, every one of the few appliances and sticks of furniture that did arrive with cart off within hours by some other visitor to the landfill: one man's trash, apparently, is another man's treasure" (Rathje and Murphy 2001, p. 189).

[5] "Entrepreneurial alertness refers to an attitude of receptiveness to available but hitherto overlooked opportunities. The entrepreneurial character of human action refers not simply to the circumstance that action is taken in an open ended, uncertain world, but also to the circumstance that the human agent is at all times spontaneously on the lookout for hitherto unnoticed features of the environment present or future... and entrepreneurial attitude is one which is always ready to be surprised, always ready to take the steps needed to profit by such surprises" (Kirzner, 1997, p. 70).

Effectuation focuses on controlling aspects of an unpredictable future (Sarasvathy, 2011). Sarasvathy leans toward the notion that entrepreneurial opportunities are created, not discovered, and that entrepreneurial thinking makes the difference. As the physical aspect of these opportunities are tied to notions of making do, combining resources and using resources at hand, they fit neatly under the banner of bricolage for the sake of our taxonomy.

6.2.7. *Cohen and Winn*

Responding to Venkataraman's (1997) call for further research into the sources of entrepreneurial opportunity, Cohen and Winn postulate that market failure creates opportunity. In their 2007 paper, "Market Imperfections, Opportunity and Sustainable Entrepreneurship," they describe opportunities that arise from four specific market failures: "(1) firms are not perfectly efficient; (2) externalities exist, (3) pricing mechanisms work imperfectly, and (4) information is not perfectly distributed" (Cohen and Winn, 2007). Resolving any of these market failures through entrepreneurial work would, they claim, manifest sustainable entrepreneurship.[6]

The first opportunity described here, INEFFICIENT FIRMS, is a fascinating one that imagines one firm's or society's waste as the input for another agent's value-creating process. This section of their paper is inspired by Benyus' (1997) biomimicry, with specific reference to "waste equals food," a concept that is very well explained in a far more deliberate setting by McDonough and Braungart (2003). Attractive as Cohen and Winn's ad hoc industrial ecology paradigm is, it will not make our list as a standalone category, because Baker and Nelson had precedent (Graedel and Allenby, 1995). Thus, it is seen in Table 6.1 these two strongly related concepts in the same cell entitled, WASTE EQUALS FOOD.

Cohen and Winn's second category is EXTERNALITIES. Because we believe that Dean and McMullen's (2007) contemporary paper does a more robust job of incorporating the environmental economist's likely prescription, we will defer elaboration on this new category until Section 6.2.8. Finally, Cohen and Winn's third and fourth suggested categories, IMPERFECT PRICING and IMPERFECT INFORMATION, fall directly into the arms of Hayek, and therefore do not appear on our consolidated list.

6.2.8. *Dean and McMullen*

Like the coincident paper of Cohen and Winn, Dean and McMullen's, "Toward a Theory of Sustainable Entrepreneurship: Reducing Environmental Degradation

---

[6]"...we define *sustainable entrepreneurship* as the examination of, 'how opportunities to bring into existence future goods and services are discovered, created and exploited, by whom, and with what economic, psychological, social, and *environmental* consequences (Cohen & Winn 2007)."

- Public Goods   => Assign Rights
- Externalities   => Trade
- Monopoly Power   => Innovate
- Subsidies, etc. => Lobby
- Imperfect information => Find & Inform

Figure 6.1. Dean and McMullen's prescriptions for action.

Through Entrepreneurial Action," describes entrepreneurial opportunity rising from the ruins of market failure. Dean and McMullen call out five specific market failures, two of which are shared with Cohen and Winn: EXTERNALITIES and IMPERFECT INFORMATION. Informed by an expertise in the field of environmental economics,[7] they go so far as to prescribe certain entrepreneurial actions related to each of these market failures that they believe promise both profit and increased sustainability. Notably, for these authors, sustainable entrepreneurship encompasses not only a focus on the reduction of environmental degradation but "also addresses issues such as inequality, poverty, and disease" (Dean and McMullen, 2007), the social leg of the sustainability three-legged stool. Their list of five market failures and associated opportunities for entrepreneurial action are depicted in Figure 6.1.

A direct quote from this text does a complete job of explaining the authors' approach to the PUBLIC GOODS opportunity. See Table 6.1 for examples of such activity:

In recognition of Nobel Prize winning economist Ronald Coase's (1974) study of "The Lighthouse in Economics," we refer to entrepreneurs who develop property rights regimes for previously non-excludable public goods as Coasian entrepreneurs. Coasian entrepreneurs translate public goods into excludable private ones through both political and technological mechanisms (Dean and McMullen, 2007).

Later calling their protagonists "institutional entrepreneurs," because of the institutional change they effect, Dean and McMullen (2007) also propose that, "Environmental entrepreneurs can capture economic value and reduce environmental degradation by reducing the transaction costs associated with environmentally relevant externalities." In Table 6.1, it can be seen that this activity is bundled

---

[7]"Environmental economics concludes that environmental degradation results from the failure of markets, whereas the entrepreneurship literature argues that opportunities are inherent in market failure. A synthesis of these literatures suggests that environmentally relevant market failures represent opportunities for achieving profitability while simultaneously reducing environmentally degrading economic behaviors" (Dean and McMullen, 2007).

with the similar, though less thoroughly explained, work of Cohen and Winn under the heading EXTERNALITIES. Looking now at the bottom of Dean and McMullen's list, we can see that this article offers no further unique additions to our typology: Schumpeter already covered monopoly busting with REORGANIZING AN INDUSTRY, and the last two of Dean and McMullen's suggested categories drop neatly into Hayek's almost omnipresent INFORMATION.

6.3. Discussion

Table 6.1 displays the nine different categories of entrepreneurial opportunity that survive a theoretical test of logical redundancy. Contemporary examples help to describe the real-world forms that each of these intellectual ideas might take. Naturally, in a discussion about environmental entrepreneurship, we have included only examples of such. That is not to imply that any entrepreneurial action undertaken in an effort to seize a particular opportunity or type of opportunity is going to benefit the natural environment. Taking a look around at the interaction of businesses with the natural world over the past few centuries, it is quickly obvious that much of the value-creating activity has done the opposite, having highly deleterious effects on the environment. It is then apparent that our list of entrepreneurial opportunities in Table 6.1 may be MECE, but is not yet a list of actions that are always good for the planet.

Mindful of the pragmatist's central question — "What difference would it practically make to anyone if this notion rather than that notion were true?" — we will suggest here that we can divine the Strong Opportunities (SOs) for environmental entrepreneurship from Weak Opportunities (WOs) by simply *asking if action undertaken to exploit a particular type of opportunity would be easily imagined to be good for the natural environment in general, regardless of one's intentions, slogans or political affiliations* (James, 1997; Schuessler, 2000; Krueger, 2005). Applying such an instrument to the surviving MECE categories in Table 6.1, we find that many of them are conditional; that is to say that they are easily imagined to be good for the natural environment only sometimes (as we see in the examples). Hence we would label these first six types of opportunity as weak; that includes all of Schumpeter and Hayek.

Categories seven through nine, however, do survive this test. WASTE EQUALS FOOD entrepreneurial opportunities do appear, by way of the examples and data described in the cited academic literature, to be easily imagined to be good for the natural environment in general (Baker and Nelson, 2005; Cohen and Winn, 2007). By virtue of the fact that they are borne of market failure (aka environmental problems) in the first place it is only logical that entrepreneurial opportunities that address EXTERNALITIES or PUBLIC GOODS are also strong (SOs.)

Thus we claim that pursuit of any of these three SOs represents environmental entrepreneurship in its purest form.

6.4. Conclusion

Thus we conclude our two-step process of divining SOs for environmental entrepreneurship. Our efforts to build upon the recent work of Cohen and Winn (2007), Dean and McMullen (2007), and others who sought to respond to Venkataraman's (1997) call for further research into the source of opportunity in general, and environmental entrepreneurship opportunity in particular, culminated in both a typology and a tool. The first step in this process was the assembly and consolidation of several scholars' ideas about where entrepreneurial opportunity comes from in general. Notably, this MECE typology finally populates the taxonomy Venkataraman proposed more than two decades ago:

> Research on the taxonomy and sources of opportunities, their characteristics, and the relative incidence of different opportunities in different contexts and countries, and the relative profitability of different sources of opportunities are all virgin territories for the field of entrepreneurship (Venkataraman, 1997, p. 123).

Once we had a list of nine non-overlapping types of entrepreneurial opportunities, we crafted a figurative divining stick to identify which of these activities might contribute to a more sustainable world from an environmental perspective. The pragmatic implement proposed here is to ask *if action undertaken to exploit a particular type of opportunity would be easily imagined to be good for the natural environment in general, regardless of one's intentions, slogans or political affiliations*. With the help of this instrument, three specific types of entrepreneurial opportunity were designated as strong opportunity for environmental entrepreneurship; WASTE EQUALS FOOD, EXTERNALITIES, and PUBLIC GOODS. It is our position that entrepreneurs engaged in the pursuit of such opportunities can be expected to make the world a better place in the process.

Any such bold assertion begs of more rigorous testing and analysis, i.e. logical follow-on work which is also called for in the Venkataraman quotation further up this page. We fully encourage his suggested investigation into the relative incidence of different opportunities in (1) different contexts and (2) countries and their relative profitability (3) in a triple-bottom-line sense, of course. While that charge applies to our typology in its entirety, it is obvious that our three highlighted opportunity types require an even deeper probing. We are hopeful that the readers will join us developing studies and experiments toward determining if Baker and Nelson's (2005) bricolage really is so tightly related to Cohen and Winn's (2007) WASTE EQUALS FOOD; if it is reasonable to think that bricolage is almost always good for the natural environment; or if opportunities that result from EXTERNALITIES and PUBLIC GOODS problems really do stand up to Schumpeter and Hayek as peers (Cohen and Winn, 2007; Dean and McMullen, 2007). Following this brief theoretical analysis, we believe they do, and in the spirit of academic creative destruction executed so smoothly by Cohen and Winn, we would like to close this paper with a similar permutation:

FROM: "Entrepreneurship is particularly powerful from a social welfare perspective when, in the process of pursuing selfish ends, entrepreneurs also enhance social wealth by creating new markets, new industries, new technology, new institutional forms, new jobs and net increases in real productivity" (Venkataraman, 1997).

TO: Entrepreneurship is particularly powerful from a sustainable development perspective when, in the process of pursuing selfish ends, entrepreneurs also enhance the natural environment by creating new markets, new industries, new technology, new institutional forms, new jobs and net increases in real productivity.

References

Austin, J., Stevenson, H., & Wei-Skillern, J. 2006. Social and commercial entrepreneurship: Same, different, or both? *Entrepreneurship Theory and Practice*, **30**(1), 1–22.

Baker, T., & Nelson, R. E. (2005). Creating something from nothing: Resource construction through entrepreneurial bricolage. *Administrative Science Quarterly*, **50**(3), 329–366.

Baumol, W. (1990). Entrepreneurship: Productive, unproductive, and destructive. *Journal of Political Economy*, **98**(5), 893–921.

Baxter, W. (1995). People or penguins. In C. Pierce, and D. VanDeVeer (eds.), *People, Penguins and Plastic Trees* (Belmont, CA: Wadsworth Publishing Company), pp. 381–384.

Benyus, J. (1997). *Biomimicry: Innovation Inspired By Nature* (New York: HarperCollins).

Cohen, B., & Winn, M. I. (2007). Market imperfections, opportunity and sustainable entrepreneurship. *Journal of Business Venturing*, **22**(1), 29–49.

Dean, T. J., & McMullen, J. S. (2007). Toward a theory of sustainable entrepreneurship: Reducing environmental degradation through entrepreneurial action. *Journal of Business Venturing*, **22**(1), 50–76.

Drucker, P. (1985). Purposeful innovation and the seven sources for innovative opportunity. In *Innovation and Entrepreneurship: Practice and Principles* (Harper & Row, NY: Elsevier Ltd). pp. 30–38.

Graedel, T. E., & Allenby, B. R. (1995). *Industrial Ecology* (Englewood Cliffs, NJ: Prentice Hall).

Hayek, F. A. (1945). The use of knowledge in society. *American Economic Review*, **35**(4), 519–530.

James, W. (1997). What pragmatism means. In L. Menand (ed.) *Pragmatism: A Reader*. (Toronto: Random House).

Kirzner, I. (1997). Entrepreneurial discovery and the competitive market process: An Austrian approach. *Journal of Economic Literature*, **35**, 60–85.

Krueger, N. (2005). Sustainable entrepreneurship: Broadening the definition of "Opportunity." *USASBE 2005* Best Paper, Indian Wells, CA, USA.

McDonough, W., & Braungart, M. (2003). *Cradle to Cradle: Remaking the Way We Make Things* (New York: North Point Press Imprint).

Penrose, E. T. (1995). *The Theory of the Growth of the Firm* (New York: Wiley).

Rathje, W. and Cullen, M. (2001). *Rubbish! The Archaeology of Garbage* (Tucson, AZ: The University of Arizona Press).

Sarasvathy, S. D. (2001). Causation and effectuation: Toward a theoretical shift from economic inevitability to entrepreneurial contingency. *Academy of Management Review*, **26**(2), 243–263.

Sarasvathy, S. D. (2011). What is effectuation? Available at: http://www.effectuation.org/sites/default/files/documents/effectuation-3-pager.pdf. March 30, 2019.

Schaefer, K., Doyle Corner, P., & Kearins, K. (2015). Social, environmental and sustainable entrepreneurship research. *Organization & Environment*, **28**(4), 394–413. http://doi.org/10.1177/1086026615621111.

Schuessler, A. A. (2000). *A Logic of Expressive Choice* (Princeton: Princeton University Press).

Schumpeter, J. A. (1976). *Capitalism, Socialism and Democracy* (New York: Harper and Row).

Venkataraman, S. (1997). The distinctive domain of entrepreneurship research: An editor's perspective. In J. Katz, and R. Brockhaus (eds.), *Advances in Entrepreneurship, Firm Emergence, and Growth* (Greenwich, CT: JAI Press). https://www.researchgate.net/profile/Sankaran-Venkataraman/publication/228316384_The_Distinctive_Domain_of_Entrepreneurship_Research/links/0c96052e7ccb98aa7e000000/The-Distinctive-Domain-of-Entrepreneurship-Research.pdf.

York, J. G., O'Neil, I., & Sarasvathy, S. D. (2016). Exploring environmental entrepreneurship: Identity coupling, venture goals, and stakeholder incentives. *Journal of Management Studies*, **53**(5), 695–737. http://doi.org/10.1111/joms.12198.

© 2022 World Scientific Publishing Company
https://doi.org/10.1142/9789811248863_0007

Chapter 7

Key Success Factors in Environmental Entrepreneurship: The Case of Wilderness Safaris

James E. Austin[*,¶], Megan Epler Wood[†,||] and Herman B. Leonard[‡,§,**]

[*]Harvard Business School, Boston, MA, USA

[†]International Sustainable Tourism Initiative Harvard
T.H. Chan School of Public Health, Cambridge, Massachusetts, USA

[‡]Eliot I. Snider and Family Professor of Business Administration,
Harvard Business School, Boston, MA, USA

[§]George F. Baker Jr. Professor of Public Management,
Harvard Kennedy School, Cambridge, MA, USA

[¶]jaustin@hbs.edu

[||]meganeplerwood@fas.harvard.edu

[**]dutch_leonard@harvard.edu

Abstract

This chapter analyzes the entrepreneurial conception and evolution of the Wilderness Safaris (WS) ecotourism enterprise operating in eight African countries. It illuminates a series of factors that contribute to positive environmental impact as well as financial profitability and sustainability. WS has grown to be one of the largest and most successful ecotourism enterprises internationally.

Keywords: Environmental entrepreneurship; sustainability; ecotourism; business model; climate change.

7.1. Origin and Entrepreneurial Innovation

The Wilderness Safaris (WS) company was founded in Botswana in 1983 by a South African and a New Zealander who had been safari guiding in the country for several years. They wanted to create a different approach to safari tourism that would be more beneficial to the country, its people, and its lands and wildlife. They were passionate about conservation of the animals and their habitat. Importantly, these personal environmental values of the founders became a lasting core purpose and driver of the company. Further manifesting their concern about benefiting the local communities, they set up their company in Botswana and trained locals rather than following the traditional industry approach of operating out of adjacent South Africa and traveling into Botswana.

The innovative business model that they conceived and developed over the initial years deviated from the prevailing tourism approach in several ways. First, they focused on wildlife viewing rather than the common hunting safaris. From an environmental perspective, this was shifting from a value-destroying to a value-preserving approach. Furthermore, they saw what Yang *et al.* (2017, pp. 1794–1804) refer to as "value uncaptured" in terms of a new value proposition to potential tourism clients. They believed that there was a market segment that would be attracted not only for viewing wildlife but doing this in a way that would be distinctive from current practice, and that model would enable different economic and conservation outcomes. The differentiation had multiple dimensions.

(1) Provide high-comfort accommodation and service to the tourists through specially designed and environmentally sensitive tented camps with highly trained indigenous staff.
(2) Locate them in areas where the natural environment, wildlife, and the cultural settings were spectacular. This meant obtaining land-use concessions from either governments or communities. Here WS took a very different approach to valuing land use so that total value created and returns to all stakeholders would increase. Russel Friedman, a seller of nature books who became the company's first business manager, saw this as key to their success: "The primary reason was that we were willing to take risks. I think we valued the conservation land correctly and realistically. Basically, we set precedents by being willing to pay higher 'rents' for private concession areas. In many cases our bids for concession leases exceeded existing rents by many multiples… We felt this was a fair and more realistic value, and this was an important part of the evolution of wildlife land use in Botswana" (Safaridude, 2011).
(3) Create an exclusive experience by limiting the visitors to single or small numbers of client groups. This combination gave rise to a highly distinctive and often unique service for which the entrepreneurs believed that a certain segment of the market would pay previously unreached premium prices.

In fact, this pioneering model proved highly successful, leading one Botswanan tourist industry observer to note that WS "changed the perception of what luxury tourism was, and how conservation should be done" (Spenceley and Snyman, 2016, pp. 52–67). This demonstrated dual opportunity recognition and synergistic financial and conservation goals.

7.2. Strategic Framework: Quadruple Bottom Line

As the company grew and evolved, its business model became expressed as a multipurpose sustainable framework encompassing a quadruple bottom line of 4Cs: Commerce, Conservation, Community, and Culture, which it adopted from the Zeitz Foundation. Management conceived of each of these four purposes as individually important and collectively interdependent. The CEO of WS, Keith Vincent, stated, "First and foremost, we believe we're a conservation business. Many people say that being sustainable isn't profitable, but our belief is that we can be a profitable company but still do good. Tourism pays for conservation ... Even if there is a viable business proposition, we cannot justify an investment that does not address the other 3Cs." The purposes are viewed as holistic, integrative, and synergistic. The WS' 4C approach appears to fit Schaltegger *et al.*'s (2016, p. 6) definition of a business model for sustainability: "a conceptual approach that helps describing, analysing, managing and communicating what sustainable value a company proposes to its existing and potential customers, and all other stakeholders, how it creates and delivers this value, and how it captures economic value for the company while maintaining or regenerating natural, economic and social capital beyond the organization's boundaries."

Integral to the realization of these 4Cs were various forms of collaboration with the relevant stakeholders. Austin and Seitandi (2012) conceptualized different collaborative arrangements as four stages on a Collaboration Continuum: *philanthropic* (charitable donor–recipient relationship), *transactional* (doing a specific project or activity with mutual resource and value exchange), *integrative* (fusing each organization's capabilities and purposes), and *transformational* (system-changing). As we will describe in this chapter, WS has moved along this continuum as its aspirations — and, correspondingly, its needs for resources beyond its current grasp — continuously evolved.

7.2.1. *Commerce and conservation*

There are vital synergies among the model's purposes. On the Commerce–Conservation link, Chief Marketing Officer Chris Roche observed, "If we don't protect it, we can't sell it"; one of the company's mottos was: "Without wilderness there is no Wilderness." The model's interdependencies reveal that the value-creation paths were different from that proposed by others. For example, Schaltegger and Wagner (2011, pp. 222–237) assert that social innovation in sustainable models needs to be aimed at the mass market. While that may be appropriate in some situations, the WS model seeks a select segment that can and will pay more, because fewer clients mean a smaller environmental footprint. To further their Conservation Purpose, their decision rule for when client demand exceeds their existing facilities' capacity is to raise prices rather than increase physical capacity. Less is better. Lüdeke-Freund *et al.* (2016) suggest that inclusive pricing models are desirable, but for WS, exclusive pricing is preferred. It has the highest prices (US$250 to US$4,400 per person night) and the lowest bed-to-nature area ratio (1 bed per every 11,312 acres) in the industry. The company is viewed as a leader in the industry, having won many international tourism awards.

Contributing to the Conservation Purpose is a driver of company actions in its own right, beyond direct commercial benefits. WS puts US$5 from every bednight charge into a Sustainability Fund that it directs into conservation activities — e.g. WS spent US$1.3 million in 2016 directly on biodiversity conservation in addition to a considerable amount for in-kind assistance. WS CEO Keith Vincent noted, "We decided right up front that we wanted to play an active role in the total conservation of any piece of land under our lease or influence." These conservation efforts included monitoring (particularly of the threatened and "critically endangered" species); anti-poaching efforts; preventing changes in land use; vegetation rehabilitation and native species regeneration; supporting research; and reintroducing depleted species, with a major effort on reintroducing black and white rhinos into Botswana where they had been extinct since 1900. This involved close cooperation with the governments from South Africa, Zimbabwe, and Botswana, which were examples of transactional business–government collaborative relationships focused on a specific project and objective.

To further its Conservation Purpose, in the late 1980s, WS established the non-profit Wilderness Wildlife Trust as a legally separate entity with its own independent board of directors. About 90% of its funding came from WS guests and travel agents, with WS providing 9% of the trust's funds as well as significant in-kind contributions. In effect, WS arranged for additional "revenue capture" from its clients by encouraging them to support a related but distinct entity. The Trust supported research (77%), anti-poaching management (16%), and community empowerment and education (6%), with 1% for administration. While the Trust worked closely with WS in its conservation efforts, it also operated in areas where WS did not. This can be considered an organizational form of hybridity, wherein the corporate philanthropic activities are delegated to a non-profit, but in this case, the collaborative relationship is integrative. The Trust is an organizational extension of the company's Conservation Purpose that enables additional activities and broadens the geographical scope.

Beyond the biodiversity preservation efforts, WS broadened its sustainability perspective to encompass Environmental Management Systems. Dr. Sue Snyman, Group Sustainability Manager, explained, "It doesn't matter how much biodiversity you're conserving if you are negatively impacting the environment in any number of ways. And that goes from the start of how we build our camps. The selection of sites is always done with environmental impact assessments and management plans. The camps are all built so that they can be taken down, never having permanent structures. In terms of physical footprint, WS has 1.7 square kilometers of temporary camp facilities on 25,472 square kilometers of land [1 square kilometer is about .39 square miles]. To reduce our CO_2 emissions, we have invested over $3.8 million in solar installations, which have allowed us to reduce emissions by 18% since 2012. To lower water usage, we use a reverse osmosis purification system, and the amount of plastic bottled water that was saved was huge (77%)."

Derek de la Harpe, Commercial Director and Chief Sustainability Officer, commented on the degree of synergy between the sustainability investments and financial returns: "It is a common-sense judgment we're making here. We can't actually demonstrate that clients will be swayed by sustainability investments. When we started making solar investments and eliminating the use and transport of diesel for generators in the camps, the then high price of oil meant a payback of the investment in 4 to 5 years. Now oil is one-third the price and the payback period would more than double. Eleven of our camps are 100% solar and 29 have solar-inverter hybrids reducing generator usage 50%. Even if the purely financial returns are lower than previously, we are convinced that we should continue to invest in solar."

7.2.2. *Community*

WS divides its third C, Community, into two parts: **External and Internal Communities**.

7.2.2.1. *External community*

Externally, the company considers as key stakeholders neighboring communities, governments, NGOs, academia, and media. The adjacent communities are critical to the sustainability model. They often control the lands and wildlife thereon, without which there is no commerce to be had, so this is an *input-intrinsic synergy*. In a basic sense, access to these distinctive ecological sites is the company's most differentiated and uncopiable asset and competitive advantage. Similarly, without the company's distinctive operating competencies that bring the tourists, the communities' lands would remain an undervalued asset, so this is an *enabling synergy*. Each side is bringing key and complementary assets to the partnership. These company–community collaboration opportunities arose because of important contextual changes in land-use rights throughout Southern Africa. With independence in Botswana, Zimbabwe, Zambia, and Namibia came new legislation ceding land and wildlife ownership or usage rights to local communities. Previously, tourism was constrained to government parks or reserves that constituted just 17% of the region's land, so the new laws opened vastly expanded tourism usage partnerships with communities (Bond et al., 2004, p. 29).

These remote communities often had very constrained economic opportunities, limited skill sets, and low incomes. High-end ecotourism expanded the opportunity set. WS has about three dozen community partnerships for operating camps with a variety of financial arrangements: fixed annual lease fees, fixed per bednight fees, percentage of annual revenue, and joint equity ownership, with most having a mix of guaranteed and performance-related revenue. In one instance in Namibia, WS gifted 20% ownership of the camp venture to the community annually between years 10–15, and after the community's ownership reached 100%, they sold 60% back to WS and retained 40% in the joint venture. With vested interests in conserving its wildlife, communities have an incentive to prevent poaching and habitat destruction, thereby contributing to the Conservation Purpose.

Managing the interface between the company and communities was seen by management as important, complicated, and demanding. CEO Vincent observed, "I've stressed the importance of being able to interact and talk in the villages, but quite often you can get caught between the community's agenda, the government's agenda, an NGO's agenda, and our agenda. Sometimes it's a mess. One real risk has come from the NGOs who got into these community areas and created unviable expectations for the communities themselves. That puts the business under huge risk and stress as unrealistic promises are made by well-meaning people, but with no on-the-ground experience of how to make a business or how to make a partnership with a community and a private sector business actually work." CFO Amy Anzoulay indicated one WS approach to handling these issues: "The challenge is to get a better understanding of the commercial realities in those specific areas. Engaging with the community, being open and transparent with them, and make them understand that they are part of this business."

The company's Code of Conduct requires close interaction and participation with communities: "Wilderness Safaris will encourage the development of tourism projects with relevant authorities, facilities and infrastructure, which are economically, environmentally and socially sustainable and which secure the future of rural communities. Wilderness Safaris will, where relevant, ensure community involvement and participation in all stages of tourism projects: planning, development, implementation and maintenance." The collaboration is more an integrative relationship than just transactional.

Beyond these revenue streams that enable communities to fund a range of needed community projects, they garner additional skills about how to manage economic enterprise and their wildlife resources. WS hires its camp staff preferentially from these communities and, also, incorporates community producers into their supply chains as providers of food and other supplies and services. Another major form of engagement was via the independent NGO Children in the Wilderness (CITW), which WS formed in 2001 as another hybrid organizational extension of WS. CITW provided environmental education to 2,500 community children per year, as well as hosting an additional 500 children in WS camps so that they could experience what the tourists do. WS saw these efforts, costing US$387,000 in 2016, as strengthening relationships and as long-term investments in instilling greater conservation knowledge and commitment in the future leadership of the communities, and therefore a continuity insurance policy.

(1) Governments

Governments are a key part of WS' external constituency, and its cross-sector interactions with governments were vital and multifaceted. As with the external communities, governments were essential to gaining access to wildlife sites either via concessions or entry fees to national parks. Other interaction areas included anti-poaching actions and conservation of endangered species. Government regulatory, financial, and developmental roles affected tourism promotion and operations. CEO Vincent set forth the company's approach to the cross-sector collaboration with governments: "I think the first step above all is how to communicate what the company's goals and aspirations are and make sure that they're aligned before you go in with the longer-term aspirations of a country. We do a lot of homework on a strategic vision of a country as far as wildlife and conservation and job creation goes. We try to make sure that our 4Cs are aligned with this. Once we're established and trusted as partners, we are often invited to help shape the strategic direction in the country in the future by having a seat at the table."

Over the decades, WS' relationship with the Botswana government had evolved through various stages on the previously described "Collaboration Continuum," as WS' pioneering efforts led to dramatic changes in the tourist industry and government's approach to it. Early on, WS' extensive and highly regarded training of its local guides led the government to request that the company be the government's principal trainer for guide certification and provide the government with the training methodology. The company happily did this, in effect, making their training expertise open source. It built the industry and they also received tax credits for the training efforts. Over time, the relationships with government officials from the President on down became close, collegial, and collaborative. In 2015, WS was recognized with the receipt of the Presidential Order of Meritorious Service Award. As WS expanded across multiple countries, its political contexts and governmental relations became increasingly complex.

(2) Internal community

Three-fourths of the company's almost 2,500 **employees** (47% of them female) came from the communities adjacent to the WS camps, thereby further tightening the larger company–community collaboration. For most, this was their first permanent job, and they typically arrived with little or no service experience and skills. The company invested heavily in continual training on-site and online, as its value proposition of luxury service required this. Thus, skill enhancement was an important micro-level benefit accruing to community members. Reciprocally, the company obtained a nearby workforce knowledgeable about the local ecosystem and the village contextual realities and forces. On average, each employee's wages supported seven family members, and for 60% of the staff, their jobs were the only income for their entire family (Snyman, 2017, pp. 247–268). These economic well-being and distributive social benefits further strengthened the linked interests between the company, its camps, and the community.

A second vital internal community group was about 2,000 **independent travel agents** specializing in African Safaris in the source markets (50% US, 30% UK and Europe, and the rest Australia and Asia). Chief Sales Officer Dave Bennett considered this group vital to the company's success: "We choose our core agent partners very, very carefully. They are required to come out and visit us in country to experience our products, to fly in our airplanes, to go in our jeeps, and that gives us the confidence that when they get back into the marketplace and they're selling to their consumers they're well qualified to sell them the exact experience that will match what we can offer on the ground. Many of these agents we have worked with for decades, and so it is almost like a passion for them. Our business is based on relationships, trust, credibility, and authenticity."

In its business model, unlike most of its competitors, WS does not do direct booking and passes on all requests (about 30%) to its agents. It has its own fee-based travel support unit, primarily based in South Africa, that works daily with the agents to craft the final itineraries, which often are circuits involving stays at multiple camps in a single country or countries. The company also engages several promotional firms abroad to publicize WS, sometimes jointly with their travel agents. Currently, WS is studying incorporating online direct customer booking.

A related important component of the business model is **vertical integration**. Its own airline deploys 38 planes to ensure transport to its remote and exclusive camps, and its local tour operators in each country take care of ground transportation and accommodations to ensure client convenience and logistical certainty. This also gives more cost control to the company in creating the pricing for its travel packages.

7.2.3. Culture

This fourth C involved values of respect for, and appreciation of, cultural differences and fostering cultural exchange and understanding. This has intrinsic value as a larger societal purpose, but it also has synergistic links with the other 3Cs within the model. With 40 different ethnic groups among its staff and collaborating communities, cross-cultural understanding and harmony are essential to effective interaction. Additionally, there are many cultural determinants of conservation that are important inputs to action plans. Lastly, there is a growing interest among tourists for cultural learning and exchange. Hence, experiential interaction of clients and communities presents an enriched value proposition to both.

Cultural interaction can be a complicated area fraught with potential misunderstandings and conflict. Hence, attending to it is also a form of risk management within the WS model. To deal with this, WS created a Cultural Ethics Charter with 22 objectives. These include fostering cultural awareness, mutual understanding, appreciation, respect, worth, identity, aesthetics, customs, traditions, and heritage, among others. These objectives apply to guests, staff, host communities, and other stakeholders. The intention is to ensure authentic experiences and avoid cultural commodification. The tourist visits also open additional income opportunities to the villages, including the sale of their crafts. To guide the implementation of the forgoing principles, the company also has set forth Cultural Codes of Conduct that cover: (1) critical preparatory actions for guests and communities prior to visits to villages to ensure mutual understanding and expectations; (2) appropriate behavior and acceptable actions during visits to achieve satisfying experiences for all; and (3) periodic independent evaluations of the cultural tourism experiences.

The realization of the Cultural Purpose requires a very close collaboration between the company, communities, and guests. The resulting deepened cultural understanding and appreciation has an integrative effect on the collaboration and fosters deeper trust among the partners.

7.3. Performance Measurement and Integrated Reporting

The need for monitoring and reporting outcomes on all dimensions of multipurpose businesses is increasingly recognized and WS does this through Integrated Reporting that assesses performance on each of its 4Cs. The Republic of South Africa, uniquely in the world, designates sustainable development as a human right in its constitution, and publicly listed corporations are obligated to report on it. What is optional in one context can be obligatory in another. WS' efforts, however, go far beyond the legal minimum and even more ample than the international GRI sustainability standards, South Africa's King Code of Corporate Governance's robust reporting norms (King IV, 2016), and the International Integrated Reporting Council's framework.

The company invests an exceptional amount of time monitoring operations, collecting relevant data, and then reporting on a series of specifically designed key indicators measuring its financial, conservation, community, and cultural performance. These are assembled into its Annual Integrated Report that is about 200 pages, and which was recognized as the fifth best integrated report in the world by the 2017 Corporate Register Reporting Awards.

In addition to providing transparency to the company's multiple external stakeholders, CEO Vincent pointed to internal benefits from the process of producing and having the report: "I think from an environmental point of view, it allowed us to become incredibly more disciplined and ensure that we were better measured in all forms of what we were promising that we wanted to achieve. Where we're not doing well, it allows us to set goals for the future to allow us to do better. Interestingly, it's become the glue amongst our staff to feel that we're doing better than anyone else and it's made a desire for us to even do better in the future, and be more environmentally conscious and measure it more properly than ever before. It's now completely ingrained." Hence, it is a feedback learning vehicle, a harmonizer of values, a standards enforcer, and a motivator. Enhancing internal knowledge and commitment thus increases external impact.

Measuring progress on social, environmental, and cultural problems is complicated due to problems of "nonquantifiability, multicausality, temporal differences, perception differences of the social impact created" (Austin *et al*., 2006, pp. 1–22), as well as attribution (Ebrahim & Rangan, 2014, pp. 118–141). Nevertheless, WS continually tries to improve its indicators. While performance measurement and reporting are demanding, they have organizational value by fostering purpose cohesion and internal and external accountability.

7.4. Collaboration Mindset

It is clear from the foregoing analyses that collaboration across stakeholders is integral to the WS multipurpose model's design and its implementation. Essential to the effectiveness of its collaborative engagements was the management's mental map (Austin and Seitanidi, 2014, pp. 60–63). Our interviews revealed a common emphasis on the importance of collaboration to the success of the firm. Five mindset dimensions, among others, emerged: mutuality, alignment, expectations, reinvestment, and competitor collaboration.

7.4.1. *Mutuality*

CMO Chris Roche expressed mutual interests this way: "Collaboration is absolutely critical. In our environment, the African continent, it's just impossible not to have collaborations, not to have mutual benefit, not to have some kind of symbiotic bond that holds you together, because without those things, you're doomed to failure."

7.4.2. Alignment

CFO Anzoulay observed that alignment is essential: "There are three significant parties: communities, governments, and our agent network. All of those have to be aligned, and understand the business model, our purpose, and our objective. And the reality is that if any of these are unhappy it's a serious risk for the business. If there isn't ongoing communication, ongoing dialog, and transparency from a long-term point of view, that puts the business at a significant risk. The reality is that these parties have to be sitting around the table effectively and be part of our purpose."

7.4.3. Expectations

Dereck de la Harpe noted that expectations have to be kept grounded and realistic: "The biggest challenge is managing expectations and what we call expectation creep, which seems to be a factor of these long-term relationships. The need to outperform the alternative uses to which land can be put is, in the long-term, the real challenge facing this business."

7.4.4. Reinvestment

Sue Snyman sees sustaining reinvestment in core assets as an essential element of sustainability: "What makes us unique is that the understanding that you have to invest in your product, and our product is conservation and communities in terms of the business and the success of the business."

7.4.5. Competitor collaboration

Another significant aspect of the mindset is how the company views competition and its relationship with competitors. Traditional business models stress the importance of gaining competitive advantage. More recently, benefits of cooperation with competitors ("coopetition") have been identified. WS views competitor collaboration as contributing to its multiple purposes and actively pursues positive interaction. CEO Vincent explained, "More and more we see our model being copied throughout various areas of Africa, which is fantastic...If you've got more people singing the same hymn tune, the marketing audience becomes so much greater around the world... We collaborate with several of our main competitors incredibly closely on conservation and community." In effect, WS sees such collaboration as helping stimulate primary demand for the industry. They compete with the quality of their specific offerings to stimulate selective demand for the company. The collective actions expand conservation areas and strengthen communities, which are shared purposes among the competing companies.

7.5. The International Dimensions

WS grew steadily within Botswana and then recruited other experienced guides to set up operations in the Republic of South Africa (1993), Namibia (1993), Malawi (1994), Zimbabwe (1995), and Zambia (2000). Vincent, who joined the company in 1992, explained this early expansion process: "Basically WS was originally built by five or six individuals that were given incredibly free rein to be an entrepreneur and just build a business. It was always about wildlife. We were able to attract an incredible number of really passionate wildlife and conservation-oriented people into our business. Until 1996 we operated as individual countries when we joined the group together. We chucked all our businesses into a pot, made some rudimentary valuations, and split the equity basically amongst us."

A critical salient feature of this process was the congruency of values regarding conservation among the new personnel that entered the company and subsequently rose to constitute the current leadership after the original founders had moved on. Conservation became embedded early on as a core value through this self-selection process. Personnel selection has been indicated as a mechanism for obtaining harmony in hybrid organizations (Battilana and Lee, 2014). As the company expanded, management used its intensive training programs to ensure that new personnel understood the multiple purposes and core values of the company.

Continued growth of the company's operations was driven by both the Conservation and Commerce purposes. Chris Roche stated, "Ultimately, the vision of Wilderness Holdings is to have a continental impact or a pan-African impact in multiple biomes [distinct ecological areas in which specific flora and fauna have evolved]. It's irresponsible for our industry not to attempt to evolve our model out of the savanna and into biomes like the rain forest." Additionally, concerns about growing saturation of their Southern Africa markets led them to look at East Africa, a long-established wildlife safari tourist market, led by Kenya. WS was also attracted by Rwanda, as Vincent explained: "Rwanda is the home of 220 of the 880 mountain gorillas left alive. We felt an urge to play a role in making sure we could contribute to the protection of those 220 mountain gorillas. There are few better-run countries in Africa than Rwanda right now in the form of good governance, no corruption, the desire to do well and to do it properly."

After two years of full-time, in-country study of Kenya, Wilderness Holdings acquired 51% of Governors', the biggest, best-reputed, award-winning tourism company in Kenya, for US$6.1 million. In this collaboration, Governors' would continue to manage the operations. The two companies shared common values on conservation and communities, but there was a fundamental contrast in business models. In contrast to WS's high price–low volume model, Governors' and the Kenyan safari industry in general operated on a lower price–higher volume model, primarily accessing government parks. Consequently, the issue of possible sustainable business model compatibility problems remains an open issue.

In 2017, the company partnered with a local community to open a new lodge for gorilla-watching in Rwanda with a 49-year lease on a completely deforested site. Chief Sales Officer Bennett laid out the vision and how it connected to WS' larger purposes: "The lodge will be simple, luxurious, and really fancy, but actually the purpose is not to build a lodge, the purpose is to rehabilitate rainforest in that part of the world. And the lodge is just like a byproduct of that. It's like a means to an end. I think it's just making a difference in this world and being part of something bigger." This Bisate lodge soon became a sought-after destination site and was fully booked. WS worked with the government and local communities to develop another lodge in a government preserve where rare chimpanzee species existed. This would give tourists another site in addition to the gorillas and prolong their stay in the country with the corresponding economic benefits.

The evolution of the company into a multi-country operation multiplied its managerial and financial complexity. At various times, political and economic turmoil erupted in one or more countries, disrupting tourism flows. By having a portfolio of countries, WS was able to endure difficulties in one country by relying on successful operations in others. Thus, it preserved its reserves and camps and retained personnel until stability returned.

Given that its clients were international tourists, it had the financial benefit of receiving its revenues in hard currencies and spending operating funds in local currencies generally more subject to devaluation. However, disruptions to the international tourism flows remain a risk. For example, financial downturns in the US or Europe dampen the tourist flow. Public health eruptions such as Ebola or COVID-19 can shut down international tourism.

WS expanded incrementally to encompass operations in eight countries. The company is part of a global market for its clients. This carries significant implications for the economics of the business as well as the exposure to external phenomenon affecting tourism such as Ebola, COVID-19, or political turmoil.

7.6. Organization and Governance

WS is particularly interesting because of the evolution of its organizational and ownership structure. From a single-country operation, it added semi-independent multiple operations in other nations, each being another entrepreneurial undertaking. This led to the creation of Wilderness Holdings to consolidate ownership, which was followed by taking the organization public with an IPO and public listing. This brought in new capital from local and international corporate investors, enabling further growth but also formalizing decision-making structures and processes. Most recently, the company has replaced the existing corporate owners with two new impact investors and has delisted. This was a form of entrepreneurial governance that facilitated greater decision-making flexibility and environmental impact alignment.

7.6.1. *The shift to public ownership*

A critical point in the organizational evolution of WS occurred in 2010 when the company grouped together its various country operations into Wilderness Holdings and registered it on the Botswana Stock Exchange with a secondary listing on the Johannesburg Exchange. Whereas IPOs are generally pursued to raise capital, that was not the motivation for WS, as explained by Vincent: "In essence, you had ten 'white people' who owned WS and we were looking after nine million acres of land across multiple countries. That was not sustainable in the long term. We felt that by listing we allowed citizens in a variety of countries to have ownership and that would give us much better long-term security. It was not a capital-raising initiative." In effect, this was a context-driven, political risk management initiative.

The action did, however, bring important organizational changes, involving new investors, governance structure, and administrative processes, along with a capital infusion. It raised the interesting issue of whether a publicly owned company can simultaneously meet the demands of shareholders while pursuing a sustainable quadruple bottom line model. Wilderness Safaris (Holdings) appears to provide an affirmative example. The model's many-dimensioned synergies and co-creation of collaboration value discussed above have produced positive financial results. On a consolidated basis, turnover rose from US$82 million in 2013 to US$106 million in fiscal year 2017, with net profit after taxes rising from US$2.9 million to US$6.1 million. CFO Amy Anzoulay indicated that the company aimed to achieve a 20%–24% EBITDA return on revenue (Earnings Before Interest, Taxes, Depreciation, and Amortization, a measure of the operating profitability of a business). Dividends were about US$107,000 in 2015, US$118,000 in 2016, and US$335,000 in 2017. The company made US$1.3 million of investments in 2016, with two-thirds going to maintenance of existing facilities and one-third for expansion.

The IPO attracted international companies. The Travel Corporation, a large international travel company via its South African company, Wine Investments, which had made an earlier investment in the company to help in its expansion, increased its stake to 34%. PUMA SE, a German multinational sporting apparel company headed by Jochen Zeitz, a pioneering advocate of integrating environmental impact into corporate strategy and the formulator of the quadruple bottom line framework, was attracted by WS' sustainability platform; Puma and its parent company Kering bought 25%. By 2017, individuals, including WS employees, owned 23%, in part via a 4C performance-related stock reward program. The Botswana Public Officers Pension Fund held 16% and Trusts held 10% of the

231,882,451 issued shares. The Wilderness Holdings market capitalization as of 2017 was about US$160 million.

Importantly, management believed that the new investors were reasonably aligned with the multiple purposes, recognized the synergies among them, and believed in "the wider business and its impact," as Derek de la Harpe stated. The 13-person board of directors consisted of independent directors, including representatives of the major corporate investors, one of which was Jochen Zeitz. The company's CEO, CFO, and Director of Sustainability also sat on the board, which included a Social, Ethics, and Sustainability Committee in addition to the standard set of board committees. The board had oversight responsibility for the company, but management indicated that they seldom intervened explicitly in company operations. Nonetheless, the more formalized governance requirements did represent an abrupt change for company personnel, as noted by Dave Bennett, Chief Sales Officer: "Writing board reports and having all the committees, for a lot of us was a massive cultural shock. But in hindsight, to have that level of governance and checks and balances is really comforting and necessary. With 2,500 employees and an average dependency ratio of seven family members to each staffer in our business, we have a massive responsibility to make sure that this business is very successful going into the future." The company also brought on new staff with the professional skills required of a listed company and that were lacking among the existing top management, who mostly had guiding and ecotourism backgrounds. There was a shared view that the formalization helped develop a more disciplined and efficiently run organization.

Although the commitment to conservation, community, and culture remained firm, there was acknowledgment that the pressure for financial returns had increased. Tensions among the multiple purposes did occur. For example, at different times, adverse political or economic conditions, including fluctuating exchange rates in some of the countries or internationally, caused downturns in tourism, resulting in losses in some countries and camps. Closing down those operations could be seen as being financially prudent under many business models, but WS chose not to do so as not to harm its staff and the communities, as well as the wildlife, fulfilling its commitments toward all. Management's longer-term time frame also supported this preservation approach. Given that the sites were vital to their competitive advantage, not abandoning them was a key asset preservation strategy.

A related financial issue arose among camps within countries. Of the company's 40 camps, some were the key money-makers while others lost money. However, to close the unprofitable sites would hurt the company's conservation goals. Furthermore, if one takes the circuit of camps generally used by clients as the more appropriate unit of analysis, then the presence of even the loss-making camps within a circuit contribute to more attractive total experiences for the guests and to overall circuit profitability. This is where the portfolio concept is applicable, with different camps and circuits serving different functions, contributing distinctly to each of the four purposes, and enabling different mixes to achieve optimum outcomes. The portfolio approach also became even more applicable across countries as the company expanded.

7.6.2. *The shift to impact investors*

WS' capital structure was designed to enable it to operate successfully in a complex political context and with a modest time horizon (where investments in a newly developed site could be expected to show returns within a period of 5–10 years). WS began to realize, however, that conservation efforts at scale would have to involve not only preserving the small amount of remaining wilderness in Africa — an effort it had already been heavily invested in — but would also have to include the much more expensive process of reclaiming lands that had been exploited for other interests (e.g. through logging operations). As it contemplated making the much larger investments with much longer time frames and with social and economic returns across a wider variety of dimensions that would be required to extend conservation to reclamation, the aspirations of its management group came to be less aligned with the interests of its majority owners. In July 2018, WS announced that its two principal corporate owners had been bought out by two US social impact investment companies. The RISE Fund, recognized as the largest private impact fund in the US, purchased a 34% share, and another 24% went to African Wildlife Holdings, an affiliate of family-owned FS Investors, a private equity investment firm. Impact investors seek enterprises that produce both positive financial returns and social impact. Impact investment was estimated in 2019 at US$502 billion globally; while there is a wide diversity of investors, 62% are asset investors like RISE and FS Investors (Mudaliar and Dithrich 2019).[1]

The acquisition took several years of mutual scrutiny and interaction between the investors and WS management. For the impact investors, the company's quadruple purposes and clear commitment to conservation, supported empirically by its Integrated Report, were instrumental to their analyses. The imputed value of carbon sequestration due to averted deforestation on the company's preserved lands was deemed a major positive environmental impact as was the protection of wildlife. Providing economic opportunities for its employees and the collaborating communities was also viewed as significant. WS CEO Keith Vincent believed that the new investors' orientation toward environmental and longer-term impact was more aligned with management's strategy of obtaining and preserving significantly larger and threatened reserves in their existing operating countries and new ones. As Vincent observed, "Natural wild lands are becoming harder and harder to get your hands on … we need to go and take land that is being depleted and recreate it, which takes a longer-term mindset of investing. We aim to double the land we are managing and protecting."

7.7. Corporation or Social Enterprise?

There is no doubt that the entrepreneurial WS has been a profit-making corporation benefiting investors. However, its explicit multiple purposes aimed at generating environmental and societal good gives it characteristics of social entrepreneurship (Austin *et al.*, 2006, pp. 1–22; Doherty *et al.*, 2014, pp. 417–436). It meets the criteria set forth by Upward and Jones (2016, pp. 97–123) as a Strongly Sustainable Business Model, as well as those described by Yunus *et al.* (2010, pp. 308–325) for Social Business Models. In both instances, the model must generate profits and simultaneously contribute to environmental and social betterment.

WS is clearly a hybrid organization. Hahn and Ince (2016, pp. 33–52) as well as Haig and Hoffman (2012, pp. 126–134) contend that both profit and growth are means to achieving sustainability and social impact goals, and the entrepreneurs' driving motivations are non-monetary. The potential for tensions among purposes in hybrid organizations is significant (Battilana and Lee, 2014; Seigner *et al.*, 2017), but in WS the integrated and permanent centrality of the multiple purposes produces significant synergies. WS manifests corporate social entrepreneurship (Austin and Reficco, 2009, pp. 86–92) and hybridity.

7.8. Final Reflections on Key Effectiveness Factors

We conclude the chapter by highlighting some key factors that emerge from the foregoing analyses as contributing significantly to the effectiveness of WS as a successful entrepreneurial environmental enterprise.

Purpose Synergies. Management has created a model in which the distinct purposes have a synergistic relationship with each other and evolved that model significantly as conditions changed. The greater those positive interdependencies, the more cohesive will be the constellation of purposes. At the most integrated level, the mutual dependency is imperative; one purpose cannot be achieved without the others. In this case, one should not view the purposes hierarchically, but rather as complementary and interdependent. They function as a whole. To achieve one but not the others, or at the expense of the others, would not be deemed a successful outcome.

Purpose Tensions. Battilana and Lee's (2014) research led to the useful observation that it is important to recognize that, across social enterprises, there is a continuum in the degree of compatibility or tension between the economic and social purposes. This would also hold for multipurpose corporate businesses, such as WS. A conceptual refinement of such a compatibility continuum across firms or within a firm and for each of the purposes would be to conceive of it as a dynamic rather than static analytical tool. The inevitability of changing circumstances means that the degree of purpose compatibility, synergy, and parity may vary over time, across places, and among purposes. In effect, context-driven dynamism becomes an important mediator of purpose compatibility. The hybridity of social enterprises and multi-purpose businesses carries the risks of organizational tensions among personnel being tugged in the various purposes' directions, particularly with regard to the financial versus the non-financial sides. Finding mechanisms to ameliorate or manage these tensions is an important managerial exigency for multipurpose businesses. While WS has managed these tensions on a case-by-case basis as they have emerged across its many diverse operating sites, it has in general given primacy to the conservation goal and embedded that in its organizational values. Commitment to conservation is a de facto filter for screening new employees. It is a glue that creates cohesion in the organizational culture.

Value Synergies. Economic, social, environmental, and cultural purposes each have distinct forms of value, but their interdependencies and interactions also can create blended values (Emerson, 2003, pp. 35–51) or shared values (Porter and Kramer, 2006, pp. 78–92; 2011, pp. 62–77; Dembek *et al.*, 2016, pp. 231-267). At the heart of WS' value creation model is the synergistic relationship of its 4Cs. They all interact and reinforce each other, a form of mutual enabling synergy.

Innovation. At the heart of environmental entrepreneurship is often an innovation that creates a distinctive and more effective model for addressing a sustainability problem profitably (Pedersen *et al.*, 2016). Of particular significance for value creation is when those innovations find ways to create greater synergies among multiple purposes. The more linkages there are and the stronger those linkages are among the purposes, the greater will be the value-creating synergisms in the model. WS' ability to create new value propositions for clients and other stakeholders is an ongoing key innovative capability.

Collaboration. With each new purpose, the number of relevant stakeholders multiply, and collaboration with them is an operational imperative (Breuer and Lüdeke-Freund, 2017; Lowitt, 2013; Rohrbeck *et al.*, 2013, pp. 4–23; Zott and Amit, 2013, pp. 403–411). Bocken *et al.* (2015, p. 67) asserted, "A sustainable society cannot be achieved if individual agents advance their own interests independently." Gray and Stites (2013) point to collaborations as key vehicles for achieving sustainability. WS management recognizes its multiplicity of stakeholders and the imperative of having effective collaborative relationships with all. They are able to find common goals, identify the distinctive and complementary resources that each party brings to joint effort, and then ensure that the resulting value created is shared equitably. Achieving this alignment requires a collaboration mindset, creativity in discovering mutual interests, and strong communication abilities. This mirrors the challenge of political coalition-building: as coalitions get larger, they can become more powerful, but they also tend to become more diverse in their interests, so a major challenge of growing coalitions lies in finding mutual interests and persuasively arguing for the importance of the common interests while finding ways to de-emphasize the interests that are not in common.

Time Perspective. The managers' time perspective is also important. A longer-run horizon is more amenable to many environmental and social actions that require a longer time to produce positive outcomes because of the inherent nature of the change processes involved (Slawinski and Bansal, 2012, pp. 1537–1563). Short-termism can overlook both risks and opportunities that require longer-term investments to strengthen the enterprise's ongoing sustainability (Bower and Paine, 2017, pp. 50–59). WS management takes a long-term view, has the capacity to envision systemic change and formulate bold strategies to accomplish the goals, and has developed a capital structure that has a long time horizon and can assume the corresponding significant risks.

A long-term focus does, of course, bring its own risks: since the intended impacts are long in the future and denominated in different units, we could be fooling ourselves in the short run about whether we are making progress toward those goals. This is where the performance metrics discipline built into WS — first through its need to formalize reporting and governance when it went public, and then again reinforced by its sharp-penciled impact investor partners — plays a critical role in keeping WS on track in balancing short-term spending against long-term benefits. Most social businesses will intrinsically be an intertemporal and interdimensional play — with heavy investment in the short term designed to produce long-term benefits, often in a different "currency." Crafting a capital structure that understands and enables this — i.e. finding impact investors who are willing to accept that temporal pattern of returns and who value social returns in different dimensions, is a key challenge for social entrepreneurs.

Implementation Capabilities. Fundamental to the organization's effectiveness are the managerial skills to implement the business model and strategies. Among these capabilities are training its staff to deliver world class services, developing environmental management systems to reduce impact, and collecting and utilizing performance indicators for its multiple purposes.

In their comprehensive analysis of conservation tourism in Africa, Snyman and Spenceley (2019, p. 216) conclude,

> In the final analysis, a huge amount of responsibility rests on the sustainable management of tourism in conservation areas ... with investment focused on finding and ensuring the implementation of sustainable, environmentally friendly developments with positive socioeconomic and sociocultural impacts.

While every company has its distinctive characteristics, WS manifests the exercise of this responsibility and offers an opportunity to learn from its rich and effective ongoing journey of environmental entrepreneurship.

References

Austin, J., Epler Wood, M., & Leonard, H. (2018). Wilderness Safaris: Entrepreneurial Ecotourism. Harvard Business School.

Austin, J. & Reficco, E. (2009). Corporate social entrepreneurship. *International Journal for Not-for-Profit Law*, **11**(4), 86–92.

Austin, J., & Seitanidi, M. (2014). *Creating Value in Nonprofit-business Collaborations: New Thinking and Practice* (San Francisco, CA: Jossey-Bass).

Austin, J., & Seitanidi, M. M. (2012). Collaborative value creation: A review of partnering between nonprofits and businesses, part 1. *Nonprofit and Voluntary Sector Quarterly*, **41**(5), 723–755.

Austin, J., Stevenson, H., & Wei-Skillern, J. (2006). Social and commercial entrepreneurship: Same, different or both? *Entrepreneurship Theory and Practice*, **30**, 1–22.

Battilana, J., & Lee, M. (2014). Advancing research on hybrid organizing: Insights from the study of social enterprises. *The Academy of Management Annals*, **8**(1), 397–441.

Bocken, N. M. P., Rana, P., & Short, S. W. (2015). Value mapping for sustainable business thinking. *Journal of Industrial and Production Engineering*, **32**(1), 67–81.

Bond, I., with Child, B., de la Harpe, D., Jones, B., Barnes, J., & Anderson, H. (2004). Private land conservation in South Africa. In B. Child (ed.), *Parks in Transition* (South Africa: IUCN), p. 29.

Bower, J. L., & Paine, L. S. (2017). The error at the heart of corporate leadership. *Harvard Business Review,* May–June, 50–59.

Breuer, H., & Lüdeke-Freund, F. (2014). Normative innovation for sustainable business models in value networks. In K. Huizingh, S. Conn, M. Torkkeli, and I. Bitran (eds.), *The Proceedings of XXV ISPIM Conference: Innovation for Sustainable Economy and Society* (Dublin, Ireland: Lappeenranta University of Technology Press), pp. 1–17.

Dembek, K., Singh, P., & Bhakoo, V. (2016). Literature review of shared value: A theoretical concept or a management buzzword? *Journal of Business Ethics*, **137**, 231–267.

Doherty, B., Haugh, H., & Lyon, F. (2014). Social enterprises as hybrid organizations: A review and research agenda. *International Journal of Management Reviews*, **16**, 417–436.

Ebrahim, A. & Rangan, V.K. (2014). What impact? A framework for measuring the scale and scope of social performance. *California Management Review*, **56**(3), 118–141.

Emerson, J. (2003). The blended value proposition: Integrating social and financial returns. *California Management Review*, **45**(4), 35–51.

Gray, B., & Stites, J. P. (2013). Sustainability through partnerships: Capitalizing on collaboration. Network for Business Sustainability, January. Available at: https://s3.van1.auro.io/v1/AUTH_63f3dc66246c4447ad749fa1da8b5736/sophia/blox/assets/data/000/000/127/original/NBS-Systematic-Review-Partnerships.pdf?1492527925. Accessed November 21, 2017.

Hahn, R., & Ince. I. (2016). Constituents and characteristics of hybrid businesses: A qualitative, empirical framework. *Journal of Small Business Management*, **54**(S1), 33–52.

Haigh, N., & Hoffman, A. J. (2012). Hybrid organizations. *Organizational Dynamics*, **41**(2), 126–134.

Lowitt, E. (2013). *The Collaboration Economy* (San Francisco, CA: Jossey-Bass).

Lüdeke-Freund, F., Massa, L., Bocken, N., Brent, A., & Musango, J. (2016). Main report: Business models for shared value. Network for Business Sustainability, South Africa. Available at: https://nbs.net/p/main-report-business-models-for-shared-value-4122f859-2499-4439-824e-7535631a14ed. Accessed November 21, 2017.

Mudaliar, A., & Dithrich, H. (2019). Sizing the impact investing market. Global Impact Investing Network. Available at: https://thegiin.org/assets/Sizing%20the%20Impact%20Investing%20Market_webfile.pdf. Assessed on July 12, 2020.

Pedersen, E. R. G., Gwozdz, W., & Hvass, K. K. (2016). Exploring the relationship between business model innovation, corporate sustainability, and organisational values within the fashion industry. *Journal of Business Ethics*. doi:10.1007/s10551-016-3044-7.

Porter, M. E., & Kramer, M. R. (2006). Strategy and society: The link between competitive advantage and corporate social responsibility. *Harvard Business Review*, **84**(12), 78–92.

Porter, M. E., & Kramer, M. R. (2011). Creating shared value. *Harvard Business Review*, **89**(1/2), 62–77.

Rohrbeck, R., Konnertz, L., & Knab, S. (2013). Collaborative business modelling for systemic and sustainable innovations. *International Journal of Technology Management*, **63**(1/2), 4–23.

Safaridude (2011). Available at: http://safaritalk.net/topic/6729-russel-friedman-founding-partner-of-wilderness-safaris/. Accessed on June 18, 2017.

Schaltegger, S., Lüdeke-Freund, F., & Hansen, E. G. (2016). Business models for sustainability: Origins, research, and future avenues. *Organization & Environment*, **29**(1), 3–10.

Schaltegger, S. & Wagner, M. (2011). Sustainable entrepreneurship and sustainability innovation: Categories and interactions. *Business Strategy and the Environment*, **20**, 222–237.

Seigner, M., Pinske, J., & Panwar, R. (2017). Managing tensions in a social enterprise: The complex balancing act to deliver a multi-faceted but coherent social mission. *Journal of Cleaner Production*. doi:10.1016/j.jclepro.2017.11.076.

Slawinski, N., & Bansal, P. (2012). A matter of time: The temporal perspectives of organizational responses to climate change. *Organizational Studies*, **33**(11), 1537–1563.

Snyman, S., & Spenceley, A. (2019). *Private Sector Tourism in Conservation Areas in Africa* (Oxford, UK: CABI).

Snyman, S. (2017). The role of private sector ecotourism in local socio-economic development in southern Africa. *Journal of Ecotourism*, **16**(3), 247–268.

Spenceley, A., & Snyman, S. (2016). Can a wildlife tourism company influence conservation and the development of tourism in a specific destination? *Tourism and Hospitality Research*, **17**(1), 52–67.

Upward, A., & Jones, P. (2016). An ontology for strongly sustainable business models: Defining an enterprise framework compatible with natural and social science. *Organization & Environment*, **29**(1), 97–123.

Yang, M., Evans, S., Vladimirova, D., & Rana, P. (2017). Value uncaptured perspective for sustainable business model innovation, *Journal of Cleaner Production*, **140**, 1794–1804.

Yunus, M., Moingeon, B., & Lehmann-Ortega, L. (2010). Building social business models: Lessons from the Grameen experience. *Long Range Planning*, **43**, 308–325.

Zott, C. & Amit, R. (2013). The business model: A theoretically anchored robust construct for strategic analysis. *Strategic Organization*, **11**, 403–411.

Part II

Social Entrepreneurship and Impact

© 2022 World Scientific Publishing Company
https://doi.org/10.1142/9789811248863_0008

Chapter 8

Societal Attitudes Toward Corporate Responsibility and Social Entrepreneurship

Sumita Sarma[*,†,§] and Sharon A. Simmons[‡,¶]

[†]*California State University, Bakersfield, CA, USA*

[‡]*Jackson State University, Jackson, MS, USA*

[§]*ssarma@csub.edu*

[¶]*sharon.simmons@jsums.edu*

Abstract

A number of ecosystem factors influence the entry and engagement decisions of individual entrepreneurs — societal attitudes being one of them. Prior research in this area has focused on societal attitudes that shape the mode of entry — such as beliefs about gender roles or stigmas of business failure. Research is lacking on the effects of different societal attitudes and the resulting entrepreneurial behaviors of individuals. Drawing on Situationism Theory, we test for relationships between societal attitudes about corporate social responsibility and individual-level engagement in social entrepreneurship. To test our hypotheses, we constructed a unique dataset for 26 countries built from the Global Entrepreneurship Monitor, Flash Eurobarometer, and World Bank Doing Business Reports. We find evidence of positive correlation between being well-informed and likelihood of individual-level engagement in social entrepreneurship, which can have important theoretical and practical implications.

Keywords: Societal attitudes; corporate social responsibility; situationism theory; social entrepreneurship; ecosystems.

---

[*]Corresponding author.

8.1. Introduction

An entrepreneurial ecosystem is a "set of interdependent actors and factors coordinated in such a way that they enable productive entrepreneurship" (Stam, 2015, p. 1765). Entrepreneurial ecosystem researchers have gathered an impressive body of empirical data on the mechanisms that implicate regional and business ecosystems (Acs *et al.*, 2017). Prior ecosystem studies have provided comparisons of the framework conditions of local (e.g. Kabia *et al.*, 2016; Wirtz and Volkmann, 2015), and national entrepreneurial ecosystems (e.g. Chung, 2014; Villeneuve-Smith & Temple, 2015). In these studies, a limited number of ecosystem framework conditions presently receive most of the attention in these entrepreneurship studies — i.e. market accessibility, labor supply and demand, resource dependencies, accessible markets, government and regulatory structure, and access to support services (Acs *et al.*, 2017).

We believe that two perspectives are missing from prior studies of entrepreneurial ecosystems. The first perspective is an understanding of relationships between different social cues that are framework conditions of entrepreneurial ecosystems (Isenberg, 2010; 2011; Feld, 2012; Spigel, 2017) and decisions to select into different types of entrepreneurial careers. The second perspective focuses on the relationships between the social framework conditions of entrepreneurial ecosystems and the supply of different groups of entrepreneurs (Jack and Anderson, 2002), such as those who engage in entrepreneurial activities with a social purpose.

Within an ecosystem, the pool of individual entrepreneurs (potential, nascent, experienced) in a society, knowingly or unknowingly receive social cues about the desirability and necessity of different forms of entrepreneurship. Some scholars have already begun to examine these relationships (Autio *et al.*, 2013; Wennekers *et al.*, 2002; Zahra *et al.*, 2008). Some of the social cues that have been examined in these studies pertain to societal perceptions of family or network ties, of prior work and life experiences and how these social cues that correlate to entrepreneur career decisions (Shumate *et al.*, 2014; Cavazos-Arroyo *et al.*, 2017). Other social cues examined are cultural biases and stigmas about the entrepreneurial engagement of different groups of entrepreneurs, such as those with prior failures (Simmons *et al.*, 2014).

In this study, we explore how the relationship between two social cues affect the social impact of corporations and decisions to engage in social entrepreneurship. From earlier studies, we understand that there is a need to know more about how entrepreneurial processes differ across social contexts (Lumpkin *et al.*, 2013). The first attitude is how informed citizens feel about what companies do to behave responsibly toward society. The second attitude is what citizens believe the overall influence of companies on society to be. For purposes of our study, we refer to individuals who engage in entrepreneurial activities with a social purpose as "social entrepreneurs." This broad definition of social entrepreneurs encompasses individuals who engage in social ventures primarily to protect and promote the well-being of others (Grant and Rothbard, 2013) or themselves.

We believe that societal attitudes toward the social impact of corporations may influence the supply of social entrepreneurs in an entrepreneurial ecosystem. For our study, we equate the social impact of corporations to Corporate Social Responsibility (CSR) — a familiar concept in the management literature (Jamali *et al.*, 2017). The CSR activities of corporations build trusting relationships among corporate stakeholders beyond employees and customers (Jenkins, 2006). The general CSR literature suggests that socially responsible corporate activities are motivated by corporate efforts to improve relations and impact customers, investors, suppliers, employees, and community stakeholders' groups (Aguilera *et al.*, 2007; Carroll, 1991).

In national-level ecosystems, information about CSR activity is made available through informal mechanisms such as networks and industry norms, and through formal mechanisms such as news and regulatory reports (Floridi, 2006). Using a situationism approach, we examine whether perceptions of the incidence and impact of this CSR activity correlate to the levels of individual-level engagement in social entrepreneurship observed in national ecosystems. In the social psychology literature, situationism theory is used to explain the influence of the external environment or the situation on individual-level behaviors. We believe that this theory is applicable to the context of social entrepreneurship because the framework conditions of entrepreneurial ecosystems can shape individual awareness of broad social needs — which in turn can shape engagement in activities to better public welfare (Balasubramanian *et al.*, 2005).

The term "situationism," coined as part of the "person–situation" debate (Mischel, 1968), refers to human behavior as determined by the specific characteristics (i.e. values, ideas, knowledge, institutions, and practices) of the environment in which an individual is embedded rather than by personal qualities or intrinsic attributes. We hypothesize that situationism with respect to CSR perceptions evoke a concern for social improvement and a need to care for society in individuals (Balasubramanian *et al.*, 2005). A perceived awareness of the possibility for engagement may help aspiring entrepreneurs discover different interpretations of social opportunities (Herdova and Kearns, 2017) in the national ecosystem in which they are geographically embedded (Moore, 1993). We also hypothesize that there can be a bystander effect if citizens feel that established corporations are already addressing social needs.

To test our hypotheses, we constructed a unique dataset of 26 countries and 85,958 individuals from the Global Entrepreneurship Monitor, Flash Eurobarometer, and World Bank Doing Business report projects. Our unique database comprised indicators on national-level social attitudes toward CSR, various economic and social ecosystem control variables, and individual-level decisions about entry and engagement in social entrepreneurship. We find interesting and significant correlations between societal attitudes and engagement in social entrepreneurship activity that support our hypotheses.

This study contributes to the emerging conversation on the effects of national entrepreneurial ecosystems on individual decisions to engage in social entrepreneurship. While societal attitudes are recognized as an integral part of national entrepreneurial ecosystems (Acs *et al.*, 2014), cross-national studies are sparse (Simmons *et al.*, 2014), particularly with regards to social entrepreneurship.[1] Furthermore, a limitation of this body of literature, however, is the dominant focus on commercial entrepreneurship and high-growth entrepreneurial ventures, to the exclusion of contexts such as social entrepreneurship.

We draw attention to some important societal attitudes that influence individual awareness and actions to pursue entrepreneurial opportunities with a social purpose. Although social attitudes are slow to change, our findings make the case for national policies with the dual aim of increasing the visibility of CSR activities and informing citizens of additional opportunities to address social problems via social entrepreneurship.

We also believe that this is the first study to use situationism to empirically test correlations between national-level societal attitudes about CSR and social entrepreneurial activity at the individual-level. Situationism plays an important role in invoking social awareness, primarily manifested by individuals who possess compassion for others, and which requires actions like noticing, feeling, and sense-making. Our findings in this regard contribute back to CSR literature by illuminating correlations between societal perceptions of the social impact of corporations and the organizing of new firms in national ecosystems. Our study also extends what we know about the impact of CSR from the management literature to the developing field of social entrepreneurship and provides insight into situational considerations of CSR activities as the framework conditions for different entrepreneurial ecosystems (Karam and Jamali, 2017).

8.2. Situationism and Social Entrepreneurial Engagement

Situationism theory suggests that external environments and surrounding behavioral contexts help to define individual behaviors (Herdova and Kearns, 2017). Within social psychology, various experiments have been conducted to provide evidence in support of situationism theory, including the well-known Stanford Prison Experiment (Zimbardo, 1971), which demonstrates the power of the social environment.

---

[1] A Google search of "national social entrepreneurial ecosystems" on February 26, 2021, returned 1 result. In contrast, a search of "national entrepreneurial ecosystems" returned 2070 results.

Situational factors in the environment (e.g. noise, number of bystanders) that are external to the individual are found to influence helping behavior (Lefevor *et al.*, 2017). Experimental results suggest that individuals, knowingly or not, are influenced by situations, and that behaviors are attributable to the consistency of situations. The topic of situationism remains vibrant even today, with scholars suggesting that situations, and not personal traits, are more important in influencing prosocial behavior (Lefevor *et al.*, 2017).

As per the situationism theory, individual behavior is highly situation-specific, and response patterns of behavior can be causally linked to stimuli present in the environment (Bowers, 1973). A situation is a context that is external to the respective phenomenon and enable or constrain it and affect individual behavior (Welter, 2011). For instance, while a layperson may view an individual as "honest," a situationist might say that telling the truth is under the control of the situation or circumstances in which it occurs (Bowers, 1973). Situationism deals with the "where" context (e.g. the country context in which a particular theory is applied) (Welter, 2011).

Situationism theory ties back to the experimental paradigm in social psychology with famous socio-psychological experiments like the Honesty Experiment and the Milgram Experiment demonstrating the influence of situational variations on human behavior, especially radical human behaviors (Kristjánsson, 2012). In the social psychology literature, various situational variables have been examined — incentive for advocacy, hurry, number of onlookers, proximation of authority, etc., and how these variables influence behaviors such as attitude repor, bystander interventions, and obedience, respectively (Funder and Ozer, 1983; Darley and Latane, 1968). For example, the number of onlookers can inversely affect bystander intervention, i.e. the more the number of onlookers in a crisis situation, the less the help expected from a potential helper (Funder and Ozer, 1983). Similarly, the behavior of obedience or defiance was found to be influenced by a situational variable, namely, proximity of the commanding authority to the subject in the Milgram experiments (Milgram, 1974a; Milgram, 1974b). In the entrepreneurship literature, situational theories have been emerging which showcase the influence of entrepreneurial ecosystems (Spigel, 2017) or other situational contexts which influence new venturing (Welter, 2011). However, situational variables and their influence in evoking social entrepreneurial behaviors have received scant attention in the entrepreneurship literature.

To address the breach, we draw on two situational variables. The first is being well informed about CSR activities of corporations that influence individual philanthropy, which can increase the likelihood of individual-level engagement in social entrepreneurship. The second is the perception of positive corporate influence on society, which can give rise to bystander apathy that deter individual-level engagement in social entrepreneurship.

In this chapter, we equate the "situation" to the entrepreneurial ecosystem that encompasses physical conditions, circumstances, social norms, and attitudes within a country. Within entrepreneurial ecosystems, individuals create social ventures around opportunities derived from societal problems such as poverty, healthcare, energy, private education, and water purification (Zahra et al., 2014). These social ventures often work side by side or in partnerships with not-for-profit, government agencies, community organizations, and NGOs in delivering their products and services. Successful commercial companies often use the resources of social ventures to address social issues or needs of particular interest to them (e.g. providing education and schooling infrastructure for children in remote areas) (Zahra et al., 2008, 2009).

Research on social entrepreneurship has rapidly gained traction (Estrin et al., 2013) and new insights are emerging on the "what" and "how" of individual-level motivation as an antecedent to becoming a social entrepreneur. Germak and Robinson (2014), through interviews with self-identified nascent social entrepreneurs in the US, found that personal fulfillment, helping others, non-monetary focus, achievement orientation, and closeness to social problems were key drivers of social entrepreneurial activity for individuals. On the other hand, Christopoulos and Vogl (2015) focused on the need for social entrepreneurs to play multiple roles — such as economic, political, and civic agents — with each role having its own relevance to the various tenets of social entrepreneurship, including provision of innovative solutions to economic problems, maximization of public utility, or enhancement of social welfare.

Because ecosystem factors influence entrepreneurial engagement (Acs et al., 2014b), the Kauffman Foundation (Auerswald, 2014) suggests that policies and regulations that have different effects on incumbent corporations and new entrepreneurial ventures should be better understood. Along these lines, there has been an emerging stream of research examining the influence of informal institutional factors like cultural and social determinants in studying social entrepreneurship intentions and activities. We strive to join that conversation using the situationism theory in the realm of social entrepreneurship. Hechavarria et al. (2017) considered the role of a national-level variable, culture (e.g. post-materialism), and gender as antecedents to entrepreneurs' value-creation goals — be they economic, social, or environmental. Witte (2013) examined the fear of failure at the individual level, and factors such as confidence in public sector at the national level, as cultural determinants of social entrepreneurship. These studies demonstrate the importance of situational variables that drive social entrepreneurial behaviors in individuals.

8.3. Hypotheses Development

8.3.1. *Situationism and perception of being adequately informed (activation of the community through information)*

Within an opportunity-centric view of entrepreneurship (Alvarez and Barney, 2007), an aspiring social entrepreneur shapes a social enterprise opportunity through affective and cognitive processes when he or she identifies an unmet social need, with the goal of developing an innovative solution to create social value (Yitshaki and Kropp, 2016). To recognize an opportunity, the entrepreneur needs access to special information and knowledge. Entrepreneurs take action based on opportunity perception as well as the perceptions of being adequately informed about potential opportunities.

Just as the core insight of situationism theory is that individuals do not act in a vacuum but are influenced by their context, so it is argued here that certain external stimuli that activates a community can empower and spur individuals to engage in social actions. One way to activate the citizens of a country is by providing information about the social activities being carried out by the corporations in that country to create awareness and knowledge in the individuals about social activities or prevalent social needs. Societal expectations about access to CSR initiatives originate from a growing number of interest groups, including shareholders, employees, governments, NGOs, consumers, and local communities in which these businesses operate.

In the existing literature, the impact of CSR-related information has been examined in the context of investors, board of directors, and governments (UNCTAD, 2003). However, the influence of CSR-related disclosure on the general public has not yet been formally investigated. Such an investigation is required as the scope of CSR encompasses the direct effects of companies' actions *and* the spillover effects they may have on society; in this chapter, we are addressing the latter topic.

Different stakeholders (e.g. investors, employees, consumers, NGOs, etc.) perceive CSR information in different ways. It is argued here that the individual citizens in a country will view CSR-related information in two ways. First, information about social activities carried out by corporations legitimizes those activities and problem areas in the mind of the recipient, and second, the information creates entrepreneurship-related knowledge and awareness or "knowledge spillover" to the recipient. The concept of knowledge spillover is linked rather narrowly to technology-related regional social networks (Owen-Smith and Powell, 2004; Acs and Varga, 2005). However, if the dissemination of knowledge is to all the citizens of a country, then the knowledge spillover effect could be applied more broadly to national levels of analysis. By extension, the dissemination of information on prosocial activity (Stephan et al., 2016) by corporations to the wider public might also provide both "legitimation" and "knowledge spillover" to potential social entrepreneurs.

Knowledge of CSR activities may provide *legitimacy* to social entrepreneurship. Specifically, receipt of information on socially responsible activities (e.g. through CSR reports, media reporting on national socially responsible awards) can trigger recognition of the social value of prosocial interventions, social acclaim associated with such social welfare activities, and more importantly, the areas that need such interventions. These, in turn, acknowledge and confer normative legitimacy to the social problems and needs within which potential social entrepreneurs are embedded (Jack and Anderson, 2002).

We argue that knowledge of CSR activities may provide *knowledge spillover* to social entrepreneurship in several ways. Socially responsible information can contain information about social needs, about potential resources — key potential stakeholders such as potential influencers and partners — and about viable social business models. Equipped with such knowledge, an individual will be more likely to recognize social opportunities and feel empowered to take actions. Socially responsible information also may include requests for open inquiry or tender from companies or individuals to fulfill the gap in expertise or skills in implementing prosocial projects.

In addition, we reason that commercial companies often use the resources of social ventures if they lack the necessary skills or expertise to address social issues or needs of particular interest to them and/or to burnish their corporate reputation by association (see Zahra *et al.*, 2008 for examples). Clear information pertaining to these by the existing corporations can reduce information asymmetry between aspiring social entrepreneurs and the gaps in existing socially responsible activities and subsequently help potential social entrepreneurs shape prosocial opportunities, either in partnership with corporations, or by filling gaps in provision.

For example, Steel Authority of India Limited, a company in India recently reported in its CSR report that it has provided access to water infrastructure to people living in far-flung areas by installing 5,153 water sources, thereby providing drinking water access to 4 million people. In addition, each of the company's plant ensured that villages within the radius of approximately 10–12 miles of its township has access to potable water.

Such advocacy for providing drinking water in the remote areas of developing nations can have several outcomes: first, the information establishes the fact that non-availability of drinking water in the rural areas is a genuine social need that should be addressed. This information promotes detection and seizing of viable social opportunities by the aspiring social entrepreneurs. Second, the fact that large and established corporations are engaging in this activity implies that the existing social innovation model, including the infrastructural design and processes used for providing potable water for human consumption, could be replicated in other areas where drinking water is not available. Third, interested individuals can seek help and support from the said corporations and enter into a contract with them to address these special needs in remote areas. Fourth, addressing this particular need can be a viable social opportunity with the potential to generate greater social return (e.g. satisfaction in helping others in need) to an individual than private returns in terms of monetary gains.

The desirability and feasibility of a social entrepreneurial action by individuals may be increased through the mechanisms of legitimation and knowledge spillover, and therefore dissemination of CSR activities. Being informed is the notion of being primed through activation of the knowledge structures in the individual citizens through the information about social responsible activities that the corporations disseminate to the public (Garcia et al., 2002). In this regard, the importance of information will depend on various factors such as whether the semantic content allows an individual to elaborate propositional knowledge (Floridi, 2006). The behavior of an individual encompasses the situation wherein the individual construes, interprets, and transforms the stimulus in a dynamic reciprocal interaction with the social world (Mischel, 1968). Hence, we argue that a society that feels positively informed about CSR of companies will trigger and empower individuals therein to engage in social entrepreneurial activities (Figure 8.1).

Generalizing,

H1: The more positive the societal attitudes about being informed of socially responsible activities of established companies in a country, the higher the likelihood of individual-level SE.

8.3.2. *Situationism and bystander apathy effect (deactivation of the community)*

As seen earlier, the information disclosure by corporations about their CSR activities create an impact on society, which can invoke voluntary commitment to address the social needs by individuals. CSR information disclosure by corporations act as a mechanism to manage social perceptions and expectations on the social role and utility of a business in a society beyond its core function of selling commodities at a profit (Wang et al., 2016). Being informed about what companies do to behave responsibly can trigger individuals to engage in social entrepreneurship. However, individual citizens' actions are influenced by the presence of others who might be

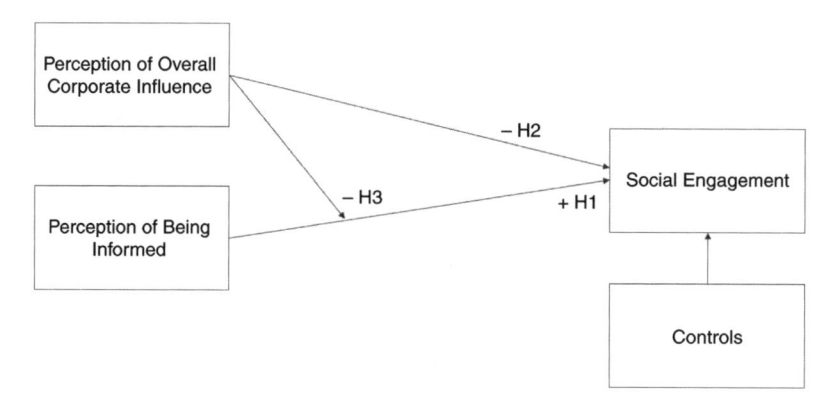

Figure 8.1. Hypothesized model.

better endowed to meet the needs of the society than they can. In social psychology, the bystander apathy effect has been developed to explain the individual-level phenomenon in which a potential helper in a situation where others are present and available to help, is slower and less likely to help than a person who knows that he or she is the only one aware of the distress (Darley and Latane, 1968; Garcia et al., 2002; Latané and Darley, 1970).

The literature describes three possible explanations of the bystander effect. The first is referred to as pluralistic ignorance — i.e. the thought that if others are not helping, then probably help is not needed (Prentice and Miller, 1996). This assumption explains why, for instance, in an emergency situation, if other people appear calm and are just standing around, then the individual might assume that help has already been given, or help has been solicited and is on the way, or maybe the situation is not an actual emergency. The second explanation refers to the fear of standing out, making a mistake, or overblowing the situation (Prentice and Miller, 1996). It has been reasoned that humans have a strong instinct not to stand out from the crowd, especially if they perceive that the action that needs to be taken is already the responsibility of another, more legitimate actor that is already present (Garcia et al., 2012). Finally, the third possible explanation is that each individual feels less compelled and responsible to help as the number of onlookers increases (Darley and Latane, 1968).

It has been observed that most of the situational studies have been conducted in the context of emergency or crisis situations (Bowers, 1973; Darley and Latane, 1968). However, as Garcia et al.'s (2002) study asserts, bystander apathy effects can occur even in a "non-situational" instance; it is not mandatory that an emergency situation or any other situation in which immediate help from others is required. In such a non-situational case, the authors found that it is possible to affect social perception and behavior by activating individuals' knowledge regarding the presence of others, which in turn leads to an implicit bystander apathy effect as suggested by research on priming (Garcia et al., 2012).

Drawing from this literature, we argue that interested individuals who are aware of a high prevalence of positive activities by corporations for society around them may be inhibited from engaging in prosocial behavior themselves. In the case of prosocial activity, within societies where corporations are perceived as a force for good in society, the additional resources available to corporations and their greater legitimacy as institutions (Zahra et al., 2014) increases the likelihood of occurrence of this phenomenon. In such societies, individuals may be more likely to believe that others who are better equipped to address social needs than them are already doing so. Garcia et al. (2002) found that the bystander apathy effect does not depend on the calculational effort (calculations pertaining to the presence of other persons who might help) but rather it is one that can be brought about by priming the individual about the presence of groups and the resulting mental state that is induced.

Prior research has established that social attitudes toward entrepreneurship, manifested in both formal and informal institutions, affect the propensity to act entrepreneurially (Hechavarria, 2016, Simmons *et al.*, 2014). The differences in the prevalence of social entrepreneurship across countries can be attributed to the prevalent situation dependent on both formal and informal institutions that encompass the economic, political, social, and cultural environment of the area (Pelucha *et al.*, 2017). In a study investigating the link between national culture and venture performance, Laskovaia *et al.* (2017) elaborated on how national culture influences entrepreneurship through individual-centric, collective, and societal mechanisms.

The third mechanism — societal — is understood to work through formal and informal institutions that are based on cultural norms and behavioral patterns. Informal institutions, cultural norms (Hoogendoorn, 2016), and social institutions such as family and religion have been found to positively relate to collectivism, which, in turn, decrease the prevalence of social entrepreneurship (Hartog and Hoogendoorn, 2011). Stephan *et al.* (2015) carried out an empirical study examining the effects of both formal and informal institutions on social entrepreneurship across countries. Within the boundary of informal institutions, cognitive institutional context represented by post-materialism as an aggregate cultural value of a country's population was found to influence social entrepreneurship. More specifically, they argued that citizens of a country are more likely to engage in social entrepreneurship when there is a greater social need and demand, and when post-materialism is high. Additionally, socially supportive cultural (SSC) norms were found to be positively correlated with social entrepreneurship.

In another study, Stephan and Uhlaner (2010) focused on cultural practices and how they influence entrepreneurship, specifically by analyzing national-level aggregates to investigate the relationship between "socially supportive culture" and "performance-based culture" to tease out the national-level entrepreneurship rates. Autio *et al.* (2013) replicated and built on Stephan and Uhlaner's (2010) study to examine the effect of macro-level factors on micro-level individual behaviors through the conceptualization of entrepreneurship as a fundamentally individual-level endeavor. The macro-level factors they investigated were the three societal-level constructs of institutional collectivism, uncertainty avoidance, and performance orientation.

Similar to culture, societal attitudes can be viewed as informal institutions that denote common patterns of shared beliefs and attitudes that impact individual-level behavior. As Stephan and Uhlaner (2010) showed that culture shapes the decision-making logic and behaviors of individuals, so can we argue that societal attitudes can mold an individual's decision to engage in social entrepreneurship activity. Qureshi *et al.* (2016) used the lens of social network theory to understand the growth of social entrepreneurship in China and found that entrepreneurs who are associated with more pluralistic networks are more likely to reject conformism and act innovatively. Hoogendoorn (2016) found that an institutional void (defined as limited government support for social programs) spurred individuals to become social entrepreneurs.

This provides validation of our argument that when citizens of a country perceive corporations to have a positive impact on society, these citizens could assume all social needs and problems being taken care of by these corporations. If people in a society feel that companies are a negative force in society, they could be more likely to perceive opportunities to solve the social problems, i.e. to believe that since it is unlikely that corporations will solve the problems, then they must do so themselves. In short, it is possible that societal perceptions that corporations are having an overall positive effect on society can inculcate false assurance to the individual citizens that social needs are being taken care of adequately, which, in turn, might prevent individuals from addressing unmet social needs.

Generalizing,

H2: The more positive the societal attitude about the overall influence of established companies on society, the lower the likelihood of individual-level SE.

In an entrepreneurial ecosystem, societal attitudes coexist and will have balancing or counterbalancing effects on entrepreneurial engagement. In this case, we suspect that the bystander effect from the perception of positive corporate influence may weaken the positive effects of "being informed" of the CSR activities of companies. Generalizing,

H3: Societal attitudes about the overall influence of established companies on society negatively moderates the effects of being informed on individual-level SE such that the lower the overall corporate influence, the stronger the effect of being informed.

8.4. Data and Method

8.4.1. *Research design and sample*

To test our hypotheses, we constructed a unique dataset built from the Global Entrepreneurship Monitor (GEM) 2015, and the European Union Flash Barometer (Flash EB) 363 of 2012. The GEM Project is an ongoing cross-national study of the entrepreneurial intentions, attitudes, and activities of a random sample of the population in study countries (Kwon and Arenius, 2010). Table 8.1 provides a list of the 26 countries included and details of the sample. The Flash EB measures the entrepreneurial mindsets of individuals in a country. Our final sample has 85,958 GEM respondents across 26 countries.

Table 8.1. Sample size and focal variable statistics by country.

Country	Total sample size	CSR informed	Corporate influence
Belgium	2020	−0.46	0.16
Brazil	1991	0.13	0.74
Bulgaria	1984	−0.46	0.03
China	3286	−0.81	0.42
Croatia	1981	−0.24	−0.61
Estonia	1975	−0.42	0.58
Finland	1991	0.01	0.83
Germany	3794	−0.22	0.17
Greece	2000	−0.59	−0.35
Hungary	1958	−0.15	−0.15
India	3378	0.51	0.69
Ireland	1959	−0.29	0.38
Israel	1988	−0.45	−0.01
Italy	1990	−0.36	−0.29
Latvia	1999	−0.53	0.27
Luxembourg	1929	−0.26	0.51
Netherlands	1745	0.03	0.61
Poland	1855	−0.46	0.21
Portugal	2002	−0.22	0.36
Romania	1996	−0.38	0.02
Slovakia	1968	−0.33	0.02
Slovenia	1980	−0.2	−0.33
Spain	24242	−0.73	0.09
Sweden	3610	−0.01	0.6
UK	7719	−0.24	0.16
US	2618	0.38	0.28

8.4.2. *Variables and measures*

Dependent Variable: *Entrepreneurial Activity with a Social, Environmental or Community Objective*. The dependent variable is constructed from the GEM study. Respondents were asked the question "are you, alone or with others, currently trying to start or currently leading any kind of activity, organization or initiative that has a particularly social, environmental or community objective? This might include providing services or training to socially deprived or disabled persons, activities aimed at reducing pollution or food-waste, organizing self-help groups for community action, etc." The dependent measure is a dichotomous variable (with 1 = intentions to start or have already started an entrepreneurial activity with a social, environmental, or community objective).

Independent Variable: Informed about socially responsible activities of established companies. Our first independent variable is a perceptual measure from the Flash EB, aggregated at the national level, of how informed individuals feel about socially responsible activities of established companies in a country. We use the following question from the Flash EB 363: "Do you feel very well informed/fairly well informed/not very well informed/not at all informed about what companies do to behave responsibly towards society in your country?" The response choices were from "very well informed," "fairly well informed," "not very well informed," and "not well informed at all," which we respectively assigned scores of 2, 1, −1, and −2. We reverse-coded the response categories such that a highly positive perception of overall corporate influence had higher scores. Finally, we calculated a single score per question at the national level by multiplying each scale score for the four categories with the respective percentage of responses and aggregating them up (Simmons *et al.*, 2014).

Independent Variable: Corporate Influence. Our second independent variable and moderator is a perceptual measure aggregated at the national level that pertains to citizen perceptions of the overall influence of companies in society. This variable consists of the question: "Do you think that the overall influence of companies on society in your country is very positive, somewhat positive, somewhat negative or very negative?" The response choices were from "very positive" to "very negative" on a scale from −2 to 2. We reverse-coded the response categories such that a highly positive perception of overall corporate influence had higher scores. Finally, we calculated a single score per question at the national level by multiplying each scale score for the four categories with the respective percentage of responses and aggregating them up (Simmons *et al.*, 2014).

Control variables: To strengthen our results, we controlled for several individual-level variables drawn from the GEM 2015 dataset. An individual's age, gender, and educational attainment (Arenius and Minniti, 2005) have been found to influence their propensity to engage in entrepreneurship. At the national level, we controlled for GDP per capita, GDP per capita growth, and Total Early-Stage Entrepreneurial Activity (TEA). GDP and GDP per capita growth have been used as proxies for the availability of growth opportunities (Simmons *et al.*, 2014).

8.4.3. *Descriptive statistics*

The descriptive statistics and correlations are shown in Table 8.2. The resulting sample consists of 85,958 individual respondents from 26 countries. Among these, 42,727 are males (49.71%) and 43,231 are females (50.29%). Their age ranged from 18–64

Table 8.2. Descriptive statistics.

Variable	Mean	S. D.	Min	Max	1	2	3	4	5	6	7	8
1. CSR informed	−0.366	0.34	−0.81	0.51	1.00	—	—	—	—	—	—	—
2. Corporate influence	0.19	0.30	−0.61	0.83	0.44*	1.00	—	—	—	—	—	—
3. Age	41.4	13.1	18	64	−0.064*	−0.05*	1.00	—	—	—	—	—
4. Education	0.76	0.42	0	1	0.014*	−0.002	−0.14*	1.00	—	—	—	—
5. Gender	0.50	0.50	0	1	0.001	0.004	−0.021*	0.014*	1.00	—	—	—
6. GDP per capita	0.34	0.19	0.04	1.02	0.09*	0.203*	0.047*	0.10*	0.003	1.00	—	—
7. GDP per capita growth	−3.05	3.97	−12.9	8.7	0.09*	0.442*	−0.069*	−0.07*	0.003	−0.19*	1.00	—
8. Involve in TEA	0.079	0.269	0	1	0.047*	0.06*	−0.06*	0.05*	0.06*	−0.032	0.048*	1.00

Note: N = 85,958 (Breakdown by gender: Males = 42,727 and Females = 43,231).
*p<0.05.

years. The education level of 75.84% (65,187) respondents are secondary education and higher, while the remaining 24.16% do not have a secondary education.

8.4.4. *Mixed logit regression models*

As the dependent variable was binary and at the individual level of analysis, and the explanatory variables were at the national level, we validated the research hypotheses using multilevel logistic regression models (melogit function in the Stata 14.2) for fitting mixed-effects models for binary/binomial responses. The multilevel model estimated a random intercept for the Level 2 country variables and fixed effects for the explanatory covariates. This multilevel approach could take into account cross-level interactions used in the study. The estimation technique facilitated the nesting of the individual-level decisions of the entrepreneurs within the context of national-level variables and the examination of the effects across levels (Guo and Zhao, 2000).

We estimated the models using adaptive quadrature with nine integration points. The equation for the null model is described in Equation (8.1), where the intercept β_0 is shared by all 26 country contexts and the random effect u_{oj} is specific to the country j. The random effect is assumed to follow a normal distribution with the expected value 0 and the variance σ^2_{uo}:

$$\log [p_{ij}/(1 - p_{ij})] = \beta_0 + u_{oj} \tag{8.1}$$

Table 8.3. Regression results.

DV = Social	Model 1	Model 2	Model 3	Model 4
Control Variables				
Age	—	1.001 (0.001)	1.0 (0.001)	1.0 (0.001)
Gender	—	1.073 (0.046)	1.067 (0.048)	1.067 (0.048)
Education	—	1.829*** (0.211)	1.837*** (0.218)	1.837*** (0.218)
GDP per capita	—	2.592* (0.002)	3.313* (1.64)	2.318* (0.977)
GDP per capita growth	—	1.023 (0.027)	1.053* (0.026)	1.053* (0.025)
TEA (Total Early-stage Entrepreneurial Activity)	—	3.322*** (0.334)	3.301*** (0.35)	3.30*** (0.35)
Main effects				
CSR informed — H1	—	—	2.249* (0.969)	12.567*** (8.41)
Corporate influence — H2	—	—	0.52* (0.20)	0.204** (0.09)
Interaction effects				
CSR informed x Corporate influence — H3	—	—	—	0.012** (0.011)
Random Effects (Country)	—	—	—	—
Constant	0.066*** (0.009)	0.023*** (0.008)	0.036*** (0.013)	0.074*** (0.031)
ICC (Intra-Class Correlation Coefficient)	0.14 (0.032) or 14%	0.113 (0.035) or 11.3%	—	0.069 (0.022) or 6.9%
Wald Chi2	—	443.6***	603.58***	1999.36***
Log pseudo likelihood	−19239.11	−18655.79	−17471.74	−17,467.74
Number of observations	91,832	91,832	85,958	85,958
Number of groups	29	29	26	26

*$p<0.05$.
**$p<0.01$.
***$p<0.001$.

The null Model 1 in Table 8.3 suggests that social venturing intentions of the GEM respondents in the study vary significantly across countries. To check the suitability of a mixed model, we calculated the intra-block group correlation coefficient (ICC) using Equation (8.2), where p is the ICC coefficient, $\tau 00$ is the between country variance from level 2, and σ^2 is the level 1 variance fixed to the variance of a standard logistic distribution, $\sigma^2 = \pi 2/3 = 3.29$.

$$p = \tau 00/(\tau 00 + \sigma^2) \qquad (8.2)$$

The resulting ICC was 14% in the null model, which justifies the random effect or a mixed model analysis. The hypothesized model was more explanatory and parsimonious compared to the alternative models. The ICC indicates that variability in the dependent variable at the individual level behavior is accounted for by the national-level aggregated perceptions. The ICC for national-level variance predicting social behavior was 14%. The greater-than-zero ICCs for the dependent variable supported the assumptions that macro-level societal perceptions influence micro-level behaviors.

We introduced the controls in Model 2. While not hypothesized, it is worth noting the significant odds ratio for education (OR = 1.83, $p < 0.001$), GDP (OR = 2.5, $p < 0.001$), and TEA (OR = 3.32, $p < 0.001$). At the individual level, the odds ratio of 1.83 for education suggests that the odds of being engaged with social entrepreneurship activities for the citizens with post-secondary education is 1.83 times that of those citizens with no secondary education. At the national level, the odds ratio of 2.5 for GDP per capita implies that the odds of citizens engaging in social entrepreneurship activities is more likely to occur as the GDP increases. Hence, these ratios suggest that these variables play significant roles in citizens' intentions and/or decision to engage in entrepreneurship with a social goal.

8.5. Results

Hypothesis 1 states that the more positive the societal attitudes about being informed of socially responsible activities of established companies in a country, the greater the prevalence of individuals will engage in social entrepreneurial activity. From models 3 and 4 (Table 8.3), we find that the odds ratio of being informed about socially responsible activities of corporations is greater than 1 and significant (OR = 2.25, $p < 0.05$; and OR = 12.57, $p < 0.001$). Hypothesis 1 is supported.

Hypothesis 2 states that the more positive the societal attitude about the overall influence of established companies on society, the lower the prevalence of individuals engaging in social entrepreneurial activity. The lesser than 1 and significant odds ratio of overall corporate influence (OR = 0.52, $p < 0.05$; and OR = 0.204, $p < 0.01$) in models 3 and 4 imply that the odds of citizens of a country engaging in social entrepreneurial activities decrease as the perception of positive corporate influence on society increases. Hypothesis 2 is supported.

Hypothesis 3 states that societal attitudes about the overall influence of established companies on society negatively moderates the effects of perceptions about being informed of socially responsible corporate activities on social entrepreneurial activity. From model 4 (Table 8.3), we find that the odds ratio of the interaction term between corporate influence and being informed is less than 1 and significant (OR = 0.012, $p < 0.01$). To interpret the nature of the interaction, the relationship was plotted on a y-axis the individual-level likelihood of engaging in social entrepreneurship, and an x-axis of being informed about CSR activities of corporations. The nature of the interaction is illustrated in Figure 8.2. As can be

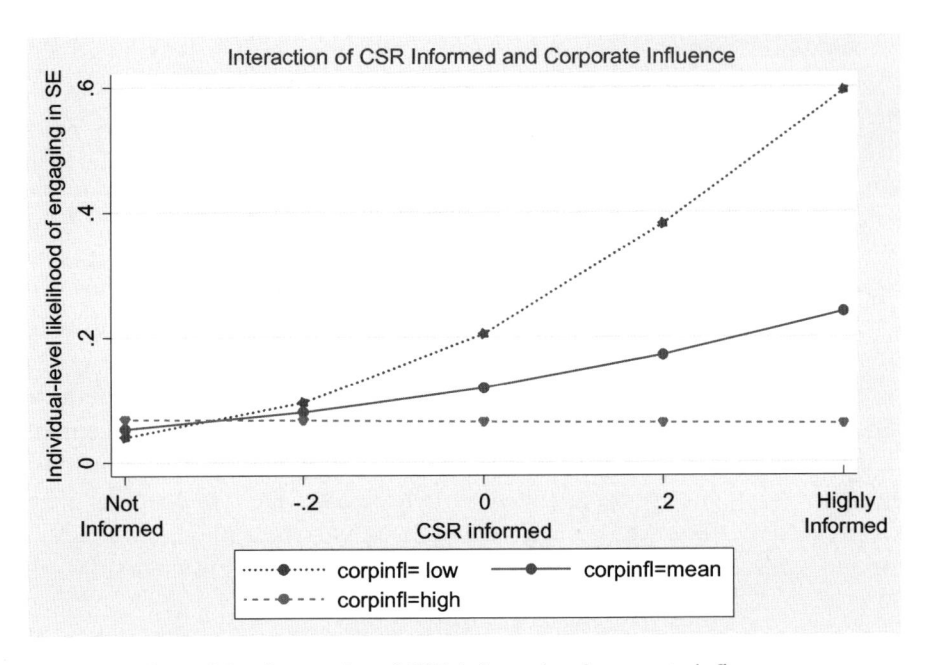

Figure 8.2. Interaction of CSR informed and corporate influence.

seen from the interaction plot (Figure 8.2), the slope between the likelihood of individuals engaging in social entrepreneurship and being informed significantly increases when corporate influence is low compared to when corporate influence is high. This finding supports hypothesis 3.

8.6. Discussion

As pointed out in the literature, the current trend is to measure and operationalize social impact in various ways such as "social performance," "environmental impact," and "environmental efficiency" (Rawhouser *et al.*, 2019), but the literature falls short when it comes understanding the effects of what society thinks of the CSR initiatives of corporations. To fill this gap, this study draws upon situationism theory to examine societal attitudes about corporate CSR activities at the national level and their influences at the individual-level engagement in social entrepreneurial activities.

We find that in countries where citizens feel adequately informed about socially responsible activities of the established corporations, individuals are more likely to engage in social entrepreneurship. This finding may suggest that keeping citizens informed of CSR activities may help to activate community engagement in social entrepreneurship. While our data does not allow prescriptive conclusions, we suspect that some of these effects may stem from the legitimization and created awareness of opportunities for social entrepreneurship.

We also find that in countries where citizens perceive the overall influence of corporations to be positive, there is evidence of a bystander apathy effect that might be associated with individuals being deterred from starting social entrepreneurial activity. We also find that this bystander effect may be more prevalent in societies where individuals feel more informed about corporate CSR activities. To overcome such bystander effects, careful targeting of socially responsible content, including messages on what more needs to be done, could help individuals to sense the need for their personal involvement and giving through social entrepreneurship.

Collectively, our study findings contribute to the growing stream of research that examines relationships between ecosystem framework conditions and individual agency in recognition and exploitation of entrepreneurial opportunities with a social purpose. Our study findings also illuminate the need for research on "national social entrepreneurial ecosystems" that complements the existing projects, such as the global entrepreneurship index, which focuses on the commercial entrepreneurship ecosystem and the mix of attitudes, resources, and infrastructure (GEDI). In short, if a culture of prosocial entrepreneurship is to be stimulated, then a better understanding of the social cues of corporate CSR activities and impact is needed. How these social cues are managed in an entrepreneurial ecosystem may determine whether individual entrepreneurs come forward to start social ventures (Stam, 2015).

8.7. Limitations and Future Research

This chapter attempted to examine the correlation between the spillover effects of CSR information disclosure to the general populations and its influence on individual behaviors in their decision to take up a social focus. The externalities of CSR information are still being debated upon (UNCTAD, 2003), as efforts are directed toward the content and method of dissemination of CSR information and reporting. Though the content of CSR information and the mode of its relay to the population is beyond the scope of this study, in future, research could be conducted to investigate the relationship between the content of CSR information and how it influences micro-level (individual) behaviors for engagement in social entrepreneurship by citizens of a country.

The present study establishes only correlations between societal perceptions and engagement or intentions to engage in social entrepreneurship. Our data did not allow for causal relationships to be established. Future studies can attempt to establish causal relationships through collection of longitudinal data. In this chapter, we used secondary data.

Growth of social entrepreneurship initiatives is urgently required in developing countries, which are fighting multiple dimensions of poverty and lack of basic necessities like access to safe drinking water, education to all, health services, hygiene, and sanitation. Local businesses as well as multinational companies undertake CSR activities in these developing countries to address poverty and unemployment and to increase the general quality of life. Various areas of development like environmental protection, philanthropy, urban development, and involvement in social causes such as human rights awareness and AIDS have been taken up by the established corporations in these countries.

In future research, it would be interesting to collect and analyze data from developing and underdeveloped nations, both about the transparency and accountability of corporations' social and environmental initiatives and about the present state of social entrepreneurship in those countries. CSR-related information, through stakeholder dialogues, can create conditions for better consultation and engagement of the general population. Further, CSR information can be an antidote to corruption by indirectly influencing governments to follow the same transparency and accountability in their governance systems.

Additionally, in our study, we only considered two focal variables related to being informed and overall corporate influence but did not take into account the cultural determinants (Hofstede, 1984) or specific country laws. Studies examining moderating effects of these factors can provide additional insights.

8.8. Conclusion

Macro-level ecosystem factors influence micro-level individual entrepreneurial behaviors. Societal attitudes and public opinion is a major component of the entrepreneurial ecosystem framework that can directly impact an individual's entrepreneurial behaviors, intentions, and actions. Our findings indicate that corporations play a crucial role in shaping an entrepreneurial ecosystem through the formation of public opinions and attitudes. These societal attitudes and perceptions, in turn, influence the individual citizens in their decisions to engage in social venturing.

We have examined CSR information disclosure in the context of corporations' direct impacts on society and how that can improve the enterprises' brand name and financial outcomes. However, it has not been formally hypothesized or tested whether CSR's scope also encompasses the spillover effects on the society, such as knowledge spillover, that can trigger individuals to launch into social entrepreneurship.

Our study demonstrates that companies' information about their corporate social activities can empower individual citizens by creating an environment where they naturally start making decisions for themselves in the context of social entrepreneurship activities. The CSR information disclosure can act as true empowerment for individuals leaving space, creating trust, and pointing out genuine gaps that someone else can rise to the challenges themselves.

References

Acs, Z. J., Estrin, S., Mickiewicz, T., & Szerb, L. (2014a). The continued search for the solow residual: The role of national entrepreneurial ecosystem. https://www.econstor.eu/bitstream/10419/106598/1/dp8652.pdf.

Acs, Z. J., Szerb, L., & Autio, E. (2014b). National systems of entrepreneurship: Measurement and policy implications. *Research Policy*, *43*(3), 476–494.

Acs, Z. J & Varga, A. (2005). Entrepreneurship, agglomeration and technological change. *Small Business Economics*, **24**(3), 323–334.

Acs, Z. J., Stam, E., Audretsch, D. B., & O'Connor, A. (2017). The lineages of the entrepreneurial ecosystem approach. *Small Business Economics*, 1–10.

Aguilera, R. V., Rupp, D. E., Williams, C. A., & Ganapathi, J. (2007). Putting the S back in corporate social responsibility: A multilevel theory of social change in organizations. *Academy of Management Review*, *32*(3), 836–863.

Alvarez, S. A., & Barney, J. B. (2007). Discovery and creation: Alternative theories of entrepreneurial action. *Strategic Entrepreneurship Journal*, *1*, 11–26.

Arenius, P., Minniti, M., 2005. Perceptual variables and nascent entrepreneurship. *Small Business Economics*, **24**(3), 233–247.

Auerswald, P. E. (2014). Enabling entrepreneurial ecosystems. *The Oxford Handbook of Local Competitiveness*. Oxford, UK: Oxford University Press, GMU School of Public Policy Research Paper (3).

Autio, E., Pathak, S., & Wennberg, K. (2013). Consequences of cultural practices for entrepreneurial behaviors. *Journal of International Business Studies*, *44*(4), 334–362.

Autio, E., & Thomas, L. (2014). *Innovation ecosystems*. The Oxford handbook of innovation management, pp. 204-288.

Balasubramanian, N. K., Kimber, D., & Siemensma, F. (2005). Emerging opportunities or traditions reinforced? An analysis of the attitudes towards CSR, and trends of thinking about CSR, in India. *Journal of Corporate Citizenship*, *17*, 79–92.

Barney, J. B. (2001). Resource-based theories of competitive advantage: A ten-year retrospective on the resource-based view. *Journal of Management*, *27*(6), 643–650.

Baumol, W. J. (1990). Entrepreneurship: Productive, unproductive, and destructive. *Journal of Political Economy*, *98*, 893–921.

Baumol, W. J. (1996). Entrepreneurship: Productive, unproductive, and destructive. *Journal of Business Venturing*, *11*(1), 3–22.

Bowers, K. S. (1973). Situationism in psychology: An analysis and a critique. *Psychological Review*, **80**(5), 307.

Carroll, A. B. (1991). The pyramid of corporate social responsibility: Toward the moral management of organizational stakeholders. *Business Horizons*, *34*(4), 39–48.

Cavazos-Arroyo, J., Puete-Diaz, R. & Agarwal, N. (2017). An examination of certain antecedents of social entrepreneurial intentions among Mexico residents. *Revista Brasileira De Gestão De Negócios*, **19**(64), 180–199.

Christopoulos, D., & Vogl, S. (2015). The motivation of social entrepreneurs: The roles, agendas and relations of altruistic economic actors. *Journal of Social Entrepreneurship*, **6**(1), 1–30.

Chung, C. (2014). *Lighting the Way: A Report on the Social Enterprise Landscape in Morocco* (London: Social Enterprise UK).

Cohen, B. (2006). Sustainable valley entrepreneurial ecosystems. *Business Strategy and the Environment*, **15**(1), 1–14.

Darley, J. M., & Latane, B. (1968). Bystander intervention in emergencies: Diffusion of responsibility. *Journal of Personality and Social Psychology*, **8**, 377.

Estrin, S., Michiewicz, T., & Stephan, U. (2013). Entrepreneurship, social capital, and institutions: Social and commercial entrepreneurship across nations. *Entrepreneurship Theory & Practice*, **37**, 479–504.

Estrin, S., Mickiewicz, T. and Stephan, U. (2016). Human capital in social and commercial entrepreneurship. *Journal of Business Venturing*, **31**, 449–467.

Feld, B. (2012). *Startup Communities: Building an Entrepreneurial Ecosystem in Your City* (Colorado, Boulder: Wiley).

Floridi, L. (2006). The logic of being informed. *Logique Et Analyse*, **49**(196), Nouvelle Serie, 433–460.

Funder, D. C., & Ozer, D. J. (1983). Behavior as a function of the situation. *Journal of Personality and Social Psychology*, **44**(1), 107–112.

Garcia, S. M., Weaver, K., Moskowitz, G. B., & Darley, J. M. (2002). Crowded minds: the implicit bystander effect. *Journal of Personality and Social Psychology*, **83**(4), 843.

Gartner, W. B. (1988). "Who is an entrepreneur?" is the wrong question. *American Journal of Small Business*, **12**(4), 11–32.

Gartner, W. B. (1989). Some suggestions for research on entrepreneurial traits and characteristics, *Entrepreneurship Theory and Practice*, **14**(1), 27–37.

The Global Entrepreneurship and Development Institute. Available at: https://thegedi.org/global-entrepreneurship-and-development-index/.

Germak, A. J., & Robinson, J. A. (2014). Exploring the motivation of nascent social entrepreneurs. *Journal of Social Entrepreneurship*, **5**(1), 5–21.

Grant, A. M., & Rothbard, N. P. (2013). When in doubt, seize the day? Security values, prosocial values, and proactivity under ambiguity. *Journal of Applied Psychology*, **98**(5), 810.

Guo, G., Zhao, H. 2000. Multilevel modeling for binary data. *Annual Review of Sociology*, **26**, 441–462.

Hartog, C., & Hoogendoorn, B. (2011). Prevalence and determinants of social entrepreneurship at the macro-level. EIM Business and Policy Research No. H201022.

Hayek, F. A. (1945). The use of knowledge in society. *The American economic review*, **35**(4), 519–530.

Hechavarria, D. M. (2016). The impact of culture on national prevalence rates of social and commercial entrepreneurship. *International Entrepreneurship and Management Journal*, **12**(4), 1025–1052.

Hechavarría, D. M., Terjesen, S. A., Ingram, A. E., Renko, M., Justo, R., & Elam, A. (2017). Taking care of business: The impact of culture and gender on entrepreneurs' blended value creation goals. *Small Business Economics*, **48**(1), 225–257.

Herdova, M., & Kearns, S. (2017). This is a tricky situation: Situationism and reasons-Responsiveness. *The Journal of Ethics*, **21**(2), 151–183.

Hofstede, G. (1984). *Culture's consequences: International differences in work-related values* (Vol. 5). sage.

Hoogendoorn, B. (2016). The prevalence and determinants of social entrepreneurship at the macro level. *Journal of Small Business Management*, **54**, 278–296.

Isenberg, D. J. (2010). How to start an entrepreneurial revolution. *Harvard Business Review*, **88**(6), 40–50.

Isenberg, D. (2011). The entrepreneurship ecosystem strategy as a new paradigm for economic policy: Principles for cultivating entrepreneurship. Institute of International European Affairs, Dublin, Ireland.

Jack, S. L., & Anderson, A. R. (2002). The effects of embeddedness on the entrepreneurial process. *Journal of business Venturing*, **17**(5), 467-487.

Jamali, D., Karam, C., Yin, J., & Soundararajan, V. (2017). CSR logics in developing countries: Translation, adaptation and stalled development. *Journal of World Business*, **52**(3), 343–359.

Jenkins, H. (2006). Small business champions for corporate social responsibility. *Journal of Business Ethics*, **67**(3), 241–256.

Kabia, M., Goodall, K., & Ross, R. (2016). From the ground up: Defining social enterprise systems in the U.S. Available at: https://halcyonhouse.org/sites/default/files/2016_seer_report.pdf [halcyonhouse.org]. Last Accessed February 26, 2021.

Karam, C. M., & Jamali, D. (2017). A cross-cultural and feminist perspective on CSR in developing countries: Uncovering latent power dynamics. *Journal of Business Ethics*, **142**(3), 461–477.

Kristjánsson, K. (2012). Situationism and the concept of a situation. *European Journal of Philosophy*, **20**(S1).

Kwon, S. W., & Arenius, P. (2010). Nations of entrepreneurs: A social capital perspective. *Journal of Business Venturing*, **25**(3), 315–330.

Laskovaia, A., Shirokova, G., & Morris, M. H. (2017). National culture, effectuation, and new venture performance: global evidence from student entrepreneurs. *Small Business Economics*, **49**(3), 687–709.

Latané, B., & Darley, J. (1970). *The Unresponsive Bystander* (New York: Appleton-Century Crofts).

Lefevor, G. T., Fowers, B. J., Ahn, S., Lang, S. F., & Cohen, L. M. (2017). To what degree do situational influences explain spontaneous helping behaviour? A meta-analysis. *European Review of Social Psychology*, **28**(1), 227–256.

Lumpkin, G. T., Moss, T. W., Gras, D. M., Kato, S., & Amezcua, A. S. (2013). Entrepreneurial processes in social contexts: how are they different, if at all? *Small Business Economics*, **40**(3), 761–783.

Milgram, S. (1974a). *Obedience to authority: An experimental view*. (New York, NY: Harper & Row).

Milgram, S. (1974b). We are all obedient. *The Listener*, **99**, 567–568.

Mischel, W. (1968). *Personality and assessment*. (New York, NY: John Wiley & Sons, Inc.).

Mischel, W. (2013). *Personality and assessment*. (New York: Psychology Press).

Moore, J. F. (1993). Predators and prey: A new ecology of competition. *Harvard Business Review*, **71**(3), 75–83.

Owen-Smith, J., & Powell, W. (2004). Knowledge networks as channels and conduits: The effects of spillovers in the Boston biotechnology community. *Organization Science*, **15**(1), 5–21.

Pelucha, M., Kourilova, J., & Kveton, V. (2017). Barriers of social entrepreneurship development — A case study of the Czech Republic. *Journal of Social Entrepreneurship*, **8**(2), 129–148.

Prentice, D. A., & Miller, D. T. (1996). Pluralistic ignorance and the perpetuation of social norms by unwitting actors. *Advances in Experimental Social Psychology*, **28**, 161–209.

Qureshi, I., Kistruck, G. M., & Bhatt, B. (2016). The enabling and constraining effects of social ties in the process of institutional entrepreneurship. *Organization Studies*, **37**(3), 425–447.

Rawhouser, H., Cummings, M., & Newbert, S. L. (2019). Social impact measurement: Current approaches and future directions for social entrepreneurship research. *Entrepreneurship Theory and Practice*, **43**(1), 82–115.

Sarasvathy, S. D. (2001). Causation and effectuation: Toward a theoretical shift from economic inevitability to entrepreneurial contingency. *Academy of Management Review*, **26**(2), 243–263.

Shumate, M., Atouba, Y., Cooper, K.R. and Pilny, A. (2014). Two paths diverged: Examining the antecedents to social entrepreneurship. *Management Communication Quarterly*, **28**(3), 404–421.

Simmons, S. A., Wiklund, J., & Levie, J. (2014). Stigma and business failure: implications for entrepreneurs' career choices. *Small Business Economics*, **42**(3), 485–505.

Spigel, B. (2017). The relational organization of entrepreneurial ecosystems. *Entrepreneurship Theory & Practice,* **41**(1), 49–72.

Stam, E. (2015). Entrepreneurial ecosystems and regional policy: A sympathetic critique. *European Planning Studies*, **23**(9), 1759–1769.

Stephan, U., & Uhlaner, L. M. (2010). Performance-based vs socially supportive culture: A cross-national study of descriptive norms and entrepreneurship. *Journal of International Business Studies*, **41**(8), 1347–1364.

Stephan, U., Uhlaner, L.M. & Stride, C. (2015). Institutions and social entrepreneurship: The role of institutional voids, institutional support, and institutional configurations. *Journal of International Business Studies*, **46**, 308–331.

Stephan, U., Patterson, M., Kelly, C. and Mair, J. (2016). Organizations driving positive social change: A review and an integrative framework of change processes. *Journal of Management*, **42**(5), 1250–1281.

Swanson, D.L. (2014). *Embedding CSR into Corporate Culture: Challenging the Executive Mind* (London: Palgrave Macmillan).

United Nations Conference on Trade and Development. Available at: http://unctad.org/en/docs/iteteb20037_en.pdf [unctad.org]. Last Accessed February 26, 2021.

Villeneuve-Smith, F. & Temple, N. (2015). *State of Social Enterprise Survey 2015* (London: Social Enterprise UK).

Wang, H., Tong, L., Takeuchi, R., & George, G. (2016). Corporate social responsibility: An overview and new research directions thematic issue on corporate social responsibility. *Academy of Management Journal*, **59**(2), 534–544.

Welter, F. (2011). Contextualizing entrepreneurship—conceptual challenges and ways forward. *Entrepreneurship Theory and Practice*, **35**(1), 165–184.

Wennekers, S., Uhlaner, L., & Thurik, R. (2002). Entrepreneurship and its conditions: a macro perspective. *International Journal of Entrepreneurship Education (IJEE)*, **1**(1), 25–64.

Wirtz, M. & Volkmann, C. (2015). Do social business cities foster sustainable urban development? *Social Business*, **5**(2), 157–175.

Witte, C.T. (2013). Cultural Determinants of Social Entrepreneurship. Master's Thesis, Erasmus University Rotterdam, Rotterdam, The Netherlands.

Yitshaki, R., & Kropp, F. (2016). Motivations and opportunity recognition of social entrepreneurs. *Journal of Small Business Management*, **54**(2), 546–565.

Zahra, S. A., Rawhouser, H. N., Bhawe, N., Neubaum, D. O., & Hayton, J. C. (2008). Globalization of social entrepreneurship opportunities. *Strategic Entrepreneurship Journal*, **2**, 117–131.

Zahra, S. A., Gedajlovic, E., Neubaum, D. O., & Shulman, J. M. (2009). A typology of social entrepreneurs: Motives, search processes and ethical challenges. *Journal of Business Venturing*, **24**(5), 519–532.

Zahra, S., Newey, L. and Li, Y. (2014). On the frontiers: The implications of social entrepreneurship for international entrepreneurship. *Entrepreneurship: Theory and Practice*, **38**, 137–158.

Zimbardo, P. (1971). The Stanford Prison Experiment: A Simulation Study of the Psychology of Imprisonment. Stanford University, Stanford Digital Repository, Stanford.

© 2022 World Scientific Publishing Company
https://doi.org/10.1142/9789811248863_0009

Chapter 9

How Social Entrepreneurs' Metacognition Shapes Socioeconomic Change Toward Sustainability-as-Flourishing

Katrin Schaefer,[*,†,§] Patricia Doyle Corner[‡,¶] and Kate Kearins[†,∥]

[†]*Faculty of Business, Economics and Law, Auckland University of Technology, Auckland 1142, New Zealand*

[‡]*Faculty of Management, University of British Columbia, Kelowna BC V1V 1V7, Canada*

[§]*katrin.schaefer@posteo.nz*
[¶]*trish.corner@ubc.ca*
[∥]*kate.kearins@aut.ac.nz*

Abstract

Our empirical study explores how social entrepreneurs' metacognition — awareness and regulation of thoughts and feelings — affects the entrepreneurial process of social and environmental value creation that supports positive socioeconomic change toward sustainability-as-flourishing (defined below). We use an inductive design that yields patterns across five German cases of social entrepreneurship at different levels of analysis. Findings at the individual level reveal social entrepreneurs' metacognitive abilities facilitated awareness of discontent about

---

[*]Corresponding author.

social and environmental problems. These abilities included perspective-taking, empathy, suspending rushed judgment, seeing a bigger picture, and reducing ego-defensiveness. The discontent then activated a creative social entrepreneurial response. Findings at the enterprise level show how social entrepreneurs resolved conflicts with recalcitrant external stakeholders by calming stakeholders' anxieties and negativity. At a societal level, social entrepreneurs were shown to co-create change by consciously investing in and empowering external stakeholders. We induce theory that depicts how the individual, enterprise, and societal levels interact, thus drawing a more complete picture of the social and environmental value creation process. By considering entrepreneurs' metacognition, this study extends the predominant research focus from external, objective entrepreneurial phenomena to the internal, subjective dimension of social entrepreneurs. It offers insight into the process of how enterprises could potentially contribute to a flourishing future for humans and the planet.

Keywords: Social entrepreneurship; entrepreneurial value creation process; metacognition; self-awareness; self-regulation; sustainability-as-flourishing; socioeconomic change.

9.1. Introduction

Sustainability-as-flourishing is an aspirational vision of a possible future where humans and the planet thrive indefinitely (Ehrenfeld, 2008). The vision is seen to materialize through self-actualized individuals, positive relationships, prospering enterprises (Laszlo *et al.*, 2014), and a thriving Earth (Ehrenfeld and Hoffman, 2013). Scholars maintain advancing sustainability-as-flourishing requires profound socioeconomic change in society in general (Ehrenfeld and Hoffman, 2013; Moore, 2015), and in business in particular (Laszlo *et al.*, 2012; Schaefer *et al.*, 2015). But how might such profound change come about?

Social entrepreneurship has been discussed as a promising and useful business approach to bring about such change. Scholars suggest it can challenge the unsustainable status quo of modern society and collectively help engender socioeconomic change toward sustainability-as-flourishing (Haigh and Hoffman, 2014; Laszlo *et al.*, 2014). Previous work has praised social entrepreneurs for addressing societal problems innovatively, being unwilling to submit themselves to conventional economic beliefs, and seeing the bigger picture of unsustainable circumstances (Elkington and Hartigan, 2008). However, there has been little investigation into how such entrepreneurs are able to find creative, novel solutions; think unconventionally; challenge the status quo; and see societal problems from a wider perspective.

One suggestion is that metacognition may enable entrepreneurs to approach issues creatively. Scholars say metacognition helps entrepreneurs overcome habitual, no-longer-useful cognition, emotions, and behavior (Haynie and Shepherd, 2009; Haynie et al., 2010; Pavlovich and Corner, 2014). Metacognition — *awareness and regulation of patterns in thoughts and feelings* (Flavell, 1976; Shimamura, 2000) — is thus conjectured to be a mechanism that engenders more effective ways of thinking and decision-making in organizations (Kudesia, 2017). It supports entrepreneurs in solving various challenges that come with founding and growing responsible enterprises (Laszlo et al., 2014; Pavlovich and Corner, 2014) and enables socioeconomic change (Corner and Pavlovich, 2016). Unfortunately, empirical research on social entrepreneurship's potential to stimulate socioeconomic change has employed an external, objective perspective at the organizational and societal levels (Wry and Haugh, 2018) and focused on outwardly discernible facts and social entrepreneurs' *actions* to innovatively solve pressing problems (Dwivedi and Weerawardena, 2018).

The purpose of this research is to focus instead on the inner subjective world of individual social entrepreneurs. This focus has received little attention in the literature (Pavlovich and Corner, 2014), despite its promise to reveal how entrepreneurs identify creative solutions (Karp, 2006). In particular, social entrepreneurs' metacognition remains underexplored despite the fact that scholars identify metacognition as a key to creativity and innovation (Andriopoulos and Lewis, 2010; Lorenz et al., 2018) that ultimately can bring about societal change (Corner and Pavlovich, 2016).

The present study therefore develops a more complete and theoretically rich understanding of the role of social entrepreneurs' metacognition in the entrepreneurial process of generating socioeconomic transformation. In this chapter, we ask the research question, *how does social entrepreneurs' metacognition shape socioeconomic change toward sustainability-as-flourishing?* To explore this "how" question, we employed an inductive, theory-building, multiple-case study design. We selected five cases of social entrepreneurship that engendered socioeconomic change. Collected data included field interviews and supplemental secondary data (Eisenhardt, 1989).

This chapter contributes to the literature in three ways. First, it extends entrepreneurship research in general, and social entrepreneurship in particular, by offering a more comprehensive view of the process of socioeconomic change. Unlike other studies, it considers social entrepreneurs' metacognition as an internal, subjective human-centered factor that can ripple out and influence enterprises and, ultimately, industries and communities. Second, as an extension of this contribution, our work expands social entrepreneurship and wider sustainability research by applying a multilevel examination of how societal transformation can come about. There is limited research that links all three levels — individual, enterprise, societal — when examining the creation of change at the macrosocietal level (for an exception see Tracey *et al.*, 2011). Third, this study enriches the business and sustainability literature by empirically researching the components, such as social entrepreneurship, that might move us closer to the vision of sustainability-as-flourishing.

The chapter begins by reviewing the literature on sustainability-as-flourishing, metacognition, and social entrepreneurship. It then describes the inductive methodology we employ. Next, we identify three patterns that capture how social entrepreneurs' metacognition shaped the process of generating socioeconomic change. These patterns emerged at the levels of the individual social entrepreneur, the enterprise, and society. We conclude by discussing the process of how metacognition influenced change creation.

9.2. Background Literature

9.2.1. *Sustainability-as-flourishing*

The concept of sustainability-as-flourishing emerged in the strategic management and corporate sustainability literature (Grant, 2012; Laszlo *et al.*, 2012; Ehrenfeld and Hoffman, 2013; McGhee and Grant, 2016; Upward and Jones, 2016). The notion of flourishing may move us beyond simply surviving (Ehrenfeld, 2012), and, as such, may function as an inspiring societal aim and target of business strategy (Cooperrider and Fry, 2012; Grant, 2012; McGhee and Grant, 2016). Thus, the vision of sustainability-as-flourishing is seen to go beyond merely reducing social and environmental unsustainability discussed by most existing research (Grant, 2012; Haigh and Hoffman, 2014; Upward and Jones, 2016). It appears very pertinent at a time when the unsustainable state of the world can seem worrying, and for some frightening (Worldwatch Institute, 2017).

Creating the conditions for flourishing is seen to imply a holistic and fundamental shift for society at large and business in particular (Upward and Jones, 2016). It requires a profound change in our cultural — including business — beliefs and values (Upward and Jones, 2016) and ensuing actions. Scholars contend two important beliefs exist that undergird the possibility for sustainability-as-flourishing. The first belief is that authentic human behavior rests upon caring for ourselves, other humans, and the natural environment (Fromm, 1976; Ehrenfeld and Hoffman, 2013). Caring implicates being aware of our interrelationship with others and nature (Heidegger, 1996; Laszlo *et al.*, 2012). The second belief recognizes that the world functions as an integrated and dynamic system composed of many interconnected parts (Gladwin *et al.*, 1995; Collins and Kearins, 2010; Ehrenfeld and Hoffman, 2013). This understanding involves acknowledging that the physical economy and society are nested in, and reliant on, the ecological system that sustains life (Costanza *et al.*, 2013; Upward and Jones, 2016).

However, there is a tendency in our modern culture to adhere to habitual ways of thinking and acting that, in many cases, differ strongly from the two beliefs described above (Fromm, 1976; Senge and Krahnke, 2013). Psychology research has found that routinized ways of perceiving and acting are resistant to change because of the greatly automatic nature of thought processes (Haidt, 2001; Reynolds, 2006). The majority of thought processes, feelings, and ensuing actions flow habitually and reflexively without conscious awareness (Haidt, 2001; Reynolds, 2006). These ordinary cognitive processes have been, and continue to be, conditioned by individuals' social context (Anderson and Miller, 2003), including previous experiences in childhood, cultural norms, societal values, and assumptions. In other words, the "socio-cultural milieu" that individuals are embedded in (Haynie *et al.*, 2010) shapes their habitual perceptual filters and beliefs.

9.2.2. *Metacognition*

For individuals to overcome habitual cognition and associated emotions, psychology scholars currently recommend metacognition (Flavell, 1979; Ochsner *et al.*, 2002; Brown *et al.*, 2007). Formally, metacognition is defined as *awareness of cognitive content, cognitive processes, and related emotions, and regulation thereof* (Flavell, 1979; Shimamura, 2000). Put differently, metacognition signifies the introspective monitoring or knowledge of patterns in thoughts and thought processes (Nelson, 1996), and associated feelings (Ochsner *et al.*, 2002). It can facilitate non-habitual thoughts and the transformation of emotions (Ochsner *et al.*, 2002). Management research has referred to metacognition as "second-order thinking" that involves critical self-reflection to re-frame one's deep-seated assumptions (Lewis, 2000, p. 764). Across individuals, there is a spectrum of aptitudes in being aware of and regulating thought processes and feelings (Brown and Ryan, 2003; Haynie *et al.*, 2010). It is believed that individuals may enhance these aptitudes through practice over time (Brown and Ryan, 2003).

Conceptual knowledge is accumulating about how metacognition can give rise to metacognitive abilities that may support socioeconomic change (Corner and Pavlovich, 2016). For example, research shows that metacognition enables the pro-social ability to empathize with other beings (Vago and Silbersweig, 2012). Empathy and the ability to take others' perspectives is seen to enhance interpersonal skills (Brown *et al.*, 2007; Miller *et al.*, 2012) by enabling a "collaborative mind-set" (Williams, 2002) and finding "common ground for solution building" (Pavlovich and Krahnke, 2012). These capabilities are regarded as essential in co-creating large-scale generative change for a flourishing future (Waddock, 2013; Waddell et al., 2015). Similarly, metacognition can facilitate the capability to take a more complex, systems view (Brown, 2012; Senge and Krahnke, 2013). Seeing the bigger picture of a large dynamic system can, in turn, enable identifying the root causes of social and environmental problems, instead of just looking at the mere symptoms (Ehrenfeld and Hoffman, 2013; Senge and Krahnke, 2013). Therefore, in this chapter, we argue that metacognition and resulting metacognitive abilities are important for change toward sustainability-as-flourishing. However, in general, little is known about how actors interested in working toward socioeconomic change employ these abilities in their work.

9.2.3. *Social entrepreneurship and metacognition to promote sustainability-as-flourishing*

We define social entrepreneurship as *a process to create social and environmental value beyond private economic gain* (Seelos and Mair, 2005) *that can engender socioeconomic change by challenging assumptions in predominant business and sustainability discourse and practice* (Haigh and Hoffman, 2014). Recent research suggests that social entrepreneurship is based on novel beliefs and practices as it integrates a social and environmental mission with commercial activities (Battilana and Dorado, 2010; Battilana and Lee, 2014; McMullen and Warnick, 2016; York et al., 2016). This unconventional entrepreneurial orientation, in turn, might pose challenges to, and engender change in, historical assumptions and practices ingrained in strategic management and orthodox business (Haigh and Hoffman, 2014). We see potential in social entrepreneurship to advance socioeconomic change despite its challenges in scaling-up impact to effect large-scale change (Hockerts and Wüstenhagen, 2010; Laszlo et al., 2014).

Research on the entrepreneurial process of social and environmental value creation has analyzed and identified useful approaches to socioeconomic change at the enterprise and societal levels (Wry and Haugh, 2018). While scholars have started to investigate how novel social entrepreneurial approaches may influence wider society (Tracey et al., 2011; Ruebottom, 2013; Waldron et al., 2016), research on the origins of such novel approaches at the individual level, such as on metacognition, remains sparse.

Researchers have begun to explore a self-aware and self-regulatory mindset and its part in empowering entrepreneurs to alter less useful ways of doing things (Haynie et al., 2010), and to think beyond preconceptions ingrained in prevalent cognitive patterns (Haynie et al., 2012). Being able to cognitively adapt seems especially important for social entrepreneurs who face complex changing environments (Goldstein et al., 2008; Waddock, 2013). Metacognition may also foster innovativeness, which is relevant when tensions need to be overcome

(Andriopoulos and Lewis, 2010; Lorenz *et al.*, 2018), such as in the simultaneous creation of social/environmental and economic value (Smith *et al.*, 2013). It has been argued that metacognitive capabilities, such as intuition or seeing nuances outside of habitual thinking processes, may help generate new ideas (Corner and Pavlovich, 2016). Innovativeness seems to be essential for entrepreneurs who aim to develop novel business models and products to address social and environmental challenges (Schaltegger and Wagner, 2011; Hall *et al.*, 2012). As another benefit, metacognition facilitates human and planetary flourishing, as it supports a transformation of our unsustainable social institutions, including modern culture (Fromm, 1976; Rimanoczy, 2013), by enabling individuals to break their unsustainable, limiting habitual patterns in thinking and behaving (Senge and Krahnke, 2013; Moore, 2015).

In regards to social entrepreneurship, there is single case study evidence contending that an entrepreneur's awareness of her thoughts shapes enterprise characteristics that, in turn, generate social and environmental value (Pavlovich and Corner, 2014). This research is deemed potentially useful, because psychologists attest a strong connection between people's subjective, internal metacognition and their decisions and actions (Nelson, 1996; Ochsner *et al.*, 2002; Reynolds, 2006) that can influence the enterprise and beyond. We, therefore, seek to fill the gap by empirically exploring how social entrepreneurs' metacognition affects the value creation process and ultimately change toward sustainability-as-flourishing.

9.3. Method

9.3.1. *Research design and setting*

We analyzed five cases of social entrepreneurship to induce theory. Using multiple cases facilitated a replication logic whereby each case served to examine emerging theoretical insights (Yin, 2009). This research design enabled a close correspondence between theory and data, grounding the emergent theory in the case data. A criterion sampling method was applied to purposefully gather a sample of German social entrepreneurship cases. Recent conceptual work suggests that an ideal enterprise geared to contribute to sustainability-as-flourishing would avoid harm, generate social value while regenerating the environment, and be financially viable (Upward and Jones, 2016, p. 103). To select cases that proxied such ideal enterprises, we developed criteria. Selected enterprises had to exhibit the following: (1) an environmental and/or social organizational purpose; (2) a business model that generated revenue; (3) financial (or near) sustainability; and (4) visible changes at the socioeconomic level. To be able to study the effect of metacognition, we included a fifth criterion — the founder of the enterprise was still involved with it. To allow depth, we limited the number to five selected cases. Table 9.1 offers expanded detail on the cases and lists the data sources. The unit of analysis is the

Table 9.1. Description of social entrepreneurship cases.

Case	Founder(s) and age range	Enterprise description	Focus of value creation	Age and size of enterprise at interview	Scaling-up of concept beyond initial location	Primary and secondary data sources
Eden	Emil, late 50s	Platform for social integration between people with and without disabilities	Social	More than 25 years old, 10–15 employees	More than 20 franchisees in nearly 20 countries worldwide	1 interview with founder, field notes, enterprise website, report and promotional material, internet profile, several YouTube videos, 2 online articles
Apollo	Anton, mid 50s	Transparent citizen stock company for a regional, just and organic agriculture that enables shareholder participation	Ecological, social	8 years old, 2 employees, more than 20 partner organizations	Several affiliated German regions and 1 European region	1 interview with founder, field notes, enterprise website, internet profile, several YouTube videos, 1 online article
Freyja	Frieda + 2 others, early 50s	Socioecological model for urban greening and social inclusion of marginalized	Ecological, social	4 years old, 2 managing directors, a few contractors	Dissemination of knowhow to over 70 communities in Germany and other countries	1 interview with founder, field notes, enterprise website, internet profile, several online articles
Gaia	Georg, late 60s	Organic mail order business; later: organic retail and wholesale business supporting a healthy nature and just world	Ecological, social	Almost 40 years old, 500–550 employees	Dissemination of knowhow to about 1000 independent organic retail outlets in Germany	1 interview with founder, field notes, enterprise website/documentation/promotional material, 5 online articles, 1 YouTube video
Hera	Heide + several others, early 60s	Citizen-owned cooperative electricity supplier; later also green energy provider for nuclear-free, climate-friendly energy	Ecological	20 years old, around 100 employees	Dissemination of knowhow to many municipalities nationally and internationally, affiliation with other municipalities	1 interview with founder, field notes, enterprise website, internet profile, documentary film, 2 online articles

social entrepreneurial process at three levels: (1) individual entrepreneur, (2) social enterprise, and (3) societal level.

9.3.2. *Data collection*

The first author collected primary and secondary data (see Table 9.1). The main source was semi-structured interviews with five German social entrepreneurs — one founder for each of the five selected social enterprises. Interviews were conducted and later analyzed in German by the first author as part of a larger study. All interviews but one were conducted on-site at the enterprises' premises. Interviews, lasting between 60 and 100 minutes, were audio-recorded, and transcribed. The founders were asked about their thoughts and emotions during the process of social and environmental value generation, spanning the time before enterprise foundation through to more recent events. Consequently, the interviewees' answers yielded retrospective and real-time data on the social entrepreneurial process.

This research regards participants as meaning-makers who self-report their interpretation of their thoughts, emotions, and entrepreneurial experiences, in contrast to objectively observable facts (Warren, 2002). The participants' introspective reports of their internal processes are subjective and valuable. Thus, we do not report the social entrepreneurs' actual metacognition, but how they made sense of their internal and external experiences and saw fit to share it at the time of the interview. We also acknowledge our subjectivity in interpreting the participants' accounts.

Field notes supplemented interview data and comprised the first author's impressions of nonverbal cues and the general atmosphere at the organizational premises. In three cases, field notes also contained more detailed observations from tours of premises. Secondary data included organizational documentation and publicly available articles, YouTube videos, and enterprise websites (see Table 9.1). These documents added rich insight into the cases and were used to verify the chronology of social entrepreneurship cases. The secondary data also provided further perspectives on the social entrepreneurial process, in particular at the organizational and societal level.

9.4. Data Analysis

Data analysis employed familiar methods for inductive theory building (Eisenhardt, 1989; Yin, 2009; see Creswell, 2013). It involved a thematic analysis of the interview data for each case, through the lens of the research question: *how does social entrepreneurs' metacognition shape socioeconomic change toward sustainability-as-flourishing?* Secondary data were helpful in confirming events external to the social entrepreneurs (organizational/societal level).

For the thematic analysis, we proceeded through a set of analytical devices to progress "from the raw data to more abstract themes and patterns" (Singh *et al.*, 2015, p. 155). These devices included open and expanded coding, margin notes, analytic memo-ing, and theme-ing (Richards, 2005; Creswell, 2013). The initial open codes reflected the research question. The open codes sought to get up off the data and see cumulative evidence mirroring a larger process (Richards, 2005; Richards and Morse, 2007). The analytical objective was to identify patterns within each case in regard to the research question.

In the ensuing cross-case analysis, we cross-checked patterns emerging within one case for their presence in other cases. Patterns reported in the findings persisted across all five cases. Tables were used to track and summarize emergent patterns across cases. As a final step in the data analysis, we generated a figure of a process model to summarize and integrate the identified patterns. During the theory-building process and interpretation of the patterns, we iteratively compared the case data, emerging theory, and extant concepts in the literature.

9.5. Findings

9.5.1. *Metacognition shaping socioeconomic change*

The research focused on the question, *how does social entrepreneurs' metacognition shape socioeconomic change toward sustainability-as-flourishing?* Case data revealed three patterns linking metacognition to enterprise capabilities, and ultimately to societal change. Figure 9.1 integrates the three patterns (displayed in bold) and summarizes the process model that emerged from analysis of the cases. We offer a detailed description of the patterns (including Tables 9.2–9.4) after this section.

The model encompasses three different levels — the social entrepreneur, the enterprise, and wider society. Regarding the first level, data suggests that microlevel characteristics of social entrepreneurs affected more macrolevels. More precisely, evidence reveals social entrepreneurs' metacognition shaped enterprise capabilities that, in turn, created change at the societal level. Data show the process of shaping societal level change started with social entrepreneurs' metacognition and ensuing metacognitive abilities at the individual level, well before the enterprise was founded, as depicted in the box in the top left corner of Figure 9.1. Although entrepreneurs' metacognition differed across cases, all entrepreneurs shared an awareness of and ability to overcome some of their limiting thought patterns and biases. Entrepreneurs also mentioned the awareness of their feelings, such as a feeling of antipathy toward conventional responses to social and environmental issues. Participants reported metacognition activated a creative social entrepreneurial response. For instance, in the case of Eden, its founder Emil stated that his awareness of limiting thought patterns engendered insights and emotional discontent in the face of marginalization of people with disabilities and the

Social entrepreneur

Metacognitive abilities
- Empathy
- Perspective taking
- Seeing bigger picture
- Suspending rushed judgment
- Reducing ego-defensiveness

↓ facilitate

Creative discontent
- through the mechanisms
- discontent
- creative response to discontent

→ enables

Social enterprise

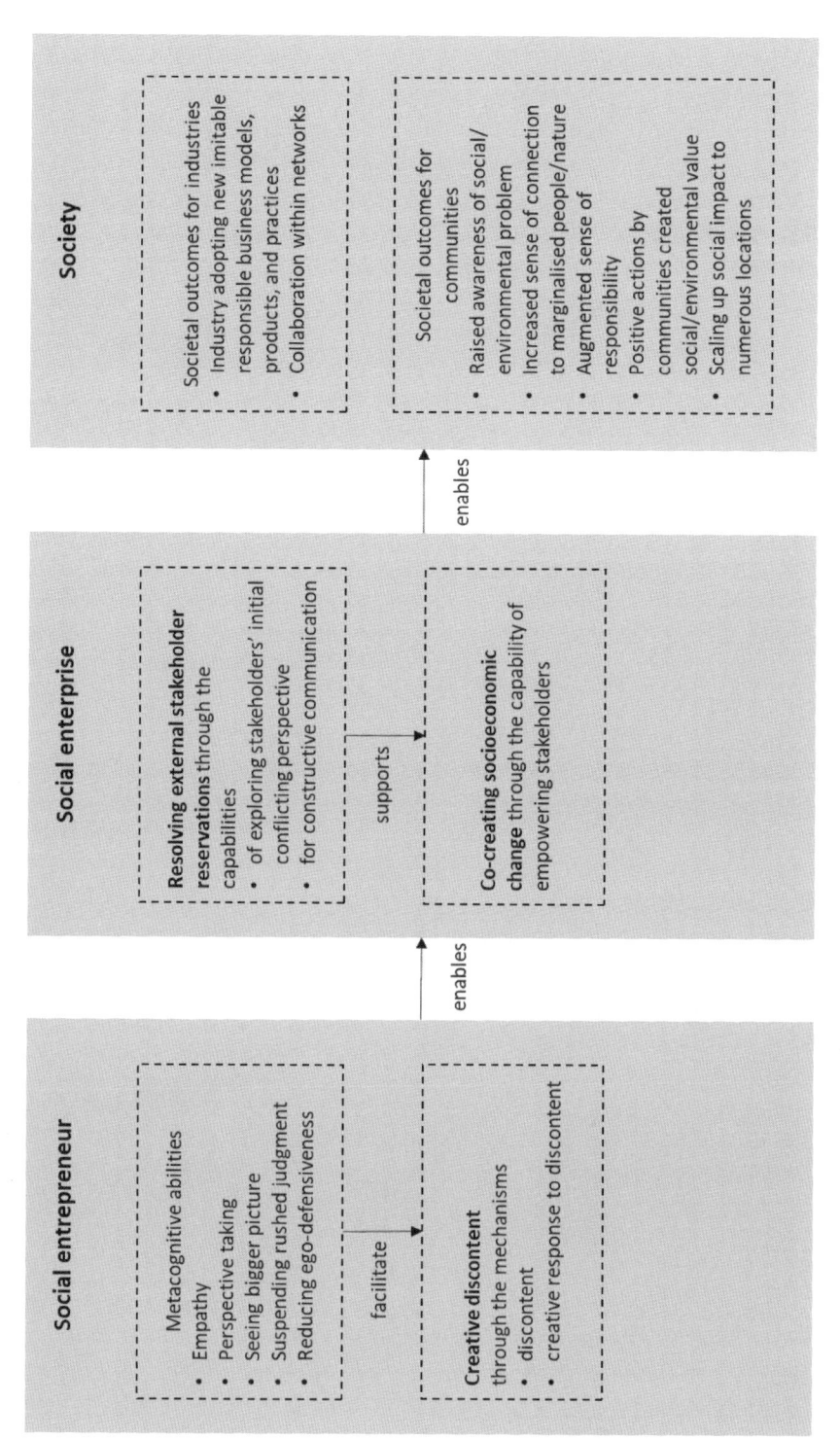

Resolving external stakeholder reservations through the capabilities
- of exploring stakeholders' initial conflicting perspective
- for constructive communication

↓ supports

Co-creating socioeconomic change through the capability of empowering stakeholders

→ enables

Society

Societal outcomes for industries
- Industry adopting new imitable responsible business models, products, and practices
- Collaboration within networks

Societal outcomes for communities
- Raised awareness of social/environmental problem
- Increased sense of connection to marginalised people/nature
- Augmented sense of responsibility
- Positive actions by communities created social/environmental value
- Scaling up social impact to numerous locations

Figure 9.1. Metacognition ultimately shaping socioeconomic change.

Table 9.2. Pattern of metacognitive abilities enabling creative discontent.

Case Founder	Metacognitive abilities generate insights	→ Mechanism 1: Discontent	→ Mechanism 2: Creative response to discontent
Eden Emil	• Suspending rushed judgment when interacting with disabled person led to scrutiny of prejudices about disabled people • Empathy allowed realization of commonalities with them	• Discontent about discrimination and authorities' bureaucratic, risk averse responses • Felt frustrated about insufficient interventions of authorities to include marginalized people	• Suddenly left old job and registered an enterprise to explore ways that support inclusion
Apollo Anton	• Suspending rushed judgment when studying accounting led to questioning beliefs about being a "victim" of unbalanced accounting rules • Openness to alternatives enabled seeing accounting rules as human constructs that could be changed	• Discontent with unbalanced financial statements neglecting environmental/social returns and lack of capital investment for regional organic agriculture • Felt "angry" about unacknowledged social and environmental values generated in his organic farm	• Developed new accounting rules that considered social/environmental/financial returns • Initiated think tanks with like-minded people to ideate alternative capital flows and value chains
Freyja Frieda	• Empathy with citizens/nature enabled awareness of maltreatment of the environment and people • Open-mindedness enabled seeing life as effortless flow instead of struggle	• Discontent with ecologically harmful practices and social exclusion • Felt "sad" about people's inaction in her city	• Joined forces with two like-minded people to collaborate in delivering ecosocial sustainable urban design
Gaia Georg	• Openness to alternatives and seeing interconnectedness of human well-being, environmental sustainability and food industry during illness allowed noticing wholesome nutrition as key for well-being	• Discontent with unethical practices in food industry • Felt unsatisfied with lack of healthy food options	• Engaged in conversations with alternative practitioner to explore options to offer healthy organic products
Hera Heide	• Seeing bigger picture facilitated insight that appropriate action in response to a nuclear catastrophe could only come from citizens like herself and not from authorities • Empathy increased concern for humans/environment	• Discontent about the energy sector's monopolistic structures and environmentally detrimental practices • Felt concerned about own and other citizens' wasteful energy consumption.	• Collaborated with other citizens to found an association that empowered citizens to educate about environmental protection

Social Entrepreneurs' Metacognition & Sustainability-as-Flourishing 237

Table 9.3. Pattern of resolving external stakeholder reservations.

Case Founder	Instance of stakeholder anxiety/ negativity/conflict	Capability of exploring stakeholders' initial conflicting perspective	Capability of communicating constructively	Outcomes
Eden Emil	Conflicts with franchisees due to non-payment of license fees or consulting services	• Approached franchisees who did not pay with curiosity and sincere willingness to help • Scrutinized own shortcomings	• Empathetic dialogues • Collaboration to design solution • Transfer of knowhow	• Constructive solution to conflict • Strengthened enterprise/ stakeholder relationship
Apollo Anton	Citizen investors felt anxious due to reduced short-term financial security when not receiving monetary dividends immediately, which then triggered aggressiveness toward entrepreneur	• Met investors in many personal conversations with non-judgment to understand anxieties and entrenched thought patterns	• Empathetic, peaceful conversations that consider others' mindsets and fears • Patience and objectivity when explaining long-term benefits of financial investment over and over	• Trusting relationships with citizen investors and accountants • Investors scrutinized their old beliefs about profit shares
Freyja Frieda	Citizens and local authorities were anxious about and resisted greening communal spaces and including marginalized people	• Came from a place of love and connection with people • Approached resistant citizens and authorities with curiosity and sincere willingness to understand anxieties	• Empathetic questions and deep listening • Collaboration with diverse stakeholders to get people onboard and design green urban spaces	• Local authorities' and citizens' resolved resistance • Trust in new pathways of designing the urban environment
Gaia Georg	Bankers' negativity about the enterprise's value to invest in employees long term led to problems to secure funding	• Courageously and assertively approached bankers despite him feeling vulnerable about lack of financial reserves	• Honest conversation about enterprise values • Patience when explaining vision	• Bankers' resolved resistance to investment in employees • Good long-term relationship with bankers
Hera Heide	There was conflicts with citizens who did not trust that the new enterprise could provide non-nuclear energy steadily	• With a friendly disposition visited all households to explore citizens' anxieties	• Respectful interactions from a place of authenticity and vulnerability • Peacefully explained strategy for energy supply and invited people to join them	• Trusting relationships with citizens who supported the entrepreneurs' endeavors to buy the local energy grid

Table 9.4. Pattern of co-creating socioeconomic change.

Case Founder	Empowering diverse stakeholders e.g. through disseminating knowledge formally and informally, collaborating with them	Outcomes at societal level e.g. for industries, communities
Eden Emil	• Spreading product knowledge via franchise system and industry contacts • Empowering local franchisees by giving up control of the concept • Empowering people with disabilities through employing them	• Created quality jobs for people with disabilities • Scaled up social impact to 19 international locations • Improved inclusion of people with disabilities in several communities
Apollo Anton	• Spreading knowledge through freely sharing intellectual property with affiliated regions and other imitators • Empowering citizen investors to inform themselves about social/environmental impact of their investment through new transparent and holistic accounting rules • Enabling sustainable small growers by investing in/mentoring them	• Raised awareness of holistic value creation in organic agriculture • Increased local stakeholders' (citizen investors and consumers) sense of connection to and responsibility for their region • Expanded sustainable agricultural practices in region • Scaled up regional citizen stock company to 4 additional regions
Freyja Frieda	• Empowering citizens and local authorities through disseminating knowledge via organizational structure, books, TV, newspapers, events • Enabling external partners through long-term trusting collaboration • Empowering long-time unemployed people by training and employing them as permaculture assistants	• Raised connection to nature and awareness of environmental issues • Heightened sense of responsibility and care for urban edible gardens • Increased inclusion of unemployed and migrant people • Augmented demand for cities with high quality of life • Disseminated concept to over 70 communities in Germany and beyond
Gaia Georg	• Empowering suppliers by fairly collaborating long-term • Empowering customers [store owners] by educating them in-house and offering to adopt successfully branded store concept/products with image for trust and high organic quality • Enabling consumers by offering wholesome food	• Heightened awareness of benefits of organic food and helped establish organic food as mainstream in Germany • Increased appreciation of ecological and ethical organizational practices within industry • Helped spread 1,000 organic wholefood shops in Germany
Hera Heide	• Empowering citizens and local authorities by offering education about energy production/savings and climate protection, initiating referendums, environmental activism which fostered a nationwide community • Disseminating expertise through affiliates and non-profit organization	• Decreased customers' energy consumption • Freedom of electricity from nuclear/coal-fired plants and of overpowering monopolist structures for local community • Contributed to liberalization of energy market in Germany (achieved) • Contributed to nationwide energy shift to green energy (in progress) • Raised awareness/ action for alternative energy in several countries

insufficient initiatives of authorities. He then responded creatively to his emotional discontent as he was inspired to found a social enterprise that addresses the social problem (pattern "metacognitive abilities enabling creative discontent," Table 9.2). The creative response then led to social entrepreneurial actions at the organizational level. The box in the top left corner of Figure 9.1 lists entrepreneurs' metacognitive abilities (e.g. empathy, perspective-taking, suspending rushed judgment) that shaped their entrepreneurial actions.

At the second level, social entrepreneurs' metacognitive abilities influenced the process of working with external stakeholders when creating a social enterprise. Entrepreneurs described how, after founding their social enterprises, they encountered conflicts with recalcitrant external stakeholders that had to be overcome (pattern "resolving external stakeholder reservations"; see Table 9.3 and the top box in the middle column of Figure 9.1). Social entrepreneurs' metacognitive abilities led to the development of enterprise capabilities designed to explore and constructively communicate about stakeholders' conflicting perspectives. We note that sometimes individual entrepreneurial decisions and enterprise-level capabilities are not as clearly distinguishable as pictured in the diagram and tables but overlap.

On the third level, enterprise capabilities facilitated positive, trusting relationships with stakeholders. These relationships meant that other partners beyond enterprise boundaries actively engaged with the enterprise to collaboratively engender social change (pattern "co-creating socioeconomic change"; see Table 9.4 and bottom box in middle column of Figure 9.1). The societal level change can be seen in Figure 9.1 (right column). For example, enterprise Hera founder Heide shared how engaging other partners to work toward the same goal and empowering them through sharing knowledge raised awareness even in other countries:

> We have invested in similar ventures [that give power over energy production back to citizens] and shaped their business model, for example in that they also engage citizens or only sell renewable energy... Every week we have visitors from Japan [that we educate], and we encourage them to change direction [away from nuclear energy] after Fukushima.

In sum, the model depicts how social entrepreneurs' metacognition ultimately shaped substantial change in perceptions and practices of the wider public, apparently in line with flourishing humans and a thriving planet. The following sections provide a more comprehensive description of *how social entrepreneurs' metacognition shapes socioeconomic change toward sustainability-as-flourishing*.

9.5.2. *Activation of a creative social entrepreneurial response*

A pattern emerged that we label "metacognitive abilities enabling creative discontent." This pattern illustrates the connection of metacognition with social entrepreneurial decisions and actions at the individual level. In all cases, the pattern appeared at the inception stage, well before the actual enterprise creation. Metacognitive abilities facilitated insight as supported by details in Table 9.2.

Metacognition is illustrated by social entrepreneurs reporting a growing awareness of some of their limiting habitual ways of thinking and related feelings. Self-awareness enabled challenging these patterns and generated insights. Eden's founder Emil recalled that he used to think "Disabled people have no quality of life." However, when Emil got to know a person with disabilities, he "was blown away by his optimism." He suspended rushed judgment to realize he had to "realign in this area [of thinking]" by scrutinizing his stereotypes about people with disabilities. Emil stated that "The encounter with this gentleman with special needs was a kind of turning point in my life." He began to see that people with disabilities "have strengths and needs" as he does. Also, Anton, who founded Apollo, noted he became aware of a less useful habitual way of thinking before founding his enterprise. He described how he tended to think that he and his former organic agricultural business "had more or less become a victim of the process of making organic farming more conventional." He thought the unfavorable accounting rules that did not acknowledge the social and environmental benefits his organic farm produced were "constitutional law or God given." However, when he used the metacognitive ability of suspended rushed judgment, he "could challenge" his beliefs. Openness to find a way out of the situation supported his insight that, while the "society had shaped and legally consolidated the accounting rules," the rules were "flawed" and could be revised.

Metacognition embraced two mechanisms: "discontent" and "creative response to discontent" (see Table 9.2). Discontent reflects how participants' fresh insights and new patterns of thought, more in line with human and planetary flourishing, raised awareness of social and environmental problems. These newly acknowledged problems, in turn, created emotional discontent in participants. The Eden case offers an example of the first mechanism (see Table 9.2). Founder Emil's realization of a likeness between himself and people with disabilities raised awareness of discrimination more widely and led to a feeling of discontent about the "mediocrity of the management" at his former employer, an institution that supported people with disabilities. He had a sense of "frustration" with their excessive "bureaucracy and risk averseness." Case Freyja provides an additional illustration of the first mechanism. Frieda's insight that "life in the garden is so simple" heightened her discontent with "the ecological problems in her city." She experienced a sadness that also activated her — the second mechanism that is discussed in more depth below: "This passivity [of the citizens] makes [me] sad. Passivity makes sick! And sometimes you really have to make a stand against passive masses that could actually be active and much happier."

The second mechanism, i.e. "creative response to discontent," reflected participants' ability to be aware of emotional discontent and be activated by it to initiate social entrepreneurial actions. The Gaia case highlights the mechanism (see Table 9.2). Gaia's creator Georg described how the unethical practices in the food and agricultural industries mobilized him to respond in a creative and useful way. At first, he kept "thinking and was emotionally moved." He remained consciously aware of, and constructively engaged with, his negative thoughts and emotional discomfort. This engagement ultimately led to something beneficial as he described in this quote: "I was discontent, and then something new and positive emerged." What emerged was the social entrepreneurial decision to create a more conscious and responsible enterprise. He then talked with his "alternative practitioner" to "get inspired about new wholesome products" he could sell. Similarly, before Apollo's founding, Anton became aware of "a feeling of doom" and anger in the face of investors who merely focused on the financial success of agricultural enterprises and neglected the creation of environmental and social value. These uneasy feelings prompted him to discuss with other passionate and knowledgeable people the issue of unacknowledged social and environmental values and possible solutions. Anton realised he could "create a tool," an enterprise that would give him "a lever in his hand ... to really make a difference and generate change." In combination, the two mechanisms revealed how metacognition at the individual level shaped a social entrepreneurial response to social and environmental problems. This involved reflection on, and scrutinizing of, entrenched thought patterns, the emergence of new insights, as well as a creative and active response to emotional discontent due to social injustice and environmental degradation.

9.5.3. *Resolution of conflicts with recalcitrant external stakeholders*

Cases revealed a second pattern that we label "resolving external stakeholder reservations." This pattern shows the influence of social entrepreneurs' metacognitive abilities on capabilities at the organizational level and outcomes beyond the enterprise. Table 9.3 characterizes the pattern for each of the cases. The pattern emerged in the building phase after founding the enterprise and reflects how participants' decisions and actions at the individual level shaped social and environmental value creation at the organizational level (see Figure 9.1). At times, the social enterprises' novel and unconventional solutions triggered anxieties in stakeholders beyond organizational boundaries, like franchisees, investors, citizens, or bankers, who then resisted the entrepreneurial efforts. Stakeholders' negativity led to interpersonal tensions.

Entrepreneurs and their teams calmed stakeholder anxieties and negativity and resolved the tensions by engaging two capabilities: "exploring stakeholders' initial conflicting perspective" and "communicating constructively." The cases revealed how participants drew on metacognitive abilities to respond peacefully and helpfully to conflict. Participants reported that through resolving the conflicting situation at the enterprise level, they also were able to generate positive outcomes at the socioeconomic level, including strengthened, trusting relationships with stakeholders. Positive external relations are essential for different entrepreneurial phases, including founding, building, managing an enterprise, and for shaping socioeconomic change (Corner and Ho, 2010; Montgomery et al., 2012; de Bruin et al., 2017; Lumpkin and Bacq, 2019).

Case Freyja provides an example for the first enterprise capability "exploring stakeholders' initial conflicting perspective." Frieda mentioned that local authorities and some citizens initially were negative about establishing communal gardens. She described drawing upon her metacognitive abilities of empathy and perspective-taking to resolve these conflicts. Frieda shared:

> When there is resistance, I always ask people, "You really have to tell me, what are your arguments?" Then it is best to listen very closely to where the anxieties stem from.... Then I get a chance to show them that [my socioecological concept of greening the city] works, and the resistance dissolves ... You have to love humans and nature, then it works.

The case of Apollo is another illustration of "exploring stakeholders' initial conflicting perspective." The entrepreneur reported decreasing his self-centered cognition and premature judgment, which enabled him to understand that aggression originated from anxieties and ingrained beliefs:

> When faced with questions that are so existential for an individual like money, capital, assets, and one does not fit into their thinking patterns, people [investors] become aggressive ... They cannot think it [grasp the concept] ... Sometimes, they felt let down because they received no money dividend ... I try to understand the aggression of the vis-à-vis person, to see what leads him to become aggressive.

Case Apollo also offers an example for the second enterprise capability "communicating constructively." Anton reported an ability to stay anchored in the big picture and draw on facts even in highly emotional arguments with citizen investors who, sometimes, became personal and unfair in their attacks. Anton shared:

> I have to deal with them [emotional and aggressive investors] every day and explain in many, many dialogues that value is being built in the long run. I have developed an ability to persuade based on objectivity with dispassion. When I explain my ideas, I aim to stay calm, not to apportion any blame. And then, new images, new thoughts, new connections emerge within individuals.

In addition, Hera's case exemplifies constructive communication capabilities. The metacognitive capabilities of capabilities of reducing ego-defense and perspective-taking helped Heide and her co-founders avoid creating conflict in the phase before enterprise founding. When the entrepreneurs won two direct votes (plebiscites) regarding the ownership of the energy grid, the citizens were entitled to acquire the grid. However, some of the citizens initially did not support the idea of buying the local grid from the monopolist energy supplier. These citizens did not trust in the capabilities of the new enterprise and feared an erratic supply of energy. By reducing their ego-defense and taking the perspective of those citizens, the entrepreneurs were able not to offend them. Heide recalled:

> We made a big effort not to flaunt that we were the winners [of the plebiscites] ... We really tried to be fair winners, not to be triumphant, and instead to get them [people who voted against the citizens' acquisition of the energy grid] back on board ... We walked from household to household and talked to all people.

Heide mentioned that in her conversations with citizens, she showed up authentic and vulnerable. She highlighted what was at risk for her and her family in case she was not telling the truth. Her attitude and behavior convinced many fellow citizens to let go of the reservations, trust her, and embrace the plan to buy the grid.

Exploring conflicting perspectives and engaging constructively with stakeholders facilitated outcomes at the socioeconomic level — positive external relations and acceptance of new ideas. Case Hera exemplifies how constructive dialogues were critical in achieving public acceptance of the novel idea that ordinary citizens could own and run an energy company. In the end, Hera enterprise was able to gather a "strong base of support in the local community." This, in turn, facilitated successfully building the citizen-owned energy enterprise in the municipality. Also in the Apollo case, interpersonal and communicative skills enabled positive results at the socioeconomic level. Anton and his team achieved that shareholders and other stakeholders revised their preconceptions about their capital gains and conventional accounting methods. Anton reported:

> Awareness rises, a particular development has been achieved ... The last two shareholder meetings have been great, money only played a relative role ... And in the last three years, I have not had any conversation with an auditor, tax consultant, or economist in which they didn't agree with me that we need to internalize [externalized social and environmental costs].

Overall, entrepreneurs reported capabilities that reflect metacognition or an awareness of habitual thought patterns. These entrepreneurs disengaged from self-concern using metacognitive capabilities such as perspective-taking, empathy, and suspending rushed judgment (Brown *et al.*, 2007; Pavlovich and Krahnke, 2012).

The metacognitive capacities were useful to overcome conflicts and challenges and resolve stakeholder reservations by enabling relational skills, such as to engage with curiosity, love, respect, peace, patience, and honesty. Through these skills, social entrepreneurs and their teams were able to build trust and positive relationships with external stakeholders, importantly at times when the new business model or product was not yet seen as legitimate. Evidence shows incidences in which entrepreneurs were successful in their attempt to alter wider public perceptions. Participants skillfully and gently invited people beyond the organizations' boundaries to scrutinize their limiting thought patterns and then gradually embrace new patterns of thought apparently more in tune with a flourishing world.

Despite the data in support of participants' metacognitive abilities, the cases also evidence occasional moments when social entrepreneurs applied unhelpful tendencies of thinking and related emotions, such as frustration, that did not lead anywhere positive. For example, Anton admitted:

> When it comes to concrete implementation [of a new balance sheet valuation], I am sometimes a lone wolf. Although people understand that internalization is vital, they don't follow through on their understanding to consequently re-evaluate the annual financial statement. This is when I reach a point of despair. [...Them] not following through agitates me again and again.

Participants shared that, from time to time, they resorted to old cognitive habits that predated their metacognitive abilities that enabled all these processes described in the findings.

9.5.4. *Shaping socioeconomic change*

Case data suggested a final pattern — "co-creating socioeconomic change." The pattern reflects how the social enterprises supported a shift at the societal level by investing in collaborators (see Figure 9.1). Table 9.4 documents this pattern across cases. The pattern consisted of an enterprise capability called "empowering diverse stakeholders" as well as resulting outcomes in the wider environment. Social entrepreneurs realized scaling-up wider change in industries and communities required joined efforts with a range of internal and external stakeholders. It seems that entrepreneurs' individual metacognitive abilities and their enterprise capability to resolve conflicts with stakeholders facilitated collaboration with partners beyond the organization. In every case, the enterprise engaged in several activities to enable diverse stakeholders to facilitate change. Empowering activities included, e.g. spreading knowledge about their business model, products, and processes (sometimes at no charge); long-term collaboration; and employment of disadvantaged individuals.

For example, in Gaia's case, Georg reported his enterprise's capability of developing retail customers and suppliers into resilient, powerful co-creators by "making them strong." He shared that Gaia invested in their customers by offering extraordinary free education and holistic management advice in their own academy, teaching about natural food and enterprise management. Georg said, "It is fun to observe that new customers [organic retailers], who switch from one of our competitors to us, usually improve their balance sheet within two years." In addition, Gaia strengthened their suppliers, including farmers, by maintaining long-term trusting relations with them as well as planning purchase quantities well in advance to "be a predictable partner for suppliers."

Freyja's case exemplifies how marginalized citizens were first empowered and then were able to support the socioecological project of greening the city. Frieda shared:

> We educate long-time unemployed people with a disability as permaculture assistants. They become the creators of a beautiful city ... We have had a very high societal impact through our ecological projects ... Citizens helped to look after the gardens, no more vandalism or feces in public spaces.

Eden sheds light on the enterprise's ability to disseminate knowledge and hand over control to their external stakeholders. In a report, an executive team member declared that the enterprise spread knowledge through an "innovative" franchise structure. She said:

> We give the franchisees our know-how, and then there is a local translation. We are not important any more ... We give up control of the concept. This local strength is one of the key factors of our success.

The empowerment of stakeholders engendered various societal-level outcomes for industries and communities. The outcomes were often a result of more than one activity. Case Eden illustrates the enterprise's capability to hand over power to more than 20 independent franchisees and to entrust them with the concept (i.e. "enabled" people meet people with special needs in a special environment). This empowerment led franchisees to adapt the concept to local cultures, propagate it, and raise awareness internationally. Some of Eden's end-customers who encountered people with disabilities testified to the enterprise's ability to address root causes of marginalization by challenging people's prejudices. Their product elevated awareness and changed stereotypes around disability. End-customers stated (in YouTube videos) how "life-changing" this "experience of humanity" was, or that it helped them "empathize and connect with others in the community."

The Gaia case also offers an example of how the enterprise's capability to empower their organic retailer customers and organic farmers engendered positive outcomes for industry and communities. Georg reported that he received feedback reflecting that "[Gaia] caused other wholesalers [in the industry] to become more customer oriented and to raise their organic standards." Furthermore, he was pleased that their ability to encourage retail customers to become co-creators led to them having about 1,000 largely successful organic retailers in Germany at the time. The visibility of organic food stores throughout the country then promoted Gaia's mission by contributing to increased awareness of and demand for organic produce.

In addition, Freyja's case highlights environmental outcomes of the enterprise's capability to empower diverse stakeholders. Frieda shared the result that, "in the edible gardens ... with diverse wild plants and butterfly meadows... vandalism and pollution" almost completely disappeared. This evidenced a heightened sense of responsibility for the gardens. She underlined that citizens, especially the long-term unemployed people who were educated as permaculture assistants, looked after the urban gardens well. Overall, the social entrepreneurs reported that their enterprises had achieved to create more social inclusion of marginalized people, a wider spread of organic agriculture, as well as fair and respectful working conditions and broader use of renewable energy. Their achievements seem to be in line with progress toward sustainability-as-flourishing.

9.6. Discussion and Conclusion

This chapter empirically examines the role social entrepreneurs' metacognition plays in shaping entrepreneurial value creation and engendering change toward sustainability-as-flourishing. More precisely, we explored how awareness of thought patterns, feelings, and associated behaviors engendered mechanisms, capabilities, and outcomes at three levels — individual, enterprise, and wider society. As such, we addressed the research question, *how does social entrepreneurs' metacognition shape socioeconomic change toward sustainability-as-flourishing?*

We used a multiple-case study design to induce theory, given the current lack of empirical research investigating the connection of social entrepreneurs' metacognition to the value creation process (Pavlovich and Corner, 2014) and to wider socioeconomic change (Corner and Pavlovich, 2016). The induced theory sheds light on how society might move toward the possibility of sustainability-as-flourishing (Laszlo *et al.*, 2012). Specifically, we identified patterns connecting metacognition to social enterprise capabilities, and ultimately to changes in industries and communities that are in line with change toward sustainability-as-flourishing. Our research thus offered initial evidence that social entrepreneurs' metacognition helped shape the process of transformation at the societal level.

Findings have implications for literature and practice. First, findings extend current literature (Haigh and Hoffman, 2014; Upward and Jones, 2016) by encompassing three levels of analysis — individual, enterprise and societal — and thus drawing a more complete picture of the factors involved in a transformation of industries and communities in line with sustainability-as-flourishing. In addition, empirical findings support conceptual work suggesting that, for sustainability-as-flourishing to start manifesting, substantial changes in our cultural beliefs and practices are necessary (Ehrenfeld, 2012; Grant, 2012; Ehrenfeld and Hoffman, 2013). They indicate mechanisms whereby individual actors' metacognition facilitates changes in thought patterns, which then induce changes at the societal level. Thus, this study lays the groundwork for further research that investigates the role of internal, individual-level transformation in contributing to a substantial shift in cultural perceptions and actions in keeping with the possibility of thriving humans and a thriving planet. A thriving future can serve as an ideal and inspiring target of business strategy (Cooperrider and Fry, 2012; Grant, 2012).

Second, findings illustrate the potential insights gained by taking a subjective, bottom-up perspective in research design. Findings revealed metacognitive capabilities relevant to social and potentially commercial entrepreneurship. We showed how social entrepreneurs' metacognition, feelings, perceptions, decisions, and interactions can give rise to higher-level phenomena (Kozlowski and Klein, 2000). We propose that such findings are the result of viewing the value creation process as having its "theoretical origin" at the individual level (Kozlowski and Klein, 2000, p. 5). Moreover, findings provide rare empirical corroboration of conceptual research suggesting that entrepreneurial and management processes are subjective processes influenced by individuals´ metacognition (Bryant, 2009; Hodgkinson and Healey, 2011; Dheer and Lenartowicz, 2018; Lorenz et al., 2018; Murnieks et al., 2019). Our hope is that these initial findings encourage future research that reflects a bottom-up theorizing process. Such a process would be in contrast to the bulk of organizational research which adopts a top-down perspective, examining how contextual factors at higher levels (e.g. industrial or institutional forces) limit and impinge on lower-level phenomena (e.g. individual social entrepreneurs) (Kozlowski and Klein, 2000, p. 5; Lenox and York, 2012).

Third, of interest to both the wider entrepreneurship and social entrepreneurship literature, the chapter develops theory on the entrepreneurial process by offering rich detail on a particular entrepreneurial mechanism in the start-up phase — creative discontent. Evidence suggests that participants' metacognition enabled them to endure emotional discontent in the face of pressing problems. Research acknowledges highly complex social or environmental problems can seem daunting because they have many interrelating elements and lack verified solutions (Metcalf and Benn, 2013). The social entrepreneurs in this study seemed to be resilient and resourceful (Brendel and Bennett, 2016). They appeared to see the problems and experience much of the resulting emotional discontent without suppressing it. Despite the cultural bias that prompts people to avoid unpleasant experiences (Hayes et al., 2011), the entrepreneurs used their uneasiness as a "healthy call-to-change" that initiated social transformation (Davies, 2012). In the analyzed cases, awareness of thoughts and feelings allowed actors to be vulnerable to, and moved by, social and environmental distress. The vulnerability seemed supportive in the activation of a creative pro-social response to the problems instead of glossing over them. We find this notion of creative discontent, as an impetus for value creation, as potentially useful to explore in further research in both social and commercial entrepreneurship. Interestingly, the mechanism of becoming creative as a response to emotional discontent was unexpected, given commercial entrepreneurship research that finds negative emotions influence both opportunity evaluation and opportunity exploitation negatively; in other words, it dampens entrepreneurial activity (Grichnik et al., 2010) and encourages rigid thinking (Baron, 2008). Future research thus could examine whether the concept of creative discontent is more prominent in social entrepreneurship than in commercial entrepreneurship.

Fourth, our identification of enterprise capabilities that support the resolution of external stakeholder reservations expands organizational theory around cooperation. Overcoming challenges and tensions enabled participants to effectively generate change across enterprise boundaries (Williams, 2002). The unconventional business models and products of the enterprises in the study provoked initial resistance in external stakeholders. The ability of entrepreneurs to be compassionate and understanding appeared to "create fertile ground" for others to overcome resistance (Brown, 2012, p. 571) and become partners. Collaborating with stakeholders is key in creating social and environmental value, but "the path to fruitful cooperation is often highly complex" (Lumpkin and Bacq, 2019, p. 387). A challenge when co-creating change with diverse groups of stakeholders is that each group takes decisions and actions based on different underlying assumptions, beliefs, and values (Lumpkin and Bacq, 2019). Our evidence shows how important metacognitive abilities are in becoming aware of such assumptions and in developing positive relationships beyond organizational boundaries to co-create larger scale change (Waddell et al., 2015). We thus propose further studies that empirically investigate the role of metacognition, ensuing relational capabilities and resulting socioeconomic change toward human and planetary flourishing.

For practice, our findings encourage entrepreneurs to enhance their metacognitive abilities. Existing literature points to practices that can, over time, further develop metacognition. Practices include, but are not restricted to, yoga and mindfulness meditation (Brown and Ryan, 2003; Corner and Pavlovich, 2016). Present findings promote future work that explores the extent to which these practices expand the metacognitive abilities identified in the present study.

The current study has two limitations. First, findings from an inductive study of five cases may be limited in generalizability, however revelatory (Pavlovich and Corner, 2014). Case data served to help extend the mostly conceptual existing theory by offering a more complete description of the role of metacognition in the social entrepreneurial process toward sustainability-as-flourishing. The possible interrelationships of elements in the revealed patterns can then be tested in future research (Pavlovich and Corner, 2014).

Second, the study's design is built, in part, on retrospective data. In three cases, the enterprise foundation reached back several decades (between 20 and 39 years). We acknowledge the general risk that a retrospective research design might affect interviewees' ability to recall information accurately. However, like others, we do not consider this potential recall bias as "overly problematic" (Cope, 2011; Singh *et al.*, 2016, p. 22). Studies indicate that critical events in an individual's life can still be remembered well, even after many years (Berney and Blane, 1997; Chell, 2004). We maintain that founding an enterprise with a meaningful social or environmental purpose can be considered as a critical event.

In conclusion, we aimed to build theory regarding the role social entrepreneurs' metacognition plays in shaping the entrepreneurial value creation process and ultimately change toward sustainability-as-flourishing. We see our most important contribution as providing insight on how an individual's metacognitive abilities can play a substantial role in the generation of wider socioeconomic change toward a flourishing world. This study reminds us that we humans are powerful beings and the way we shape our reality and the environment around us is influenced by our awareness of our own thoughts, potential biases, and feelings. Yes, our external environment can condition and influence us, but it is our choice if we unconsciously react or consciously respond to it.

References

Anderson, A. R., & Miller, C. J. (2003). "Class matters": Human and social capital in the entrepreneurial process. *Journal of Socio-Economics*, **32**(1), 17–36.

Andriopoulos, C., & Lewis, M. W. (2010). Managing innovation paradoxes: Ambidexterity lessons from leading product design companies. *Long Range Planning*, **43**(1), 104–122.

Baron, R. A. (2008). The role of affect in the entrepreneurial process. *Academy of Management Review*, **33**(2), 328–340.

Battilana, J., & Dorado, S. (2010). Building sustainable hybrid organizations: The case of commercial microfinance organizations. *Academy of Management Journal*, **53**(6), 1419–1440.

Battilana, J., & Lee, M. (2014). Advancing research on hybrid organizing: Insights from the study of social enterprises. *Academy of Management Annals*, **8**(1), 397–441.

Berney, L., & Blane, D. (1997). Collecting retrospective data: Accuracy of recall after 50 years as judged against historic records. *Social Science & Medicine*, **45**(10), 1519–1525.

Brendel, W., & Bennett, C. (2016). Learning to embody leadership through mindfulness and somatics practice. *Advances in Developing Human Resources*, **18**(3), 409–425.

Brown, B. C. (2012). Leading complex change with post-conventional consciousness. *Journal of Organizational Change Management*, **25**(4), 560–575.

Brown, K. W., & Ryan, R. M. (2003). The benefits of being present: Mindfulness and its role in psychological well-being. *Journal of Personality and Social Psychology*, **84**(4), 822–848.

Brown, K. W., Ryan, R. M., & Creswell, J. D. (2007). Mindfulness: Theoretical foundations and evidence for its salutary effects. *Psychological Inquiry*, **18**(4), 211–237.

Bryant, P. (2009). Self-regulation and moral awareness among entrepreneurs. *Journal of Business Venturing*, **24**(5), 505–518.

Chell, E. (2004). Critical Incident Technique. In C. Cassell, and G. Symon (eds.), *Essential Guide to Qualitative Methods in Organizational Research* (Thousand Oaks, CA: Sage), pp. 45–60.

Collins, E. M., & Kearins, K. (2010). Delivering on sustainability's global and local orientation. *Academy of Management Learning and Education*, **9**(3), 499–506.

Cooperrider, D. L., & Fry, R. (2012). Mirror flourishing and the positive psychology of sustainability. *Journal of Corporate Citizenship*, **46**(1), 3–12.

Cope, J. (2011). Entrepreneurial learning from failure: An interpretative phenomenological analysis. *Journal of Business Venturing*, **26**(6), 604–623.

Corner, P. D., & Ho, M. (2010). How opportunities develop in social entrepreneurship. *Entrepreneurship Theory & Practice*, **34**(4), 635–659.

Corner, P. D., & Pavlovich, K. (2016). Shared value through inner knowledge creation. *Journal of Business Ethics*, **135**(3), 543–555.

Costanza, R., Alperovitz, G., Daly, H., Farley, J., Franco, C., Jackson, T., & Victor, P. (2013). Building a sustainable and desirable economy-in-society-in-nature. In L. Starke, E. Assadourian, and T. Prugh (eds.), *State of the World 2013: Is Sustainability Still Possible?* (Washington, DC: Island Press/Worldwatch Institute), pp. 126–142.

Creswell, J. W. (2013). *Qualitative Inquiry & Research Design: Choosing Among Five Approaches*, 3 edn. (Thousand Oaks, CA: Sage).

Davies, J. (2012). *The Importance of Suffering: The Value and Meaning of Emotional Discontent* (London: Routledge).

de Bruin, A., Shaw, E., & Lewis, K. V. (2017). The collaborative dynamic in social entrepreneurship. *Entrepreneurship & Regional Development*, **29**(7–8), 575–585.

Dheer, R. J. S., & Lenartowicz, T. (2018). Multiculturalism and entrepreneurial intentions: Understanding the mediating role of cognitions. *Entrepreneurship Theory and Practice*, **42**(3), 426–466.

Dwivedi, A., & Weerawardena, J. (2018). Conceptualizing and operationalizing the social entrepreneurship construct. *Journal of Business Research*, **86**, 32–40.

Ehrenfeld, J. R. (2008). *Sustainability by Design: A Subversive Strategy for Transforming our Consumer Culture* (New Haven, CT: Yale University Press).

Ehrenfeld, J. R. (2012). Beyond the brave new world: Business for sustainability. In P. Bansal, and A. J. Hoffman (eds.), *The Oxford Handbook of Business and the Natural Environment* (Oxford: Oxford University Press), pp. 611–619.

Ehrenfeld, J. R., & Hoffman, A. J. (2013). *Flourishing: A Frank Conversation About Sustainability* (Stanford, CA: Stanford University Press).

Eisenhardt, K. M. (1989). Building theories from case study research. *Academy of Management Review*, **14**(4), 532–550.

Elkington, J., & Hartigan, P. (2008). *Power of Unreasonable People: How Social Entrepreneurs Create Markets that Change the World* (Cambridge, MA: Harvard Business Press).

Flavell, J. H. (1976). Metacognitive aspects of problem solving. In L. B. Resnick (ed.), *The Nature of Intelligence* (Hillsdale, NJ: Erlbaum), pp. 231–236.

Flavell, J. H. (1979). Metacognition and cognitive monitoring: A new area of cognitive-developmental inquiry. *American Psychologist*, **34**(10), 906–911.

Fromm, E. (1976). *To Have or To Be?* (New York: Harper & Row).

Gladwin, T. N., Kennelly, J. J., & Krause, T.-S. (1995). Shifting paradigms for sustainable development: Implications for management theory and research. *Academy of Management Review*, **20**(4), 874–907.

Goldstein, J. A., Hazy, J. K., & Silberstang, J. (2008). Complexity and social entrepreneurship: A fortuitous meeting. *Emergence: Complexity & Organization*, **10**(3), 9–24.

Grant, G. B. (2012). Transforming sustainability. *Journal of Corporate Citizenship*, **46**, 123–137.

Grichnik, D., Smeja, A., & Welpe, I. (2010). The importance of being emotional: How do emotions affect entrepreneurial opportunity evaluation and exploitation? *Journal of Economic Behavior & Organization*, **76**(1), 15–29.

Haidt, J. (2001). The emotional dog and its rational tail: A social intuitionist approach to moral judgment. *Psychological Review*, **108**, 814–834.

Haigh, N., & Hoffman, A. J. (2014). The new heretics: Hybrid organizations and the challenges they present to corporate sustainability. *Organization & Environment*, **27**(3), 223–241.

Hall, J. K., Matos, S., Sheehan, L., & Silvestre, B. (2012). Entrepreneurship and innovation at the base of the pyramid: A recipe for inclusive growth or social exclusion? *Journal of Management Studies*, **49**(4), 785–812.

Hayes, S. C., Villatte, M., Levin, M., & Hildebrandt, M. (2011). Open, aware, and active: Contextual approaches as an emerging trend in the behavioral and cognitive therapies. *Annual Review of Clinical Psychology*, **7**, 141–168.

Haynie, J. M., Shepherd, D., Mosakowski, E., & Earley, P. C. (2010). A situated metacognitive model of the entrepreneurial mindset. *Journal of Business Venturing*, **25**, 217–229.

Haynie, J. M., & Shepherd, D. A. (2009). A measure of adaptive cognition for entrepreneurship research. *Entrepreneurship Theory & Practice*, **33**(3), 695–714.

Haynie, J. M., Shepherd, D. A., & Patzelt, H. (2012). Cognitive adaptability and an entrepreneurial task: The role of metacognitive ability and feedback. *Entrepreneurship Theory & Practice*, **36**(2), 237–265.

Heidegger, M. (1996). *Being and Time: A Translation of Sein und Zeit* (translated by Joan Stambaugh) (Albany, NY: State University of New York Press).

Hockerts, K., & Wüstenhagen, R. (2010). Greening Goliaths versus emerging Davids: Theorizing about the role of incumbents and new entrants in sustainable entrepreneurship. *Journal of Business Venturing*, **25**(5), 481–492.

Hodgkinson, G., & Healey, M. (2011). Psychological foundations of dynamic capabilities: Reflexion and reflection in strategic management. *Strategic Management Journal*, **32**(13), 1500–1516.

Karp, T. (2006). The inner entrepreneur: A constructivistic view of entrepreneurial reality construction. *Journal of Change Management*, **6**(4), 291–304.

Kozlowski, S., & Klein, K. (2000). A multilevel approach to theory and research in organizations. In K. Klein and S. Kozlowski (eds.), *Multilevel Theory, Research, and Methods in Organizations: Foundations, Extensions, and New Directions* (San Francisco: Jossey-Bass), pp. 3–90.

Kudesia, R. S. (2017). Mindfulness as metacognitive practice. *Academy of Management Review* [online].

Laszlo, C., Brown, J. S., Ehrenfeld, J., Gorham, M., Pose, I. B., Robson, L., ... Werder, P. (2014). *Flourishing Enterprise: The New Spirit of Business* (Stanford, CA: Stanford Business Books).

Laszlo, C., Brown, J. S., Sherman, D., Pose, I. B., Boland, B., Ehrenfeld, J., & Werder, P. (2012). Flourishing: A vision for business and the world. *Journal of Corporate Citizenship*, **46**(1), 31–51.

Lenox, M., & York, J. G. (2012). Environmental entrepreneurship. In P. Bansal and A. J. Hoffman (eds.), *The Oxford Handbook of Business and the Natural Environment* (Oxford: Oxford University Press), pp. 70–82.

Lewis, M. W. (2000). Exploring paradox: Toward a more comprehensive guide. *Academy of Management Review*, **25**(4), 760–776.

Lorenz, M. P., Ramsey, J. R., & Richey, R. G. (2018). Expatriates' international opportunity recognition and innovativeness: The role of metacognitive and cognitive cultural intelligence. *Journal of World Business*, **53**(2), 222–236.

Lumpkin, G. T., & Bacq, S. (2019). Civic wealth creation: A new view of stakeholder engagement and societal impact. *Academy of Management Perspectives*, **33**(4), 383–404.

McGhee, P., & Grant, P. (2016). Teaching the virtues of sustainability as flourishing to undergraduate business students. *Global Virtue Ethics Review*, **7**(2), 73–117.

McMullen, J. S., & Warnick, B. J. (2016). Should we require every new venture to be a hybrid organization? *Journal of Management Studies*, **53**(4), 630–662.

Metcalf, L., & Benn, S. (2013). Leadership for sustainability: An evolution of leadership ability. *Journal of Business Ethics*, **112**(3), 369–384.

Miller, T. L., Grimes, M. G., McMullen, J. S., & Vogus, T. J. (2012). Venturing for others with heart and head: How compassion encourages social entrepreneurship. *Academy of Management Review*, **37**(4), 616–640.

Montgomery, A., Dacin, P., & Dacin, M. (2012). Collective social entrepreneurship: Collaboratively shaping social good. *Journal of Business Ethics*, **111**(3), 375–388.

Moore, H. L. (2015). Global prosperity and sustainable development goals. *Journal of International Development*, **27**(6), 801–815.

Murnieks, C. Y., Arthurs, J. D., Cardon, M. S., Farah, N., Stornelli, J., & Michael Haynie, J. (2019). Close your eyes or open your mind: Effects of sleep and mindfulness exercises on entrepreneurs' exhaustion. *Journal of Business Venturing* [advance online publication] 1–19.

Nelson, T. O. (1996). Consciousness and metacognition. *American Psychologist*, **51**(2), 102–116.

Ochsner, K. N., Bunge, S. A., Gross, J. J., & Gabrieli, J. D. E. (2002). Rethinking feelings: An fMRI study of the cognitive regulation of emotion. *Journal of Cognitive Neuroscience*, **14**(8), 1215–1229.

Pavlovich, K., & Corner, P. D. (2014). Conscious enterprise emergence: Shared value creation through expanded conscious awareness. *Journal of Business Ethics*, **121**(3), 341–351.

Pavlovich, K., & Krahnke, K. (2012). Empathy, connectedness, and organization. *Journal of Business Ethics*, **105**(1), 131–137.

Reynolds, S. J. (2006). A neurocognitive model of the ethical decisionmaking process: Implications for study and practice. *Journal of Applied Psychology*, **91**(4), 737–748.

Richards, L. (2005). *Handling Qualitative Data: A Practical Guide* (Thousand Oaks, CA: Sage).

Richards, L., & Morse, J. (2007). *Readme First For a User's Guide to Qualitative Methods*, 2nd edn. (Thousand Oaks, CA: Sage).

Rimanoczy, I. (2013). *Big Bang Being: Developing the Sustainability Mindset* (Sheffield: Greenleaf Publishing).

Ruebottom, T. (2013). The microstructures of rhetorical strategy in social entrepreneurship: Building legitimacy through heroes and villains. *Journal of Business Venturing*, **28**(1), 98–116.

Schaefer, K., Corner, P. D., & Kearins, K. (2015). Social, environmental and sustainable entrepreneurship research: What is needed for sustainability-as-flourishing? *Organization & Environment*, **28**(4), 394–413.

Schaltegger, S., & Wagner, M. (2011). Sustainable entrepreneurship and sustainability innovation: Categories and interactions. *Business Strategy and the Environment*, **20**(4), 222–237.

Seelos, C., & Mair, J. (2005). Social entrepreneurship: Creating new business models to serve the poor. *Business Horizons*, **48**(3), 241–246.

Senge, P., & Krahnke, K. (2013). Transcendent empathy: The ability to see the larger system. In K. Pavlovich and K. Krahnke (eds.), *Organizing Through Empathy* (New York: Routledge), pp. 185–202.

Shimamura, A. P. (2000). Toward a cognitive neuroscience of metacognition. *Consciousness and Cognition*, **9**(2), 313–323.

Singh, S., Corner, P. D., & Pavlovich, K. (2015). Failed, not finished: A narrative approach to understanding venture failure stigmatization. *Journal of Business Venturing*, **30**(1), 150–166.

Singh, S., Corner, P. D., & Pavlovich, K. (2016). Spirituality and entrepreneurial failure. *Journal of Management, Spirituality & Religion*, **13**(1), 24–49.

Smith, W. K., Gonin, M., & Besharov, M. L. (2013). Managing social-business tensions: A review and research agenda for social enterprise. *Business Ethics Quarterly*, **23**(3), 407–442.

Tracey, P., Phillips, N., & Jarvis, O. (2011). Bridging institutional entrepreneurship and the creation of new organizational forms: A multilevel model. *Organization Science*, **22**(1), 60–80.

Upward, A., & Jones, P. (2016). An ontology for strongly sustainable business models: Defining an enterprise framework compatible with natural and social science. *Organization & Environment*, **29**(1), 97–123.

Vago, D. R., & Silbersweig, D. A. (2012). Self-awareness, self-regulation, and self-transcendence (S-ART): A framework for understanding the neurobiological mechanisms of mindfulness. *Frontiers in Human Neuroscience*, **6**, 1–30.

Waddell, S., Waddock, S. A., Cornell, S., Dentoni, D., McLachlan, M., & Meszoely, G. (2015). Large systems change: An emerging field of transformation and transitions. *Journal of Corporate Citizenship*, **58**(6), 5–30.

Waddock, S. A. (2013). The wicked problems of global sustainability need wicked (good) leaders and wicked (good) collaborative solutions. *Journal of Management for Global Sustainability*, **1**, 91–111.

Waldron, T. L., Fisher, G., & Pfarrer, M. (2016). How social entrepreneurs facilitate the adoption of new industry practices. *Journal of Management Studies*, **53**(5), 821–845.

Warren, C. A. B. (2002). Qualitative interviewing. In J. F. Gubrium and J. A. Holstein (eds.), *Handbook of Interview Research: Context and Method* (Thousand Oaks, CA: Sage), pp. 83–101.

Williams, P. (2002). The competent boundary spanner. *Public Administration*, **80**(1), 103–124.

Worldwatch Institute. (2017). *EarthEd: Rethinking Education on a Changing Planet* (Washington, DC: Island Press).

Wry, T., & Haugh, H. (2018). Brace for impact: Uniting our diverse voices through a social impact frame. *Journal of Business Venturing*, **33**(5), 566–574.

Yin, R. K. (2009). *Case Study Research: Design and Methods*, 4th edn. (Thousand Oaks, CA: Sage).

York, J. G., O'Neil, I., & Sarasvathy, S. D. (2016). Exploring environmental entrepreneurship: Identity coupling, venture goals, and stakeholder incentives. *Journal of Management Studies*, **53**(5), 695–737.

© 2022 World Scientific Publishing Company
https://doi.org/10.1142/9789811248863_0010

Chapter 10

How a Prosocial Personality is Helpful in Predicting Social Entrepreneurial Intentions

Preeti Tiwari

*School of Management and Entrepreneurship,
IIT Jodhpur, Rajasthan, India*

preeti.tiwari@tapmi.edu.in

Abstract

The aim of the present study is to identify the role of prosocial personality traits (empathy, moral obligation, and sense of responsibility) on the formation of social entrepreneurial intentions among the students of a premier multi-campus technical university in India using Theory of Planned Behavior (TPB) as the research framework. The sample represents 77% of the male respondents and 23% female, and the average age of the respondents was 20 years, belonging to various disciplines. Empathy was found to be the strongest affecting antecedent followed by social responsibility. Findings of this research will be helpful in predicting how the prosocial personality traits affect the formation of the intention of Indian students.

Keywords: Social ventures, social entrepreneurial intention; theory of planned behavior; prosocial personality traits, new venture creation.

10.1. Introduction

The entrepreneurship study takes three approaches: functional, personality, and behavior. The first conceptualizes the interaction between the entrepreneur and his/her environment; the second focuses on the unique characteristics of entrepreneurs; and the third centers on the actions of the entrepreneur (Cope, 2005). This study is part of the second approach as it focuses on the personality traits of social entrepreneurs. The importance of deepening the knowledge of the entrepreneurial personality is highlighted by Johnson (1990), who mentions that the study of the individual's role is critical, including his or her psychological profile, given that it is the individual who drives the entrepreneurial process. In this sense, Shane *et al.* (2003) state that the entrepreneurial process depends on the decisions of entrepreneurs and these decisions are influenced by their personal characteristics. Thus, the personality would be fundamental to realizing the intention to start an enterprise.

At present, the reason that enables or hinders social entrepreneurship and what motivates people to become social entrepreneurs seems inadequate. This leads to a more specific question: why do people become social entrepreneurs? In this sense, Short *et al.* (2009) question: "What triggers the search for and exploitation of opportunities in some, but not in others?" Short *et al.* (2009) is still of relevance, particularly in the new field of social entrepreneurship. Many anecdotal works on social entrepreneurship outline the passion the entrepreneurs develop for their cause, often pointing out the selflessness of their deeds (e.g. Bornstein *et al.*, 2004). This commitment to addressing social injustice is considered a sign of prosocial behavior and suggests the existence of a prosocial personality. Penner and Finkelstein (1998) define a prosocial personality. The prosocial personality is made up of the traits moving people to act in a way benefiting other people than themselves (Dreesbach, 2010; Penner *et al.*, 2005). This phenomenon and related behavior have been treated extensively in social psychology research to date (Dreesbach, 2010). One finding has been that there seems to be a prosocial personality, which is consistent over time (Eisenberg *et al.*, 2002). These characteristics cause a person to act when the distress of others arouses him/her (Penner *et al.*, 2005). A prosocial personality is associated with helping, social responsibility, care orientation, consideration of others, and sympathy (Eisenberg *et al.*, 2002). In line with the definitions of the social entrepreneurial and entrepreneurial personality above, this study understands prosocial personality to be a combination of stable traits common to prosocial actors but uncommon within the rest of the population, which causes them to act the way they do.

This chapter identifies the core elements influencing people to become social entrepreneurs. Therefore, this study focuses on identifying how social entrepreneurship is created and is conducted in India. As academic literature in the field of social entrepreneurship is very limited, the main focus of this study is to identify the effect of prosocial personality traits in predicting social entrepreneurial intention among the young Indian population by using the Theory of Planned Behavior (TPB) as its research framework.

10.2. Social Entrepreneurship in India

Social entrepreneurs are considered the key players in delivering basic services and opportunities to the untouched sector of India. Some are employing innovative, cost-efficient, and often technology-driven business models that put forward essential services to those who are short of access. Others are working hard at removing barriers that prevent access (Intellecap, 2012). These social entrepreneurs are recognized not only in India but also on a global level. Many of these organizations work on an impressive scale — serving millions of low-income households and transforming their quality of life (Khanapuri and Khandelwal, 2011). Social entrepreneurship culture in India is young but very aggressive. There are various social enterprises that are working toward one mission, i.e. "Better India."

India's current total population is 1.32 billion, and by 2020 it has also witnessed the world's second-largest labor force of 516.3 million people. Despite the hourly wage rates in India having more than doubled over the last couple of years, the latest World Bank report states that approximately 350 million people in India currently live below the poverty line. This implies that every third Indian is deprived of even basic necessities like nutrition, education, and healthcare, and many are still wracked by unemployment and illiteracy (Shaw *et al.*, 2013). Social entrepreneurs can prove helpful in eradicating these issues by placing those with fewer fortunes on a pathway toward a meaningful life (Lans *et al.*, 2014). India is set to become the world's youngest country demographically, with 64% of its population in the working-age group. If this major chunk of the young population in India is encouraged to take up social entrepreneurship, it will impact the Indian economy significantly by not only addressing the problem of unemployment but also several social problems in an affordable manner.

This motivated the author to investigate what factors affect the intentions formation process so as to encourage the young generation toward social entrepreneurship. Social entrepreneurship in the Indian context is still an understudied topic, with limited research studies which usually fall short of supporting empirical data. Research studies that are so far conducted in India mostly used case studies or a storytelling approach and were more focused toward the concept of social innovation through incubators and government initiatives (Sonne, 2012) and with cases of the social entrepreneur in rural development (Yadav and Goyal, 2015).

Table 10.1. Individual loadings, composite reliabilities, and AVE.

Antecedents	Items	Loading	Composite reliability	AVE
Attitude toward becoming social entrepreneur	ATB1	0.69	0.845	0.523
	ATB2	0.66		
	ATB3	0.79		
	ATB4	0.82		
	ATB5	0.64		
Subjective norms	SN1	0.89	0.852	0.660
	SN2	0.86		
	SN3	0.67		
Perceived behavioral control	PF1	0.78	0.866	0.591
	PF2	0.71		
	PF3	0.81		
	PF4	0.67		
	PF5	0.84		
Empathy	Emp1	0.88	0.928	0.684
	Emp2	0.82		
	Emp3	0.78		
	Emp4	0.83		
	Emp5	0.85		
	Emp6	0.80		
Moral obligation	MO1	0.92	0.916	0.733
	MO2	0.79		
	MO3	0.86		
	MO4	0.85		
Social responsibility	SR1	0.72	0.844	0.577
	SR2	0.85		
	SR3	0.69		
	SR4	0.77		
Social entrepreneurial intentions	SEI1	0.92	0.954	0.806
	SEI2	0.87		
	SEI3	0.89		
	SEI4	0.88		
	SEI5	0.93		

Selective research studies conducted in India in the field of social entrepreneurship are shown in Table 10.1.

Most of the literature available in the field of entrepreneurial intentions, or more specifically social entrepreneurship, were from Europe and other Western countries. Despite most of the renowned social enterprise initiatives being based in the South Asian continent, empirical research in this part of the continent is almost negligible. Social set-up and environmental factors affecting the process of social entrepreneurship is very different in this part of the world as compared to the factors covered in the existing research studies. The most familiar socio-cultural factors influencing entrepreneurship are education, religion, caste, family background, and social background. In their article, Shradha *et al.* (2005) stated that sociocultural factors, such as education, religion, caste, family support, and social background were important in the Indian environment for starting a business, and empirical results confirm that socio-cultural factors are important in the creation of entrepreneurial intentions. Therefore, instead of comparing India to other countries, this research study concentrates on how social entrepreneurship intentions are generated in India. Therefore, identifying the validity of the antecedents affecting social entrepreneurial intentions in the West and other developed European countries need to be investigated before adopting it in the Indian context.

The objectives of this study are:

- To empirically test the effect of prosocial personality traits on social entrepreneurial intentions.
- To develop and validate a conceptual model depicting the role of the TPB as a mediator in predicting social entrepreneurial intentions.

In the present study, the sample population of young undergraduates of a premier technical university in India is taken. Next, an extensive literature review is performed to understand the emergence of social entrepreneurship and various theories underlying entrepreneurship intentions.

10.3. Theoretical Background

Research dealing with the factors that affect the prosocial actions of the person has a long and diversified history in the area of both personality and social psychology. In general terms, prosocial behavior is the deliberate act determined to help others. The term "prosocial personality" is defined as acting in a certain way in order to benefit others and society as a whole (Penner *et al.*, 2005), and has attracted the attention of various researchers.

Eisenberg (2002) pointed out that a prosocial personality remains constant over time and the effect of these traits is that the person acts in certain way when the agony of others provokes them. Early research on prosocial personality traits were more focused on determining why people engage in prosocial activities (Penner *et al.*, 2004). Penner and Finkelstein (1998) defined a prosocial personality as. Therefore, it is clear from this definition that a prosocial personality is rotating around the idea of helping and benefiting others. In entrepreneurial traits studies, the prosocial personality was not studied much. There are some prominent researchers like Penner *et al.* (1995) and Eisenberg *et al.* (2002) that tried to relate this concept to the idea of entrepreneurship. The following paragraphs discusses in detail the various studies related to the personality traits of social entrepreneurs.

In order to increase the tendency of social entrepreneurship, Leadbeater (1997) conducted a qualitative research study. In his research study, Leadbeater used case studies of seven social entrepreneurs and tried to determine the distinguishing personality traits of social entrepreneurs. Despite the research study lacking empirical validation and conclusion, it highlighted the three important aspects of the social entrepreneur personality. Leadbeater defined the social entrepreneur as a person with different genes and a strong desire to change the world and proposed three adjectives for them i.e. *entrepreneurial, innovative, and transformative.*

After Leadbeater (1997), Barendsen and Gardner (2004) conducted a qualitative study to determine the personality traits that differentiate social entrepreneur with for-profit entrepreneurs. Gartner used the sample of social entrepreneurs, business entrepreneurs, and service professionals. The major finding of the Gartner study was that social entrepreneurs are similar to service professionals as they consider themselves an "outsider," but their qualities of providing innovative solutions and thinking out of the box is similar to the business entrepreneurs. Gartner further identified the traits of social entrepreneurs as being energetic and risk-takers. Although this research study proved helpful in the field of social entrepreneurship research, it failed to identify the source of these qualities. Mair and Noboa (2006) first attempted to develop a model that could capture social entrepreneurial intention formation. In their model, they used individual variables to measure intentions and suggested that the intention to start a social enterprise develops from perception of desirability, which was affected by **cognitive-emotional** dimensions, consisting of empathy as an emotional factor, and perceived feasibility, which was affected by **enablers** consisting of self-efficacy & Social Support prosocial traits, viz. moral obligation and empathy as the antecedents of perceived feasibility. They measured the effects of these variables on social entrepreneurial intentions. Antecedents that distinguish this model from traditional entrepreneurial models are empathy and moral judgment. While researchers cannot deny that everyone who possess empathy and moral judgment do not become a social entrepreneur, a certain level of empathy and moral judgment is required to trigger the social entrepreneurial intention process (Mair and Martí, 2006).

The only empirical study conducted in India in the field of social entrepreneurship is by Vasakarla (2008). In her study, Vasakarla (2008) used a sample of 75 social entrepreneurs in India. The major research findings of this quantitative research study were that the many traits, such as innovativeness, the need for achievement, and risk-taking propensity exhibited by the social entrepreneur, are similar to that of the business entrepreneur, but the major differentiating trait is that social entrepreneurs feel an emotional connection toward social issues. Hwee Nga and Shamuganathan (2010) conducted a research study in Malaysia, where they tested the effect of personality traits in predicting the characteristics of social entrepreneurship on a sample of 181 Malaysian students. However, the Big-Five personality theory used in their study that did not really prove useful in order to predict the characteristics of social entrepreneurs. Ernst (2011) carried out another research study to test social entrepreneurial intentions on a sample of 203 students from four different German universities. She used prosocial factors as antecedents to predict social entrepreneurial intention. Effect of these antecedents was mediated by variables of the TPB. In the study, Ernst (2011) failed to find any link between empathy and social entrepreneurial intentions.

Later, some researchers came up with related models. Hockerts (2015, 2017) made an attempt to validate the model of Mair and Noboa. He modified the model by removing the mediating variables (perceived desirability and perceived feasibility) and tested the direct effect of moral obligation, entrepreneurial self-efficacy, empathy, and perceived social support on social entrepreneurial intention. Hockerts (2015) further added prior experience in the model, and the effect of prior experience was mediated by the above-mentioned four antecedents. He carried out this research study on three different samples and determined that some positive relationship existed with the social entrepreneurial intentions.

Although few research studies try to empirically test the effect of antecedents on social entrepreneurial intentions, these studies are more or less replications of each other. Antecedents used in intentions studies change with time. While most of the studies based in the international context focus on individual cases offering individual-level analysis, they overlook the antecedents and prerequisites that are necessary to encourage the social entrepreneurial activities in those regions (Thompson et al., 2000).

Based on above-discussed literature, it is evident that personality traits such as creativity, risk-taking propensity, and innovativeness are required by both entrepreneurs and social entrepreneurs. The unique traits that are different in social entrepreneurs are the prosocial personality traits. As of now, only Ernst's (2011) study indirectly tried to measure the effect of prosocial personality on social entrepreneurial intentions. Thus to validate the role of prosocial personality traits, it is very important to conduct an empirical study in the Indian context as the nature and scope of every research study are different. Therefore, the main objective of this research study is to determine the relationship between three important prosocial personalities traits — viz. empathy, moral obligation, and social responsibility — with social entrepreneurial intentions. We do so by using a sample of undergraduate students of a premier technical university in India. On the basis of Ernst (2011) and Mair and Noboa (2006) studies, we propose the following theoretical framework to test social entrepreneurial intentions among Indian students (Figure 10.1).

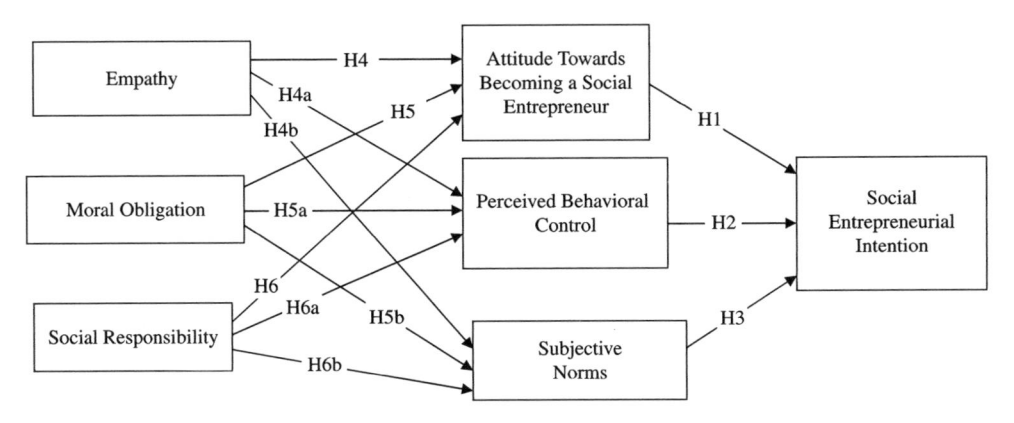

Figure 10.1. Proposed social entrepreneurship intention model.

10.4. Hypothesis Development

Social entrepreneurial intentions can be heeded as a psychological behavior of human beings that persuade them to gather knowledge, perceive the idea, and execute social business plans to become a social entrepreneur (Mair et al., 2006). In the field of entrepreneurial intentions research, various intentions models were used to study the development of intentions. These include the model proposed by Bird (1988) and developed by Boyd and Vozikis (1994), Shapero (1975), Shapero and Sokol (1982); the model tested by Krueger (1993); and the Davidsson (1995) variation, which was used and modified by researchers to test university situation. These popular models are more or less similar in the sense that they all emphasize the pre-entrepreneurial stage and integrate attitude and behavior theory (Ajzen, 1991) and self-efficacy and social learning theory (Bandura and Bandura, 1997). Therefore, intentions are used as a mediator between influencing factors and behavior (Krueger, 2000). Researchers emphasized that these antecedents do not directly affect intention but they affect attitude and which later influence intentions (Krueger, 2006). These factors/antecedents are categorized as cognitive, motivational/non-motivational or situational (Venkataraman, 2000; Shane et al. 2003; Liñán and Chen, 2009).

Shook et al. (2003) suggested researchers should try to examine and integrate different intention models. The two most used models in the field of entrepreneurial intentions are TPB and Shapero's Theory of Entrepreneurial Event. In TPB, Ajzen (1991) stated that actions are followed by conscious judgments to act in a certain way. According to Ajzen, there are three determinants of the intention to act: "attitude toward the behaviour," "subjective norm," and "perceived behavioural control." In contrast, Shapero and Sokol's (1982) model of the entrepreneurial event presents a process model of new enterprise formation. In relation to the theory, the three major factors estimated to influence an individual's intentions to act in a certain way are "perceived desirability," "perceived feasibility," and "propensity to act." Researchers pointed out that these two models are more or less similar. Shapero's construct of perceived desirability is the combination of Ajzen's attitude toward behavior and subjective norms. Perceived feasibility explained by Shapero is similar to perceived behavioral control of TPB. Here, TPB is adopted as a research framework, and the major advantages of the TPB is explained in the latter part of the chapter. The advantage of TPB is that by splitting perceived desirability into two different variables, viz. attitude toward behavior and subjective norms, TPB provides extra information as desirability is viewed in a more deferential manner (Mueller, 2011). Therefore, here, TPB is adopted as a mediator to measure the result between antecedents and social entrepreneurial intentions.

10.5. TPB

In the field of entrepreneurial intention research, one of the most adopted and used models is Ajzen's TPB (Engle *et al.*, 2010). TPB is based on the idea that an intention to carry out specific behavior is shaped by a person's attitude toward behavior and their ability to carry out that behavior (Ajzen, 1991). He also mentioned that these intentions were the outcome of attitudes developed through past experience and individual characteristics (Ajzen, 1996). According to Ajzen, there are three determinants of the intention to act. These are:

(1) Attitude toward the behavior (the degree to which a person has a good or bad assessment or evaluation of the behavior in question);
(2) Subjective norm (the perceived social pressure to execute or not to execute the behavior); and
(3) Perceived behavioral control (the individual's perception of how easy or hard performance of the behavior is going to be.)

Although TPB was initially developed in the field of psychology, due to the wider scope and extensive applicability, it is very well adapted and used in various other fields (Krueger and Carsrud, 1993; Krueger, 1993; Iakovleva and Kolvereid, 2009).

Modification in the standard TPB model is an essential prerequisite because the nature and scope of each study are different (Kolvereid, 1996). As pointed by researchers, these antecedents only affect intentions indirectly (Krueger and Carsrud, 1993). Therefore, this research study uses a theory-driven approach to testing how exogenous factors (empathy, moral obligation, and social responsibility) affect attitudes, intentions, and behavior. The classical model of TPB is shown in Figure 10.2.

```
                ┌─────────────────────────┐
                │ Attitude towards behavior│
                │   (Behavioral belief)    │
                └─────────────────────────┘
                ┌─────────────────────────┐     ┌────────────┐     ┌──────────┐
                │    Subjective norms     │────▶│ Behavioral │────▶│ Behaviour│
                │    (Normative belief)   │     │ Intentions │     │          │
                └─────────────────────────┘     └────────────┘     └──────────┘
                ┌─────────────────────────┐
                │Perceived behavioral control│
                │    (Control Belief)     │
                └─────────────────────────┘
```

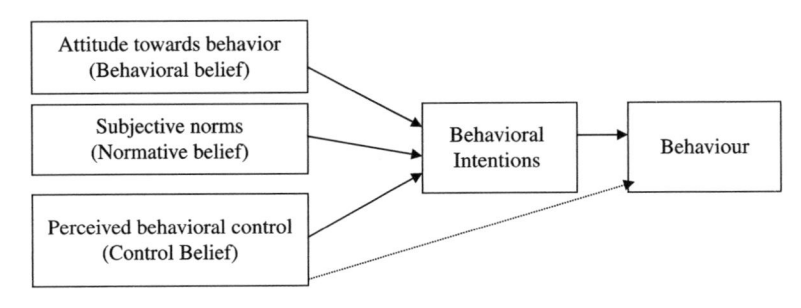

Figure 10.2.   Classical model of Theory of Planned Behavior.
Source: Ajzen (1991).

10.6. Attitude Toward Becoming a Social Entrepreneur

The variable Attitude Toward Behavior (ATB) refers to the degree to which a person has a good or bad assessment or evaluation of the behavior in question. ATB refers to one's personal pull toward particular target behavior. The most sought out construct of intention in TPB is ATB. According to Ajzen and Fishbein (1970), ATB is a "person's good or bad assessment toward performing or not to perform certain behaviour." Thus, attitude is different from the traits with respect to the evaluative nature toward certain specific intention (Armitage and Conner, 2001). In the entrepreneurial intention studies, ATB proved to be an important factor that affects intention in a positive manner (Erikson, 1998; Koçoğlu and Hassan, 2013). In many studies, ATB proved as the strongest or second strongest predictor of entrepreneurial intentions, followed by perceived behavioral control (Krueger and Brazeal, 1994). Therefore, for the purpose of this research study, we adopt ATB as an attitude toward becoming a social entrepreneur, i.e. the degree to which person possesses positive or negative assessment toward social entrepreneurship as a career option. Therefore, the following hypothesis formed:

H1: Attitude toward becoming a social entrepreneur has a positive effect on social entrepreneurial intentions.

10.6.1. Subjective norms

Subjective norms (SN) refer to the perceived social pressure to execute or not execute the behavior and comprises the pressure of family, friends, and other important people. In the social entrepreneurial intention study, Ernst (2011) also found the insignificant relationship between SN and the antecedents used in the study. However, a direct relationship between SN and social entrepreneurial intentions was found to be significant in her study. India is a society with clear collectivistic traits; this means that high preference is given to the social framework.

Family, friends, and various other associated sub-groups affect individual decision-making process. Thus it is very important to measure whether subjective norms will be helpful in predicting social entrepreneurial intentions. Therefore, the researcher formed the following hypothesis:

H2: Subjective norms have a positive effect on social entrepreneurial intentions.

10.6.2. *Perceived behavioral control*

Perceived behavioral control (PBC) can be considered as the antecedent to the actual levels of control (Armitage and Conner, 2001). More specifically, PBC is the individual belief about his/her ability to carry out a certain task. In entrepreneurial intention studies, there is an ongoing debate about the fact that self-efficacy and PBC are the same as they both measure the ability to carry out a particular activity. In a similar fashion, Ajzen (2002) considers self-efficacy as a subset of PBC. In this research study, self-efficacy is not considered as equivalent to PBC. However, for the purpose of this study, self-efficacy is identified as task-specific (Krueger and Dickson, 1994), whereas PBC is a broader concept. As defined by Ajzen (2002), PBC is the perceived acceptance or difficulty in performing the behavior, therefore it includes various activities required to perform that task. Hence in this study, self-efficacy and PBC are used and measured separately.

Therefore following hypothesis formed on the basis of the above explanation:

H3: Perceived behavioral control has a positive effect on social entrepreneurial intentions.

10.6.3. *Empathy*

Empathy is defined as a person's ability to access another person state of mind in particular circumstances (Mcdonald and Messinger, 2013). Mair and Noboa (2006) described empathy as an antecedent of attitude toward the behavior. According to the social cognition theory of Bandura (1999), empathy can be divided into two parts: emotional and cognitive empathy. Emotional empathy is dealing with the emotional response a person has toward others, whereas in the latter, an empathetic person imaginatively acquires the role of the other and is able to calculate the feelings and actions of others (Bandura and Bandura, 1997).

Social entrepreneurship is all about understanding the difficulties faced by other people and converting that social problem into an opportunity for the betterment of the people (Prahalad, 2009). Therefore, in order to predict social entrepreneurial intentions, empathy is considered an important antecedent. In this research study, we used cognitive empathy, i.e. the capability to understand others' emotional state of mind (Hockerts, 2015). Based on the literature, the authors formed the following hypothesis:

H4: Empathy is positively related to attitude toward becoming a social entrepreneur.
H4a: Empathy is positively related to subjective norms.
H4b: Empathy is positively related to perceived behavioral control.

10.6.4. *Moral obligation*

Moral obligation has multiple meanings. In general, moral obligation is defined as a belief of a person by the virtue of belief in order to perform a set of tasks (Bryant, 2009). Mair and Noboa (2006) first used moral obligation in their proposed model for social entrepreneurial intention. Roberts and Woods (2005) stated that a social entrepreneur should have high moral values. There are individuals who are more motivated by a sense of duty toward society. In a similar fashion, social entrepreneurs are born within normal people in the urge of doing good for the betterment of the society and for the development of the nation on a whole (Thompson, 2008). Boschee (1995) mentioned that social entrepreneurs are those who can balance "moral imperatives and the profit motive." In this study, we measure moral obligation at the societal level, not at the individual level. Therefore on the basis of literature authors formed the following hypothesis:

H5: Moral obligation is positively related to attitude toward becoming a social entrepreneur.
H5a: Moral obligation is positively related to subjective norms.
H5b: Moral obligation is positively related to perceived behavioral control.

10.6.5. *Social responsibility*

Bierhoff (1996) defined social responsibility as the characteristics that result in a sense of commitment toward those who are in pain or distress. It can be described as acting with compassion and sympathy toward the underprivileged and disadvantaged in the field of social entrepreneurial research; however, this antecedent in not much explored and tested. Prominent researchers in the field of social entrepreneurship like Dees (2001) mentioned the self-sacrificing behavior of social entrepreneurs. Mair and Noboa (2006) identified social entrepreneurs as social change agents with strong ethical traits. Therefore, it is advisable to measure the sense of social responsibility in relation to social entrepreneurs. In her research study, Hwee Nga and Shamuganathan (2010) determined that social responsibility is the main trait that differentiates social entrepreneurs from business entrepreneurs. In the literature on social entrepreneurial intention formation, at the time of writing, only Ernst (2011) tried to measure the effect of social responsibility on the intention formation. In her research study, social responsibility showed a significant relationship with attitude toward becoming a social entrepreneur and subjective norms. However, the relationship between social responsibility and perceived behavioral control were not tested in this research study. Therefore, on the basis of literature, the following hypotheses were formed

H6: Social responsibility is positively related to attitude toward becoming a social entrepreneur.
H6a: Social responsibility is positively related to subjective norms.
H6b: Social responsibility is positively related to perceived behavioral control.

10.6.6. *Social entrepreneurial intention*

According to TPB, individual behavior could be predicted from its consequent intentions (Ajzen and Fishbein, 1970). Researchers have described intentions in many different ways. Bird (1998) defines intention as a state of mind that motivates the person toward a certain goal or path (Bird 1998). Intention can be considered as a precondition that governs planned behavior (Souitaris *et al.* 2007). According to Krueger (1994), "Entrepreneurial intention can be defined as the commitment of a person towards some future behavior, which is projected toward starting, a business or an organisation." Various research studies emphasize the importance of intentions as one of the crucial variables in predicting planned behavior (Krueger and Brazeal, 1994). Thus, researchers posit that entrepreneurial intention is an indispensable tendency for the formation of enterprise, and it has become an emerging research area that is attracting a substantial amount of research. The configuration of social entrepreneurial intention is an area that is barely touched by the researchers. Ziegler (2009) mentioned that the prerequisites contributing to people's motivations to act as a social entrepreneur are yet to be explored. Thus, identifying the factors that facilitate an individual to opt for social entrepreneurship still requires a lot of research.

10.7. Research Methodology

10.7.1. *Data collection and sample*

After an extensive literature survey, quantitative methods were used to examine the effect of exogenous variables on social entrepreneurial intention. In order to select the sample for the research study, the researcher followed Kruger's (1993) suggestion that, for an accurate measurement of entrepreneurial intentions, the sample should be selected from those currently facing major career decisions. Although various entrepreneurial intention studies used a sample of undergraduate students, no prior Indian study sampled undergraduate students in order to measure social entrepreneurial intentions.

For this research study, primary data were collected by distributing the questionnaire to the students of one of the premier private universities in India. The type of research sampling used is systemized random sampling. Responses were collected from final-year students of engineering and management, as they are clearer about their professional choices. In the questionnaire, there was an additional test regarding the privacy of the response and to highlight the meaning of social entrepreneurship. Besides this, the researcher also explained the meaning of terms such as social enterprise, social entrepreneurship, and social entrepreneurial intentions to the participants. The survey was personally administered by the researcher. The questionnaire contained 37 items representing antecedents used in the study, including the control variable (age, gender, entrepreneurial education, and family business). A total of 1,550 questionnaires were distributed to the students, out of which we received 975 completed questionnaires corresponding to a 62.90% response rate. About 77% ($N = 751$) of the respondents were male and 23% ($N = 224$) were female, and the average age of the respondents was 20 years.

10.7.2. *Measures*

10.7.2.1. Social entrepreneurial intention

In the literature on entrepreneurial intentions, there are various scales that measure intentions. For this study, the 6-item scale used was adopted from Krueger *et al.*'s (2000) study. The items were measured on a 7-point Likert's scale from 1 = strongly disagree and 7 = strongly agree. Cronbach's alpha value was $\alpha = 0.88$.

(i) Independent variable:
(a) Attitude toward becoming a social entrepreneur
To measure the attitude toward becoming social entrepreneur, the authors used scales developed by Ajzen (2002b) and EIQ (Liñán and Chen, 2007, 2009). Pretest of theses scale reduced the items, and the final scale comprised five items. Cronbach's alpha value was $\alpha = 0.73$.

(b) Subjective norms
To measure subjective norms, authors used EIQ (Liñán and Chen, 2007, 2009). EIQ consists of two sets of three items that measured the normative belief and

motivation to comply. To measure these, two sets were multiplied and divided by three to generate an average score (Rueda et al., 2015). Cronbach's alpha value was $\alpha = 0.69$.

(c) Perceived behavioral control
To measure perceived behavioral control, researchers used the 5-item scale developed by Liñán and Chen (2009) and modified by Ernst (2011). The items were measured on a 7-point Likert scale from 1 = strongly disagree and 7 = strongly agree. Cronbach's alpha value was $\alpha = 0.85$.

(d) Moral obligation and empathy
Hockerts (2015b) developed the Social Entrepreneurial Antecedent Scale (SEAS) in order to measure moral obligation, empathy, previous experience in social activities, and social entrepreneurial self-efficacy. It is a newly developed scale in the field of social entrepreneurial research. Various social intention studies (Ernst, 2011; Hwee Nga and Shamuganathan, 2010; Forster and Grichnik, 2013; Hemingway, 2005) were considered while forming this scale. The SEAS scale was validated in three different samples (Hockerts, 2015). Therefore, in order to measure these two constructs, viz. moral obligation and empathy, the researcher used SEAS. Reliability and validity of the scale were checked.

To measure moral obligation, a 4-item scale was used. Cronbach's alpha value was $\alpha = 0.78$. For empathy, a 6-item scale was used. A sample item to measure empathy was: "When thinking about socially disadvantaged people, I try to put myself in their shoes," and Cronbach's alpha value was $\alpha = 0.84$.

(e) Social responsibility
To measure social responsibility, we followed the standard questionnaire of Bierhoff and Schülken (1999) and Ernst (2011). The final three items were chosen based on the relevance of their content and high factor loading. Cronbach's alpha value was $\alpha = 0.80$.

10.8. Data Analysis

For data analysis, SPSS version 20 is used, and the researcher used the same software to test Cronbach's Alpha Reliability and validity of the questionnaire.

10.8.1. *Exploratory factor analysis*

An exploratory factor analysis of the sample confirmed the six-factor model. Factorability of data is tested using Bartlett's Test of Sphericity and the Kaiser–Meyer–Olin (KMO) test to measure sampling sufficiency. In EFA, KMO value of 0.810 was derived and significant value of Bartlett's test (χ^2 =357, df = 395, $p < 0.000$) was generated to depict the adequacy of sampling (Child, 1990).

10.8.2. *Reliability of the scales*

According to the rule of thumb, if Cronbach's alpha is equal or higher to 0.70, then it is considered as good reliability. All independent variables are in good reliability. Cronbach's alpha values were calculated for attitude toward becoming a social entrepreneur ($\alpha = 0.815$), subjective norms ($\alpha = 0.621$), perceived behavioral control ($\alpha = 0.874$), empathy ($\alpha = 0.783$), moral obligation ($\alpha = 0.841$), and social responsibility ($\alpha = 0.756$). The dependent variable, viz. social entrepreneurial intention, also showed tremendous reliability result, with Cronbach's alpha value of 0.915. Thus the alpha values show the internal consistency of the items authenticates the reliability of scales used in the study.

10.9. Results

Descriptive statistics and correlation are shown in Table 10.2. These statistics show that the hypothesis is partially supported. Attitude toward becoming a social entrepreneur ($r = 0.38, p < 0.01$), subjective norms ($r = 0.41, p < 0.01$), perceived behavioral control ($r = 0.45, p < 0.01$), empathy ($r = 0.36, p < 0.01$), moral obligation ($r = 0.32, p < 0.01$), and social responsibility ($r = 0.27, p < 0.01$) were positively correlated with social entrepreneurial intention, showing provisional support.

10.9.1. *Convergent and discriminant validity*

Convergent validity reflects the extent to which two measures capture a common construct (Chell, 2007). The average variance extracted is used as an indicator. Composite reliability and average variance extracted (AVE) were tested in order to examine the internal reliability of the scales shown in Table 10.1, i.e. individual loadings, composite reliabilities, and AVE.

Table 10.2. Measurement model.

S. No	Model fit		Absolute measures			Incremental fit measures		Parsimonious fit measures	RMSEA
Model 1	χ^2	χ^2/df	RMR	GFI	AGFI	CFI	TLI	PCFI	
	570.43	1.817	0.021	0.872	0.811	0.835	0.877	0.066	0.059

As shown in Table 10.1, the AVE value is above 0.50. Fornell (1981) stated that an AVE value higher than 0.50 is considered to be a more representative indicator of the construct. Convergent validity is measured using AVE. The summary of derived statistics for the measurement model is shown in Table 10.2.

As shown in the proposed model, the social entrepreneurial intention is influenced by prosocial personality traits, viz. empathy, moral obligation, and social responsibility of students, and these effects are mediated by three mediators, viz. attitude toward becoming a social entrepreneur, subjective norms, and perceived behavioral control. The first model tests the relationship between the mediators, viz. attitude toward becoming a social entrepreneur, subjective norms, and perceived behavioral control with social entrepreneurial intention. The hypothesis (H1) i.e. attitude toward becoming a social entrepreneur showed the positive significant relationship of medium value ($\beta = 0.28***$). Subjective norms (H2) highlighted the positive significant relationship of small size ($\beta = 0.13***$). The result of subjective norms was similar to previous entrepreneurial intention studies (Engle et al., 2010; Heuer and Liñán, 2013; Rueda et al., 2015), where subjective norms showed the lowest effect on entrepreneurial intention. Perceived behavioral control (H3) disclosed the strongest impact on social entrepreneurial intention ($\beta = 0.37***$). Therefore, TPB factors explained the moderate percentage of social entrepreneurial variance ($R^2 = 0.30$). Alternative Model 1 showed acceptable fit to the data ($\chi^2/df = 2.94$; RMSEA = 0.044; SRMR = 0.066; NNFI = 0.88; CFI = 0.87; AGFI = 0.83).

The Alternative Model 2 (Figure 10.3) was used to test the relationship between empathy (H5), moral obligation (H6), and sense of responsibility (H7) and the attitude toward becoming a social entrepreneur. Empathy showed a strong positive

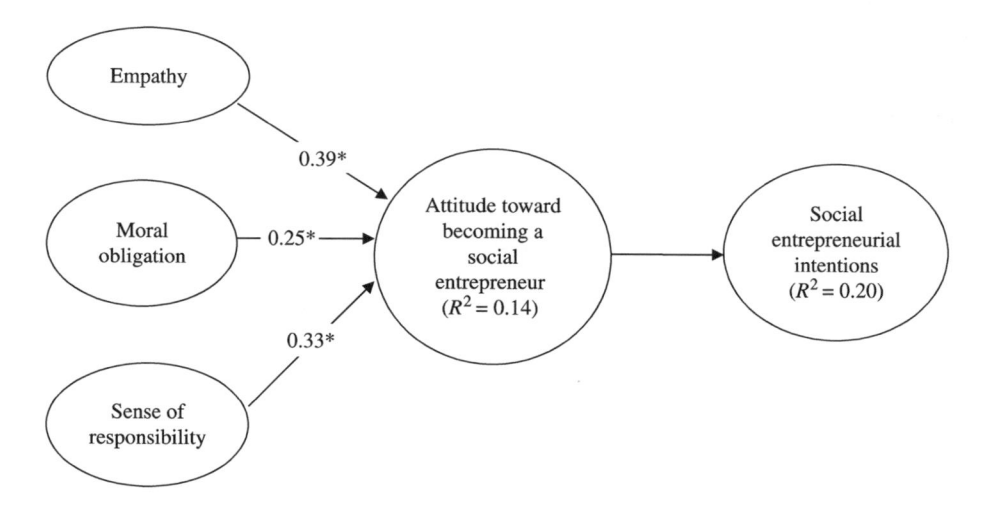

Figure 10.3. The relationship between antecedents and attitude towards becoming a social entrepreneur.

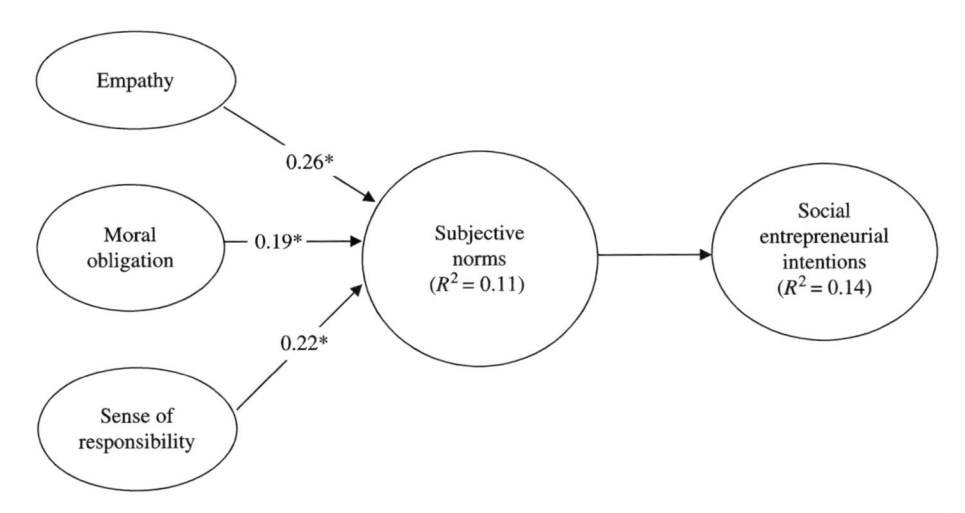

Figure 10.4. The relationship between antecedents and subjective norms.

significant relationship with attitude toward becoming a social entrepreneur ($\beta = 0.39^{**}$, $p < 0.01$), followed by social responsibility ($\beta = 0.33^{**}$, $p < 0.01$) and moral obligation ($\beta = 0.25^{**}$, $p < 0.01$). The Alternative Model 2 showed an acceptable fit to the data (χ^2/df = 5.77; RMSEA = 0.051; SRMR = 0.063; NNFI = 0.81; CFI = 0.92; AGFI = 0.86).

The Alternative Model 3 (Figure 10.4) was used to test the relationship between empathy (H5a), moral obligation (H6a), and social responsibility (H7a) and the subjective norms. Empathy showed a strong positive significant relationship with subjective norms ($\beta = 0.26^{**}$, $p < 0.01$), followed by social responsibility ($\beta = 0.22^{**}$, $p < 0.01$) and moral obligation ($\beta = 0.19^{**}$, $p < 0.01$). The Alternative Model 3 showed an acceptable fit to the data (χ^2/df = 4.19; RMSEA = 0.048; SRMR = 0.061; NNFI = 0.85; CFI = 0.87; AGFI = 0.88).

The Alternative Model 4 (Figure 10.5) was used to test the relationship between empathy (H5b), moral obligation (H6b), and social responsibility (H7b) and perceived behavioral control. Again empathy showed a strongest positive relationship with perceived behavioral control ($\beta = 0.40^{**}$, $p < 0.01$) followed by moral obligation ($\beta = 0.28^{**}$, $p < 0.01$) and social responsibility ($\beta = 0.16^{**}$, $p < 0.01$). The Alternative Model 4 showed acceptable fit to the data (χ^2/df = 7.25; RMSEA = 0.056; SRMR = 0.069; NNFI = 0.91; CFI = 0.83; AGFI = 0.85).

As shown in Figures 10.3–10.5, all the antecedents used in the study showed a positive significant relationship with the attitude toward becoming a social entrepreneur, subjective norms, and perceived behavioral control. Hence all hypotheses are accepted.

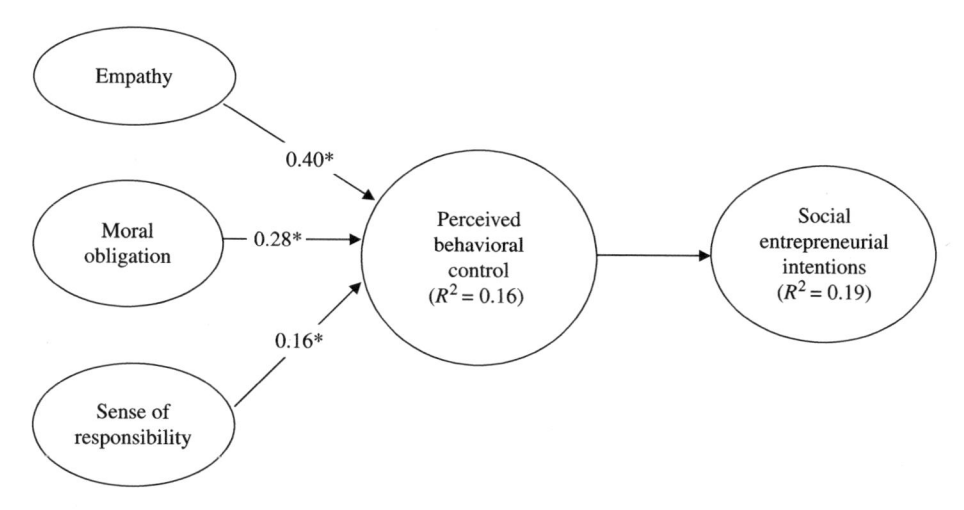

Figure 10.5. The relationship between antecedents and perceived behavioral control.

10.10. Discussion

10.10.1. *TPB*

According to Kruger (1993), antecedents do not directly affect intention but they affect attitude, which later influence intentions. Therefore, in this research study, authors used TPB as the research framework. The result of TPB is in line with similar studies from entrepreneurship: "attitude toward becoming a social entrepreneur" and "perceived behavioral control" show high significant positive effects on social entrepreneurial intentions. This implies that the students who are expected to develop a social entrepreneurial intention are those who have positive perception toward becoming a social entrepreneur. The result of the study also suggests that subjective norms also affect social entrepreneurial intentions. Findings regarding the result of subjective norms are contradictory to the previous study of Ernst (2011), where subjective norms did not show any significant relationship with the social entrepreneurship intention. Therefore, the role of subjective norms should be explored further in a collectivist country like India, where there exist strong family ties. Pressure exerted by important people and close surroundings do affect the decision-making process. Hence, for the future research, subjective norms should be taken as the central factor that not only affects the intentions process but also controls other factors' interaction.

10.10.2. *Effect of prosocial personality trait*

Empathy showed the strongest relationship with attitude toward becoming a social entrepreneur. This suggests that an ability to put yourself in other's situation means that the individual will also be capable of performing in a way that solves other's problems. This shows that empathy plays an important role in developing attitude and intentions. Empathy and social responsibility showed a strong relationship with subjective norms. In simple terms, it is suggested that individuals who want to "do good" are looking for those career opportunities that enable them to follow this passion. The strong relationship of social responsibility with subjective norms also suggests that social responsibility is often considered as the trait which a person inherent from his/her upbringing. All the three antecedents of prosocial personality trait, viz. empathy, moral obligation, and social responsibility, showed a significant relationship with the perceived behavioral control. Hence, the ability to put yourself in other's shoes, a moral obligation to help marginalized people, and a sense of responsibility proved helpful in developing the perceived ability of the person in order to start his/her own social venture. This is the first study that tried to measure the direct link between prosocial personality traits with perceived behavioral control.

The results of this research study contrast with the previous studies of Forster and Grichnik (2013) and Ernst (2011), in which empathy not only showed an insignificant relationship but also showed a negative effect. The result shows that the proposed model in the present study explains 53% of the variance. To our knowledge, this research study is considered to be the first that tried to determine the effect of prosocial personality traits on social entrepreneurial intentions.

10.11. Theoretical Implications

Social entrepreneurs engage in the activity of solving a social problem. Therefore, it is important to analyze whether an individual's personality traits affect his/her decision-making processes. In this research, the study authors tried to determine an indirect effect of prosocial personality traits on students' intention to opt for social entrepreneurship as their career choice. Ernst (2011) was the first research study in the area of social entrepreneurship that tried to determine the effect of prosocial personality traits on social entrepreneurial intention formation by adopting TPB as the mediator. In Ernst's (2011) research study, both empathy and moral obligation did not show any relationship with the attitude toward becoming a social entrepreneur and subjective norms. This research study extends the Ernst (2011) study by testing the effect of empathy, moral obligation, and social responsibility on perceived behavioral control.

In previous studies of Foster (2013) and Hockerts (2015), empathy showed a positive effect on intention formation, whereas in Ernst (2011), it showed a negative influence on ATB. In this research study, empathy showed a strong relationship with the attitude toward becoming a social entrepreneur. This study contributes to the growing body of the empirical literature on social entrepreneurship by synthesizing results from the literature on entrepreneurial intentions. This is the first empirical study conducted in India in the field of social entrepreneurship. It used a sample of 975 students to perform a quantitative analysis of the factors identified in the literature. Therefore, this is research study can be helpful in developing regions, where social entrepreneurship as a phenomenon is growing at tremendous speed but research in this field is still lagging behind.

10.12. Practical Implications

Based on the study findings, efforts should be made by policy-makers and universities to start such courses that can be helpful in developing social responsibility and belongingness among students. Ashoka University started an initiative known as "Ashoka Empathy Initiative" that facilitates schools to participate in a collaborative initiative to indulge young students with the feeling of empathy. Concretely, interested business schools should engage in and try to measure the effect of service-learning that exposes students to social problems first hand and can start some programs that increase the empathetic behavior of the students. The findings also suggest that interventions could be aimed at eliciting empathy with disadvantaged groups, as well as highlighting the availability of support systems. Stressing society's moral obligation seems to be less important. Moreover, the results also suggest that interventions that bring individuals in direct contact with social problems are likely to elicit an increase in social entrepreneurial intentions.

References

Ajzen, I. (1991). The theory of planned behaviour. *Organisational Behaviour and Human Decision Processes*, **50**(2), 179–211.

Ajzen, I. (1996). The social psychology of decision-making. In *Social Psychology: A Handbook of Basic Principles* (New York: Guilford Press), pp. 297–325.

Ajzen, I. (2002). Residual effects of past on later behavior: Habituation and reasoned action perspectives. *Personality and Social Psychology Review*, **6**(2), 107–122.

Ajzen, I., & Fishbein, M. (1970). The prediction of behaviour from attitudinal and normative variables. *Journal of Experimental Social Psychology*, **6**(4), 466–487.

Ajzen, I., & Thomas, M. J. (1986). Prediction of goal-directed behaviour: Attitudes, intentions, and perceived behavioral control. *Journal of Experimental Social Psychology*, **22**(5), 453–474.

Anderson, J. C., & Gerbing, D. W. (1988). Structural equation modelling in practice: A review and recommended a two-step approach. *Psychological Bulletin*, **103**(3), 411.

Armitage, C. J., & Conner, M. (2001). Efficacy of the Theory of Planned Behaviour: A meta-analytic review. *The British Journal of Social Psychology*, **40**(4), 471–499.

Austin, J., Stevenson, H., & Wei-Skillern, J. (2006). Social and commercial entrepreneurship: Same, different, or both? *Entrepreneurship Theory and Practice*, **30**(1), 1–22.

Baker, T., & Nelson, R. E. (2005). Creating something from nothing: Resource construction through entrepreneurial bricolage. *Administrative Science Quarterly*, **50**(3), 329–366.

Bandura, A. (1999). Social cognitive theory of personality. In *Handbook of Personality*, pp. 154–196.

Bandura, A., & Bandura, A. (1997). *Guide for Constructing Self-efficacy Scales*, pp. 307–337.

Barendsen, L., & Gardner, H. (2004). Is the social entrepreneur a new type of leader?. *Leader to Leader*, **2004**(34), 43.

Bull, M. (2008). Challenging tensions: Critical, theoretical and empirical perspectives on social enterprise. *International Journal of Entrepreneurial Behavior & Research*, **14**(5), 268–275.

Bird, B. (1998). Implementing entrepreneurial ideas: The case for intention. *Academy of Management Review*, **13**(3), 442–453.

Bierhoff, H. W. (1997). Prosocial behaviour. In *Social Psychology* (Berlin, Heidelberg: Springer), pp. 395–420.

Bierhoff, H. W., & Schülken, T. (1999). *Motives of volunteer helpers: comparison of volunteers, social pedagogues, community service providers and professional helpers*. Ruhr-Univ., Fac. For Psychology.

Bocken, N. M. P., Short, S. W., Rana, P., & Evans, S. (2014). A literature and practice review to develop sustainable business model archetypes. *Journal of Cleaner Production*, **65**, 42–56.

Boons, F., & Lüdeke-Freund, F. (2013). Business models for sustainable innovation: State-of-the-art and steps towards a research agenda. *Journal of Cleaner Production*, **45**, 9–19.

Bornstein, G., Kugler, T., & Ziegelmeyer, A. (2004). Individual and group decisions in the centipede game: Are groups more "rational" players?. *Journal of Experimental Social Psychology*, **40**(5), 599–605.

Boschee, J. (1995). Social entrepreneurship: Some nonprofits are not only thinking about the unthinkable, they're doing it — Running a profit. *Across the Board, The Conference Board Meeting*, **32**(3), 1–25.

Boyd, N. G., & Vozikis, G. S. (1994). The influence of self-efficacy on the development of entrepreneurial intentions and actions. *Entrepreneurship Theory & Practice*, **18**, 63–63.

Bryant, P. (2009). Self-regulation and moral awareness among entrepreneurs. *Journal of Business Venturing*, **24**(5), 505–518.

Child, D. (1990). *The essentials of factor analysis*. (Washington, DC: Cassell Educational).

Chowdhury, I., & Santos, F. M. (2010). Scaling social innovations: The case of gram vikas. *Director*, 0–35.

Cope, J. (2005). Toward a dynamic learning perspective of entrepreneurship. *Entrepreneurship Theory and Practice*, **29**(4), 373–397.

Datta, P. B., & Gailey, R. (2012). Empowering women through social entrepreneurship: Case study of a women's cooperative in India. *Entrepreneurship: Theory and Practice*, **36**(3), 569–587.

Davidsson, P. (1995). Determinants of entrepreneurial intentions. In *RENT XI Workshop*. https://eprints.qut.edu.au/2076/1/RENT_IX.pdf.

Dees, J. G. (1998). The meaning of "social entrepreneurship." 1–6.
Defourny, J., & Nyssens, M. (2010). Conceptions of social enterprise and social entrepreneurship in Europe and the United States: Convergences and divergences. *Journal of Social Entrepreneurship*, **1**(1), 32–53.
Eisenberg, N., Guthrie, I. K., Cumberland, A., Murphy, B. C., Shepard, S. A., Zhou, Q., & Carlo, G. (2002). Prosocial development in early adulthood: a longitudinal study. *Journal of Personality and Social Psychology*, **82**(6), 993.
Engle, R. L. et al. (2010). Entrepreneurial intent: A twelve-country evaluation of Ajzen's model of planned behavior. *International Journal of Entrepreneurial Behaviour & Research*, **16**(1), 35–57.
Ernst, K. K. (2011). Heart over mind — An empirical analysis of social entrepreneurial intention formation on the basis of the theory of planned behavior (Doctoral). *Schumpeter School of Business and Economics, University of Wuppertal–Bergische Universität Wuppertal*.
Eisenberg, N., Fabes, R. A., Guthrie, I. K., & Reiser, M. (2000). Dispositional emotionality and regulation: their role in predicting the quality of social functioning. *Journal of Personality and Social Psychology*, **78**(1), 136.
Fitzsimmons, J. R., & Douglas, E. J. (2011). The interaction between feasibility and desirability in the formation of entrepreneurial intentions. *Journal of Business Venturing*, **26**(4), 431–440.
Forster, F., & Grichnik, D. (2013). Social entrepreneurial intention formation of corporate volunteers. *Journal of Social Entrepreneurship*, **4**(2), 153–181.
Ghani, E., Kerr, W. R., & O'Connell, S. (2013). Spatial determinants of entrepreneurship in India. *Regional Studies*, **48**, 1071–1089.
Harding, R. (2004). Social enterprise: The new economic engine? *Business Strategy Review*, **15**(4), 39–43.
Hemingway, C. A. (2005). Personal values as a catalyst for corporate social entrepreneurship. *Journal of Business Ethics*, **60**(3), 233–249.
Hendry, J. (2004). *Between Enterprise and Ethics: Business and Management in a Moral Society* (Oxford University Press).
Heuer, A., & Liñán, F. (2013). Testing alternative measures of subjective norms in entrepreneurial intention models. *International Journal of Entrepreneurship and Small Business*, **19**(1), 39–49.
Hirsch, P. M., & Levin, D. Z. (1999). Umbrella advocates versus validity police: A life-cycle model. *Organization Science*, **10**(2), 199–212.
Hockerts, K. (2015a). Determinants of social entrepreneurial intentions determinants of social entrepreneurial intentions. *Academy of Management Annual Meeting Proceedings* (January).
Hockerts, K. (2015b). The Social Entrepreneurial Antecedents Scale (SEAS): A validation study. *Social Enterprise Journal*, **11**(3), 260–280.
Hu, L., & Bentler, P. M. (1998). Fit indices in covariance structure modelling: Sensitivity to unparameterized model misspecification. *Psychological Methods*, **3**(4), 424–453.

Hwee Nga, J. K., & Shamuganathan, G. (2010). The influence of personality traits and demographic factors on social entrepreneurship start up intentions. *Journal of Business Ethics*, **95**, 259–282.

Iakovleva, T., & Kolvereid, L. (2009). An integrated model of entrepreneurial intentions. *International Journal of Business and Globalisation*, **3**(1), 66.

Intellecap (2012). On the path to sustainability and scale: A study of India's social enterprise landscape. *Intellecap Report*, (April), 66.

Johnson, B. R. (1990). Toward a multidimensional model of entrepreneurship: The case of achievement motivation and the entrepreneur. *Entrepreneurship Theory and Practice*, **14**(3), 39–54.

Khanapuri, V. B., & Khandelwal, M. R. (2011). Scope for fair trade and social entrepreneurship in India. *Business Strategy Series*, **12**(4), 209–215.

Koçoğlu, M., & Hassan, M. U. (2013). Assessing entrepreneurial intentions of university students : A comparative study of two different cultures: Turkey and Pakistan. *European Journal of Business and Management*, **5**(13), 243–252.

Koe, J., Nga, H., & Shamuganathan, G. (2010). The influence of personality traits and demographic factors on social entrepreneurship start up intentions. *Journal of Business Ethics*, **95**(2), 259–282.

Kolvereid, L. (1996). Prediction of employment status choice intentions. *Entrepreneurship Theory & Practice*, **21**(1), 47–57.

Krueger, N. (2000). Entrepreneurial intentions are dead: Long live. In A. L. Carsrud & M. Brännback (eds.), *Understanding the Entrepreneurial Mind, International Studies in Entrepreneurship* (Springer Science+Business Media), pp. 51–72.

Krueger, N. (2006). So you thought the intentions model was simple? Cognitive style and the specification of entrepreneurial intentions models cognitive style and the specification of entrepreneurial intentions models. *SSRN Electronic Journal*, **10** (2006).

Krueger, N. (1993). Title: The impact of prior entrepreneurial exposure on perceptions of new venture feasibility and desirability. *Entrepreneurship Theory & Practice*, **18**(1), 315–330.

Krueger, N. F., & Brazeal, D. V. (1994). Entrepreneurial potential and potential entrepreneurs. *Entrepreneurship Theory & Practice*, **18**, 91–104.

Krueger, N., & Dickson, P. R. (1994). How believing in ourselves increases risk taking: Perceived self-efficacy and opportunity recognition. *Decision Sciences*, **25**(3), 385–400.

Krueger, N. F., & Carsrud, A. L. (1993). Entrepreneurial intentions: Applying the theory of planned behaviour. *Entrepreneurship & Regional Development*, **5**, 315–330.

Krueger, N. F., Reilly, M. D., & Carsrud, A. L. (2000). Competing models of entrepreneurial intentions. *Journal of Business Venturing*, **15**(5–6), 411–432.

Lans, T., Blok, V., & Wesselink, R. (2014). Learning apart and together: Towards an integrated competence framework for sustainable entrepreneurship in higher education. *Journal of Cleaner Production*, **62**, 37–47.

Leadbeater, C. (1997). The rise of the social entrepreneur, Report No. 25, Demos.

Leonard, H. B., Mcdonald, S., & Rangan, V. K. (2008). The future of social enterprise. Working Paper, Harvard Business School.

Light, P. C. (2006). Reshaping social entrepreneurship. *Stanford Social Innovation Review*, **4**(3), 47–51.

Liñán, F. (2004). Intention-based models of entrepreneurship education. *Piccolla Impresa/Small Business*, **3**, 11–35. Available at: http://congreso.us.es/gpyde/DOWNLOAD/a9.pdf (Accessed November 20, 2014).

Liñán, F., & Chen, Y. W. (2006). Testing the entrepreneurial intention model on a two-country sample. https://idus.us.es/bitstream/handle/11441/60716/Testing_the_entrepreneurial_intention_model.pdf?sequence=1.

Liñán, F., Urbano, D., & Guerrero, M. (2011). Regional variations in entrepreneurial cognitions: Start-up intentions of university students in Spain. *Entrepreneurship and Regional Development*, **23**(3–4), 187–215.

Liñán, F., & Chen, Y. (2009). Development and cross-cultural application of a specific instrument to measure entrepreneurial intentions. *Entrepreneurship Theory and Practice*, **33**(3), 593–617.

Mair, J. (2008). Social entrepreneurship: Taking stock and looking ahead. *World Entrepreneurship Forum, IESE Business School*, pp. 1–17.

Mair, J., & Martí, I. (2006). Social entrepreneurship research: A source of explanation, prediction, and delight. *Journal of World Business*, **41**(1), 36–44. Available at: http://linkinghub.elsevier.com/retrieve/pii/S1090951605000544 (Accessed July 9, 2014).

Mair, J., & Noboa, E. (2003). Working Paper. 3(521).

Mair, J., & Noboa, E. (2006). Social entrepreneurship: How intentions to create a social venture are formed. In *Social entrepreneurship* (pp. 121–135). Palgrave Macmillan, London.

Mair, J., Robinson, J., & Hockerts, K. (2006). *Social Entrepreneurship*, Available at: http://www.palgraveconnect.com/doifinder/10.1057/9780230625655.

Mcdonald, N. M., & Messinger, D. S. (2013). On the development of empathy: How, when and why. In *Free Will, Emotions, and Moral Actions: Philosophy and Neuroscience in Dialogue*, pp.1–36.

Mulgan, G. (2006). The process of social innovation. *Innovations*, **1**(2), 145–162.

Mueller, S. (2011). Increasing entrepreneurial intention: effective entrepreneurship course characteristics. *International Journal of Entrepreneurship and Small Business*, **13**(1), 55–74.

Penner, L. A., Dovidio, J. F., Piliavin, J. A., & Schroeder, D. A. (2005). Prosocial behaviour: Multilevel perspectives. *Annual Review of Psychology*, **56**, 365–392.

Penner, L. A. (2002). Dispositional and organisational influences on sustained volunteerism: An interactionist perspective. *Journal of Social Issues*, **58**(3), 447–467.

Penner, L. A., & Finkelstein, M. A. (1998). Dispositional and structural determinants of volunteerism. *Journal of Personality and Social Psychology*, **74**(2), 525.

Penner, L. A., Fritzsche, B. A., Craiger, J. P., & Freifeld, T. R. (1995). Measuring the prosocial personality. *Advances in Personality Assessment*, **10**, 147–163.

Penner, L. A., Dovidio, J. F., Piliavin, J. A., & Schroeder, D. A. (2004). Prosocial behavior: Multilevel perspectives. *Annu. Rev. Psychol.*, **56**, 365–392.

Peterman, N. E., & Kennedy, J. (2003). Enterprise Education: Influencing students' perceptions of entrepreneurship. *Entrepreneurship Theory and Practice*, **28**(2), 129–144.

Phillips, W., Lee, H., Ghobadian, A., O'Regan, N., & James, P. (2015). Social innovation and social entrepreneurship: A systematic review. *Group & Organization Management*, **40**(3), 428–461.

Prabhu, G. N. (1999). Social entrepreneurial leadership. *Career Development International*, **4**(3), 140–145.

Prahalad, C. K. (2009). *The fortune at the bottom of the pyramid*. Wharton School Publishing, Philadelphia, pp.1–7.

Ridley-Duff, R. (2008). Social enterprise as a socially rational business. *International Journal of Entrepreneurial Behavior & Research*, **14**(5), 291–312.

Roberts, D., & Woods, C. (2005). Changing the world on a shoestring: The concept of social entrepreneurship. *University of Auckland Business Review*, **7**(1), 45–51.

Rueda, S., Moriano, J. A., & Liñán, F. (2015). Validating a theory of planned behaviour questionnaire to measure entrepreneurial intentions. In A. Fayolle, P. Kyrö, & F. Liñán (eds.), *Developing, Shaping and Growing Entrepreneurship* (Cheltenham, United Kingdom: Edward Elgar Publishing Ltd), pp. 60–78.

Seelos, C., & Mair, J. (2005). Social entrepreneurship: Creating new business models to serve the poor. *Business Horizons*, **48**, 241–246.

Seth, S., & Kumar, S. (2011). Social entrepreneurship: A growing trend in Indian business. *Entrepreneurial Practice Review*, **1**(3), 4–16. Available at: http://www.entryerson.com/epr/index.php/jep/article/viewFile/66/49.

Shane, S., Locke, E. A., & Collins, C. J. (2003). Entrepreneurial motivation. *Human Resource Management Review*, **13**(2), 257–279. Available at: http://linkinghub.elsevier.com/retrieve/pii/S1053482203000172.

Shradha, S., Mukherjee, S., & Sharan, R. (2005). Structural interventions for favourable sociocultural influences on India entrepreneurs. https://scholar.google.com/scholar?hl=en&as_sdt=0%2C39&q=Structural+interventions+for+favourable+socio cultural+influences+on+India+entrepreneurs&btnG=.

Shapero, A. (1975). The displaced, uncomfortable entrepreneur. *Psychology Today*, **9**(6), 83–88.

Shapero, A., & Sokol, L. (1982). The social dimensions of entrepreneurship. *University of Illinois at Urbana-Champaign's Academy for Entrepreneurial Leadership Historical Research Reference in Entrepreneurship*. https://papers.ssrn.com/sol3/papers.cfm?abstract_id=1497759.

Shaw, E., & Carter, S. (2007). Social entrepreneurship. *Journal of Small Business and Enterprise Development*, **14**(3), 418–434. Available at: http://www.emeraldinsight.com/doi/abs/10.1108/14626000710773529 (accessed November 18, 2014).

Shaw, E., Gordon, J., Harvey, C., & Maclean, M. (2013). Exploring contemporary entrepreneurial philanthropy. *International Small Business Journal*, **31**(5), 580–599.

Shook, C. L., Priem, R. L., & McGee, J. E. (2003). Venture creation and the enterprising individual: A review and synthesis. *Journal of management*, **29**(3), 379–399.

Short, J. C., Moss, T. W., & Lumpkin, G. T. (2009). Research in social entrepreneurship: Past contributions and future opportunities. *Strategic Entrepreneurship Journal*, **3**(2), 161–194.

Shukla, M. (2012). Introduction to social entrepreneurship. *SSRN Electronic Journal*, 1–3.

Sonne, L. (2012). Innovative initiatives supporting inclusive innovation in India: Social business incubation and micro venture capital. *Technological Forecasting and Social Change*, **79**(4), 638–647. Available at: http://dx.doi.org/10.1016/j.techfore.2011.06.008.

Spear, R. (2005). Social enterprise for work integration in 12 European countries: A descriptive analysis. *Annals of Public and Cooperative Economics*, **76**(2), 195–231.

Thompson, J., Alvy, G., & Lees, A. (2000). Social entrepreneurship — A new look at the people and the potential. *Management Decision*, **38**, 328–338.

Thompson, J. L. (2008). Social enterprise and social entrepreneurship: Where have we reached? *Social Enterprise Journal*, **4**(2), 149–161.

Tracey, P., Phillips, N., & Jarvis, O. (2011). Bridging institutional entrepreneurship and the creation of new organisational forms: A multilevel model. *Organization Science*, **22**(1), 60–80.

Vasakarla, V. (2008). A study on social entrepreneurship and the characteristics of social entrepreneurs. *ICFAI Journal of Management Research*, **7**(4), 32–40.

Venkataraman, S. S. (2000). The promise of entrepreneurship as a field of research. *The Academy of Management Review*, **25**(1), 217–226.

Waddock, S. A., & Post, J. E. (1991). Social entrepreneurs and catalytic change. *Public Administration Review*, **51**(5), 393–401.

Yadav, V., & Goyal, P. (2015). User innovation and entrepreneurship: Case studies from rural India. *Journal of Innovation and Entrepreneurship*, **4**(1), 1–20.

Young, D. R. (1980). *Entrepreneurship and the behaviour of nonprofit organisations: Elements of a theory*. Institution for Social and Policy Studies, Yale University.

Zahra, S. A. *et al.* (2009). A typology of social entrepreneurs: Motives, search processes and ethical challenges. *Journal of Business Venturing*, **24**(5), 519–532.

Zeyen, A. *et al.* (2012). Social entrepreneurship and broader theories: Shedding new light on the "bigger picture." *Journal of Social Entrepreneurship*, (August 2015), 1–20.

Ziegler, R. (2009). An introduction to social entrepreneurship: Voices, preconditions, contexts. In R. Ziegler (ed.), *An Introduction to Social Entrepreneurship — Voices, Preconditions, Contexts* (Cheltenham, UK; Northampton, MA, USA: Edward Elgar Publishing Ltd), pp. 1–18.

Appendix

Table A.1. Social entrepreneurial studies in India.

S. No.	Author(s)/Year	Nature of Study
1	Mair & Ganly (2009)	Case study analysis of Gram Vikas in Orissa, India.
2	Seth & Kumar (2011)	An explorative case study regarding social entrepreneurial ecosystem in India.
3	Khanapuri & Khandelwal (2011)	Qualitative research study dealing with Fair Trade and scope of social entrepreneurship in India.
4	Shukla (2012)	Working paper dealing with the contextual framework of social entrepreneurship in India.
5	Datta & Gailey (2012)	Case study analysis of women cooperatives in India.
7	Chowdhury & Santos (2010)	Case study analysis of Gram Vikas in India.
8	Sonne (2012)	A case study of social business incubators like Villgro and Aavishkaar.

Table A.2. Descriptive statistics of the variables used in the study.

Construct	Mean	SD	ATB	SN	PBC	Emp	MO	SR	SEI
ATB	6.02	0.50	**(0.710)**	—	—	—	—	—	—
SN	5.67	0.52	0.256**	**(0.718)**	—	—	—	—	—
PBC	7.65	0.64	0.538**	0.146*	**(0.721)**	—	—	—	—
Emp	5.11	0.45	0.439**	0.298*	0.226*	**(0.649)**	—	—	—
MO	5.19	0.49	0.18**	0.341**	0.582**	0.562*	**(0.834)**	—	—
SR	6.26	0.44	0.176	0.294*	0.385**	0.149**	0.421	**(0.693)**	—
SEI	6.27	0.59	0.389**	0.414**	0.454**	0.363**	0.321**	0.271*	**(0.871)**

Note: Diagonal values are the square root of AVE between the variables and their items and off-diagonal elements are correlations. To measure discriminant validity, diagonal values should be higher than off-diagonals values in the same row and column.

Abbreviations: ATB: attitude toward becoming a social entrepreneur; SN: subjective norms, PBC: perceived behavioral control; Emp: empathy; MO: moral obligation; SR: social responsibility; SEI: social entrepreneurial intentions.

*$p < 0.001$; **$p < 0.05$.

© 2022 World Scientific Publishing Company
https://doi.org/10.1142/9789811248863_0011

Chapter 11

Changing the World Under Limitations: The Role of Resource in Social Enterprise

Wentong Liu

*School of Business Administration,
Zhongnan University of Economics and Law, Wuhan, China*

wliuf@outlook.com

Abstract

Social entrepreneurship has been attracting more attention from practices and scholars as a valuable process in terms of solving social problems in the past decades. However, social entrepreneurs face more serious resource challenges than other types of entrepreneurs because they are not or not only keen on the financial return. Therefore, in order to gain entrepreneurial success and avoid potential failure, the pioneers try to access every resource and combine various resources in an innovative way for stimulating social changes or meeting social needs. The purpose of this chapter is to summarize the overall framework of the resource mobilization in social entrepreneurship operations. We try to show readers a detailed analysis of the social enterprise and social entrepreneurship literature regarding the resource issues. This chapter contains four parts: resource typology, resource strategy, antecedent of resource acquisitions and outcomes of resource mobilization. We hope you can gain more knowledge and understanding about resource acquisitions and mobilization in social enterprises through this chapter, and that it inspires you to thinking more along these lines.

Keywords: Resource typology; resource strategy; resource acquisition; resource mobilization; social enterprise performance.

11.1. Introduction

Social Enterprise (SE), Social Entrepreneur (SEneur), and Social Entrepreneurship (SEship) have been increasingly gaining the attention of academics and practitioners (Bacq and Janssen, 2011; Dees, 1998; Mair and Martí, 2006; Nicholls, 2008; Weerawardena and Mort, 2006), and studies in these areas have grown exponentially in the past decades, as research in related areas has become independent (Mair and Martí, 2006; Newth and Woods, 2014). Thus, social entrepreneurship and social enterprise research as an emerging field have been embraced by authors from various disciplines (Johnson, 2000; Thompson et al., 2000; Weerawardena and Mort, 2006). The studies on SE, SEneur, and SEship have been recognized as areas of potential deep research in social science disciplines (Leadbeater, 1997; Mair and Martí, 2006; Muñoz, 2010). However, it should be noticed that social entrepreneurship research is in a pre-paradigmatic state, particularly for established epistemology (Lehner and Kansikas, 2013). As Short *et al.* (2009) note, research on social entrepreneurship is still at a very early stage, and the development of social entrepreneurship in academia is slower than that in practice (Dearlove, 2004; Mair and Martí, 2006). Figure 11.1 shows, according to Google Scholar, that there is an observable increase in the number of publications on social entrepreneurship since 1954, with research rapidly increasing from 1980s onward.

Social entrepreneurship has existed for a long time worldwide (Dart, 2004; Roberts and Woods, 2005). The number and the types of social entrepreneurship have also rapidly increased (Thompson and Doherty, 2006). For example, in the 19th century, the British pioneer Florence Nightingale strived to improve hospital conditions during the Crimean War. In Pakistan, Kashf Foundation works toward improving the living conditions of women through thousands of micro-credit

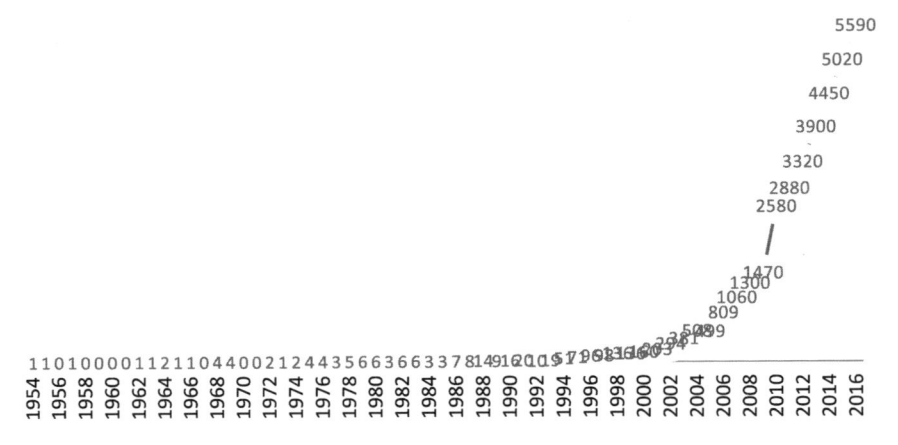

Figure 11.1. Number of publications per year (1954–2016) containing the exact search phrase "social entrepreneurship" according to Google Scholar in May 2017.

financial institutions. Nowadays, more institutions and organizations have been started to support social entrepreneurship on the both side of the Atlantic, such as Ashoka (1980), the Skoll Foundation (1999), the Manhattan Institute's Social Entrepreneurship Initiative (2001) in the US, The School of Social Entrepreneurs in the UK, Canadian Social Entrepreneurship Foundation, and others (Bacq and Janssen, 2011). According to the Global Entrepreneurship Monitor survey in 2005, there are an estimated 1.2 million social entrepreneurs in the UK. This number represents 3.2% of the working-age population and shows that social entrepreneurship is as important as commercial business with the passage of time. Till 2007, it was estimated that there were more than 62,000 social enterprises in the UK based on the ASBS survey published by government. With the development of social entrepreneurship, the importance of these organizations has been recognized in that they could act as an instrument for the government and a source of solutions to certain illnesses plaguing our modern society.

In the past decades, social entrepreneurship has attracted more attention from scholars and practitioners as a valuable process in terms of solving social problems worldwide (Bornstein, 2007; Mair and Martí, 2006). Social entrepreneurs have tried to combine various resources in an innovative way to stimulate social change or meet social needs (Mair and Martí, 2006; Waddock and Post, 1991). The resources of social entrepreneurship ventures contribute to a competitive advantage if these resources are rare and valuable. However, social entrepreneurship is more likely to exist within severely resource-constrained environments (Griffiths *et al.*, 2013) because of their unique characteristics.

Social entrepreneurship enterprises always face challenges in resource mobilization since they serve low-interest clients and survive in difficult markets, thus social entrepreneurships require resources to a much greater degree than traditional firms, although both depend on resources in the same way (Tan and Yoo, 2015). Furthermore, social entrepreneurships need financial and non-financial resources to make their business sustainable and then achieve their social mission in the end. As a result, social entrepreneurs should know what resources they require (such as financial, local, natural, cultural, and social resources), how to access them, what resource acquisition strategy is effective, and what factors will influence them to obtain these resources. In Section 11.2, we will provide a detailed introduction and analysis of the above questions.

11.2. Resources in Social Entrepreneurship: An In-Depth Study

Are all entrepreneurships purely profit-driven? Are all socially oriented organizations totally non-profit organizations? Absolutely not. Social entrepreneurship, as a rapidly developing form of enterprise, has been recognized to combine social and economic goals and are widely acknowledged in delivering positive socio-economic impact to the community, tackling social problems, and meeting unfulfilled social needs (Doherty *et al.*, 2014). Social entrepreneurship enterprises work by mobilizing various resources to explore opportunities and then create value. Social entrepreneurship has become an important pillar in the society, complementing the functions of the public, private, and third sectors (Mair and Martí, 2006; Santos, 2012). Social entrepreneurs identified potential entrepreneurial areas in the society that pose major challenges now, including healthcare, unemployment, environment protection, betterment of living conditions, and poverty (Baines *et al.*, 2010; Hall *et al.*, 2012a; Hall *et al.*, 2012b; Boluk and Mottiar, 2014; Gupta *et al.*, 2015). Despite social entrepreneurship becoming much more important now, the majority of these companies still face resource-scarcity problems. Venture resources identified as the valuable assets and competencies under the control by organizations, when strategically marshalled, can create a competitive advantage (Barney, 1991). Resource acquisition plays a critical role for the development and success of any organization (Katz and Gartner, 1988) and include tangible or intangible (Barney, 1991) and monetary or non-monetary resources (Kistruck *et al.*, 2013). In short, securing the necessary resources is fundamental for social entrepreneurship, as it can help them compete in the marketplace (Hynes, 2009; Sharir *et al.*, 2009).

In the following sections, the analysis is divided into four parts:

(1) Resource Typology: An in-depth analysis is conducted, focusing on financial, tangible, and intangible resources. We analyze and conclude the sources of financial support for social entrepreneurship by scanning published papers. In terms of tangible resources, this section includes infrastructure and material resources. With regard to intangible resources, there is a wide range of categories, such as organizational governance and structure, different skills and knowledge, market issues, social and human capital, as well as networks.
(2) Resource Strategy: There are various approaches and strategies for social entrepreneurship to acquire and manage resources.
(3) Antecedent factors of resource acquisitions: This section focuses on why some social entrepreneurs or social entrepreneurship enterprises are more capable of gaining resources or attention compared to others and the role of institution on resource acquisition. It includes two forms — institutional analysis and macro-context analysis.
(4) Outcomes: This is the final part of the cross-analysis section.

11.2.1. *Resource Typology*

As mentioned earlier, financial and non-financial resources are necessary for social entrepreneurship. Since social entrepreneurships enterprises have been acknowledged as dual-mission driven, they must rely on community-based rather than internally based resources (Austin et al., 2006). Although social entrepreneurships have a wider range of funding sources than commercial entrepreneurships, social entrepreneurships have more pressure to make them financially independent and sustainable. The resource typology analysis focuses on three types of resources — financial, tangible, and intangible resources.

11.2.1.1. Financial resources

Many entrepreneurs, irrespective of whether they are traditional or social entrepreneurs, are struggling with their fundraising methods. A UK report mentioned that the lack of appropriate financing is the single most significant constraint for the development of social entrepreneurships. Therefore, social enterprises have to depend on grants and diversify their sources of funding such as loans, debts, or commercial activities to secure their finance in a sustainable manner (Sunley and Pinch, 2012). According to the Table 11.1, obviously social entrepreneurship has very wide range of financial sources now, but the most important channel is government support, and the majority of scholars have focused on government or community source for social entrepreneurship (Hines, 2010). Social entrepreneurial activities mainly still depend on government support (McCarthy, 2008), and Elson and Hall (2012) found that the government is the primary source of financing for social enterprises, followed by individuals and foundations (Table 11.1).

As the most important source of financing for social entrepreneurship, government support provides social enterprises with various channels to attract monetary resources. Fisac and Moreno-Romero (2015) found that social entrepreneurship in Spain acquired medium to high support from the government compared to other sources. Many researchers (Flockhart, 2005; Chan et al., 2011; Sunley and Pinch, 2012; Barraket et al., 2016; Zasada and Zasada, 2017) identified that governments have grants for social entrepreneurships, such as in Scotland (Hare et al., 2007). Because social entrepreneurships have social goals, which may help the government to solve social issues or meet social needs, government funding can, for specific or general purposes, provide support to social entrepreneurships (Barraket et al., 2016). Social entrepreneurship may receive state support through direct funding with no obligations (Hazenberg et al., 2016), such as the European Social Fund (Gawell, 2013). Social entrepreneurship can also gain support from local communities (Campin et al., 2013). Besides capital from government, Amin (2009) identified Neighborhood Renewal Funding, set up by the UK government, which is a method for social entrepreneurship to obtain financial support as well.

Sometimes, social entrepreneurships could sell their services or products to the public sector or government to earn trading income. This special trading

Table 11.1. Source of funding for social entrepreneurship enterprises.

Government	Government	McCarthy (2008)
		Mair & Martı (2009)
		Di Domenico et al. (2010)
		Datta & Gailey (2012)
		Thompson (2012)
		Elson & Hall (2012)
		Hall et al. (2012a)
		Katre & Salipante (2012)
		Desa & Basu (2013)
		Sarpong & Davies (2014)
		Gras & Mendoza-Abarca (2014)
		Gupta et al. (2015)
		Walske & Tyson (2015)
		Smith & Woods (2015)
		Fisac & Moreno-Romero (2015)
		Zhao & Lounsbury (2016)
		Hazenberg et al. (2016)
	Government grants	Flockhart (2005)
		Hare et al. (2007)
		Chan et al. (2011)
		Sunley & Pinch (2012)
		Gawell (2013)
		Barraket et al. (2016)
		Zasada & Zasada (2017)
	Community	Campin et al. (2013)
	Neighborhood renewal funding	Amin (2009)
	Government procurement	Muñoz (2009)
		Sunley & Pinch (2012)

behavior is called government procurement (Muñoz, 2009). Social enterprises can, through government procurement, earn income to develop, while the government can achieve best value in these trading activities. Sunley and Pinch (2012) identified a social entrepreneurship named DWP that engaged in contract work with the local health sector to earn commercial income.

In short, public funds provide a crucial pathway for social entrepreneurship to gain funds to survive. Yet, governments have concurrently reduced the direct funding for social entrepreneurship, with their development shadowed in the background of the worldwide financial crisis (Defourny and Nyssens, 2010; Peattie and Morley, 2008), social entrepreneurship has to increase the income of commercial activities to sustain themselves (Chell, 2007; Dees, 1998) (Table 11.2).

Table 11.2. Alternate sources of funding for social entrepreneurship.

Charitable funds	Philanthropy funds	Flockhart (2005)
		Di Domenico *et al.* (2010)
		Diochon (2010)
		Chan *et al.* (2011)
		Mauksch (2012)
		Hall *et al.* (2012b)
		Thompson (2012)
		Elson & Hall (2012)
		Gawell (2013)
		Maclean *et al.* (2013)
		Liu *et al.* (2013)
		Acs & Boardman (2013)
		Ingstad *et al.* (2014)
		Gras & Mendoza-Abarca (2014)
		Smith & Woods (2015)
		Gupta *et al.* (2015)
		Imperatori & Ruta (2015)
		Fisac & Moreno-Romero (2015)
		Walske & Tyson (2015)
		Haski-Leventhal & Mehra (2016)
		Barraket *et al.* (2016)
		Zhao & Lounsbury (2016)
	International foundation/investment	Mair & Martı (2009)
		Mauksch (2012)
		Elson & Hall (2012)
		Scott & Laine (2012)
		Nelson *et al.* (2013)
		Barinaga (2013)
		Maclean *et al.* (2013)
		Wilson & Post (2013)
		Sarpong & Davies (2014)
		Walske & Tyson (2015)
		Akemu *et al.* (2016)
		Bhatt & Ahmad (2017)
	Lottery funding	Tjornbo & Westley (2012)
		Sarpong & Davies (2014)
		Zasada & Zasada (2017)

As Table 11.2 shows, charitable foundations are a crucial funding source in the financial resource mobilization for social entrepreneurship (Mauksch, 2012). Fisac and Moreno-Romero (2015) found that philanthropic support was medium to high in Spain. Philanthropic venture capital is an intermediate investment in social enterprises that exhibit a potential for a high social impact (Scarlata and Alemany, 2010). They provide social entrepreneurs with financial and non-financial resources (Maclean et al., 2013; Ingstad et al., 2014). In particular, during the early stages, social entrepreneurships rely on international or national charitable foundations (Bhatt and Ahmad, 2017). The Border Foundation, established between Finland and Russia, is a special funding source in Scott and Laine (2012)'s research. With the development of social entrepreneurship, an increasing number of foundations have provided grants for these firms (Nelson et al., 2013; Barraket et al., 2016). Some international foundations have launched incubation investment programs (Akemu et al., 2016). Some national third-sector organizations have engaged social entrepreneurships to provide more services to citizens: e.g. NHS in the UK have invested several healthcare social enterprises to improve the social welfare system (Hall et al., 2012). In previous research studies, three papers mentioned about lottery funding for social entrepreneurship (Sarpong and Davies, 2014; Tjornbo and Westley, 2012; Zasada and Zasada, 2017), which could also help social entrepreneurships access financial support, citing case studies from the UK.

However, it should be noticed that if social entrepreneurship is reliant on donor funds to operate, without considering interest or cashback, it will become as a charity or non-profit organization (Acs et al., 2013) (Table 11.3).

Virtual donation sites are a useful channel for social entrepreneurs, such as crowdfunding websites (Mauksch, 2012). Crowdfunding is an important channel for financing, especially for young entrepreneurs as they are more familiar with information technology: e.g. a fairphone company in Central Africa utilized a crowdfunding website to seek financial support (Akemu et al., 2016). Research from Lehner (2014) indicated that the fundraising targets of most social entrepreneurial crowdfunding projects were lower than US$30,000. Only very few rewards from social entrepreneurships were monetary; more than half were tangible rewards, and intangible rewards comprised nearly half. Bernardino and Santos (2016) analyzed the personality traits that influenced social entrepreneurs' decision to use crowdfunding platforms in Portugal and identified openness, conscientiousness, extraversion, agreeableness, and neuroticism as the major traits. In addition, an orientation toward sustainability will affect the entrepreneurs' ability to acquire financial resources through crowdfunding platforms (Calic and Mosakowski, 2016). Crowdfunding websites can make these social entrepreneurships more visible to customers or governments, allowing them to attract interest and build networks.

However, social entrepreneurships are increasingly seeking support from banks and venture capitalists, but unlike commercial entrepreneurs, the vast majority of social entrepreneurs seem not to prefer borrow money from banks or other institutions — they are typically seen as the "last resort" (Steiner and Teasdale, 2016). An earlier research study by Kistruck and Beamish (2010) also

Table 11.3. Other external sources of funding for social entrepreneurship enterprises.

Other external sources	Crowdfunding	Mauksch (2012) Lehner (2014) Lehner & Nicholls (2014) Chandra (2016) Bernardino & Santos (2016) Akemu *et al.* (2016) Calic & Mosakowski (2016) Parhankangas & Renko (2017)
	Donor agency	Moore *et al.* (2012) Wilson & Post (2013) Gupta *et al.* (2015)
	Debt/loans	Zhao & Lounsbury (2016) Elson & Hall (2012) Sunley & Pinch (2012) Kistruck & Beamish (2010) Hare *et al.* (2007) Barraket *et al.* (2016) Wilson & Post (2013)
	Fundraising activities	Gras & Mendoza-Abarca (2014) Haski-Leventhal & Mehra (2016) Sarpong & Davies (2014) Katre & Salipante (2012) Yann *et al.* (2014)
	Credit union	Elson & Hall (2012)
	Business competition	Walske & Tyson (2015)
	Friend/Family member	Steiner & Teasdale (2016) Imperatori & Ruta (2015) Hare *et al.* (2007) Wilson & Post (2013)
	Sponsorship/ advertisement	Gupta *et al.* (2015) Haski-Leventhal & Mehra (2016)

suggested that only very few social entrepreneurships borrowed funds from banks in Zimbabwe. Soft loans from their friends or family members may be a non-preferable option as well. Wilson and Post (2013) mentioned that personal sources for financing, such as loans from friends, family, and the local church could also be acknowledged by social entrepreneurs.

Most social entrepreneurships still depend on donations of necessary materials and supplies (Diochon, 2010; Whitelaw and Hill, 2013); in cases where some social entrepreneurs lack social networking skills to gain attention from the government or foundations, donor agencies can help them (Gupta *et al.*, 2015).

Moore et al. (2012) identified some social finance agencies in Canada that provide assistance in this regard.

Fundraising activities are a supplementary source for social entrepreneurship to obtain money. Social entrepreneurs could organize events to attract potential customers or donors, and they could perform some trading activities in the events (Yann Ching Chang et al., 2014). Social entrepreneurs could join some venture capital pitch conferences to obtain financial support; such events also serve as a source of fundraising. Similar to fundraising activities, business competition will benefit social entrepreneurship in attracting the attention of capitalists and media (Walske and Tyson 2015). Credit unions, mentioned by Elson and Hall (2012), are also noteworthy as they represent an untapped source of financing for social entrepreneurship in Canada.

Some banks have invested in non-profit foundations for social entrepreneurship ventures — e.g. Thompson (2012) mentioned Halifax Bank of Scotland Community Foundation. Some traditional enterprises are interested in sponsoring social entrepreneurships to help their fundraising (Haski-Leventhal and Mehra, 2016) — e.g. Mercedes-Benz formed a partnership with a healthcare enterprise in Africa to raise money (Gupta et al., 2015) (Table 11.4).

Social entrepreneurship is social mission driven, but it should simultaneously have economic goals. There are many limitations when social entrepreneurships receive donations or government support — e.g. the money could only be used for the specific programs indicated by the fund providers. Market-based income is flexible for social entrepreneurships, since it can be used unencumbered for any social missions. If a social entrepreneurship receives only public support or other direct funding without any trading activities, it will function akin to a charity or non-profit organization. Therefore, many social entrepreneurships access financial support through commercial behaviors or trading activities (Gras and Mendoza-Abarca, 2014; Haski-Leventhal and Mehra, 2016b; Sunley and Pinch, 2012; Zhao and Lounsbury, 2016). Jenner (2016) suggested that for-profit social enterprises are likely to be more reliant on earned income streams than their non-profit organization counterparts. In other words, earning income through commercial activities can help social entrepreneurships reduce their reliance on government funding or donations, which will make them more sustainable. Self-reliance involves the social entrepreneurs investing their own money in the organizations as well, as evidenced by Omorede's (2014) study of a social enterprise in Nigeria. Furthermore, some social entrepreneurs put their own money in the business to avoid borrowing money from other institutions. Actually, social entrepreneurs prefer for-profit entrepreneurship to self-reliance as they do not consider the latter to be a good choice (Di Domenico et al., 2010; Gras and Mendoza-Abarca, 2014).

For some particular types of social entrepreneurships, their goal involves attracting as many members as possible (Mair and Martı, 2009; Kistruck and

Table 11.4. Internal sources of funding.

Internal sources	Commercial/trading activities	Zhao & Lounsbury (2016) Gras & Mendoza-Abarca (2014) Sunley & Pinch (2012) Haski-Leventhal & Mehra (2016) Imperatori & Ruta (2015) Chan *et al.* (2011) Sarpong & Davies (2014) Barth *et al.* (2015) Barraket *et al.* (2016)
	Self-reliance	Datta & Gailey (2012) Di Domenico *et al.* (2010) Gras & Mendoza-Abarca (2014) Omorede (2014) Imperatori & Ruta (2015) Wilson & Post (2013) Chan *et al.* (2011)
	Membership fee	Chan *et al.* (2011) Lyon & Fernandez (2012) Mair & Martı (2009) Kistruck & Beamish (2010) Barraket *et al.* (2016)
	Gaming income	Gras & Mendoza-Abarca (2014)
	Speculation	McCarthy (2008)
	Investment income	Gras & Mendoza-Abarca (2014)

Beamish, 2010). Thus, membership fees contribute as a major source of funds in these social entrepreneurships' financing process. When social entrepreneurships expand in size, they will have enough capability to take some investment decisions (Gras and Mendoza-Abarca, 2014). However, these investments may sometimes seem like gaming (Gras and Mendoza-Abarca, 2014) or speculation (McCarthy, 2008). However, if successful, such activities can provide social entrepreneurships with relatively better income.

To sum up, social entrepreneurship relies more on external financial support than commercial entrepreneurship, and they have a wider range of funding sources. The government plays a critical role in financing resources required for social entrepreneurships, not merely because social enterprises are dual-mission driven. Creating economic value is not the most important aspect for social enterprises, therefore these organizations seek funds from charitable foundations rather than traditional venture capital. Social entrepreneurs prefer to receive donations rather than borrow money from outside sources because the risk of social entrepreneurial activities is higher than that of traditional entrepreneurships. In order to achieve sustainable development, trading and commercial activities will become much more crucial for social entrepreneurships' financial resource acquisition.

11.2.1.2. Tangible

Apart from the importance of financial resources in social entrepreneurship, tangible resources are also significant for them to create a competitive advantage. Without these tangible resources, social entrepreneurships cannot engineer social change or realize their social mission. In this section, tangible resources will be separated into two main parts — infrastructure and materials (Table 11.5).

Social entrepreneurs have to make the most of available resources to gain outside resources and lower costs. Hence, social entrepreneurship needs to find suitable infrastructure for them to engage in different types of work according to their different target markets or missions. For example, educational social entrepreneurship needs classroom as their space (Tasavori et al., 2016), musical event entrepreneurship needs stadiums or sites for conducting festivals (Tasavori et al., 2016). Sonnino and Griggs-Trevarthen (2012) explored a food service social entrepreneurship in UK — this company needed enough land for growing cereals. Of course, an office is the fundamental infrastructure for many social entrepreneurships. Tillmar (2009) described that social networks help social entrepreneurships obtain help and support from local authorities.

Beyond that, social entrepreneurs may obtain initial materials from their social networks or other resources. Software or some information technological

Table 11.5. Tangible resources: Infrastructure.

Infrastructure	Space	Munoz et al. (2015)
		Vestrum & Rasmussen (2013)
		Tasavori et al. (2016)
	Land	Sonnino & Griggs-Trevarthen (2012)
	Office	Di Domenico et al. (2010)
		Tillmar (2009)
Materials	Software	Desa (2012)
		Desa & Basu (2013)
		Halme et al. (2012)
		Barinaga (2013)
		Kistruck et al. (2013)
	Hardware	Desa (2012)
		Desa & Basu (2013)
		Hall et al. (2012a)
		Ceranic et al. (2013)
		Di Domenico et al. (2010)

applications have been mentioned by several researchers (Desa, 2012; Desa and Basu, 2013; Halme *et al.*, 2012; Kistruck *et al.*, 2013) — e.g. the Internet facilitates access to information and helps understand the client requirements. Halme *et al.* (2012) introduced a social entrepreneurship in Africa named VilCo, an intrapreneurship of Nokia. The manager bricolaged resources from their parent company to obtain the necessary software at zero cost. Barinaga (2013) explored a microfinance pilot project incubated by a Swedish bank — this project also obtained software from the parent bank.

Hardware or raw materials are defined by several scholars as well (Ceranic *et al.*, 2013; Desa, 2012; Desa and Basu, 2013; Di Domenico *et al.*, 2010; Hall *et al.*, 2012a). For those social enterprises engaged in the manufacturing industry, natural materials are required (Ceranic *et al.*, 2013) — for instance, Hall *et al.* (2012a) identified bicycles were as one type of resource in a social enterprise.

11.2.1.3. Intangible

The range of intangible resources is wider than that of tangible resources and mainly include institutional governance, structure, necessary skills and knowledge, human capital, social capital, and network. Intangible resources are positively related to the relative attention to social goals for social entrepreneurship (Stevens *et al.*, 2015), similar to commercial entrepreneurship. However, social entrepreneurship has its own special distinguishing features with regard to intangible resources, since these organizations need to survive in a competitive marketplace to achieve their social mission (Table 11.6).

Table 11.6. Intangible resources: Governance and structure.

Governance	Style	Datta and Gailey (2012)
		Overall *et al.* (2010)
		Cato *et al.* (2007)
		Diochon (2010)
		Haugh & Talwar (2016)
		Nwankwo *et al.* (2007)
	Association	Whitelaw & Hill (2013)
	Democratically	Tillmar (2009)
		Levander (2010)
Structure	Management structure	Cato *et al.* (2007)
		Costanzo *et al.* (2014)
		Henry (2015)
		Elson & Hall (2012)
	Marketing channel	Chan *et al.* (2011)
	Distribution channel	Gupta *et al.* (2015)

Governance is generally defined as the relationship among participants to decide the future direction and strategy of organizations. Social entrepreneurship is associated with public, private, and voluntary organizations, thus the governance is more specific and complex. Many scholars like Cato *et al.* (2007) have been interested in the governance and management structure of social enterprises and their impact on their social value. Moreover, since social entrepreneurship has a dual mission, which involves blending governance and management structure to achieve their social goals (Costanzo *et al.*, 2014), governance strategy is linked to their success. For example, Haugh and Talwar (2016) explored a case in the Indian context and found that the members of this social entrepreneurship can attend meetings to make decision — this governance style empowers each member and engages them as stakeholders. Levander (2010) termed this as "everybody in power."

Some social entrepreneurs do not want to be bosses, and they try to run the company in a democratic manner (Tillmar, 2009). Whitelaw and Hill (2013) found that, in Finland, social entrepreneurships aimed at older people were mainly supported by the public sector and worked as an integrative function, and their governance was more likely an "association" model with focus on volunteering — the cases from Sweden are similar as well. The informal voluntary model is practiced in Greenland communities. But in Scotland, social entrepreneurship prefers to follow company governance.

Many scholars like Cato *et al.* (2007) and Costanzo *et al.* (2014) were interested in the governance and management structure of social enterprises and its impact on their social value. Similar to commercial entrepreneurship, some social enterprises need to build their marketing and distribution channels as well, as they will enhance the financial independence of these organizations and facilitate increased trading income. But research on this topic is very rare — with only Chan *et al.* (2011) and Gupta *et al.* (2015) having mentioned these research areas (Table 11.7).

Steiner and Teasdale (2016) found there is a trend that social entrepreneurs should be considered as "superhuman," characterized by their "can do" approach. Social entrepreneurs should regard social business as a desirable career choice and be involved in their activities (Bacq *et al.*, 2016); they also need the relevant skills to manage a business in a resource-constrained environment. Moreau and Mertens (2013) illustrated that the skillset of entrepreneurs include strategic, business, interpersonal, and cognitive skills. According to previous research, social entrepreneurs should have the following specific capabilities: skills for international resource mobilization (Lough and McBride, 2013), identification of the potential resources and facilities (Chang *et al.*, 2014), building social network with others (Ko and Liu, 2015), leadership abilities (Maak and Stoetter, 2012), identification and/or creation of support networks (Perrini *et al.*, 2010), self-confidence and maturity (Denny *et al.*, 2011), and management skills (Hare *et al.*, 2007).

Table 11.7. Intangible resources: Skills.

Skills		
Skills	Entrepreneurs' skills	Desa (2012)
		Desa & Basu (2013)
		Parhankangas & Renko (2017)
		Estrin *et al.* (2016)
		Zhao & Lounsbury (2016)
		Jenner (2016)
		Steiner & Teasdale (2016)
		Denny *et al.* (2011)
		Nelson *et al.* (2013)
		Moreau & Mertens (2013)
		Hare *et al.* (2007)
		Yann *et al.* (2014)
		Ko & Liu (2015)
		Sharir & Lerner (2006)
		Perrini *et al.* (2010)
		Bacq & Eddleston (2016)
		Maak & Stoetter (2012)
		Lough & McBride (2013)
		Bacq *et al.* (2016)
	Language	Chandra (2016)
		Seanor *et al.* (2008)
		Ruebottom (2013)
		Parkinson & Howorth (2008)
		Jones *et al.* (2008)
	Technology application	Liu *et al.* (2013)
		Desa (2012)
		Mulloth *et al.* (2016)
	Organizational capability	Jenner (2016)
	Marketing capability	Liu *et al.* (2013)
		Thompson (2012)
		Tillmar (2009)
		Jenner (2016)
		Miles *et al.* (2014)

In addition, the entrepreneurs' skills can be used to persuade stakeholders to be involved in their social enterprise business and help them in various ways (Bacq and Eddleston, 2016).

As for language skills, Chandra (2016) proposed that social entrepreneurs should use rhetoric strategy to influence stakeholders and persuade them to attend their fundraising programs — rhetorical strategy can build legitimacy and attract the attention of potential stakeholders (Ruebottom, 2013). Narrative construction of social entrepreneurship is crucial, in particular for crowdfunding. When social entrepreneurs introduce themselves or their business to others, "community" was the most popular word, followed by "we," "social," and "funding." In addition, Seanor et al. (2008) suggested that communication skills could help social enterprises forge better network connections.

As mentioned earlier, technical skills have become much more significant since the rapid development of IT technology. Social entrepreneurs have to know well how to utilize technical application to solve challenges (Desa, 2012; Liu et al., 2013; Mulloth et al., 2016). Jenner (2016) demonstrated that organizational capability is one of the necessary skills for social entrepreneurs. This skill may help social entrepreneurships become more effective and united, as seen when they organize some large-scale events in a systematic and clear manner.

Miles et al. (2014) suggested that social enterprises may benefit by leveraging their marketing capabilities to better serve their beneficiaries and stakeholders. Since many social entrepreneurships are based in difficult environments, learning and applying marketing strategy makes a considerable impact. Social entrepreneurs who can apply media resources to expand their social influence will more easily gain attention, such as Incredible Edible filmed by BBC (Thompson, 2012), a fair phone company which, through media marketing strategy, gained attention in Africa (Akemu et al., 2016) (Table 11.8).

Unlike marketing capability, which utilizes related skills in practice, marketing knowledge in this situation emphasizes on learning "what" and "how." Social entrepreneurs and staff need to acquire marketing knowledge and then could devise marketing plans and routines to promote their business (Powell and Osborne, 2015). Environmental knowledge can help social entrepreneurship develop disaster relief and business capabilities to mitigate risks (Gray et al., 2014) — e.g. Nwankwo et al. (2007) identified a multinational corporation that acquired local knowledge before they entered the Nigerian market to deliver water

Table 11.8. Intangible resources: Knowledge.

Knowledge	Marketing knowledge	Liu et al. (2013)
		Powell & Osborne (2015)
		Nwankwo et al. (2007)
	Natural/environment	Gray et al. (2014)
		Hall et al. (2012)
	Leadership	Gupta et al. (2015)
		Maak & Stoetter (2012)
		Moreau & Mertens (2013)
	Creative/technological knowledge	Cato et al. (2007)
		Gupta et al. (2015)
		Ghauri et al. (2014)

Table 11.9. Intangible resources: Market orientation.

Market	Desa (2012)
	Di Domenico et al. (2010)
	Zhao & Lounsbury (2016)
	Gras & Mendoza-Abarca (2014)
	Baines et al. (2010)
	Mair & Martı (2009)
	Gray et al. (2014)
	Minard (2009)
	Gupta et al. (2015)
	Tukamushaba et al. (2011)
	Mulloth et al. (2016)
	Halme et al. (2012)

resources. Social ventures in the tourism industry need to acquire geographic and cultural knowledge to mobilize resources effectively (Hall *et al.*, 2012a).

Leadership knowledge needs more attention because it will influence the performance of organizations. In Nelson *et al.*'s (2013) case study, the founder Susan Murcott studied leadership in MIT, and it prompted her to overcome challenges and achieve final goals. Technological knowledge is also very important for social entrepreneurship, especially for those social ventures that need to apply high-tech to their trading activities. Ghauri *et al.* (2014) demonstrated that multinational social entrepreneurships collaborate with local non-government organizations to learn technical knowledge from them to better understand the local market (Table 11.9).

Social entrepreneurship is not merely a for-profit venture but emphasizes on creating social value, solving social problems, meeting social needs, and tackling social issues. Therefore, identifying sustainable market opportunities is the initial step for social entrepreneurs (Gray *et al.*, 2014). Social enterprises can blend non-profit and private resources to overcome the barriers that commercial enterprises face when they want to enter a new market, such as lack of partnership, financial support, and policy challenges. Many social enterprises fail because of market failure (Minard, 2009). Creating markets is a research tendency for scholars who are interested in the social entrepreneurship research field (Gupta *et al.*, 2015). Prezi is an example of a social entrepreneurship that identified an untapped market — they provide services for non-government organizations with IT resources (Mulloth *et al.*, 2016). Some multinational organizations prefer to launch different brands in different markets (Halme *et al.*, 2012). For instance, an international social entrepreneurship created a sub-project in Uganda by educating customers to create a new market (Tukamushaba *et al.*, 2011) (Table 11.10).

Table 11.10. Intangible resources: Human capital.

Human capital	Volunteer	Desa (2012)
		Liu *et al.* (2013)
		Desa & Basu (2013)
		Barth *et al.* (2015)
		Whitelaw & Hill (2013)
		Sunley & Pinch (2012)
		Zasada & Zasada (2017)
		Hare *et al.* (2007)
		Vickers & Lyon (2014)
		Ko & Liu (2015)
		Tan & Yoo (2015)
	Manager	Ingstad *et al.* (2014)
	Stakeholder/membership	Royce (2007)
		Ko & Liu (2015)
		Ramus & Vaccaro (2014)
	Oversight committee	Smith & Woods (2015)
	Loan officer	Zhao & Lounsbury (2016)
	Seasonal	Elson & Hall (2012)
	Casual employee	Barth *et al.* (2015)
	Part-time	Zasada & Zasada (2017)
		Hynes (2009)
		Barth *et al.* (2015)
	Contract	Elson & Hall (2012)
		Hynes (2009)
	Foreign employee	Gupta *et al.* (2015)
	Labor	Desa (2012)
		Desa & Basu (2013)
		Estrin *et al.* (2013, 2016)
		Amin (2009)
		Sharir & Lerner (2006)
		Ceranic *et al.* (2013)
		Tillmar (2009)
		Diochon (2010)
		Gawell (2013)
		Cooney (2013)
		Ko & Liu (2015)
		Barth *et al.* (2015)
		Bhatt & Ahmad (2017)
		Katre & Salipante (2012)
		Bacq *et al.* (2016)
		Sunley & Pinch (2012)

Social entrepreneurships have a higher number of employees compared to traditional enterprises (Bacq *et al.*, 2013). Managers, committees, full-time staff, part-time staff, and volunteers are the main types of labor for social enterprises. However, Amin (2009) mentioned that some coordinators, sub-contractors, secondments, consultants, and supervisors can be found in social ventures as well. Because social entrepreneurships aim at creating social value, the volunteer category supports in providing services to their clients, especially for those social entrepreneurships with a strong and professional employment, training, and linkage aspect in their social mission. On the other hand, social entrepreneurships cannot provide their staff with good salaries like traditional companies at the early stage, hence many social businesses prefer employing part-time staff or seek volunteers; some social entrepreneurs even choose to run part-time businesses.

In short, volunteering is a key resource for social entrepreneurship (Tan and Yoo, 2015) due to potential differentials in salary and career development (Austin *et al.*, 2006; Dacin *et al.*, 2011). Thus, the ability to mobilize appropriate human resources is salient for social entrepreneurship. They cannot be reliant on volunteer labor since this does not represent a secure long-term strategy for the sector (Hynes, 2009) — even volunteer labor is a strength for social entrepreneurship when they compete with commercial ventures.

Some social entrepreneurships have become much more international in the past few years and can hire executives with professional degrees like MBA or who have graduated from top-tier education institutions (Gupta *et al.*, 2015). In some underdeveloped countries, social entrepreneurships have to hire few foreign employees (Gupta *et al.*, 2015) with professional skills to help them achieve their social missions. During this time, social entrepreneurships could receive help from the government or some labor markets when they want to hire or train staff (Katre and Salipante, 2012). Philanthropic venture capital companies need to find and hire managers with professional knowledge and skills with a related background. Mass media provides a good channel for these companies to hire the right people (Ingstad *et al.*, 2014).

Besides part-time employees, "contract" and seasonal staff are prevalent in social entrepreneurships. Contract or seasonal workers are not like official employees — their salaries are normally lower than full-time staff and they would not receive any income from social enterprises without the activities organized by these organizations (Elson and Hall, 2012). Although these workers need to be trained before they work, to call them employees in the standard sense is also not accurate. The reason for social entrepreneurship to hire contractors or seasonal staff is the same as with finding volunteers — due to lack of enough funds to pay for many full-time staff. To lower the costs or because of the unique structure, many social entrepreneurships provide positions for their stakeholders or members. They function as volunteers, enhancing their engagement and involvement in the social enterprises.

Table 11.11. Intangible resources: Social capital.

Social capital	Estrin *et al.* (2013)
	Minard (2009)
	Rotheroe & Miller (2008)
	Scheiber (2014)
	Curtis *et al.* (2010)
	Bhatt & Ahmad (2017)
	Crispen *et al.* (2012)
	Jenner & Oprescu (2016)
	Lewis (2016)

There are some special types of staff in social entrepreneurships. For example, microfinance companies have to hire loan officers. These officers often have university degrees and professional skills (Zhao & Lounsbury, 2016). Another type of staff in microfinance companies is the oversight committee. Many social venture capital companies have designated this position as well because they act as mentors and supervise monetary trading to avoid losses (Smith and Woods, 2015). According to research from Barth *et al.* (2015), social entrepreneurships in the cultural industry prefer to hire casual artists, similar to part-time staff.

Interestingly, Diochon (2010) suggests that residents who have occupational backgrounds and can access financial or educational resources are likely to start their business in an unstable environment, similar to social entrepreneurs (Table 11.11).

Social entrepreneurship mainly started as an entity with social capital trust, cooperation, and collective need (Minard, 2009). Social capital has become as important as financial capital in any context for social entrepreneurship (Kerlin, 2009). Coleman (1988) identified social capital as networks of relationship, reciprocity, trust, and social norms. Social capital could enforce trust and resource mobilization for social entrepreneurship. Many researchers explored the influence and effectiveness of social capital for social ventures in different contexts. Bhatt and Ahmad (2017) focused on social capital in the Indian context and analyzed how social entrepreneurs enhance social capital to make their entrepreneurial activities successful. Crispen *et al.* (2012) explored a healthcare social enterprise in Africa and demonstrated that it involves a complex network of people and institutions within the entire community. In various research studies, scholars suggested social entrepreneurs should learn how to identify social capital, especially youth entrepreneurs who have little experience and nascent networks (Friedman and Desivilya, 2010). Moreover, when members, clients, and donors, who are seen as stakeholders of social entrepreneurship, participate in the entrepreneurial process, it will enhance the social capital (Rotheroe and Miller, 2008). It is good for social entrepreneurs to maintain sustainable development (Table 11.12).

Table 11.12. Intangible resources: Network resources.

Network	Stakeholder	Estrin et al. (2013)
		Di Domenico et al. (2010)
		Desa & Basu (2013)
		Gupta et al. (2015)
		Hazenberg et al. (2016)
		Moreau & Mertens (2013)
		Hlady Rispal & Servantie (2017)
		Imperatori & Ruta (2015)
		McNamara et al. (2018)
		Seanor et al. (2008)
	Agency	Mauksch (2012)
		Ghauri et al. (2014)
	Entrepreneurs	Di Domenico et al. (2010)
		Seanor et al. (2008)
		Nelson et al. (2013)
		Desa & Basu (2013)
		Hlady Rispal & Servantie (2017)
		Shaw & Carter (2007)
		Hechavarría et al. (2017)
	Social actors	Meyskens et al. (2010)
		Hockerts (2015)
		Thompson (2012)
		Marshall (2011)
	Donor	Kistruck & Beamish (2010)
		Maclean et al. (2013)
		Scarlata et al. (2016)
		Smith & Woods (2015)
	Family/kin	Di Domenico et al. (2010)
		Overall et al. (2010)
		Hockerts (2015)
		Steiner & Teasdale (2016)
	Collaboration/social alliance	McCarthy (2008)
		Huybrechts & Nicholls (2013)
		Liu et al. (2016)
		Jenner & Oprescu (2016)
	Client	Barth et al. (2015)
	Staff	Diochon (2013)
	Expert	Ko & Liu (2015)
	Non-profit organization	Tillmar (2009)
		Hockerts (2015)
		Nwankwo et al. (2007)
	Membership	Datta and Gailey (2012)
		Smith & Woods (2015)

Social capital embodies the trust, networks, and mutual obligations that develop in social relationships (Putnam, 1993). Following social capital, social network needs to be analyzed in detail. All enterprises are embedded in a network of relations that impact their performance (Conway and Jones, 2012). Network is a new avenue of resource mobilization (Shaw and Carter, 2007), and entrepreneurs can create network embeddedness by building their own networks (Johannisson & Sexton, 2000). These networks are viewed as a critical aspect of small business success and growth (Shaw and de Bruin, 2013). The question of how to effectively develop such networks is therefore an important research issue (Dacin et al., 2011).

Social entrepreneurs need to communicate with different people and institutions to enhance their networks (McNamara et al., 2018); their resources may affect their organization's resources (Hechavarría et al., 2017). At the initial stage, social entrepreneurs mainly rely on their personal network for resources (Hlady Rispal and Servantie, 2017), such as friends or family members, to access finance (Steiner and Teasdale, 2016). Kin relationships can help social entrepreneurs find more potential customers and survive (Overall et al., 2010). Within the context of social entrepreneurship, it can thus be assumed that individuals will assess the degree to which they will be backed up and supported in their endeavor by people in their personal network (Hockerts, 2015). Some social entrepreneurs may have had some experience in working for non-profit organizations or voluntary work, thus they could build some social networks within these people and partnerships (Curtis et al., 2010) — e.g. Scarlata et al. (2016) explored the effect of founders' experience on the performance of philanthropic venture capital firms.

Since non-profit organizations have a longer history in practice, and the regulations are more complete in many contexts, they can maintain good relationships with the authorities and gain help from policymakers. As a new entrant, social entrepreneurships that build good networks with non-profit organizations can help them to connect with government (Tillmar, 2009). Social enterprise–corporate collaborations can be found in several regions (Huybrechts & Nicholls, 2013), sometimes termed as "social alliance." Collaboration can be seen as a vital component of sustainable social entrepreneurial development in McCarthy (2008)'s research. Liu et al. (2016) demonstrated that the performance of a social alliance was impacted by their management structure and governance.

For multinational social entrepreneurships, they cannot get every resource from different countries on their own, so they need to cooperate with local organizations, even agencies, to access the resources sometimes (Ghauri et al., 2014). Some agents provide social entrepreneurs with funding support and network meantime (Mauksch, 2012).

For example, a water service company in Nigeria became involved in the donation activities hosted by a local charity and gained attention from the government (Nwankwo et al., 2007). Conversely, the government will play a significant role in supporting social entrepreneurships build a strong network by organizing conferences or events (Jenner and Oprescu, 2016; McNamara *et al.*, 2018). In the UK, the Community Foundation Network comprises 55 foundations and helps social entrepreneurs seek funding or gain knowledge (Maclean *et al.*, 2013). Compared to traditional enterprises, the relationships among different social entrepreneurships are more like friends rather than foes. Participation in networks provides access to new customers and market information and allows social entrepreneurs to exchange ideas, discuss similar challenges they may encounter, and identify solutions to those challenges (Shaw and Carter, 2007). They can support each other through acts such as introducing resources or sharing information without profit competition. A "win-win" model has become a common view when social entrepreneurs work with stakeholders. To build and maintain a sustainable and durable relationship with stakeholders can lead social enterprises to survive and reach higher levers of success (Imperatori and Ruta, 2015). However, social entrepreneurs should take the leading role in stakeholder network and maintain a high level of stakeholders engagement (Ramus and Vaccaro, 2017).

Other human resources required for social entrepreneurships to maintain good networks include experts who could give social entrepreneurship tips and access to funding (Ko and Liu, 2015). Clients, members, staff, and donors are stakeholders of social entrepreneurships, but their networks can also be utilized by organizations to acquire resources or information. As a common destiny, social entrepreneurs should build and use their personal networks, meanwhile, they also need to access the wider resource channels of their stakeholders (Barth *et al.*, 2015; Diochon, 2013).

11.2.2. *Resource strategy*

Non-profits face greater challenges than other entities, such as limited access to talent and capital, when advocating for social causes. Resource acquisition plays a critical role for social entrepreneurship to support their dual-mission while striving to scale up and become financially sustainable. Effective resource mobilization can be especially important to achieve the social mission. Some scholars have found that social entrepreneurships or social enterprises operate in resource-scarcity contexts, and the resources they need are expensive. Thus, such social entrepreneurs have to find a suitable way to mobilize the essential resources. Sonnino and Griggs-Trevarthen (2012) highlight the capacity of social entrepreneurs to empower the local communities through resources mobilization. The capability of deciding on a resource strategy is as crucial as the other skills of social entrepreneurs (Table 11.13).

Many scholars have emphasized on the bricolage strategy for social entrepreneurship (Desa, 2012; Di Domenico *et al.*, 2010; Bacq *et al.*, 2015; Bhatt & Ahmad, 2017). Bricolage is defined as applying combinations of existing resources to solve new problems and/or find new opportunities. Social entrepreneurships that are mostly confronted with unfavorable institutional environments and constraints engage in bricolage to reconfigure their existing resources.

Table 11.13. Intangible resources: Social capital.

Approach		
	Bricolage	Desa (2012)
		Di Domenico et al. (2010)
		Desa & Basu (2013)
		Sunley & Pinch (2012)
		Bhatt & Ahmad (2017)
		Steiner & Teasdale (2016)
		Mair & Martı (2009)
		Kang (2017)
		Bacq et al. (2015)
		McNamara et al. (2018)
		Sunduramurthy et al. (2016)
		Wulleman & Hudon (2016)
		Halme et al. (2012)
	Ingenieur	Sunduramurthy et al. (2016)
	Allocation	Chalmers & Balan-Vnuk (2013)
	Partnership	Muñoz (2009)
		Gupta et al. (2015)
		Meyskens & Carsrud (2013)
	Acquisition	Zhao & Lounsbury (2016)
		Calic & Mosakowski (2016)
		Henry (2015)
	Optimization	Desa & Basu (2013)

Resource constraints push the social entrepreneurship into finding innovative ways of using the existing resources and acquiring new resources in order to achieve both financial sustainability and generate social outcomes. Bricolage can help social entrepreneurs mitigate the lack of institutional support. There are three different bricolages: material, labor, and skills. Many researchers (Baker and Nelson, 2005; Garud and Karnoe, 2003; Johannisson & Olaison, 2007) have been interested in using the concept of bricolage to address resource-scarcity problems in the entrepreneurship study field. Social entrepreneurs should adopt a more nuanced conception of bricolage to survive in a particular context. Resorting to bricolage often leads to ventures satisfying as opposed to maximizing to achieve their goals (Duymedjian and Rüling, 2010). Moreover, intrapreneurial social entrepreneurship prefer to apply the bricolage strategy because they have the strong background of the parent organization, especially multinational corporations (Halme et al., 2012).

Optimization and bricolage involve significantly different approaches to the structuring and bundling of resources. The optimization approach involves acquiring standard resources for specific application but bricolage is defined as "making do by applying combinations of resources already at hand" (Baker and Nelson, 2005, p. 33). Optimization of the mobilized resources seems much easier to fulfill, and social entrepreneurship can enhance their reputations via this strategy. However, social entrepreneurs should consider outside sources sometimes because they may obtain resources from different channels. In terms of human capital, volunteer labor plays a vital role in the bricolage process of social entrepreneurship (Desa, 2012; Liu et al., 2013) — e.g. the Grameen Bank (Desa and Basu, 2013). However, in an optimization approach, a social entrepreneurship would prefer to hire the person who has particular skills suitable for the specific position.

Unlike bricolage, the optimization approach is a goal-directed resource-acquisition method (Desa and Basu, 2013). The ventures utilizing optimization would like to purchase standardized existing materials, hire proper salaried employees to produce their products or offer professional services, and then achieve their goals. According to the research from Desa and Basu (2013), organizational prominence shows a positive association with the use of an optimization approach. The degree of environmental munificence has a U-shaped effect with the use of the bricolage approach. Besides, Sunduramurthy et al. (2016) illustrated that "ingenieur" strategy was applied by some social entrepreneurships, which use resources more intensely for commonly intended purposes.

Maintaining a good partnership with the public sector is a useful resource strategy for social enterprises (Muñoz, 2009). Moreover, these partnerships will provide some professional support, such as management skills for new social entrepreneurs and those who lack experience to avoid schoolboy errors (Muñoz, 2009). By applying a resource-based view, Meyskens and Carsrud (2013) pointed that resources mobilized do not mediate the relationship between partnership diversity and success as measured by venture development, value creation, and venture innovation (Meyskens and Carsrud, 2013). However, partnership diversity and resources mobilized are related to venture development. In addition, social ventures can leverage the visibility through large-scale events to create positions of mutual dependence. It will help these social ventures broadly get support from outside. From large-scale events, social entrepreneurship may mobilize resources with soft power attraction and inducement. In addition, social entrepreneurships utilizing any soft power strategies should depend on their mission and the relationship with external resource providers (McNamara et al., 2018).

In summary, the organizations' social mission acts a heuristic tool to help them formulate their resource allocation strategy (Chalmers and Balan-Vnuk, 2013), and social entrepreneurs need to consider a range of situations to choose a suitable resource strategy (Mair and Martı, 2009). Social enterprises thereby acquire advantageous resource effectively and develop in a healthier way.

11.2.3. *Antecedent*

After analyzing resource typologies and strategy, it is noteworthy to focus on the antecedent of resource acquisitions. Many factors may affect social entrepreneurships' ability to acquire resources and their resource acquisition performance among various social enterprises. What make some more capable of attracting resources than others? This is the question we focus on in this section, which is divided into two parts: the first part analyzes from micro view and second from environmental factor to consider the antecedent factors for social entrepreneurship (Table 11.14).

Culture is a vital asset for social entrepreneurship (Overall *et al.*, 2010) and plays a pivotal role in development success (Datta and Gailey, 2012). Indigenous enterprises will be affected by the regional culture when they choose the governance model. For example, the Maori culture is strongly collective or kin based. Different social entrepreneurships has different common values and cultures. It will attract human resources or donors through stating the companies' culture. Moreover, the culture factor can influence the management structure and governance structure in an organization and is linked to cohesion and future success.

Table 11.14. Antecedent factors of social enterprising.

Institution	Culture	Datta and Gailey (2012)
		Estrin *et al.* (2013, 2016)
		Zhao & Lounsbury (2016)
		Overall *et al.* (2010)
		Monroe-White *et al.* (2015)
		Munro & Belanger (2017)
	Ownership	Yu (2013)
	Governance	Monroe-White *et al.* (2015)
		Imperatori & Ruta (2015)
		Ridley-Duff (2010)
		Huybrechts (2010)
		Costanzo *et al.* (2014)
		Cornée (2017)
		Montesano Montessori (2016)
	Institutional environment	Amin (2009)
		Heike Johansen (2014)
		Monroe-White *et al.* (2015)
		Perrini *et al.* (2010)
		Gawell (2013)
	Organizational prominence	Desa & Basu (2013)
	Infrastructure	Desa (2012)

Not every social entrepreneur wants to be boss (Yu, 2013); the ownership of social entrepreneurship may affect the networks and governance of organizations. Similar to traditional companies, social entrepreneurship ventures have a wide range of ownership, like social firms (Costanzo *et al.*, 2014), workers' cooperatives, non-profit organizations, stakeholders, democratic, stewardship, and co-optation (Imperatori and Ruta, 2015). As for governance, it broadly refers to the institutions and processes involved in regulating and managing an organization (Yu, 2013). The size of the social enterprise sector will be larger in countries with a strong civil society sector, strong governance system, low uncertainty avoidance and collectivist values, high economic competitiveness, and more international aid (Monroe-White *et al.*, 2015). Scholars identified many different governance types in social entrepreneurship practice, such as participatory governance structure (Chell, 2007), club (Montesano Montessori, 2016), teams (Lewis, 2013), and communitarian governance (Ridley-Duff, 2010).

In addition, scholars mentioned institutional environment, organizational prominence, and infrastructure as three other factors that may influence the resource acquisition of social entrepreneurship. Based on a case study from Bristol, Amin (2009) suggested that the institutional environment played an important role in facilitating numerical expansion of the social entrepreneurship and helping them succeed (Table 11.15).

The past decades have witnessed the blossoming of social entrepreneurship worldwide, and scholars have explored the development of social enterprises in different regions — in Asia: China (Yu, 2011), Hong Kong and Taiwan (Chan *et al.*, 2011), South Korea (Jeong, 2015), Vietnam (Jenner and Oprescu, 2016), Japan (Kaneko, 2013), Indonesia (Idris and Hijrah Hati, 2013), Cambodia (Khieng and Dahles, 2015), Singapore (Maak and Stoetter, 2012); in Europe: Czech Republic (Pelucha *et al.*, 2017), Belgium (Huybrechts, 2010), Spain (Fisac and Moreno-Romero, 2015), Italy (Scarlato, 2012), Austria (Lehner, 2011), the UK (Nelson *et al.*, 2013); in Oceania: Australia (Mason and Barraket, 2015); in Africa: South Africa (Urban, 2008), Central Africa (Akemu *et al.*, 2016), Ghana (Nelson *et al.*, 2013); in North/South America: Mexico (Wulleman and Hudon, 2016), Brazil (Siqueira *et al.*, 2014), Paraguay (Maak and Stoetter, 2012), and Chile (Gatica, 2015). Irrespective of achieving social entrepreneurship success or sustainable development, it is important to understand the regional political environment. The topics these research studies covered include governance, culture, business policy, non-profit organization development, and economic transition. It shows that the regions with a longer history of social entrepreneurship have more complete environment and regulation for social enterprises, and social entrepreneurships can easily gain access to government support for resources. Meanwhile, in some rapidly developing countries, although social entrepreneurial activity has had a short history, social entrepreneurs could identify

Table 11.15. Institutional factors of social enterprising.

Context		
	History	Fisac & Moreno-Romero (2015)
		Jeong (2015)
		Gatica (2015)
		Chan *et al.* (2011)
		Kaneko (2013)
		Curtis (2011)
		Idris & Hijrah Hati (2013)
		Siqueira *et al.* (2014)
		Yang *et al.* (2015)
		Pelucha *et al.* (2017)
		Lehner (2011)
	Government support	Muñoz (2009)
		Gawell (2013)
		McCarthy (2012)
		Hörisch *et al.* (2017)
		Chan (2015)
		Bacq & Eddleston (2016)
		Stephan *et al.* (2015)
	Regulation/Policy	Estrin *et al.* (2016)
		Baines *et al.* (2010)
		Cato *et al.* (2007)
		McCarthy (2008)
		Whitelaw & Hill (2013)
		Minard (2009)
		Hazenberg *et al.* (2016)
		Mason (2012)
		Gawell (2013)
		Jenner & Oprescu (2016)
		Somers (2005)
		Fisac & Moreno-Romero (2015)
		Jeong (2015)
		Bidet & Eum (2011)
		Huybrechts (2010)
		Yu (2011)
		Mason & Barraket (2015)
		Mendoza-abarca *et al.* (2015)
		McCarthy (2012)
		Barraket *et al.* (2016)
		Bacq *et al.* (2017)
		Hörisch *et al.* (2017)
		Muñoz (2011)
		Simón *et al.* (2017)

Table 11.15. (*Continued*)

		Akemu *et al.* (2016) Yang *et al.* (2015) Mair *et al.* (2012) Bhatt *et al.* (2017) Vansandt *et al.* (2009) Idris & Hijrah Hati (2013)I Scarlato (2012) Wulleman & Hudon (2016) Teasdale *et al.* (2013)
	Political issue	Desa (2012) Estrin *et al.* (2013) Mason (2012) Mason & Barraket (2015) Jeong (2015) Gatica (2015) Nelson *et al.* (2013) Mendoza-abarca *et al.* (2015) Urban (2008) Griffiths *et al.* (2013) Mair *et al.* (2012) Maak & Stoetter (2012) Jenner & Oprescu (2016) Khieng & Dahles (2015)

potential markets or uncover domestic social needs and receive resources through various avenues, not only just from host countries.

Government support plays an important role in the development of social entrepreneurship. There are varied forms of government support. In the UK, the government has invested significant resources into social enterprise infrastructure, partly to increase the capacity of social enterprises to deliver or replace public services (Teasdale *et al.*, 2013). The government has organized some events for social entrepreneurs, such as workshops, meetings, or dinners (Muñoz, 2009). These activities will enhance the cooperation between social entrepreneurs and help improve their entrepreneurial capabilities, including resource mobilization. Government activism is one form of government support (Stephan *et al.*, 2015). Government effectiveness affects social entrepreneurship resource mobilization (Monroe-White *et al.*, 2015). In other words, an effective government will be beneficial for a social entrepreneurship's resource acquisitions and development — e.g. the Canadian government provides prompt social support for social entrepreneurship (Chan, 2015). In fact, attracting government support is dependent on the social entrepreneurs' capability and their networks (Bacq and Eddleston, 2016).

Some public service provider enterprises are policy-dependent entrepreneurships. Government policies affect founding rates by enhancing the legitimacy of a different registration forms through regulations and tax policies, demand stimulation, or through direct subsidies for certain types of organization. Social entrepreneurship will also create social value to enhance social development (McCarthy, 2008). The UK policy on social entrepreneurship is still in the initial stage, although the UK is the most developed country for social entrepreneurship. From 2002 to 2008, the UK government focused on defined the meaning and form of social entrepreneurships. During that period, social entrepreneurship played a very small role in the government's third sector (Mason, 2012). As a result, the policy framework for social enterprise in the UK prioritizes the organization as the enterprising entity rather than the individual entrepreneur, as one might find in the US (Somers, 2005). In many developing countries, social entrepreneurial activities are not recognized by the law, which means that they are operating outside its formal reach (Minard, 2009). Social enterprises draw legitimacy from their social purpose (Dart, 2004), representing potential competitive advantage in the marketplace for these ventures (Dacin *et al.*, 2011). Hence, legitimacy has particular relevance to the success of social ventures (Dacin *et al.*, 2011; Doherty *et al.*, 2014) with access to resources "directly linked to the venture's ability to gain legitimacy" (Sharir *et al.*, 2009, p. 78). In 2005, Mexico became one of the first countries to attempt to implement a specific law for social enterprises through the Law of Social and Solidarity Economy (LESS) (Wulleman and Hudon, 2016). Suitable and completed regulation aids social entrepreneurship, as it will make them identify their form and legitimacy, which will consequently influence their resource acquisition and mobilization.

The contextual political environment is more macro than policy. Some countries still suffer from wars, some countries provide a completed welfare system, while some countries are divided. Social entrepreneurships should possess a deep understanding about the political environment of their host countries, and it is important for them to find their sources of resources. For instance, Friedman and Desivilya (2010) have stated that the college institution is an underutilized resource in divided societies (Table 11.16).

There are several small but important contextual factors that affect resource acquisitions. One is the governance of a country. Many countries are poverty stricken, and the majority of their citizens live in absolute poverty, especially in countries such as Nigeria in Africa. Omorede (2014) pointed that economic deficiency influenced social entrepreneurs' resource mobilization in Nigeria, and this problem motivated social entrepreneurs to set up their own businesses. Some countries are civil societies, where the size of social entrepreneurship may be larger than that in other societies (Monroe-White *et al.*, 2015). This is to say the

Table 11.16. Contextual factors of social enterprising.

Context		
Context	Governance	Yu (2011, 2013) Gatica (2015) Bertotti *et al.* (2014)
	Culture	Fisac & Moreno-Romero (2015) Gatica (2015) Scott & Laine (2012) McCarthy (2012) Bacq *et al.* (2017) Yang *et al.* (2015) Mendoza-abarca *et al.* (2015) Griffiths *et al.* (2013) Idris & Hijrah Hati (2013) Khieng & Dahles (2015) Bhatt *et al.* (2017)
	Religious	Zhao & Lounsbury (2016) Omorede (2014) Miles *et al.* (2014) Munro & Belanger (2017)
	Economic deficiency	Omorede (2014) Fisac & Moreno-Romero (2015) Griffiths *et al.* (2013) Khieng & Dahles (2015)
	Macro-environmental munificence	Desa & Basu (2013) Gawell (2013) Bhatt *et al.* (2017)
	Government spending	Mendoza-abarca *et al.* (2015)
	Income	Ghauri *et al.* (2014)
	Population density	Gupta *et al.* (2015) Smith *et al.* (2014) Hall *et al.* (2012) Munro & Belanger (2017) Scheiber (2014) Bacq *et al.* (2017) Mendoza-abarca *et al.* (2015) Urban & Kujinga (2017)
	Urbanization	Gupta *et al.* (2015) O'Shaughnessy (2008) Bhatt & Ahmad (2017)
	Education	Estrin *et al.* (2016) Omorede (2014) Munro & Belanger (2017)

(*Continued*)

Table 11.16. (Continued)

		Friedman & Desivilya (2010)
		Hörisch et al. (2017)
		Mair et al. (2012)
		Bhatt et al. (2017)
	Language	Munro & Belanger (2017)
		McCarthy (2012)
	Technology regulation	Desa (2012)
		Yang et al. (2015)

civil society is friendly for social entrepreneurship to access resources and develop (Scott and Laine, 2012). Economic situations and revolutions will affect social entrepreneurship as well. An innovative social enterprise was created in Paraguay influenced by the socio-economic revolution (Maak and Stoetter, 2012). Because of the regulations in China, social entrepreneurships have found it increasingly easier to gain attention and survive (Yang et al., 2015); the same case can be found in Vietnam since the country is undergoing an economic transition (Jenner and Oprescu, 2016). In addition, spatial location is also an important factor influencing founding rates — it refers to the characteristics of the geographical location in which the populations exist (Aldrich, 1999). Social entrepreneurship will also be influenced by spatial location factors when they need to find resources, as Bacq et al. (2017) explored the geographical context influence for social entrepreneurship in India.

Culture may influence funding by affecting the way entrepreneurs in each community perceive the opportunities in their environment. For example, Chile has a relatively low level of individualism (Gatica, 2015), similar to China (Yang et al., 2015). Regions with high level of power distance will create barriers for social entrepreneurship to access resources, but for the US, which is a low-power-distance country, entrepreneurs find it easier to acquire resources. Griffiths et al. (2013) studied the role of culture and influence of gender patterns in entrepreneurial activities. Language may affect resource acquisitions (Munro and Belanger, 2017). Although some previous research studies have demonstrated the importance of communication for funding purposes, the role of linguistic style has been largely ignored in entrepreneurial finance research area. Because social entrepreneurship first developed in English-speaking countries, if the social entrepreneurs' native language is not English, it will pose a challenge for them to gain resources from international foundations. Since social entrepreneurship in developing countries still face some challenges, such as imbalanced population density and low urbanization (Gupta et al., 2015), social entrepreneurs have to gather resources based on these unique environments. Besides, some minority languages create a big challenge for social entrepreneurs. Because some social entrepreneurships are located in poverty-stricken areas, some local people may use different minority languages, and social entrepreneurships may find it difficult to extend the market and receive resources from the local communities (McCarthy, 2012).

Education level is also important for social entrepreneurs when they start their business. As social entrepreneurship is gaining institutional support, an increasing number of educational interventions are being designed, aimed at encouraging more people to engage in social entrepreneurial behavior (Smith and Stevens, 2010). If an environment is business friendly, with lower taxes and encouragement of high-technology development, social entrepreneurship can certainly gain benefits from it (Hörisch et al., 2017). In short, information technology can be the catalysts for social entrepreneurship (Vansandt et al., 2009), especially when more and more youth entrepreneurs prefer to acquire resource from the Internet without considering the distances involved. The next factor is religion. Social entrepreneurs should learn and understand local beliefs, as it will help them find potential resources. Omorede (2014) explored the Nigerian context, where he found that social entrepreneurs believe in God, that social entrepreneurial activities can get help from God, and that they will be rewarded by God for their virtuous behavior.

11.2.4. Outcomes

Since social entrepreneurships aim to achieve social and economic missions simultaneously, after obtaining the necessary resources, they need to try their best to achieve their goals. Are the performance outcomes from different sources same or different? What are the strengths and weakness of each method? In this section, we will summarize the outcomes and performance of resource acquisition by social entrepreneurships (Table 11.17).

Dees (2001) suggested entrepreneurs mobilize all available resources to achieve their ends — for social entrepreneurship, social value and impact are more important than stockholders' interest returns. That is why many researchers have interest in the outcomes of social entrepreneurship through resource mobilization. Social enterprises that seek to operate across multiple contexts to achieve desired outcomes require substantial reliance upon social capital (Jenner and Oprescu, 2016). Social entrepreneurship is like a change agent whose original intention is to create social value and improve the society through resource mobilization (Gawell, 2013). Empowerment is concerned with removing inequalities in the capacity of an actor to make choices, and any attempt to increase empowerment will involve disrupting the existing status quo and moving from a position of being unable to exercise choice to a position of doing so (Haugh and Talwar, 2016). Social empowerment results in increasing the status of the underprivileged in the community; and political empowerment originates from increased participation in

Table 11.17. Factors influencing the performance of social enterprises.

Performance	Empowerment	Datta & Gailey (2012) Pless & Appel (2012) Haugh & Talwar (2016)
	Well-being	Campin et al. (2013)
	Innovation	Meyskens & Carsrud (2013) Padilla-Meléndez et al. (2014) Mulloth et al. (2016)
	Change agent	Minard (2009) Gawell (2013) Montesano Montessori (2016) Hervieux & Voltan (2016)
	Social trust	Minard (2009) Curtis et al. (2010) Gupta et al. (2015)
	Sustainable	Whitelaw & Hill (2013) Gray et al. (2014) Gupta et al. (2015) Powell & Osborne (2015) Meyskens & Carsrud (2013) Jenner & Oprescu (2016) Weerawardena et al. (2009)
	Survive	Gras & Mendoza-Abarca (2014)
	Scaling/international	Gupta et al. (2015) Fisac & Moreno-Romero (2015)
	Social value/social impact	Liu et al. (2013) Minard (2009) Gupta et al. (2015) Chan et al. (2011) Bacq et al. (2015) Hazenberg et al. (2016) Weerawardena et al. (2009) Haski-Leventhal & Mehra (2016) Ormiston & Seymour (2011) Easter & Conway Dato-On (2015)
	Economic	Liu et al. (2013) Chan et al. (2011) Meyskens & Carsrud (2013) Bacq & Eddleston (2016)

public life. Many unemployed men and women have achieved social empowerment through social entrepreneurial activities (Pless and Appel, 2012) and breaking the vicious circle of poverty. Social entrepreneurship can build strong social trust among different groups. They can access financial support from social trust and forge closer and better relationships by building social trust.

Those social entrepreneurships that are reliant not only on donations but also trading income can become more independent and sustainable (Gray *et al.*, 2014). Because social enterprises are not charities or non-profit organizations, they have to find a stable source of income to support their social mission (Gupta *et al.*, 2015). Along this route, social entrepreneurship can scale their business and even go global (Fisac and Moreno-Romero, 2015). Social impact and value are hard to measure but they are the outcomes of social entrepreneurship. Bricolage strategy can be seen as a driver of scaling social impact (Bacq *et al.*, 2015). At the same time, internal resources and the role of networks will influence social value as well (Ormiston and Seymour, 2011). Some multinational social entrepreneurship and foundations gain international influence through reports of their entrepreneurial activities (Fisac and Moreno-Romero, 2015). Their performance largely depends on the extent of social entrepreneurship focus on market-based opportunities. Low to moderate levels of market-based income decrease the likelihood of firm exit, whereas high levels increase this likelihood (Gras and Mendoza-Abarca, 2014). Although market-based income can decrease the traditional financial dependency of social entrepreneurship, when it exceeds half of the proportion of funds received, social entrepreneurship will depend more on commercial markets and will increase the probability of exit.

Social entrepreneurships mostly confronted with unfavorable institutional environments and constraints engage in bricolage to reconfigure their existing resources. Resource constraints push social entrepreneurship to find innovative ways of using existing resources and acquiring new ones in order to achieve financial sustainability and generate social outcomes. Crowdfunding for social entrepreneurship provides additional legitimacy and will create a strong investment signal to other players. Such legitimacy and signals have high value for social entrepreneurs because they can promote these programs to the market, societies, and the public (Kerlin, 2009; Lehner, 2014).

This review research provides a better understanding of theoretical research before, points a direction for future research topics, provides an in-depth or detailed examination of how countries/industries differ, analyzes the development of industries or institutions across periods and regions, evaluates the empirical measurements in different countries, and compares various international datasets. This study uses descriptive statistics/analysis to define and explain the research phenomenon and practical activities, thereby providing a macro view of social entrepreneurship to contribute to the evolution and subsequent development of this field.

References

Acs, Z. J., Boardman, M. C., & McNeely, C. L. (2013). The social value of productive entrepreneurship. *Small Business Economics*, **40**(3), 785–796. http://www.springerlink.com/index/f1253h13m8648868.pdf

Akemu, O., Whiteman, G., & Kennedy, S. (2016). Social enterprise emergence from social movement activism: The Fairphone case. *Journal of Management Studies*, **53**(5), 846–877. https://doi.org/10.1111/joms.12208

Aldrich, H. E. (1999). Organizations evolving. *Contemporary Sociology*, **31**(2), 150–151.

Amin, A. (2009). Extraordinarily ordinary: Working in the social economy. *Social Enterprise Journal*, **5**(1), 30–49. https://doi.org/10.1108/17508610910956390

Austin, J., Stevenson, H., & Wei-Skillern, J. (2006). Social and commercial entrepreneurship: Same, different, or both? *Entrepreneurship: Theory and Practice*, **30**(1), 1–22. https://doi.org/10.1111/j.1540-6520.2006.00107.x

Bacq, S., & Eddleston, K. A. (2016). A resource-based view of social entrepreneurship: How stewardship culture benefits scale of social impact. *Journal of Business Ethics*, 1–23. https://doi.org/10.1007/s10551-016-3317-1

Bacq, S., Hartog, C., & Hoogendoorn, B. (2013). A quantitative comparison of social and commercial entrepreneurship: Toward a more nuanced understanding of social entrepreneurship organizations in context. *Journal of Social Entrepreneurship*, **4**(1), 40–68. https://doi.org/10.1080/19420676.2012.758653

Bacq, S., Hartog, C., & Hoogendoorn, B. (2016). Beyond the moral portrayal of social entrepreneurs: An empirical approach to who they are and what drives them. *Journal of Business Ethics*, **133**(4), 703–718. https://doi.org/10.1007/s10551-014-2446-7

Bacq, S., & Janssen, F. (2011). The multiple faces of social entrepreneurship: A review of definitional issues based on geographical and thematic criteria. *Entrepreneurship & Regional Development: An International Journal*, **23**(5–6), 373–403. https://doi.org/10.1080/08985626.2011.577242

Bacq, S., Janssen, F., & Kickul, J. R. (2016). In pursuit of blended value in social entrepreneurial ventures: an empirical investigation. *Journal of Small Business and Enterprise Development*, **23**(2), 316–332. https://doi.org/10.1108/JSBED-04-2015-0047

Bacq, S., Janssen, F., & Noël, C. (2017). What happens next? A qualitative study of founder succession in social enterprises. *Journal of Small Business Management*, **57**(3), 820–844. https://doi.org/10.1111/jsbm.12326

Bacq, S., Ofstein, L. F., Kickul, J. R., & Gundry, L. K. (2015). Bricolage in social entrepreneurship: How creative resource mobilization fosters greater social impact. *International Journal of Entrepreneurship and Innovation*, **16**(4), 283–289. https://doi.org/10.5367/ijei.2015.0198

Baines, S., Bull, M., & Woolrych, R. (2010). A more entrepreneurial mindset? Engaging third sector suppliers to the NHS. *Social Enterprise Journal*, **6**(1), 49–58. https://doi.org/10.1108/17508611011043057

Baker, T., & Nelson, R. E. (2005). Creating something from nothing: Resource construction through entrepreneurial bricolage. *Administrative Science Quarterly*, **50**(3), 329–366. https://doi.org/10.2189/asqu.2005.50.3.329

Barinaga, E. (2013). Politicising social entrepreneurship — Three social entrepreneurial rationalities toward social change. *Journal of Social Entrepreneurship*, **4**(3), 347–372. https://doi.org/10.1080/19420676.2013.823100

Barney, J. (1991). Firm resources and sustained competitive advantage. *Journal of Management*, **17**(1), 99–120. https://doi.org/10.1177/014920639101700108

Barraket, J., Furneaux, C., Barth, S., & Mason, C. (2016). Understanding legitimacy formation in multi-goal firms: An examination of business planning practices among social enterprises. *Journal of Small Business Management*, **54**(S1), 77–89.

Barth, S., Barraket, J., Luke, B., & McLaughlin, J. (2015). Acquaintance or partner? Social economy organizations, institutional logics and regional development in Australia. *Entrepreneurship and Regional Development*, **27**(3–4), 219–254.

Bernardino, S., & Santos, J. F. (2016). Financing social ventures by crowdfunding: The influence of entrepreneurs' personality traits. *International Journal of Entrepreneurship and Innovation*, **17**(3), 173–183.

Bertotti, M., Han, Y., Netuveli, G., Sheridan, K., & Renton, A. (2014). Governance in South Korean social enterprises. *Social Enterprise Journal*, **10**(1), 38–52. https://doi.org/10.1108/SEJ-05-2013-0020

Bhatt, B., Qureshi, I., & Riaz, S. (2019). Social entrepreneurship in non-munificent institutional environments and implications for institutional work: Insights from China. *Journal of Business Ethics*, **154**(3), 605–630. https://doi.org/10.1007/s10551-017-3451-4

Bhatt, P., & Ahmad, A. J. (2017). Financial social innovation to engage the economically marginalized: Insights from an Indian case study. *Entrepreneurship & Regional Development*, **29**(5–6), 391–413.

Bidet, E., & Eum, H.-S. (2011). Social enterprise in South Korea: History and diversity. *Social Enterprise Journal*, **7**(1), 69–85. https://doi.org/10.1108/17508611111130167

Boluk, K. A., & Mottiar, Z. (2014). Motivations of social entrepreneurs: Blurring the social contribution and profits. *Social Enterprise Journal*, **10**(1), 53–68. https://doi.org/10.1108/SEJ-01-2013-0001

Bornstein, D. (2007). *How to Change the World: Social Entrepreneurs and the Power of New Ideas* (Oxford: Oxford University Press).

Calic, G., & Mosakowski, E. (2016). Kicking off social entrepreneurship: How a sustainability orientation influences crowdfunding success. *Journal of Management Studies*, **53**(5), 738–767. https://doi.org/10.1111/joms.12201

Campin, S., Barraket, J., & Luke, B. (2013). micro-Business community responsibility in Australia: Approaches, motivations and barriers. *Journal of Business Ethics*, **115**(3), 489–513. https://doi.org/10.1007/s10551-012-1396-1

Cato, M. S., Arthur, L., Smith, R., & Keenoy, T. (2007). So you like to play the guitar? Music-based social enterprise as a response to economic inactivity. *Social Enterprise Journal*, **3**(1), 101–112. https://doi.org/10.1108/17508610780000725

Ceranic, T. L., Montiel, I., & Cook, W. S. (2013). Grenada Chocolate Company: Big decisions for a young social enterprise on a small island. *Journal of Business Ethics Education*, **10**(June), 327–337. https://doi.org/10.5840/jbee20131016

Chalmers, D. M., & Balan-Vnuk, E. (2013). Innovating not-for-profit social ventures: Exploring the microfoundations of internal and external absorptive capacity routines. *International Small Business Journal*, **31**(7), 785–810. https://doi.org/10.1177/0266242612465630

Chan, A. N. W. (2015). Social support for improved work integration perspectives from Canadian social purpose enterprises. *Social Enterprise Journal*, **11**, 47–68. https://doi.org/10.1108/SEJ-07-2014-0033

Chan, K., Kuan, Y., & Wang, S. (2011). Similarities and divergences: Comparison of social enterprises in Hong Kong and Taiwan. *Social Enterprise Journal*, **7**(1), 33–49.

Chandra, Y. (2016). A rhetoric-orientation view of social entrepreneurship. *Social Enterprise Journal*, **12**(2), 161–200. https://doi.org/10.1108/sej-02-2016-0003

Chang, J. Y. C., Benamraoui, A., & Rieple, A. (2014). Stimulating learning about social entrepreneurship through income generation projects. *International Journal of Entrepreneurial Behaviour and Research*, **20**(5), 417–437. https://doi.org/10.1108/IJEBR-10-2012-0111

Chell, E. (2007). Social enterprise and entrepreneurship: Towards a convergent theory of the entrepreneurial process. *International Small Business Journal*, **25**(1), 5–26. https://doi.org/10.1177/0266242607071779

Coleman, J. S. (1988). Social capital in the creation of human capital. *American Journal of Sociology*, **94**, S95–S120.

Conway, S., & Jones, O. (2012). Entrepreneurial networks and the small business. In Carter, S. & Jones Evans, D. (eds.), *Enterprise and the Small Business: Principles, Practices and Policy*. Financial Times, 3rd edn. (Harlow: Pearson), pp. 338–361.

Cooney, K. (2013). Examining the labor market presence of US WISEs. *Social Enterprise Journal*, **9**(2), 147–163. https://doi.org/10.1108/SEJ-01-2013-0006

Cornée, S. (2017). The relevance of soft information for predicting small business credit default: Evidence from a social bank. *Journal of Small Business Management*. https://doi.org/10.1111/jsbm.12318

Costanzo, L. A., Vurro, C., Foster, D., Servato, F., & Perrini, F. (2014). Dual-mission management in social entrepreneurship: Qualitative evidence from social firms in the United Kingdom. *Journal of Small Business Management*, **52**(4), 655–677.

Crispen, K., Toledano, N., Karanda, C., & Toledano, N. (2012). Social entrepreneurship in South Africa: a different narrative for a different context. *Social Enterprise Journal*, **8**(3), 201–215. https://doi.org/http://dx.doi.org/10.1108/17508611211280755

Curtis, T. (2011). "Newness" in social entrepreneurship discourses: The concept of "Danwei" in the Chinese experience. *Journal of Social Entrepreneurship*, **2**(2), 198–217. https://doi.org/10.1080/19420676.2011.621444

Curtis, T., Herbst, J., & Gumkovska, M. (2010). The social economy of trust: Social entrepreneurship experiences in Poland. *Social Enterprise Journal*, **6**(3), 194–209.

Dacin, M. T., Dacin, P. A., & Tracey, P. (2011). Social entrepreneurship: A critique and future directions. *Organization Science*, **22**(5), 1203–1213.

Dart, R. (2004). The legitimacy of Social Enterprise. *NonProfit Management and Leadership*, **14**(4), 411–424. https://doi.org/10.1002/nml.43

Datta, P. B., & Gailey, R. (2012). Empowering women through social entrepreneurship: Case study of a women's cooperative in India. *Entrepreneurship: Theory and Practice*, **36**(3), 569–587.

Dearlove, D. (2004). Interview: Jeff Skoll. *Business Strategy Review*, **15**(2), 51–53. http://onlinelibrary.wiley.com/doi/10.1111/j.0955-6419.2004.00314.x/full

Dees, J. G. (1998). The meaning of social entrepreneurship. *The Social Entrepreneurship Funders Working Group*, 1–6. https://doi.org/10.2307/2261721

Defourny, J., & Nyssens, M. (2010). Conceptions of social enterprise and social entrepreneurship in Europe and the United States: Convergences and divergences. *Journal of Social Entrepreneurship*, **1**(1), 32–53. https://doi.org/10.1080/19420670903442053

Denny, S., Hazenberg, R., Irwin, W., & Seddon, F. (2011). Social enterprise: evaluation of an enterprise skills programme. *Social Enterprise Journal*, **7**(2), 150–172. https://doi.org/10.1108/17508611111156619

Desa, G. (2012). Resource mobilization in international social entrepreneurship: Bricolage as a mechanism of institutional transformation. *Entrepreneurship: Theory and Practice*, **36**(4), 727–751. https://doi.org/10.1111/j.1540-6520.2010.00430.x

Desa, G., & Basu, S. (2013). Optimization or bricolage? Overcoming resource constraints in global social entrepreneurship. *Strategic Entrepreneurship Journal*, **7**(1), 26–49.

Di Domenico, M. L., Haugh, H., & Tracey, P. (2010). Social bricolage: Theorizing social value creation in social enterprises. *Entrepreneurship: Theory and Practice*, **34**(4), 681–703. https://doi.org/10.1111/j.1540-6520.2010.00370.x

Diochon, M. (2013). Social entrepreneurship and effectiveness in poverty alleviation: A case study of a Canadian First Nations community. *Journal of Social Entrepreneurship*, **4**(3), 302–330. https://doi.org/10.1080/19420676.2013.820779

Diochon, M. C. (2010). Governance, entrepreneurship and effectiveness: Exploring the link. *Social Enterprise Journal*, **6**(2), 93–109.

Doherty, B., Haugh, H., & Lyon, F. (2014). Social enterprises as hybrid organizations: A review and research agenda. *International Journal of Management Reviews*, **16**(4), 417–436. https://doi.org/10.1111/ijmr.12028

Duymedjian, R., & Rüling, C. C. (2010). Towards a foundation of bricolage in organization and management theory. *Organization Studies*, **31**(2), 133–151. https://doi.org/10.1177/0170840609347051

Easter, S., & Conway Dato-On, M. (2015). Bridging ties across contexts to scale social value: The case of a Vietnamese social enterprise. *Journal of Social Entrepreneurship*, **6**(3), 320–351. https://doi.org/10.1080/19420676.2015.1049284

Elson, P. R., & Hall, P. V. (2012). Canadian social enterprises: Taking stock. *Social Enterprise Journal*, **8**(3), 216–236.

Estrin, S., Mickiewicz, T., & Stephan, U. (2013). Entrepreneurship, social capital, and institutions: Social and commercial entrepreneurship across nations. *Entrepreneurship: Theory and Practice*, **37**(3), 479–504. https://doi.org/10.1111/etap.12019

Estrin, S., Mickiewicz, T., & Stephan, U. (2016). Human capital in social and commercial entrepreneurship. *Journal of Business Venturing*, **31**(4), 449–467. http://www.sciencedirect.com/science/article/pii/S0883902616300192

Fisac, R., & Moreno-Romero, A. (2015). Understanding social enterprise country models: Spain. *Social Enterprise Journal*, **11**(2), 156–177. https://doi.org/10.1108/SEJ-02-2014-0012

Flockhart, A. (2005). Raising the profile of social enterprises: The use of social return on investment (SROI) and investment ready tools (IRT) to bridge the financial credibility gap. *Social Enterprise Journal*, **1**(1), 29–42. https://doi.org/10.1108/17508610580000705

Friedman, V. J., & Desivilya, H. (2010). Integrating social entrepreneurship and conflict engagement for regional development in divided societies. *Entrepreneurship and Regional Development*, **22**(6), 495–514.

Garud, R., & Karnoe, P. (2003). Bricolage vs. breakthrough: Distributed and embedded ageny in technology entrepreneurship. *Research Policy*, **32**(2), 277–300. https://doi.org/10.1016/S0048-7333(02)00100-2

Gatica, S. (2015). Understanding the phenomenon of Chilean social enterprises under the lens of Kerlin's approach. *Social Enterprise Journal*, **11**(2), 202–226. https://doi.org/10.1108/SEJ-02-2014-0013

Gawell, M. (2013). Social entrepreneurship — innovative challengers or adjustable followers? *Social Enterprise Journal*, **9**(2), 203–220. https://doi.org/10.1108/SEJ-01-2013-0004

Ghauri, P., Tasavori, M., & Zaefarian, R. (2014). Internationalisation of service firms through corporate social entrepreneurship and networking. *International Marketing Review*, **31**(6), 576–600. https://doi.org/10.1108/IMR-09-2013-0196

Gras, D., & Mendoza-Abarca, K. I. (2014). Risky business? The survival implications of exploiting commercial opportunities by nonprofits. *Journal of Business Venturing*, **29**(3), 392–404.

Gray, B. J., Duncan, S., Kirkwood, J., & Walton, S. (2014). Encouraging sustainable entrepreneurship in climate-threatened communities: A Samoan case study. *Entrepreneurship & Regional Development*, **26**(5–6), 401–430. https://doi.org/10.1080/08985626.2014.922622

Griffiths, M. D., Gundry, L. K., & Kickul, J. R. (2013). The socio-political, economic, and cultural determinants of social entrepreneurship activity. *Journal of Small Business and Enterprise Development*, **20**(2), 341–357. https://doi.org/10.1108/14626001311326761

Gupta, S., Beninger, S., & Ganesh, J. (2015). A hybrid approach to innovation by social enterprises: lessons from Africa. *Social Enterprise Journal*, **11**(1), 89–112. https://doi.org/10.1108/SEJ-04-2014-0023

Hall, J., Matos, S., Sheehan, L., & Silvestre, B. (2012a). Entrepreneurship and innovation at the base of the pyramid: A recipe for inclusive growth or social exclusion? In *Journal of Management*. http://onlinelibrary.wiley.com/doi/10.1111/j.1467-6486.2012.01044.x/full

Hall, K., Miller, R., & Millar, R. (2012b). Jumped or pushed: What motivates NHS staff to set up a social enterprise? *Social Enterprise Journal*, **8**(1), 49–62. https://doi.org/10.1108/17508611211226584

Halme, M., Lindeman, S., & Linna, P. (2012). Innovation for inclusive business: intrapreneurial bricolage in multinational corporations. *Journal of Management Studies*, **49**(4), 743–784. https://doi.org/10.1111/j.1467-6486.2012.01045.x

Hare, P., Jones, D., & Blackledge, G. (2007). Understanding social enterprise: a case study of the childcare sector in Scotland. *Social Enterprise Journal*, **3**(1), 113–125. https://doi.org/10.1108/17508610780000726

Haski-Leventhal, D., & Mehra, A. (2016). Impact measurement in social enterprises: Australia and India. *Social Enterprise Journal*, **12**(1), 78–103. https://doi.org/10.1108/SEJ-05-2015-0012

Haugh, H. M., & Talwar, A. (2016). Linking social entrepreneurship and social change: The mediating role of empowerment. *Journal of Business Ethics*, **133**(4), 643–658. https://doi.org/10.1007/s10551-014-2449-4

Hazenberg, R., Bajwa-Patel, M., Mazzei, M., Roy, M. J., & Baglioni, S. (2016). The role of institutional and stakeholder networks in shaping social enterprise ecosystems in Europe. *Social Enterprise Journal*, **12**(3), 302–321. https://doi.org/10.1108/SEJ-10-2016-0044

Hechavarría, D. M., Terjesen, S. A., Ingram, A. E., Renko, M., Justo, R., & Elam, A. (2017). Taking care of business: The impact of culture and gender on entrepreneurs' blended value creation goals. *Small Business Economics*, **48**(1), 225–257. https://doi.org/10.1007/s11187-016-9747-4

Heike Johansen, P. (2014). Green Care: Social entrepreneurs in the agricultural sector. *Social Enterprise Journal*, **10**(3), 268–287.

Henry, C. (2015). Doing well by doing good: Opportunity recognition and the social enterprise partnership. *Journal of Social Entrepreneurship*, **6**(2), 137–160. https://doi.org/10.1080/19420676.2014.997780

Hervieux, C., & Voltan, A. (2018). Framing social problems in social entrepreneurship. *Journal of Business Ethics*, **151**(2), 279–293. https://doi.org/10.1007/s10551-016-3252-1

Hines, F. (2010). Viable social enterprise: An evaluation of business support to social enterprises. *Social Enterprise Journal*, **1**(1), 13–28.

Hlady Rispal, M., & Servantie, V. (2017). Business models impacting social change in violent and poverty-stricken neighbourhoods: A case study in Colombia. *International Small Business Journal: Researching Entrepreneurship*, **35**(4), 427–448.

Hockerts, K. (2015). The Social Entrepreneurial Antecedents Scale (SEAS): A validation study. *Social Enterprise Journal*, **11**(3), 260–280. https://doi.org/10.1108/SEJ-05-2014-0026

Hörisch, J., Kollat, J., & Brieger, S. A. (2017). What influences environmental entrepreneurship? A multilevel analysis of the determinants of entrepreneurs' environmental orientation. *Small Business Economics*, **48**(1), 47–69.

Huybrechts, B. (2010). The governance of fair trade social enterprises in Belgium. *Social Enterprise Journal*, **6**(2), 110–124.

Huybrechts, B., & Nicholls, A. (2013). The role of legitimacy in social enterprise-corporate collaboration. *Social Enterprise Journal*, **9**(2), 130–146. https://doi.org/10.1108/SEJ-01-2013-0002

Hynes, B. (2009). Growing the social enterprise — Issues and challenges. *Social Enterprise Journal*, **5**(2), 114–125.

Idris, A., & Hijrah Hati, R. (2013). Social entrepreneurship in Indonesia: Lessons from the past. *Journal of Social Entrepreneurship*, **4**(3), 277–301. https://doi.org/10.1080/19420676.2013.820778

Imperatori, B., & Ruta, D. C. (2015). Designing a social enterprise: Organization configuration and social stakeholders' work involvement. *Social Enterprise Journal*, **11**(3), 321–346.

Ingstad, E. L., Knockaert, M., & Fassin, Y. (2014). Smart money for social ventures: an analysis of the value-adding activities of philanthropic venture capitalists. *Venture Capital*, **16**(4), 349–378.

Jenner, P. (2016). Social enterprise sustainability revisited: an international perspective *Social Enterprise Journal*, **12**(1), 42–60. https://doi.org/10.1108/SEJ-12-2014-0042.

Jenner, P., & Oprescu, F. (2016). The sectorial trust of social enterprise: Friend or foe? *Journal of Social Entrepreneurship*, **7**(2), 236–261. https://doi.org/10.1080/19420676.2016.1158732

Jeong, B. (2015). The developmental state and social enterprise in South Korea. *Social Enterprise Journal*, **11**(2), 116–137. https://doi.org/10.1108/SEJ-01-2014-0005

Johannisson, B., & Sexton, D. L. (2000). Networking and entrepreneurial growth. *Journal of Business Venturing*, **2008**, 368–386. https://doi.org/10.1111/b.9780631215738.1999.00023.x

Johannisson, B., & Olaison, L. (2007). The moment of truth — Reconstructing entrepreneurship and social capital in the eye of the storm. *Review of Social Economy*, **65**(1), 55–78. https://doi.org/10.1080/00346760601132188

Johnson, S. (2000). Literature review on social entrepreneurship. *Canadian Centre for Social Entrepreneurship*, **16**(23), 96–106.

Jones, R., Latham, J., & Betta, M. (2008). Narrative construction of the social entrepreneurial identity. *International Journal of Entrepreneurial Behaviour and Research*, **14**(5), 330–345. https://doi.org/10.1108/13552550810897687

Kaneko, I. (2013). Social entrepreneurship in Japan: A historical perspective on current trends. *Journal of Social Entrepreneurship*, **4**(3), 256–276. https://doi.org/10.1080/19420676.2013.799085

Kang, T. (2017). Bricolage in the urban cultural sector: The case of Bradford city of film. *Entrepreneurship & Regional Development*, **29**(3–4), 340–356. https://doi.org/10.1080/08985626.2016.1271461

Katre, A., & Salipante, P. (2012). Start-up social ventures: Blending fine-grained behaviors from two institutions for entrepreneurial success TL — 36. *Entrepreneurship Theory and Practice*, **36 VN-r**(5), 967–994. https://doi.org/10.1111/j.1540-6520.2012.00536.x

Katz, J., & Gartner, W. B. (1988). Properties of emerging organizations. *Academy of Management Review*, **13**(3), 429–441. https://doi.org/10.5465/amr.1988.4306967

Kerlin, J. A. (Ed.). (2009). *Social enterprise: A global comparison*. Tufts University Press, Lebanon, NH.

Khieng, S., & Dahles, H. (2015). Commercialization in the non-profit sector: The emergence of social enterprise in Cambodia. *Journal of Social Entrepreneurship*, **6**(2), 218–243. https://doi.org/10.1080/19420676.2014.954261

Kistruck, G. M., & Beamish, P. W. (2010). The interplay of form, structure, and embeddedness in social intrapreneurship. *Entrepreneurship: Theory and Practice*, **34**(4), 735–761. https://doi.org/10.1111/j.1540-6520.2010.00371.x

Kistruck, G. M., Beamish, P. W., Qureshi, I., & Sutter, C. J. (2013). Social intermediation in base-of-the-pyramid markets. *Journal of Management Studies*, **50**(1), 31–66. https://doi.org/10.1111/j.1467-6486.2012.01076.x

Ko, W W, & Liu, G. (2015). Understanding the process of knowledge spillovers: Learning to become social enterprises. *Strategic Entrepreneurship Journal*, **9**(3), 263–285. https://doi.org/10.1002/sej.1198

Leadbeater, C. (1997). The rise of the social entrepreneur (No. 25). Demos.

Lehner, O. M. (2011). The phenomenon of social enterprise in Austria: A triangulated descriptive study. *Journal of Social Entrepreneurship*, **2**(1), 53–78. https://doi.org/10.1080/19420676.2011.555775

Lehner, O. M. (2014). The formation and interplay of social capital in crowdfunded social ventures. *Entrepreneurship and Regional Development*, **26**(5–6), 478–499.

Lehner, O. M., & Kansikas, J. (2013). Pre-paradigmatic status of social entrepreneurship research: A systematic literature review. *Journal of Social Entrepreneurship*, **4**(2), 198–219. https://doi.org/10.1080/19420676.2013.777360

Lehner, O. M., & Nicholls, A. (2014). Social finance and crowdfunding for social enterprises: a public-private case study providing legitimacy and leverage. *Venture Capital*, **16**(3), 271–286.

Levander, U. (2010). Social enterprise: Implications of emerging institutionalized constructions. *Journal of Social Entrepreneurship*, **1**(2), 213–230. https://doi.org/10.1080/19420676.2010.511815

Lewis, K. V. (2013). The power of interaction rituals: The Student Volunteer Army and the Christchurch earthquakes. *International Small Business Journal*, **31**(7), 811–831. https://doi.org/10.1177/0266242613478438

Lewis, Kate V. (2016). Identity capital: An exploration in the context of youth social entrepreneurship. *Entrepreneurship and Regional Development*, **28**(3–4), 191–205.

Liu, G., Eng, T.-Y., & Takeda, S. (2013). An investigation of marketing capabilities and social enterprise performance in the UK and Japan. *Entrepreneurship Theory and Practice*, **39**(2), 267–298. https://doi.org/10.1111/etap.12041

Liu, G., Ko, W. W., & Chapleo, C. (2018). How and when socially entrepreneurial non-profit organizations benefit from adopting social alliance management routines to manage social alliances? *Journal of Business Ethics*, **151**(2), 497–516. https://doi.org/10.1007/s10551-016-3231-6

Lough, B. J., & McBride, A. M. (2013). The influence of solution-focused reflection on international social entrepreneurship identification. *Journal of Social Entrepreneurship*, **4**(2), 220–236. https://doi.org/10.1080/19420676.2013.777361

Lyon, F., & Fernandez, H. (2012). Strategies for scaling up social enterprise: Lessons from early years providers. *Social Enterprise Journal*, **8**(1), 63–77. https://doi.org/10.1108/17508611211226593

Maak, T., & Stoetter, N. (2012). Social entrepreneurs as responsible leaders: "Fundación Paraguaya" and the case of Martin Burt. *Journal of Business Ethics*, **111**(3), 413–430. https://doi.org/10.1007/s10551-012-1417-0

Maclean, M., Harvey, C., & Gordon, J. (2013). Social innovation, social entrepreneurship and the practice of contemporary entrepreneurial philanthropy. *International Small Business Journal*, **31**(7), 747–763. https://doi.org/10.1177/0266242612443376

Mair, J., & Martı, I. (2009). Entrepreneurship in and around institutional voids: A case study from Bangladesh. *Journal of Business Venturing*, **24**(5), 419–435. http://www.sciencedirect.com/science/article/pii/S0883902608000517

Mair, J., Battilana, J., & Cardenas, J. (2012). Organizing for society: A typology of social entrepreneuring models. *Journal of Business Ethics*, 1–21. https://doi.org/10.1007/s

Mair, J., & Martí, I. (2006). Social entrepreneurship research: A source of explanation, prediction, and delight. *Journal of World Business*, **41**(1), 36–44. https://doi.org/10.1016/j.jwb.2005.09.002

Marshall, R. S. (2011). Conceptualizing the international for-profit social entrepreneur. *Journal of Business Ethics*, **98**(2), 183–198. https://doi.org/10.1007/s10551-010-0545-7

Mason, C. (2012). Up for grabs: A critical discourse analysis of social entrepreneurship discourse in the United Kingdom. *Social Enterprise Journal*, **8**(2), 123–140. https://doi.org/10.1108/17508611211252846

Mason, C., & Barraket, J. (2015). Understanding social enterprise model development through discursive interpretations of social enterprise policymaking in Australia (2007-2013). *Social Enterprise Journal*, **11**(2), 138–155. https://doi.org/10.1108/SEJ-02-2014-0010

Mauksch, S. (2012). Beyond managerial rationality: Exploring social enterprise in Germany. *Social Enterprise Journal*, **8**(2), 156–170. https://doi.org/10.1108/17508611211252864

McCarthy, B. (2008). Case study of an artists' retreat in Ireland: An exploration of its business model. *Social Enterprise Journal*, **4**, 136–148. https://doi.org/10.1108/17508610810902020

McCarthy, B. (2012). From fishing and factories to cultural tourism: The role of social entrepreneurs in the construction of a new institutional field. *Entrepreneurship and Regional Development*, **24**(3–4), 259–282.

McNamara, P., Pazzaglia, F., & Sonpar, K. (2018). Large-scale events as catalysts for creating mutual dependence between social ventures and resource providers. *Journal of Management*, **44**(2), 470–500.

Medina Munro, M., & Belanger, C. (2017). Analyzing external environment factors affecting social enterprise development. *Social Enterprise Journal*, **13**(1), 38–52.

Mendoza-abarca, K. I., Anokhin, S., & Zamudio, C. (2015). Uncovering the influence of social venture creation on commercial venture creation : A population ecology perspective. *Journal of Business Venturing*, **30**(6), 793–807.

Meyskens, M., & Carsrud, A. L. (2013). Nascent green-technology ventures: A study assessing the role of partnership diversity in firm success. *Small Business Economics*, **40**(3), 739–759. https://doi.org/10.1007/s11187-011-9400-1

Meyskens, M., Carsrud, A. L., & Cardozo, R. N. (2010). The symbiosis of entities in the social engagement network: The role of social ventures. *Entrepreneurship and Regional Development*, **22**(5), 425–455.

Miles, M. P., Verreynne, M. L., & Luke, B. (2014). Social enterprises and the performance advantages of a Vincentian marketing orientation. *Journal of Business Ethics*, **123**(4), 549–556. https://doi.org/10.1007/s10551-013-2009-3

Minard, C. S. L. (2009). Valuing entrepreneurship in the informal economy in Senegal. *Social Enterprise Journal*, **5**(3), 186–209.

Monroe-White, T., Kerlin, J. A., & Zook, S. (2015). A quantitative critique of Kerlin's macro-institutional social enterprise framework. *Social Enterprise Journal*, **11**(2), 178–201.

Montesano Montessori, N. (2016). A theoretical and methodological approach to social entrepreneurship as world-making and emancipation: Social change as a projection in space and time. *Entrepreneurship & Regional Development*, **28**(7–8), 536–562. https://doi.org/10.1080/08985626.2016.1221229

Moore, M.-L., Westley, F. R., & Brodhead, T. (2012). Social finance intermediaries and social innovation. *Journal of Social Entrepreneurship*, **3**(2), 184–205. https://doi.org/10.1080/19420676.2012.726020

Moreau, C., & Mertens, S. (2013). Managers' competences in social enterprises: which specificities? *Social Enterprise Journal*. **9**(2), 164–183. https://doi.org/10.1108/SEJ-01-2013-0005

Mulloth, B., Kickul, J. R., & Gundry, L. K. (2016). Driving technology innovation through social entrepreneurship at Prezi. *Journal of Small Business and Enterprise Development*, **23**(3), 753–767. https://doi.org/10.1108/JSBED-08-2015-0111

Muñoz, S.-A. (2011). Health service provision through social enterprise: Opportunities and barriers identified by social entrepreneurs and procurement professionals in the UK. *International Journal of Entrepreneurship and Innovation*, **12**(1), 39–53. https://doi.org/10.5367/ijei.2011.0014

Munoz, S.-A., Farmer, J., Winterton, R., & Barraket, J. (2015). The social enterprise as a space of well-being: an exploratory case study. *Social Enterprise Journal*, **11**(3), 281–302. https://doi.org/10.1108/SEJ-11-2014-0041

Muñoz, S. (2009). Social enterprise and public sector voices on procurement. *Social Enterprise Journal*, **5**(1), 69–82. https://doi.org/10.1108/17508610910956417

Muñoz, S. A. (2010). Towards a geographical research agenda for social enterprise. *Area*, **42**(3), 302–312. https://doi.org/10.1111/j.1475-4762.2009.00926.x

Nelson, T., Ingols, C., Christian-Murtie, J., & Myers, P. (2013). Susan Murcott and Pure Home Water: Building a sustainable mission-driven enterprise in Northern Ghana. *Entrepreneurship: Theory and Practice*, **37**(4), 961–979. https://doi.org/10.1111/j.1540-6520.2011.00448.x

Newth, J., & Woods, C. (2014). Resistance to social entrepreneurship: How context shapes innovation. *Journal of Social Entrepreneurship*, **5**(2), 192–213. https://doi.org/10.1080/19420676.2014.889739

Nicholls, A. (2008). *Social entrepreneurship: New Models of Sustainable Social Change* (Oxford: Oxford University Press).

Nwankwo, E., Phillips, N., & Tracey, P. (2007). Social investment through community enterprise: The case of multinational corporations involvement in the development of Nigerian water resources. *Journal of Business Ethics*, **73**(1), 91–101. https://doi.org/10.1007/s10551-006-9200-8

O'Shaughnessy, M. (2008). Statutory support and the implications for the employee profile of rural based Irish work integration social enterprises (WISEs). *Social Enterprise Journal*, **4**(2), 126–135.

Omorede, A. (2014). Exploration of motivational drivers towards social entrepreneurship. *Social Enterprise Journal*, **10**(3), 239–267.

Ormiston, J., & Seymour, R. (2011). Understanding value creation in social entrepreneurship: The importance of aligning mission, strategy and impact measurement. *Journal of Social Entrepreneurship*, **2**(2), 125–150. https://doi.org/10.1080/19420676.2011.606331

Overall, J., Tapsell, P., & Woods, C. (2010). Governance and indigenous social entrepreneurship: when context counts. *Social Enterprise Journal*, **6**(2), 146–161.

Padilla-Meléndez, A., Rosa Del Aguila-Obra, A., & Lockett, N. (2014). All in the mind: understanding the social economy enterprise innovation in Spain. *International Journal of Entrepreneurial Behavior & Research*, **20**(5), 493–512. https://doi.org/10.1108/IJEBR-10-2013-0164

Parhankangas, A., & Renko, M. (2017). Linguistic style and crowdfunding success among social and commercial entrepreneurs. *Journal of Business Venturing*, **32**(2), 215–236.

Parkinson, C., & Howorth, C. (2008). The language of social entrepreneurs. *Entrepreneurship & Regional Development*, **20**(3), 285–309. https://doi.org/10.1080/08985620701800507

Peattie, K., & Morley, A. (2008). Eight paradoxes of the social enterprise research agenda. *Social Enterprise Journal*, **4**(2), 91–107. https://doi.org/10.1108/17508610810901995

Pelucha, M., Kourilova, J., & Kveton, V. (2017). Barriers of social entrepreneurship development — A case study of the Czech Republic. *Journal of Social Entrepreneurship*, 1–20. https://doi.org/10.1080/19420676.2017.1313303

Perrini, F., Vurro, C., & Costanzo, L. A. (2010). A process-based view of social entrepreneurship: From opportunity identification to scaling-up social change in the case of San Patrignano. *Entrepreneurship and Regional Development*, **22**(6), 515–534.

Pless, N. M., & Appel, J. (2012). In pursuit of dignity and social justice: Changing lives through 100% inclusion-how gram vikas fosters sustainable rural development. *Journal of Business Ethics*, **111**(3), 389–411. https://doi.org/10.1007/s10551-012-1415-2

Powell, M., & Osborne, S. P. (2015). Can marketing contribute to sustainable social enterprise? *Social Enterprise Journal*, **11**(1), 24–46.

Putnam, R. (1993). The prosperous community. *The American Prospect*, **4**(13), 35–42.

Ramus, T., & Vaccaro, A. (2017). Stakeholders matter: How Social Enterprises address mission drift. *Journal of Business Ethics*, **143**(2), 307–322. https://doi.org/10.1007/s10551-014-2353-y

Ridley-Duff, R. (2010). Communitarian governance in social enterprises: Case evidence from the Mondragon Cooperative Corporation and School Trends Ltd. *Social Enterprise Journal*, **6**(2), 125–145. https://doi.org/10.1108/17508611011069266

Roberts, D., & Woods, C. (2005). Changing the world on a shoestring: The concept of social entrepreneurship. *University Auckland Business Review*, **Autumn**, 45–51. http://www.uabr.auckland.ac.nz/files/articles/volume11/v11i1-asd.pdf

Rotheroe, N. C., & Miller, L. (2008). Innovation in social enterprise: Achieving a user participation model. *Social Enterprise Journal*, **4**(3), 242–260. https://doi.org/10.1108/17508610810922721

Royce, M. (2007). Using human resource management tools to support social enterprise emerging themes from the sector. *Social Enterprise Journal*, **3**, 10–19. http://www.emeraldinsight.com/doi/abs/10.1108/17508610780000718

Ruebottom, T. (2013). The microstructures of rhetorical strategy in social entrepreneurship: Building legitimacy through heroes and villains. *Journal of Business Venturing*, **28**(1), 98–116. https://doi.org/10.1016/j.jbusvent.2011.05.001

Santos, F. M. (2012). A positive theory of social entrepreneurship. *Journal of Business Ethics*, **111**(3), 335–351. https://doi.org/10.1007/s10551-012-1413-4

Sarpong, D., & Davies, C. (2014). Managerial organizing practices and legitimacy seeking in social enterprises. *Social Enterprise Journal*, **10**(1), 21–37.

Scarlata, M., & Alemany, L. (2010). Deal structuring in philanthropic venture capital investments: Financing instrument, valuation and covenants. *Journal of Business Ethics*, **95**(suppl. 2), 121–145. https://doi.org/10.1007/s10551-011-0851-8

Scarlata, M., Zacharakis, A., & Walske, J. (2016). The effect of founder experience on the performance of philanthropic venture capital firms. *International Small Business Journal: Researching Entrepreneurship*, **34**(5), 618–636.

Scarlato, M. (2012). Social enterprise and development policy: Evidence from Italy. *Journal of Social Entrepreneurship*, **3**(1), 24–49. https://doi.org/10.1080/19420676.2012.659675

Scheiber, L. A. (2014). Social capital and the target population. *Social Enterprise Journal*, **10**(2), 121–134.

Scott, J. W., & Laine, J. (2012). Borderwork: Finnish-Russian co-operation and civil society engagement in the social economy of transformation. *Entrepreneurship & Regional Development*, **24**(3/4), 181–197. https://doi.org/10.1080/08985626.2012.670912

Seanor, P., Meaton, J., Thompson, J., Doherty, B., Peattie, K., & Morley, A. (2008). Learning from failure, ambiguity and trust in social enterprise. *Social Enterprise Journal*, **4**(2), 202–228. https://doi.org/10.1108/17508610810877713

Sharir, M, & Lerner, M. (2006). Gauging the success of social venture initiated by individual social entrepreneurs. *Journal of World Business*. **41**(1), 6–20. http://www.sciencedirect.com/science/article/pii/S1090951605000568

Sharir, M., Lerner, M., & Yitshaki, R. (2009). Long-term survivability of social ventures: qualitative analysis of external and internal explanations, In Robinson, J., Mair, J. & Hockerts, K. (eds.), *International Perspectives of Social Entrepreneurship*, Palgrave Macmillan, Basingstoke.

Shaw, E., & Carter, S. (2007). Social entrepreneurship: Theoretical antecedents and empirical analysis of entrepreneurial processes and outcomes. *Journal of Small Business and Enterprise Development*, **14**(3), 418–434. https://doi.org/10.1108/14626000710773529

Shaw, E., & de Bruin, A. (2013). Reconsidering capitalism: The promise of social innovation and social entrepreneurship? *International Small Business Journal*, **31**(7), 737–746. https://doi.org/10.1177/0266242613497494

Short, J. C., Moss, T. W., & Lumpkin, G. T. (2009). Research in social entrepreneurship: Past contributions and future opportunities. *Strategic Entrepreneurship Journal*, **3**(2), 161–194. https://doi.org/10.1002/sej.69

Simón, G., Fernando J., T. G.-C., & Contreras-Pacheco, O. (2017). Policies to enhance social development through the promotion of SME and social entrepreneurship: A study in the Colombian construction industry. *Entrepreneurship & Regional Development*, **29**(1–2), 51–70. http://rsa.tandfonline.com/doi/abs/10.1080/08985626.2016.1255437

Siqueira, A. C. O., Mariano, S. R. H., & Moraes, J. (2014). Supporting innovation ecosystems with microfinance: Evidence from Brazil and implications for social entrepreneurship. *Journal of Social Entrepreneurship*, **5**(3), 318–338. https://doi.org/10.1080/19420676.2014.927388

Smith, B. R., & Stevens, C. E. (2010). Different types of social entrepreneurship: The role of geography and embeddedness on the measurement and scaling of social value. *Entrepreneurship and Regional Development*, **22**(6), 575–598. https://doi.org/10.1080/08985626.2010.488405

Smith, L., & Woods, C. (2015). Stakeholder engagement in the social entrepreneurship process: Identity, governance and legitimacy. *Journal of Social Entrepreneurship*, **6**(2), 186–217. https://doi.org/10.1080/19420676.2014.987802

Smith, R., Bell, R., & Watts, H. (2014). Personality trait differences between traditional and social entrepreneurs. *Social Enterprise Journal*, **10**(3), 200–221. https://doi.org/10.1108/SEJ-08-2013-0033

Somers, A. B. (2005). Shaping the balanced scorecard for use in UK social enterprises. *Social Enterprise Journal*, **1**(1), 43–56. https://doi.org/10.1108/17508610580000706

Sonnino, R., & Griggs-Trevarthen, C. (2012). A resilient social economy? Insights from the community food sector in the UK. *Entrepreneurship & Regional Development*, **5626**(June), 1–21. https://doi.org/10.1080/08985626.2012.710268

Steiner, A., & Teasdale, S. (2016). The playground of the rich? Growing social business in the 21st century. *Social Enterprise Journal*, **12**(2), 201–216. https://doi.org/10.1108/SEJ-12-2015-0036

Stephan, U., Uhlaner, L., & Stride, C. (2015). Institutions and social entrepreneurship: The role of institutional voids, institutional support, and institutional configurations. *Journal of International*. http://www.ingentaconnect.com/content/pal/jibs/2015/00000046/00000003/art00003

Stevens, R., Moray, N., & Bruneel, J. (2015). The social and economic mission of social enterprises: Dimensions, measurement, validation, and relation. *Entrepreneurship: Theory and Practice*, **39**(5), 1051–1082. https://doi.org/10.1111/etap.12091

Sunduramurthy, C., Zheng, C., Musteen, M., Francis, J., & Rhyne, L. (2016). Doing more with less, systematically? Bricolage and ingenieuring in successful social ventures. *Journal of World Business*, **51**(5), 855–870.

Sunley, P., & Pinch, S. (2012). Financing social enterprise: Social bricolage or evolutionary entrepreneurialism? *Social Enterprise Journal*, **8**(2), 108–122. https://doi.org/10.1108/17508611211252837

Tan, W.-L., & Yoo, S.-J. (2015). Social entrepreneurship intentions of nonprofit organizations. *Journal of Social Entrepreneurship*, **6**(1), 103–125. https://doi.org/10.1080/19420676.2014.954260

Tasavori, M., Ghauri, P. N., & Zaefarian, R. (2016). Entering the base of the pyramid market in India: A corporate social entrepreneurship perspective. *International Marketing Review*, **33**(4), 555–579.

Teasdale, S., Lyon, F., & Baldock, R. (2013). Playing with numbers: A methodological critique of the social enterprise growth myth. *Journal of Social Entrepreneurship*, **4**(2), 113–131. https://doi.org/10.1080/19420676.2012.762800

Thompson, J. (2012). Incredible Edible — Social and environmental entrepreneurship in the era of the "Big Society." *Social Enterprise Journal*, **8**(3), 237–250. https://doi.org/10.1108/17508611211280773

Thompson, J., Alvy, G., & Lees, A. (2000). Social entrepreneurship — A new look at the people and the potential. *Management Decision*, **38**, 328–338. https://doi.org/10.1108/00251740010340517

Thompson, J., & Doherty, B. (2006). The diverse world of social enterprise: A collection of social enterprise stories. *International Journal of Social Economics*, **33**(5/6), 361–375. https://doi.org/10.1108/03068290610660643

Tillmar, M., & Assoc, P. D. (2009). Societal entrepreneurs in the health sector: Crossing the frontiers. *Social Enterprise Journal*, **3**(5), 282–298. https://doi.org/10.1108/17508610911004340

Tjornbo, O., & Westley, F. R. (2012). Game changers: The big green challenge and the role of challenge grants in social innovation. *Journal of Social Entrepreneurship*, **3**(2), 166–183. https://doi.org/10.1080/19420676.2012.726007

Tukamushaba, E., Orobia, L., & George, B. (2011). Development of a conceptual model to understand international social entrepreneurship and its application in the Ugandan context. *Journal of International Entrepreneurship*, **9**(4). https://doi.org/10.1007/s10843-011-0079-9

Urban, B. (2008). Social entrepreneurship in South Africa: Delineating the construct with associated skills. *International Journal of Entrepreneurial Behaviour and Research*, **14**(5), 346–364. https://doi.org/10.1108/13552550810897696

Urban, B., & Kujinga, L. (2017). The institutional environment and social entrepreneurship intentions. *International Journal of Entrepreneurial Behavior & Research*, **23**(4), 638–655. https://doi.org/10.1108/IJEBR-07-2016-0218

Vansandt, C. V., Sud, M., & Marme, C. (2009). Enabling the original intent: Catalysts for social entrepreneurship. *Journal of Business Ethics*, **90**(3), 419–428. https://doi.org/10.1007/s10551-010-0419-z

Vestrum, I., & Rasmussen, E. (2013). How community ventures mobilise resources: Developing resource dependence and embeddedness. *International Journal of Entrepreneurial Behaviour and Research*, **19**(3), 283–302. https://doi.org/10.1108/13552551311330183

Vickers, I., & Lyon, F. (2014). Beyond green niches? Growth strategies of environmentally- motivated social enterprises. *International Small Business Journal*, **32**(4), 449–470. https://doi.org/10.1177/0266242612457700

Waddock, S. A., & Post, J. E. (1991). Social entrepreneurs and catalytic change. *Public Administration Review*, **51**(5), 393. https://doi.org/10.2307/976408

Walske, J. M., & Tyson, L. D. (2015). Built to scale: A comparative case analysis, assessing how social enterprises scale. *The International Journal of Entrepreneurship and Innovation*, **16**(4), 269–281. https://doi.org/10.5367/ijei.2015.0197

Weerawardena, J., Mcdonald, R. E., & Sullivan, G. (2009). Sustainability of nonprofit organizations: An empirical investigation. *Journal of World Business*. https://doi.org/10.1016/j.jwb.2009.08.004

Weerawardena, J., & Sullivan Mort, G. (2006). Investigating social entrepreneurship: A multidimensional model. *Journal of World Business*, **41**(1), 21–35. https://doi.org/10.1016/j.jwb.2005.09.001

Whitelaw, S., & Hill, C. (2013). Achieving sustainable social enterprises for older people: Evidence from a European project. *Social Enterprise Journal*, **9**(3), 269–292.

Wilson, F., & Post, J. E. (2013). Business models for people, planet (& profits): Exploring the phenomena of social business, a market-based approach to social value creation. *Small Business Economics*, **40**(3), 715–737. https://doi.org/10.1007/s11187-011-9401-0

Wulleman, M., & Hudon, M. (2016). Models of social entrepreneurship: Empirical evidence from Mexico. *Journal of Social Entrepreneurship*, **7**(2), 162–188. https://doi.org/10.1080/19420676.2015.1057207

Yann Ching Chang, J., Benamraoui, A., & Rieple, A. (2014). "Stimulating learning about social entrepreneurship through income generation projects," *International Journal of Entrepreneurial Behavior & Research*, **20**(5), 417–437. https://doi.org/10.1108/IJEBR-10-2012-0111.

Yang, R., Meyskens, M., Zheng, C., & Hu, L. (2015). Social entrepreneurial intentions: China versus the USA — Is there a difference? *The International Journal of Entrepreneurship and Innovation*, **16**(4), 253–267. https://doi.org/10.5367/ijei.2015.0199

Yu, X. (2011). Social enterprise in China: Driving forces, development patterns and legal framework. *Social Enterprise Journal*, **7**(1), 9–32.

Yu, X. (2013). The governance of social enterprises in China. *Social Enterprise Journal*, **9**(3), 225–246.

Zasada, M., & Zasada, M. (2017). Entrepreneurial activity in community health promotion organisations: Findings from an ethnographic study. *Social Enterprise Journal*, **13**(2), 144–162. http://www.emeraldinsight.com/doi/abs/10.1108/SEJ-07-2016-0030

Zhao, E. Y., & Lounsbury, M. (2016). An institutional logics approach to social entrepreneurship: Market logic, religious diversity, and resource acquisition by microfinance organizations. *Journal of Business Venturing*, **31**(6), 643–662. https://doi.org/10.1016/j.jbusvent.2016.09.001

Zheng, C., Sunduramurthy, C., Rhyne, L., Musteen, M., & Francis, J. (2016). Doing more with less, systematically? Bricolage and ingenieuring in successful social ventures. *Journal of World Business*, **51**(5), 855–870.

Part III

Social Entrepreneurship and Impact

© 2022 World Scientific Publishing Company
https://doi.org/10.1142/9789811248863_0012

Chapter 12

Sustainability Leadership: Innovation in Governance and Gender[*]

Anne H. Reilly

*Quinlan School of Business,
Loyola University Chicago, Chicago, IL, USA*

areilly@luc.edu

Abstract

This empirical study examines sustainability leadership in n=194 U.S.-based global companies across fifteen industries. The focus is multidisciplinary, exploring the intersection of sustainability leadership, innovative corporate governance, and gender diversity, using metrics compiled from corporate social responsibility (CSR) reports, 10-K documents, company websites, and the Global Reporting Initiative (GRI). We explore company engagement in sustainability reporting through CSR reports and GRI participation, as well as key elements of sustainability governance and leadership: the presence of board-level committees with specific mandates for sustainability oversight, the proportion of women chairs of those committees, the number of chief sustainability officers present across firms, and whether men or women hold those positions. Results, implications, and recommendations are discussed.

Keyword: Sustainability leadership; corporate social responsibility; gender diversity; corporate governance; board of directors.

---

[*] An earlier version of this paper was presented at the 24th *Annual World Forum of the International Association of Jesuit Business Schools*, Seattle University, in July 2018.

12.1. Sustainability Leadership: Innovation in Governance and Gender

In recent years, corporate performance metrics have been expanded to include sustainability and corporate social responsibility (CSR) measures along with financial performance in assessing a firm's effectiveness. Multiple metrics allow for the recognition of healthy environmental and social returns — such as addressing climate change and supporting educational opportunities — as well as economic profits (Vickers and Lyon, 2014). Sustainability is frequently conceptualized as a triple bottom line, with environmental, social, and economic elements, the "3Ps" of planet, people, and profit, or the three "ESG" components: Environment, Social, and Governance. A recent report by Bank of America Merrill Lynch noted that ESG-driven investing is becoming increasingly popular (Reinicke, 2019), as a growing body of research has linked corporate strategies that support sustainability with positive performance outcomes (Ameer and Othman, 2012). For example, an 18-year study of 180 companies by Eccles *et al.* (2014) found the companies they characterized as high sustainability (90/180 firms) outperformed the low-sustainability firms (the remaining half) in terms of both stock market and accounting measures. Furthermore, a highly publicized August 2019 statement of purpose by The Business Roundtable (a non-profit association whose members are CEOs of major companies) called on top corporate leaders to consider the societal impact of their strategic planning, addressing concerns of all stakeholders.

Corporate engagement in the sustainability domain may take various forms. One indication of a company's commitment is its sustainability reporting: whether it regularly publishes a sustainability or CSR report (Reilly and Hynan, 2014). Such reports are optional and not mandated by SEC regulations, as are annual 10-K documents. CSR reports that include specific metrics, such as greenhouse gas emissions and gender diversity, provide more compelling evidence about a firm's sustainability engagement compared to vague claims about resource priorities in company reports (Reilly and Hynan, 2014). These reports share common elements with company codes of ethics, which are familiar strategic components in many corporations. Research suggests that if an ethical code is clearly communicated and embedded in a firm's culture, it can shape ethical behavior (Stevens, 2008, p. 607). Just as with a code of ethics, a CSR report should be in alignment with the organization's performance goals for sustainability and its ESG behavior.

Another sustainability engagement measure is a firm's voluntary participation in the Global Reporting Initiative (GRI). GRI is an independent, international, non-profit organization established in 1997 that seeks to make sustainability reporting a standardized practice. Many experts agree that GRI measures have long been considered the "de facto standard" for third-party sustainability reporting (*cf.* Herzig and Schaltegger, 2011; Fernandez-Feijoo *et al.*, 2014).

Both published CSR reports and participation in GRI are voluntary initiatives and thus suggest proactive engagement in sustainability-related activities.

Furthermore, sustainability engagement is a strategy that generally requires an innovative, entrepreneurial approach to leadership. Previous research has noted that such leadership requires creating something new, rather than replicating existing enterprises or practices (Austin *et al.*, 2006). Wiengarten *et al.* (2015) noted that companies have responded by addressing sustainability not only with operational changes but also through structural changes in executive governance. As corporate sustainability strategies have evolved, the Chief Sustainability Officer (CSO) role has been added to C-suite teams worldwide (Miller and Serafeim, 2015; Gerdeman, 2014). These shifts in governance have had measurable impacts — e.g. companies with a CSO in their top management teams were three times more likely to be included in the Dow Jones Sustainability Index than corporations with none (Strand, 2013).

Sustainability leaders support transformational innovations that address business opportunities as well as societal challenges (Wiengarten *et al.*, 2015). These positions require a wide range of strong technical competencies as well as entrepreneurial skills, such as the ability to work under rapidly changing conditions (Schuler *et al.*, 2011). CSOs perform a critical risk management function (Reinicke, 2019), identifying opportunities and threats as well as providing informed perspectives on longer-term shifts in the global context (Lueneburger and Goleman, 2010). In this regard, the evolution of the CSO position may reflect both a process model of organizational change (Mohr, 1982), reflecting shifts in leadership roles over time, as well as a contingency model, in which a firm responds to its context (e.g. climate change).

In addition, sustainability executives almost invariably serve as entrepreneurial change agents, integrating sustainability within core businesses in order to drive innovation. One intriguing element about the emerging CSO position is the role of gender diversity. Research by Catalyst has found that "leaders who embrace a more holistic view of diversity, equity, and inclusion can build a more innovative and collaborative workforce" (Daley, 2019, p. 2). As global companies move toward sustainability in their operations and strategies, it appears that women leaders may be catalysts in shaping this shift (McElhaney and Mobasseri, 2012). These female innovators are guiding companies in developing sustainability policy and in allocating resources toward sustainability initiatives.

Because sustainability leadership is relatively new, prior research in this domain is meager. This empirical study contributes to the literature by examining sustainability engagement and leadership among 194 global companies across multiple industries. The study considers these companies' general sustainability engagement through reviewing their CSR reporting and GRI participation. In addition, the intersection between sustainability governance, leadership, and gender diversity is examined using data from the sample firms' websites, CSR reports, and 10-K documents, plus additional information from *Bloomberg, Forbes, Newsweek's* Green Rankings, and the GRI.

12.2. Sustainability Leadership: An Evolving Role with Multiple Responsibilities

Despite the growing impact and scope of CSR issues, many companies have no designated sustainability executives. Instead, the senior management is charged with sustainability oversight as an add-on to the multiplicity of other responsibilities. Some firms allocate sustainability responsibility to their Boards of Directors (Tonello, 2013), often through a Board Committee whose mandate includes some element of sustainability, perhaps as an element of safety and health, regulatory and compliance, or under the auspices of some dimension of corporate citizenship such as community relations or philanthropy. Similar to the development of C-suite roles such as Chief Technology Officer, Chief Talent Officer, and Chief Public Relations Officer, the evolving CSO position illustrates how executive governance roles change in response to shifts in the corporate landscape (Groysberg *et al.*, 2011). Svejenova and Alvarez (2017) argue that the proliferation of C-suite positions — currently an average of 10 per company — is linked to the ever-broader and more complex institutional environments in which business organizations operate. Chief Officer positions are hence actively constructed by firms in response to strategic shifts in institutional, market, and organizational complexity. For example, the increasing accountability and transparency around sustainability is reflected in more C-suite positions such as chief risk, ethics, sustainability, and compliance officers (Svejenova and Alvarez, 2017).

Companies differ in where they place their sustainability leaders in the corporate hierarchy, reflecting variance in the position's perceived power and influence (Miller and Serafeim, 2015). Miller and Serafeim (2015) also reported that the CSO's authority and responsibility varied depending on the stage of the organization's commitment to sustainability. Substantial research has identified the importance of fundamental business knowledge and entrepreneurial leadership skills more than narrow technical expertise among effective C-suite executives (Groysberg *et al.*, 2011; Austin *et al.*, 2006). Thus, like any member of a company's top management team, the CSO position may involve a wide range of activities. Table 12.1 illustrates examples of the different titles held by C-level executives serving in sustainability leadership positions, drawn from this study's sample of firms.

Preliminary research suggests that CSOs come from multiple different backgrounds, reflecting the evolution of sustainability into a complex, multifaceted field. As with any C-suite position, the career path to CSO has varied by industry, company, and individual. Some sustainability leaders migrated from engineering

Table 12.1. Examples of titles for highest-ranking sustainability executives.

Chief Sustainability Officer
Chief Sustainability Officer & Vice President
Senior Vice President, Corporate Responsibility
Group Executive, Corporate Affairs
Executive Vice President of Corporate Affairs
Executive Vice President of Public Policy
Chief Philanthropy Officer
Executive Vice President, Global Talent & Sustainability
Senior Vice President & Chief Diversity Officer
Chief Human Resources & Global Diversity Officer
Senior Vice President, Chief Diversity & Inclusion Officer
Vice President of Diversity & Inclusion Officer

positions, shifting their technical focus to the environmental disciplines (Gerdeman, 2014). Others arrived via a marketing path, drawing on the CSO's heavy engagement in external and internal communication (Reilly and Hynan, 2014). Still other sustainability executives were recruited from non-profit or non-governmental organizations with a commitment to CSR issues (Miller and Serafeim, 2015). These varied backgrounds suggest the need to assess the fundamental skill sets required for a sustainability leader, given the ongoing evolution of this new position coupled with its multiple roles.

Overall, as sustainability strategies have expanded, so has the scope of the CSO position, and prior research has noted several overarching responsibilities for this role.

Positioning sustainability within corporate strategy. According to Greenbiz's State of the Profession 2018, a majority of high-level sustainability professionals has consistently reported over time that developing strategy is a top priority (Greenbiz, 2018, p. 15). Indeed, a sustainability officer's strategy work may begin by influencing busy C-suite executives to recognize the importance of the sustainability agenda itself, in that "an issue becomes strategic when top management believes that it has relevance for organizational performance" (Dutton and Ashford, 1993, p. 397). Sustainability management involves changing strategy, operations, and products to support more responsible types of economic value creation (Hesselbarth and Schaltegger, 2014). Thus, CSOs often identify sustainable efficiency goals, such as reducing energy and water use, which improve the firm's bottom line while also protecting its reputation (Gerdeman, 2014). In some organizations, sustainability directors are charged with critical resource allocation decisions and large budgets, which allow them to initiate important sustainability-related projects (Crider, 2014). In other companies, however, CSO-driven projects may be invisible because they are embedded within the firm's core businesses (Bader, 2015).

In many companies, the CSO role has transitioned from focusing on the tactical implementation of specific sustainability initiatives toward a more entrepreneurial approach that concurrently emphasizes business value and stakeholder collective benefits (Weinreb Group, 2014). Most CSOs do not work alone. The very nature of their cross-functional, multidisciplinary mandate requires effective partnering with colleagues. According to one of the CSOs interviewed by Longsworth et al. (2012, p. 13), "you can come to sustainability with almost any background, but you have to compensate with those around you." Not only must a sustainability leader develop her firm's internal operations, she also must encourage corresponding changes among key external constituencies as well.

Overseeing a critical risk management function. CSOs operate in the risk management domain, in particular for ESG risks, or opportunities, that are not immediately obvious. According to Anderson (2006, p. 74), "Sustainability strategies can decrease sustainability risk costs, augment competitive positions, protect reputations and improve bottom lines." A Fall 2019 report by Bank of America Merrill Lynch (see Reinicke, 2019) found that ESG ratings are effective in signaling future risk as well providing an estimate of future cost of capital (i.e. higher ESG scores linked with lower cost of capital).

Sustainability leaders thus play an important strategic role within their firms, providing informed perspectives on trends and shifts over the medium to long term (Bader, 2015; Lueneburger and Goleman, 2010). According to Unruh (2015), sustainability directors may act as "social radar," targeting key emerging issues to place before organizational decision-makers. Selling the sustainability agenda to top executives gets their attention and drives action on these issues (Dutton and Ashford, 1993). In addition, a CSO may help her executive teammates in visualizing sustainability goals and aligning the resultant vision with the company's business strategy — including tracking results and monitoring accountability (Lubin and Esty, 2010). Gerdeman (2014) quotes Serafeim in suggesting that the CSO may be charged with identifying how the future is developing and how regulations and the business environment are shifting, so the company may prepare for change.

The firm's point person for sustainability. Third, sustainability directors are perceived as the designated sustainability liaison, charged with sharing the company's sustainability agenda with key organizational stakeholders both within and outside the organization (Crider, 2014; Weinreb Group, 2014). The CSO is a role model, communicating sustainability values as well as modeling sustainability leader behavior (Stevens, 2008). As Lubin and Esty (2010) suggest, CSOs must work regularly with multiple constituencies, including shareholders, customers, interest groups, and the community, as firms are increasingly held responsible for the sustainability impact of their entire supply chain. According to Groysberg et al. (2011, p. 8), sustainability is becoming a business imperative for executives who are charged with managing the supply chain function via transparency and collaboration. CSOs promote the company's sustainability vision and make the business case for sustainability initiatives (Lueneburger and Goleman, 2010); they report at meetings, benchmark with other firms, and serve as evangelists for the sustainability agenda (Unruh, 2015; Van der Heijden et al., 2012).

To fulfill this point person role, sustainability leaders also benefit from skills in communication and marketing, as most CSOs are extensive users of both external and internal communication (Reilly and Hynan, 2014). Any organization must engage its target audiences, but the sustainability agenda has the additional challenge of effective translation. Stakeholders must recognize and understand the firm's sustainability values before supporting its initiatives. Indeed, Longsworth et al. (2012, p. 22) study of CSOs reports that communication is cited most frequently as the predominant skill needed to successfully advance the sustainability agenda.

Change agents for sustainability. One of the sustainability leader's most fundamental roles is that of organizational change agent and entrepreneur: recognizing, using, and creating opportunities to craft innovative responses to sustainability challenges. Hesselbarth and Schaltegger (2014, p. 26) propose the following definition:

> A change agent for sustainability is an actor who deliberately tackles social and ecological problems with entrepreneurial means to put sustainability management into organizational practice and to contribute to a sustainable development of the economy and society.

They suggest further that such change agents require three essential components: knowledge (about ecological concepts, environmental management systems, and social justice concepts); skills (for communication, negotiation, critical analysis, and change management); and attitudes (toward questioning, reflecting, and challenging their own views). Through integrating sustainability within core businesses, CSOs drive transformational innovations within the firm that also address societal challenges (Gerdeman, 2014; Wiengarten et al., 2015; Marshall, 2007). This same emphasis on innovation is echoed in the CSO survey results compiled by PwC (2012, p. 25): "Sustainability has enabled a new, independent, and creative thought process through the organization, challenging employees to think outside the box."

According to Lueneburger and Goleman (2010), sustainability initiatives require different leadership competencies compared to other forms of organizational change. Because sustainability involves both operational reality and public perceptions, CSOs must be skilled at managing both elements, which requires collaboration and influence as well as a deep knowledge of the commercial enterprise (Lueneburger and Goleman, 2010). Also critical is recognizing the importance of individual attitudes and organizational culture in driving sustainability shifts. Like any effective change agent, a sustainability leader must understand what motivates people to change (Glass and Cook, 2017; Gerdeman, 2014; Ely *et al.*, 2011). According to Svejenova and Alvarez (2017), the overlapping domains of actions and tasks among C-suite officers — including the CSO — reflect both differing responsibilities and jockeying for power in the C-suite, thus also impacting the change process. Bader (2015) suggests that if a CSO has a seat at the table where major corporate decisions are made, then s/he is in a position to effect real organizational change.

12.3. Sustainability Leadership and Gender

A plethora of prior studies continues to show limited progress in appointing female top executives in any domain — e.g. Noland *et al.*'s (2016) global survey of 22,000 firms, which found over half of these firms had neither female board members nor women executives in C-suite positions. However, the gender diversity landscape appears more encouraging in sustainability-related executive roles, and an intriguing dimension of the emerging CSO position is gender. The first designated CSO in a US-based, publicly traded firm was a woman, Linda Fisher, who was appointed at DuPont in 2004 (Bader, 2015). As global firms move toward sustainability in their operations and strategies, it appears that women leaders may be catalysts in shaping this shift (McElhaney and Mobasseri, 2012; Boynton, 2013). Although their numbers are small, the proportion of women pursuing sustainability leadership careers is markedly higher than women in other executive officer positions, who typically represent about 25% of executive/senior-level officials and managers at S&P 500 firms (Catalyst, 2016). According to Greenbiz (2018, p. 27), the proportion of women was well over 50% of the sustainability managers and directors responding to their 2018 survey, and 48% of sustainability vice presidents were female. These women leaders are guiding companies in developing sustainability policy and in allocating resources toward sustainability initiatives, illustrating benefits of diversity in driving innovative strategy.

A growing body of research has documented the importance of women leaders to the sustainability agenda. According to a longitudinal study of US-listed companies by Wiengarten *et al.* (2015), adding a sustainability director to a firm's top management team (TMT) supported financial performance, especially if the appointee was female with a CSR functional background. Boynton (2013) also noted a positive correlation between a gender-diverse top management team and strong company CSR performance, even if the women executives were not in sustainability-related positions. According to McElhaney and Mobasseri (2012), firms with greater numbers of women board members were more proactive in managing their ESG performance. Galbreath (2011) reported links between women on boards of directors and several measures of organizational performance; see also Glass et al.'s (2016) study of the relationship between women CEOs, the proportion of women on boards, and their board interlinks with sustainability performance. GRI has noted that gender is an important but often overlooked issue in sustainability and CSR, and women sustainability officers may be a critical force in the transition toward a sustainable world view.

Preliminary research has examined several possible reasons why women leaders may be more concerned with sustainability outcomes than their male counterparts. There is some indication that women's attitudes and behaviors toward sustainability are different from those of men, in that women express more concern about sustainability and its related issues of CSR (Li et al., 2019). McCright (2010) found modest but enduring gender differences on climate change knowledge and concern within the US general public, while prior research about the developing world has found gender differences in approaches to sustainability (see Meinzen-Dick et al., 2014, for a review). According to Prior (2014), women investors may be more likely to consider ESG issues when making their investment decisions. In a survey of high-net-worth individuals, about half of the respondents said that the social and environmental impact of their investments was important, but the response was 73% for women and millennials. Similar results were reported by Bank of America Merrill Lynch (Reinicke, 2019): the top three groups noting current or intended ESG investing were millennials, high-net-worth individuals, and women.

Women executives may bring a different skillset (Noland et al., 2016) as well as values to top management teams, including openness to new paradigms such as sustainability (Marshall, 2007). In their analysis of gender and sustainability, Casimir and Dutilh (2003, pp. 321–322) build on Hofstede's work in their distinction of citizen versus consumer: "The long-term oriented, more collective attitude [of citizen] correlates with more feminine cultures, which give priority to care and collectivity, and to environmental protection over economic growth." Holmes and Chhotray (2015) note that as more women are involved in investment and executive decision-making, they are contributing to a shift toward incorporating sustainability as the new norm, while Miles and Niethammer (2009) argue that gender diversity at company upper echelons may foster organizational transparency, social justice, and full participation in decision-making (see also Daley, 2019). As discussed earlier, sustainability initiatives require organizational change, and some research suggest that women leaders may hold important competencies as change agents (*cf.* Glass and Cook, 2017; Ely et al., 2011).

12.4. Research Propositions

This empirical study contributes to the literature by examining the intersection between sustainability engagement, leadership, and gender diversity in a sample of US-based global companies across multiple industries. Based on prior research (e.g. Ameer and Othman, 2012; Reilly and Hynan, 2014), it is predicted that sustainability engagement will differ across industry, and that women leaders will be present in sustainability executive governance, acting as entrepreneurial catalysts for the sustainability agenda for the many potential reasons discussed above (Glass *et al.*, 2016). Three research propositions are outlined below.

(1) Company engagement in the sustainability agenda will vary across industry and firm, as measured through voluntary participation in two dimensions of sustainability reporting:
 (a) producing a Sustainability or CSR report
 (b) requesting a rating by the GRI.
(2) Sustainability executive governance will differ across industry and firm, as measured through two elements:
 (a) a Board of Director's (BOD) committee charged with sustainability oversight
 (b) a designated sustainability leader, often a CSO.
(3) Women are more likely than men to hold high-level sustainability leadership positions.
 (a) More women than men will hold the committee chair position among firms with designated BOD committees for sustainability.
 (b) More women than men will hold the CSO position among firms with designated CSOs.

12.5. Method

This empirical study considered sustainability leadership in $n = 194$ US-based, publicly traded global firms drawn from 15 industries. The target industries were chosen based on variance in firm sustainability metrics, executive gender diversity, and representation in *Newsweek's* 2016 "Green Rankings." *Newsweek's* annual Greenest Companies rankings, published since 2009, provide an independent assessment of sustainability performance. Sustainability engagement was measured in two ways: a firm's proactive sustainability/CSR reporting, and its voluntary participation in the GRI at June 2016. Governance and sustainability leadership variables measured for each company included the CEO's gender, the proportion of women members on each company's Board of Directors, the presence of BOD committees charged with sustainability oversight, the gender of

Table 12.2. Industries in sample.

Industry	Number of Firms (June 2016)	Company Examples
Aerospace & Defense	11	Boeing, General Dynamics, L-3 Communications
Electric Utilities	12	Edison Intl, Avangrid Inc., Exelon Corp, PPL Corp
Food	15	Hershey, Tyson, Kellogg, ConAgra, Kraft
Healthcare Providers	15	Humana, Aetna, Cardinal Health, McKesson
Hotels, Restaurants, and Leisure	13	Starbucks, Las Vegas Sands, Carnival PLC, Hilton
Insurance	17	Aflac, MetLife, FNF Group, Progressive
IT Services	18	Fiserv, Xerox, PayPal, Visa, IBM, First Data Corp
Machinery	10	Cummins, Snap-On, Deere, Dover Corp
Media	15	Sirius XM, CBS Corp, Viacom, Time Warner
Medical Equipment	7	Baxter, Stryker, St. Jude Medical, Abbott Labs
Multi-Utilities	11	WEC Energy, PG&E Corp, CMS Energy, SCANA
Pharmaceuticals	11	Mylan, Pfizer, Bristol-Meyers Squibb, AbbVie
Semiconductors and Equipment	12	NVIDIA, Intel, Micron Technology, Xilinx
Software	16	Oracle, Adobe, Microsoft, Electronic Arts
Specialty Retail	11	Best Buy, L Brands, Ulta, Tiffany & Co, Lowe's

these committees' chairs, the presence of designated sustainability officers, and their gender. Sustainability engagement, leadership, and gender data were drawn from the individual companies' websites, their CSR reports, and 10-K documents, with additional metrics from *Bloomberg*, *Forbes*, and the GRI. The study was intentionally limited to companies headquartered in the US, due to different legislation mandating executive gender diversity across nations (in particular, the European Union). Table 12.2 lists the 194 companies in the sample organized by industry, with some representative firms from each industry.

12.6. Results

The aggregate data across industries for sustainability engagement, governance, leaders, and gender diversity are summarized in Tables 12.3 and 12.4. As shown, the results illustrate an uneven commitment to sustainability issues, coupled with a continuing lack of female executives across industries. It was expected that women played a bigger role in these sectors' general executive governance as

Table 12.3. Sustainability engagement by industry.

Industry	Publish CSR Report (at June 2016)	Some Level of GRI Ranking (6/16)
Aerospace & Defense	7/11 64%	2/11 18%
Electric Utilities	11/12 92%	7/12 58%
Food	15/15 100%	8/15 53%
Healthcare Providers	11/15 73%	3/15 20%
Hotels, Restaurants, and Leisure	9/13 69%	6/13 46%
Insurance	13/17 76%	6/17 35%
IT Services	8/18 44%	4/18 22%
Machinery	6/10 60%	1/10 10%
Media	10/15 67%	2/15 13%
Medical Equipment	7/7 100%	3/7 43%
Multi-Utilities	10/11 91%	4/11 36%
Pharmaceuticals	9/11 82%	4/11 36%
Semiconductors and Equipment	10/12 83%	7/12 58%
Software	10/16 63%	5/16 31%
Specialty Retail	8/11 73%	6/11 55%
Total	144/194	68/194
Average	74%	35%
	Industry Leaders	**Industry Laggards**

well as sustainability leadership, given multiple consumer-focused industries and (for many) high employment of women. Overall, the most visible differences found in sustainability commitment and gender-diverse leadership were by industry.

As shown in Table 12.3, results showed that sustainability engagement varied by both reporting metric and industry, providing support for Research Propositions 1(a) and 1(b). In terms of voluntary CSR reports, sustainability engagement was strong, with 144 of the 194 companies in the sample (74%) engaging in this activity. Participation differed across industry — e.g. 100% of the 15 food and 7 medical equipment firms provided such reports, but only 44% of the 18 IT services companies did so. The strongest performers ("Industry Leaders") in terms of the percentage of companies publishing CSR/sustainability reports were food, medical equipment, electric utilities, and multi-utilities. (Note that as regulated entities, many utilities are mandated to produce reports summarizing their environmental sustainability performance.) "Industry Laggards" (for this metric, < 65%) were IT services, machinery, software, and aerospace & defense.

Results for sustainability engagement were much lower overall for the voluntary GRI participation: only 35% (68/194) of the sample engaged in some level of GRI reporting, again with cross-industry variance. One explanation for this difference may be that GRI standards require following strict reporting guidelines, while CSR reports have no standardized metrics — and sometimes may represent more infomercial than unbiased reporting. Industry leaders (> 50% of companies demonstrating some level of GRI ranking) included electrical utilities, semiconductors, specialty retail, and food, perhaps reflecting high direct engagement with consumers. Industry laggards (< 25% of companies in the industry) were machinery, media, aerospace, healthcare providers, and IT services (again).

Table 12.4 notes that the presence of designated sustainability governance positions was limited and again varied by industry as well as across firms, supporting Research Propositions 2(a) and 2(b). For example, 11/15 (73%) of the food companies had designated sustainability leaders and one-third reported a Board committee with sustainability oversight. In contrast, one-quarter of the 16 software firms had a CSO position but not a single company had a sustainability-related BOD committee; although software companies may lead in innovative products, they lag in sustainability executive governance. Table 12.4 illustrates that overall, slightly more than one in five companies (22%) reported BOD committees with specific sustainability governance accountability. Industry leaders (at > 36% with designated committees) were pharmaceuticals, multi-utilities, and specialty retail; laggards (at zero) were media and software. In terms of designated sustainability leaders, the results were slightly more encouraging at 50/194 firms (26%) with CSOs. Industry leaders (> 28% with sustainability executives in high-ranking positions) were food, hotels/restaurants, specialty retail, and IT services. Five industries were laggards in terms of sustainability leaders, with zero reported among the 56 companies in aerospace, healthcare providers, medical equipment, pharmaceuticals, and semiconductors.

Table 12.4. Sustainability governance, leaders, and gender by industry.

Industry	Woman CEO	Women on BOD (mean)	Sustainability BOD Committee	Woman Chair	CSO Role	Woman in CSO Role
Aerospace & Defense	2/11	23%	3/11	2/3	0/11	0/0
Electric Utilities	1/12	23%	1/12	0/1	2/12	2/2
Food	3/15	24%	5/15	4/5	11/15	6/11
Healthcare Providers	0/15	23%	2/15	1/2	0/15	0/0
Hotels, Restaurants, and Leisure	0/13	27%	4/13	2/4	9/13	5/9
Insurance	0/17	18%	4/17	2/4	6/17	5/6
IT Services	1/18	20%	6/18	4/6	5/18	1/5
Machinery	1/10	21%	1/10*	0/1	2/10	1/2
Media	0/15	17%	0/15	0/0	4/15	3/4
Medical Equipment	0/7	26%	1/7	1/1	0/7	0/0
Multi-Utilities	2/11	22%	4/11	1/4*	2/11*	2/2
Pharmaceuticals	1/11	20%	6/11	4/6	0/11	0/0
Semiconductors and Equipment	0/12	20%	1/12	0/1	0/12	0/0
Software	1/16	20%	0/16	0/0	4/16	3/4
Specialty Retail	2/11	32%	4/11	2/4	5/11	4/5
TOTAL	14/194		42/194	23/42	50/194	32/50
Average	7%	22%	22%	55%	26%	64%

Industry Leaders | Industry Laggards

Note: Data at June 2016.
*Information n.a. for one firm in each of these industries.

Table 12.4 also indicates the continuing dearth of women among chief executives and boards of directors found in much prior research (e.g. Catalyst, 2016). In this sample of 194 US-based global firms, only 14 (7%) had women CEOs, and fewer than one in four (22%) had female members on their Boards of Directors. Again, however, gender diversity was much higher in sustainability leadership positions. Among the 42 firms with BOD sustainability committees, 23 (55%) of the committee chairs were women. For the 50 firms with CSOs, 32 (64%) were women. These numbers, while small, provide support for Research Propositions 3(a) and 3(b): women are taking on the opportunity for leadership in sustainability. Compared to women's ongoing limited representation in other executive governance roles (at about 25% of executive/senior level officials and managers, according to Catalyst [2016]), these results suggest that women executives are making measurable strides in leading sustainability progress.

12.7. Discussion and Implications

Given the ongoing environmental, economic, and social challenges confronting today's world, sustainability is a strategic and competitive priority offering the opportunity for innovative approaches to corporate leadership. Specific metrics such as GRI participation and number of women sustainability executives provide more compelling evidence about a firm's engagement than vague claims about resource priorities in company reports (Reilly and Hynan, 2014). Study results indicated that although sustainability leadership and innovation are critical for the future, many firms remain lacking in engagement, despite their rhetoric. In addition, the study supported prior research in suggesting that benchmarking sustainability performance by industry may be most effective (Ameer and Othman, 2012). This research also proposed that, as firms integrate the sustainability agenda into their operations and strategies, women leaders are playing a key part in supporting this shift (Glass *et al.*, 2015). The low numbers of women executives overall in the sample were disappointing in their implications for gender diversity, and they also constrained data analysis. However, while generalizability was limited by the small numbers of women in C-suite roles — including sustainability officers — the proportion of female leaders in this domain may represent progress in diversity and inclusion regarding these important roles.

The findings that women are strongly represented in sustainability leadership positions may be interpreted in different ways. Concluding that women leaders are indeed critical contributors to the sustainability agenda is the most encouraging explanation. However, as with most executive positions, there is an ongoing pay gap between top male and female sustainability executives, as documented by Greenbiz (2018). With a study design that permits correlation but not causality, a competing explanation is that progressive companies support *both* sustainability and gender diversity. That is, the high-performing firms in this sample allocate resources toward both strategies, reflecting the environmental and social elements of the sustainability triple bottom line. One illustration is Metlife Insurance, which was #8 in *Newsweek*'s 2016 Green Rankings and listed by *Working Mother* among its top 100 places to work in 2015, 2016, 2017, 2018, and 2019.

There is yet another alternative explanation for these results that should not be ignored. If the sustainability agenda is perceived as peripheral to the organization's strategy, naming a CSO may be merely a symbolic action for a position with no real power or influence (Miller and Serafeim, 2015). Even for those firms with women in their top management teams, Meinzen-Dick *et al.* (2014) point out that simply including women in positions of power does not ensure that they influence decision-making. Ely *et al.* (2011) cite a "glass cliff phenomenon" in noting that women are often selected as change agents in high-risk situations — such as many sustainability positions. Perhaps the proportionately greater number of female CSOs in this research indicates that male executives are simply not interested in the CSO position. And if so, are women executives being channeled into this role as symbolic "window-dressing," perhaps another form of "greenwashing"? Learning more about the roles of high-ranking female change agents for sustainability offers multiple promising avenues for future research.

Another topic meriting additional study is exploring which talent management factors (e.g. career paths, training, and backgrounds) appear most salient for effective sustainability leadership — especially for women. Scholars and practitioners alike have noted that more female leaders are needed throughout the corporate world, as they contribute diverse ways of thinking, problem-solving, and collaborating to an organization's talent management pool (Casimir and Dutilh, 2003; Noland et al., 2016). Indeed, women's leadership development has been targeted by the United Nations' Principles for Responsible Management Education (PRME) initiative, and PRME has created a Working Group on Gender Equality, bringing together academics and employers in order to provide support and resources for integrating gender issues and awareness into management education, business school curricula, and related research. The long-term challenges of sustainability — from climate change to community development — mean that companies will require every resource possible in meeting these challenges.

As discussed above, the development of sustainability leadership involves multiple factors, ranging from proactive corporate decisions (e.g. adding a CSO position) to reactions to contextual shifts (e.g. responding to regulatory changes). From a theoretical perspective, future research about sustainability governance could benefit from using process models as well as variance models of change to examine how these leadership outcomes develop over time (Mohr, 1982). Process theories encourage focus on events and time-ordering, rather than precursor conditions. For example, a process model might ask, Given that all business organizations operate in a world confronting climate change, what events and processes cause some (but not all) companies to change their sustainability governance structures in response? Future research could also draw on process theory to assess the performance outcomes of a sustainability officer's intra-organizational career path, in terms of self-selection versus corporate appointment into this role. These different career progressions may yield different results in terms of sustainability governance, strategic alignment, and corporate performance.

12.8. Recommendations

As sustainability is an emerging strategic issue for many companies, it offers the opportunity for new approaches and innovative leadership, opening the door for women executives to make a significant contribution. The study results have many implications for business practice as well. For those companies seeking to support gender diversity among sustainability leaders, the following recommendations may be helpful.

(1) For guidance, benchmark high performers in the sustainability domain by learning how they are managing these challenges. Leading US-based global companies among this sample, such as Hershey, Biogen, Coca-Cola, and MetLife offer highly visible examples to follow.
(2) Benchmark with companies headquartered in regions that support gender diversity and sustainability initiatives (e.g. a number of European nations, including France, Finland, Iceland, Norway, and Spain, have mandated female representation on corporate boards).
(3) Support a variety of career paths (beyond engineering and business) to the CSO position, and use mentoring and cross-disciplinary assignments to support development of sustainability-related expertise. Diverse mentors may open doors for diverse younger colleagues who may be interested in sustainability leadership.
(4) As for any C-suite position, intentionally target high-potential women for sustainability executive roles, beginning early in their careers (*cf.* Noland *et al.*, 2016). For example, consider developing an intra-company network of colleagues interested in sustainability careers with a particular emphasis on recruiting women (Ely *et al.*, 2011).
(5) Learn about the growth of formal external training in sustainability, such as sustainability MBAs and certificate programs.

In summary, although many large companies continue to lag in gender-diverse executive governance, this study's results suggest that, in sustainability-focused firms, women leaders are present and active. Learning more about how these women contribute to their firms' corporate social responsibility initiatives is a useful contribution to the literature, with particular links to leadership and entrepreneurial development. Further, broadening our knowledge about the responsibilities of the CSO role may assist in expanding this position's impact on important corporate strategies and outcomes for the future. Some scholars and practitioners have noted that if corporate social responsibility becomes "everyone's issue," a separate CSR office would disappear (Unruh, 2015), and CSOs might work themselves out of this job as the firm's sustainability efforts blossom (Gerdeman, 2014).

Acknowledgments

Financial support provided by Loyola University's Gannon Center for Women and Leadership is gratefully acknowledged, as is the assistance of Matthew Braatz and Anna Chudzinski in data collection.

References

Ameer, R., & Othman, R. (2012). Sustainability practices and corporate financial performance: A study based on the top global corporations. *Journal of Business Ethics*, **108**, 61–79.

Anderson, D. (2006). The critical importance of sustainability risk management. *Risk Management*, **53**(4), 66–74.

Austin, J., Stevenson, H., & Wei-Skillern, J. (2006). Social and commercial entrepreneurship: Same, different, or both? *Entrepreneurship Theory and Practice*, **30**(1), 1–22.

Bader, C. (2015). What do chief sustainability officers actually do? *The Atlantic*, May 6.

Boynton, J. (2013). 35 female CSR leaders you've (possibly) never heard of. *TriplePundit*, January 17. Available at: http://www.triplepundit.com/2013/01/women-in-csr/. Retrieved May 8, 2016.

Casimir, G. & Dutilh, C. (2003). Sustainability: A gender studies perspective. *International Journal of Consumer Studies*, **27**(4), 316–325.

Catalyst (2016). *Pyramid: Women in S&P 500 Companies* (New York: Catalyst), July 26, 2016.

Crider, K. G. (2014). Chief sustainability officers: The growing role of the sustainability manager. Ecotech institute, November 5. Available at: https://www.ecotechinstitute.com/ecotech-news/chief-sustainability-officers-the-growing-role-of-the-sustainability-manager

Daley, L. P. (2019). Women and the future of work. Catalyst. Available at: https://www.catalyst.org/research/women-future-work-report

Dutton, J. E., & Ashford, S. J. (1993). Selling issues to top management. *Academy of Management Review*, **18**(3), 397–428.

Eccles, R. G., Ioannou, I., & Serafeim, G. (2014). The impact of corporate sustainability on organizational processes and performance. *Management Science*, **60**(11), 2835–2857.

Ely, R. J., Ibarra, H., & Kolb, D. M. (2011). Taking gender into account: Theory and design for women's leadership development programs. *Academy of Management Learning & Education*, **10**(3), 474–493.

Fernandez-Feijoo, B., Romero, S., & Ruiz, S. (2014). Effect of stakeholders' pressure on transparency of sustainability reports within the GRI framework. *Journal of Business Ethics*, **122**(1), 53–63.

Galbreath, J. (2011). Are there gender-related influences on corporate sustainability? A study of women on boards of directors. *Journal of Management & Organization*, **17**, 17–38.

Gerdeman, D. (2014). Who is the chief sustainability officer? Harvard Business School *Working Knowledge*, October 8. Available at: https://hbswk.hbs.edu/item/who-is-the-chief-sustainability-officer, Retrieved May 22, 2016.

Glass, C., Cook, A., & Ingersoll, A. R. (2016). Do women leaders promote sustainability? Analyzing the effect of corporate governance composition on environmental performance. *Business Strategy and the Environment*, **25**(7), 495–511.

Glass, C., & Cook, A. (2017). Do women leaders promote positive change? Analyzing the effect of gender on business practices and diversity initiatives. *Human Resource Management*, **57**(4), 823–837.

Greenbiz (2018). *State of the Profession*. Available at: www.greenbiz.com

Groysberg, B., Kelly, L. K., & MacDonald, B. (2011). The new path to the C-suite. *Harvard Business Review*, **89**(3), March. https://hbr.org/2011/03/the-new-path-to-the-c-suite. Retrieved March 10, 2021.

Herzig, C. and Schaltegger, S. (2011). Corporate sustainability reporting. In J. Godemann, and G. Michelsen (eds.), *Sustainability Communication: Interdisciplinary Perspectives and Theoretical Foundations* (Dordrecht: Springer Science+Business Media B.V.), pp 151–169.

Hesselbarth, C., & Schaltegger, S. (2014). Educating change agents for sustainability — learnings from the first sustainability management master of business administration. *Journal of Cleaner Production*, **62**, 24–36.

Holmes, T., & Chhotray, S. (2015). How female investors can lead the way to a low-carbon world. GreenBiz. Available at: https://www.greenbiz.com/article/how-female-investors-can-lead-way-low-carbon-world. Retrieved May 8, 2016.

Li, D., Zhao, L., Ma, S., Shao, S., & Zhang, L. (2019). What influences an individual's pro-environmental behavior: A literature review. *Resources, Conservation & Recycling*, **146**, 28–34.

Longsworth, A., Doran, H., & Webber, J. (2012). The Sustainability Executive: Profile and Progress. pwc.com/sustainability. https://growthorientedsustainableentrepreneurship.files.wordpress.com/2016/07/od-chief-sustainability-officer.pdf Retrieved May 8, 2016.

Lubin, D. A. & Esty, D. C. (2010). The sustainability imperative. *Harvard Business Review*, May.

Lueneburger, C. & Goleman, D. (2010). The change leadership sustainability demands. *MIT Sloan Management Review*, **51**(4), 49–55.

Marshall, J. (2007). The gendering of leadership in corporate social responsibility. *Journal of Organizational Change Management*, **20**(2), 165–181.

McCright, A. M. (2010). The effects of gender on climate change knowledge and concern in the American public. *Population and Environment*, **32**(1), 66–87.

McElhaney, K. A. & Mobasseri, S. (2012). Women create a sustainable future. Center for Responsible Business, UC Berkeley, October.

Meinzen-Dick, R., Kovarik, C., & Quisumbing, A. R. (2014). Gender and sustainability. *Annual Review of Environment and Resources*, **39**, 29–55.

Miles, K. & Niethammer, C. (2009). Embedding gender in sustainability reporting: A practitioner's guide. *International Finance Corporation (World Bank) and Global Reporting Initiative Topics Series*. 28. https://www.semanticscholar.org/paper/Embedding-gender-in-sustainability-reporting-%3A-a-Niethammer-Miles/551769ea3137474e69afd2d00c838bb0e75cbbc4 Retrieved March 10, 2021.

Miller, K. P. & Serafeim, G. (2015). Chief sustainability officers: Who are they and what do they do? In R. Henderson, R. Gulati, and M. Tushman (eds.), *Leading Sustainable Change* (Oxford, UK: Oxford University Press), pp. 196–221.

Mohr, L.B. (1982). *Explaining Organizational Behavior* (San Francisco: Jossey-Bass).

Noland, M., Moran, T., & Kotschwar, B. (2016). Is gender diversity profitable? Evidence from a global survey. *Peterson Institute for International Economics,* Working Paper 16, February.

Prior, I. (2014). ESG investing goes mainstream. *U.S. Trust Capital Acumen.* Available at: http://www.ustrust.com/publish/ust/capitalacumen/winter2014/features/ESG-mainstream.html

Reilly, A. H., & Hynan, K. A. (2014). Corporate communication, sustainability, and social media: It's not easy (really) being green," *Business Horizons,* **57**(6), 747–758.

Reinicke, C. (2019). Bank of America: The top ten reasons investors and companies should care about ESG investing. *Business Insider*, September 26. Available at: https://markets.businessinsider.com/news/stocks/10-reasons-to-care-about-esg-investing-bank-of-america-2019-9-1028557439. Retrieved December 19, 2019.

Schuler, R. S., Jackson, S. E., & Tarique, I. (2011). Global talent management and global talent challenges: Strategic opportunities for IHRM. *Journal of World Business*, **46**(4), 506–516.

Stevens, B. (2008). Corporate ethical codes: Effective instruments for influencing behavior. *Journal of Business Ethics*, **78**, 601–609.

Strand, R. (2013). The chief officer of corporate social responsibility: A study of its presence in top management teams. *Journal of Business Ethics*, **112**(4), 721–734.

Svejenova, S., & Alvarez, J. L. (2017). Changing the C-suite: New chief officer roles as strategic responses to institutional complexity. In G. Krucken, C. Mazza, R.E. Meyer, and P. Walgenbach (eds.), *New Themes in Institutional Analysis: Topics and Issues from European Research* (Cheltenham, UK: Edward Elgar Publishing), pp. 135–161.

Tonello, M. (2013). Sustainability in the boardroom. The Conference Board, *Director Notes*, March, 1–17.

Unruh, G. (2015). What does a corporate responsibility manager do? *MIT Sloan Management Review*, August 11.

Van der Heijden, A., Cramer, J. M., & Driessen, P. P. J. (2012). Change agent sensemaking for sustainability in a multinational subsidiary. *Journal of Organizational Change Management*, **25**(4), 535–559.

Vickers, I., & Lyon, F. (2014). Beyond green niches? Growth strategies of environmentally-motivated social enterprise. *International Small Business Journal*, **32**, 449.

Weinreb Group (2014). CSO back story II: The evolution of the Chief Sustainability Officer, Fall.

Wiengarten, F., Lo, C. K. Y., & Lam, J. Y. K. (2015). How does sustainability leadership affect firm performance? The choices associated with appointing a chief officer of corporate social responsibility. *Journal of Business Ethics*, **138**, 1–17.

© 2022 World Scientific Publishing Company
https://doi.org/10.1142/9789811248863_0013

Chapter 13

The Language of Entrepreneurship: An Exploratory Gender-Coding Study

Rosanna Garcia
University of Denver, Denver, CO, USA
Rosanna.Garcia@du.edu

Abstract

Women are less likely to engage in entrepreneurial activity. This study examines the role of language in promoting this phenomenon. Using a sample of entrepreneurs and non-entrepreneurs of both genders, we examine how success in business is linguistically expressed. University entrepreneurship programs' webpages are then assessed for gender-coding. Results suggest that gender is not the delineating factor in masculine and feminine approaches to entrepreneurship; instead a strong distinction exists between entrepreneurs, who have a more masculine viewpoint, and non-entrepreneurs, who have a balanced viewpoint. In addition, universities provide a more balanced gender approach in webpage text than in visuals.

Keywords: Women in entrepreneurship; gender diversity; masculine and feminine; self-efficacy; entrepreneurship education.

13.1. Introduction

Within the US, the average rate of entrepreneurial activity for men from 1996–2013 was 37%, while the average rate for women was substantially lower at 23% (Fairlie, 2014). Evidence has shown that these patterns extend to the enrollment of women in entrepreneurship programs in university settings (Menzies and Tatroff, 2006). The persistent disparity in men and women entrepreneurial activity in education and practice makes it important to understand why fewer women, compared to men, choose to become entrepreneurs. Women's lower propensity to engage in entrepreneurship has been attributed to fear of failure, occupational segregation, and gender inequality (Elam, 2008; Klyver et al., 2013; Hechavarría et al., 2018) and their lack of entrepreneurial self-efficacy (Wilson et al., 2007), among other factors.

From an academic perspective, Wilson et al. (2007) found that female MBA students already enrolled in entrepreneurial programs possessed less self-efficacy compared to their male counterparts. Wilson et al.'s findings suggest that, because of the strong role higher education plays in piquing the interest of women in starting their own ventures, access to entrepreneurship education is especially important for fueling the pipeline of aspiring women entrepreneurs. However, making programs accessible may not be enough. Recent studies show that language can have a significant impact on how women and men are treated in the field of entrepreneurship (Kanze et al., 2018; Malmström et al., 2017). Little is known about how universities may be contributing to this bias. This exploratory study investigates the language of entrepreneurship based on gender and the language public universities use to describe their entrepreneurship programs. We seek to understand whether unintended gender-coding within the online marketing of such programs further reinforces women's gender schema that discourages involvement in entrepreneurship. Specifically, we evaluate whether the language used to market public universities' entrepreneurial programs may be gender-biased.

There has been a call to approach research on gender not as an explanatory variable, which views gender as "something as *is*," but instead using constructionist research where gender-coding is "something that is *done*" (Ahl, 2006, p. 612). Is there "something being done" by society that keeps the representation of women in entrepreneurship below that of men? In addition, in higher education, educators and mentors must understand whether they are "doing something" that negatively impacts female students' choices in selecting an entrepreneurship major (Hughes et al., 2012). We take a constructionist approach in conducting a two-part study using gender schema, gender-coding, and gendered-linguistics theories to evaluate the prevalence of gender biases in the language used to describe entrepreneurial success.

Gupta et al. (2009) claim that there is a lack of research on whether men and women in contemporary society see entrepreneurship as more masculine or feminine. In the first part of this study, we seek to identify whether men and women describe themselves using gender schema and whether gender-coding has an impact on how successful entrepreneurs are identified. Through this study, we close some of the gaps in the understanding of gender biases around entrepreneurship and the role of universities in propagating these biases.

Our findings suggest that: (1) gender schemas do exist in US society; (2) gender schema in entrepreneurship exists as the entrepreneurs in our study viewed themselves more masculine compared to non-entrepreneurs; (3) the current theory of gender-coding in entrepreneurship should be revisited using today's contemporary social setting as we did not find gender to be a differentiating factor on how success in entrepreneurship is expressed; and (4) universities do not promote gender-coding in entrepreneurship through the language on their websites, but neither are they alleviating the gender bias in entrepreneurship.

Section 13.2 of this chapter provides a theoretical background into gender schema theory, gender-coding, and gendered-linguistic structures as they relate to entrepreneurship and education. We then explain our empirical approach using both quantitative and qualitative analyses to test our hypotheses. After reporting on our results, we provide normative suggestions for universities to minimize gender-coding within the marketing of their entrepreneurship programs.

13.2. Theoretical Background

We draw on three different theories in order to explore our question of whether public universities in the US may be having a negative impact on the pipeline of women in entrepreneurship programs across campuses. Gender schema theory sets the stage to understand whether men and women in the US self-identify using gender-specific scales. We then use the theory of gender-coding to determine if men and women code entrepreneurship as a masculine activity in the language and perceptions they hold about success in entrepreneurship. Next, the theory of gendered-linguistic structures provides a foundation to explore the language used by public universities to market their entrepreneurship programs.

13.2.1. *Gender schema theory*

The gender schema theory proposes that individuals become gender-stereotyped in the society by how gender-identity (sex typing) characteristics are maintained and transmitted by members of a culture. Bem (1981), a pioneer in gender schema theory, argues that one's concept of self becomes assimilated to sex typing, which is the process by which "society transmutes male and female into masculine and feminine characteristics," maintained by a society. The universality and importance of sex typing is reflected in psychological theories that elucidate how the developing child learns sex-appropriate behaviors (Bem, 1981). Societies allocate adult roles based on sex and socialize their children to fulfill these roles. This theory suggests that, as the child evaluates and assimilates new information, he/she will apply self-concept attribution of sex typing to him/herself. "The child, in short, learns to process information in terms of an evolving gender schema, and it is this gender-based schematic processing that constitutes the heart of the present account of sex typing" (Bem, 1981, p. 355).

Bem (1981) stresses that the gender schema theory is a theory of process, not content. Schematic processing enables the individual to impose structure and meaning onto a vast array of new information and incoming stimuli. "As children learn the contents of the society's gender schema, they learn which attributes are to be linked with their own sex, and hence with themselves" (Bem, 1981, p. 355). Simultaneously, the child also learns to evaluate his or her adequacy as a person in terms of the gender schema, to match his or her preferences, attitudes, behaviors, and personal attributes against the prototypes stored within. It is the *process* of how a student self-conceptualizes or self-identifies with cognitive recognition based on gender that is important in gender schema theory. "The readiness with which an individual invokes one schema rather than another is referred to as the cognitive availability of the schema (Nisbett & Ross, 1980; Tversky & Kahneman, 1973, 1974)" (Bem, 1981, p. 355).

In the US, there is evidence that cognitive availability of gender stereotypes exists where there is a shared belief about the characteristics and attributes associated with each sex (Fiske and Taylor, 1991; Powell and Graves, 2003). "Women are commonly believed to have more communal qualities (expressiveness, connectedness, relatedness, kindness, supportiveness, timidness) whereas men are associated with more agentic qualities (independence, aggressiveness, autonomy, instrumentality, courage)" (Gupta *et al.* 2009, p. 399). Not surprisingly, Miller and Budd (1999) show these gender stereotypes are facilitated by parents, schools, peers, and the mass media.

Bem (1981) created a masculinity and femininity index, a set of characteristics that describe either masculine or feminine traits (see Appendix A for this index). Despite some controversy, Bem's index has become the culturally accepted norm of what is masculine and what is feminine in the gender schema theory (Hoffman and Border, 2001). We suggest that, within the US, a gender schema exists where men will identify more with masculine qualities and women will identify more with feminine qualities. Thus, we hypothesize:

H1. Women and men self-identify using language in alignment with the masculine-feminine scale.

13.2.2. *Gender-coding in entrepreneurship*

If indeed the cognitive recognition of gender stereotype exists, as suggested by the gender schema theory, it should also manifest in entrepreneurship. Indeed, a male gendered theory of entrepreneurship has been observed (Bird and Brush, 2002; Chell *et al.*, 1991; Mirchandani, 1999). Extant studies have shown the entrepreneur as an unusual and extraordinary figure with levels of achievement orientation, optimism, self-efficacy, internal locus of control, cognitive skills, and tolerance for ambiguity above the ordinary (Shane and Venkataraman, 2000). Entrepreneurship and creation of organizations have been identified as a "man's" domain (Bird and Brush, 2002). Schumpeter (1934/1983) describes the entrepreneur as a man of "daring and decisiveness" driven by a will to conquer; Hébert and Link (1988) celebrate the "key man," and Collins and Moore (1964) describe *The Enterprising Man.* More recent studies have shown that the characteristics essential for success in business tend to be masculine (e.g. Heilman, 2001).

From a female perspective, Jennings and Brush (2013) found that (1) women are less likely than men to be involved in entrepreneurial activities; (2) enterprises headed by women tend to be financed at lower levels compared to those owned by men, and (3) women are more likely to see their businesses not as a separate economic entity but rather as integral to their familial structures. In her review of the entrepreneurship literature, Ahl (2006) suggests that disparity in entrepreneurial intentions between men and women is a reflection of socially learned and culturally produced boundaries imposed by gender stereotypes rather than psychological differences in women. Gender-coding, where cultural influences and gender stereotypes influence how men and women are encouraged to take masculine and feminine roles in society, encourages a masculine perception to entrepreneurship. Thus, we hypothesize:

H2: Women and men will both identify success in entrepreneurship using more of a masculine than feminine scale.

There is considerable empirical research indicating that cultural influences drive expectations on stereotypical behavior of men and women (Carli and Eagly, 1999). Social relations are embodied as a gender code that is transmitted through the structures and processes of social interactions, such as through education, which affect an individual's gender identity, experience, and property (Arnot, 2002). In an effort to identify the latent differences in men and women entrepreneurs, Bird and Brush (2002) identified five dimensions in the entrepreneurial process that may differ across genders: concept of reality, time, action, power, and ethics. They suggest that masculine views of the entrepreneurial process are "focus, analysis, goal-direction, control through knowledge, and rapid growth" (Bird and Brush, 2002, p. 57). Generalizing, men are thought to be more rational in their business strategy and take a traditional approach that focuses on the economic, political, and technical approaches to new value creation. Feminine approaches, typically taken by women, are "diffused awareness, deep feeling, spiraling pathways, caring knowledge, affiliation, and balanced ...lifestyle business ventures" (Bird and Brush, 2002, p. 57). Again generalizing, because of the emotional attachment females have toward their business — e.g. an emphasis on caring, balanced lifestyles, empowered workforces, social responsibility, and charitable actions (Bird and Brush, 2002) — it is suggested that women operate at a more personal level, infusing emotional decisions into value creation. Bird and Brush are careful to emphasize that gender — male or female — is likely *not* the delineating factor to determine if an entrepreneur employs masculine and feminine approaches as either gender may use a combination of approaches. However, Cliff *et al.* (2005) reveal that business owners tend to *talk* as if they organize and manage their firms in different (and gender-stereotypic) ways, even though they may not do so in practice. We, thus, hypothesize:

> H3: *Men will describe entrepreneurial success as instrumental, rational, and autonomous compared to women who will describe it from a personal, existential, emotional perspective.*

13.2.3. *Gendered-linguistic structures and gender-coded education*

Language has been shown to be the instrument through which individuals understand their roles in society and make decisions (Boroditsky, 2010, 2011; Gumperz and Levinson, 1996). Furthermore, "the fundamental building blocks of a culture begin with language whose categories and vocabulary reflect the cumulative experience of a society" (North, 2005, p. 39). Linguistic relativity theory emerged to describe how the structure of languages shape the thoughts and behaviors of its speakers (Whorf *et al.*, 1956) and it suggests that gendered-linguistic structure asymmetries (e.g. the number of pronouns to identify gender in a language) may create and reinforce gender stereotypes and inequalities (Cameron, 1998; Prewitt-Freilino *et al.*, 2012). In their study on entrepreneurship, Hechavarría *et al.* (2018) found that gendered-linguistic structures reinforce gender stereotypes and discourage entry by women in entrepreneurship. They found a greater gender gap in entrepreneurship activity in countries where the dominant language's structure incorporated sex-based systems and gender-differentiated pronouns.

Ahl (2006) found heavy usage of masculine characteristics in the language to describe entrepreneurs and also found that Bem's terms describing femininity did not match the list of entrepreneur words used by scholars. In fact, Ahl suggested that feminine words are antonyms of entrepreneurial descriptions. For example, words such as "affectionate," "sympathetic," and "understanding" are not entrepreneurial descriptors. Ahl (2006, p. 601) too draws the conclusion that "entrepreneur is a masculine concept, i.e. it is not gender neutral." If gendered-linguistic structure asymmetries are a cultural phenomenon, we would expect all members of a culture to see entrepreneurs in a similar light and describe the successful entrepreneur using the same masculine language. To test whether gendered-linguistic structure may not be gender-specific, we examine the language of entrepreneurship compared to non-entrepreneurs as opposed compared by gender. We thus hypothesize that:

H4: Both non-entrepreneurs and entrepreneurs use predominately masculine language for describing successful entrepreneurs.

Social and cultural reproduction theory offers an understanding of the inequalities in relationship across social class, race, and gender relations in education. Studies on gender in educational contexts have shown that social relations are produced, reproduced, and transmitted through schooling (Arnot, 2002). The "assumption underlying most of the 'reproduction' theories is that education plays a mediating role between the individual's consciousness and society at large..." (MacDonald, 1977, p. 60). "The transfer of femininity, for example, from the student to the school subject and back again to the student exemplifies the process of objectification and embodiment" (MacDonald, 1980, p. 37). If educational systems are responsible for propagating gender-coding, it will be evident in the language and images that they use to discuss entrepreneurship programs and activities. We thus hypothesize that:

H5: The language and visual cues used by public US universities to describe their entrepreneurship programs is predominately on a masculine scale.

13.3. Data and Methodology

Our study was conducted in two stages. First, a survey to test for self-identified sex typing (gender schema) and to collect written responses on how entrepreneurial success is described by men and women (gender-coding) was distributed. Second, a content analysis of the text and images of US public universities' entrepreneurial programs was conducted to evaluate gendered-linguistic structures. In the first part of the study, we solicited individuals from a survey call to a US southeast regional entrepreneurial community and an undergraduate marketing lab where students were given course credit for participation. We sought a mix of participants with and without entrepreneurial experience. After removing respondents who did not complete the survey, we obtained a sample of 49 men and 75 women for a total respondent pool of $n = 124$. The occupational split overall was 71% entrepreneurs ($n = 88$) and 29% non-entrepreneurs ($n = 36$). The average length of time of business ownership for the entrepreneurs was 5.45 years, with a range of less than a month to 35 years. Demographics of the overall sample broken out by gender are shown in Table 13.1(a). Table 13.1(b) shows the demographics for just the entrepreneurs broken out by gender.

In testing Hypothesis 1, we used the Bem Sex Role Inventory (BSRI; Bem, 1981b) (see Appendix A) to determine how respondents ($n = 124$) self-identify on the masculine–feminine scale. The BSRI is an instrument that categorizes individuals based on their self-ratings of personal attributes. Respondents were asked

Table 13.1(a). Demographics of $n = 124$.

Mean	Male	Female
Average Age	30	25
Entrepreneur	83.7%	52.6%
Minority	14.3%	24.3%
College Degree (Bachelors or higher)	55.1%	41.3%
Income	US$125,000	$100,000

Table 13.1(b). Demographics of entrepreneurs $n = 88$.

	Male	Female
For Profit	83.3%	52.2%
Not for Profit	2.8%	6.5%
Government Sponsored	5.6%	6.5%
Benefit Corp	8.3%	10.9%
Not Incorporated	0	23.9%
Average Age of Co. (years)	6.44	4.58
Number of Employees	1.91	2.52

to indicate — on a 7-point scale of "never" to "always" — how well each of 60 attributes described him/herself. Of the 60 attributes, 20 reflected the US' cultural definition of masculinity, 20 reflected femininity, and 20 were neutral. A masculinity and a femininity score was calculated for each respondent using the mean of the scores for the 20 masculine attributes, the mean of the 20 feminine attributes, and the mean of the 20 neutral attributes.

To test Hypotheses 2–4, we asked each of the survey respondents to describe a successful entrepreneur in their own words, using a guiding prompt: "What personality characteristics do you think makes a person successful at launching their own business?" There was no mention of entrepreneurship in this question in order not to prime the responses to a masculine or feminine schema or introduce a gender-bias that has been reported regarding entrepreneurship (Gupta *et al.*, 2009). In order to analyze the responses, we used QSR International's NVivo 11 software for Windows, Pro Edition (2015). The software was used to develop a corpus of words relating to a masculine and a feminine scale of entrepreneurship based on the masculinity/femininity words of BSRI, Ahl (2006), and Bird and Brush (2002).

Building on Bem's (1981a) work on gender schema, Ahl (2006) utilized the BSRI scale to create a list of masculine words and phrases. Similarly, she created a list of words and phrases seen as the opposite of entrepreneurship to create a feminine perspective. For this study, we utilized Ahl's words specifically related to entrepreneurship for gender-coding analysis. The phrases were translated into single words to build a corpus of masculine and feminine words relating to entrepreneurship. Ahl's translation from the BSRI words to entrepreneurship words and our subsequent translation of Ahl's phrases are shown in Appendix B. Similarly we took the Bird and Brush gender perspectives on the entrepreneurial process (see Appendix C) and translated those words and phrases then added them to the BSRI/Ahl list of words. To translate Bird and Brush, each author of this chapter separately generated their own corpus that was then compared, discussed, and agreed upon as a group. The resulting entrepreneurship corpus resulted in 68 masculine words and 68 feminine words based on the extant studies of Bem, Ahl, and Bird and Brush. This final list is shown in Appendix D. We identify this inventory of words as the GAH[1] corpus in future references.

Survey responses ($n = 124$) were entered into NVivo as follows: (1) text responses for all 124 respondents, (2) text responses for females only, (3) text responses for males only, (4) text responses for entrepreneurs, both genders, and (5) text responses for non-entrepreneurs, both genders. For each grouping, a word frequency count was created, editing out words with less than four letters, prepositions, and conjunctions, using the "stop word" functionality in NVivo. Word clouds and cluster maps were created to assist in identifying the most frequently occurring words in the text passages.

The word frequencies of each of the five categories previously described were evaluated to compare how the GAH words were used by the respondents. In addition, the nodes or themes created by the initial word frequencies were run through a cluster analysis to determine the relationships attributed to the words in the text. Subsequently, these analyses were used to test H2–H4.

To test Hypothesis 5, we identified public US-based universities that offer academic undergraduate entrepreneurship programs; 11 fit the criteria. We chose public institutions as a comparison to the host institution of the author(s), which is a state university that promotes entrepreneurship across campus and regionally. We used human intelligence to identify all webpages directly related to an institution's entrepreneurial programs/curricula. This ensured that the data captured in November 2016 was relevant to our study. Using a proprietary scraping tool, we gathered the text from 38 websites or 142 webpages, and downloaded 81 images containing people that appeared on these websites. The scrapers captured all the text and images on the website. There was an average of 488 words per webpage. The results of our analyses are based on 70,332 total words and 72 images. The full text from each website was compiled into a single PDF document, which was entered into NVivo software. Stop words, proper nouns (e.g. College of Business), and web-based directions (e.g. "click here") were eliminated from the

---

[1] Initial of author(s).

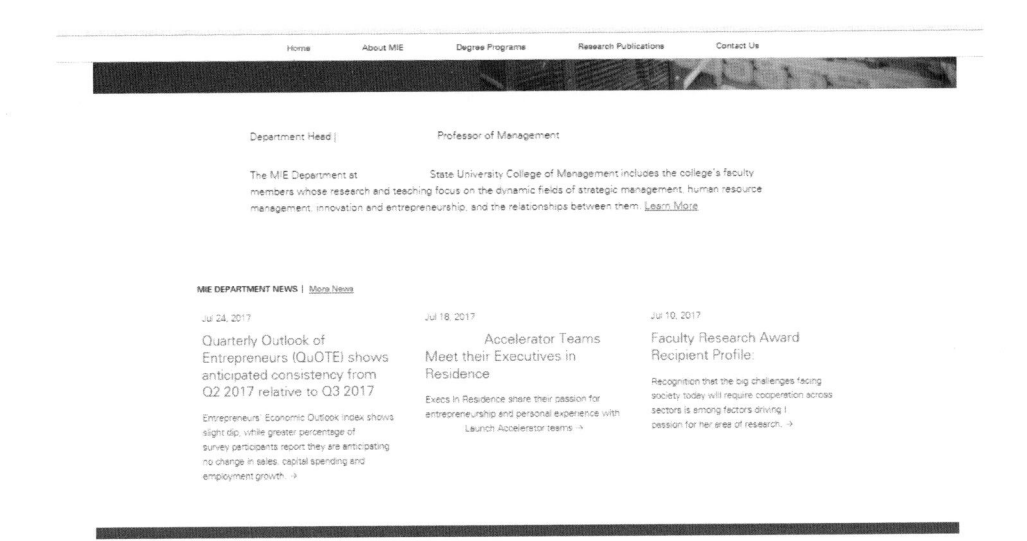

Figure 13.1. Example of university website marketing entrepreneurship.

Note: All identifying logos have been removed.

text. Word frequency counts were run on the full text, using stemmed word filters (e.g. "success" and "successful" would be grouped together). In this way, we were able to capture the gendered-linguistics of a university entrepreneurship webpage by comparing the GAH corpus to the text in the university webpages. Similarly, we calculated a score for image gender-coding by counting the number of times a male was represented in an image and the number of times a female was represented in an image on these sites. Figure 13.1 is a screenshot of from the host institution's entrepreneur website (dated August 2017).

13.4. Results

Using ANOVA, we analyzed the mean difference in the self-reported BSRI masculinity and femininity scales between men and women respondents (see Appendix A for a list of characteristics in each scale). Hypothesis 1 is supported as men rated higher on the masculinity scale compared to women ($F = 12.26$, $p \leq 0.001$) and women scored higher on the femininity scale compared to men ($F = 9.53$, $p \leq 0.002$). There was no significant difference between the two groups on the neutrality scale ($F = 1.80$, $p \geq 0.182$) as shown in Table 13.2. These results align with gender schema theory that men identify on a more masculine scale and women identify on a more feminine scale.

Subsequently, although not hypothesized, we also evaluated differences between entrepreneurs and non-entrepreneurs. Entrepreneurs scored higher on the masculinity scale compared to non-entrepreneurs ($F = 8.25$, $p \leq 0.005$), but there

The Language of Entrepreneurship: An Exploratory Gender-Coding Study 367

Table 13.2. BSRI Sex Inventory Scales.*

Mean	Male	Female	Entrepreneur	Non-Entrepreneur
Masculine Scale	**5.30**	**4.93**	**5.17**	**4.84**
Feminine Scale	**4.41**	**4.69**	4.56	4.61
Neutral Gender Scale	4.48	4.40	4.44	4.39

Note: *Only men are compared to women and entrepreneurs compared to non-entrepreneurs in determining significance. Comparison in bold are significant, others are not significant.

(a) *Word cloud for females*   (b) *Word cloud for males*

Figure 13.2. Word clouds from descriptions of success in entrepreneurs.

was no significant difference between entrepreneurs and non-entrepreneurs on the femininity ($F = 0.209$, $p \geq 0.648$) or the neutrality scale ($F = 0.686$; $p \geq 0.409$). In this study, entrepreneurs (both males and females) were more likely to identify themselves along the masculine BSRI scale. The suggestion by Ahl (2006) and others that entrepreneurship is a masculine concept is empirically supported.

To test Hypothesis 2, that both genders use more masculine words than feminine to describe success in entrepreneurship, responses from the open question were entered into QSR NVivo software. Word clouds for each gender were generated separately for the 50 most frequently occurring words using stemming (i.e. "talk" and "talking" would be grouped together). As can be seen from the word clouds of Figures 13.2(a) (female respondents) and 13.2(b) (male respondents), the word most frequently used by females to describe success is the verb NEED and the most frequently occurring word used by males is TAKE. The other nine most frequently occurring words in descending order are as follows [feminine word indicated by (F) and masculine word indicated by (M) based on the GAH corpus]:

Female: BUSINESS (M), SUCCESS/FUL, ABILITY/ABLE (M), TAKE, DETERMINATION, PERSON, WILLING, INNOVATIVE, RISK (M)

Male: ABILITY (M), BUSINESS, HARD, WILLING (M), WORK/ING, PERSON, RISK (M), THINKING, AMBITION[2], CREATIVE DRIVE, PERSISTENCE, SOMEONE, SUCCESS/FUL

From these results of frequently occurring words, it was interesting to note that both females and males use the non–gender-specific PERSON and SOMEONE when describing an entrepreneur, implying that both genders are keenly aware of the need for neutrality in an overt context. Thus when using the GAH corpus, Hypothesis 2 is supported that both genders use more masculine words when describing the success of entrepreneurs as no feminine words were identified.

Hypothesis 3 (H3) suggests that men will talk about entrepreneurship focused on rational, goal-oriented actions that empower them as the master of their company. Women will talk about entrepreneurship from an emotional, communal perspective seeking a balanced lifestyle. These feminine views of entrepreneurship will be diffused-communal awareness, deep feeling, spiraling pathways, caring, emotional, and balanced. To test H3, we again used the text from the open question on success first culling those words with less than 0.50% weighting. Using weighting as the cut-off as opposed to frequency of word accounts for the difference in sample size between men and women. This resulted in 75 unique words (shown in Table 13.3) — 28 were used by both genders, 26 words used only by males, and 21 words used only by females. We label this corpus of 75 words originating from this study as the "language of entrepreneurs" (LOE). It is important to note that the LOE corpus is separated by gender (male/female) and not gender type (masculine/feminine) as is the GAH corpus. It is interesting to note that, in the LOE corpus, no feminine words from the GAH corpus were used by the respondents, although 22 masculine words were used.

To test H3, which proposes that men take a more authoritative approach to entrepreneurship whereas women take a more communal approach, we reviewed the word cloud looking for words related to these themes. Indeed, men used authoritative words such as AMBITION, CONFIDENT, ORIENTED, and SELF, but they also used words such as BALANCE, COMMUNICATION, LISTEN, OPEN, and PATIENCE, which take more of a feminine approach. Females used communal words such as POSITIVE, GIVE, and PERSONALITY, but they also relayed authoritative concepts such as LEADERSHIP, IDEA, MANAGEMENT, ORDER, and ORGANIZED.

We next utilized a cluster analysis to look for latent themes not evident in the word cloud. Cluster analysis displays the words as a horizontal dendrogram where words that co-occur are clustered together. In order to ease interpretation of the clusters, we further reduced our data set to frequently cited words using a weighting greater than 0.80% as it reduced the corpus to a manageable grouping that

---

[2] The last five words in this list were equally weighted so there are more than nine.

Table 13.3. Language of Entrepreneurs (LOE) Corpus — weighting ≥ 0.50%.*

Used by both Genders	Used only by Males	Used only by Females
Ability/able (M)	Ambition (M)	Even
Business (M)	Answer	Focus (M)
Creative	Balance (M)	Give
Determination	Characteristics	Idea
Drive/n	Communication	Important
Entrepreneur	Confident/confidence (M)	Keep
Fail/failure	Courage (M)	Leadership (M)
Flexibility	Criticism	Lot
Goals (M)	Curiosity	Making
Hard	Ethic	Management/manger (M)
Innovative	Good	Order
Launch/launching	Know/knowledge (M)	Organized (M)
Learn	Listen	Personality
Motivate, motivation	Market	Positive
Need	Network	Set
Passion	Never	Something
People	New	Start
Perseverance (M)	Open	Strong (M)
Persistence (M)	Optimism (M)	Times
Person	Oriented	Want (M)
Product	Patience	Well
Risk (M)	Realism/realistic (M)	—
Someone	Self (M)	—
Success/successful	Service	—
Take (M: take a risk)	Vision (M)	—
Tenacity	Way	—
Willing (M: willing to take a stand)	—	—
Work/working	—	—

Note: *Those marked (M) are in the masculine GAH corpus; there are no feminine GAH words.

could be interpreted. The 0.80% resulted in 19 words for females and 23 words for males, as shown in Figure 13.3. After evaluating different cluster sizes, we selected four clusters as it explained the data the best. Major themes revealed from these clusters for the women were: business, creative risk-taker, determined innovator, able & passionate; and for the men were: determined, risk-taker, hardworking & creative, business. Themes are very similar across the two genders.

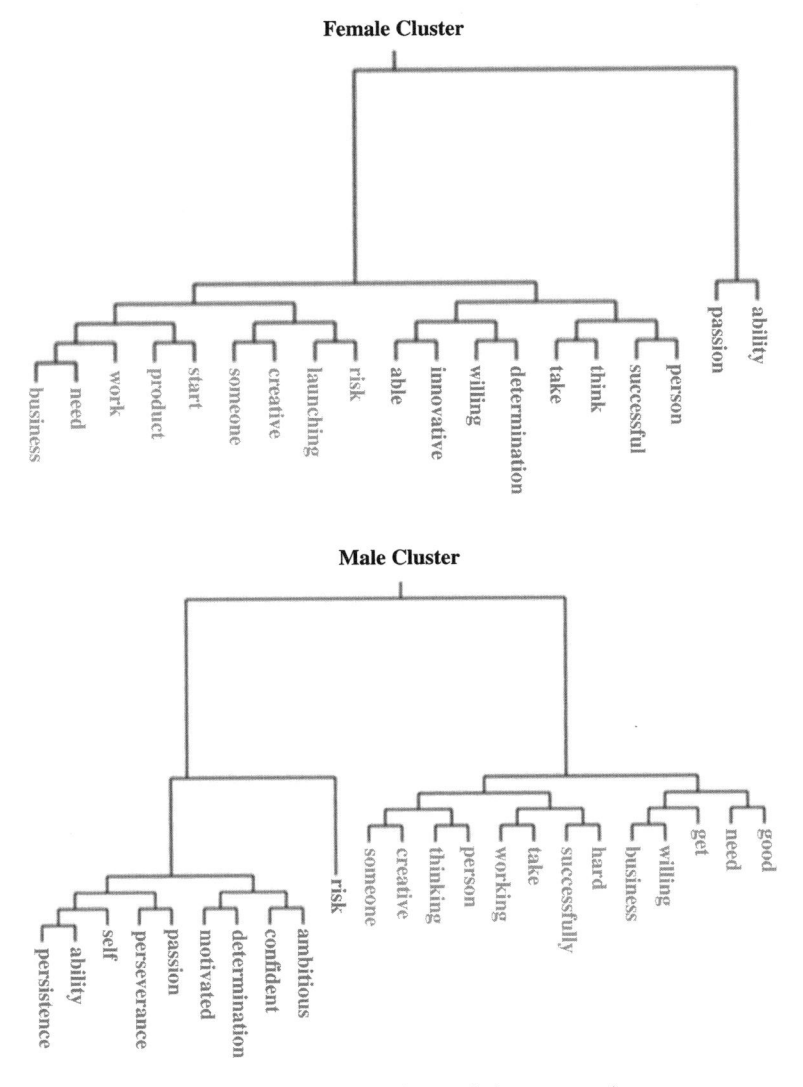

Figure 13.3. Female/male word cluster groupings.

Thus, there is no support for H3 that a differentiated masculine or feminine approach to entrepreneurial value creation is used in describing success in entrepreneurship. Our results, however, do support Bird and Brush's gender maturity concept that entrepreneurs use a conscious integration of both masculine and feminine traits for gender balance when discussing the success of entrepreneurs.

We reviewed the word clouds and conducted a cluster analysis on the two groups separately with NVivo to test Hypothesis 4, which proposes that, across populations, a gender-coding exists where both entrepreneurs and

The Language of Entrepreneurship: An Exploratory Gender-Coding Study 371

non-entrepreneurs perceive entrepreneurs to have predominately masculine traits. The 0.80% cutoff for the cluster analysis resulted in 20 unique words for entrepreneurs and 19 words for the non-entrepreneurs. After evaluating different cluster sizes, we selected five clusters as it explained the data the best. We evaluated the word cloud and clusters against the GAH and the LOE corpora. In Figures 13.4(a)–(b), GAH masculine words are marked with an asterisk; M^{LOE}

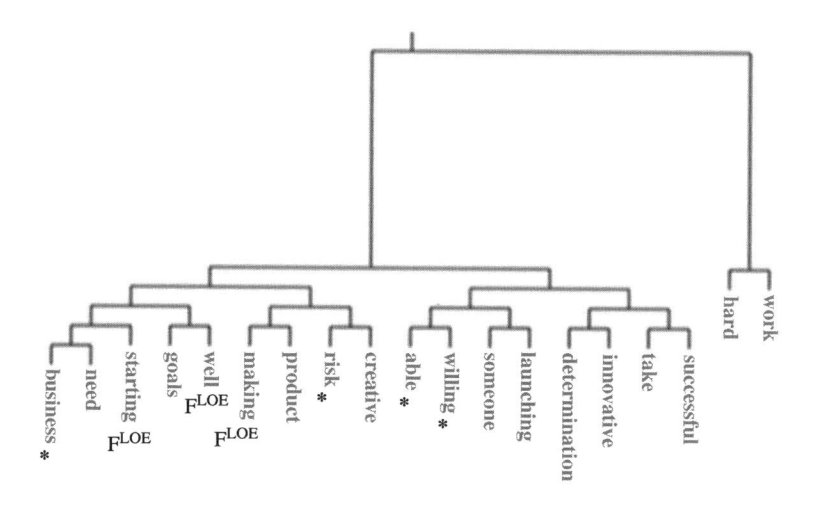

(a) Non-Entrepreneur (GAH masculine words with *, LOE female words with F^{LOE})

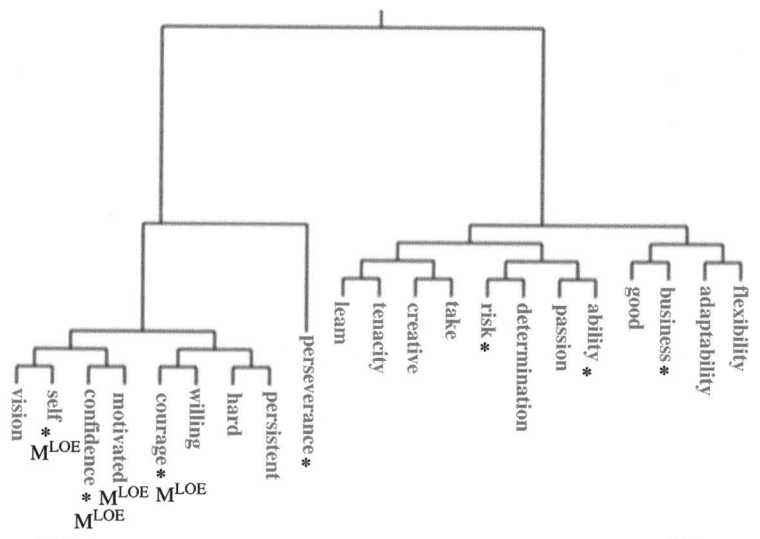

(b) Entrepreneur (GAH masculine words with *, LOE male words with M^{LOE})

Figure 13.4. Entrepreneur/non-entrepreneur word clusters.

indicates LOE male words; F^{LOE} indicates female words. Entrepreneurs used eight masculine/male words (7 from GAH and 1 unique one from LOE) compared to no feminine/female words; non-entrepreneurs used four GAH masculine words and three LOE female words. Hypothesis 4 is thus not supported. Entrepreneurs use a more masculine gender type when discussing success in entrepreneurship, and non-entrepreneurs use a more balanced perspective. We had predicted they would both take a masculine approach.

It became clearly evident that because non-entrepreneurs use a more balanced scale, these words cluster in a very different fashion compared to entrepreneurs. We then evaluated the word relationships within clusters each for non-entrepreneurs and entrepreneurs, as shown in Table 13.4. Text from the responses are shown next to each cluster. Major grouping for non-entrepreneurs were interpreted as: goal-oriented, inventor, dedicated, tenacious, and hardworking. For entrepreneurs, they were: motivated, courageous, persevere, risk-taker, and adaptive. There is some overlap in concepts with "goal-oriented" and "motivated" being similar and "tenacious" and "persevere" being similar.

To further understand the differences, we next identified the top differentiating word stems to reveal where the most extreme differences lay in the words used between the two groups. Using the method suggested by Sylwester and Purver (2015), the frequency of a word cited by a single group (entrepreneurs vs. non-entrepreneurs) is divided by the sum of number of uses of the word by both groups to calculate the probability of occurrence. In addition, to account for missing probability mass due to unobserved events, we smoothed the data by adding 50 to all counts before conducting the calculations. (For example: NEED was mentioned 0 times by entrepreneurs; it was mentioned 37 times by non-entrepreneurs, resulting in $prob(NEED)_{entrepreneurs} = (0 + 50)/(50 + 87) = 0.365$ and $prob(NEED)_{non-entrepreneurs} = 87/137 = 0.635$). We then took the absolute difference between the two probabilities ($diff(NEED) = |0.365 - 0.635| = 0.270$) and sorted from largest to smallest, as shown in Table 13.5. The top five differentiating words were NEED, SUCCESSFUL, INNOVATIVE, BUSINESS, LAUNCHING, and SOMEONE, with the last two sharing the fifth place. "Successful," "innovative," and "launching" were words never used by entrepreneurs, which is interesting as these seem to be fundamental terms around entrepreneurship. "Someone" was also never used by entrepreneurs, which is indicative that non-entrepreneurs use a third-person description to identify others but not themselves. "Business" was used seven times more by non-entrepreneurs compared to entrepreneurs. Although not hypothesized, these results indicate there is strong evidence that entrepreneurs talk about success in entrepreneurship very differently compared to those who do not consider themselves entrepreneurs.

To address Hypothesis 5, the full text from each university website, as previously described, was compiled into a single PDF document and entered into NVivo software. We first ran the website text through the GAH masculine/

Table 13.4. Word cluster analysis.

Non-Entrepreneurs		
Cluster Grouping	**Words in Cluster**	**Example Text**
C1. Goal-oriented	starting, needs, business, well, goals	"They also need to be well rounded because starting a new business fresh requires you to know all aspects of it fully and know how to play each role"
C2. Innovator	creative, risk, product, making	"Someone who is innovative, creative, willing to take risk"
C3. Dedicated	launching, someone, willing, able	"To successfully launch a business, [some]one must be driven, dedicated, and willing to put the business before all other priorities"
C4. Tenacious	innovative, determination, successful, take	"In business you need equal parts innovation, determination and ruthlessness"
C5. Hardworking	work, hard	"Someone should be ambitious, hardworking, a self-starter, flexible"

Entrepreneurs		
Cluster Grouping	**Words in Cluster**	**Example Text**
C1. Motivated	motivated, confidence, self, vision	"Motivated, determined, brave, confident, good at what they do, curious, flexible, resourceful"
C2. Courageous	persistent, hard, willing, courage	"Tolerance for risk, to believe so deeply in their mission that they are willing to endure all of the frustration, doubt uncertainty and keep showing up and being positive"
C3. Persevere	perseverance	"Ambitious, confidence, naivety, perseverance, persistence, grit, extroversion"
C4. Risk-taker	ability, passion, determination, risk, take, creative, tenacity, learn	"…willingness to take a risk, ability to learn from mistakes."
C5. Adaptive	flexibility, adaptability, business, good	"to see ahead, evaluate and adapt quickly"

feminine corpus. A total of 47 masculine words and 17 feminine words appeared in the webpages. Frequency of usage was 317 for the masculine words (72%) and 123 for the feminine words (28%), as shown in Table 13.6. The most frequently occurring masculine word was COMPETITIVE, while its counterpart on the feminine side was TEAM.

Table 13.5. Top 20* most differentiating word stems between Entrepreneurs (Entre) and Non-Entrepreneurs (Non-Entre) obtained with 50-smoothing.

	Entre Word Count	Weighted % Entre	Non-Entre Word Count	Weighted % Non-Entre	Difference in Frequency Probability
need	0	0.00	37	3.81	0.270
successful	0	0.00	29	2.99	0.225
business	5	0.99	36	3.71	0.220
innovative	0	0.00	17	1.75	0.145
launching	0	0.00	16	1.65	0.138
someone	0	0.00	16	1.65	0.138
passion	11	2.17	0	0.00	0.100
product	0	0.00	10	1.03	0.091
take	10	1.98	21	2.16	0.084
persistent	9	1.78	0	0.00	0.083
work	4	0.80	13	1.34	0.077
goals	0	0.00	8	0.82	0.074
making	0	0.00	8	0.82	0.074
starting	0	0.00	8	0.82	0.074
well	0	—	8	—	0.0741
characteristics	0	—	7	—	0.0654
idea	0	—	7	—	0.0654
tenacity	7	—	0	—	0.0654
flexibility	6	—	0	—	0.0566
important	0	—	6	—	0.0566
learn	6	—	0	—	0.0566
order	0	—	6	—	0.0566
perseverance	6	—	0	—	0.0566
set	0	—	6	—	0.0566
strong	0	—	6	—	0.0566
times	0	—	6	—	0.0566
wants	0	—	6	—	0.0566

Note: *There are 27 words listed here as the last nine were equally represented.

We next ran the text through the LOE male/female corpus of 75 words; 10 male-LOE words appeared and 10 women-LOE words were utilized in websites' text. Frequency of usage was 63 for the male words (24%), and 203 for the female words (76%). This is in exact contrast to the GAH analysis. Using the LOE

Table 13.6. GAH word count in university websites.

Masculine	Count	Feminine	Count
Competitive	63	Team	40
Business-oriented	62	Connected	23
Leadership	49	Systemic thinker (eco-system)	18
Realistic (real)	27	Familial (family)	16
Futuristic	22	Understanding	7
Focused	21	Fairness	5
Committed	11	Follower/Following	5
Goals	11	Present	5
Knowledge	11	Personal	4
Active	6	—	—
Law	6	—	—
Manage	6	—	—
Strong-willed	4	—	—
Achiever	3	—	—
Visionary	3	—	—
Independent	2	—	—
Intelligent	2	—	—
Risk-taking	2	—	—
Ability	1	—	—
Ambitious	1	—	—
Analyst/Analytical	1	—	—
Consistent	1	—	—
Master	1	—	—
Organizer	1	—	—
TOTAL	**317**		**123**

corpus, the most frequently occurring male word was NETWORK, while its counterpart on the feminine side was IDEA. Table 13.7 displays the words and their frequency of appearance as well as the count for words cited by both genders, which made up the majority of words in the text analysis.

We also assessed the images that were portrayed on each webpage at the time of data capture, as we believe that visual communication also has power on academic webpages. Results showed that there were 81 total images of people across 142 webpages devoted to university entrepreneurship. Of these, 21% ($n = 17$) were of single males, and 6% were images of single females ($n = 5$). All male groups (two or more males, with no females) represented 20% of the

Table 13.7. LOE word count in university websites.

Used by both Genders	Count	Used only by Males	Count	Used only by Females	Count
Entrepreneur	106	Network	21	Idea	54
Entrepreneurial	86				
Entrepreneurship	404				
Learn	80	Know/knowledge	11	Leader/leadership	49
Business	62	Market	11	Give/giving	37
Success/successful	35	Ethic	5	Focus	21
Work/working	33	Good	5	Well	11
Need	25	Vision	3	Making	9
Launch/launching	21	Never	2	Important	6
People	17	Communication	2	Management/manger	6
Innovative	16	Answer	2	Want	6
Product	15	Ambition	1	Strong	4
Goals	11	—	—	—	—
Creative	11	—	—	—	—
Passion	7	—	—	—	—
Ability/able (M)	6	—	—	—	—
Fail/failure	3	—	—	—	—
Drive/driven	2	—	—	—	—
Motivate, motivation	2	—	—	—	—
Risk (M)	2	—	—	—	—
TOTAL	**949**		**63**		**203**

images ($n = 16$), while female groups (two or more females, with no males), represented 6% of the images ($n = 5$). We also found mixed groups, which represented the largest percentage of images of people (47%, $n = 38$). Within the mixed groups, there were certain characteristics of image. We found that there were "crowd" photos, where everyone appears to be given equal stake in the photo (similar to a large selfie), and then "small group" photos, where activity is happening, such as a lecture, or group work is being conducted. In the small group shots, the key players were predominately male (lecturer, group leader, etc.) and active, while the women in the photos are passive. There were only four small group shots where the female was taking on an active role and appeared visually dominant (10.5% of total group images). However, it must be pointed out that the mixed group shots feature predominately females over males. In addition, it was interesting to note if a photo featured a pitch competition winning team, a male was always holding the check. Thus, we find mixed support for H5 that university websites are gender-biased. A more balanced approach is taken when evaluating the text using the up-to-date LOE corpus of this study and examining group photos, however, a more masculine approach is taken when examining single-person photos and using the GAH corpus, built from the literature and authors' interpretation of the literature.

13.5. Discussion

The impetus for this project was the analysis of multiple studies on the topic of female entrepreneurship, together with anecdotal evidence, that although energy is currently high in the US for entrepreneurial spirit, and governmental support is increasing, the culture is not yet supportive to women-led companies. Based on recent evidence that language can have a significant impact on how men and women are treated in entrepreneurial roles (Kanze et al., 2018; Malmström et al., 2017), we focused on gendered-linguistics in entrepreneurship to determine if universities promote gender-coding in entrepreneurial programs. We first tested for gender schemas and then searched for gender-coding in entrepreneurship to set the foundation for evaluating gendered-linguistics in the language of entrepreneurs. During this process, we developed two corpora for the language of entrepreneurship that were used to evaluate the text in university websites.

Indeed, in testing for a gender schema in our sample population, we found that men identify higher on the BSRI masculinity scale and women identify higher on the femininity scale. With this gender schema in place, it was not surprising that our results showed support of the existence of a gender-coding in entrepreneurship where men operate businesses in a different fashion compared to women. Demographics in the first stage of this study revealed that, even though there were fewer men in the sample, men made up the majority of the entrepreneurs. In addition, more men owned for-profit businesses (83.3% compared to 52.2% for women). Interestingly, 24% of women-owned businesses were unincorporated; this figure was 0% for men. Overall, women in the study were more likely to utilize different types of incorporations beyond profit-driven, were more likely to have a benefit corporation structured company, and maintained a higher number of employees than men, all of which support the communal approaches to entrepreneurship taken by women (Gupta et al., 2009; Bird and Brush, 2002). In addition, entrepreneurs identify strongly with a masculine scale, whereas non-entrepreneurs were more balanced, showing no differences between masculine and feminine traits, further supporting gender-coding in entrepreneurship. Our results support Ahl (2006), Bird and Brush (2002), Heilman (2001), and others' findings that entrepreneurship is seen in contemporary society as a masculine domain with an agentic approach.

The primary focus of our study was on gendered linguistics in entrepreneurship or "the language of entrepreneurs." In evaluating the words used by men and women to describe success in business, it was found they used similar words, however, the frequency of use of words differed. For example, the most frequently occurring word in the female text was NEED, while in the male text, its equivalent was TAKE. *Webster's Dictionary* defines NEED as: necessary duty and obligation; lack of something requisite; requirement for well-being; condition requiring supply or relief; and lack of means of subsistence. Summarizing all these definitions, one interpretation of the use of the word NEED by females would be that of void and passivity. In contrast, the word TAKE is defined by *Webster's* in many ways, such as: getting possession, power, or control over; seizing; winning; acquiring; catching; attacking; imposing oneself upon; and accepting burden or consequence of. Therefore the use of the verb TAKE by male respondent implies activity and action, even aggression. A masculine domain in entrepreneurship was also supported in the prevalence of "masculine" words and the absence of any "feminine" words in both genders' word clouds using the GAH corpus compiled from extant studies dating from 1981 to 2006.

Furthering the theory on gendered-linguistics in entrepreneurship, we developed an updated corpus of words, labeled LOE, based on the open-ended survey question for this study. Linguistic analyses revealed evidence of gender language maturity (Bird and Brush, 2002) on the part of both females and males in the way in which they describe success using similar terms with more than 37% of the words in this study being used by both genders. This contradicts the results using the older GAH corpus. The balanced approach of the LOE corpus may be a reflection of the changing demographics and social/political discussions surrounding entrepreneurship in current times. A closer evaluation of the language of entrepreneurs evolving over time is warranted and is suggested for future research.

Adding to our knowledge of gendered-linguistics in entrepreneurship, we found self-identification as an entrepreneur, not gender self-identification, to be a differentiating factor in the language used to denote success in business. Entrepreneurs used masculine words to describe success whereas non-entrepreneurs used more balanced words. Cluster analyses on the words showed entrepreneurs describe the successful entrepreneur as a courageous, adaptive, persistent risk-taker; non-entrepreneurs described the successful entrepreneur as a goal-oriented, hardworking, tenacious innovator. In fact, entrepreneurs did not use words such as INNOVATE, LAUNCH, PRODUCT, MAKE, GOALS, START, and non-entrepreneurs did not use words such as PASSION, PERSISTENT, TENACITY, and FLEXIBILITY. Entrepreneurs have a more passion-driven perspective and non-entrepreneurs appear to have a more grounded view of entrepreneurial success. These finding suggest that the Ahl (2006) perspective of entrepreneurship as a purely masculine endeavor is likely outdated. This balanced approach has been suggested in extant research (e.g. Gupta *et al.*, 2009) but not empirically tested to our knowledge. This too warrants future research.

We evaluated the gendered-linguistics in university websites to determine whether universities may introduce gender-coding coding into entrepreneurship programs. Gender-coding biases exist in the language of these webpages when the "dated" GAH corpus of masculine and feminine terms were used to analyze the text. However, when the language taken from the contemporary LOE corpus is used, current language structures show a much greater weight on balanced than on either masculine or feminine scales. In this case, universities are to be applauded for keeping abreast of linguistic developments in the entrepreneurship space, and for achieving a sense of gender maturity in marketing language.

We, however, did find some evidence of gender bias in a visual capacity on university webpages that promote entrepreneurship programs. The discrepancy in the visual images on the webpages could be explained by the tendency of marketing departments and web developers to use stock images, due to the time and expense needed to photograph various settings around campus and events with current students. It may not reflect actual demographics of the universities' entrepreneurship programs, but the editorial choices being used by web designers.

One of our goals of this study was to discover whether public universities may be doing something that keeps female representation lower than male. The visual data collected in this study suggests that to be the case when it comes to small groups and individual portrayed in photos, and care should be taken to rethink visuals. Millennials and younger incoming students are heavily visually oriented (e.g. Instagram, Snapchat). It is arguable whether visuals would be a deciding factor in whether an incoming student would choose one school over another, but it is certainly worth taking that variable out of the decision process by providing more gender equality in the images that are selected.

Because of the evidence that gender schemas and gender-coding exists in entrepreneurship, it is important to understand how societies, and universities in particular, promote a culture of entrepreneurship. We found that universities, although not egregiously promoting gender-coding using gendered-linguistics, still have much they can do to promote a more balanced perspective of entrepreneurship. One way that they can begin to alleviate the masculine identification in entrepreneurship is to use the language used by women as identified in the LOE corpus in Table 13.3. In addition, universities can better present entrepreneurship from a more balanced perspective, emphasizing communal approaches, including benefit corporations, non-profits, and social entrepreneurship structures, which more women seem to undertake. This balanced approach also appeals to non-entrepreneurs who presumably are the target audience for growing university programs — those students who have not thought of themselves as entrepreneurs due to cultural gender-coding, yet, given the opportunity, could excel in this area. Changing the language used on university websites is a first step in reducing the gender-coding prevalent in the American culture that entrepreneurship requires masculine thinking and management styles. Normative suggestions we provide are: (1) universities should stay current with language changes used by younger entrepreneurial communities; (2) visual images should be selected from current classrooms and activities that reflect the changing nature and face of student entrepreneurs; and (3) universities should proactively promote balanced approaches to entrepreneurship.

There are limitations with our study. Our sample population of respondents represents a region of the US southeast where gender schemas and gender-coding may be more prevalent compared to other US regions. Accordingly, our LOE corpus reflects the linguistics of this region. Future studies should include other regions of the US. In addition, as our study was exploratory in nature, our natural language processing methodology relied on word counts and clustering, which can miss the subtleties of a language. Additional text is needed to uncover the latent differences between genders and between entrepreneurs and non-entrepreneurs. Access to accelerator program applications may be an interesting set of text to mine.

13.6. Conclusion

We believe this study is timely and important, given the recent media regarding the discrimination of women in entrepreneurial communities (Lyons, 2017; Zetlin, 2017). However, our results showed less of a difference between men and women toward entrepreneurship than between entrepreneurs and non-entrepreneurs. Although we expected to see major differences in how men and women talk about entrepreneurship, this was not the outcome in our study. Our results do support the theoretical and practical notion that entrepreneurship is a masculine endeavor. Yet, we advance theory by making an important distinction that, in concordance with Bird and Brush (2002), *gender* is not the delineating factor if an entrepreneur employs masculine and feminine approaches in entrepreneurship; instead a strong difference was found between entrepreneurs and non-entrepreneurs. Entrepreneurs in our study had a more masculine viewpoint of entrepreneurship, while non-entrepreneurs had more of a balanced viewpoint, suggesting that the *culture* of entrepreneurship maybe the root of gender-coding, not gender as previously prescribed. Recent media (Lyons, 2017) has spoken about the "bro" culture in entrepreneurship, which deserve further attention by academic researchers.

The results of this study call for additional research to update the language of entrepreneurship. An unanswered question is "how can language be changed to encourage more women to recognize entrepreneurship as a career choice and reduce the masculine gender-coding prevailing in the entrepreneurship culture?"

Another question that must be asked is "do entrepreneurs just inherently have masculine traits or are they taught to see entrepreneurship this way?" Gupta et al. (2009) claim that there is a lack of research on whether men and women in contemporary society see entrepreneurship as more masculine or feminine. Our results show that it is seen as more masculine. Future research should be conducted to determine if this viewpoint can be changed.

References

Ahl, H. (2006). Why research on women entrepreneurs needs new directions. *Entrepreneurship Theory and Practice*, **30**(5), 595–621.

Arnot, M. (2002). *Reproducing Gender: Critical Essays on Educational Theory and Feminist Politics* (Londay, New York: Routledge).

Bem, S. L. (1981a). Gender schema theory: A cognitive account of sex typing. *Psychological Review*, **88**(4), 354.

Bem, S. L. (1981b). *Bem Sex Role Inventory: Professional Manual* (Palo Alto, CA: Consulting Psychologists Press).

Bird, B., & Brush, C. (2002). A gendered perspective on organizational creation. *Entrepreneurship Theory and Practice*, **26**(3), 41–66.

Boroditsky, L. (2011). How language shapes thought. *Scientific American*, **304**(2), 62–65.

Carli, L. L. & Eagly, A. H. (1999). Gender effects on social influence and emergent leadership. In Powell, and N. Gary (eds.), *Handbook of Gender and Work* (Thousand Oaks, CA, US: Sage Publications), pp. 203–222.

Cameron, D. (1998). Gender, language, and discourse: A review essay. *Signs: Journal of Women in Culture and Society*, **23**(4), 945–973.

Chell, E., Haworth, J., & Brearley, S. (1991). *The Entrepreneurial Personality: Concepts, Cases and Categories* (London: Routledge).

Cliff, J. E., Langton, N., & Aldrich, H. E. (2005). Walking the talk? Gendered rhetoric vs. action in small firms. *Organization Studies*, **26**(1), 63–91.

Collins, O. F., & Moore, D. G. (1964). *The Enterprising Man*, Vol. 1 (Lansing, MI: Michigan State University Press).

Elam, A. B. (2008). *Gender and Entrepreneurship: A Multilevel Theory and Analysis* (Cheltenham, UK: Edward Elgar).

Fairlie, R. W. (2014). *2013 Kauffman Index of Entrepreneurial Activity* (Ewing Marion Kauffman Foundation, Kansas City, MO).

Fiske, S. T., & Taylor, S.E. (1991). *Social Cognition* (New York: Mc-Graw Hill).

Gumperz, J. J., & S. C. Levinson. (1996). *Rethinking Linguistic Relativity*. Cambridge University Press, Cambridge, UK.

Gupta, V. K., Turban, D. B., Wasti, S. A., & Sikdar, A. (2009). The role of gender stereotypes in perceptions of entrepreneurs and intentions to become an entrepreneur. *Entrepreneurship Theory and Practice*, **33**(2), 397–417.

Hechavarría, D. M., Terjesen, S. A., Stenholm, P., Brännback, M., & Lång, S. (2018). More than words: do gendered linguistic structures widen the gender gap in entrepreneurial activity?. *Entrepreneurship Theory and Practice*, **42**(5), 797–817.

Hébert, R. F., & Link, A. N. (1988). *The Entrepreneur: Mainstream Views & Radical Critiques*. (Praeger Publishers).

Heilman, M. E. (2001). Description and prescription: How gender stereotypes prevent women's ascent up the organizational ladder. *Journal of Social Issues*, **57**, 3–26.

Hoffman, R. M., & Borders, L. D. (2001). Twenty-five years after the Bem Sex-Role Inventory: A reassessment and new issues regarding classification variability. *Measurement and Evaluation in Counseling and Development*, **34**(1), 39.

Hughes, K. D., Jennings, J. E., Brush, C., Carter, S., & Welter, F. (2012). Extending women's entrepreneurship research in new directions. *Entrepreneurship Theory and Practice*, **36**(3), 429–442.

Jennings, J. E., & Brush, C. G. (2013). Research on women entrepreneurs: challenges to (and from) the broader entrepreneurship literature? *Academy of Management Annals*, **7**(1), 663–715.

Kanze, D., Huang, L., Conley, M. A., & Higgins, E. T. (2018). We ask men to win and women not to lose: Closing the gender gap in startup funding. *Academy of Management Journal*, **61**(2), 586–614.

Klyver, K., Nielsen, S. L., & Evald, M. R. (2013). Women's self-employment: An act of institutional (dis)-integration? A multilevel, cross-country study. *Journal of Business Venturing*, **28**(4), 474–488.

Lyons, D. (2017). Jerks and the start-ups they ruin. *New York Times*, April 1.

MacDonald, M. (1980). Schooling and the reproduction of class and gender relations. In Barton, L., Meighan, R., and Walker, S. (eds.), *Schooling, ideology and the curriculum*. (Barcombe, Sussex: Falmer Press), pp. 29–49.

MacDonald, M. (1977). *The Curriculum and Cultural Reproduction* (Milton Keynes, England: Open University Press).

Malmström, M., Johansson, J., & Wincent, J. (2017). We recorded VCs' conversations and analyzed how differently they talk about female entrepreneurs. *Harvard Business Review*. https://www.diva-portal.org/smash/get/diva2:1096776/FULLTEXT01.pdf

Menzies, T. V., & Tatroff, H. (2006). The propensity of male vs. female students to take courses and degree concentrations in entrepreneurship. *Journal of Small Business & Entrepreneurship*, **19**(2), 203–223.

Miller, L., & Budd, J. (1999). The development of occupational sex-role stereotypes, occupational preferences and academic subject preferences in children at ages 8, 12 and 16. *Educational Psychology*, **19**(1), 17–35.

Mirchandani, K. (1999). Feminist insight on gendered work: New directions in research on women and entrepreneurship. *Gender, Work and Organization*, **6**(4), 224–235.

Nisbett, R. E., & Ross, L. (1980). *Human Inference: Strategies and Shortcomings of Social Judgement* (Englewood Cliffs, NJ: Prentice-Hall).

North, D. C. (2005). Institutions and the process of economic change. *Management International*, **9**(3), 1.

NVivo (2015). Qualitative Data Analysis Software; QSR International Pty Ltd. Version 11.

Powell, G. N., & Graves, L. M. (2003). *Women and Men in Management* (Thousand Oaks, CA: Sage).

Prewitt-Freilino, J. L., Caswell, T. A., & Laakso, E. K. (2012). The gendering of language: A comparison of gender equality in countries with gendered, natural gender, and genderless languages. *Sex Roles*, **66**(3), 268–281.

Schumpeter, J. A. (1934/1983). *The Theory of Economic Development*, Reprint 1971 ed. (New Brunswick: Transaction Publishers).

Shane, S., & Venkataraman, S. (2000). The promise of entrepreneurship as a field of research. *Academy of Management Review*, **25**(1), 217–226.

Sylwester, K., & Purver, M. (2015). Twitter language use reflects psychological differences between democrats and republicans. *PloS one*, **10**(9), e0137422.

Tversky, A., & Kahneman, D. (1973). Availability: A heuristic for judging frequency and probability. *Cognitive Psychology*, **5**, 207–232.

Tversky, A., & Kahneman, D. (1974). Judgment under uncertainty: Heuristics and biases. *Science*, **185**, 1124–1131.

Whorf, B. L., Carroll, J. B., Levinson, S. C., & Lee, P. (1956). *Language, Thought, and Reality: Selected writings of Benjamin Lee Whorf* (Boston, MA: MIT Press).

Wilson, F., Kickul, J., & Marlino, D. (2007). Gender, entrepreneurial self-efficacy, and entrepreneurial career intentions: implications for entrepreneurship education. *Entrepreneurship Theory and Practice*, **31**(3), 387–406.

Zetlin, M. (2017). Silicon Valley reeling after 24 female entrepreneurs speak out about sexual harassment. *Inc.* June 30. Available at https://www.inc.com/minda-zetlin/sex-for-funding-silicon-valley-reeling-after-24-fe.html. Accessed August 26, 2017.

Appendix

Appendix A. BSRI Sex Inventory Scales.

BSRI Femininity	BSRI Masculinity	BSRI Neutral
Rate yourself on each item on a scale of 1–7:	Rate yourself on each item on a scale of 1–7:	Rate yourself on each item on a scale of 1–7:
– yielding	– self reliant	– helpful
– cheerful	– defends own beliefs	– moody
– shy	– independent	– conscientious
– affectionate	– athletic	– theatrical
– flatterable	– assertive	– happy
– loyal	– strong personality	– unpredictable
– feminine	– forceful	– reliable
– sympathetic	– analytical	– jealous
– sensitive to other's needs	– leadership ability	– truthful
– understanding	– willing to take risks	– secretive
– compassionate	– makes decisions easily	– sincere
– eager to soothe hurt feelings	– self-sufficient	– conceited
– soft spoken	– dominant	– likable
– warm	– masculine	– solemn
– tender	– willing to take a stand	– friendly
– gullible	– aggressive	– inefficient
– childlike	– acts as a leader	– adaptable
– does not use harsh language	– individualistic	– unsystematic
– loves children	– competitive	– tactful
– gentle	– ambitious	– conventional

Appendix B. Masculinity and femininity corpus of words.

Masculinity Corpus of Words

Masculinity words (Bem, 1981a)	Entrepreneur (Ahl, 2006)	Entrepreneur (This Study)
Self-reliant	Self-centered, internal locus of control, self-efficacious, mentally free, able	Self-centered, Influencer, self-efficacy, free spirit, ability, controlling
Defends own beliefs	Strong willed	Strong-willed, Stand firm
Assertive	Able to withstand opposition	Stand firm
Strong personality	Resolute, firm in temper	Resolute, Consistent
Forceful, athletic	Unusually energetic, capacity for sustained effort, active	High-energy, Persistent, Active
Has leadership abilities	Skilled at organizing, visionary	Organizer, Visionary
Willing to take risks	Seeks difficulty, optimistic, daring, courageous	Risk-taking, Optimistic, Daring, Courageous
Makes decisions easily	Decisive in spite of uncertainty	Decisive
Self-sufficient	Independent, detached	Independent, Detached
Dominant, aggressive	Influential, seeks power, wants a private kingdom and a dynasty	Influential, Authoritative, Dynastic
Willing to take a stand	Stick to a course	Persevere,
Act as a leader	Leading economic and moral progress, pilot of industrialism, manager	Leadership, Manage
Individualistic	Detached	Detached
Competitive	Wants to fight and conquer, wants to prove superiority	Fighter, Conqueror, Superior
Ambitious	Achievement oriented	Achiever
Independent	Independent, mentally free	Independent, Free-thinking, Progressive
Analytical	Exercising sound judgment, superior business talent, foresighted, astute, perceptive, intelligent	Balanced, Business-oriented, Foresight, Astute, Perceptive, Intelligent

(Continued)

Appendix B. (*Continued*)

Femininity Corpus of Words

Femininity Scale (Bem, 1981a)	Opposites of Entrepreneur (Ahl, 2006)	Opposite of Entrepreneur (This study)
Gentle	Cautious	Cautious
Loyal	Follower, dependent	Follower, Dependent
Sensitive to the needs of others	Selfless, connected	Selfless, Connected
Shy	Cowardly	Cowardly
Yielding	Yielding, no need to put a mark on the world, subordinate, passenger, irresolute, following, weak, wavering, external locus of control, fatalist, wishy-washy, uncommitted, avoids power, avoids struggle and competition, self-doubting, no need to prove oneself	Yielding, Unambitious, Subordinate, Passenger, Irresolute, Following, Weak, Wavering, Blamer, Fatalist, Wishy-washy, Uncommitted, Power-averse, Risk-averse, Non-competitive, Flight, Self-doubt, Apprehensive, Self-effacing, Retiring
Gullible	Gullible, blind, shortsighted, impressionable, making bad judgments, unable, mentally constrained, stupid, disorganized, chaotic, lack of business talent, moody	Gullible, Blind, Shortsighted
Impressionable, Unable, Narrow-minded, Stupid, Disorganized, Chaotic, Moody	(No match)	
Sympathetic, affectionate, understanding, warm, compassionate, eager to soothe hurt feelings, soft spoken, tender, loves children, does not use harsh language, cheerful, childlike, flatterable		Sympathetic, Affectionate, Understanding, Warm, Compassionate, Fixer, Soft-spoken, Tender, Parental, Mild-mannered, Cheerful, Childlike, Flatterable

Appendix C. Gender perspective on the entrepreneurial process.

Corpus this Study

	Masculine	Feminine
Concept of Reality	Focused consciousness	Diffuse awareness
	Analysis	Appreciation
	Separable nature	Interconnected nature
	Knowledge as control	Knowledge as caring
Time	Future	Present
	Faster pace	Slower pace
	Linear	Circular or spiral
Action	Rational	Emotional
	Strategic, grounded in goals and reason	Personable, influenced by familial history and biology
	Competitive	Cooperative, caring
	Aggressive, violent	Harmonizing, calming
	Distant	Empathic
Power	Mastery over others	Self-mastery
	Used for self	Used for others
	Centralized	Shared
Ethics	Responsibility as control over self	Responsibility as a response to others, circumstances
	Restrain aggression/limit behavior	Preserve relationships/repair harm
	Right and laws	Caring and fairness

Bird and Brush (2002)

	Masculine	Feminine
Concept of Reality	Focused, conscientious, realistic	Aware
	Analytical	Appreciative
	Separable, Disconnected	Connected
	Knowledge, control	Care, caring
Time	Futuristic	Present
	Fast	Slow, relaxed
	Linear thinker	Systemic thinker
Action	Rational	Emotional
	Goals, reasoning	Personable, personal, familial
	Competitive	Cooperative
	Aggressive, violent	Harmonizing, calming
	Distant, aloof	Empathic, empathy, understanding, compassionate
Power	Master	Team
	Self	Others
	Self-focused	Team-focused
Ethics	Aggressive, boundaries	Preserve, community
	Constrained	Apologetic, apology
	Law, legal	Fairness, compromise

Source: Bird and Brush (2002), Table 1, p. 47.

Appendix D. Complete GAH corpus.

Masculine	Feminine
Ability	Affectionate
Achiever	Appreciative
Active	Apprehensive
Aggressive	Apologetic, apology
Aloof	Aware
Ambitious	Blamer
Analyst/Analytical	Blind
Astute	calming
Authoritative	Care/Caring
Balanced	Cautious
Boundaries	Chaotic
Business-oriented	Cheerful
Competitive	Childlike
Committed	Compassionate
Confident	Compromise, compromising
Conqueror	Connected
Conscientious	Cooperative
Consistent	Cowardly
Constrained	Dependent
Control/controlling	Disorganized
Courageous	Emotional
Daring	Empathic/empathy
Decisive	Fairness
Detached	familial (family)
Disconnected	Fatalist
Distant	Fixer
Dynastic	Flatterable
Fast	Flight
Fighter	Follower/Following
Focused	Gullible
Foresight	Harmonizing
Free spirit	Impressionable
Free-thinking	Irresolute
Futuristic	Mild-mannered
Goals	Moody

Appendix D. (*Continued*)

Masculine	Feminine
High-energy	Narrow-minded
Independent	Non-competitive
Influencer/Influential	Others
Intelligent	Parental
Knowledge	Passenger
Law	Personable
Leadership	Personal
Legal	Power-averse
Linear thinker	Present
Manage	Preserve
Master	Relaxed
Optimistic	Retiring
Organizer	Risk-averse
Perceptive	Self-doubt
Persevere	Self-effacing
Persistent	Selfless
Progressive	Shortsighted
Soft-spoken	Slow-paced
Rational	Stupid
Realistic (real)	Subordinate
Reasoning	Sympathetic
Resolute	Systemic thinker (eco-system)
Risk-taking	Team
Self/Self-focused	Tender
Self-centered	Unable
Self-efficacy	Unambitious
Separable	Uncommitted
Stand firm	Understanding
Strong-willed	Warm
Superior	Wavering
Violent	Weak
Visionary	Wishy-washy
Willingness	Yielding

© 2022 World Scientific Publishing Company
https://doi.org/10.1142/9789811248863_0014

Chapter 14

Where to Fall Dead: A Comparative Analysis of the Death Care Industry

Gladis Cecilia Villegas-Arias
Universidad de Medellín,
Carrera 87 No 30-65, Medellín, Colombia
gcvillegas@udem.edu.co

Abstract

The death care industry satisfies the ritualistic and technical needs associated with human death, providing ceremonial services such as the tribute, the disposition of remains, and memorialization (Industry Focus: Death Care, 2016). However, although from a technical point-of-view and according to the Basel Convention, human remains are nothing but a type of hazardous anatomical waste, sociocultural factors affect the availability of choice between separate specific disposal options (Technical Guidelines on the Environmentally Sound Management of Biomedical and Healthcare Wastes, 2003) that drive social, ecological, and economic costs.

Keywords: Death; death care industry; sustainability; funerary ethos; environmental impact; economic impact; social impact.

> *"Every city like Laudomia has another city by its side whose inhabitants are all called by the same names: It is the Laudomia of the dead, the cemetery."*
>
> — Italo Calvino, *Invisible Cities*

14.1. Introduction

This chapter describes the current trends in the funeral business model and compares the death care industries in the US, Spain, and Colombia according to the evolution of services provided and the resources demanded according to each alternative. The comparative analysis applied (Yin, 2013) includes the following elements.

(1) The evolution of sociocultural factors related to death services (Robben, 2018; Thomas, 1980) is reviewed.
(2) The traditional and innovative services provided by the death care industry (Beard and Burger, 2017) is presented. The business model is also reviewed in order to understand the source of profits (Osterwalder *et al.*, 2010). Traditionally, death was a desirable event for the industry since income was derived from the sale of goods and services. Today, [Over 50's Life Insurance] insurance guarantees that the beneficiary makes prepayment for his funeral, thereby releasing loved ones from the burden (Choi-Allum, 2007) of paying for death care services. This change in the business model represents a significant social innovation that enabled some individuals who previously had nowhere to "fall dead" to be able to prepay for somewhere to do so (Pijl van der, 2015) and moved the industry toward an insurance-driven business in which the realization of the insured event is not welcomed; in this case, the later the better.
(3) A comparative sustainability analysis of the aforementioned national industries in Spain, the US, and Colombia is conducted.
(4) Conclusions regarding the foreseeable future of the death care industry — given the certainty of death, the scientific struggle to keep humans alive (More, 2013), world population growth (World Population Prospects, 2017), and the amount of resources demanded for death services, some of which have already become an environmental burden, as represented by the amount of land dedicated to abandoned cemeteries all over the planet that cannot be deployed to other uses (BBC News, 2015) — is presented.

14.1.1. *Purpose*

Proposing that social values are the key factors that affect decisions regarding the disposal of human remains, this chapter assesses current trends in the death care industry as well as the impact of those factors on the industry.

14.1.2. *Approach*

A business model analysis as well as a comparative industry analysis is conducted. A trend analysis is also performed on the death care industry, considering the resources consumed and its cultural evolution. In addition, three national death care industries — the US, Spain, and Colombia (Sundale Research, 2018; PANASEF, 2017; Fenalco Antioquia, 2015) — are compared using available statistics, studies, and reports regarding their business models, economic indicators, and social and ecological impacts.

14.1.3. *Findings*

- Land is scarce, which implies that the individual and social costs of burial are rapidly increasing, to the point that some cities prohibit burial of the dead (Rothstein, 2018).
- The air contamination and energy consumption (Rothstein, 2018) caused by the cremation process are some of the environmental costs that affect the continued sustainability of the death care business.
- The conservation of human remains for ritualistic or logistical processes also implies ecological impacts that affect the long-term survival of the business (Krupar, 2018).
- The values of society are moving from slow to a fast pace in every aspect of human routine, including mourning, changing the needs that the industry strives to satisfy (Dobscha, 2015). Consequently, innovation in the industry depends on understanding cultural changes as related to death and designing services that respond to that understanding in a sustainable way (Krupar, 2018).
- Because of the above reasons, the funeral business encompasses all that is social in business since there is nothing more social than death, its primary subject matter.

14.1.4. *Research limitations*

This analysis is based on secondary economic, social, and environmental information as recorded by government agencies. Future studies should focus on ethnographic research of human behavior because the key variables of the study are sociocultural in nature (Goodwin-Hawkins and Dawson, 2018).

14.1.5. *Research contribution*

The theoretical relevance of this research lies in proposing that culture is a mediating variable that affects the sustainability of the death care industry. However, this is a preliminary theorization that could also extend to other industries in which culture is perceived as a determinant not only of market demands but also of their satisfaction costs.

14.2. Evolution of Sociocultural Factors Related to Death Services

Death is a defining condition of living. Up until now (even though humankind continues the quest for immortality (Bostrom, 2005)), everyone that has been born, must eventually die, and as the poem states: "what you call being born is to begin to die" (De Quevedo, 1976, p. 135). Texts as ancient as *Genesis* (22) mention death as a result of disobeying God: "And the Lord God said, the man has now become like one of us, knowing good and evil. He must not be allowed to reach out his hand and take also from the tree of life and eat, and live forever." Being aware of death defines the human condition (Becker, 2007) and dealing with death is a universal characteristic of culture (Thomas, 1980).

The three principles that have moved history include burial, religion, and marriage (Vico, 1948). About burial, archeology has discovered that the Neanderthals, as long as 50,000 years ago, already buried their dead, demonstrating that even these progenitors of humanity showed an emotional concern for the treatment of corpses (Rendu *et al.*, 2014). Later, when human groups settled in one place (a process called "sedentism" in the field of cultural anthropology), along with building houses and farming the fields, people also dug graves (Bar-Yosef, 1998). This process linked the group's identity and sense of belonging to the land in which their ancestors were interred, ground which then was considered to be sacred (Balkan, 2015). Subsequently, starting in the later 17th century, funerals evolved to become a display of wealth and power (Mytum, 2017). This is how the disposition of human remains, the burial places, and the corresponding rituals that have existed from the beginning of time gave rise to a professional service industry dedicated to caring for the dead (Habenstein and Lamers, 1985).

On the side of the bereaved, mortuary rituals are conceived as rites of passage that allow survivors to begin the mourning process (Robben, 1991). It is the survivors who attend such events and use cemeteries, tombs, gravestones, and now even digital art, to preserve the memory of the dead.

As for the cost of funerals, this last public appearance of the deceased is where wealth and power are put on display. In antiquity, embalming was a process reserved only for the very rich and powerful (Aranda and Molina, 2006), while consumerism was the way survivors dealt with loss, grief, and transition during the 18th century (Mytum, 2017). Today, services are customized to the preferences of the clientele. People have choices that range from lower-cost funerals to very expensive, upscale rituals for those who want to pay for them.

The purchaser of funerary services has changed from the grieving being the individual that pays for funeral arrangements (at-need) to each person providing for his or her own funeral bill (pre-need) through a collection of alternatives such as the 80+, pre-need funeral, burial insurance, among other choices.

Options for the disposal of human remains vary from ground burial, cremation, immurement, to other less common alternatives such as a relatively new method called alkaline hydrolysis (resomation), with the cost of each being variable and dependent on the availability of the required resources. For instance, cremation demands a high consumption of energy (1400–1800°F for an average 90-minute process for one adult body) while ground burial involves the high cost of increasingly scarce land (an 8 feet long by 2.5 feet wide cemetery plot requires approximately 20 square feet per body). While in the past, family cemeteries existed, the availability of public cemeteries and the high cost of keeping a private family plot thrust public graveyards — that are running out of space in today's crowded world — into favor.

Memorialization has evolved over time from simple stones placed on top of a tomb to crosses labeled with names, to engraved gravestones, to funerary art, to digital immortality and the recreation of death using digital media (Bell and Gray, 2001).

Besides technical, economic, legal, and political considerations, culture is the key driver of choice amongst alternative mortuary rituals (Metcalf and Huntington, 1991). It is because of religious beliefs that cremation may not be possible, or, on the other hand, that it may be the only choice. Moreover, different groups may demand burial grounds that are exclusive, such as for military, magicians, circus artists, certain families, or Jews, in addition to a long list of other exclusive criteria (Tarlow and Shultz, 2013).

14.3. Business Model Analysis

Applying business model categories, as synthesized by Osterwalder *et al.* (2010), the death care industry is characterized by the following features. Below an analysis of the various elements of the death care industry, with a focus on the three main service areas discussed below.

14.3.1. *Value proposition*

14.3.1.1. *Customers' problems solved or needs satisfied*

The needs satisfied by the death care industry consist of handling matters related to death for bereaved customers. The three main services provided by the industry are: (1) disposition of remains, (2) arranging ceremony and tribute, and (3) memorialization of the deceased.

(1) **Disposition of Human Remains**. The human body is considered to be hazardous biological anatomical waste (Basel Convention's Technical Guidelines on the Environmentally Sound Management of Biomedical and Healthcare Wastes, 2003) that decomposes rapidly if it is not embalmed. Disposing of corpses using incineration, entombment, immurement, or any other method is a service rendered by the death care industry that generates a high environmental impact.

(2) **Ceremony and Tribute (Funeral or Memorial Service)**. Humans are cultural beings for whom symbolism gives meaning to life and death. Each human group conducts different mortuary rituals to send members off after death, start the grieving process, and escort the departed to the threshold of the afterlife (Young *et al.*, 1996). Funeral homes provide the service of customized funerary rites for diverse social groups.

(3) **Memorialization**. Memorials are objects — such as gravestones, mausoleums, monuments, plaques, funerary art, graveyard architecture, or online memorials — designed to commemorate the life of the deceased. The latest memorialization methods even digitally resurrect the dead through augmented virtual reality features. Manufacturers create the physical components of the service such as coffins, tombstones, and urns, while digital designers may create memorial websites or avatars.

14.3.1.2. *Products and services offered to various customer segments*

- Processing the necessary paperwork,
- Picking the corpse up and transporting it to the funeral home,
- Preparing the corpse for mortuary rituals and the final disposition of the body,
- Disposing of the body according to the arrangements agreed upon with the customer,
- Holding the mortuary ritual, and
- Arranging for memorialization (i.e. tombstone, plaque, etc.) as negotiated.

14.3.1.3. *Value delivered to the customer*

Organizing and executing mortuary rituals in a planned, customized manner relieves the family and loved ones who survive the deceased from the stress of coping with such tasks.

14.4. Revenue Streams[1]

People pay for services related to death including burial, ritual, memorialization, and paperwork. There are several options for each of these aspects and they are frequently interrelated. Burial, ritual, and memorialization are culturally mediated, including different protocols for diverse ethnicities, social groups, families, religions, and beliefs. The paperwork refers to the legal requirements that can be fulfilled more or less easily depending on the specific circumstances. For instance, trans-boundary movement of cadavers requires a sophisticated legal puzzle that involves international law, logistics, and infrastructure. Burial may become a hassle if ground burial is prohibited in a certain location, such as in locales around the world that have run out of space for burial. Likewise, cremation may be prohibited because of the impact on air quality and the amount of energy consumed (Achawangkul *et al.*, 2016). Scarce resources imply higher costs that lower-income individuals cannot afford or the displacement of the problem to another location.

New value-added innovation in the industry is taking place in terms of payment methods that enable people to plan and pay for their death rituals in advance, a process known as pre-need arrangement. Other advancements include the simplification of the process, reduction in the time required, enabling telepresence at funerary events through the Internet, shortening delay times, streamlining activities (e.g. making the wake optional), reducing environmental damage (through green alternatives without caskets or embalming), digital memorialization, and customization of the service to provide unconventional rituals, such as rendering services for the death of animals.

Another innovation in the death industry is the rise of the pre-need funeral arrangement, or the pre-payment for funeral services. This larger contribution to overall revenue has recently prompted the industry to incorporate new financial activities, such as accepting savings or selling insurance, which has changed the overall business model. The listing of such types of contracts, their language, and their parameters may change according to the specific country or seller (Frank, 1996).

---

[1] See Roberts (1997).

14.4.1. *Consumer decision-making process*

The consumer buying process includes acknowledging a need or problem, searching for information, evaluating alternatives, deciding, purchasing, consuming, and appraising the experience for repurchase decisions (Nicosia, 1966). As previously discussed, death is one of the most psychological-*cum*-sociocultural experiences, which implies that economic rationality may not be a decisive factor in the consideration of funerary services. It is important to identify the decision-makers for each stage of the buying process and for each payment arrangement (i.e. at-need, pre-need), and the decision criteria for each of the three components of funerary service: the disposition of human remains, the ritualization, and the memorialization of the deceased.

The disposition of human remains is affected by religious beliefs and practices. Ritualization is a farewell experienced by the survivors but not by the departed, the definition of which may be open to innovation. Memorialization is a process that honors the life of the deceased and can be improved with new technologies that preserve their memory in more reliable ways.

14.4.2. *The influence of religious beliefs on purchase decision criteria*

Religion is: "(1) a system of symbols which acts to (2) establish powerful, pervasive, and long-lasting moods and motivations in men by (3) formulating conceptions of a general order of existence and (4) clothing these conceptions with such an aura of factuality that (5) the moods and motivations seem uniquely realistic" (Geertz, 1966, p. 90). Scholars on the study of religion have listed the largest religious groups by the number of adherents worldwide. Known as "The Big Five," Christianity, Islamism, Judaism, Hinduism, and Buddhism (Smart, 1998), are the religions that have the most members.

Scholars have established the influence of religious beliefs and practices on decisions regarding the purchase of goods and services (Bailey and Sood, 1993; Delener, 1994), including the choice for the final disposition of corpses (Technical Guidelines on the Environmentally Sound Management of Biomedical and Healthcare Wastes, 2003). Since the conception of life, death, and the afterlife are the main constituents of religious belief, it is known that the choice of mortuary services will be influenced by one's doctrine regarding the afterlife (Hirschman, 1982; Kellehear, 2007; Kundu, 2019); by the use of the body (i.e. is there a place for the body in the afterlife through resurrection, or is it a disposable shell with no meaning?); by send-off ritualization and mourning; and by the importance of honoring the memory of the dead in society (are ancestors a meaningful, living part of society with whom one wants to maintain a bond? [Klass *et al.*, 2014]). See Table 14.1 for

Table 14.1. The influence of religious beliefs as decision criteria on the purchasing process.

Religion	Disposition of human remains	Funeral	Memorialization
Christianism (Catholic, Protestant Christian)	1963 ban on cremation was lifted by the Pope (Holy Office, 1963) Christian protestants allow cremation	1997 the funeral could take place before the ashes (Holy Office, 2016)	"the ashes of the faithful must be laid to rest in a sacred place" (Holy Office, 2016)
Judaism (14.7 million people as of 2019) (The Jewish People Policy Institute, 2019; Goodman, 2003)	Cremation is forbidden	Brief funeral at the burial ground or cemetery	Memorialization through prayer and visiting the grave
Islamism (1.9 billion as of 2020) (Kutty, 1991; https://www.pewforum.org/2011/01/27/the-future-of-the-global-muslim-population/)	Cremation is forbidden	Brief collective prayer	Very few or not memorialization
Buddhism (Ladwig & Williams, 2012)	Cremation is mandatory. Ashes may be scattered.	Long funeral with prayers and procession	Memorial services the third, seventh, forty-ninth, and hundredth day after cremation
Hinduism (Sahoo, 2014)	Cremation is mandatory	No funeral, the ashes are consecrated to a river or the sea	A meal with invited relatives and friends

a summary of how each religion affects the decision-making criteria of the three stages of the funerary process: disposition, ritualization, and memorialization.

14.4.3. Key actors in the purchasing process for at-need and pre-need funerary arrangements

As for the decision-makers, following the description of Bonoma (1982), Table 14.2 describes the roles of the key actors — initiator, gatekeeper, influencer, decider, purchaser, and user — in the funerary purchasing process for at-need and pre-need arrangements. For at-need arrangements, survivors must decide very quickly, using whatever information they have at hand, and might be highly influenced by difficult, raw emotions. For pre-need arrangements, the purchaser has the

Table 14.2. Actors in the buying process for at-need and pre-need funerary arrangements.

Role in the decision	At-need (emotional, compulsory, rushed decision)	Pre-need (rational, planned, wider window of opportunity)
The Initiator acknowledges the need.	Survivor.	Beneficiary or interested parties.
The Gatekeeper knows information about the funeral industry (offerings and providers).	Sellers, advisors, web, trusted persons, advertising, face-to-face attention in boutiques.	Sellers, advisors, web, trusted persons, advertising.
The Influencer "has a say" in whether a purchase is made and about what is bought.	Interested parties.	Trusted people, interested parties, affected people (including funders).
The Decider says yes or no to the purchase.	Payers.	Beneficiary or interested parties.
The Purchaser obtains the product or service.	Payers, funeral directors.	Beneficiary, the payer, or anyone acting on their behalf.
The User consumes the product or service.	For the disposition of human remains, the users are society and the environment. For ritualization and memorialization, the users are the interested parties.	Beneficiary.

benefit of sufficient time, being relaxed, economic rationality, and the user is usually both the decision-maker and purchaser.

14.4.4. *Conditions of business operation*[2]

Because the ritualization of death is a universal cultural practice (Palgi and Abramovitch, 1984), continued demand is a certainty. However, the size of the market for at-need arrangements depends on the potential number of funerals, as measured by the mortality rate, while determining the demand for pre-need arrangements depends on the estimated adult population.

The demand for funerary services is relatively inelastic to price because service offerings are very similar at specific price ranges, which means that switching suppliers will not enable the customer to benefit from a major reduction in price or a significant improvement in value, while the window of opportunity for making a purchase is very narrow. In other words, the cost of switching outweighs its potential benefit (Kopp and Kemp, 2007; Market Research Vision, 2019).

A funerary purchase decision is culturally mediated and is a once-in-a-lifetime choice. When not planned, as in the case of at-need buying, it is immediate, emotional, and compulsory because, at a minimum, the human remains must be dealt immediately with as hazardous anatomical biological waste.

Trends in the death industry include cremation as a growing alternative choice for the final disposition of corpses. This tendency is driven by the reduction in cost represented by cremation, as compared to other alternatives (cremation can cost up to 90% less than ground burial), speed of the process, personalization, decrease in religious influence or restraint (as in the case of the acceptance of cremation by the Catholic Church in 1963), and growing environmental awareness.

Property in the industry is dispersed amongst small, family-owned, traditional firms, except in the US, where there is a consolidation process in progress that aims to reduce costs by taking advantage of economies of scale. Consequently, detailed information about public issues such as the number, type, and location of cemeteries, crematoriums, or other burial resources is dispersed and hard-to-find in several countries.

One of the most important challenges of this business is reducing the environmental impact of its processes, which can be quite high in the case of embalming due to the use of hazardous chemicals. The process of entombment is likewise environmentally cost-intensive, requiring at least 20 square feet of land for a standard cemetery plot. Incineration also has a heavy environmental impact, releasing about 540 pounds of carbon dioxide (CO_2) into the atmosphere per body (Achawangkul *et al.*, 2016). In summary, embalming uses hazardous chemicals,

---

[2] See Research and Markets (2018) and Sundale Research (2019).

entombment secludes land, and cremation releases particulates and greenhouse gases (Rothstein, 2018). For instance, a study by *La Fondation des Services Funéraires Ville de Paris* (2017) demonstrated that the environmental impact of an interment equals 3.6 cremations as measured by the greenhouse effect (kilograms of CO_2 equivalent); 2.9 as measured by the consumption of non-renewable resources (Megajoules, MJ), and 3.8 as measured by the consumption of rare resources (kilograms of antimony equivalent).

The supply chain of the industry includes logistics of transporting the body, preparation of the cadaver, execution of mortuary rituals, disposition of human remains, memorialization, legal support, and handling of payment alternatives. In some countries, the occupation of funeral director is dedicated to coordinating all the activities of the supply chain, from picking up the body to disposing of it (Hyland and Morse, 1995).

Given the degree of development of the industry in the US, the segmentation of its market is representative of what it could become anywhere else and is characterized by criteria such as operations (funeral homes, cemeteries); payment arrangements (at-need, pre-need); and by-products and services (caskets and vaults, facility rentals, embalming and cosmetic preparation, and urns, among others). The distribution channels in the US include boutiques, warehouses, retail stores, and recently, e-commerce stores. However, until today, the boutique channel is the one preferred by the customers.

14.4.5. *Trends*

In a globalized world, some cultural features are becoming universal. One of those that affect mortuary rituals is the perception of time. People go through life at a rapid speed, particularly in urban areas. They want any activity, no matter how sacred, to proceed quickly — even funerals. In response, some funeral homes now offer extreme means of memorialization, including novel services such as drive-thru funerals (Dobscha, 2015).

Another universal issue is the global concern for environmental impact. Environmentally conscious consumers prefer more sustainable choices that include eco-friendly caskets, natural burials, green burials (e.g. burials without caskets, metal, toxic materials, or chemicals), alkaline hydrolysis/resomation (water cremation), immurement in vertical cemeteries (the tallest in the world being *Memorial Necropole Ecumenica* in Santos, Brazil, with 16 stories and 16,000 graves) (Krupar, 2018), or multiple-depth companion plots, among others.

Customization is another universal trend that is reflected in prices, with more expensive services featuring the use of scarce resources such as the property in cemeteries; time-consuming events like high-end processions and wakes; and the use of facilities such as reception rooms, kitchen space and equipment, adequate parking, and banquet spaces. Or, for clients that want to save money, there are simpler options, such as direct cremation with or without an accompanying memorial service. The average service ranges between US$2,000 for direct cremation and US$15,000 for a traditional service complete with a viewing and cemetery burial (Beard and Burger, 2020).

The trend of digitization paved the road to the integration of online services that facilitate such novel services such as the payment of last respects from afar, the design of online memorials to keep and make accessible the deceased's life story, and even the re-creation of a deceased's likeness using virtual reality (Bell and Gray, 2001). Finally, pet humanization inspired the innovation of providing mortuary services for animals (Chur-Hansen, 2011).

Lastly, considering that aging is the main foreseeable cause of death, demographic information forecasts a sustained business opportunity for death care services. The global population that is aged 60 years or older is expected to reach 2 billion, doubling from 12% to 22% of the total population between 2015 and 2050, according to organizations such as The World Health Organization (WHO), The World Economic Forum (WEF), and The Global Coalition on Aging.[3]

14.5. Comparative Analysis of the Death Care Industries, in Spain, the US, and Colombia[4]

The business model previously described is very similar for companies in the death care industry located in the US, Spain, and Colombia. The US is the world leader in managerial practices, with the National Funeral Directors Association (NFDA) being the international reference for the entire industry worldwide. See Table 14.3 for a comparison of the key figures in the death care industry in the US, Spain, and Colombia.

Consumption, as measured by the death rate per 100,000 of population, shows similarities between the US (728.8) and Spain (880.16), with a lower index for Colombia (463.87). The difference in this index may reflect that, while in peaceful environments, the main cause of death is aging, social conditions for this period in Colombia were unusually peaceful and in the presence of a young population of survivors of past violence. Assuming that burial is the only choice, the impact of entombment on land use would appear to be extreme (requiring 20 square feet

---

[3] See WHO, https://www.who.int/ageing/en/; The World Economic Forum, https://intelligence.weforum.org/topics/a1Gb0000000LHRxEAO; and The Global Coalition on Aging globalcoalitiononaging.com.
[4] Sundale Research (2018); *Asociación Nacional e Servicios Funerarios* (PANASEF) (2017); FENALCO Antioquia (2015).

Table 14.3. Comparison of death care business figures from the US, Colombia, and Spain.

Variable	United States	Colombia	Spain	Comments
2016 Death Rate deaths/100,000 population (square feet of cemetery land if buried)	728.8 (14,576)	463.87 (9,277.4)	880.16 (17,603.2)	Each standard plot measures about 8 feet long and 2.5 feet wide (about 20 square feet), which makes cemeteries a growing environmental liability.
Annual Revenue (Industry) (2016)	US$14.2 billion	US$0.33 billion	US$1.29 billion	Almost steady income, low growth rate
Number of Competitors	22,818 (15,818 funeral homes, and about 7,000 crematoriums and cemeteries)	2,155 companies	1,404 companies	Small, intensely local, family-owned businesses. The trend in the US is toward consolidation.
Revenue (Industry) as a percentage of GDP	0.08% of GDP	0.12% of GDP	0.13% of GDP	• GDP is gross domestic product.
• Cremations/Burials (%)	• 48.6%/51.4%	• 67%/33%	• 40.33%/59.67%	• Cremation is a very strong alternative among burial choices. In Colombia, it is the first choice.
• Employees (women/men)	• 105,668 (27,791/77,877)	• 9,477 (not available)	• 11,176 (2,911/8,215)	• The industry is labor-intensive, with the number of employees paralleling the size of the market. Industry employment is dominated by men (26% rate of women to men).
• Pre-Need (millions)	• 4.62 M (1.43% of population)	• 18 M (37.3% population)	• 21 M (45.1% population)	• Pre-need clients are family groups in Colombia and Spain while they are mainly individuals in the US.

Source: Data were taken from Sundale Research (2018); *Asociación Nacional de Servicios Funerarios* (PANASEF) (2017); and *Fenalco Antioquia* (2015).

per body), while the impact on the quality of air, although inferior, would be not be negligible either (releasing 540 pounds of carbon dioxide per body).

The annual revenue of the death care industry for 2016 was the lowest for Colombia (US$0.33 billion), while it was the highest for the US (US$14.2 billion), the last being about 10 times the revenue of the entire industry in Spain (US$1.29 billion). The revenue for the period in all three cases had a very low growth rate. However, no matter how wide the comparative gap between the three countries, given that this industry is local, the level of income makes it a good business to compete for nationally.

Property in this industry is dispersed between small, intensely local, family-owned businesses. The US features 22,818 companies, including funeral homes, 7,000 crematoriums, and cemeteries; in Spain there are 1,404 companies; while in Colombia there are only 2,155. The US market shows some tendency toward industry consolidation that is not present in the other countries, with five current major vendors in the death care industry, including Service Corporation International (SCI), Hillenbrand, StoneMor, Carriage Services, and NorthStar Memorial Group.

The gross domestic product (GDP) of the death care industry was low and about the same in all three countries: 0.08% for the US, 0.12% for Colombia, and 0.13% for Spain, which implies that the industry is not among the most relevant for any of these economies.

Concerning consumer preferences, when comparing cremation to burial, the former is a very strong choice in all three cases, being the preferred choice in Colombia 67/33 (203%), and the second choice in the US 48.6/51.4 (95%) and Spain 40.33/59.67 (68%). The reduced cost, reduced environmental impact, and recent acceptance by some religions might be contributing to the increasing adoption of cremation.

The number of employees in each country parallels the difference in the number of companies in the industry, demonstrating that death care processes are labor-intensive. In the death care industry, there are 105,668 people employed in the US, 11,176 in Spain, and 9,477 in Colombia. In addition, the ratio of women to men working in the industry in the US and Spain is about 26%, indicating the fact that the death care industry is male-dominated. There is no data for Colombia.

Finally, pre-need is the payment arrangement for 45.1% of the population in Spain, 37.3% of the population in Colombia, and only 1.43% of the population in the US. Collectivist thinking may explain the difference between Spain and Colombia as compared to the US, since market reports state that, in Spain and Colombia, pre-need is a family or group choice while in the US, the policyholders are mostly individuals. For instance, in Colombia, pre-need payments were a significant social innovation that allowed family groups to have a dignified burial for their loved ones — so much so that statistics for 2018 indicate that pre-need is the insurance with the highest affiliation in the entire country *(Banca de Oportunidades,*

Fasecolda, & Superitendencia Financiera de Colombia, 2018). In addition, it is well known that elderly women are the most common initiators, influencers, deciders, or purchasers of pre-need payment arrangements for death care services. For all other characteristics, the business model is very similar in all three countries, with the main differences between figures accounting for differences in the respective scales of operations in the three countries.

14.6. Conclusion

Cultural anthropology and marketing scholars have proven that religion is a key driver of decision-making with regard to mortuary services. Results of this analysis demonstrate that the business model of the death care industry is very standard and includes the disposition of the corpse, ritualization, and memorialization. Disposition of human remains is the component of the service that causes a significant degree of environmental impact related to ground burial, which affects land use, and cremation, which expels greenhouse gases into the atmosphere.

In recent years, a number of factors — the religious acceptance of cremation, the drastic reduction in cost (an estimated 90% less than the cost of a ground burial), and the reduction in environmental impact — is driving cremation to become the preferred alternative for the disposal of human remains. However, other technologies with a lower impact are also being explored, e.g. water cremation by means of a process called alkaline hydrolysis.

Payment arrangements have also recently evolved from at-need disbursement by the deceased's survivors to pre-need instalments by the individuals or groups that plan their own funerals in advance. This change in payment process has prompted the business from selling goods and services to collecting savings as its primary source of revenue. Pre-need payments have become an important social innovation in locales such as Colombia where families might not be able to afford high-cost funerals, especially when deaths were mounting during times of violence and when incomes were suppressed. One interesting cultural characteristic of pre-need clients is that in collectivist cultures, they often consist of groups and in the case of Colombia, elderly women are the key actors in purchasing decisions. On the other hand, because the world population is aging, the funeral business looks promising for any of its payment options.

Ritualization is a process that benefits the living survivors and it is the component of the business most influenced by cultural trends such as personalization, an acceleration in the pace of life, pretense of wealth, narcissism, or a propensity toward selfishness. However, the industry has customized death care services to cater to a diversity of tastes by creating a combination of options that produces different ranges of prices and features from which customers may choose.

Memorialization has evolved from simple gravestones and funerary art to digital options that may document, maintain, and make accessible the deceased's life story. Such innovative technology may even evolve to recreate the deceased using advanced virtual reality (Lilley, 2012).

The foreseeable future of the death care industry implies that there is an imminent change regarding the mediation of culture moving away from just the disposition of the corpse and more toward the memorialization process. Ecological reasons will most probably define future choices in disposition alternatives, with traditional funerary rituals becoming more of a luxury, while digital memorialization will grow as the price of technology decreases, creating a whole new market for digital ritualization of the ages-old human custom of burying the dead to honor the deceased's life (Krupar, 2018).

This research used secondary data sources to describe the business model and industry trends, the mediation of cultural variables in the purchasing of funerary services, and the ecological impacts of the various choices. Future research should conduct fieldwork through which the role that culture plays in determining consumer behavior can more fully be described and should also model its influence on the death care industry.

References

Achawangkul, Y., Maruyama, N., Hirota, M., Chaichana, C., Sedpho, S., & Sutabutr, T. (2016). Evaluation on environmental impact from the utilization of fossil fuel, electricity and biomass producer gas in the double-chambered crematories. *Journal of Cleaner Production*, **134**, 463–468.

Aranda, G., & Molina, F. (2006). Wealth and power in the Bronze Age of the south-east of the Iberian Peninsula: The funerary record of Cerro de la Encina. *Oxford Journal of Archaeology*, **25**(1), 47–59.

Asociación Nacional de Servicios Funerarios (PANASEF) (2017). *Radiografía del Sector Funerario*. PANASEF.

Bailey, J. M., & Sood, J. (1993). The effects of religious affiliation on consumer behavior: A preliminary investigation. *Journal of Managerial Issues*, **5**(3), 328–352.

Bar-Yosef, O. (1998). The Natufian culture in the Levant, threshold to the origins of agriculture. *Evolutionary Anthropology: Issues, News, and Reviews: Issues, News, and Reviews*, **6**(5), 159–177.

Balkan, O. (2015). Burial and belonging. *Studies in Ethnicity and Nationalism*, **15**(1), 120–134.

Banca de Oportunidades, Fasecolda, & Superitendencia Financiera de Colombia (2018). *Estudio de Demanda de Seguros* (Bogotá: Puntoaparte).

BBC News (2015). The world is running out of burial space, 13 March. Available at: https://www.bbc.com/news/uk-31837964 (Accessed 2 November 2018).

Beard, V. R., & Burger, W. C. (2017). Change and innovation in the funeral industry: A typology of motivations. *OMEGA-Journal of Death and Dying*, **75**(1), 47–68. https://doi.org/10.1177/0030222815612605.

Beard, V. R., & Burger, W. C. (2020). Selling in a dying business: An analysis of trends during a period of major market transition in the funeral industry. *OMEGA — Journal of Death and Dying*, **80**(4), 544–567. https://doi.org/10.1177/0030222817745430.

Becker, E. (2007). *The Denial of Death* (Massachusetts: Simon and Schuster).

Bonoma, T. V. (1982). Major sales-Who really does the buying. *Harvard Business Review*, **60**(3), 111–119.

Bell, G., & Gray, J. (2001). Digital immortality. *Communications of the ACM*, **44**(3), 28–31.

Bostrom, N. (2005). A history of transhumanist thought. *Journal of Evolution and Technology*, **14**(1), 1–25.

Choi-Allum, L. (2007). Funeral and Burial Planners Survey Report. Available at: https://www.aarp.org/money/estate-planning/info-2007/funeral_survey.html.

Chur-Hansen, A. (2011). Cremation services upon the death of a companion animal: Views of service providers and service users. *Society & Animals*, **19**(3), 248–260.

De Quevedo, F. (1976). *Quevedo Dreams* (New York: Barron's Educational Series Incorporated).

Delener, N. (1994) Religious contrasts in consumer decision behaviour patterns: Their dimensions and marketing implications. *European Journal of Marketing*, **28**(5), 36–53.

Dobscha, S. (Ed.). (2015). *Death in a Consumer Culture* (London: Routledge).

Fenalco Antioquia (2015). Gestión de la Prestación del Servicio Funerario y Exequial Simposio Funerarias y Servicios Exequiales Ficha Técnica. Available at: https://www.fenalcoantioquia.com/sites/default/files/pictures/estudio_sep_2015_sector_de_funerarias_y_servicios_exequiales.pdf (Accessed 2 November 2018).

Frank, J. A. (1996). Preneed funeral plans: The case for uniformity. *Elder Law Journal*, **4**, 1.

Geertz, C. (1966). *Religion as a Cultural System* (London: Tavistock), 45 pp.

Goodman, A. M. (2003). *A Plain Pine Box: A Return to Simple Jewish Funerals and Eternal Traditions* (New York: KTAV Publishing House, Inc.)

Goodwin-Hawkins, B., & Dawson, A. (2018). Life's end: Ethnographic perspectives. *Death Studies*, **42**(5), 269–274.

Habenstein, R. W., & Lamers, W. M. (1985). *The History of American Funeral Directing* (Tennessee: Ingram).

Hirschman, E.C. (1982), Religious affiliation and consumption processes: A preliminary paradigm, in Sheth, J. (ed.), *Research in Marketing*, Vol. 6 (Chicago, IL: JAI Press), pp. 131–170.

Holy Office, Instruction (1963). *Piam et costantem*: AAS 56 (1964) 822, 5 July.

Holy Office, Instruction (2016). *Ad resurgendum cum Christo*, 2 March.

Hyland, L., & Morse, J. M. (1995). Orchestrating comfort: The role of funeral directors. *Death Studies*, **19**(5), 453–474.

Industry Focus: Death Care (2016). Available at: https://2016.export.gov/build/groups/public/@eg_main/@byind/@healthtech/documents/webcontent/eg_main_113189.pdf.

Tarlow, S., & Stutz, L. N. (eds.). (2013). *The Oxford handbook of the archaeology of death and burial*. (OUP Oxford).

Kellehear, A. 2007. *A Social History of Dying*. (Cambridge: Cambridge University Press).

Klass, D., Silverman, P. R., & Nickman, S. (2014). *Continuing Bonds: New Understandings of Grief* (Abingdon: Taylor & Francis).

Kopp, S. W., & Kemp, E. (2007). The death care industry: A review of regulatory and consumer issues. *Journal of Consumer Affairs*, **41**(1), 150–173.

Krupar, S. R. (2018). Green death: Sustainability and the administration of the dead. *Cultural Geographies*, **25**(2), 267–284.

Kundu, D. (2019). Transacting death: José Saramago's Death at Intervals and the politics of the death industry. *Thanatos*, **8**(2), 203–221.

Kutty, A. (1991). *Islamic Funeral Rites and Practices* (Toronto: Islamic Foundation of Toronto).

La Fondation des Services Funéraires Ville de Paris (2017). Analyse environnementale comparative du rite de la crémation et de l'inhumation en Ile-de-France (París: Durapole/Verteego).

Ladwig, P., & Williams, P. (2012). Introduction: Buddhist funeral cultures. In P. Williams & P. Ladwig (Eds.), *Buddhist Funeral Cultures of Southeast Asia and China* (pp. 1–20). Cambridge: Cambridge University Press. doi:10.1017/CBO9780511782251.002.

Lilley, S. (2012). *Transhumanism and Society: The Social Debate Over Human Enhancement* (Berlin: Springer Science & Business Media).

Market Research Vision. (2019). Global Death Care Services Market Report 2019. Retrieved from https://www.marketresearchvision.com/reports/206752/death-care-services-market.

Metcalf, P., & Huntington, R. (1991). *Celebrations of Death: The Anthropology of Mortuary Ritual* (Cambridge: Cambridge University Press).

More, M. (2013). The philosophy of transhumanism. In More, M., & Vita-More, N. (Eds.). The Transhumanist Reader (pp. 3–17). Oxford: John Wiley & Sons. https://doi.org/10.1002/9781118555927.ch1.

Mytum. H. (2017). Mortuary culture, In C. Richardson, T. Hamling and D. Gaimster (eds.), *The Routledge Handbook of Material Culture in Early Modern Europe* (Farnham: Routledge), pp. 154–167.

Nicosia, F. M. (1966). *Consumer Decision Processes; Marketing and Advertising Implications* (New Jersey: Prentice-Hall).

Osterwalder, A., Pigneur, Y., Clark, T., & Smith, A. (2010). *Business Model Generation: A Handbook for Visionaries, Game Changers, and Challengers* (New Jersey: John Wiley & Sons).

Palgi, P., & Abramovitch, H. (1984). Death: A cross-cultural perspective. *Annual review of Anthropology*, **13**(1), 385–417.

Pijl van der, Patrick. (2015). The business model of death — Business Models Inc. Retrieved November 2, 2018, from https://www.businessmodelsinc.com/the-business-model-of-death/.

Rendu, W., Beauval, C., Crevecoeur, I., Bayle, P., Balzeau, A., Bismuth, T., ... & Tavormina, C. (2014). Evidence supporting an intentional Neandertal burial at La Chapelle-aux-Saints. *Proceedings of the National Academy of Sciences*, **111**(1), 81–86.

Research and Markets (2018). Death Care Market in US_Industry Outlook and Forecast 2018–2023.

Robben, A. C. (Ed.). (2018). *A Companion to the Anthropology of Death*. (John Wiley & Sons)

Robben, A. C. (Ed.). (1991). *Death, mourning, and burial: A cross-cultural reader*. (John Wiley & Sons).

Roberts, D. J. (1997). *Profits of Death: An Insider Exposes the Death Care Industries* (Byron Center, MI: Five Star Publishing).

Rothstein, K. (2018). The new civic–sacred: Designing for life and death in the modern metropolis. *Design Issues*, **34**(1), 29–41.

Sahoo, K. (2014). Rituals of death in Odisha: Hindu religious beliefs and socio-cultural practices. *International Journal of Language Studies*, **8**(4).

Smart, N. (1998). *The World's Religions* (Cambridge: Cambridge University Press).

Sundale Research. (2019). State of the Industry Report: Funeral and Cremation Services and Supplies in the U.S.(14th edition). 27 pages.

Technical Guidelines on the Environmentally Sound Management of Biomedical and Healthcare Wastes (2003). Available at: http://www.basel.int/Portals/4/Basel Convention/docs/pub/techguid/tech-biomedical.pdf.

The Jewish People Policy Institute (2019). *Annual Assessment of the Situation and Dynamics of the Jewish People* (Jerusalem: Jewish People Policy Institute).

Thomas, L. V. (1980). *Anthropology of Death I, II* (Belgrade: Prosveta Publishing House).

Vico, G. (1948, orig. pub. 1725). *The New Science*, T. G. Bergin & M. H. Fisch (trans.) (Ithaca, NY: Cornell University).

World Population Prospects: The 2017 Revision | Multimedia Library — United Nations Department of Economic and Social Affairs. (n.d.). Available at: https://www.un.org/development/desa/publications/world-population-prospects-the-2017-revision.html (Accessed 2 November 2018).

Yin, R. K. (2013). *Case Study Research: Design and Methods* (California: Sage Publications, Inc.).

Young, B., Parkes, C. M., & Laungani, P. (1996). *Death and Bereavement Across Cultures* (London and New York: Routledge).

© 2022 World Scientific Publishing Company
https://doi.org/10.1142/9789811248863_bmatter

Index

A
active and passive stakeholders, 6
adaptability, 12
agency, 120, 147
agentic qualities, 360
ANOVA, 366
authoritative approach, 368

B
B-corporation, 7
benchmarking, 13
bias, 358
board of directors, 178, 189, 205
bricolage, 12, 165–168, 171, 305–307, 317
business model, 2, 52, 58, 66, 71, 76–78, 176–177, 182, 185, 187, 191, 231, 244, 392–393, 395, 397, 403, 406–407
business model innovations, 59

C
carbon capture, 18, 22–24, 29
chief sustainability officer, 12
civic wealth creation, 8, 12
clean energy, 2
climate change, 2
climate change mitigation, 50–54, 56–57, 75, 77–78, 120, 122, 124, 134
cluster analysis, 365, 368, 370
cluster maps, 365
co-create, 11
commitment, 12
communal approach, 368
communal qualities, 360
comparative case analysis, 13
competitor collaboration, 184–185
contextuality, 3
corporate governance, 12, 54, 337
corporate social, 139
corporate social performance, 11
corporate social responsibility, 12, 50, 338
corporate stakeholder orientation, 9
corporate sustainability, 63, 91–92, 135, 139, 143, 145, 228, 339
CSR, 51, 53, 78, 201, 206, 217, 339–340, 345, 353
CSR activities, 202–203, 206–207, 210, 215, 217–218
CSR initiatives, 205, 216
CSR report, 59, 206, 347, 349
CSR reporting, 346
cultural influences, 361

D
death care industry, 13, 391–392
death industry, 401
different registration forms through, 312
diminishing returns, 10

E
early stage venturing, 6
ecological value creation, 139, 143, 145, 148

economic efficiency, 1
ecosystems, vii, 18, 30–31, 37, 123, 200–203, 217
ecotourism, 10, 162, 180, 189
ecotourism enterprise, 10
entrepreneurial action, 1–2, 10
entrepreneurial activity, 357
entrepreneurial ecosystem, 8–9
entrepreneurial intention, 12, 210, 258–268, 270–271, 273–275, 361
entrepreneurial opportunity, 10, 158–160, 166–171
entrepreneurial programs, 377
entrepreneurial success, 363
entrepreneurship corpus, 365
environmental entrepreneurship, 1, 3, 9–10, 121, 132, 135, 138, 140, 145–147, 158–159, 161, 170–171, 192–193
environmental impact, 11, 55–56, 78, 112, 121, 124–125, 128, 132, 134, 136–137, 140, 143, 146–148, 179, 188, 190, 216, 238, 396, 401–402, 405–406
exploratory qualitative approach, 9

F
female entrepreneurship, 377
female-led entrepreneurship, 13
feminine approach, 370
feminine scale, 364, 367
feminine words, 373
femininity, 362, 364, 367
femininity index, 360
femininity scale, 366
field research, 2
financial innovation, 9
financial, physical human & social capital, 6
Flash Eurobarometer, 11
funeral business model, 392

G
GAH corpus, 366, 368, 377
gender, 358
gender balance, 370
gender bias, 364, 377, 379

gender-coding, 358–359, 361, 363, 365–366, 370, 377, 379–380
gender diversity, 12–13, 337–339, 344–347, 350–351, 353
gendered-linguistic, 358–359, 362–363, 366, 377–379
gender equality, 379
gender-identity, 359
gender inequality, 358
gender language maturity, 378
gender maturity, 370
gender perspectives, 365
gender schema, 358–360, 364, 366, 377, 379–380
gender stereotypes, 360–362
gender-stereotypic, 362
gender type, 372
Global Entrepreneurship Monitor, 11
global warming, 18–23, 26–27, 32, 37–39, 133
grand challenges, 51, 89
greenhouse gas, 9

H
higher education, 358
horizontal dendrogram, 368

I
identity, 3
inequalities, 363
institutional level, 11
insurance-driven business, 392

L
language of entrepreneurship, 358
legitimacy, 2
linguistic relativity, 362
low carbon economy, 8

M
manufacturing industry, 295
masculine, 370
masculine and feminine entrepreneurship, 13
masculine approach, 372
masculine domain, 378

masculine–feminine scale, 363
masculine Scale, 367
masculine traits, 381
masculine words, 373
masculinity, 360, 364
masculinity scale, 366, 377
metacognition, 11–12, 227–231, 233–234, 239–241, 243, 246–249
microfoundations, 6
mission drift, 8
motivation, 3

N
non–gender-specific, 368
non-profit, 2

O
organizational alignment, 8

P
planned behavior, 267
prosocial, 12
prosocial personality, 12, 256–257, 259, 261, 271, 274
public-private partnership, 9

Q
qualitative analysis, 9

R
reinvestment, 184–185
resource acquisition, 285–286, 294, 307–309, 312, 314–315
resource typology, 12, 286–287

S
scalability, 3
scarce resources, 397
scraping tool, 365
self-regulation, 93
sex typing, 359, 363
situationism, 201–205
situationism theory, 11, 216
social enterprise, 8
social enterprise resource typology, 12
social entrepreneurial intentions, 12

social entrepreneurship, 1–3, 11–12
social impact, 2–4, 6, 184, 190–191, 200–201, 216, 290, 317
social norms, 3
social problem, 6
social value, 6
social venture, 3, 6
social welfare, 1
societal attitudes, 201–202, 207, 209–210, 215–216, 218
socioeconomic change, 226–230, 233–234, 238–239, 242, 246, 248
stakeholder and entrepreneurial action, 11
stakeholder anxiety and negativity, 11
stakeholder management, 3, 8, 10, 12
stakeholder orientation, 9, 91–92, 100, 108, 113
stakeholders, 2–3
strategic alliances, 7
strategic leadership perspective, 8
supply chain, 9, 51–52, 54, 402
sustainability, 3
sustainability and environmental entrepreneurship, 9
sustainability-as-flourishing, 11, 157, 226–228, 230, 234, 239, 246, 248–249
sustainability leadership, 12, 337, 339–340, 344, 346, 348, 350–353
sustainable business model, 9, 50
sustainable business practices, 9
sustainable entrepreneur, 10
sustainable entrepreneurship, 121, 136, 139–141, 158, 168–169
sustainable farming, 3
sustainable value creation, 52

T
taxonomy, 10
theory of planned behavior, 12

U
university webpages, 379
university websites, 377
UN Sustainable Development Goals, 2

V

value creation, 10–11, 53–54, 56–57, 73, 92, 120, 136, 143, 166, 178, 192, 204, 230–232, 238, 241, 246–249, 307, 341, 361

value-destroying & value-preserving, 11

W

word cloud, 365, 367, 370–371

World Bank Doing Business Report, 11